Jill Ker Conway

In Her Own Words

WOMEN'S MEMOIRS FROM AUSTRALIA,
NEW ZEALAND, CANADA,
AND THE UNITED STATES

Jill Ker Conway was born in Hillston, New South
Wales, Australia, graduated from the University of
Sydney in 1958, and received her Ph.D. from Harvard
University in 1969. From 1964 to 1975 she taught at
the University of Toronto and was vice president there
before serving for ten years as president of Smith College. Since 1985 she has been a visiting scholar and professor in M.I.T.'s Program in Science, Technology, and
Society, and she now lives in Boston, Massachusetts.

In Her Own Words

WOMEN'S MEMOIRS FROM AUSTRALIA, NEW ZEALAND, CANADA, AND THE UNITED STATES

Edited and with an Introduction by
Jill Ker Conway

VINTAGE BOOKS
A DIVISION OF RANDOM HOUSE, INC.
NEW YORK

A VINTAGE ORIGINAL, MARCH 1999

FIRST EDITION

Copyright © 1999 by Jill Ker Conway

Library of Congress Cataloging-in-Publication Data
In her own words : women's memoirs from Australia, New Zealand,
Canada, and the United States / edited and with an introduction by
Jill Ker Conway. — 1st ed.
p.   cm.
"A Vintage original".
Includes bibliographical references (p.   ).
ISBN 0-679-78153-6
1. Women—Biography.   2. Biography—20th century.
3. Autobiographies.   I. Conway, Jill K., 1934–   .
CT3235.I5   1999
920.72—dc21   98-44745
CIP

Page 612 constitutes an extension of this copyright page.

Book design by Robert Bull Design

www.randomhouse.com/vintage

Printed in the United States of America
10 9 8 7 6 5 4 3 2 1

CONTENTS

PART FOUR
The United States
*Somehow I would tell the world
how things were as I saw them*

INTRODUCTION

The autobiographer writes a narrative where subject and object are intermingled—where knower and the known are part of the same consciousness. This makes for riveting reading when the narrator can move seamlessly between the self as object and speaker, providing text which conveys both inner life and external events. That is why we often use memoirs as windows on the worlds the writers inhabit. They are social documents as well as literary texts—one reason why historians quote them so frequently.

This anthology is a window on the lives of talented women from the old British colonial world and their twentieth-century counterparts in the United States. Nine of the twelve authors represented are successful writers, a predominance suggestive of the extent to which the colonial experience is a forcing ground for women's literary consciousness.

A product of the pre-1950 British Commonwealth world, I have lived my adult life in Canada and the United States. This means I have often played the game of wondering what life might have been like had I stayed in my native Australia, and during journeys home, I have reflected on the various ways in which being a woman in one segment or another of the English-speaking world is different yet the same. This anthology is an exploration of that difference and sameness.

We learn a great deal about the social and cultural context of an autobiographer's life, because at every stage in the story the writer must tell us whether she or he is responding to the world around them in ways that were typical of or deviant from her or his society and times. A subtext of any such story then is the life plot the writer assumes is to be expected, and not in need of explanation. A striking aspect of the memoirs in this collection is the extreme sense of deviance the authors report, and the trouble they had finding a life plan which both fit their experience and was even marginally acceptable to those around them.

Because of this difficulty, memoirs are invaluable documents for the historian for the patterns of culture they delineate, even

though memoirs are invariably shaky sources of factual information about the writer's life. Our memories are deceptive. People,
events, life circumstances change depending on the point in life
from which we choose to view them. Because, of course, the structure of the autobiographer's narrative is shaped by the end point
toward which the story leads. The factual record is something a
biographer may compile after a life's end point is known, but only
the autobiographer can tell us what that experience felt like and
seemed to be about at a given point in the life history.

Four women in this selection chose expatriation for all or part
of their lives. Their journeys from colony to metropolis are instances of a near universal phenomenon for British colonial intellectuals and leaders, a theme as marked in the lives of men as of the
women selected here. Gabrielle Roy, doubly colonized as a French-
Canadian living in English-speaking Manitoba, had to experience
France and England before she could see her French-Canadian
world straight. Dorothy Livesay found her métier on a journey to
England, and tested her newfound independence as a widow on a
journey to Africa. Robin Hyde and Janet Frame, two outstanding
creative talents from New Zealand, endured acute alienation from
a world that perceived their creativity as a form of madness. They
took flight for Europe and the dream of a more congenial cultural
environment, a flight from the frontier to complexity, a reverse version of the American flight to the frontier to escape the confines of
settled society. Both Hyde and Frame were able to mine their experience of New Zealand mental institutions to make the predicament
of madness the vantage point for seeing the world with dazzling
clarity, but Hyde's travels, in contrast to Frame's liberating ones,
underline the dangers of travel for the solitary and impoverished
woman with few resources to withstand the dangers of deep depression. Frame's and Hyde's journeys have their origin in the same
alienation which sent countless male Australians and New Zealanders to Europe. What is different about their stories is how much
harder it was for a woman to get together the money to get away,
and how vulnerably alone she was on reaching the fabled England.

Rosemary Brown and Shirley Chisholm both kept the counter-
world of their native Jamaica and Barbados, where women were
strong and influential leaders, in their inner mind's eye as they followed their political vocations in Canada and the United States.
Brown's years as a leader in British Columbia politics and on the

national Canadian scene emphasize the value of travel and expatriation for women. The newcomer, from outside the society, is less disturbing to its social and political hierarchies when she seeks power than the local woman, who occupies a clearly defined place in society's kin and status networks.

Lillian Hellman and Ellen Chernin each have extraordinary kin networks to reckon with, Hellman's a colorful New Orleans family, Chernin's a committed left radical family whose love of Russia and dialectical materialism sent their daughter toward poetry and mysticism. Sally Morgan's discovery of her Australian aboriginal kin network is a story unique to Australia, yet her drive to understand her mother and grandmother's story is not unlike Chernin's effort to understand her Jewish family and its lost history in Eastern Europe.

Dorothy Hewett's early rebellion against her bourgeois Western Australian family, and her voluntary expatriation, not abroad but into the working-class life of the rank and file of the Australian Communist Party, means that she, like Dorothy Livesay in Canada, deferred her serious writing career into midlife in the interests of practicing the socialist realism required by the Party.

What the life histories of the Australian, New Zealand, and Canadian women make clear is that for rebellious and ambitious Commonwealth women, almost the only escape from family and the requirements of respectable society was into political commitment to left politics. Whereas the spectrum of occupations, avant-garde circles, and institutions was broader for Americans, as Hellman's Hollywood years or Chernin's escape from family in residential university life demonstrate. Gabrielle Roy's education by nuns and the strong figure of her heroic Maman at the center of a powerful French-Canadian extended family also meant that Roy was not easily recruited into the political extremes of the 1930s, even though her first love was a fervent anti-Communist and Nazi sympathizer, and even though she had come to see the survival codes of her French-Canadian culture as narrow and limiting. The contrast of Roy's and Hewett's stories is striking, because Roy was able to return to her French-Canadian roots and celebrate Quebec's working-class life, while Hewett's rage at the pretenses of her Perth family never diminished.

One of the great themes of Roy's writing about her Manitoba childhood is her love of the light on the prairies, the extended views of sun, and subtle contours of land that come from seeing late-slanting sunshine cast a golden haze over immense space. At her loneliest in her exploration of Paris, Roy can be comforted by a glimpse of a distant sunset seen across the expanse of the Place de la Concorde—the light seeming to be a blessing coming to her from her beloved prairies.

Patsy Adam-Smith has the same talent for making the Australian landscape not a backdrop but a deep emotional presence in her story of a childhood beside her hardworking parents, living on the farthest reaches of Victoria's early railroad networks. The 1939–45 war arrives just in time to liberate Adam-Smith from life in outback Australia. It gives her the reason to leave without guilt, which Gabrielle Roy could not escape in her flight from her isolated rural Manitoba. But for Adam-Smith the larger world does not offer many institutions besides the army medical service where she can put down roots and develop her talents. So her intellectual and creative life, like Livesay's, is temporarily set to one side by an ill-assorted and unhappy marriage.

Lauris Edmond's memoir must be the archetypal story of the gifted woman swamped by a conventional marriage in the immediate postwar years of the 1940s and 1950s. The six children, the distant and unsympathetic husband, the series of New Zealand country towns to which her husband's school-teaching career takes the family, and her slowly developing awareness that she craves more from life, and that the more has to do with her own intellect and passion for poetry, have no real counterpart in Australian or Canadian women's memoirs. There is no Hollywood or literary New York to flee to, so Edmond's slow liberation has to be achieved by an achingly lonely struggle.

As a group, the lives of the Commonwealth women underline the absence in Australia, Canada, and New Zealand of the women's institutions which were so often staging places for creative rebellion on the part of American women, leaving only left politics with its assertively male values as the first stage in quest for intellectual passion and critical awareness. This absence of sustaining institutions outside the family left women like Frame and Hyde no shelter but mental institutions, or led women like Livesay and Edmond to make the marriages which deferred their creative lives for many decades.

What is gripping about the twelve stories in this volume is the

risks each woman was prepared to take to get away, the unquenchable creative drive which kept them returning to their passion for
writing despite the many unproductive paths their initial rebellion
had set them upon, and the quiet authority with which the women
politicians set about building their base of power. They tell their
stories as quests, doubly complicated quests for women in colonial
settings because life at the margins can never be completely understood without testing the metropolis, and because the artist's or
politician's vocation necessitates claiming a personal history, a life
lived for the calling rather than for the conventional bonds of family and maternity. When we listen to Gabrielle Roy's and Janet
Frame's words about their isolation and their need to leave, we can
feel their internal exile, and imagine the voice that will resonate in
a larger world. Speaking of the French-Canadian Manitoba world
to which she was tied by deep bonds of family obligation, Roy
writes:

> It didn't escape me that our life was an inward-looking one,
> which led inescapably to a kind of withering. The watchword was
> survival, and the principal standing order, though it was never
> formally pronounced, was not to fraternize with the outside
> world. I seemed to feel a little more of my lifeblood escaping
> every day.

For Frame, the loneliness produced a sense of personal extinction, a "nowhereness" within which she was sustained only by literature:

> It is strange to think of my life being lived as I then lived my 'real
> life', so much within and influenced by English and French litera-
> ture, with my daily adventures the discovery of a paragraph or a
> poem and my own attempts to write. It was not an escape in the
> sense of a removal from the unhappiness I felt over the sickness at
> home and my own feeling of nowhereness. . . . There was simply
> the other world's arrival into my world, the literature streaming
> through it like an array of beautiful ribbons through the branches
> of green growing tree, touching the leaves with unexpected
> light. . . .

These points of departure give us the knower being known in
the perspective of poetry and tragedy. We have the sense of suffocating confinement, producing a literary voice the more powerful
for the narrowness of the writer's escape.

PART ONE

Australia

I've heard the real train blow

Patricia Jean Adam-Smith

(1924–)

Patricia Jean Adam-Smith, author, was born in Melbourne and raised as the daughter of a railroad fettler and his station mistress wife. *Hear the Train Blow* chronicles her early life accompanying her peripatetic parents around the remote railroad stations of Victoria, the traditional Australian working-class battle with economic and environmental hardship, her backcountry childhood quest to overcome limited educational opportunity, and her escape to a larger world as a volunteer nurse during the 1939–45 war.

The memoir is rich in scene language and imagery of the irrepressible Australian battler (male or female), always irreverent about the rich, about authority or formality, proud of the powers of endurance honed by heat, drought, and backbreaking labor. Adam-Smith represents nature through British imperial eyes as in harsh contrast to an idealized British landscape.

Adam-Smith's world is not shattered by war, and as her 1995 memoir *Goodbye Girlie* shows, service as an army nurse brings her sociability, freedom from her parents' stern Catholic morality, temporary stagnation in an unhappy marriage, followed by a life of adventure, travel, and successful journalism. Like her railroad parents, she always has itchy feet, ready to set out for a new adventure at a moment's notice.

From 1954 to 1960 she was the first woman radio operator on an Australian merchant vessel, for nearly a decade she served as an Adult Education Officer in Hobart, before becoming Manuscript Field Officer for the State Library of Victoria, traveling the state to collect and preserve the records of its settlement. Thereafter she has traveled extensively to write about Australian military history, Australia's railroads, and the heroism of outback settlers. Awarded the Order of the British Empire in 1980 for her services to Australian literature, she lives in Melbourne.

A product of the Depression and the 1939–45 war, Adam-Smith gives an account of her life almost untouched by feminist ideas. The hero and heroine of *Hear the Train Blow* live in the conventional pattern of a working-class marriage, uncommented upon by their otherwise observant daughter. The later narrative of her life

is organized around the shifting patterns of her relationships with
men, with female friendship only briefly important during her life
as an army nurse. The narrative structure and voice of her work
are those of the internalized male, who has achieved relative freedom in life by becoming "one of the boys," a typical style of female
adaptation to Australia's culture focused upon celebrating male
endurance and heroism.

HEAR THE TRAIN BLOW

All our closest friends lived and worked on railways; three of my
aunts, my mother's sisters, were in charge of railway stations
or post offices in places as isolated as were we, and other aunts
waited on small, hungry farms in Gippsland for their railway-fencer
husbands to come home from the little cabin on wheels shunted
into a lonely siding. . . .

Dad's father and his brothers (there were eight boys until
World War I) were said to have cut more railway sleepers than any
other family in Australia. 'Those Smith boys were all born with a
broad axe in their hands,' they used to say in the Gippsland forests
back of Neerim. . . . My parents were railway people and we lived
beside the tracks all our life.

My mother was station and postmistress of lonely places where
often our house was all there was of the town named on the railway
signpost. Sometimes our four-roomed wooden cottage was on the
platform and as we lay asleep the great steam engines crunched by
like nailed boots crossing our bedroom floor. . . .

Dad worked on the line as a fettler*; his section was the flat
long miles skirting the Hattah Desert country at Nowingi. My
mother was station-mistress cum postmistress at Nowingi. This
office served Kulkyne cattle station, twelve miles away. As far as the
eye could see there was only one house besides ours, that of another
fettler and his wife. This woman looked after the office when Mum
was in Melbourne. In the crowded, laughter-filled days of childhood I never thought it strange that Mum should go down only one
day before my arrival and return as soon as I could travel. She

---

* A person responsible for maintaining the railroad track. Ed.

wrote to Dad from Melbourne. Two days later the engine-driver
pulled his train up when he saw the gang at the side of the track.

'Where's Albert Smith?' he called. A letter had come in the
mailbag and the fettler's wife at Nowingi had sent it up to him.
Everyone knew he was awaiting news of the baby. The driver
climbed down from his hot cab onto the track and delivered the letter. He waited while Dad read it aloud.

Squatting beside the railway line on the red soil of that red,
dusty land where the desert meets the acres man has claimed, he
read from my mother's letter to his mates, some standing nearby
rolling cigarettes, another tinkering with the motor of the Casey
Jones.

'The baby,' he read, 'was born on the thirty-first of May, has
black, curly hair, weighs eight pounds, and should not be upset by
the long journey home.' The man laughed. 'When are you going to
wet its head, Albert?' My father wasn't a drinking man, but today
was different. He asked the driver to bring him a billy of beer on the
run back the next day. 'I'll fix you up for it then.' Fettlers never carried money, or, as Dad said, never had any to carry.

Next day on the way back the engine was pulled up and the
driver and guard climbed down carrying a black billy of beer each.
The fireman followed them, mopping his neck with his sweat-rag.
'It's as hot as the hobs of hell up there today,' he said, and nodded
up to where the heat shimmered in his cab. When all the mugs were
full Kelly the ganger lifted his and said, 'To Albert's son. May he be
half the man his father is.' 'Good luck to you, Albert,' the others
toasted him. They drank the flat, warm beer, one mug apiece, and
the driver and fireman climbed back on the engine. The guard stood
beside the track ready to jump onto the step when his van came
by. . . .

When Mum arrived and they found I was a girl they were just
as happy.

'A little dancing partner,' the bachelor ganger said. Any sort of
baby was a novelty to them. There wasn't another white infant for
twenty miles. . . .

The Mallee, that stretch of country in north-west Victoria, was
being turned into a dust bowl by steam-driven 'mallee-rollers' and
tree trunks dragged behind horse teams with heavy chains. They
rolled down every tree, shrub, bush and plant and then grubbed out
the stumps of the stunted trees and sold them in the cities as

'mallee-roots', leaving the top-soil to be blown away by the willy-willies, the Cock-Eye-Bobs that swept in off the desert during the hot summer months. The hot, dry winds whirled the dust up high as the sky where it travelled until it reached the coastal cities and fell on the streets and houses, and women ran around shutting doors and windows crying, 'Quick! It's a Mallee dust storm!' . . .

The olive-green mallee scrub disappeared and left a land where emus, kangaroos and lizards up to six feet long were the only permanent residents in a temperature that could hover around 112°F for days at a time. . . .

Nowingi was Mum's first post as station and postmistress. . . .

Rain came grudgingly here. Out on the sand where the construction navvies worked boys were employed to run water to the parched men when they called: a sort of Australian version of Gunga Din.

At our railway house at the siding the contents of our two galvanised iron tanks were of such concern and the word 'tank' used so often that babies used the word at an early age. All through summer the clok-clok of knuckles rapping the rims of the tanks could be heard. Dad said that if ever we Smiths had a coat of arms it would be a closed fist raised to rap an iron tank. Everyone as they passed would rap the tanks to see how they were holding. As the dry months rolled by, lower and lower sank the rings that echoed hollowly until there were only a few at the bottom of the tanks that echoed with the weight of water. When we got to this stage we would apply to the Railways Department to send us up a tanker. At times we were down to the last rim before this arrived. Every drop other than for drinking purposes had to be agreed to by Mum. The tap was turned off so tightly that we children couldn't move it, sometimes a padlock was placed on it, and always a tin dish was left on the ground beneath the tap to catch any errant drop that might fall. For ordinary daily attentions we washed in the tin dish on the tank-stand made of sleepers. In summer we never threw this dish of water out after use in case someone else might want to wash in it. We used fresh water only to wash our faces. . . .

But often we were too low in water for the luxury of a bath. Things were like this the day Mum shot at the camel.

Far from shops, we were on the trade route of the Afghan-Indian hawkers, those turbaned traders who brought a colour and *exotique* along with the calico aprons, print dresses, cotton 'bodies', dungaree trousers and 'stuff' for dresses. This was the late 1920s and cars hadn't yet come to the bush in numbers. A moving ball of dust on the horizon announced the coming of the 'Ghan in his horse-drawn wagon. Further out the hawkers used camels, but they only came to our place this once.

Dad was away and Mum was alone. When she saw them coming, the turbaned hawker and his three camels, she knew intuitively what had driven him from his habitual route into strange territory. The drought was everywhere. The railways were so pressed by their commitments to their outback workers that their few tankers could hardly cope with the calls for water. We had waited four weeks. Further west in the wasteland near the South Australian border the position must be desperate.

'Stay inside,' Mum ordered Mick* and me. 'Lock the door when I go out.' She took Dad's rifle down from behind the door and loaded it.

The hawker didn't ask for water. He led his animals directly to the tank and put our wash dish under the tap. Inside the house, we girls pressed our faces to the window. Mum rested the rifle across the top of the empty tank. It was a low tank and she stood on the wooden sleepers on which it rested on the ground.

'If you touch that tap,' Mum said, 'I'll shoot your camel.' She sighted along the barrel. I once saw her bring down a crow on the wing. The hawker didn't know this. To him she was a gentle little woman with her protecting man far away.

'My camels must drink, missus,' he said, and turned the tap. As he did, Mum fired. There was the most awesome, reverberating explosion and the leading camel fell to the ground. The empty tank had magnified the sound many times and sent it richocheting round and round the iron cylinder.

'You shoot my camel!' the man screamed.

'I'll shoot you if you don't turn that tap off,' she said, facing the Indian. He turned the tap off.

'I didn't shoot your camel. I fired in front of his nose. A good inch in front.' She was right. The camel had fallen from fright. Weakness had prevented it from bolting. . . .

'That jolly tank frightened me nearly as much as it did the

---

* Adam-Smith's half sister. Ed.

camel! I had no idea it would do that. I nearly fell over backwards when it went bang!' . . .

Dad was a runner, footballer and axeman. He followed sports meetings around the bush in the way a city man might follow horseraces. This Saturday he had gone up to Carwarp on the goods train in the morning. Mum was to follow in the jinker* with us two children after she had attended to the 'down' train.

By the time we trotted into the paddock that had become a sports ground for the day, the Married Ladies' Race was being announced.

'Hold the reins,' Mum told Mick, and she sprang to the ground. In a few minutes she was racing down the unmarked track, her shoes in one hand, the other holding her hat on her head. Sixteen women were in the race. The men came over from the wood-chopping arena to watch. We could hear Dad shouting, 'Come on, Birdie! You little beauty!' And Mum had won. Then she came back to the jinker, took up the reins and drove over to the post-and-rail enclosure where harness horses could be rested.

'Put your hat straight,' she reprimanded me. 'Wherever will people think we've come from!' . . .

By the time I was five years old we began moving in earnest. For the rest of our childhood we were never in one place longer than two years. Often our stay was only for a few months. . . .

Moving was fun. There was the packing, the arrival at the siding of the trucks that would take our goods, the preparation of cages for our chooks† to travel in, coaxing the cow into the cattle truck, and Billy our white horse into the loose-box truck and lashing the jinker onto a flat-top, locking the white cockatoo into a cage where he protested non-stop at the indignity, getting the Major Mitchell cockatoo into a box so we could carry her with us—'Poor little Chew-Chew can't travel alone'—and then getting the dog to the guard's van, where she lay with her head on her paws and moaned with loneliness until we released her at the end of the journey. . . .

Waaia was not on any map. We had to go there before we knew where it was. . . .

---

* A light, two-wheeled horse-drawn conveyance. Ed.
† Chickens. Ed.

No matter how often we had to go to a new school, that first day was always frightening. We were on guard. We had both already been to several schools and knew we had to be ready for almost anything. At Waaia we got on better than anywhere else. When the twenty-odd pupils had marched in and sat down the teacher sized Mickie and me up where we stood by his desk holding our slates and lunch bags. We, in turn, sized him up. Would he be a shouter, a strap man, a kind but useless teacher, a martinet, a weeper? We had had them all. Schoolmasters at an early age—this one was twenty years old—they must teach eight grades, with an average of six subjects to each class, with no one to refer to should they strike trouble. This responsibility developed big personalities or worried them to uselessness.

This man didn't hurry us, he let us take our time. After a while we were satisfied and returned his grin.

'Are you any good at anything?' he asked Mick. Honest Mick said, no, she wasn't.

'Oh well,' he said. 'No good worrying about something we can't mend.' Mickie grinned from ear to ear. They were friends.

I was in the third grade. Moving from school to school did not trouble me as it did some children; instead, the different methods of teaching seemed to me to stimulate application. . . .

The school was next to the Waaia recreation ground, a great paddock containing a fine football field, cricket oval, two tennis courts, a basketball court and a rounders* field. There was vigour in the little one-pub, one-store town. We could use all these playing fields; indeed a wooden stile was built over the school fence to make access easier. As well, our own school ground was a quarter of a mile long and had basketball and tennis courts. Though I was useless at all sports this extravagant abundance didn't upset me. After all, one has to be bad not to gain a place in a team where there are only nineteen children in the school. Using every girl we had we still must impress boys to get a basketball team and opposition. And in turn, the boys press-ganged us girls in eight-a-side football and cricket. My sister Mickie was one of the best footballers in the school. . . .

Going to church was as much a social event as a religious expe-

---

* A game played with a bat and ball, similar to baseball. Ed.

rience in the bush. There were few other places to which one could wear a pretty hat and a frilly dress. There was no Catholic church at Waaia. Ten miles down the line at Numurkah there was one and ten miles up the line at Nathalia was another, so church-going there was a sort of safari.

Because it was not a simple matter for us to attend church we never took the services lightly, as one grown too familiar with them may. Each contact claimed our devout and painstaking attention. . . .

There was only one other Catholic family at Waaia, the Youngs. The father was a wheat-buyer, the mother a London-trained dressmaker; their son Kevin was my age. Inevitably our two families became friends. Kevin shared the only real friendship I had during my childhood. . . .

He and I were friends until we were adults and he died. We were both musical, and what was termed 'quick' at school. We planned there at Waaia what we would do with our lives. I wrote then, I would always write. He would become a doctor. And so it came to pass. We talked out our plans there beside the wheat stacks long before we told anyone else. Such aspirations, we knew, would be considered freakish in our circumstances. . . .

Waaia was on the line to Picola, which is the same as saying it was on the line to nowhere. Yet we had enough travellers to amuse us, and when there was no one else we amused ourselves. . . .

Sometimes a railway 'home on wheels' was shunted off onto our siding and in this would live a fencer and his mate or two painters. These men who lived a lonely life usually played an instrument or had some other method of entertaining that made them welcome at bush homes. My Uncle Frank, the husband of Mum's eldest sister, used to work on the railways as fencer and he played the fiddle 'wondrous gay'. There is the world of difference between a fiddler and a violinist that only those who had heard a fiddler know. When Uncle Frank played the fiddle you wanted to leap and dance and sing and laugh and live.

Out Barmah way where mighty red gums grew, gangs of sleeper-cutters lived in the bush. Every quarter of the year these men came in to Waaia station to sell their sleepers* to the Victorian Rail-

---

* A wooden beam forming part of a railroad track, a support for the rails. Ed.

ways. A railway inspector came up from Melbourne to examine their red, redolent pile in the station yard. Sometimes the men might have to wait a week, so they camped in the lee of the wheat stacks or up in the big grain shed. Almost to a man they played the gumleaf, getting a variety of tones and pitches from different leaves. They were gregarious and wanted to talk to everyone.

Waaia State School Mothers' Club always had a raffle going for something or other and the day these men got their cheques I'd take my raffle book over and they'd say, 'How much the lot?' and take the whole book between them. I made the transaction last as long as I could because I'd only be permitted to go to their camp this once and it was the only chance I had to watch them work. They used broad axes like the one the executioner used to cut off the head of Mary Queen of Scots, razor-sharp 'trimming' axes to trim the chosen sleepers. The condemned sleepers were sold in the yard, and Dad often could buy them for as little as three pence each. They made the best burning of all and burnt to a hot ash.

We once had a trip to see the sea. Mum, as president of the Mothers' Club, organised this and coaxed Dalton Beswick from the hotel to take us down on his flat-top truck. We travelled all through the night, wrapped in rugs at our mothers' feet while they sat on backless wooden forms. As daylight broke, the truck pulled up and we all climbed stiffly down and stared. As far as eyes reached there was this shimmering, silver, rippling water. Some of us sifted sand through our fingers but our eyes never left that shimmering mass that rolled over the horizon. At last Billy Wilson broke our trance. 'What a bloody lot of water,' he marvelled.

Aborigines no longer roamed this land although they must have been numerous here once because all the places in the district were named by the blacks before the coming of the white man: Picola, Nathalia, Numurkah, Barmah, Barwoo, and of course Waaia, which meant water that Aborigines found at Broken Creek. On the New South Wales side of the Murray was the Aboriginal settlement of Cummeragunja where full-bloods and half-castes lived in humpies made of flattened-out kerosene tins. When any of our numerous relatives would visit us we'd take them to this settlement, crossing the Murray on an old cable punt. The men would go fishing along the banks of the river, the women would set up a picnic lunch under the gums, and we kids would play with the Aboriginal children. There were still paddle-steamers on the Murray and the crew and passengers would wave to us as they churned by, and we white kids would try to look as much like blacks as possible by turning our knees in and clasping our hands and putting our heads on the side and giggling shyly as we waved so we too could be thought curious to be examined by the passing parade.

I had a full-blood friend there whose name sounded like Dollery, so I called her Dolly. One night Mum's sister Sadie who played the accordion came up and we had music and singing and dancing on the banks of the Murray in the light of a big fire and the moon, and Dolly sang,

> You may not be an angel,
> But still I'm sure you'll do . . .

and she danced a little behind the fire as the women of her tribe used to do while the men leapt in the forefront of the playabout dancers in the days before we came with our sophistication and weight of numbers. Dolly would sing to me in her language and try to teach me words, but I was not adept and we would roll and giggle helplessly with our arms round each other when I attempted to repeat the lesson. We decided, the two of us, that when she was old enough she would come to work at the Waaia Hotel, as many black girls did, and we would then be close to one another. The Murray has run many a banker since then, and the little black girl who ate bite for bite with me the food I secreted from the packed-away baskets as we sat behind the gums in the dark has no doubt had the sad battle of most of the girls of that place. I hope she remembers that we kissed when we parted at the close of those visits because we were such good friends and only had to look at one another to start laughing. Memory might make clear to her that we are not born with colour prejudice, that she and I did not have it when we were kids together. . . .

There was plenty of social life for us. Dad had been fond of tennis all his life and here at Waaia he put down a court on the sun-baked red ground and painted lines on it with whitewash and encircled it with wire netting, which also served for the net. Neighbours came from far and near to play on this court, more for the company of lively Dad and the hospitality of Mum than the game. It was too hot to play during the heat of the day; Kevin often came over of a morning and he and I would play from 6 A.M. to 7 A.M., then no one would play until the sun dropped lower around about

6 P.M. From then until night fell the court was never vacant. People arrived in jinkers, on horseback, by push-bike and in tin-lizzies. Mum in mid-summer bought cases of bottled cordials and we kept these in our Coolgardie safe (a wooden frame enclosed by hessian* down which water trickled from strips of flannel leading from a dish of water on the top), and when each set finished those four players came in for a drink. . . .

Waaia was not rich in bird life because of the scarcity of trees and water, but we learnt to call those we knew up to us. Alex Walker, now known throughout Australia as the 'Birdman', taught us. Alex was an odd-job man. He was a cross-country rider, boot-mender and wheat-lumper—he'd have a go at anything—but his great love was birds. He trained our school (fourteen on the roll at that time) to whistle and call curlews, cockatoos, crows, magpies, pallid cuckoos, kookaburras and many others, and then he took us down to Shepparton radio station where we went on the air.

The parents all piled into our house back at Waaia to listen in while we first sang 'Bird of Wilderness', and then went into our repertoire.

'Jean Smith,' said the announcer, 'will now imitate the pallid cuckoo and the blackbird.' Kevin with the morepork followed. Oh, we were big time that night, all right!

School concerts were another opportunity for us to show off. I always gave lots of items, not because I was a better performer than the others but because the teacher knew he could depend on Mum to dress me well. If it were a toss-up between a new dress for herself or a stage costume for me Mum didn't hesitate. I was a jester in crimson and gold, a pied piper in red and yellow, a 'sweet queen of loveliness and grace' in blue brocade, and Ted Jorgenson sang to me 'dressed in your gown of blue brocade' and we trod a measure or two of a minuet. We thought it was all very aesthetic. . . .

Of course we didn't stay at Waaia too long. After two years Mum had itchy feet.

'You want to get on the wallaby, Birdie?' Dad asked. 'Is there anything going?' There was never any difficulty in getting a trans-fer. The foot-loose fettler and the station-master with wanderlust moved from one area to another and 'the Heads' knew they took

---

* Burlap. Ed.

with them new methods of work and, as well, injected an impetus and social vigour into isolated outposts stagnating in the wet blanket of the Depression.

In his work the railwayman built up a tradition of service that only he and his immediate community knew of. It was a tradition that was born of a complete sense of being part of a great movement. 'The Great Family of Railway Workers' Harold Clapp called them (and they, in their turn, called him the greatest transport man Australia had known).

'Is there anything going?'

There was a small caretaker-and-fettler station vacancy in Gippsland and within three weeks we were there. . . .

Monomeith had no pub, no shop, nothing but us. The railway station was post office too, as it had been at Nowingi. . . .

This line was a busy one, but not many of the trains stopped at our station; most of them went to the coal town of Wonthaggi direct, not stopping at any of the little stations in between. Our house was up on the platform itself and in the nights when you were in bed you could feel the crunch, crunch, crunch of the passing trains like nailed boots walking across your bedroom floor. I soon learnt to distinguish full trucks from empty ones, and the different kinds of wagons, coal trucks, cattle trucks and passenger coaches.

'There was something wrong with the early train going up this morning,' I told my father at breakfast one day. 'It seemed unfinished.'

That night Dad told me he had spoken to the driver on his return trip and told him what I'd said.

'We'd coupled a flat-top behind the guard's van to shunt off at Caldermeade,' the driver had said. 'Therefore she couldn't "get" the van and the train would sound incomplete.' I certainly knew my trains.

Sometimes a train would pull up and shunt trucks into our siding; then you would see tarpaulins lift and heads pop out while men 'jumping the rattler' looking for work tried to get their bearings. If they saw us kids looking they'd put their fingers to their lips conspiratorially and disappear back under the tarp. Dad knew we knew of this illegal traffic. He said, 'Try not to see it, but try not to forget it when you have full and plenty.'

One day the train pulled up and they weren't shunting. Lying awake in my bed I couldn't work out what they were doing. I got up and looked out the window. A man was walking along the platform forcing the guard to undo the lashings holding the tarps down. He was after the illegal passengers, but as fast as he climbed in one side of a truck men sprang over the other side and sprinted into the low, wet, swampy scrub and disappeared. The guard did no more than he was ordered to do by the 'head'. I thought at first that the men were negroes: they were all black from travelling in the coal trucks.

Suddenly one of the men was trapped. He hadn't been able to squeeze out the other side and had jumped onto the platform. The 'head' had his back to him trying to hustle the guard in his task. The guard looked up and saw the man as he jumped. He would be unable to get away because the gates to this platform were locked each night. The guard quickly motioned with his head towards our house gate and as he looked up saw my face at the window. The man ran in the gate through our rose garden and round the back of the house. When the 'head' gave up and went back to the van, the guard motioned me to put the window up.

'Tell your dad,' he said softly, nodding towards the back of the house.

At Monomeith I went to school by train each day to the next 'town', Caldermeade, travelling free in the guard's van. This day I was told by the guard that I was to travel in the passenger coach, and as I stepped in I saw a figure bolt from our gate into the van. He looked like Dad; he was dressed in clothes very like Dad's old suit, which I never saw after that day. Strange times when a man who could have been one's own father was on the run because he'd committed the crime of not being able to find a job.

On Melbourne Cup day the gang would work near the station so they could listen to the broadcast of the great race. On our first Cup day at Monomeith the goods train pulled in just before 3 P.M. and the driver, seeing the trikes pulled off the side of the track, came in to listen too, beckoning the guard after him. Dad saw a tarpaulin on a truck lift up a little so he opened the windows and the door wide and turned the great trumpet towards the train to enable the men on the 'rattler' to hear too. . . .

I would travel to Caldermeade station by train then walk a mile along the road to Caldermeade school between sweet hedges of may. At night I must walk all the way home for there was no suitable train, but sometimes as I'd plod along beside the 'five-foot' gauge an unscheduled goods train would pull up and I'd be hauled up on the footplate or into the guard's van and given the run of the crib tins while we rattled homewards. On one memorable occasion the Commissioner's car actually pulled up and took me home. This vehicle was an ordinary car with the rubber tyres replaced by flanged steel wheels and with the steering wheel removed. It was used by 'head' only. It gave Mum, as she later declared, 'quite a turn' to see the Commissioner's car pulling up unexpectedly at her station and then to see Harold Clapp himself handing her child up onto the platform. . . .

I was at the 'awkward age', an aptly named period of clumsy manoeuvres more of the mind than the body, an urgent awareness of the world and everything in it coupled with an inability to articulate. Paddy Einsedel the horse-breeder was one of the few people who could approach a child at that age as an equal, on a level of comprehension. One Saturday I watched him leaving for the races at Caulfield. I had saved two shillings to spend on our annual holiday.

'Give it to me and I'll win you a ten-bob note,' he suggested. I handed it over immediately and that night when he got off the train he handed me a ten-shilling note and my own two shillings back. Waltzing Lily had come home at five to one.

Paddy named his horses after people who worked for him. His best filly, Waltzing Lily, was named after Lily Walters, his housemaid. One night the housekeeper had caught Lily creeping in late from a dance and in the morning hauled her in front of Paddy.

'What were you doing to that hour?' he asked.

'Waltzing,' answered the girl.

'Waltzing,' the old man said with a reminiscent smile. 'Waltzing Lily.' When the next filly was born its name was registered as just that. . . .

Then we were on the wallaby again. Mum and Dad pored over the *Gazette* every time it arrived and laconically discussed the vacancies. The one issue had the place we were all looking for: Waaia station was 'up' again.

Waaia welcomed us back with sunshine and many friends waiting on the platform for our train to arrive.

Dad said to the gang assembled to meet him, 'Well, I'm back.'

'About time,' they said to him.

There was a thin, nasty woman schoolteacher now, but even she couldn't spoil that school. Ted Jorgenson and Alan Thornton were ready for me.

'Are you as stupid as ever?' they wanted to know. We were all in grade seven now. . . .

Louey Marsh, the new schoolteacher, couldn't abide me; the feeling was mutual.

I handed her an envelope Mum had given me containing my birth certificate on the first day I returned to school.

'What is your name?' she asked.

'Patricia Jean Smith,' I replied. 'I am usually called Jean.'

'Smith?' she said. 'Smith?' Looking down at the birth certificate in her hand. I have never seen this, it was always sealed by Mum before she handed it to me.

'Smith?' she asked again.

A fear grabbed me and my heart shook. 'Smith is my name, isn't it?' I appealed to the kids, who of course remembered me.

'Yes,' they chorused. 'That's her name.'

I was still standing in front of the teacher's desk; she had not allotted me a place.

'So this is the clever little girl?' said this strange woman, attacking again. I was very frightened, but I stared straight back at her and said, 'Yes.'

She was extremely angry about that, and fear of her and rage at her battled within me. Goodness knows what she had been told about me.

I had never met a teacher like this one. At Caldermeade we'd had a man who would chase the boys up and down the aisles between the desks lashing at them with a strap of leather as they ran. This woman was coldly, surely insanely, cruel. Not for her the temper of heat.

I wrote a note on my slate later to Ted Jorgenson.

'Is she always mad?'

'Yes,' he wrote back. 'She takes a fit and hates a person. She hates anyone clever like Dorothy Fowler.'

In a matter of hours I saw clearer evidence of this when she went directly to the frail child and hit her across chilblain-covered legs. This girl had the worst chilblains I ever saw, and I saw plenty because many children seemed to suffer with them in those days. Mostly they occurred on the hands only, but Dorothy had them on her legs, and her poor feet were so swollen with them that they wouldn't fit into shoes. To protect the broken sores her mother bound her feet into an old pair of felt slippers that had belonged to an adult.

When the teacher hit her Dorothy just stood and stared, petrified. Big tears rolled silently down her cheeks.

'Put out your hands,' the teacher said.

Instead of putting them out the girl lifted them dully in front of her eyes, the hands covered with fingerless mittens, the fingers sticking out of the ends like blue sausages marbled, repulsive. Perhaps, as sometimes happens with bad chilblains, the pain was so intense that they were numb and dead.

'Put out your hands,' the woman said again. We were all watching, silent. Suddenly, quietly, Ted Jorgenson stood up.

'I'll take them,' he said.

It was the time-honoured rule that if an older child offered to take the cuts for a younger the offer must be accepted. Miss Marsh gave Ted ten of the best for his chivalry.

Children have great loyalty to a teacher; perhaps it is more to the dedicated profession they represent than the individual. We did not tell our parents about Louey Marsh, but we spoke about her calmly among ourselves without any of the rancour most teachers receive at some time in their career from thoughtless children. We knew this woman was sick. Mostly we supported one another against her, sometimes she made sure this would not be possible. She provided sweets for the whole school once to ensure their alienation from Kevin and me.

We two were the only Catholics at the school. This day a minister of religion came out from Numurkah to give instruction to the children. Because our parents had ordered us not to attend this class Louey Marsh sent Kevin to empty the two lavatory pans, and me to scrub the seats of the boys' and girls' lavatories. Before the other kids could rally to our defence she announced, 'A lolly scramble for the Bible class!' She knew that many of those children had sweets only at Christmas and would not be able to resist her bribe.

It was still the 1930s, a time when men were on top of the world today and in the bankruptcy court tomorrow.

At Waaia when the effects of the Depression hit people we were surprised. At Monomeith we saw the effects regularly as men from the country jumped the rattler heading down to the Big Smoke to look for work and men from the city headed for the country, equally sure there must be work there for willing hands. Waaia being on the track to nowhere, no one came through looking for work. Men merely left the place. But the Depression took its toll here as everywhere, and this affected us all as every man was part of the whole life in this small, isolated community. . . .

One Saturday going into Numurkah on the Casey, Dad saw the car of a friend of ours near a bridge and slowed down, thinking to have a talk with the man. Then he saw our friend . . . and revved the motor up fast, hoping Mum had not seen what he had seen, and went on into the town to report to the police that Reg Dillon was lying dead beneath the bridge with a rifle barrel in what was left of his mouth.

That night at home, Dad said, 'If a man could only have a mate to talk to at these times. It's a mate you need for just those few moments when there seems to be no other way out. But such is life.'

The next blow fell very close. Kevin Young's family went bank-rupt. 'Just like that,' the grown-ups repeated over and over again. We children couldn't understand. We stared in disbelief at their colonial-style home and solid British-made furniture that Mum had told us was now seized and would be sold. We wandered through their garden with its trellises weighed down by vines under which we would lie and eat grapes in the cool of the night while our parents sat in canvas chairs relaxing after the heat of the day. There were the chicken hatcheries and the poultry pens that housed thousands of laying hens—sidelines to wheat-buying—where we'd watched chickens hatch and gathered eggs with the workmen, and the gristing mill where each morning Kevin's father would process the newly garnered wheat into meal for the morning's porridge.

All this was to go under the hammer. Kevin and I walked dis-consolately round the places we loved. The front of the house had been a shop before the wheat-buying became big business, and the size and wealth of that new business were evident in the stock still left in the store which there had been no need to realise on when the golden grain brought such a fortune. Kevin and I played shop there and sold to one another rolls and reels of ribbons and laces and broderie anglaise, cottons, needles and tins of goods. There were scales for weighing things, counters with rulers let into them to measure materials, a till that 'pinged' when we put our cardboard money in it. Now this would all go.

We went over to the workman's cottage empty beside the bamboo plantation; we had used this as a make-believe home whenever it was unoccupied, and we wished now to take away and keep a picture we had used to decorate the wall. Kevin held the picture in his hands and as we walked out the cottage door big 'Bull' Marvel grabbed him by the arm.

'Don't try that,' he snarled. 'Trying to sneak things.' He swore at Kevin and called him a dirty name and said his father was no longer the 'big boss cocky'. It was the only time I ever heard anyone speak poorly to that boy. I cried and went home. Dad told me we must forgive 'Bull' his hate because he had never had love, family, a proper home or money to spend.

'These are strange times to be living through,' he said. 'All we can hope to do is lend a hand when someone needs it.' Dad wasn't to know how soon he would need a hand himself and how readily help would be forthcoming because of the many times his own tough, callused hand had stretched out towards others. But this was later.

Kevin at times would be grave with concern for his parents—he could see that they were distressed—but at other times he would be a young boy and forget. One such time was when his mother scolded him.

'I shan't stop with you,' he said. 'I'll go where my friends are.' He packed a bag with pyjamas, a packet of biscuits and his old teddy-bear which he hadn't taken to bed for many a year, and came to us. Mum sent Mickie across to tell Mrs Young he was safe and would bed down at our house. But when it grew dark he began to fidget and then he said, 'I think I'd better have a look and see if Mum and Dad are all right.' And off he went with his bag on his back.

The family were allowed to keep only those things necessary to continue to exist—a bed each and little more. All else must be sold.

'How are things going?' Mrs Young asked Kevin and me when we came inside during the sale, which was held in the grounds.

With the thoughtlessness of children we said, 'Wonderful. They're selling things for almost nothing.' We had seen a cedar cabinet go for five shillings, a chest of drawers the family had brought out from England via India for ten shillings.

'It doesn't matter,' she said. 'Nothing matters.'

They went to Melbourne to look for work. The father, used to employing many men, now took a job as a carpenter's mate and shortly after fell from high scaffolding and broke his neck. Mrs Young, a skilled dressmaker who had done her apprenticeship to the trade in Europe, opened a high-class salon in the city and soon was dressing many of Melbourne's socialites. One night, visiting a friend in hospital, she was knocked over by a car driven by an unlicenced youth and was partly crippled. At that time an outbreak of 'infantile paralysis' was ravaging Australian cities, so Kevin was left to live with us at Waaia until that should ease.

I was twelve. . . .

I still sat between Ted Jorgenson and Alan Thornton, but we had a new teacher. He was a type unknown to us and we distrusted him at first; he didn't hit girls! And he encouraged us to read—even to read newspapers—and to enter sports contests with other schools. He bought us a radio with Mothers' Club money so that we could listen to Schools Broadcasts which were then only beginning.

Soon I idolised him. He opened up for me a new world of learning—*and* under his guidance I won my first race. . . .

Ted and Alan still gave me larry-dooley.* I was twelve and they were fourteen years old and we were all going to sit for the Merit exam. Their size and weight made me defer to them, my size and weight led them to bully me, but when the day came for us to go to another little bush school to do the exam we were all equal in our nervousness. Alan Thornton drove the three of us in the shay-cart his family came to school in, and we put our lunch bags under the flap, jogged off and hardly said a word the whole way.

Three weeks later the results came back. We had all passed. Ted and Alan would leave school and go to work. I wanted to learn much more.

'What is there to learn now?' said the boys. 'We've got our Merit.'

---

* Rough teasing. Ed.

I had sat for three scholarships and was awarded all three. '[Not until] my dying day,' Mum said as I stamped out, laughing hard, shouting, 'I don't care! I didn't want them anyway!' because I never let anyone know when I was hurt beyond speech, 'Till my dying day I will never forgive them. The advertisements were lies, all of them. "Free scholarship!" Now she's won them they tell us they aren't free! She can't go, and they lied.'

It was no use Mr Schmidt telling her that no, the colleges had not lied, but they were totally unaware of the financial straits of a family living on the 'emergency reduction of wages' that had been dropped on wage earners like a threatening hand on 12 February that year.

'Free?' she said. 'And here on the letters they list the costs of uniforms and all the other things.'

'The scholarships are for tuition only,' Mr Schmidt explained.

'But how can a country girl whose father earns £2 19s 4d a week, whose mother gets nothing except the house rent-free for running the station for twelve hours a day six days a week, how can she get uniforms and travel and "the extras" they mention . . . and there's only one of them offers her a bed!' Mum had been loud, but now she became still and silent, staring at the papers spread on the kitchen table; then she spoke so quietly I could hardly hear her. 'She won't be able to go and she's tried and tried. How can they . . . the thing is, they don't know how people are hanging on out here in the bush. They don't know about us.'

Out at the stunted-for-water nectarine tree I heard the terrible noise begin, the deep sobbing that would humiliate her to have been caught in front of anyone at all. The teacher came out. 'You should go to your mother.' He put his arm around my shoulder and it felt like a log. 'Her hurt is as bad as yours.'

Mum stopped crying when I came in and turned on me in frustration. All the hard years, the pride in never letting on that they were hard years, boiled over. 'You and your Little Miss-Muck scholarships!'

I took the papers from the kitchen table, tore them up and threw the pieces in the wood-fire stove. 'I didn't want to go to their flash schools anyhow!'

This new teacher had made my mind sit up and look around for the first time. Perhaps I might even . . . I whispered and the teacher had to bend to hear . . . perhaps even the university . . . then I became embarrassed and pretended that I hadn't meant it and was fooling; I hadn't heard those words spoken in any school I had attended; I hadn't known what one could do in a university until this teacher told me of the open, unfenced plain of learning one could embark on there. But to blurt out that I of all people wanted to go—they'd all laugh at me for sure.

'University!' said Mr Schmidt. 'University?' He looked unseeing at me, thinking.

Then, 'Yes, why not! You can do it. You do it and take all of us along with you, because you'll do correspondence lessons here at the school.'

When the first lessons arrived everyone in the school crowded round to have a look. The first papers to be taken out of the package were the French lessons. That fixed it. I was a scholar.

Mr Schmidt looked at the programme to see when the French lessons were broadcast. I sat staring at the radio. The voice was speaking slowly, loudly, but I had no idea what it was saying. The other kids giggled at the alien sound of the voice, but naturally I didn't, I was a scholar! And I was learning French! The truth of the matter is that as time went by I learnt to read and write the language a little, but to this day I can neither 'hear' nor speak it, this being the fault, I believe, of learning by eye and not at all by ear.

Learning at an advanced stage by correspondence is not easy. The teacher helped me when he could, but his first consideration must be to his eight school curriculum grades, and sometimes weeks would pass and he'd not be able to spare time for me. The great benefit of doing the lessons in a schoolroom was the timetable and the enforced silence which one could not get in one's own home. A drawback to the whole scheme was the mailing of work for corrections. This week's work might not be returned until the week after next, by which time I'd be busy with a different problem and would have no interest in the work I'd done so long ago, not even to look at the corrections.

Because of the drawbacks of this system of learning I was told that an extra year of study would be added onto my time before I could take the Leaving for matriculation. Correspondence education is not the best means of gaining knowledge, but when there is nothing else it is the very best. . . .

This year summer came in with a blast like an open oven door. Swaggies limped by, sweat staining the backs of their shirts where the swag rubbed. Often before they came up to the house seeking hot water for their billies they would rest for a time under the shade of the big gum in our horse paddock where Sylvia and I had met the day we played swaggies. One said to my mother as she boiled water for his billy, 'You can trace my footsteps from here to Cunnamulla, missus. There's not been a breath of wind nor a drop of rain for twelve months to wipe them out.' Birds came in wearily to rest in the drooping greenery of our pepper-corn trees. On Sundays when we must study our catechisms we would sit under those trees and the birds would nosey down to see what we were doing. Now they perched listlessly, their chattering only half the volume it was in the days of rain showers. The only breeze we got was an occasional willy-willy that swirled the red dust round covering everything and creeping in everywhere. That Christmas a small freak shower came out of the blue cloudless sky and disappeared within minutes leaving the sky blue and cloudless as before. . . .

January continued hot. The stillness and heat were sombre. The rail men made inspection runs back along the line after each steam train passed to ensure that no errant spark could start a fire. The wheat was golden and tinder-dry. The grass on the side of the line was the same. The men were trying to burn it off, working mostly at night.

For four days in succession the thermometer read 105 in the shade. On that fourth day Dad lay on the track with his broken face resting on the rail that now seared flesh, his poor shattered body exposed to this killing heat. Five hours passed before his unconscious body was found.

He had been home late before, but this night he wasn't ten minutes overdue when Mum began to fidget. 'Go and see if your father's trike's in the shed,' she said to me. No, there was no sign of him. 'You might just look up the line and see if he's coming.' But he wasn't coming. In a while, 'Go and put your ear to the rail. See if you can hear anything.' There was no sound or vibration in that blistering, mirage-washed heat. 'He isn't coming,' I reported.

Mum set our tea for us and left to walk a few miles of the track in case he had broken down. It was too late to phone Nathalia or Picola railway stations, in the direction from which he should be travelling home. The stations would be closed and the phones could not be heard from the houses. It was 8 P.M. when Mum came back, alone. We sensed the despair in her. 'It's nearly dark. He should be home.' She sent us girls to the hotel to tell them there that Dad wasn't home. 'Then he's in trouble,' Dalton Beswick said. 'I'll get the truck cranked up. Get your mother and we'll look for him.'

His truck . . . was a 1924 model and Mick and I stood on the tray at the back, hanging on to the top of the cabin while Mum sat in front with Dalton. The road ran level with the rail track and he steered the truck with one hand and beamed a flashlight across on the rails with the other. Six miles further on the headlights of a car approached us. 'That's them,' said Mum. 'Who?' 'They've found him,' she replied with certainty. 'Pull up.' She walked across to the other car as it came abreast of us, and the driver guessed who she would be. 'Hop in, Mrs Smith,' he said. Then he got out and came across to Dalton. 'Take her kids home,' he said. 'He won't go for an hour or so yet, so she mightn't be home till morning.'

'As bad as that?' Dalton asked.

'They're putting the pieces of his trike into sugar-bags.'

Dalton knew we heard. He sat us in the front of the truck with him. He did things on the way home in an attempt to make us forget what we had heard. He sang, whistled, drove fast, drove slow, silly things to keep our numbed thoughts from that solid iron and hardwood motor-trike that was now fragmented and bundled into sugar-bags. At the hotel he put us to bed and made lumpy cocoa. 'You don't want to worry,' he said. 'You don't want to worry.' But he was only seventeen and he was crying too, so he put the lamp out and left us.

All the next day Mick and I had no word. I had never communicated easily, neither had she. Now we couldn't ask if he were still alive and no one thought to tell us. I prayed and Mick prayed and when we finished our gentle pleading entreaties I continued savagely in silence: 'If You kill him I'll kill You.' . . .

Five weeks after he was carried in Dad opened his one remaining eye and said, 'Hello, Birdie. How long have I been here?' For answer she laid her head beside his and thanked God over and over again.

All the while he had been unconscious little had been done to mend his broken body. At first they waited for him to die. Then it was all they could do to keep him alive. Now the Railways Department at their own expense sent up a Melbourne specialist. This man examined him and thought it might be worth an attempt to get him to Melbourne for a series of operations. . . .

The engine-driver looked in and said, 'We'll take it easy, mate, you'll be right.' Then the steam whistle blew on the engine and the train began to jolt slowly forward. . . .

Dad stayed in hospital in Melbourne for six months and came home walking, sane and with two sighted eyes. His absent eye was discovered undamaged beneath his cheekbone. To us he looked wonderful. Like the lovers in the enchanted cottage who could not see one another's defects we were so happy to be together again that we didn't notice any change in his looks.

There was change we did notice. Dad couldn't work. The Railways Department allowed Mum to stay on as station-mistress. Her wage was fifteen shillings a week with the house rent-free. She tried to keep out of debt. The piano was still being paid-off.

'Let it go,' the relatives urged her. 'Why put yourself in debt for *her*?' That was me.

'We'll manage,' Mum said. . . .

I had not been confirmed in the Church and as I was twelve years old the time was ripe for this 'giving of the Holy Ghost'. This ceremony was so important and we were so far from religious instruction that it was decided I should be cared for at the convent in Numurkah and attend classes there. This came to be one of the happiest periods of my life.

The convent at Numurkah was not a boarding school but merely a large house wherein lived the nuns who taught at the day school there. I had a wonderful time with them and I think they had the same with me. . . .

Far from having to hide books, here they were thrust on me. I read every spare minute and I had plenty.

'A most intelligent little girl,' the nuns told the priest when he called to see how I was getting along. 'Reads all day.' Rarely can starvation have been mistaken for intelligence as it was here.

The ordered days were a delight. At 6 A.M. a nun would come into my room and touch my cheek, begin a prayer and leave the room when my sleepy voice took over from her. The nuns filed down the corridor to their chapel for prayers, smiling at me as they passed. Out in a vestibule on a tray a glass of warm milk awaited me before a radiator, my book lay on the table ready for me to read until breakfast was served. . . .

At last confirmation day was upon me. The night before I'd had a bath, washed my hair and gone into the chapel to pray and had put on the light and startled out of their wits the six nuns who were praying there in the dark. Hot with embarrassment I knelt there, not knowing whether to turn off the light or leave it on. Old Mother Superior solved that by coming to me and putting her arm round my shoulders.

'You'll get your death of cold in here after a hot bath,' she said. 'Come and I'll tuck you into your bed.'

'But I haven't said my rosary.'

'Say it in bed then.'

Mum would never believe me if I told her that! . . .

How Mum must have scraped and done without herself to do this for me . . . a white silk dress, white stockings and black patent leather shoes with big silver buckles, white tulle veil and coronet of flowers. When the sponsor stood behind me, her hand on my shoulder, I was asked the name of the patron saint I had chosen. Because I'd been away from home and no one had remembered to prepare me for this.

'Bridget,' I said, without hesitation, my mother's real name. . . .

Not for a year did Mum speak to me of the things my grandmother had ordered her to speak of. Then she began diffidently, her words becoming muddled.

'I know,' I interrupted her, 'I know.' I walked out the kitchen door. She followed me.

'How do you know?'

'I've always known,' I lied.

She didn't speak of it again for a long time. Then, one day when I was cornered in the kitchen and couldn't get past her without actually pushing her away:

'Do you know who your parents are?'

'Of course.'

'You don't.'

I stared at her insolently, hoping to stop her. But she wouldn't stop.

'Don't you ever wonder?'

'No.' I had thought of it a little since that night, more in rage at their intrusion in my life and between Mum and Dad and me than from any desire to know them.

'You see your mother occasionally. She is one of my sisters.'

I wasn't interested. Mum thought this was a ruse, but it wasn't. I just didn't care.

'Blood is thicker than water,' Mum said. Fearfully she looked at me. 'Sometimes I've wondered if you haven't felt attracted to her rather than to me. It would be natural. Blood is thicker than water. Think of your aunts. Isn't there one you feel kin to?'

No, there wasn't. Suddenly: 'Not Auntie . . . ?' I mentioned the one I was not particularly fond of.

'No.'

Thank goodness!

'She is one of my younger sisters.'

Good. It must be Aunt Sadie. I liked her tartness and incisive brain. She drove a semi-trailer in a trucking business with her husband.

So I tried to look casual. 'Is it Aunt Sadie?'

No, it wasn't. Mum was bewildered. 'I was sure you would know your own mother,' she said.

I longed to tell her not to be silly, that she was my mother. When she spoke the name of the woman who had borne me it moved me not at all.

'Oh, her,' I said.

'She and your real father,' Mum began, but I had heard enough and I pushed her aside and ran past her.

'If you want to get rid of me then I'm big enough to go,' I called back, cruelly, so she would realise she must say no more. She never mentioned it to me again. All I knew of my father were the barbed remarks I could remember from the past. I realised now that it was his decision not to spend the rest of his life with this family that made me, his child, the target for the barbs. I didn't care what he had done, whether it had been right or wrong; my only regret was that I had to know of it at all.

It was this knowledge and the constant whispering and the knowing looks whenever learning, art, music or books were mentioned that ended my childhood and made me uncertain for so long, made me look for love and affection when all the time I had it more than most will ever know. I remembered with hate the schoolteacher Louey Marsh hesitating over the name on my birth certificate: I had sensed something amiss that day; I was embarrassed when I thought of the kindness of that good man Kelly and his gang, at Nowingi, to the strange baby their mate had brought home; I thought of the many times I had been cruel and hurtful to Mum and Dad, taking for granted that I could hurt them because they were my parents; I thought of the times I'd complained to out-siders about Mum's restrictions, been disloyal to her.

As for religion, I no longer was fettered by it. I had striven to learn liturgical Latin in an endeavour to more fully participate in the service. But now I recalled a remark my crabbed aunt had passed, 'You and your fancy Latin. You're not even entitled to be a Catholic.' (*He* wasn't; whispers made it clear that he was a Freema-son.) Now I thought of that remark as a passport to freedom. I was not bound to anything. I was free. I felt so free I longed for the chains of belonging to bind me tight again; but it was too late. I had fallen too hard.

'The bigger they are the harder they fall,' Dad used to shout above the noise of the Casey Jones on our Saturday morning trips. All the wheels of all the trains on all the journeys we had made never sounded so loud as the turmoil within my head.

Dad began work again, but the heat of Waaia was too much for him and we must move to a cooler climate. This time we knew we were leaving Waaia forever. Mum went to her packing with a sto-lidity that was unusual in her.

'I think we'll have to get on with it, Birdie,' Dad had to gently remind her the day the trucks arrived at the siding to take on our goods. She wandered about, talking of the times we'd all sat up through the night with half our neighbours in the lounge listening to the Test match being played in England, amazed that we could hear such a thing from the other side of the world.

'Of course, it's all for the best,' she said brightly. We knew she didn't mean it any more than we did.

On my last day at school the fourteen children presented me with a crystal powder bowl. I have never used it for fear that it might break.

'Goodbye, dreamer,' Mr Schmidt wrote on the card. 'Don't let them stop you from that. You're never beaten while you've a dream.' . . .

The presentation to my parents in the Waaia hall was gay with music and dancing. Old Bill Leaf presented Dad and Mum with a most elegant canteen of cutlery and said that it was like seeing the horse-drawn wagons leave the roads to see the Smiths go from Waaia.

'You'll not be forgotten at Waaia,' he said. 'And we know you will not forget Waaia.'

They had us stand in the middle of the hall and they all stood about us in a circle and joined their hands.

'Oh no . . .' Mum said. They had already started to sing those words that must have wrenched more hearts than any others: 'Should auld acquaintance be forgot . . .' I didn't know till then why people weep when it is sung.

Next day the platform was crowded with people to watch the Smiths go. A royal send-off for a railway fettler and his family. We travelled in the guard's van; all our furniture was in the trucks ahead on the long goods train. At the last moment Mum remembered some instruction she had meant to leave for the new station-mistress who would come on the morrow; the fettlers came into the van for a last word with old Nip in his box with bars across the front.

The driver and guard didn't bustle us, but the time came when we must go. As the train began to roll, Bill Leaf on the platform called, 'Three cheers for Albert and family. Hip hip . . .' We waved from the windows in the van till they were out of sight. We had scarcely sat down when an explosion went off under the wheels, then another and another, bang bang bang as the wheels ran over the rails. It was detonators, used normally by the men to warn the guard of danger on the line. Now they put them along the track to farewell their mate on his way.

Penshurst is in the Western District, a stony land twenty miles from Hamilton. This was the last part of our continent to settle down, and rocks from the time of upheaval haven't yet decayed. They lie around in such profusion that stone walls, houses, public buildings and miles of stone fences have been made with them. Penshurst itself grew up beside the crater of a dead volcano, Mount Rouse. It was quite a big town by the standards of anywhere else we had lived. . . .

I went along to the local State school. It was a big school, at least eighty children; a frightening rabble it seemed to me, used as I was to a maximum of twenty schoolmates. The headmaster could offer me no more than a desk if I wished to do correspondence lessons here.

I went home. 'I'd never learn quickly enough there.' . . .

Money seemed scarcer than ever here, because of course there was more to spend it on. I went out to work. I was fourteen. At first I kept the books and did the accounts of a butcher, and in this way learnt the practical application of accounting; but such work could not fill my day now. As though smitten by some disease that gnawed the walls of the mind, exciting it to take in more and more, I applied myself to the limit. Calmly I set about studying whatever was available to me, without actually speaking of this to anyone, yet my urgency was such that it was conveyed to others. All sorts of people, unasked, offered to help me.

The town's policeman offered to teach me typing.

'I use two fingers,' he said, 'but I did learn to touch-type once and I'll teach you.'

Then I wanted to learn shorthand. 'I can't remember any of it, but I'll learn it again as I teach you,' he offered. Each day at 5 P.M. I'd tramp to the police station and apply myself to this dullest of all trades taught to women but, as I knew, one of the few occupations in business open to them.

The local priest offered to teach me Latin, surely the most beautiful of all languages. On Saturday mornings I'd cycle up to him for a two-hour lesson.

The correspondence lessons still came and these I did at night.

I had been learning music in a desultory manner for years from anyone who set up to be a teacher, but I had never had a good tutor. We had been at Penshurst for a few weeks only when Mum came hurrying home from a Progress Association meeting.

'There's an excellent teacher comes here once a week,' she told me. 'I'll send you to her.'

Madame Sherman was not only talented, she was a fanatic. Music was her whole life.

'You'd better learn the violin too,' she told me. 'It will give you a wider appreciation of music.' She lent me a squeaky, cheap violin and each morning and evening as well as most of each weekend I practised these two instruments. (We had no near neighbours.) Under this musical martinet I sat the exams of the Music Examinations Board, the London College of Music and the Trinity College of London, gaining diplomas from them all for the piano and advanced passes for the violin and theory. In one month, May 1939, I sat for and passed five examinations. I was as indefatigable as Madame. We punished one another with our perseverance and labour.

Because the work I had begun was tedious and because I wanted to earn more money than the fifteen shillings a week offered for book-keepers, as well as wanting to have more time to study, I set up in business on my own, a freelance you might say. Mum advanced me the money for a secondhand typewriter and with this I tendered to do the monthly accounts of three shops—two butchers and a baker. I arranged that I was to work when and for as long as I pleased so long as I had the accounts out by the first of each month. At 'peak' periods such as Friday nights and Christmas week I worked for a news agent, a fine chinaware shop and served at the bakery.

But the best means of earning money was playing in the dance band. The New Mayfair Dance Band was, when I was invited to join, composed of four cool sophisticated male musicians. I still wore my school clothes, my hair was dressed in shoulder-length curls, I wore cotton stockings and lace-up shoes. Our engagements were usually only on Saturday nights at the local hall, but during the shearing season we'd get several bookings from the shearing shed for 'cut out' dances, the social event of the sheep country year, held in the cleaned-up shed to celebrate the end of the shearing on each station. Dressing was formal, the women in floor-length gowns, and a certain distinction was lent by the presence of an 'official party' consisting of the matron of the local hospital (to which proceeds from the dance were donated), the doctor, squatters and their wives, a bank manager or two and the local councillors. But all this respectability could not dampen a shearers' hop and it was the bales of wool set around the walls for seats that set the atmosphere for the evening. Sometimes they danced until dawn. We were paid to play until 2 A.M.

The first 'cut out' ball I played at was in a shearing shed near Coleraine. At 2 A.M. the shearers decided the evening had only then begun so they started to take the hat around.

'We must keep the orchestra,' they said.

When the hat came to him, a smart 'gun' said, 'Aw, b-that!' and slapped a ten-shilling note on top of the old piano. Half a dozen followed suit. The little pile of money shook and trembled there near me all the while I played. At the end of the long night we musicians would share it. I knew I would have at least £2 to take home to Mum.

These young musicians were kind to me. Although my mother insisted on my appearing dressed as a child (as indeed I was), these boys knew I was dance-mad and when they'd see a young shearer look at me they'd call to him, 'Why don't you ask her for a dance?' and they'd play while I danced. But the moment the dance ended they shepherded me back into their midst like clucky hens.

The best shearers were often the best dancers and almost always the best dressed, but they were also likely to be the wildest. Sometimes, dancing by the big, open doors at the end of the shed, you could see white shirt-tails flapping as men fought in the light of the big fire built of tree trunks. One night my partner told me that there were three fights going at the same time and that four of the fighters were 'gun' shearers.*

I was book-keeping, studying piano and violin, learning Latin, taking six school subjects, playing in the dance band and now I took music pupils. I was a good piano tutor, but I was not a meticulous book-keeper and I was constantly employed thinking up quick answers to irate customers. But it was all worth it. One week during which I played with the dance band for two engagements I brought home £6 from my various projects. Mum bought herself a new pair of lace-up corsets and the sight of those formidable stays filled me with pride. . . .

Historians say that the Depression ended before the war broke out, but for the men who needed work the Depression was still on, even if it had ended for the financiers. Dad was a ganger now and we knew how badly men wanted jobs. . . .

The Western District was hard hit at this time. There were no factories here, no mills, few farms. The large sheep stations in the district had permanent staff. Even their rabbit-trappers were permanent. There was nothing here for men looking for work but the dole. . . .

Now that he was out of work again Bob† was free to wander

---

* The speediest and most skillful. Ed.
† The husband of Adam-Smith's half sister. Ed.

the streets, hold up the verandah post of the pub, or wander idly to the billiard room, but he never became apathetic about being unemployed. He was always optimistic: something would turn up. He had a go at anything. He even learnt to knit, and to pay for his keep at home he made clothes for dozens of dolls Mum was dressing for distribution to needy children that Christmas. They were fiddling little dresses, and minute booties and bonnets that tied under the dolls' chins with narrow ribbon. Bob's big, callused hands were clumsy at first, but by the time he was finished every doll was perfect because he unravelled all his work until it was just right and, as he said, the calluses soon disappeared when a man was out of work. He prowled the town every day keeping his eyes and ears open and picked up lots of odd jobs. He was one of the first to hear that a contractor was coming to open up the old quarries to get metal out for a road job. This meant that he was in the first gang to start work there. . . .

Bob had made furniture for the expected baby, a cot and a tiny table and chair all fashioned from packing cases with the rough wood sandpapered so smooth you could rub your hand over it and it felt like silk. But my sister wanted a pram.

'And,' she warned, 'I don't expect to push a packing case on wheels up the street either! I want a proper pram, a bought pram.'

So Bob left home and said he wasn't coming back until he had enough money for a bought pram.

'I'm going rabbiting,' he announced. He took Whacko the dog, Dad's bike and some borrowed traps and disappeared for three weeks. All that was visible when he returned was his face grinning in triumph; the rest of him was rabbit skins, bike and all, skins strung inside out on wire frames.

They went up to town the next day, Bob with his skins bound tightly in a bundle, Mick to wait at the post office until he returned with the money. Then they would buy the pram. We watched them go, laughing like the kids they were, Bob teasing Mickie that he could not walk with his arm around her waist any more because she no longer had a waist, and she laughingly threatening to box his ears. After they had gone a little way they held hands. They looked good. Their happiness in one another and the whole world around them that day came back to us watching them go up the road to buy the pram.

I had not truly seen the face of the Depression until I saw those two coming home that day. The Depression was something that had happened to other people, not us, I thought. But its ugly face came down that road with those two who didn't look like kids any more. Bob didn't hold Mickie's hand, they didn't even walk side by side. Instead, Bob strode out, hands in pockets, intent it seemed on the straggly gums at the roadside. Mickie was walking a few paces ahead of him, striding out a little faster than him, even though she was pregnant, and she was whistling. She looked 'brassy', as we used to call cheap girls then. Mum and Dad and I stood at the kitchen window watching them come.

'What does that girl think she's up to?' Mum said disapprovingly, and she pushed up the window to tell my sister to behave herself. Dad stopped her.

'Leave them alone,' he said. 'Come away from the window. Don't let them know we've been watching for them.' Dad knew what had happened.

'I reckon the dealers wouldn't buy Bob's skins. I thought they mightn't. He had them pegged out wrongly.'

Buyers could pick and choose in a period when it seemed that every second man in creation was out rabbiting. . . .

He was resigned, but resignation and unbounded optimism can go hand in hand when you're young—along with high spirits. The high spirits of him and a score of other young dole boys in the town bubbled up in April of that year, 1939, when they crept out at midnight and decorated the war memorial on Anzac eve with cabbages they stole from the priest's garden.

'I don't see what the caterwaulin's all about,' the old Irishman said the next day when the 'desecration' was being decried all over town.

'After all, they were my cabbages, and I'm not complaining. If it gave the boys a bit of fun, surely they get little enough of it.'

I wonder if any of the citizens of that little town ever look at the new names on the ugly little stone memorial and remember the boys who prematurely decorated their own tombstone that year with cabbages. Bob's name is there now and Gus Schramm's too, and numbered among the other names are most of the lads who drew the dole with Bob in those other hungry years. . . .

It was the evening of Sunday, 3 September. We sat in front of the fire listening to the radio. The old wireless with the big flower-like trumpet had gone; this was the latest model. But we had never listened so intently, not even when we listened to our first broadcast back in the old days.

All afternoon Dad had sat in the house waiting for this. He said abruptly when we began to fool, 'Keep quiet!' Mick and Bob were visiting and we sobered, hearing Dad severe one of the few times in our lives. Then the message came through. The static crackled but the words were clear. We were at war.

Not one of us spoke until after the playing of 'God Save the King' had ended. They had never done that before. In a play or speech, whenever he heard the call 'Three cheers for the King!' Dad would grin and we knew he was thinking of his navy days when the traditional lower-deck reply was 'Bugger the King!' Now he stood for the playing of the anthem, leaning on the mantelpiece, looking into the fire so that it would not seem affected.

I was growing up and life was now, not later, and right now there was to be a Sunday dance in the church hall and Dad had promised to take me for a short while. Now there was no doubting by the way he stood that we were not going.

Mickie broke the silence: 'They'd never take married men.'

Bob sat on the arm of her chair. 'It's a job,' he said, his voice serious, but his eyes betraying him. All the boredom, the lethargy and despondency had gone. They scintillated with excitement.

Bob and his mates were standing at the street corner the following day when the newspaper truck came in. They had heard the announcement on the radio, but this was different. The written word was the seal to the statement and there it was, on the poster on the side of the truck. One word. War.

Within a month there was hardly a young man left in the town. The boys were all 'jumping the rattler' in one direction now: Bob and his mates were on their way to the city to enlist.

Many of Australia's Sixth Division men had been on the dole. That's the way Bob and the boys like him got their first really permanent job.

In my own private world that I had thought was all the world I had been muddling on. Now there was no need for decisions. I was sheathed with patriotism. I had heard the band play and like the soldier who had spoken at that Anzac Day commemoration which I had been thrashed for attending, I had fallen in behind the music.

I would go to this war. Even to bob and float in the little whorls and eddies on the perimeter of this holocaust would be adventure enough to make my nameless, faceless fears insignificant.

To my already numerous occupations were added first-aid and home-nursing lectures and four hours a week working as nurses' aide in the local hospital. I had joined the VADs* and must have a first-aid and a home-nursing certificate as well as one hundred hours' nursing experience before I could enlist. I liked the hospital training although it consisted mainly of 'Shut your eyes and tip', advice from the training sister on the task which was for the next three years to be almost my entire contribution to the war effort— emptying pans and bottles. . . .

One obvious snag to my enlisting was my age or, to be more precise, my lack of age. This was overcome quite simply by coaxing Mum to sign the permission for me to join up and filling in the details later, in private.

'But will they take girls so young?' my mother asked. I was nearly seventeen.

'Oh yes,' I assured her. 'Look at the civilian hospitals. They had me training there.'

And then I was off, heading for Spencer Street, weighted down with the accoutrements of that war I'd not given a moment's thought to except as its being a vehicle by which I might escape from the turmoil in my mind. My peace did not come in a flash, a moment of light like the opening of a third eye. Rather, confidence stole back into me in its own sweet, meandering time. But this day saw the beginning of it as we jostled on that crowded platform.

We were not a homogeneous group yet; we hadn't rid ourselves of the secret life each of us had left behind, but we had one binding thing in common: we belonged to Australia, to the very soil of Australia. Half the population still lived in rural areas, the bush; the other half, though urban, was rural-minded, knew that the country still rode on the sheep's back, that our wealth came from what our land and our men made together. Whatever we were, the soil had made us. In the first world war and now this one, Australia had sent away armies notorious for their lack of discipline but famous for the bush-bred initiative that makes formal discipline unnecessary.

---

* Auxiliary women's medical service. Ed.

We were all here on this train, every one of us, but the drift to the cities had already begun and Australia would never see the likes of us again. If patriotism was only sheathed on me until that day it commenced now to grip my marrow.

'Do you know Spencer Street railway station?' the kindly matron had asked. Surely. It was my stamping ground, the city arena where we'd swaggered in pride in being bush-bred. Mothers soothe a fretful child with play-talk: 'Hear the train blow, love?' imitating the whistle of a steam engine. But me, I'd heard the real train blow, and spent a childhood steeped in the essence of all those things that condense and issue forth from the banshee-like wail of roaring, rushing engines. I'd slept twelve feet from the rails, heard the wheels crunch by like nailed boots crossing my bedroom floor, listened to the whistle shrieking and fading past our many outback homes, houses made into homes because wherever Mum and Dad got off the wallaby was home to us. . . .

Dorothy Hewett

(1923–   )

Dorothy Hewett, poet, playwright, and novelist, was born in Perth, Western Australia, the daughter of prosperous landowners and merchants. With the major wealth in the family in the hands of her maternal grandmother, Hewett grew up in a setting in which she saw female authority as often corrupt, especially as she became a pawn in a battle for control between her grandmother and her physically abusive mother.

Attending university in Perth in the early 1940s, Hewett's strong literary and artistic interests flowered through her contact with modernism, but her emotional life centered on a series of affairs culminating in attempted suicide. Early marriage and commitment to the Communist Party provided an escape from what she saw as the mindless affluence of her family, giving her a cause to serve and the puritanical codes of the Australian Communist Party to embrace.

Within a few years of marriage and motherhood Hewett abandoned her lawyer husband and their child for a common-law union with Les Flood, a Party member, and, to her, the authentic working-class hero her Party teachers had taught her to admire. Thereafter, she gave up creative writing to serve as a hack-journalist and Party-organizer in Sydney, until the union with Flood began to unravel as his moods deteriorated into paranoia and physical violence. Desperate to earn money to support herself and the three children she had with Flood, Hewett began writing again, producing her first successful novel, *Bobbin Up,* in 1959.

From 1959 her pent-up creative energies were released to produce nine volumes of poetry, written in a confessional romantic and occasionally bawdy mode. Alongside her poetry her extensive dramatic oeuvre is concerned with a romantic quest for identity, beginning with a naturalistic treatment of everyday Australian themes, and moving on to expressionism and an eclectic use of symbol. In both her novels and plays the dominating figures are female, bitch-goddesses or earth mothers in the conventional style of the 1950s but with an easy sensuality which is uniquely Hewett's and which prefigures later feminist interest in the explicit treatment of female sexuality.

Wild Card is a narrative which opens with a lyrical evocation of Hewett's native Western Australian wheat-farming landscape balanced by a more sinister depiction of the emotional dynamics of her family. An equally poetic but more somber depiction of bourgeois life in Perth follows before Hewett settles into more connected narrative as she describes her university years and subsequent political and personal history. The structure of the life-history is romantic, told in terms of the narrator's sexual history, with only very occasional moments of insight into her life seen from the point of view of an independent intellectual or creative artist. The story is a chilling depiction of the emotional and intellectual trap which left-political circles represented for Australian women, so chilling that the reader rejoices when Flood's abusiveness finally pries the too-willing-to-be-victimized heroine from her demon lover.

WILD CARD:
An Autobiography, 1923–1958

The first house sits in the hollow of the heart, it will never go away. It is the house of childhood become myth, inhabited by characters larger than life whose murmured conversations whisper and tug at the mind. Enchanted birds and animals out of a private ark sail out on tides of sleep, howling, whistling, mewing, neighing, mooing, baaing, barking, to an endless shimmer of wheat and cracked creek beds. Through the iron gate on the edge of Day's paddock we enter the farm, and drive past the giant she-oak split in two by a strike of lightning. The house lies in the bend of two creeks. The sheepdogs are barking from the verandahs. Beyond is the stable yard with the well in the centre where you let down the bucket to bring up fresh clear water. Large animals move there, draught horses big as the Spanish Armada champing forever at mangers full of oats, licking at rock salt, or rolling ridiculously in grey sand, hoofs waving in air. Liquid or wild-eyed, the cows file into the cow bails with curled horns and names like Strawberry, Buttercup and Daisy. The sheep jostle together in the pens, the kelpie running and snapping across their backs. The sun reflects off the corrugated iron of the shearing shed till it tilts and topples, crazy as a glasshouse. In the chaff house it makes eyes that glitter and run like mice across the floor. . . .

Near the high-wire stable gate are the murderous gallows, dripping blood and fat, where the sheep hang with their throats cut. On the other side of the gate is the blacksmith's shop with the grinder and the forge and the black anvil shooting sparks, the floor littered with curls of wood shavings. We hang them over our ears like Mary Pickford. On the left is the ant-heap tennis court where I tried to jump the tennis net and broke my arm and had to be driven fourteen miles over bush roads to the local doctor, with a deal splint my father cut from the wood heap bound round my elbow. . . .

The house is ringed with almond and fig trees. In spring the almond blossom falls in white bruised drips on the couch-grass lawn. In summer the twenty-eight parrots crack nuts over our heads till our father goes for the shotgun. At Christmas time we sit on the verandah preparing the nuts for the cake with a silver nutcracker. The twenty-eight parrots flash green and black as they fly away, the nutcracker flashes silver in the sun. . . .

The house is built with two wings, the old house and the new. The old house has two corrugated-iron rooms. In the ramshackle sleepout, my grandparents live in an old iron bedstead with silver balls for decoration. The shelves are made of butterboxes filled with paperbacks, and copies of *Bleak House* and *Little Dorrit,* with the ominous Phiz drawings. . . .

Beside the old sleepout is the little back verandah where the quinces and Jonathan apples are stored to ripen on open wooden shelves. I hide there reading *All Quiet on the Western Front,* and a paperback stolen out of the butterboxes with a cover drawing of a droopy, yellow-haired girl playing the piano, mooned over by a handsome Catholic priest. . . .

In summer we sleep in the big sleepout completely enclosed in flywire so that at night we feel as if we are floating in air above the garden and the quiet orchard, borne away by the call of the mopokes. In the morning we wake to a wash of light, a magpie perched on the clothes prop, a rooster crowing from the chook yard at the bottom of the garden. In the dim light we watch the cured hams swaying from the iron hooks above our heads. . . .

The hall is the best place to be when the temperature hits 114 in the shade. We lie on our bellies on the jarrah boards listening to

In a Monastery Garden, Cavalleria Rusticana, Humoresque and *The Laughing Policeman* on the wind-up His Master's Voice gramophone. Sometimes we play lady wrestlers, or impersonate Two-Ton Tony Galento on the strip of Persian-patterned carpet. . . .

Every spring the magpies nest in the almond tree, raising naked-necked fledglings, their beaks gaping for worms. The tomtit builds its hanging nest and lays three warm speckled eggs amongst dry grass and feathers. A wagtail balances on the top rail of the wire fence hung with dew drops, chirping 'sweet pretty creature'. The drops hang, glisten and slide. The plover nests in the furrows made by the plough. The quail settles down in the long grass over her eggs. The peewits are crying over the wheat. Rain's coming—the black cockatoos sweep down from the rock hill and collect like black rags on the gums. The racehorse goannas are racing through the orchard, switching their tails. A silver-green tree frog leaps into the pink ivy geranium hanging by the tank stand. . . .

In summer the centre of our house shifts from the kitchen to the verandahs. We sit waiting for the Albany Doctor to blow up, rippling the tops of the wattles along the creek, while the voices murmur on and on telling their endless tales of past and present. The trees lift up their roots and come closer to the house to listen. Then legendary characters stalk the Avon Valley, the ghosts of the gold miners on the road to Kalgoorlie with their wheelbarrows, riding, driving their drays, to camp at Split Rock at the bottom of our orchard; Joe Anchor, who lies buried under Joe Anchor's rock at the edge of the farm, was he seaman or drifter? . . .

We lie in the hammock flying out above stars and wind, listening as worlds coalesce, floating us down the avenues of sleep. The houses of childhood all have this mythical quality lost under the mist of time—the wooden house on the shores of the Swan River and the holiday cottage behind the sand dunes on the beach at King George's Sound. . . .

After the harvest, we travel 250 miles to the South Coast and live for two or three months in a tiny cottage of two rooms and a kitchen beside the sea. The landscape is forbidding and melancholy, with black rocks and low dark scrub lit by the occasional gleam of sunlight on granite or wave or sand dune. The places around us have magical names like Torbay, Nornalup, Nannarup and Two People Bay. Lagoon and ocean, seabird and scrub, lonely and deserted, are surrounded by great karri forests where you can drive a car through a hollow tree. . . .

Daughter, sister, lover, wife, mother, grandmother, domestic treasure, I will be suborned into all of these roles (except perhaps domestic treasure; there I am always clumsy and half-hearted), but I have my vocation. It is outside sex, and yet my sex is part of it. It is already fixed, brutal, implacable, complete. There is nothing I can do about it, except to get better at it. It shakes me, seductive as love. Words fall out, I am possessed by them.

It is 1933 and I live at the ends of the earth. This is really another country, all the wenches *are* dead, and I am a misfit, a little girl who will grow up to be a writer, brought up on a wheat and sheep farm at Malyalling via Wickepin, the Great Southern of Western Australia, New Holland, Terra Australis, the Great South Land that the Dutch explorers touched at, blown out of their way to the fabulous spice islands by the Roaring Forties. . . .

There is a Depression. Everybody talks about it. I ask my father what it means, but his explanations don't sound rational. . . .

The farms on our boundaries have been given over to the rabbits and the banks. The farmhouses fall into ruin, the fences sag; as season follows season, the bush takes over. My father says the bankrupt farmers are 'silvertails' who spent their time going to grog parties, playing golf, buying flash cars, and getting off with each other's wives. They have all been punished, working for wages down in Perth, or even, in a hushed whisper, 'on the dole'. . . .

It is my grandmother's heyday. We have liens on crops and farms. We own a cinema in Perth and grocery shops in little wheatbelt towns like Corrigin, Wickepin and Lake Yealering. We will never go broke. It is our reward for industry, thrift, morality and brains. Years later I travel through these towns reading poetry in Country Women's Association halls for Adult Education. Two old men nod sardonically in the front row, 'You're Ted Coade's granddaughter. He was always ready to lend y' money at ten per cent.'

The breath of their irony reaches out over the years. And I suppose he must share the blame. After all, he was her front man. . . .

It's four years since the last time I remember being perfectly happy, coming down the verandah singing between the old farmhouse and the new wing. I compose poems in bed and wake my parents in the middle of the night; patiently they write them down, marvelling, no doubt, that they have produced a swan. They buy me Jean Curlewis on the rules of prosody and try to make me scan. 'Tee dum diddle de dum.' How I resent it. I won't listen to the rules or let them transcribe any more. I will learn to read and write, painstakingly transcribing the lines of copperplate into my copybook.

Now I make up my poems to the drone of the separator out in the wash house, mesmerized by the underground rhythm. But sometimes they flash upon me out in the paddocks miles from home, words, images, lines tumbling out in a frenzy so that I have to run back, gasping for pencil and paper. If my sister is with me she has to remember the lines as I say them, over and over, and pity help her if she doesn't. . . .

The struggle to come to terms with my mother dominated most of my life. Her switches of mood from protective love to destructive hatred bewilder me. I learnt never to trust in her benevolence because it was sure to be followed by persecution.

Often it seems to me I have two mothers. There is the mother who lights the little night-light sweetly singing 'There's a long, long trail awinding into the land of my dreams', and wakes us in the mornings, pulling back the bedroom curtains, with:

Good morning merry sunshine
What made you wake so soon?
As yet the early rising sun
Has not attained his noon

and the mother who calls me 'a great gawk' and, frothing at the mouth, her face red and swollen, beats me with an iron-edged ruler, then clasps me to her sobbing, crying that she is 'a wicked mother to treat her little girl like this'.

These strong, dominating (even domineering) women are perpetually fuming with an excess or energy and nothing satisfactory to use it on. My mother continually admonishes us 'not to get married and have a family if you want to get on'. My grandmother is a shrewd, calculating businesswoman and without her there would have been no family fortune. But in all the years of partnership, her name never appears on the shop awning or the business letters. She is truly, although nobody believes it, 'the silent partner'. . . .

Yet in comparison to most other women of their class and time they are emancipated, unusually powerful because they are financially independent. My grandmother virtually runs the family business. 'If you want to get an answer, go to Mrs Coade. She's the real boss.' So much so that years later the image of her, senile, bewildered, resentful, sitting at the dining-room table with my mother literally guiding her hand while she signed over power of attorney, was never to leave me. Or do I imagine it? Was my grandmother really incapable by then of understanding what was happening to her? And yet I do remember it clearly, my mother's implacable face and some primitive atavistic part of my grandmother that understood only too well that abdication of power.

As the child of wealthy parents, my mother always had her own money, a separate bank account, property and shares. For years my father regularly placed the same pitiful amount of housekeeping money on the table. He had no idea of the real cost of living and she kept it hidden from him, augmenting the weekly sum from her own purse so that he, who had started with a debt of one hundred pounds to my grandfather, went on quietly amassing a considerable fortune of his own.

I take down the photograph of my mother in her wedding gown standing alone. My father always hated having his picture taken and refused to stand beside her for the traditional wedding portrait.

She poses there, uncertain: the round, sweet, vulnerable face, the large hazel eyes, the long Irish upper lip, the dark curling hair. . . .

What have these images to do with the angry overweight woman who loved cream sponges and ham sandwiches and fought a neurotic battle against fat all her life? But then I never knew my mother in those earlier days. Perhaps I don't really know her now.

Marriage destroys her. She has no talent for it, and she married the wrong man anyway. She loves company and talk and outings and travel. She is outgoing and affectionate, while he is almost a recluse, introverted and moody, a bookworm who finds it hard to show his real feelings and can never understand what she finds to do all day 'in town'—mostly window-shopping. . . .

At Lambton Downs I read the Billabong books and wish I had two brothers like Norah of Billabong. My father gets books sent from Perth and reads *The Seven Pillars of Wisdom*. A rogue horse called Jack almost kicks out his eye. He tells us how to walk long distances, stepping out heel to toe, but our mother says it's unladylike and you should point your toe first. She seems to be getting madder. She beats me often now, her face flushed red, her eyes crazy. She is menopausal at only thirty-five, but I don't understand why she hates me. My grandmother beckons me into the sleepout and I try not to go. She has betrayed me too many times already but it is so seductive, the sympathy, the bogus understanding. I know I am being used as a weapon in some deadly struggle, but I seem powerless to control it. Why do I go into the warm double bed smelling of old people? Why do I weep and show her the ruler marks on my arms and legs? . . .

Tea at night, and the men are in from the paddocks. I hear my grandmother's silky voice across the kitchen table: 'You should see what your wife has been doing to your poor little daughter today, Tom. The weals on her legs are terrible.'

I dare not raise my eyes from the mashed potatoes I hate. They stick in my throat.

'What have you been doing?' my father says.

'Nothing.'

I swallow the potato in a burning lump. My mother's terrible eyes are staring at me.

'She's a disobedient girl,' she says.

'She doesn't mean to be, do you, pet?' My grandfather is my friend and ally, the only other blond in the room. Dark, dark, dark, they all sit, relentlessly masticating their food. I try to slip away.

'I'll see you in the bedroom,' hisses my mother. She goes ahead of me, carrying the night-light. She is standing by the dressing-table, her shadow huge on the white walls. The carved heads of the griffins are grinning at me from the doors. The wind blows the curtains in and out, out and in. She is holding a tiny bottle in her hand, full of some brownish liquid. I think of *Alice in Wonderland* and the white rabbit. Her eyes blaze.

'This is poison,' she hisses. 'Tell me what you told Nan or I'll take it now.'

I lunge at her, trying to reach up and snatch it away. She holds it higher and tilts the bottle. Her eyes are watching me.

'And you'll always know you killed your mother,' she whispers.

'No, no!' I scream.

She clamps her broad hand over my mouth. I am struggling in her grasp. 'What did you say?'

I can't speak. I am choking. Why doesn't somebody come?

She takes her hand away. 'Tell me.'

I will tell her anything at all, as long as I don't have to carry this burden of guilt past her grave, because I *am* guilty. I hate my mother. I have sometimes wished she was dead.

'I told her I wished you would die,' I say, and I'm glad to say it, even though it is a lie, because her face is so shocked. She drops me. She stares. I have got through to her at last. 'Get into bed,' she says, through her teeth. I put on my flannel pyjamas. She stands watching like Judgement Day. I hide in the little bed against the wall I sleep in. My sister shares the double bed with my mother under the window. She is angry with me because I've refused to share it too. I can't breathe with big bodies beside me. I must sleep alone. It's my only independence. I wonder if my father feels the same out in his single bed in the sleepout. . . .

I am going out alone with my father to see *The Desert Song* at the Capitol Theatre. I have a toothache, but I'm not going to let on in case I have to stay home. It's almost as if I know that a signpost is about to appear in my life pointing towards a most peculiar destiny for a little bush girl living thousands of miles from the rest of the world.

I sit transfixed as the curtain rises and the Red Shadow, on the Capitol stage, rides out in his crimson cloak, mounted on a real snow-white horse. This, then, is where it has all been leading: the make-up games (as we call them), the dress parades under the salmon gums, Suzette de la Falaise, and Lucia di Lammermoor, the wax doll with her face melting under the almond trees. I have found my destiny. . . .

When the curtain falls and we go out into the streets, it seems to me that we have left the real world behind us, that this world everybody else considers 'real' is only a world of phantoms. . . .

My mother hates it all and wants to shift to Perth. The excuse she uses is that she can't teach me correspondence lessons any more because I've got 'past her'. She left school herself when she was just fourteen. . . .

The days are numbered. We can feel them passing, and everything we do seems to be haunted by . . . 'for the last time'.

I ride out on Silver and come home at dusk when that weird

primitive fear of the Aboriginality of the Australian bush shuts me out and sends me riding fast into the lighted circle of the farmhouse, that little stockade of European civilization. . . .

The farm has been leased to Tony Sartori. . . .

I have given my heart once and for all and I know I will never have another real home in the world again. I am grief-stricken but incredibly light, like a snail who has lost her shell. I float out into the world, lost and unencumbered, and write a bad poem in my poetry exercise book:

> I left you in the sunshine
> And the soft sweet breeze
> With the purple shadows lolling
> Beneath the cool green trees.

I know there's something wrong with it. It is like a bad copy of all the poems I've ever read and besides, it sounds too much like England. But one day I'll do better. I'll make legends out of this place . . . the Golden Valley of my childhood with Nim, the boy with the owl on his shoulder and the falcon on his wrist, buried at the foot of the orchard beside the chinchilla rabbit, the white pullet and the twenty-eighth parrot who took fits. . . .

Perth in 1936 is an innocent little city, not much bigger than a large country town, lost in time and distance, floating like a mirage on the banks of the Swan River. We live in a middle-class suburban street south of the river, lined with lopped-off plane trees, in a hideous, dark, liver brick bungalow I immediately christen 'The Castle of Despair'. I have never known such misery. School is a nightmare. I stand in the girls' playground, under the pines, watching the other kids play . . . French and English, fly, knucklebones, marbles, skipping games, passball. . . . I don't know any of them and am too shy and awkward to join in. . . .

I love the English lessons. When we do *The Merchant of Venice* I play Shylock, creeping crookbacked between the desks, hissing: 'Signor Antonio, many a time and oft / On the Rialto you have rated me . . .'

I've learnt to play French and English, and fly and knucklebones, but at lunch time I often sneak away to the old graveyard behind the school and sit amongst the gravestones writing poetry in my English exercise book. . . .

My father takes me to a meeting of The Fellowship of Australian Writers. We sit in a basement café with a mural of ballet dancers painted on the walls as I listen, breathless with excitement, to these heroes of Australian literature reading their works: a big, dark, handsome man from Kalgoorlie called Gavin Casey, who has won the Bulletin Short Story Competition; tall, cool, aristocratic-looking Henrietta Drake-Brockman, who has written a novel about the first settlers called *Younger Sons;* an old woman called Mollie Skinner, who looks like a boobook owl and has actually written a book, with D. H. Lawrence, called *The Boy in the Bush.*

My father sits uneasily, silent, proud and still handsome amongst these gifted paragons. Dimly I realize what a strain it is for him. He knows nobody. He doesn't fit in, but he is putting himself through all this because perhaps, in some strange way, he does believe in me, although he never says a word about it. . . .

'Seek wisdom' says the inscription on the bust of Socrates in the university quad. 'Verily it is by beauty that we come to wisdom' is chiselled into the back of the stone seat by the pool. Wisdom is all around us. Surely some of it might rub off on me. I am entranced by the university—the Spanish mission buildings in pale sandstone, the tall clock tower, the Christmas trees, orange tails blazing against green lawns, the wooden stile that leads on to the football oval with its grazing sheep from the Faculty of Agriculture—all this circled by the calm reflecting waters of the river.

I am enrolled in first-year Arts, an English Honours major, in Australia's only free university. . . .

What are we like, my generation of 1941?—romantic, idealistic, fiercely partisan about politics and equality of the sexes, determined to change our world, we are very conscious of being a radical, intellectual minority in a little Australian backwater. If our boyfriends are unlikely to survive the holocaust, then it is up to us to enjoy our youth while we have it. 'Live wildly today, forget tomorrow,' I write. We are existentialists without knowing it.

I scorn the Yanks, pasty-faced boys who seem to think that an orchid or a box of chocolates can buy them anything. I am fiercely independent. Nobody can buy me and I always insist on paying my own way. . . .

I am still a passionate pacifist, contemptuous of recruiting posters, canteens and War Loan Rallies, particularly since I've seen Lew Ayres in *All Quiet on the Western Front,* stretching his dying hand over the sandbags for the white butterfly escaping into no-man's-land. I am terrified I might be 'manpowered' and sent into a jam or munitions factory.

We are mostly the children of privilege, with well-off, middle-class parents who can afford to keep us at school and send us to university. Yet we despise them for their old-fashioned, narrow Victorian standards, their ignorance, their right-wing politics, their pathetic patriotism, their racist, male-dominated society. Between them and us, educated on Freud, Adler and Jung, there is an impassable gulf that can never be bridged again.

I have only just managed to get into university by the skin on my teeth, taking a special French translation test to qualify, but I am here, surrounded by books and paintings; prints of Michelangelo's 'Adam' in the Administration building, Diego Rivera's Mexicans in the Refectory, Gauguin's Tahitians, Van Gogh's 'Bridge at Arles' and Franz Marc's 'Red Horses' in the lecture rooms. . . .

My father . . . had wanted 'educated daughters' and now, like the serpent's tooth, I have turned against him.

The Jewish refugees are arriving in Western Australia. 'Hitler had the right idea about those Jews,' he says, folding the *West Australian* newspaper. 'They're coming in here with their fur coats and their diamond rings and taking over the country.'

His anti-Semitism disgusts me. I flare up. 'You look like a Jew yourself.'

He laughs. 'Maybe you're right. My father used to call my mother his little Jewess.'

My parents always refer to Aborigines as 'niggers'. When I protest, they jeer at me. 'What would you call them?'

'Coloured people!' My own racial attitudes are still fairly rocky.

We live in a seemingly gentle, unpolluted, isolated world of space, white beaches and long golden summers, but scratch the thin skin off the top of this utopia and you find corruption at the heart. If you are born black or poor or a woman, it is an impossible world to live in; if you are gifted, if you have a passionate, questioning intellect, it is a vicious world that blocks every avenue.

But there are advantages in belonging to a small provincial university. Our surroundings are calm and pastoral—no brutal architecture, no concrete, force-fed learning factory. . . .

I can't remember the exact moment when I became conscious of the divided self. There is the girl who moves and talks and rages and loves and there is the writer who watches and writes it down, who even in her most passionate moments is saying, 'Remember this'.

This cold, detached consciousness that always writes it down afterwards without fear or favour, who is she? Does this mean that I will never be able to experience anything fully with sincerity and passion? Whoever she is, she has come to live with me for the rest of my life—analysing, taking account of, describing everything . . . a monster? . . .

My first real success comes when I win the *Meanjin* Poetry Prize. I have seen the little magazine, with its row of Aboriginal footprints, in the university library and sent a batch of poems under the ridiculous pseudonym of Jael Paris. 'Dream of Old Love' is a Gothic lyric probably influenced by Edith Sitwell and the Chinese 'translations' of Ezra Pound.

> The sunlight hurts me like a diseased hand,
> I am the evil Chinese princess
> And you are the diseased prince,
> Ricocheting in our turret of courtesans.

The discovery that Jael Paris is an eighteen-year-old West Australian University student causes something of a stir. 'These are extraordinary poems for an eighteen-year-old,' writes editor Clem Christesen. 'All the poems sent in by Jael Paris show a distinctive poetic talent.'

I sit in the Women's Common Room, or curled up on the window seat at Ridge Street staring out at the distant river, self-absorbed, writing my poems about flame-tree women, red rooms rising over stable roofs, architects suiciding from the university tower, unaware of anything else, even the progress of the Second World War.

I am a poet. I have my vocation, and I have a secret lover. . . .

My mother tolerates him until she reads my diary. In it I describe exactly how I feel about him and the time we once spent together in his single bed in the sleepout while his parents were out visiting.

There is a terrible row and from then on we are allowed to see each other only if my parents are present. It is a nightmare sitting there on the sofa with those gimlet eyes watching every move. We can't even talk anymore. . . .

I have joined the Communist Party, recruited by a Jewish university student whose name I can't even remember. Sitting on the stone seat carved with 'Verily it is by beauty we come to wisdom', she tells me about this exciting group of people who meet clandestinely and want to change the world.

Although Hitler invaded the Soviet Union in June 1941, the Australian Communist Party has been illegal ever since the Soviet-German Non-Aggression Pact in 1939.

I go to my first cottage meeting in an ice-blue taffeta 'ballerina' with high-heeled slingback shoes. I have no idea what a 'cottage meeting' is, but soon realize I have made a serious error of judgement. Everybody else wears slacks and jumpers and is terribly serious. Someone gives a talk on Communism and there is a discussion afterwards, with wine and cheese. I understand very little of what is going on, but they are all friendly and dedicated to the Revolution and social justice. . . .

Gregor, Lloyd and Mary Bell have all enlisted to save Australia. Singapore has fallen to the Japanese and the 8th Division of the Australian Imperial Forces are imprisoned in Changi. . . .

I am working three days a week as a junior reporter on the *Daily News*. With so many male journalists enlisted as war correspondents, it is easier for women to get part-time jobs on the local papers.

I am sent mainly to cover the run-of-the-mill cases in the lower courts: a man charged with having intercourse with a cow; platinum-haired madams in big black Garbo hats charged with keeping unlicenced premises for the purpose of prostitution (the licenced brothels are across the railway line in Rowe Street); a pallid-looking woman suing for separation in the Married Women's Court on the grounds of 'unnatural sexual practices'. I have no idea what that is.

Maybe it was the Children's Court that helped me into the Communist Party, although if you were 'a rebel in thought and deed', there was nowhere else much to go. . . .

The hypocrisy sickens me. Cynically, I sit next to the teenage reporter from the yellow press *Mirror* and help him invent alliterative headlines for his lurid stories. Then I rush back to the reporters' room, type our 'my story' with two fingers on slips of copy paper, yell 'Boy!' and send it off to its fate with the sub-editors. . . .

My mother rages. My father is sarcastic but philosophical. He seems to think that it is all part of the process of growing up. Finally

I decide I'm not good or selfless enough to be a Communist, so when the romance of it wears off I just drift away. They don't try to keep me. . . .

A miracle happens. 'Testament' wins first prize in the ABC Poetry Competition. I have arrived. I am interviewed on the ABC, my poems are broadcast on the Young Artists' programme, my photograph is in the ABC Programme Guide.

On a winter's afternoon my father is sitting and talking by the gas fire with Miss Wilkins, a retired high school teacher who has become a friend of the family, I come into the room without them noticing me.

'Do you realize she might become very famous one day?' says Miss Wilkins.

'She might,' says my father dubiously. 'I don't understand a word of it. I can't read poetry. God knows where she gets it from.'

A telegram comes from the *Reader's Digest* offering me twenty-five pounds to publish 'Testament'. Breaking all the rules of the poetry fraternity, without even understanding what they are, I agree. When Clem Christesen's telegram of congratulations arrives, asking for permission to print in *Meanjin,* I have to say no. The *Reader's Digest* instead of *Meanjin*! Dimly I realize I have damned myself as a money-grubbing philistine. . . .

I decide to . . . consult a gynaecologist about the period pains that have plagued my life since I was eleven years old.

'You don't mind a bit of discomfort, do you?' he says. 'You do have an infantile womb, but everything will be fine once you get married.'

'I'm not thinking of getting married,' I say coldly.

'But when you do, your husband will expect you to be—intact.'

'It's a bit late for that,' I tell him, and his handsome jaw drops.

So I have a simple curette at The Mount Hospital and never suffer again. Home once more, I lie raging in the sleepout, thinking about all those years of pain and gin, of staggering home from school, lying on the sofa for days every month, a procession of fatherly, middle-aged doctors mouthing, 'She'll be perfectly all right once she's married.' All for the sake of this male conspiracy about virginity. . . .

Lloyd suggests we get married 'after the war', but it's 'now or never', I tell him. 'If we don't do it now I won't be here when you get back.'

Lloyd's mother is horrified. After the war she is planning to take him on a world cruise, my parents are 'in trade' and he needs to finish his law degree before he can even think about marriage. He comes to bring me the news while I wait in a crimson crepe de Chine dress with rows of red beads under the London Court clock in The Terrace.

'Mother says we can't get married,' he tells me.

I am outraged. 'What's Mother got to do with it?' I say.

Days pass. I refuse to see him again. When we finally kneel on that tatty velvet hassock in front of the altar, his leave is almost over. The Registry Office has refused to marry us at such short notice, so we are left with a special licence and a stuttering parson in a run-down Anglican church in Belmont. I think he believes he is conducting an under-age and probably 'shotgun' wedding. The witnesses are Lilla Harper and Lloyd's friend, the Rhodes scholar Sam Clarke. The wedding guests are my parents and Lesley.

Our wedding night is haunted by different memories. Lloyd has left a note confessing all to his mother. I am consumed with guilt because I know I have pushed him into this marriage and am not at all sure I'm up to it. Trying once again to keep up with the hard drinkers in the ladies' lounge in the Hotel Bohemia, I spend a great deal of that night vomiting. He sits hunched in the bedroom window, staring out over the city. I think he is crying. 'Poor little bitch,' he murmurs tenderly as he pushes me under the freezing shower in the ladies' bathroom.

Next morning at dawn he leaves for Darwin and another year in army education. Waking alone, I hear a voice calling from the corridor. 'Mrs Davies wanted on the phone downstairs.'

It takes me minutes to realize that this is actually me. Turning my wedding ring round and round on my finger I think about the past, but that seems counterproductive. I have asked myself all the questions and I have made my decision. Lloyd and I are friends and lovers. We share the same politics. He believes in the importance of Art, as I do. We are temperamentally very different but the differences seem complementary. A joyful person with a wonderful eccentric sense of humour, he believes in happiness and the new world—the socialist future.

But it is a strange wedding. Here I am going back home again to my parents' house when at least one of my reasons for getting married is to escape from my mother. I know I have come to the end of an era. The bohemian life is unliveable. It has ended in destruction—attempted suicide. Looking for some viable alternative to promiscuity. I have become a wife. . . .

A few weeks later Joan Thomas rings. She has left the *Daily News* and is editing the Communist Party weekly newspaper the *Workers' Star.* They need an extra reporter urgently. Am I interested? I report for work to the third floor of London Court, that glitzy parody of a Tudor mall where the West Australian branch of the Communist Party has its headquarters.

So my salvation will be politics and marriage, in that order. Politics first, because that commitment will last for twenty-three years. I need order in my life. I need a pattern, a systematic view of the world—and Marxism will give it to me.

Lloyd has introduced me to a whole new circle of intelligent, dedicated Communists who live in a two-storeyed wooden house in Cottesloe called 'The Kremlin'. Through those winter nights of his last leave we sat by the fire drinking claret, talking and singing songs like 'Joe Hill' and 'Harry was a Bolshie' with Grahame and Joy Alcorn, the two New Zealanders who will become our closest friends. . . .

I attend a Party school and am lectured by Grahame Alcorn on Dialectical Materialism, Political Economy and the Theory of Surplus Value. For the first time in my life I have found a philosophy that seems to make sense of the world and promises a positive future. I am like a shy convert to a new religion, but I am still divided in my allegiances, and my literary preferences are deeply suspect. I admire *Drift,* the West Australian Peter Cowan's new book of Modernist short stories. I delight in Eve Langley's poetic novel *The Pea Pickers.* My favourite poet is T. S. Eliot, who has just published his magnificent religious allegory *Four Quartets.* My favourite poem is *The Wasteland.* I admire the Imagists and read Ezra Pound, the controversial American poet and polemicist who has been imprisoned for treason.

The Angry Penguins, an avant-garde literary magazine edited by Max Harris from Adelaide, has introduced me to the Australian artists Nolan, Tucker, Vassilieff, Gleeson, Arthur Boyd, John Perceval and the European Dadaists. They have been responsible for my first overseas publication—a poem, 'Australian Sunset', in Harry

Roskolenko's magazine *Chicago*. They have published new work by Dylan Thomas and Rimbaud in translation, so that I can actually read him. When vague rumours of a Melbourne struggle between the avant-garde, led by John and Sunday Reed, and the Marxist artists, led by Noel Counihan, drift across the Nullarbor, all my natural sympathies have been with the Modernists rather than the Socialist Realists. . . .

Lloyd went back to the university to finish his law course under the post-war Commonwealth Reconstruction Training Scheme. I was allowed to re-enrol part-time, although Alec King told me he had decided I was one of those people who did better outside a university. I was still working full-time at the *Workers' Star* for £2 a week, when there was any money to pay me. We were poor enough but we had lots of parties where everybody 'brought their own', got drunk, pissed in the garden and sang bawdy student ballads—'It Was on the Good Ship *Venus*', 'Mister Winkelstein' and 'The Ball of Carrimoor'. Lloyd's favourite party piece was 'The British Workman's Grave'. He was tone deaf, but his enthusiasm always made up for his lack of tune. . . .

The first chill breath of the Cold War was beginning to blow. In March 1946 Churchill had given his Fulton speech attacking the USSR and Billy Snedden arrived drunk at the university dances, with his lawyer mates in tow, yelling 'Get the bloody Coms' and threw me across the refectory floor. Billy, a widow's son from Victoria Park, just out of air force uniform, was being groomed for stardom by the local Liberals. . . .

Somewhere, under the façade of the responsible Communist, there is still a wild girl in the heart. But part of Lloyd's hold over me is that he never issues ultimatums. I am free to make up my own mind, to do what I have to do, and it works, diffusing every half-hearted rebellion. . . .

Now that I am a married woman, my father offers to hand over the properties he has listed in my name. I can collect the rents and augment our meagre income. I agonize over the morality of this for weeks and finally take the problem to Grahame Alcorn. 'Collect the rents,' he says, 'but demand to inspect all the properties in case there is anything substandard about them. If you feel unhappy about it, you can always donate the money to the Party.'

When I deliver this ultimatum to my father, he is furious. I can accept the rentals from his hand or sign over all the property to Lesley. I sign over my capitalist birthright, feeling morally cleansed and totally justified. . . .

I have stopped writing poetry. These days I write only political articles for the *Workers' Star*. Lloyd says it's because I am always too busy working for the Party. You have to have leisure to create. But I know that isn't the real reason. I have turned myself into a political creature and dried up. I can't write poems like 'My Glorious Soviet Passport' or 'The Railsplitters Awake', so I write nothing. Everything is politically suspect and I burn the only copy of my novel *Daylight* because I consider it might have Fascist undertones. . . .

The Party is trying to clean up its image for the new struggles ahead, making itself super-respectable to fit in with its idealized view of the Australian working class. There was always a great mistrust of intellectuals, bohemians, anarchists and the unorganized lumpen-proletariat amongst the Australian Communists. No one was going to accuse them of free love, extra-marital affairs, wild and reckless behaviour or wearing the wrong clothes or the wrong hairstyles. The dictatorship of the proletariat referred only to a certain kind of worker, one who punched the bundy* without fail, brought home his pay packet to his wife and kids and mowed the lawn in a white singlet on Sunday morning.

Now all I feel are the constrictions, and I resent them. What business is it of theirs, the way I wear my hair? Why can't I write any more? What is happening to me? Does this mean that I am hopelessly bourgeoise and can never espouse the values of the sacred proletariat? Will I ever learn this new language of Socialist Realism; or do I have to remain dumb for ever? Where is the rebellious girl with the hooped earrings and the black velvet beret, who wouldn't be seen dead with her hair in a victory roll? In burying her, have I fragmented my personality so drastically that I have killed the poet in me, traded the gift of tongues for the dream of a Marxist Utopia? . . .

University friends lend me Koestler's *Darkness at Noon* and Orwell's *Animal Farm,* but this is not the time for asking awkward

---

* Time clock. Ed.

questions. This is a time to close ranks. The heroes of Stalingrad have been renamed 'the enemy' in the capitalist press, and anti-Soviet stories about Stalin's death camps are obviously only *Reader's Digest* propaganda. Refugees from Eastern Europe gather on the Esplanade to disrupt the Party platform, sometimes with violence.

My breasts swell up and, resentfully, I have to wear a bra for the first time. I have all-day morning sickness, but I won't give up. I go to work in bright patterned smocks and a huge green hat woven out of dyed reeds I buy from a craft shop in London Court. Defiantly I take off my wedding ring, and enjoy the scandalized stares at my swollen belly.

When Joan Williams and Molly Thorpe both go off to have their babies, I take over the *Workers' Star* single-handed. Joan works until the last possible moment. Molly has to go to bed and stay there, or else lose her baby. Lloyd wants to give up his law course and work as a journalist on the *Star,* but the Party needs a qualified lawyer so, reluctantly, he abandons this particular dream. He is a totally gregarious human being, but when I stagger home late from work, I am in no mood for a flat full of carousing students and, like a virago, order them outside the door. We have had these confrontations before. Once outside the Palace Hotel I smash two beer bottles poking out of his coat pocket. Lloyd is amused at my fury. 'What a terrible waste, darling,' he says, gazing ruefully into the gutter.

I write articles, paste up, choose typefaces, and work long hours on the printer's stone, putting the paper to bed. The first issues have black oversized typefaces for the leading stories, and look absurd, but gradually I learn to be more professional. . . .

Two weeks before the baby is born, Mrs Davies goes on holiday and Lloyd and I move into her house in Peppermint Grove. I have been accepted at last. I am the bearer of the new twig on the family tree, framed above the fireplace. It is a breathing space, an idyllic time for both of us. . . .

But when we take the baby back to Milligan Street, I feel drained and helpless; obsessively scrubbing out the baby's room with disinfectant every day, boiling up the endless nappies in the wood copper in the back yard. The responsibility is terrifying. I am haunted by the possibility that something may happen to him and it will be all my fault. My milk begins to dry up. Nobody warned me that this could happen. The Sister at the clinic treats me like a criminal because the baby is not putting on weight. I am ordered to drink six bottles of water a day, massage my breasts after every feed and drink a glass of stout with every meal. The baby cries louder. I walk him up and down. Lloyd walks him up and down. My baby is starving and neither of us is getting any sleep. Everything revolves around this screaming morsel of our own flesh who cries and cries.

'Put him in the room and close the door,' says Joan Williams, but I can't stand to hear him crying.

'Give him some dill water,' says Joy Alcorn. 'He's probably got two-month colic.'

I feed him his dill water and read and reread Truby King on baby care. The world has shrunk to the four walls of this dingy flat. Lloyd is away at university all day and I am imprisoned with a screaming child. I touch the soft spot on the top of his skull and weep with him.

At last I give in and we pack up and go home to my mother. Abrogating all my responsibilities, I fall asleep. My mother is always at her best in a crisis. She is in her element. Now she has not only me to look after, but the baby as well. What a relief it is, at first, to sink back again into my own childhood. The comfortable domesticity of the middle-class household folds itself around us. The meals are cooked and on the table, the nappy service is paid for and delivered to the door. I take the baby for long walks in his pram every afternoon along the river foreshores.

He is the centre of the family. Everybody dotes on him. With his golden hair and his eyes as dark brown and velvet as pansies, he sits in the garden like a fat baby Buddha, happily chewing up earth and snails, while I struggle on, trying to produce enough milk to satisfy him. The glasses of stout are beginning to make me fat. 'Better be careful or you'll have a weight problem,' says the gynaecologist at the post-natal examination. . . .

When we find the little house in the ranges, it is like an escape into Paradise. Leaving Clancy with my mother, we go up at the weekends, sleeping in the single iron bedstead on the front porch. The night is full of crickets and strange bird noises. The stars are large and glittering, the moonlight streams across the valley. A sharp, acrid, dewy smell tingles our noses. In the mornings we wake with the frost on our blankets and a row of kookaburras sitting on the top of the cement wall waiting to be fed. If we sleep too late, one old man kookaburra taps with his beak on my forehead and I wake to see his glittering eye.

When we shift into the house, it is transformed. My father and my husband have gone up at weekends, carpentering and painting. We have brought an old army hut from Disposals and added it to the dwarf's cottage. The front room of the cottage is now a small kitchen. It drops down through a little wooden gate to a cement-floored dining room with an old whitewashed fireplace and a picture window framing the valley. In winter, the stone room is a washout. It has no damp course, so everything we put into it goes mildewed and mouldy, but in the summer its thick walls cut off the blazing heat and it becomes a refuge.

The large main room of the army hut becomes our living room. An old bricklayer builds us a huge fireplace and Lloyd faces it with stone, lugging the golden blocks up from the wall and setting them in place, learning as he goes. There is a big window that takes in the whole sweep of distant blue ridges, clumps of jarrah and home-steads hidden amongst groves of trees.

At night he builds roaring whitegum fires and we sit staring into the heart of the coals, the flames dancing on the white walls, reflected in the big glass window. Outside the bush leans to listen. Great red moons rise over the valley, lifting and paling to a white globe. Frogs and crickets sing in the moonlight together. But every-thing is not always a country idyll. . . .

Lloyd is articled to a law firm in the city and I am alone all day until late in the evening, when the little steam train brings him slowly home again. 'Let's go to Sydney after your articles,' I beg him. 'You can easily get a job with a left-wing lawyer.' He writes a letter, but there are no jobs and anyway, he has a duty to the West Australian Party. . . .

'I could have joined the New Theatre,' I tell him. I am twenty-five. Time is passing and all my dreams are dissolving in dust. Soon it will be too late. I sit on the front step with Clancy, watching the lights come out across the valley, feeling intolerably lonely and iso-lated. Obviously I am not cut out to be a full-time mother. We decide to share the house with Joan Williams's young sister Laurie and her new husband. Laurie will look after the baby and I will go back to the *Workers' Star* for three days a week, I am reprieved. . . .

My first meeting with Les Flood is at a Party picnic by the river at Point Walter. I am sitting with Clancy on my knees and when I look up, he is standing there grinning at me and someone is saying, 'This is a comrade from Sydney.' What did I think of him at that fateful meeting? Brash, round-faced, with a thatch of reddish hair and pale-blue prominent eyes, he looked me up and down appraisingly until I felt as if I had been stripped in public—and found wanting. A Sydney boilermaker, he has driven across the Nullarbor from Whyalla with two English seamen who have jumped ship in Australia.

Our second meeting is at a Party school tutored by Ernie Campbell from the Central Committee, who has written *The History of the Australian Labour Movement*. I stay in the Alcorns' flat, going off to the pub most nights with the young unattached men, arguing Marxist theory and whether Bertrand Russell has sold out to the imperialists. Over pots of Swan lager in the ladies' lounge, my eyes meet the strange reckless eyes of Les Flood, who is never afraid to disagree with Ernie Campbell and say so, both in the school and out of it. The school lasts a fortnight and at the end of it I feel as if across the heady talk and argument, the Community Party texts and smeary pub tables, invisible sexual threads are pulling us tighter and tighter. . . .

Very early one Sunday morning in Western Australia the Criminal Investigation Branch swoop down on hundreds of Communist households and carry off crates of books, notes and anything else that looks suspicious to their simplistic minds. When they arrive in Darlington, Lloyd and I aren't there. I have left with Les for the Holiday Inn at Yanchep, a few miles up the coast, and Lloyd has taken Clancy and gone home to his mother.

In the empty hotel sitting room, Les is playing 'The Rustle of Spring' by ear, on an out-of-tune piano, while I try to recover from the decision I have finally made. I have moved through these last weeks like a sleepwalker, never still, travelling on buses and trains, with my head splitting and Clancy tight in my arms, unable to make up my mind. I have given myself strange ultimatums—if I am elected to the State Committee I will stay with Lloyd, but I am not elected to the State Committee.

Les tells me that we can't go on like this. He is leaving for Sydney.

'Will you write to me?'

'No, once it's over, it's over.'

I try to imagine never seeing him again, but even the thought is impossible.

Together we have stormed the Council meeting at the Midland Town Hall. Bursting through the closed doors into the sacred Council chamber with hundreds of furious citizens demanding a hospital in the district. A child has died of snakebite during the long trip by ambulance into the city. The councillors sit stunned, speechless with indignation at this affront to their dignity. Doctor Alec Jolley, the only Communist member, is sitting back grinning at us and drumming his fingers on the table. Outside, the rest of the Party Branch are still on the stairs exhorting the masses to elect a deputation and behave in a more disciplined fashion. The Lord Mayor's flabby face is pallid with fright.

'Doctor Jolley, do you know anything about this outrage?'

'No, Mr Mayor.'

'Can't you control your people?'

'They're not *my* people, Mr Mayor, they're the citizens of this municipality and they have got a legitimate grievance.'

I look across at Les in his boiler suit, with his pale hair catching the electric light, and see him as the personification of the working-class hero. Three years the Revolution, I think jubilantly, as we leave with the promise of a new district hospital. . . .

I spend the afternoon with Clancy down by the river below the university where I used to meet my lost lover. . . .

Have I made the wrong decision, underestimated the terrible primitive pull between mother and child? I will have to get away by myself somewhere and think it all out again. . . . At two o'clock in the morning, tears streaming down my face, I run back across the bridge, burst into the room I have shared with Les, find him lying on the bed smoking and staring into the dark and throw myself sobbing beside him.

'We'll go back to the big smoke,' he says. 'It's obvious that we can't stay in Western Australia. There's no possible future here for us.'

I see Clancy only once more before I leave. . . .

So consumed with guilt, I had agreed to let him [Lloyd] take Clancy, but when I tried to open up negotiations again, he was adamant, he told me, and I knew enough about the law to realize that as the absconding wife and mother I'd never stand a chance.

But in these last wild moments I have all kinds of secret plans to grab Clancy and run away where none of them will ever find us. Instead I kiss him and turn quickly and walk out of the front gate, believing that I will probably never set eyes on him again. Twenty years later, my sister asks me have I ever regretted that choice. 'I'd never leave a child for any man again,' I tell her. . . .

Sixty-five Marriott Street, Redfern, in the Cold War fifties—my very own Wigan Pier. . . .

The air is breathless with soot and smog. The knock-off whistles from the brewery, the print factory and the glassworks punctuate the day. Up on the hill, in towering blocks of concrete, the rehoused look sadly down on us from their Housing Commission flats.

The two front rooms are large, with an autumn leaf dado. The kitchen is painted a dreary railway fawn. An ancient Early Kooka stove, with one burner and a missing leg, lists drunkenly in the corner. There is no sink, so we wash up in the pitted cement tubs in the wash house; an old bath in one corner and a bricked-up wood copper in the other. . . .

Under the autumn leaf dado we type up the stencils, and print hundreds of illegal leaflets on the flatbed out in the shed. We are 'the centre' for the South Sydney section of the Australian Communist Party. There are no books or paintings in our house until we start a lending library of what we call 'working-class classics'—*The Ragged Trousered Philanthropists,* the novels of Howard Fast, Eleanor Dark and Katharine Prichard, *The Socialist Sixth of the World* by Red Dean of Canterbury.

Dark figures knock on our front door late at night, picking up their copies of the *Tribune* (the Communist newspaper) for sale at branches and factory gates. I have a *de facto* and a new baby, but we hardly spend any time alone. Our lives are devoted to the betterment of the row on row of little semis surrounding us, whose inhabitants neither know nor care. . . .

Our back room is packed full of illegal literature, and when the referendum to ban the Communist Party looks as if it will be won, we realize we will probably go to jail. We spend hours burning the dangerous stuff in the back yard. Ash floats over the roofs of Redfern. Nobody takes any notice. By the afternoon, when most of it has gone up in smoke, the referendum is lost and we breathe again. But when the news breaks that the Section secretary has gambled all the secret funds away at Thommo's Two-up School and the Labour Party representative on the Referendum Committee has stolen all the profits from the grog sold at the referendum party, the Redfern Communists are under something of a moral cloud. We have always been regarded as anarchists, or worse, by the Centre—Marx House—in the heart of the city. Everybody knows about the Redfern comrades in the Council elections who vote several times, trying on the shoes of all the dead still left on the electoral rolls. . . .

Sometimes I wake early to the baby's cry and lie for a moment watching the sunlight flush the fronts of the little semis along Marriott Street. In the evening in the sitting room, when the dust motes dance in that last luminous Sydney light before the sun goes down, I sit repainting the walls in pale pastels, hang up paintings, build bookshelves full of books in the wide alcoves beside the fireplace. 'If we do it up, they'll put up the rent,' says Les.

I have opened my house up to the world and invited them all in—the homeless, the runaways, the bludgers, the users and the dreamers all sleep on our floor and then move on. They flock to me like homing pigeons. 'It's like a bloody dollhouse,' Les Flood rages. 'Why don't you go out into the street and drag them all in?'

But I cannot get enough of them. Typewriters clatter, voices murmur into the early hours over the spitting coal, the kettle boils itself dry and is filled again. I'm obsessed. I want the front door to be permanently open, I want to invite them in and fill the house with noise. I want the talk never to stop. . . .

When my grandmother dies and leaves me some money in her will, we buy a house in Rosebery. The Redfern comrades are disgusted. 'You'll never come back,' says Snowy. 'You've deserted the working class.'

He is right, in a way. We will never see any of this again. . . .

Rosebery is a respectable, working-class suburb, further out. Gabled and liver-bricked like the rest, with a stiff dwarf pine on either side of the front porch and a blue plumbago hedge, our house is built opposite the wire factory, working day and night shift, blaring noise and light into our front bedroom.

Textured walls and autumn tonings, a gas fire in the sitting room, wall-to-wall floral carpets, cream lace and brocade curtains hanging heavily at all the windows, blocking off the air—but there is a back garden with a lawn and two peach trees with fruit fly. A line of cypresses with a resident possum marks the back fence. We buy two white leghorns and I hang a print of Van Gogh's 'Cypresses' on the dining-room wall. To our two-year-old son it is such a miracle that he buries his face in the grass on the first day and sings. . . .

I wish I had never taken my grandmother's money to buy a stranger's house full of tasteless furniture. I hate the cut moquette lounge suite, the polished veneer sideboard, the inevitable chrome smoker's stand. I miss Redfern, I miss the life and the talk and the easy frendliness. Times are hard, but there is nobody here to care or bring you a plate of soup if you are starving. Les has lost his job, the gas and the electricity are about to be cut off, and I am pregnant again. We fight bitterly, sell the house and part.

But by the end of the winter we are back together again, with a new baby, in Railway Parade, Rockdale, an old weatherboard riddled with white ants and borers, facing the railway line on the flight path to Mascot Aerodrome. . . .

I spend five days out of every week with the female lumpenproletariat of Sydney, a group of workers unorganized and unknown to the cadres of the Communist Party. I roughen my accent ('Are you a Pommy or somethin'?'), disguise my handwriting ('You're very handy with the pen there, luv') and discuss Bing Crosby, Frankie Sinatra, *True Love Stories,* sex, husbands, men, dirty postcards, comics, contraception, pregnancy, kids, dirty jokes, false teeth, the latest song hits, the ills of the flesh (female) and the old maid in Marrickville with the big Alsatian dog who gave birth to triplets with dog heads but it was all hushed up and they had to be quietly destroyed. Not much chance of masterminding the Revolution in the Alexandria Spinning Mills, nor of selling the *Tribune,* but I learn to know them all—old Bet, old Lil and Jessie, Julie, Shirl, Dawnie, Al, Beryl, Pattie, Jeannie, Gwennie, Val, Bonus Happy Maise, Curly the Horse, Greenie the leading hand, Dick the pannikin boss, Kenny his off-sider and Creeky the right-wing union organizer.

It is our fabulous year and I don't even recognize it.

'What do you and hubby do on the weekends, Skin?'

'Oh, we go walking.'

'Walking! Christ, you'll soon get over that caper when the first kid comes along.' . . .

In the summer holidays we escape to the South Coast, camping in the valley behind a beach under an overhang of black mountains.

I am delighted to be two months pregnant, but the usual all-day nausea has begun. After a week of swimming in the surf I am cured. Les sets up our tent under the giant treeferns and makes us a bed out of bush wood. The whipbirds crack overhead, at night the summer rain drums on the canvas and we wake to the chime of bellbirds, the whole valley steaming. It is like a short spell in Eden.

'You're starting to show, love,' say the girls back at the mill, as I sweat and strain over the spindles. Aime is worried. She doesn't want to be unkind, but she can't have another baby in the house. The young couple with the baby in the top flat are more than enough and *they* have a kitchenette, but her yard is always full of drying nappies and she can't get near her own copper. The housing shortage in Sydney is acute and nobody wants babies. . . .

Redfern . . . is just another place, a network of sad, inner-suburban streets in a big city, but kinder than most, with a strange, fierce loyalty to itself, a real sense of community. We begin to fit in. We are accepted as Redfernites. We are safely buried amongst the masses who have nothing to lose but their chains. Thrown out with the rubbish in Aime's wash house in Moncur Street I had found an old paperback of Louis Stone's *Jonah,* and read it, enthralled, never having even heard of it before. I read Kylie Tennant, Eleanor Dark and Ruth Park. I enter the comic world of Lennie Lower. I can recite whole sections of Slessor's *Five Bells* off by heart. Sydney is becoming once again for me the legendary city, but so different to the fantasy I had dreamt about in Western Australia.

I am creating another city for myself with its own geography and its own stories: a city of the poor and dispossessed, a city of struggle, with its smoky towers rising up through the harsh, discordant cries of paper boys, flower sellers, barrow men and the murmuring voices of lovers. . . .

I was sacked from the Alexandria Spinning Mills for being eight months pregnant, but before I left I managed two quixotic gestures. I stood up at the annual meeting of the Textile Workers' Union and demanded equal pay for women workers. There was a bit of a furore, they moved a point of order, and that was the end of it. I organized the Redfern branch of the Communist Party to Roneo and distributed a bulletin called 'Bobbin Up' outside the mill. . . .

I left the mill and never saw any of them again. Unless you lived in the same place all your days, life was like that, divided up into compartments, particularly if you were a woman. It was easy to take on the protective colouring of a different man, a different name, a different city, harder to hang on to any real sense of your own identity. And anyway, there was something oddly exhilarating about the fresh start, unburdened, homeless, with no ties or possessions and a change of name. To be someone else opened up such giddy possibilities.

I had deliberately kept away from any literary associations in Sydney, even in the Party. Once, after I had written an article for the *Tribune* under the byline 'Toddy Flood', one of the reporters had stopped me in the corridor in Marx House. 'You write a bit like that West Australian writer, Dorothy Hewett, who used to have a column in the *Workers' Star*.'

I said nothing. It was years before anybody put the two names together, probably not until *Bobbin Up* blew my cover. Why was I so obsessed with anonymity? What had happened to the girl who once wanted to be as famous as Edith Sitwell and Sarah Bernhardt, to live in a great mansion called 'Fairhaven' with a red resting room? It was the opposite end of the spectrum, that was all, and I was always an extremist.

Before the 'cult of the individual' became a Communist Party slogan, I was a devotee of the death of the ego. The ego stood for all the negatives—selfishness, vanity, corruption, bourgeois individualism—therefore it must be rooted out and replaced by this selfless servant of the masses. T. S. Eliot's line 'a condition of complete simplicity costing not less than everything' always appealed to some deeper religious sense in me, for although I had long since changed from agnostic to atheist, pacifist to militant revolutionary, the mainspring of my political belief was a utopian faith rather than any philosophical, scientific Marxism. I actually believed that Communism had saved my life. 'Teach me to feel and not to feel,' I had recited on the balcony of Mount Street Hospital—and into my life had come the theory of scientific socialism. So Marxism for me was a conversion, an act of personal salvation. The only difference was that I believed in a purely earthly heaven, a secular heaven called the Union of Soviet Socialist Republics.

I was already well on the way to becoming that most dangerous and humourless of creatures, a martyr to a cause. I actually wanted to suffer in the cause of the working class. But I couldn't help lingering in front of shop windows, lusting after the latest fashions.

Soon it would be too late and I would be too old to wear them. But then I would dismiss these thoughts as unworthy, the last twitch of a buried self. And because I had unerringly chosen the one man who would join enthusiastically in the destruction of my ego, I was in a dangerous and vulnerable position. On the other hand, I was probably lucky—only *in extremis* did I discover that ego intact and indestructible: only by going to the edge was it possible for me to find myself again. . . .

I wasn't unhappy; I even had hopes for the future. My mother had written that Clancy was probably coming to stay with her in Melbourne in the summer and she would bring him to Sydney to see me. Maybe, I thought, I could fix up the back room and he could come and stay with me for a few days, or even a week, maybe this could develop into a yearly meeting and eventually one day he might say to his father, 'I want to live with my mother.'

And then everything changed. I was about to start a new job, sorting at the printing works a few doors down the street. I had disguised my advanced pregnancy in a loose heavy coat, applied for the job and got it, when a letter arrived telling me that my mother was worried about Clancy. He had been taken out of kindergarten complaining of 'pains in his legs'. He seemed pale and listless and he didn't run or play any more. He'd had lots of tests but nobody could find anything wrong. One doctor thought he might have some form of infant rheumatism.

Immediately I sent an urgent telegram: 'What is wrong with Clancy?' Lloyd wired back, telling me it was nothing serious and he would 'keep me posted'. It was the beginning of a nightmare. Clancy's illness was eventually diagnosed as acute lymphatic leukaemia, a killer disease for which there was no known cure. I had never even heard of it before but, consumed with guilt and horror, I used money I didn't have to send urgent cables to children's clinics in the USSR and America. I rang and consulted dozens of Sydney child specialists. Each time the same answer came back, it tolled like a funeral bell. 'You must face the facts,' they said, 'that there is nothing to be done.' But I couldn't face it. . . .

During the day I never left myself time to think. If I thought, I would travel that same heartbreaking journey, up the concrete stairs, through the glass doors to the ward, the rows of neat white beds, and that one bed always waiting with the screens around it.

So I work hard to defeat the referendum. We all do—writing

leaflets, some of them illegal; cutting stencils and printing them, smudged and inky, on the flatbed in the back yard shed. Late at night we paint signs in Jack Jackson's special non-removable luminous paint, and with Joe in his bassinet, swerve down back alleys escaping from Twenty-one Division (the political squad of the police force) on their souped-up motorbikes. Through Redfern, Waterloo and Alexandria, we leaflet the letter boxes and sell *Tribune* door to door, working for a united front with the South Sydney branch of the Labour Party. Our referendum 'No' campaign, much of it emanating from the house in Marriott Street, is the most successful in the whole of Sydney—maybe in the whole of Australia. . . .

The NO vote had scraped home with a narrow margin, and democracy was safe in Australia for a little while. We wouldn't go to jail. . . .

So with a deep breath I am off again, pushing Joe through the streets of Redfern, collecting signatures against the atom bomb. . . .

Les doesn't relish living with this paragon of Communist virtue who puts the Party before everything else. The rifts in our relationship widen day by day. Once it was always possible, wordlessly, to repair the damage in bed at night. No matter what differences the day held, making love has always been our saving grace, but now even that was failing us.

We lie silently side by side in the darkness, or fall into bed at different times, both exhausted. At weekends Les takes Joe to visit his mother or the Maguires while I lead out the South Sydney comrades on yet another *Tribune* drive. Nothing can stop me. Some terrible emptiness of the heart drives me out week after week to tramp the lonely, often hostile streets, with my newspapers and petitions.

'We know who is the most important cadre in the Flood family,' says Len Donald, and my breast swells with my own self-sacrifice. Inverted vanity and pride inform everything I do. . . .

In April 1952 there is a delegation going from the Union of Australian Women to a Conference in Defence of Children in Vienna, run by the Women's International Democratic Federation. Perhaps I might like to pay my own fare and join the Sydney delegation.

'Let's both go,' I suggest to Les. 'Mum will look after Joe for me.'

At first he is less than enthusiastic, but at last he agrees, and after only a few weeks in the house at Rosebery, we travel to Melbourne to leave Joe with my mother. Les books in on the *Toscano*, one of the Lloyd Triestino line, with the rest of the delegates, but I stay with Joe in my parents' house in Heidelberg until the last possible moment. . . .

I am almost twenty-nine years old, the youngest member of the delegation on board, and my great adventure has begun. . . .

It is in Bombay that I first begin to comprehend the internationalism of the Communist movement. It is impossible ever to feel lonely or isolated again. Wherever we go throughout the world they will always be there to meet us, this shadowy army of activists who share our beliefs and our vision of world socialism—Venice, Vienna, Moscow, Leningrad, the Donbas, Peking, Shanghai, Canton, Hong Kong, Darwin. . . . There are always the hands outstretched, the welcoming banners. . . .

At the end of the conference the whole Australian delegation, invited to the Soviet Union, sets out on a long, uncomfortable journey in carriages with wooden seats, through Hungary to the border of the Union of Soviet Socialist Republics. But I don't care what the train is like. I am almost delirious with excitement, wild with anticipation. I am on my way to the workers' paradise, the socialist homeland, the earthly Utopia.

Les and I are sharing a carriage with two Sydney women—Madeleine Kempster, a schoolteacher from the New England high country, and Mary Lewis, a Sydney barmaid. Next door to us are the Chinese delegation, who nearly all speak excellent English, so it isn't long before we are invited in for a talk. . . .

Before the journey is over the four of us have been invited to visit China, travelling on a Trans-Siberian railway from Moscow to Peking with all expenses paid. A tiny ancient man with a long white beard, dressed in a skullcap and traditional robes, rises to his feet to make a formal speech in Mandarin.

'This is Comrade X from the Presidium of the Chinese People's Republic,' they tell us, 'and he is inviting you to our country.'

We are inclined to discount it all as a polite fiction, but soon after our arrival in Moscow the invitations, in gold leaf and white satin, are delivered to our rooms at the Hotel Metropole.

But before they arrive there are several inexplicable incidents that leave us all puzzled. Why are the gypsy children in this border town begging, in the Union of Soviet Socialist Republics?

'Because they are gypsies and quite incorrigible, but we have resettled them and are rehabilitating them, Comrades.'

Why do the Ukrainian peasant women, peering from the doors of their wooden hovels, glare at us with such hostile unsmiling eyes? Why do they spit after the Soviet women officials in their fur coats and fur hats and high polished boots? Why do they point and laugh, nudging and whispering behind their hands, at the black American delegate, when Paul Robeson has told her this is the one country in the world where she will be treated as an equal? Why do these people live in such abject poverty, where the only footpaths are wooden planks placed over a sea of black mud?

'This, Comrades, is the legacy of the Anti-Fascist War.'

And when the train draws into Moscow station with the banners and the flowers to greet us and the loudspeakers blaring forth 'Soviet Land', who are this trainload of prisoners, their paper-white faces pressed against the barred window, while the young Soviet soldiers lounge, smoking between the carriages, their rifles slung across their shoulders?

'A trainload of Nazi collaborators, on their way to a rehabilitation camp.'

Yet when we cross the border in the USSR and I see the armed Russian soldiers on the railway platform I remember thinking: for the first time in my life I feel really safe at last. How unforgivably naive I was. Yet how can I, in 1990, attempt to remember the dangerous innocence of that first journey; how can I hope, after thirty-eight years, to hold on to that peculiar ardent cast of mind that censored all experience and saw only what it wished to see?

There was always an undercurrent of disquiet, hidden, pushed out of sight, but undeniably there, bumping into consciousness, often at the most inconvenient moments. Or am I speaking now from hindsight, overlaying this first journey with the second, thirteen years later, when the weight of history and evidence had dissolved that radiant film of falsehood for ever? Whatever the answers, on that first night in Moscow I stand at the window of our hotel bedroom, my eyes misty with images of gilded onion domes, the red star luminous on the Kremlin spire and the dark queues patiently edging towards Lenin's tomb. . . .

Madeleine, Mary, Les and I climbed aboard the Trans-Siberian, four to a carriage, on the seven-day trip to Peking and the greatest adventure of all. It is a magical and contradictory journey. The fir forests have shaken off their mantle of snow, the ice is breaking up along the margins of the rivers, but outside the heated carriages the bitter cold numbs our lips and noses, and the sleet frosts our eyelashes.

When we stop at a Siberian station there are the inevitable ragged beggar children running alongside the train. A man sits in a doorway, naked to the waist in the terrible cold, a look of indescribable anguish on his face, a woman's arm flung across him for comfort. In the state store, smelling of unwashed bodies, footrags and sunflower seeds, a customer with furtive eyes jostles against me, muttering, trying to push something into my hand—a note, a cry for help, what is it? To my shame I shrink away and don't wait to see, outraged that a Soviet citizen should behave in this surreptitious manner. There is something about this village—the sordid, brutish, unshaven, haunted faces, the ragged clothing, the smell of misery and fear, the contempt on the faces of the Soviet officials. Are these the Nazi collaborators Tamara has warned us about? It is years before I realize that what we actually saw that day was a village of political exiles, the victims of a revolution that ate itself, turning paranoid, murderous and sour. . . .

That afternoon we pull into the station, streaming with sunlight, and, arms laden with chrysanthemums, are borne off to our rooms in the Hotel Peking. . . .

It is the best time to experience a revolution, the time of exuberance and celebration, before the contradictions have surfaced and the bitter struggles for power have begun. In 1952 the proclamation of the People's Republic of China was only three years old, still young enough to seem almost as innocent as we were.

Under silken multicoloured flags and banners, workers march to the factories and children march to school, singing revolutionary songs at the tops of their voices. In the evenings we can see the people from rooftop to rooftop doing their 'keep-fit' exercises, instructed by radios. The walls of the city are covered with posters showing enthusiastic children with fly swats and butterfly nets pursuing flies and sparrows.

Moving through the teeming streets amongst carts and trishaws and unisex pedestrians in the standard navy-blue cotton tunic, cap and trousers, we suddenly find ourselves walking hand in hand with a stranger in a spontaneous, touching gesture of friendliness.

In the schools and kindergartens the charming Chinese children climb all over us, calling us 'Uncle and Aunty Bignoses', pushing our noses comically flat on our faces to match their own. There are moments of doubt when these children, separated from their cadre parents for months at a time, seem to vie hysterically for adult attention; or when toddlers, dressed in the uniforms of the People's Liberation Army, enact a bloodthirsty Red Army charge, complete with toy bayonets and fierce yells. Perhaps, if we had read the signs correctly, we might have seen the shadow of their Red Guard future. But against this there are always the peace doves set loose above the roofs of the city, reflected in the stylized patterns on the cloisonné lamps and plates and ashtrays in the bazaars.

Our interpreters are young university students, deeply curious about our lives, determined to regard us as heroes and potential martyrs, fighting against a common capitalist enemy. One of the girls bursts into floods of tears when she leaves us at the border, before we cross over no-man's-land into Hong Kong, convinced that she is sending us to certain death. By that time we have travelled over large areas of China with these young interpreters, and they have become our friends and confidants. . . .

China is good for us. Under the gaiety and openness of Chinese life, the constant activity and adventure, the brooding has left Les's face; sometimes even the infectious grin returns for a brief moment, reminding me of what he was like three years before when we had first run away together. Hope revives. Perhaps we will discover each other again in these ancient avenues of the Forbidden City, where the jade-green Chinese lions stand guard outside the temples and the roof tiles, azure blue and gold, glitter in the sunlight, cemented together by the eggwhites brought to the city by starving peasants centuries before. The myriad clocks tick and chime in the rooms of the Dowager Empress, the mechanical nightingale opens its gilt throat to sing, and we are the bewitched Europeans wandering through these enchanted palaces and gardens, where the ancient and the new converge for one extraordinary moment in human history.

In early June we drive slowly through the streets of Hankow in open jeeps, shaking hands with the huge crowds who line the way until our fingers bruise and blister.

Cheering sailors see us off at the wharf and we sail upriver in the 'peace ship' that will transport us to a new Flood Diversion Project. Sitting in the stern at tables piled with flowers, sweets, cigarettes, oranges, apples and bananas, we watch a yellow moon rise up, outlined against the ancient square-rigged fishing boats. That night we fall asleep to the chug of the engines making upstream against the turbulent rushing of the Yangtze.

In the morning we wake to little boys skimming like small glistening Christs across the surface of the water, balanced on the backs of totally submerged buffaloes. Fishermen pass us, sitting on their decks under big red sunshades, sending out the tethered cormorants with brass rings tight round their long necks to dive for fish. Along the shore, glistening with sweat, men roped to their boats tow them upstream against the savage current. A peasant in a dark jacket, white trousers and a big straw hat is sowing seed by hand, casting it into the furrows. . . .

[After China we] are not sure of our status as former guests of an enemy country. Australian troops are still fighting the Chinese in Korea. What if our passports are impounded and we are left stateless in Hong Kong? . . .

When we touch down in Darwin at midnight for a three-hour stopover, the night air is so chilly I walk back across the tarmac to collect my coat from the baggage rack. Coming down the aisle, I interrupt the security men going meticulously through our cabin luggage.

This is my own, my native land, I think grimly. It is the first intimation of what will be waiting for us at the Mascot terminal in Sydney. Silently I take my coat and with Les, Madeleine and Mary spend the three hours sitting in the pleasant tropical living room of a big Communist wharfie. Little do I realize then the catastrophic effect this meeting will have on my future life.

At Mascot, where the vultures are waiting, we are treated like hard-drug couriers or the carriers of dangerous microbes. All our notes, posters, books, photographs and pamphlets—the cloisonné ashtrays, the china coral tree covered in white doves, the lamp base with the circling folk dancers, the straw hats with 'Down with American Imperialism', the woolen babushka, the wooden Pinocchio from Vienna—everything is impounded, to be returned intact months later. All we walk out in are our black cloth Chinese slippers and a raincoat from the People's Store in Peking. . . .

Les refuses to stay at Heidelberg until Joe gets used to us again, so we return to Sydney with a disturbed child who can't piss for two days and keeps running away down the street screaming for 'Nanna'. Eventually Les lies down on the couch with him and holds him, weeping and pissing his pants, until the crisis is over.

It is a traumatic time. . . . I have flu and a high fever, and now Les is demanding that we do our Party duty and travel to Newcastle and the northern coal fields on a speaking tour about our experiences in the Soviet Union and China. I can't face it. I want time to adjust, to get to know our son again, to recover from the flu and the jet lag, the exhaustion and the disorientation, but Les, as usual, won't listen. If I don't leave right away, he'll leave without me.

I am begging and crying. 'Just wait,' I say. 'Just give me another week, and I'll be okay,' but he only smiles, pushes some notes into my hand, and bends to kiss me. I go berserk, throw the notes back in his face, and hit him hard across the mouth, so, coolly and methodically, he beats the hell out of me. It seems to go on for ever, and I don't try to defend myself. I don't even know how to. What is the use when I am bouncing off the walls like a rag doll? When it is over, he throws me contemptuously into a corner.

'I haven't broken anything,' he says. 'Just taught you a lesson you won't forget.'

Joe is sobbing, crouched behind the furniture. I crawl over, rocking him in my arms.

'It's all right,' I say through rubbery lips. 'Mummy's all right.'

When he stops crying I get up and stagger into the bathroom—a face I hardly recognize stares back at me through swelling eyes. Les stands in the doorway.

'You'll look worse tomorrow,' he says, then he walks out of the house, slamming the front door. . . .

I have made arrangements through the Union of Australian Women to go straight to Kurri and stay with May Gregg, who shared a cabin with me on the *Toscana*. I haven't heard a word from Les since the beating, but when the train pulls into Newcastle there he is on the platform, grinning as if nothing at all has happened between us.

'I am going to May Gregg's,' I tell him. 'I don't want to see you just now, probably never again.'

He puts us on the branch line to Kurri, handing the luggage in through the open window.

'I'll see you, then,' he says, and I don't watch him walk away.

. . .

When Les rings her at the end of a fortnight to ask if he can stay for the weekend, she puts her hand over the receiver.

'Do you want him to come?'

'I don't know,' I say truthfully.

'Why don't you give him another chance?' she says. 'See how it turns out. You can have the double bedroom for the weekend.'

I wait in an open paddock with a black eye, a bruised face, and Joe beside me, for Les to disembark at the Kurri-Kurri railway station. And here he comes, walking down the slope, grinning, with that slightly jaunty swagger, the wind lifting his hair, the collar of his Chinese raincoat turned up against the cold. A slash of light parts the scurrying rain clouds and, hair and raincoat gleaming against the pale grass, he is, at the moment, illuminated in my memory for ever.

'Farver, Farver!' Pulling his hand away, Joe runs to meet him and we move together down the slope, with Joe riding on Les's shoulders, into May Gregg's weatherboard miner's cottage in the hollow.

That night in May Gregg's big bed, with the icy sheets and the starched, lace-edged pillow shams, I weep in Les's arms.

'I know I shouldn't have hit you,' I tell him. 'But look what you did to my eye.'

'You were asking for it,' he says.

'Kiss it better.'

'No,' but he does, and we are reconciled. . . .

I am working hard to bring another dream to fruition. Appointed as the official reporter for the delegation, I have sent back thousands of words describing our experiences in Vienna, the Soviet Union and China, but none of them has ever been published, simply because there is nowhere to publish them. The *Tribune* has interviewed us about the Conference but there is no room in its pages, and no real interest in the affairs of women.

The dozens of women's radical magazines I've seen in Europe have fired me with a new idea. Why not start a left-wing Australian women's journal, published quarterly under the banner of the Union of Australian Women? My enthusiasm is infectious. The

Party will put up some money, the Party press will publish it, and the UAW will raise the rest of the cost and take responsibility for distributing it. . . .

By March 1953 the first issue of *Our Women* has been coaxed and coerced into existence, but by that time my short period of happiness is over, the long nightmare has begun, and I will never again see the Les Flood I fell in love with in Perth in 1949. . . . [*Hewett's journey of discovery shows her a husband incapable of change. She's left bearing that husband's children, and facing her own self-destructive behavior. Ed.*]

The 'waiting patients' were incarcerated in a ramshackle outbuilding attached to Crown Street Women's Hospital in Surry Hills. Most of them were unmarried mothers, abandoned wives or, like myself, women who had exhausted all the possibilities of survival below the poverty line. . . .

[S]ent there by the hospital almoner, who had managed to find out a few disturbing facts about my 'situation'. I had been referred to her from the prenatal clinic because I couldn't pay the outpatient's fee, and couldn't keep to the special diet. All I could afford were potatoes and bread and cups of tea, supplemented by handfuls of raw wheat from the garage. . . .

So Betty and Rex Maguire had taken Joe to stay with them and I found myself amongst the 'waiting patients', treated like a delinquent charity case. . . . [A]t night I lay on a narrow single bed listening to the sounds of muffled weeping through the thin partitions, trying not to weep myself and wondering how I had made such a mess of my life. . . .

Michael arrived . . . blue in the face, with the cord wound tightly around his neck, a lusty eight and a half pounds, crowned with a mop of black curls. . . .

[W]e were reconciled, and came to Rockdale, picking up the threads of our lives together, building some kind of shaky structure in the ramshackle redwood house in Railway Parade, eaten out by white ants and borers.

There were no apologies, and no attempt to talk over the past or its problems. They were buried for the moment, only Les made an inordinate fuss of Michael, spoiling him and encouraging him in every act of mischief and defiance, as if he was trying to make up for the past repudiation of his own son. . . .

One morning, as I am cooking bacon and eggs for breakfast,

Les says, 'Don't bother to cook anything for me any more. I don't want to be poisoned.'

I stand paralysed by the primus, fighting for control, then slowly I turn around.

'What the hell are you talking about?'

'You heard me. I don't want to be poisoned.' . . .

Two weeks later, as we are sitting by the Cosy stove in the completed living room, Les drops another bombshell.

'I think it'd be a good idea if you and the kids went to stay with your parents for a while.'

I can't believe my ears. He could never stand my family, and never wanted any of us to have anything to do with them.

'Go away?' I say stupidly. 'But why, and how would we get there?'

'I'd drive you.'

'I don't want to go.'

But he goes on talking as if he hasn't heard me.

'It'll give me a chance to finish the house without any interruptions, and it'll be better for you and the kids. It's a strain on all of us living like this.'

I stare at him in the firelight, trying to work out what is going on behind that deadly calm, those evasive eyes. He is trying to protect us. He wants us to go away because he is afraid of what he might do if we stay. For the first time I face the truth. He is going mad. He is getting out of control, he knows it and is afraid, and I, who have done a university course in Abnormal Psychology, have refused to face the truth that has been staring me in the face for months, years, maybe always. . . .

Strangely enough, it was almost a relief to find out the truth. What had seemed deliberately cruel and destructive was explained as a sickness beyond his control, something he couldn't be blamed for. . . .

Within the week Les has driven us to Heidelberg, and my mother, smiling but bewildered, is meeting us on the stone steps edged with blue hydrangeas. The following night Les leaves for the long drive back to Sydney with a thermos of chicken noodle soup I've made up for the journey.

Two days later he is on the phone. The chicken noodle soup has poisoned him, he's been vomiting for days. One of us is mad and it is time we made an appointment to see a doctor.

I find out the name of a well-known Party psychiatrist and go to see him.

'It sounds like a well-developed paranoid schizophrenia,' he tells me. . . .

Time passed. I discovered I was pregnant again. Les rang once more.

'I think it'd be a good idea if we didn't see each other for quite a while,' he said coldly. 'I've been much better since there's nobody here to poison my food.'

'I'm having another baby,' I told him.

I found a job as a nurse's aide in the male paraplegic ward at the Austin Hospital in Heidelberg. Some days the alarm clock woke me at six and I walked to the hospital for a seven o'clock start. Other days I started late and worked night shift until ten o'clock. My mother looked after the children and taught Joe to read. Everybody was calm and supportive. Nobody said, 'I told you so.' . . .

Just before Christmas a letter came from Les: 'Dear Toddy, I think for the sake of the children we should give it another try, don't you? Love, Les.'

I went back to the clinic and asked the psychiatrist what I should do. I suppose what I was really looking for was some kind of sanction to say 'yes'.

'If you go back,' he said, 'you must remain absolutely calm at all times, and remember how important it is to try and shield him from any conflict or strain.'

I passed the Flame of Remembrance still glowing in the park, and shivered remembering that first visit months ago, but now, basking in the calm confidence of pregnancy, I felt I could accomplish anything.

The taxi from Mascot dropped us at Railway Parade. The sunflowers were out, the cicadas were already whirring in the box trees along the railway line, and the glider in the front yard of the house next door still hasn't got off the ground. Les was mowing the lawn, stripped to the waist, in an old pair of khaki shorts. Unable to bear the loneliness, he had been staying with his mother for months and the grass had grown up, dry and tall under the coconut palm. . . .

On St Patrick's night 1955 I give birth to my third son in Crown Street Maternity Hospital. . . .

[W]e call our third son Tom, after Tom Mooney, the American labour leader. . . .

In February 1956 Nikita Khrushchev denounces Stalin at the Twentieth Congress of the Communist Party of the Soviet Union. We find the printed speech pushed under the back door one summer evening when we come back from driving down the South Coast. We argue over it for weeks. Is it really genuine, or a skillful forgery by some anti-Soviet writer?

If it is genuine, the ramifications are unbelievable, the crimes monstrous, our beliefs and our lives made ludicrous, naive, even criminal, because we have lived this lie for years, and preached it everywhere—the lie of the perfection of Soviet society under its great leader, Joseph Stalin.

The Australian Communist Party does its utmost to keep the Twentieth Congress report from its members, expelling Jimmy Staples, the schoolteacher, who has dared to publish and distribute it.

Dissent and argument in the Branches, demands that the Central Committee verify or deny the report, and at last we are told the truth. The report is absolutely genuine. The crimes of Stalin are documented. The 'Cult of the Individual' is the culprit, and Stalin's body has been removed from the Mausoleum in Red Square. He will no longer lie with Lenin as one of the embalmed saints of the Revolution.

What now? Shaken but determined not to 'throw the baby out with the bath water', we will continue the struggle for socialism, but something has happened to us. Some ultimate innocence has been destroyed for ever, some uneasy voice lies at the back of the mind asking interminable questions: What if . . . ? How do we know . . . ? From now on we will never be quite so gullible again, but surely this is a good thing—to question, to learn, to discover, is one of the basic methods of dialectics. Only sometimes we long for the old settled security, the old untainted certainty before the Twentieth Congress and the deposition of the man-God Joseph Stalin, floating in fireworks over Moscow with his moustache ends dripping stars. Who now are the heroes and who the villains, after the Twentieth Congress?

Perhaps this is one of the reasons why one day we pack up our belongings, leaving Sydney, 'the big smoke' and the class struggle, all that has defined our lives for the past seven years, to go back to the bush—to 'the radical innocence of communities living close to

the earth', back to another Australian dream of 'the rugged indi-
vidualist'. A dream we never even thought we had.

'Piccaninny daylight,' says Les, as we drive away from Rockdale
in the dawn, making for Western Australia in our new second-hand
Buick, loaded to the running boards; Joe and Michael clamouring
amongst the luggage on the back seat and Pom sitting up, pink-
cheeked and cherubic, on my knee.

'Now our new life is just beginning,' says Les, and I look across
at him, beaming with excitement, wondering how long it will last
this time, trying not to be a killjoy but knowing we carry all our
problems and contradictions with us across three thousand miles of
desert, along the great Australian Bight, through the rabbit-proof
fence on to the plains of the Great Southern.

We have sold our house in Rockdale to Clarice and are on our
way to share-farm Lambton Downs with my father. I am going
home to the first house in the hollow of the heart. Surely I can at
least pretend to a confidence I no longer feel. . . .

Whatever happens, there will be protection. We won't starve,
we won't be destitute or homeless; why then do I feel this peculiar
sense of foreboding, as if we are moving into a future that darkens
as we drive? . . .

The Golden Valley of my childhood has gone for ever. I am
reliving my mother's life on the farm, finding out the difference
between illusion and reality. A child's vision has turned into a
grown-up woman's nightmare. Standing by the kitchen window,
staring out across the creek bed, I even experience the identical
loneliness my mother must have felt, the sense of hopeless entrap-
ment. We cannot stay here any longer, not with Les and my father's
hostility picking away behind my back. I remember the Melbourne
psychiatrist's advice: 'He must have absolute peace and contentment.'

When the morning sickness begins and I know I am pregnant
again, there is only one thing left to do. I go out and say goodbye to
my father, digging in the garden under the kitchen window. I can
hear the scrape of his spade against the clods of damp earth.

Feeling guilty, I kiss his cheek. 'We're going now, Dad,' I tell
him.

'You never even gave it a chance,' he grumbles.

'It wouldn't have worked.'

And so I leave him there, head bent, still digging, sour with his lost dreams. We will never run horses on the hundred acres now. He will never rechannel the salty creek through the paddocks or replant the farm with new trees.

We drive away in the late afternoon, leaving the house huddled under watery clouds, and I am not sorry. There is nothing left of the dreams of childhood. We can never relive them. Thomas Wolfe was right, you can't go home again. . . .

After driving day and night we arrive at Railway Parade. . . . [I]n Rockdale, and with a sigh of relief we settle down in our own house again.

How wonderful it is to move through these rooms knowing they are my own—the coconut palms soughing in the wind off Botany Bay, brushing against the bedroom windows; the Venetian blinds rattling as the trains rush past to Central.

But there is no money, and Les seems sublimely indifferent to getting a job. I will have to find one myself, and this time, as the breadwinner of the family, I can't afford a low-paid factory job or working for the Party for £2 a week or less.

Putting aside my ideals, I will have to sell myself to the highest bidder, but what have I got to sell? There is only one skill I have ever possessed—writing. That is how I became a 'prostitute of the pen' for Walton-Sears. . . .

Our life seems much like that of any other Sydney working-class family, but underneath the façade there are those dark moments when the shadow of madness comes closer and then recedes again. We seldom make love any more, and when we do I find myself shrinking away from him. There is some primitive part of me that cannot lie easily with a madman. Maybe it's an instinctive fear of reproducing abnormal genes. . . .

But now the miracle happens—between one catalogue and the next, while the buyers are hustling up the next lot of merchandise, the rain is splashing through the roof and the typewriters are empty, I begin to write again after ten silent years.

Sitting at my desk, pretending to be busy, I find myself typing a story about Jeanie, one of the girls at the Alexandria Spinning Mills, a story that will become the catalyst for my novel *Bobbin Up.* I can hardly believe it—are the weary years of exile over, is the long endurance of silence ended? Clumsy, awkward from disuse, the words are tumbling out of me. I am possessed again, writing wherever or whenever I can find the time or the space. I resent every time-consuming moment wasted on the wretched catalogue: writing copy, choosing typefaces, laying out the pages in millimeters so that not one line of space is wasted. Les is being extraordinarily supportive, designing a table of mathematical calculations that makes my task magically easy, even finding me a second-hand Olivetti in a hock shop.

I finish a second story, 'The Wire Fences of Jarrabin', set in the Corrigin of my childhood. There we are walking to school together with Edna and Irene McLimmens, watching their red-headed mother feed the newborn baby, watching Duncan Waldon standing at the door of the Co-op in his white apron, with the midges biting in the dusk. . . .

As a committed Socialist Realist I have given 'The Wire Fences of Jarrabin' a 'positive' ending—a strike against the Shell Oil Company led by McLimmens, the Aboriginal truck driver. When I read the story at the Realist Writers' meeting and come to McLimmens' penultimate speech—'It's my country. I been here for thirty thousand years.' . . .

For I am still a dogmatist, nothing has fundamentally changed, and I write bad sentimental stories with 'positive endings' like 'Joey' and 'Pink Blankets for Kathy and Blue', heavily loaded with sympathy for the suffering working class. They are praised, win prizes in Communist circles and are translated into foreign languages in Eastern bloc countries, so that it takes me years to realize how dishonest and saccharine they are, how the bias and propaganda distort the style.

I am still preaching Marxism in a different form, struggling to find my own ways of doing so. It's true that the rock-hard certainty of belief has trembled a little—more than a little—under the impact of the Twentieth Congress. Maybe that is the main reason why I have found my way back again to the country of the imagination.

When the *Australian Women's Weekly* advertises a short-story competition I enter 'The Wire Fences of Jarrabin', but realizing it will never be acceptable in its present form, I eliminate the strike and the 'positive ending', retitling it 'My Mother Said I Never Should'. I feel politically compromised, but Frank says it is good tactics to get yourself published, and the story has a pro-Aboriginal message anyway. The rest of the Realist Writers are not so sure, and—probably for all the wrong reasons—this is the one time when they are right. 'The Wire Fences of Jarrabin' has integrity. It is an incomparably better story than the truncated version tailor-made for the *Women's Weekly*.

When 'My Mother Said I Never Should' is chosen as one of the six finalists, and published in the magazine, my mother's friends ring her to say they didn't know she had Aboriginal blood in her family, and Aunty Daisy is upset because the grandfather of the story is the town drunk.

It is my first experience of the Australian habit of equating fiction with reality.

'My Mother Said . . . ' disappears into the ephemeral pages of the *Weekly*, but 'The Wire Fences' is anthologized in 'The Tracks We Travel', published by the Australasian Book Society. With 'The Wire Fences' I begin on a book of interrelated stories set in the wheatbelt of Western Australia. In the first story Dolly Cracker, the store-keeper's daughter, is kicking a spirit stove down the main street of Jarrabin while the local carpenter prances past on his big black stallion.

There is much that is lively, even new, in these stories, but again I spoil them with my heavy hand, twisting them out of shape. My middle-class characters are not allowed to develop under their own impetus. Without softness or humanity they are all ultimately presented as scavengers against society, giving the stories a sour, lopsided atmosphere. The copywriters at Walton-Sears read them all. Marie says I must have known a lot of nasty people in my life. . . .

In October 1956 there are demonstrations in Hungary demanding an elected democratic government. By 4 November the Soviet tanks are rumbling through the streets of Budapest, and the Australian Communist Party is torn apart by the Hungarian Revolution. The majority of its intellectuals are questioning the official Party line that the Soviets' tanks are defending socialism against the counter-revolution.

When Les and I ask questions about 'the counter-revolution in Hungary' at a Party function in Rockdale, we are told there is nothing further to talk about as the Party is now concentrating on the 'campaign against monopoly'. . . .

It never enters my head to leave the Party, because I simply cannot imagine any life outside it. Not only have I spent the last twelve years of my life defending its causes, but it has structured my whole existence, given it a special meaning. Without the Communist Party I will be adrift again, at the mercy of a hostile world, with all my old fears and inadequacies waiting to destroy me. The Communist Party once saved my life. I dare not put it aside, for maybe that way the old madness lies: the resurrection of the weeping girl with a Lysol bottle in her hand. So I tell myself there is nothing wrong with the principles of Marxism-Leninism, only deviations, human errors, that can always be rectified. I think about the Chinese Communists and their rooftop meetings in Peking. Honest unafraid criticism and self-criticism are obviously the answer, but the Australian Party leadership seems remarkably unenthusiastic about this method. . . .

In the winter of 1958 I resign from Walton's. Not long after I leave, seeing the writing on the wall, Sears withdraw all their capital and the catalogue folds. Marie has been unmasked as a secret drinker with a stash of hard liquor hidden in the women's toilets. She is dispatched, at the firm's expense, to an isolated sanatorium for alcoholics in the dark scrub at Waterfall.

There is a two-week waiting period before I start my new job, and Frank Hardy has suggested we have a 'socialist competition', both of us writing a novel for the Mary Gilmore Novel Competition. . . .

I go home and begin to write, sitting at the end of the kitchen table, listening to 'Top of the Pops' on the radio, incorporating them into the texture of the story. It is a freezing Sydney winter, but we can't afford to buy coke for the Cosy fire, so when my fingers freeze on the typewriter, I warm them over the ring on the electric stove.

As I write, the novel becomes a kind of poem to Sydney, all those places we lived in when I first arrived from Perth, the stories Les has told me over the years, the rough, slangy speech of the mill girls, weaving a web of correspondence across the city, binding this book of episodic stories together. . . .

My predictions about *Bobbins Up*'s unpopularity turn out to be untrue. The first and only Australian edition sells out in six weeks but is never reprinted. It is reprinted, however, by Seven Seas in East Berlin, and in four foreign-language editions in the Communist countries. Finally it is republished by Virago Press in London in 1985. Some male Communists maintained that it was really written by Les Flood, who 'allowed me to put my name to it.'

Working a backbreaking schedule, I finish the novel in eight weeks and dispatch it to the Mary Gilmore Novel Competition. . . .

This time I'm supposed not only to be lacing *his* tea, but drugging the children's food *and* slowly poisoning the dog. When they catch measles he says that ASIO* is using germ warfare against them. Driving in the car he tells them to keep a sharp lookout for ASIO who, he says, have developed new techniques of driving in *front* of their victims. . . .

Les has taken to whispering in the shower, or pacing up and down the hall all night, muttering, arguing with himself, as if he is possessed by two warring personalities.

'Will I kill her tonight? Will I kill her tomorrow?'

I climb into bed with Pommy, clinging to him, listening to the nightmare arguments, the steps pausing at the door, then continuing on. Surely he won't murder me as I lie in bed with our children. If he comes into the bedroom to attack me, can I possibly escape through the front door and run into the street for help? But the street is dark and empty and the neighbours never want to get involved in a 'domestic'.

Sometimes I sit out on the front verandah after midnight, shivering in my old fur fabric coat, or go walking through the Rockdale streets playing another kind of chicken with the passing cars. If suicide has ever been a solution it is always there, as a possible way out, but now I have three children to consider. If I die, what will happen to them? They will be at the mercy of a madman. Already, at eight years old, Joe is beginning to question the crazy logic of Les's theories and arguments; already he too is becoming 'the enemy' accused of being bourgeois and devious, 'just like his mother'. . . .

I ring my father from Peter Leyden's office and ask him to send me the plane fare to Western Australia, addressing the bank draft to North Sydney Post Office.

He doesn't ask any questions. 'It'll be there tomorrow,' he says. . . .

Next morning the children leave for school and kindergarten as

---

* The Australian security organization. Ed.

usual, Joe dinking Pom in front of his scooter, as I pretend to get ready for work. I stand in the bedroom doorway looking at Les, lying with the *Herald* spread out in front of his face.

'Goodbye,' I say, and cross over to kiss him, but he jerks his head away. I never see him again.

I pick up the children's clothes and catch a cab, first to the kindergarten, then to the school. . . .

We are walking across the tarmac. I am wearing the teal-blue serge Barbara gave me because it never really fitted her properly. I look back . . . and have a sudden yearning to turn and run myself, back the way I have come—all the way, to relive it and make it work this time, but of course I will never go back. Or if I do I will be somebody different who remembers this only like a long-ago horror movie I once lived through. I will weep and dream about my return, but it will never happen. It will be only a fantasy. . . .

Why am I leaving this city of dreams and nightmares, with the Harbour swinging at the end of its narrow streets? Where am I going, creeping back with my tail between my legs to watch the pitying glances, the knowing silences, the 'I told you so's' and the loneliness? What will happen to Les now that we have gone? Who will look after him, who will shield him from madness, how will he live?

The plane banks and sweeps across our back yard in Railway Parade, where he is waiting for us all to come home, but of course by this time he'll have gone to the kindergarten and school, questioning everyone, picking up the abandoned scooters he reconditioned from the Tempe Tip.

Now we are crossing the waterways of Cooks River and Botany Bay, all the places where we have wandered and driven, explored and swum, for the past nine years. The smoke from Bunnerong Power Station hangs in the wintry air and drifts across the bay. It's over and I'm going back to Western Australia—tired, defeated, sadder, older, wiser perhaps, but miraculously still alive with my children beside me. I have saved us, but we have no home—we are homeless. For the rest of my life I will dream about us walking down unknown roads together with the darkness falling, or sleeping cold, with our arms around each other in half-ruined, abandoned houses.

Night and the children sleep. Underneath lies the darkening Nullarbor with the waters of the Great Australian Bight breaking against its giddy limestone cliffs.

Perhaps now that I have nothing I can find that empty space of sunlight, 'the clean well-lighted place' in the middle of the world.

'The only unreconcilable loss,' writes Sylvia Townsend Warner, 'is the loss of one's private solitude . . . but one morning you will walk into an empty room and be cheerful.' . . .

Sally Morgan

(1951–   )

Sally Morgan was born in Perth, Western Australia, the daughter of a part-Aboriginal mother and a white ex-prisoner of war, a troubled alcoholic who commited suicide when Morgan was nine. Morgan and her four siblings were raised by their mother and maternal grandmother, two unquenchable women who conferred their zest for life on the children, even as they built a wall of silence about their Aboriginal ancestry, and the fact that they had been born on Corunna Downs, a vast property near Marble Bar, owned by a well-known grazing (ranching) family, named Drake-Brockman.

Morgan's narrative treats the family's poverty with humor, and the visible conflict of cultures between her mother and her less assimilated grandmother with affection and an inspired comic sense. She is at her most poetic in conveying her grandmother's magical sense of Australia's natural environment, a sense in dazzling contrast to the white Australian "battle with the wilderness." Much of the tension of the story comes from her own inner ambivalence about whether or not she really wants to know about her parentage, and the source of the dark skin her mother and grandmother explain as the result of "Indian" descent.

This inner story proceeds in tandem with an outer story of Morgan's personal triumphs as she negotiates school, grinding poverty, and university, all successfully. With marriage and maternity comes the inner strength to confront the past and to honor her remarkable mother and grandmother. The last part of Morgan's book ceases to be a personal history as she begins to uncover first her uncle's, then her grandmother's, and then her mother's story, and thus to chronicle the record of brutality and exploitation which took the children of white and Aboriginal unions away from their birth-mothers and placed them in institutions, where they were trained for docility and domestic service. It was this system of exploitation, still in operation, which had kept Morgan's otherwise fearless mother and grandmother unyielding in their conspiracy of silence.

True to her Aboriginal heritage, Morgan lets her characters tell their story in the first person, as they would in any oral culture, rather than asserting an omnipotent authorial voice. Nonetheless, at the end of the book, the author, as a character, has remained on center stage, and the reader is conscious that all the narratives in the book are encapsulated in Morgan's story.

Since publishing *My Place* in 1987, Morgan has continued to record the stories of her family, has published collections of Australian Aboriginal legends, and a play, *Sistergirl,* in 1992. Since 1987, however, her literary career has been overshadowed by her success as a painter, combining the free-flowing lines, strong patterns, and subtle color of Aboriginal painting with the designs and images of the European naif style. Her work is represented in the Australian National Gallery, and one of her prints appeared on a United Nations stamp in 1993.

MY PLACE

The hospital again, and the echo of my reluctant feet through the long, empty corridors. I hated hospitals and hospital smells. I hated the bare boards that gleamed with newly applied polish, the dust-free window-sills, and the flashes of shiny chrome that snatched my distorted shape as we hurried past. I was a grubby five-year-old in an alien environment.

Sometimes, I hated Dad for being sick and Mum for making me visit him. . . . My presence ensured no arguments. Mum was sick of arguments, sick and tired. . . .

Sometimes, I pretended Dad wasn't really sick. I imagined that I'd walk through The Doors and he'd be smiling at me. 'Of course I'm not sick', he'd say. 'Come and sit on my lap and talk to me.' And Mum would be there, laughing, and all of us would be happy. That was why I used to leap up and try and look through the glass. I always hoped that, magically, the view would change.

Our entry into the ward never failed to be a major event. The men there had few visitors. We were as important as the Red Cross lady who came around selling lollies and magazines.

'Well, *look* who's here', they called.

'I think she's gotten taller, what do ya reckon, Tom?'

'Fancy seeing you again, little girl.' I knew they weren't really surprised to see me; it was just a game they played. . . .

Once Mum finished having a little talk and joke with the men, we moved over to Dad's bed and then out onto the hospital verandah.

The verandahs were the nicest place to sit; there were tables and chairs and you could look over the garden. Unfortunately, it took only a few minutes for the chairs to become uncomfortable. They were iron-framed, and tacked onto the seat and across the back were single jarrah slats painted all colours of the rainbow. When I was really bored, I entertained myself by mentally re-arranging the colours so they harmonised. . . .

Dad came home for a while a couple of weeks after that, and then, in the following January, 1957, Mum turned up on the doorstep with another baby. Her fourth. I was really cross with her. She showed me the white bundle and said, 'Isn't that a wonderful birthday present, Sally, to have your own little brother born on the same day as you?' I was disgusted. Fancy getting that for your birthday. And I couldn't understand Dad's attitude at all. He actually seemed pleased David had arrived! . . .

By the beginning of second term at school, I had learnt to read, and was the best reader in my class. Reading opened up new horizons for me, but it also created a hunger that school couldn't satisfy. Miss Glazberg could see no reason for me to have a new book when the rest of the children in my class were still struggling with the old one. Every day, I endured the same old adventures of Nip and Fluff, and every day, I found my eyes drawn to the back of the class where a small library was kept.

I pestered Mum so much about my reading that she finally dug up the courage to ask my teacher if I could have a new book. It was very brave of her. I felt quite proud. I knew she hated approaching my teacher about anything.

'I'm sorry, darling', Mum told me that night, 'your teacher said you'll be getting a new book in Grade Two.'

There weren't many books at our house, but there were plenty of old newspapers, and I started trying to read those. One day, I found Dad's plumbing manuals in a box in the laundry. I could work out some of the pictures, but the words were too difficult. . . .

By the beginning of third term, I had developed an active dislike of school. I was bored and lonely. Even though the other children talked to me, I found it difficult to respond. . . .

Dad slipped in and out of our lives. He was often in hospital for periods of a few days to a month or so, and the longest he was at home at one time was about three months; usually, it was a lot less. When he first came home from hospital, he would be so doped up with drugs he wasn't able to communicate much. Then, he would seem to be all right for a while, but would rapidly deteriorate. He stayed in his room, drinking heavily, and didn't mix with us at all. And soon, he was back in hospital again.

Dad was a plumber by trade, but, when he was at home, he was often out of work. Every time he returned from hospital, he had to try and find another job. Mum provided the only steady income, with various part-time jobs, mostly cleaning. . . .

Part of the reason I was so unhappy at school was probably because I was worrying about what was happening at home. Sometimes, I was so tired I just wanted to lay my head on my desk and sleep. I only slept well at night when Dad was in hospital; there were no arguments, then.

I kept a vigil when Mum and Dad argued, so did Nan. I made a secret pact with myself. Awake, I was my parents' guardian angel; asleep, my power was gone. I was worried that, one night, something terrible might happen and I wouldn't be awake to stop it. I was convinced I was all that lay between them, and a terrible chasm.

Some nights, I'd try and understand what they were arguing about, but, after a while, their voices became indistinguishable from one another, merging into angry abandonment. It was then I resorted to my pillow. I pulled it down tightly over my head and tried to drown out the noise.

I was grateful Dad didn't belt Mum. Although, one night, he did push her and she fell. I'd been allowed to stay up late that night, and was squatting on the kitchen floor and peering around the door jamb to see what had happened. Mum just lay in a crumpled heap. I wondered why she didn't get up. I peered up at Dad, he was so tall he seemed to go on for ever. He ran his hand back through his hair, looked down at me and groaned. Swearing under his breath, he pushed roughly past Nan and staggered out to his room on the back verandah. I felt sorry for Dad. He hated himself.

Nan hurried into the hall and hovered over Mum. As she helped her up, she made sympathetic noises. Not words, just noises. I guess that's how I remember Nan all those early years—hovering, waiting for something to happen.

I sat on the kitchen floor a few minutes longer, then I crept quietly into Mum's room. I pressed my back up against the cool plaster wall, and watched as Nan made a great show of tucking in the rugs around her. Nan's eyes were frightened, and her full bottom lip poked out and down. I often saw it like that. Otherwise, she wasn't one to show much emotion.

I tried to think of something to say that would make things all right, but my lips were glued together. Finally, Nan said, 'If you haven't got anything to say, go to bed!' I fled. . . .

Things at home weren't getting any better. . . . Dad was drinking more than he was eating, he was very thin.

He had stopped even trying to get work, and was in hospital more than he was at home. . . . When he was home, he never came out of his room. The only thing he seemed interested in was the pub.

Our local pub was called the Raffles; it was situated on the banks of the Swan River, and had a Mediterranean outlook. Dad was popular at the Raffles. There was a huge group of returned soldiers who drank there. It was like a club. Give Dad a few beers down at the Raffles with his mates and he was soon in another world. He forgot about us and Mum, and became one of the boys.

We kids often went to the pub with Dad. While he enjoyed himself in the bar, we sat, bored and forgotten, in the car.

Summer was worst. Dad always wound the windows up and locked what doors were lockable in case anyone should try to steal us. He forbade us ever to get out of the car. These precautions meant that on hot summer's nights, we nearly suffocated. . . .

Whenever Dad was in hospital, Mum and Nan went out of their way to make home a nice place for us. We were allowed to stay up late, and we didn't have to worry about keeping quiet. It was much more relaxed. . . .

In April that year, my youngest sister, Helen, was born. I found myself taking an interest in her because at least she had the good sense not to be born on my birthday. There were five of us now; I wondered how many more kids Mum was going to try and squeeze into the house. Someone at school had told me that babies were found under cabbage leaves. I was glad we never grew cabbages.

Each year, our house seemed to get smaller. In my room, we had two single beds lashed together with a bit of rope and a big, double kapok mattress plonked on top. Jill, Billy and I slept in there, sometimes David, too, and, more often than not, Nan as well. I loved that mattress. Whenever I lay on it, I imagined I was sinking into a bed of feathers, just like a fairy princess.

The kids at school were amazed to hear that I shared a bed with my brother and sister. I never told them about the times we'd squeezed five in that bed. All my class-mates had their own beds, some of them even had their own rooms. I considered them disadvantaged. I couldn't explain the happy feeling of warm security I felt when we all snuggled in together.

Also, I found some of their attitudes to their brothers and sisters hard to understand. They didn't seem to really like one another, and you never caught them together at school. We were just the opposite. Billy, Jill and I always spoke in the playground and we often walked home together, too. We felt our family was the most important thing in the world. One of the girls in my class said, accusingly, one day, 'Aah, you lot stick like glue'. You're right, I thought, we do.

The kids at school had also begun asking us what country we came from. This puzzled me because, up until then, I'd thought we were the same as them. If we insisted that we came from Australia, they'd reply, 'Yeah, but what about ya parents, bet they didn't come from Australia.'

One day, I tackled Mum about it as she washed the dishes.

'What do you mean, "Where do we come from?"'

'I mean, what country. The kids at school want to know what country we come from. They reckon we're not Aussies. Are we Aussies, Mum?'

Mum was silent. Nan grunted in a cross sort of way, then got up from the table and walked outside.

'Come on, Mum, what are we?'

'What do the kids at school say?'

'Anything. Italian, Greek, Indian.'

'Tell them you're Indian.'

I got really excited, then. 'Are we really? Indian!' It sounded so exotic. 'When did we come here?' I added.

'A long time ago', Mum replied. 'Now, no more questions. You just tell them you're Indian.'

It was good to finally have an answer and it satisfied our play-mates. They could quite believe we were Indian, they just didn't want us pretending we were Aussies when we weren't. . . .

By the time I was eight-and-a-half, an ambulance parked out the front of our house was a neighbourhood tradition. It would come belting down our street with the siren blaring on and off, and halt abruptly at our front gate. The ambulance officers knew just how to manage Dad, they were very firm, but gentle. Usually, Dad teetered out awkwardly by himself, with the officers on either side offering only token support. Other times, as when his left lung collapsed, he went out on a grey-blanketed stretcher.

Jill, Billy and I accepted his comings and goings with the innocent selfishness of children. We never doubted he'd be back.

Dad hated being in hospital, he reckoned the head shrinkers didn't have a clue. He got sick of being sedated. It was supposed to help him, but it never did.

I heard him telling Mum about how he'd woken up in hospital one night, screaming. He thought he'd been captured again. There was dirt in his mouth and a rifle butt in his back. He tried to get up, but he couldn't move. Next thing he knew, the night sister was flicking a torch in his eyes and saying, 'All tangled up again are we, Mr Milroy? It's only a dream, you know. No need to upset yourself.'

Dad laughed when he told Mum what the sister had said. Only a dream, I thought. I was just a kid, and I knew it wasn't a dream.

When Dad got really bad, and Mum and Nan feared the worst, our only way out was a midnight flit to Aunty Grace's house. Other nights, the five of us were shut up in one room, and, sometimes, Mum put Helen and David, the babies of the family, to bed in the back of the van. I was so envious. I complained strongly to Mum, 'It's not fair! They have all the adventures. Why can't I sleep in the van?'

'Oh, don't be silly, Sally, you don't understand.' She was right. I never realised that if we had to leave the house suddenly, the babies would be the most difficult to wake up.

Aunty Grace was a civilian widow who lived at the back of us. Nan had knocked out six pickets in the back fence so we could easily run from our yard to hers.

It often puzzled me that we only needed a sanctuary at night. I associated Dad's bad fits with the darkness and never realised that, by dusk, he'd be so tanked up with booze and drugs as to be just about completely irrational.

Many times, we were quietly woken in the dark and bundled off to Grace's house.

'Sally . . . wake up. Get out of bed, but be very quiet.'

'Aw, not again, Nan.' It had been a bad two weeks.

'Your mother's waiting in the yard, you go out there while I wake Billy and Jill.'

I walked quickly through the kitchen, scuttled across the verandah and into the shadows, where Mum was standing with the babies.

Mum was rocking Helen to stop her from crying and David was leaning against her legs, half asleep. I shook his shoulder. 'Not yet, wake up, we'll be going soon.' Nan shuffled down the steps with Billy and Jill, and we were on our way.

'No talking, you kids', Mum said, 'and stay close.'

We followed the line of shadows to the rear of our yard. Just as we neared the gap in the back picket fence, Dad flung open the door of his sleepout and staggered onto the verandah, yelling abuse.

Oh no, I thought, he knows we're leaving, he's gunna come and get us! We all crouched down and hid behind some bushes. 'Stay low and be very quiet', Mum whispered. I prayed Helen wouldn't cry. I hardly breathed. I was sure Dad would hear me if I did. I would feel terrible if my breathing led him to where we were all hiding. I remembered all the stories Dad had told me about the camps he'd been in. Horse's Head Soup. They'd had Horse's Head Soup, fur and all. The men fought over the eye because it was the only bit of meat. I was shivering, I didn't know whether it was from nerves or cold. I remembered then that the Germans had stripped Dad naked and forced him to stand for hours in the snow. His feet were always cold, that must be why.

My heart was pounding. I suddenly understood what it had been like for Dad and his friends; they'd felt just the way I was feeling now. Alone, and very, very frightened.

For some reason, Dad stopped yelling and swearing; he peered out into the darkness of the yard, and then he turned and shuffled back to his room.

'Now, kids', Mum said. We didn't need to be told twice. With unusual speed, Billy, Jill and I darted through the gap to safety.

Within seconds, we were all grouped around Grace's wood

stove, cooking toast and waiting for our cup of tea. I felt safe, now. Had I really been so terrified only a moment ago? It was a different world.

We never stayed at Aunty Grace's long, just until Dad was back on an even keel. Prior to our return, I would be sent to negotiate with him. 'He'll listen to you', they said. I don't think he ever did.

After my mother had bedded my brothers and sisters down on the floor of Grace's lounge, Nan walked me to the gap in the picket fence. After that, I was on my own. One night, I told Nan I didn't want to go, but she replied, 'You must, there's no one else.'

If I was really worried, she stood in the gap and watched me until I reached the back verandah. She didn't have to stand there long, fear of the dark usually made my progress pretty rapid.

My father's room was the sleepout, and his light burnt all hours. I think he disliked the dark as much as me.

Our house seemed particularly menacing. It was surrounded by all kinds of eerie shadows, and I wondered if I'd find something horrible when I got there. I didn't, there was only Dad sitting on his hard, narrow bed, surrounded by empties. He always knew when I had come, quietly opening his bedroom door when he heard the creak on the back verandah.

I took up my usual position on the end of his bed and dangled my feet back and forth. The grey blanket I sat on was rough, and I plucked at it nervously.

Dad sat with his shoulders hunched. His hair, greased with Californian Poppy, curled forward, one persistent lock drooping over his brow and partly obscuring three deep parallel wrinkles. They weren't a sign of age, he had a clear sort of face apart from them. They reminded me of marks left in damp dirt after Nan had dug her spade in. It was on the tip of my tongue to ask, who dug your wrinkles, Dad? I knew it would make him cry. When Dad smiled, his eyes crinkled at the corners. It was nice. He wasn't smiling now, just waiting.

'Dad, we'll all come back if you'll be good', I stated matter-of-factly. I'd inherited none of Mum's natural diplomacy, but I sensed that Dad hated being alone, so I started from there. He responded with his usual brief, wry smile, and then gave me his usual answer, 'I'll let you all come back as long as your grandmother doesn't.' He had a thing about Nanna.

'You know we won't come back without her, Dad', I said firmly.

We both knew Mum would never agree. How would she cope with him on her own? And anyway, where would Nan go?

Dad ran his hand through his hair. It was a characteristic gesture; he was thinking. Reaching behind his back and down the side of his bed, he pulled out three unopened packets of potato chips. Slowly, he placed them one by one in my lap. I could feel the pointed corner of one pack sticking through the cotton of my thin summer dress and into my thigh. Suddenly my mouth was full of water.

'You can have them all', he said quietly, 'if . . . you stay with me.'

Dad looked at me and I looked at the chips. They were a rare treat. I swallowed the water in my mouth and reluctantly handed them back. We both understood it was a bribe. I was surprised Dad was trying to bribe me, I knew that he knew it was wrong.

'I always thought you liked your mother better than me.' He didn't really mean it, it was just another ploy to get me to stay. Deep down, he understood my decision. Reaching up, he opened the door and I walked out onto the verandah. Click! went the lock and I was alone.

I walked towards the outside door and stopped. Maybe if I waited for a while, he would call me back. Maybe he would say, 'Here, Sally, have some chips, anyway.' There was no harm in waiting. I squatted on the bare verandah, time seemed to pass so slowly. I shuddered, the air was getting cooler and damper.

Some sixth sense must have told him I was still there, because his bedroom door suddenly opened and light streamed out, illuminating my small hunched figure. Towering over me, Dad yelled, 'What the bloody hell do you think you're doing here, GET GOING!', and he pointed in the direction of Aunty Grace's house.

I shot down the three back steps and sped along the track that cut through our grass. With unexpected nimbleness, I leapt through the gap in the back picket fence and, in no time at all, arrived panting at the door of Aunty Grace's laundry.

Mum and Nan always questioned me in detail about what Dad said. It was never any different, he always said the same thing. They'd nod their heads seriously, as though everything I said was of great importance.

Once I'd finished telling them what he'd said, they'd then ask me how he seemed. I found that a difficult question to answer, because Dad was more aggressive towards them than he was towards me.

Eventually, I'd go to bed, and the following day, we generally returned home. I guess Dad slept it off.

There was only one occasion when Dad intruded into our sanctuary. We were sitting in Grace's kitchen, eating chip sandwiches, when he appeared unexpectedly in the doorway. No one had heard him come, he could move quietly when he wanted to.

We were all stunned. No one was sure what was going to happen. For some reason, Dad didn't seem to know what to do, either. He looked at all of us in a desperate kind of way, then he fixed his gaze on Mum. I heard him mumble something indistinct, but Mum didn't reply. She just stood there, holding the teapot. It was like she was frozen. I think it was her lack of response that forced him to turn to me.

'All right, Sally, which one of us do you love the most? Choose which one of us you want to live with, your mother or me.'

I was as shocked as Mum. I wanted to shout, 'Don't do this to me, I'm only a kid!', but nothing came out. I had trouble getting my mouth to work in those days.

Dad stayed a few seconds longer, then, in a resigned tone, he muttered, 'I knew you'd choose her', and left as quickly as he'd come.

That night, I found myself feeling sorry for Dad. He was so lost. I blamed myself for being too young.

It was half-way through the second term of my fourth year at school that I suddenly discovered a friend. Our teacher began reading stories about Winnie the Pooh every Wednesday. From then on, I was never sick on Wednesdays. In a way, discovering Pooh was my salvation. He made me feel more normal. I suppose I saw something of myself in him.

Pooh lived in a world of his own and he believed in magic, the same as me. He wasn't particularly good at anything, but everyone loved him, anyway. I was fascinated by the way he could make an adventure out of anything, even tracks in the snow. And while Pooh was obsessed with honey, I was obsessed with drawing.

When I couldn't find any paper or pencils, I would fish small pieces of charcoal from the fire, and tear strips off the paperbark tree in our yard, and draw on that. I drew in the sand, on the footpath, the road, even on the walls when Mum wasn't looking. One day, a neighbour gave me a batch of oil paints left over from a stint in prison. I felt like a real artist.

My drawings were very personal. I hated anyone watching me draw. I didn't even like people seeing my drawings when they were finished. I drew for myself, not anyone else. One day, Mum asked me why I always drew sad things. I hadn't realised until then that my drawings were sad. I was shocked to see my feelings glaring up at me from the page. I became even more secretive about anything I drew after that. . . .

In July, we had a surprise visit. We were all playing happily outside when Mum called us in. There was an urgency in her voice. What's going on, I thought. We don't do midnight flits during the day. I peeped into Dad's room on the way through. He was lying down, reading an old paper.

When we reached the hall, I stopped dead in my tracks. Mum grinned at me and said, 'Well, say hello, these are your cousins.' As usual, my mouth had difficulty working. The small group of dark children stared at me. They seemed shy, too. I felt such an idiot.

Just then, a very tall, dark man walked down and patted me on the head. He had the biggest smile I'd ever seen. 'This is Arthur', Mum said proudly, 'he's Nanna's brother.' I stared at him in shock. I didn't know she had a brother.

Arthur returned to the lounge-room and us kids all sat on the floor, giggling behind our hands and staring at one another. Mum slipped into the kitchen to make a cup of tea. I glimpsed her going into Dad's room. Then she returned, finished off the tea and dug out some biscuits. I helped pass them around.

Mum said, very brightly, to Arthur, 'He's asleep. Perhaps he'll wake up before you leave.' I knew she was lying, but I didn't understand why. Sleep never came easily to Dad.

After a while, they all left. I was surprised to hear Arthur speak English. I thought maybe he could speak English and Indian, whereas the kids probably only spoke Indian.

I don't remember ever seeing them again while I was a child, but the image of their smiling faces lodged deep in my memory. I often wondered about them. I wanted them to teach me Indian. I never said anything to Mum. I knew, instinctively, that if I asked about them, she wouldn't tell me anything. . . .

One morning a few weeks later, Dad emerged from his room early, we were just finishing breakfast. All the previous week, he'd been in hospital, so we were surprised by the cheery look on his face. Nan hovered near the table, intent on hurrying us along. She knew we'd seize on any pretext to miss school.

'Come on, you kids, you'll be late', she grumbled when she noticed our eating had slowed to a halt.

'Aw, let them stay home, Dais', Dad said. 'I'll look after them.' Had I heard right? I froze half-way through my last slice of toast and jam, it wasn't like Dad to interfere with anything to do with us. I'd heard him call Nan Dais before. It was his way of charming her. . . .

'All right', Nan relented, 'just Billy. Now, off you girls go!'

Billy waved at us smugly. Jill and I grumbled as we dressed. Nan had always favoured the boys in our family, and now Dad was doing the same.

By lunch-time, we'd forgotten all about Billy. Jill and I had been taken off normal classwork to help paint curtains for the school's Parents' Night, which was held at the end of each year. We were half-way through drawing a black swan family, when the headmaster came down and told us we could go home early. We were puzzled, but very pleased to be leaving before the other kids.

Nan wasn't happy when she saw us shuffling up the footpath.

'What are you kids doing here? They were supposed to keep you late at school.'

We just shrugged our shoulders, neither Jill nor I had the faintest idea what she was talking about.

'Go outside and play', Nan ordered grumpily.

Jill immediately raced out the back to play with Billy, but I decided I'd like something to eat first. I was just coming out of the kitchen with a Vegemite sandwich half-stuffed in my mouth when the familiar sound of an ambulance siren drew me to the front door. Nan stood impatiently on the porch, she had her hand over her mouth. When she saw me, she turned crossly and said, 'I told you to go out the back and play!'

Two ambulance men hurried up the path. A stretcher case, I

noted, as they walked briskly through. In a few minutes, they returned, and I watched as they carried Dad carefully, but quickly, down our faded red footpath. This time, I couldn't see his face.

Billy, Jill and David pushed up behind me, followed by Mrs Mainwaring, our neighbour. Before I knew it, she'd ushered us into the lounge-room and told us to all sit down, as she had something important to say. It was then that I noticed Mum squashed in the old cane chair in the corner of the room. Nan hovered beside her, stuffing men's handkerchiefs into her hand. It occurred to me she already had more than enough.

'What are ya crying for, Mum?' I asked, puzzled. Whenever he'd gone before, she hadn't cried. Dad was like a boomerang. Mum continued to sniffle. I tried to reassure her by saying confidently, 'He always comes back', at which she broke down completely and hid her face in a striped grey handkerchief.

'Please sit down, Sally', said Mrs. Mainwaring. 'I have something to tell you all.' I obeyed instantly. She was a nice middle-aged lady and we were a little in awe of her. Her home was very neat.

'Now . . .' she continued. 'I have some bad news for you all.' She paused and took a deep breath.

'He's dead, isn't he?' I was sure I said it out loud, but I couldn't have, because everyone ignored me.

'He's dead, isn't he?' I repeated, but still no response. My heart was pounding. Mrs. Mainwaring's lips were moving, but I couldn't hear a word. He was dead. I knew it, Dad was gone. . . .

A few months after Dad's death, Mum found out the contents of the Coroner's Report. The verdict was suicide. Mum was very upset. She had told us all that the war had killed Dad. She'd fixed it into our minds that Dad's death was due to something called War Causes.

In a way, the coroner did our family a favour. He attributed Dad's suicide to the after-effects of war, and that meant there were no problems with Mum obtaining a war pension. It was regular money at a time when we needed it.

The suicide verdict never worried me a great deal. Though, I guess like Mum, it made me feel guilty and a little responsible. I knew there was nothing any of us could do to bring Dad back, and, to a large extent, that was a relief.

Fear had suddenly vanished from our lives. There were no more midnight flits to Aunty Grace's house, no more hospitals, no more ambulances. We were on our own, but peace had returned. I was still afraid of the dark, but I didn't burrow under my pillow any more.

Dad's death crystallised many things for me. I decided that, when I grew up, I would never drink or marry a man who drank. The smell of alcohol, especially beer, had the power to make me sick. I also decided that I would never be poor. It wasn't that I was ashamed of what we had, or the way we lived, it was just that there were things I longed for that I knew only money could buy. Like art paper and paints, piano lessons, a pink nylon dress and bacon sandwiches. . . .

We saw very little of Dad's brothers during those early months. One uncle gave Mum what he thought was good advice. 'Glad', he said, 'a good-looking woman like you, in your position, there's only one thing ya can do. Find a bloke and live with him. If ya lucky, he might take the kids as well.' Another uncle turned up a few weeks later and drove off in our only asset, the 1948 Ford van. He reasoned that as Mum didn't have her driver's licence, she wouldn't be needing it.

Mum was pretty down after that. It wasn't like her. She didn't know how to assert herself, she was too confused. 'Men', she told us cynically, 'they're useless, no good for anything!'

If it hadn't been for Uncle Frank, we probably would have gone along with Mum's theory. Mind you, she wasn't too pleased when he showed up. She was sick of drinking men.

'G'day, Glad', he said when she answered the front door, 'just brought this around for ya. How ya going, kids?' he grinned as we appeared behind Mum in the doorway. 'Well, better get goin'. See ya later, kids. We'll have to go out one day, 'bye, Glad.' Mum smiled and closed the door.

'What you got there?' Nan said as she poked in the box. 'Chicken, eh? And vegetables. Who gave you that?'

'It was Uncle Frank, Nan', I said, 'do ya think we could have it tonight, do ya?'

I couldn't believe it was real chicken, such a luxury. I don't think Mum could believe it, either. Frank, of all people—she'd thought he was just another boozer.

To our surprise, Frank came around the following weeks with the same thing. Then, Mum found out that the Raffles Hotel was holding a weekly lottery. The prize was always a box of fruit and vegetables and a fresh chicken, and the winner was always Uncle Frank. His lucky run was to continue for over twelve months. . . .

I had little idea of how hard that first year was for Mum and Nan. Mum was thirty-one when Dad died, and she had five of us to rear. I was nine years old, while Helen, the youngest, was only eighteen months old.

Mum didn't like leaving us, but she knew that if we were ever to get ahead, she would have to work.

That was one thing you could say about Mum, she wasn't afraid to work. She had always kept some money coming in all the years Dad was sick, with some part-time work, but now she increased her load and took on whatever jobs were going. It was difficult to find full-time employment, so she accepted numerous part-time positions, most of which only lasted a few weeks.

Mum had an old friend, Lois, who helped out financially. Lois was an older lady who we didn't see much of, but she had befriended Mum in Mum's teenage years and, having no children of her own, considered her a daughter. She'd never liked Dad, but wasn't one to bear a grudge.

I remember, at one stage, we were really desperate. Mum and Nan kept talking in whispers. They decided to write a letter to Alice Drake-Brockman in Sydney to see if her family could lend us some money. They were really disappointed when the reply came; it said that they were broke, too, and couldn't lend us anything. Nan was very bitter. She said she didn't care that they were bankrupt, they owed her. I didn't know what she was talking about. . . .

Almost a year to the day after Dad died, I contracted rheumatic fever. Many times on the way to school, I had to stop and hold my chest until the pain had passed. Mum rushed me to the local doctor twice, but he maintained that I was merely suffering from growing pains. I had no idea that getting taller could be such agony.

Night-times were the worst. I curled myself up into a tight little ball and willed the pain to go away. I hurt too much to cry. Nan tried to help me as much as she could. I could tell by the look on her face and the sympathetic noises she made that she was worried about me. She admonished me for sleeping in such a peculiar position and then, gently, she straightened out my arms and legs, encouraging me to sleep more normally.

She spent hours wrapping wet towels and torn-off strips of sheeting around my limbs, all the time reassuring me that the pain would soon disappear. I remember a couple of nights, when I was particularly bad, she just ran her hands slowly down the full length of my body, not touching me, but saying, 'You'll be all right, I won't let anything happen to you.'

As soon as the bandages and towels had dried, she slowly unwound them and then went and wet them again. 'You're very hot, Sally', she said, 'it's not good for a child to be that hot.' By the time I finally fell asleep, I felt as stiff as a cardboard doll. When I awoke the following morning, the pain had generally gone, but not for long. I learnt a valuable lesson from being that sick, I learnt I was strong inside. I had to be to survive. My illness eventually subsided without any medical treatment. . . .

Mum was offered a job as a cleaner at our school at the beginning of the year I started Grade Six. The hours were perfect, because they fitted in with the two other part-time jobs she was doing. But she didn't accept the job straight away. First, she got us all together and asked if we would mind her taking it.

'What on earth are you talking about, Mum?' I said.

'Well, I don't want to take the job if you children would mind. I thought you might worry about what your friends would think.'

Without hesitation, I replied, 'We wouldn't mind, Mum, we'd really like it because we'd see more of you.'

Mum smiled at me. She knew how naive I was, that I didn't realise being a school cleaner carried with it very little status.

We helped after school, wiping down the boards, emptying the bins and sweeping the floors. I enjoyed the boards the most, mainly because it gave me access to the chalk. Before wiping them down, I would scrawl rude comments about school across the whole length of the wall. It gave me a great sense of power. . . .

Grade Seven was a mixture of triumphs and failures. . . .

In that last year at primary school, I developed an allergy to chalk. On one of my many trips to the doctor, Mum had naively enquired, 'Do you think it's the chalk, doctor? She seems to get an attack of hay fever every time she goes near the blackboard.'

I was amazed that, by now, Mum hadn't twigged to the fact that I was allergic to school, not chalk. To my even greater amusement, the doctor prevaricated; he was filling in for our family doctor and it was his first year out of the hospital. He'd never heard of it happening, but then, anything was possible.

The chalk allergy proved a wonderful bonus. I no longer lingered over breakfast or dragged my feet reluctantly down the footpath when it was time to leave for school. Instead, I walked cheerfully off, secure in the knowledge that, by mid-morning, I would be on my way home again. I usually managed to leave school and arrive in Manning Road just as Mum drove past in the old Vanguard on her way home from an early morning stint at her latest job, cleaning the doctor's surgery. If I was late, she'd park the car on the corner and wait for me.

Recognition came at the beginning of third term, when I won the coveted Dick Cleaver Award for Citizenship. The whole school voted, and, for some reason, I won. I wondered who Jill had bribed, she had a lot of influence in the lower grades.

My prize was a choice of any book available from the bookshops. When our headmaster, Mr. Buddee, asked me what I had in mind, I replied, without hesitation, 'A book of fairy tales please.' I think he was rather taken aback, because he told me to go away and think about it for a few days.

I stuck to my choice, even though my class teacher tried to talk me into something more suitable. My classmates thought I was potty, too, they didn't understand. I knew fairy tales were the stuff dreams were made of. And I loved dreams. . . .

It was during that final year at primary school that I noticed that whenever we brought our friends home to play after school, Nan would disappear.

'How come Nan nicks off when our friends are here?' I asked Jill one day.

'Dunno.'

'Why's she started doing it now, she never did it before, did she?'

'She's been doin' it for years.'

'I never noticed.'

'You never notice anything!'

Later that day, I asked Mum the same question and she put it down to Nan's old age. This wasn't news to me; in my mind, Nan had always been old. I couldn't imagine her actually getting older, though. She was the sort of person that would stay the same age for ever.

One day, I walked into the kitchen with one of my friends and Nan was there, making a cup of tea. She was furious with me. After my friend had left, she said, 'You're not to keep bringin' people inside, Sally. You got no shame. We don't want them to see how we live.'

'Why not?'

'People talk, you know, we don't want people talkin' about us. You dunno what they might say!'

'Okay, Nan', I agreed. It wasn't often I had friends after school, I wasn't pally with a lot of kids. . . .

That summer signalled the start of my growing up. I was very self-conscious, none of my body seemed to be in proportion. I had long legs, long arms and the bit in between was flat and skinny.

I think what I disliked most about myself, though, was the lack of pigmentation in certain patches of skin around my neck and shoulders. I always buttoned my shirts right up to the collar. If the top button happened to be missing, I pulled my collar close in around my neck and held it there with a large safety-pin.

Mum must have noticed how self-conscious I was, because she took me to see a skin specialist, who said there was nothing he could do and referred me to a cosmetician.

The cosmetician gave me different coloured batches of make-up to mix together so I could conceal my patches.

After all the trouble Mum had gone to, I didn't have the courage to tell her I had no intention of ever using the make-up. Actually, I was mad at her. It was one thing for me to stick a safety-pin in my collar, but quite another for her to drag me around to specialists, exhibiting me to the world. At the first opportunity, I wrapped my make-up in newspaper and threw it in the bin. It was a symbolic gesture. I decided that, from then on, I would bare that part of my body, and if people were repulsed, that was their problem, not mine. It was the first time my lower neck had seen the light of days for years.

Apart from my appearance, over those holidays, my main worry was high school. I kept wishing it didn't exist. For a time, I had very romantic notions about running away to join a circus. I would climb up into the small gum tree in our backyard and sit there for hours, day-dreaming about circus life. But the circus never came and, in February, 1964, I started high school.

I felt terribly old-fashioned. I still had two long plaits dangling down my back. All the other girls had short hair, and they were much more mature than me. There were about twelve hundred students at our school. I felt lost and intimidated.

As we all waited silently in line that first day, I kept wondering what stream they were going to put me in, Commercial or Professional. We'd been told there were going to be four Professional classes, denoted by the letters A to D. Only the exceptionally brainy students were permitted in the A class, everyone else was slotted into the other classes, according to their varying degrees of intelligence. I sat glumly as the teachers read through first the A list, the B and C. By the time they got to the bottom of the D list, my name still hadn't been mentioned. My hopes began to rise. Suddenly, another man, who I later found out was the principal, came over and joined our group. After a brief conversation with one of the teachers, he called out, 'Is there a Sally Milroy here?'

I slowly raised my hand.

'You're in D group, too, off you go.' I didn't know whether I wanted to laugh or cry. I hated school, yet, at the same time, I didn't want people thinking I was the sort of kid who didn't have a brain in her head. . . .

Early in the school year, I made friends with a girl called Steph. She lived seven blocks away from us, in the part they called Como, so we took to visiting each other on weekends. I was fascinated by Steph's family, they were very neat and tidy. I loved Steph's bedroom, it was decorated mainly in lilac and it reminded me of something straight off a Hollywood film set. Surprisingly, Steph was equally fascinated by my home. She loved the free and easy atmosphere, and the tall stories and jokes.

But I think my intense admiration for Steph's room caused me to become somewhat dissatisfied. I suddenly realised there was a whole world beyond what I knew. It was frightening. Sometimes when Steph's parents talked to me, my mind went blank. I always seemed to say the wrong thing, so, for fear of offending them, I began saying nothing at all, which was even worse. Steph's dog Tina had more social graces than me. . . .

When I looked at other people, I realised how abnormal I was, or at least, that's how I felt. None of my brothers and sisters seemed to be tormented by the things that tormented me. I really felt as though I just couldn't understand the world any more. It was horrible being a teenager.

Part of the reason why I hated school was the regimentation. I hated routine. I wanted to do something exciting and different all the time. I really couldn't see the point in learning about subjects I wasn't interested in. I had no long-term goals and my only short-term one was to leave school as soon as I could.

I found that the only way to cope was to truant as much as possible. Being away from school gave me time to think and relieved the pressure. I always felt better inside after I truanted. . . .

The school began enforcing stricter rules in an attempt to reduce the high rate of truancy by some of its students. Mum had been threatened with the Truant Officer many times. To her, this was as bad as having a policeman call. So she began to try and make us stay at school all day.

She was in a difficult situation, because, while she wanted us to have a good education and to get on in the world, she was also sympathetic to our claims of being bored, tired or unhappy. Also, I knew it wasn't the fact that we truanted so much that upset her, but that now and then we got caught. Getting caught inevitably brought us to the personal attention of the school staff, which also meant that, in some way, she lost face in their eyes. Like most people, I suppose, Mum liked other people, especially those who were educated, to think well of her.

She was particularly upset after one visit to our Head. He had shown her three different sets of handwriting, all purporting to be hers, and all excusing either Jill or me from a morning or afternoon at school. 'You've got to get yourselves organised', she told us crossly, 'if you're going to forge notes from me, at least do it in the same style.'

The longer I stayed at school, the more difficult I became and the more reluctant Mum became to support my truanting. She was tired of the Head and the Guidance Officer ringing her up. I sympathised with her. I was sick of visiting the Guidance Officer myself. I felt very much on the defensive in these meetings, because I knew they were based on the premise that there was something wrong with me. In my view, this was totally unfounded. Consequently, my interviews with the Guidance Officer tended to be fairly short, mainly due to my lack of response. Mum was finally advised to allow me to leave school early and let me become a shop assistant. . . .

On the fourteenth of February, 1966, Australia's currency changed from pounds, shillings and pence, to dollars and cents. According to Mum and Nan, it was a step backwards in our history. 'There's no money like the old money', Nan maintained, and Mum agreed. . . .

Then I noticed that Nan had a jar on the shelf in the kitchen with a handful of two-shilling pieces in it. Towards the end of the week, the jar was overflowing with sixpences, threepences, one-shilling and two-shilling pieces. I could contain my curiosity no longer.

'What are you saving up for, Nan?'

'Nothin'! Don't you touch any of that money!'

I cornered Mum in the bath. 'Okay, Mum, why is Nan hoarding all that money? You're supposed to hand it over to the bank and get new money.'

'Don't you say anything to anyone about that money, Sally.'

'Why not?'

'Look, that money's going to be valuable one day, we're saving it for you kids. When it's worth a lot, we'll sell it and you kids can have what we make. You might need it by then.'

I went back in the kitchen and said to Nan, 'Mum told me what you're up to. I think it's crazy.'

'Hmph! We don't care what you think, you'll be glad of it in a few years' time. Now you listen, if anyone from the government comes round asking for money, you tell them we gave all ours to the bank. If they pester you about the old money, you just say you don't know nothin'. You tell 'em we haven't got money like that in this house.'

'Nan', I half laughed, 'no one from the government is gunna come round and do that!'

'Ooh, don't you believe it. You don't know what the government's like, you're too young. You'll find out one day what they can do to people. You never trust anybody who works for the government, you dunno what they say about you behind your back. You mark my words, Sally.'

I was often puzzled by the way Mum and Nan approached anyone in authority, it was as if they were frightened. I knew that couldn't be the reason, why on earth would anyone be frightened of the government? . . .

Towards the end of the school year, I arrived home early one day to find Nan sitting at the kitchen table, crying. I froze in the doorway, I'd never seen her cry before.

'Nan . . . what's wrong?'

'Nothin!'

'Then what are you crying for?'

She lifted up her arm and thumped her clenched fist hard on the kitchen table. 'You bloody kids don't want me, you want a bloody white grandmother, I'm black. Do you hear, black, black, black!' With that, Nan pushed back her chair and hurried out to her room. I continued to stand in the doorway, I could feel the strap of my heavy schoolbag cutting into my shoulder, but I was too stunned to remove it.

For the first time in my fifteen years, I was conscious of Nan's colouring. She was right, she wasn't white. Well, I thought logically, if she wasn't white, then neither were we. What did that make us, what did that make me? I had never thought of myself as being black before.

That night, as Jill and I were lying quietly on our beds, looking at a poster of John, Paul, George and Ringo, I said, 'Jill . . . did you know Nan was black?'

'Course I did.'

'I didn't, I just found out.'

'I know you didn't. You're really dumb, sometimes. God, you reckon I'm gullible, some things you just don't see.'

'Oh . . .'

'You know we're not Indian, don't you?' Jill mumbled.

'Mum said we're Indian.'

'Look at Nan, does she look Indian?'

'I've never really thought about how she looks. Maybe she comes from some Indian tribe we don't know about.'

'Ha! That'll be the day! You know what we are, don't you?'

'No, what?'

'Boongs, we're Boongs!' I could see Jill was unhappy with the idea.

It took a few minutes before I summoned up enough courage to say, 'What's a Boong?'

'A Boong. You know, Aboriginal. God, of all things, we're Aboriginal!'

'Oh.' I suddenly understood. There was a great deal of social stigma attached to being Aboriginal at our school.

'I can't believe you've never heard the word Boong', she muttered in disgust. 'Haven't you ever listened to the kids at school? If they want to run you down, they say, "Aah, ya just a Boong". Honestly, Sally, you live the whole of your life in a daze!'

Jill was right, I did live in a world of my own. She was much attuned to our social environment. It was important for her to be accepted at school, because she enjoyed being there. All I wanted to do was stay home.

'You know, Jill', I said after a while, 'if we are Boongs, and I don't know if we are or not, but if we are, there's nothing we can do about it, so we might as well just accept it.' . . .

'You still don't understand, do you', Jill groaned in disbelief. 'It's a terrible thing to be Aboriginal. Nobody wants to know you. . . . You can be Indian, Dutch, Italian, anything, but not Aboriginal! I suppose it's all right for someone like you, you don't care what people think. You don't need anyone, but I do!' Jill pulled her rugs over her head and pretended she'd gone to sleep. I think she was crying, but I had too much new information to think about to try and comfort her. Besides, what could I say?

Nan's outburst over her colouring and Jill's assertion that we were Aboriginal heralded a new phase in my relationship with my mother. I began to pester her incessantly about our background. Mum was a hard nut to crack and consistently denied Jill's assertion. She even told me that Nan had come out on a boat from India in the early days. In fact, she was so convincing I began to wonder if Jill was right after all.

When I wasn't pestering Mum, I was busy pestering Nan. To my surprise, I discovered that Nan had a real short fuse when it came to talking about the past. Whenever I attempted to question her, she either lost her temper and began to accuse me of all sorts of things, or she locked herself in her room and wouldn't emerge until it was time for Mum to come home from work. It was a conspiracy.

One night, Mum came into my room and sat on the end of my bed. She had her This Is Serious look on her face. With an unusual amount of firmness in her voice, she said quietly, 'Sally, I want to talk to you.'

I lowered my *Archie* comic. 'What is it?'

'I think you know, don't act dumb with me. You're not to bother Nan any more. She's not as young as she used to be and your

questions are making her sick. She never knows when you're going
to try and trick her. There's no point in digging up the past, some
things are better left buried. Do you understand what I'm saying?
You're to leave her alone.'

'Okay, Mum', I replied glibly, 'but on one condition.'

'What's that?'

'You answer one question for me?'

'What is it?' Poor Mum, she was a trusting soul.

'Are we Aboriginal?'

Mum snorted in anger and stormed out. Jill chuckled from her
bed. 'I don't know why you keep it up. Why keep pestering them? I
think it's better not to know for sure, that way you don't have to
face up to it.'

'I keep pestering them because I want to know the truth, and I
want to hear it from Mum's own lips.'

'It's a lost cause, they'll never tell you.'

'I'll crack 'em one day.'

Jill shrugged good-naturedly and went back to reading her
True Romance magazine.

I settled back into my mattress and began to think about the
past. Were we Aboriginal? I sighed and closed my eyes. A mental
picture flashed vividly before me. I was a little girl again, and Nan
and I were squatting in the sand near the back steps.

'This is a track, Sally. See how they go.' I watched, entranced,
as she made the pattern of a kangaroo. 'Now, this is a goanna and
here are emu tracks. You see, they all different. You got to know all
of them if you want to catch tucker.'

'That's real good, Nan.'

'You want me to draw you a picture, Sal?' she said as she
picked up a stick.

'Okay.'

'These are men, you see, three men. They are very quiet, they're
hunting. Here are kangaroos, they're listening, waiting. They'll take
off if they know you're coming.' Nan wiped the sand picture out
with her hand. 'It's your turn now,' she said, 'you draw something.'
I grasped the stick eagerly.

'This is Jill and this is me. We're going down the swamp.' I
drew some trees and bushes.

I opened my eyes, and, just as suddenly, the picture vanished.

Had I remembered something important? I didn't know. That was the trouble, I knew nothing about Aboriginal people. I was clutching at straws.

It wasn't long before I was too caught up in my preparations for my Junior examinations to bother too much about where we'd come from. At that time, the Junior exam was the first major one in high school, and, to a large extent, it determined your future. If you failed, you automatically left school and looked for a job. If you passed, it was generally accepted that you would do another two years' study and aim at entrance to university.

Mum was keen on me doing well, so I decided that, for her, I'd make the effort and try and pass subjects I'd previously failed. For the first time in my school life, I actually sat up late, studying my textbooks. It was hard work, but Mum encouraged me by bringing in cups of tea and cake or toast and jam.

After each examination, she'd ask me anxiously how I'd gone. My reply was always, 'Okay'. I never really knew. Sometimes, I thought I'd done all right, but then I reasoned that all I needed was a hard marker and I might fail. I didn't want to get Mum's hopes up.

Much to the surprise of the whole family, I passed every subject, even scoring close to the distinction mark in English and Art. Mum was elated.

'Now, aren't you pleased? I knew you would do it. Mr Buddee was right about you.'

Good old Mr Buddee. I didn't know whether to curse or thank him. Now that I had passed my Junior, I sensed that there was no hope of Mum allowing me to leave school. I should have deliberately failed, I thought. Then, she wouldn't have had any choice. Actually, I had considered doing just that, but, for some reason, I couldn't bring myself to do it. I guess it was my pride again.

Fourth-year high school was different to third year. It was supposed to be a transitory year where we were treated more like adults and less like difficult teenagers. Even our classes were supposed to be structured to mimic the kind of organisation we might find later in tertiary institutions. I was a year older, but I was still the same person with the same problems. I felt this was also true of school. The changes were only superficial. However, some deep and important things did happen to me that year. . . .

It was about that time that I began to analyse my own attitudes and feelings more closely. I looked at Mum and Nan and I realised that part of my inability to deal constructively with people in authority had come from them. They were completely baffled by the workings of government or its bureaucracies. Whenever there were difficulties, rather than tackle the system directly, they'd taught us it was much more effective to circumvent or forestall it. And if that didn't work, you could always ignore it. . . .

I had accepted by now that Nan was dark, and that our heritage was not that shared by most Australians, but I hadn't accepted that we were Aboriginal. I was too ignorant to make such a decision, and too confused. I found myself coming back to the same old question: if Nan was Aboriginal, why didn't she just say so? The fact that both Mum and Nan made consistent denials made me think I was barking up the wrong tree. I could see no reason why they would pretend to be something they weren't. . . .

'You want to make something of yourself', Mum said to me one night when she was going on about wanting me to do well in my Leaving. She had sensed that there was more chance of me failing than passing.

I was fed up with hearing that phrase. Mum and Nan were always harping on about how us kids must make something of ourselves.

'I've got no ambitions', I replied hopelessly. 'I can't see myself doing anything.'

'You've got plenty of talents, you just haven't discovered them yet.'

'Talents? God, Mum, there are more important things than what talents you've got. I feel pressured by everything else.'

'There's no need for dramatics. You've got a good life, what's there for you to worry about?'

How could I tell her it was me, and her and Nan. The sum total of all the things I didn't understand about them or myself. The feeling that a very vital part of me was missing and that I'd never belong anywhere. Never resolve anything. . . .

At the end of first term, our Physics teacher gave the class a little talk.

'It's interesting', he said, 'only two more terms to go and I can already tell which of you will pass or fail. And I'm not just talking about Physics. In this class, most of you will pass. Then there are a few who are borderline, and one who will definitely fail.' He looked with pity at me. 'I don't know why you bother to turn up at all. You might as well throw in the towel now.'

Everyone laughed. I was really mad. Up until then, I hadn't cared whether I passed or failed. I'll prove you wrong, you crumb, I thought.

During second term, I made sporadic attempts at study. Once the August holidays were over, I began in earnest. I knew it wasn't going to be an easy task. I lacked the photographic memories of my two sisters, and I was way behind in my work. As usual, Mum tried to encourage me by bringing every snack imaginable.

Instead of having a good night's sleep before each exam, I kept myself awake by drinking strong coffee and tried to cram as much extra information into my brain as possible. By the end of the exams, I knew I'd passed English, History and Economics; I was doubtful about Chemistry and I was almost certain that I had failed Physics, Maths 1 and Maths 2.

I confided none of my fears to Mum. I figured she'd be disappointed soon enough. I needed five subjects to score my Leaving Certificate and I was confident of only three. It seemed all my hard work had been for nothing. . . .

There was only one thing to do, disappear. I volunteered to help out at some church camps for young children, it meant I would be away when the results came out. . . .

[T]he day the results came out, I received a long, mushy telegram from Mum, extolling my superior intelligence and patting me on the back for passing five subjects. By the time I returned from camp, she had convinced herself that I'd go to university and become a doctor.

She was very disappointed in my decision to never study again. I told her I was sick of people telling me what to do with my life. I wanted to work and earn some money. I wanted to be independent. . . .

Towards the end of summer, in 1969, I managed to secure a job as a clerk in a government department. It was an incredibly boring job. I had nothing to do. I begged my superiors to give me more work, but they said there was none. I just had to master the art of looking busy, like they did. A couple of weeks, I was even forced to work overtime, not that there was anything to do, but they were all working overtime and they said it would look bad if I didn't, too. In desperation, I took to hiding novels in government files; that way, I could sit at my desk and read without everyone telling me, 'Look busy, girl. Look busy!' . . .

I lasted there about six months and then I resigned. And I thought school was boring. That was my first experience of being employed and I hadn't liked it one bit. It was an important experience for me, because it taught me something about myself that I had been unaware of. I wasn't going to be satisfied with just anything. And I wasn't lazy.

I had been unemployed about four months when I decided that it was time I began looking for another job. I was sick of sitting around at home with little to do.

I found a job as a laboratory assistant. For some reason, my new employer assumed that as I had studied physics and chemistry at school, I must have known something about them.

My job was to analyse mineral samples from different parts of Western Australia for tin, iron oxide and so on.

I accidentally disposed of my first lot of samples, so, in desperation, I invented the results. My boss was quite excited. 'Hmmm', he said as he looked over my recording sheet, 'these aren't bad. Good girl, good girl!'

I felt so guilty, I imagined that, on the basis of my analysis, they might begin drilling straight away in the hope of a big strike. I took more care after that.

The women I worked with all had strong personalities. Our boss was hardly ever in so we all took extended lunch hours and had long conversations about whatever came into our heads. I was very impressed with the whole group. They were the first females I'd met who actually had something to say. . . .

One of them confided to me that she was schizophrenic. It was a confidence that failed to enlighten me, I just wondered what country she came from.

One day, I returned to the office from my lunch hour to find everyone abnormally subdued. Our office was going to be moved away from the city.

No one was keen on this, because it meant the whole company, instead of maintaining small branches here and there, would be under one roof. We would all have to knuckle under and behave. I decided to resign.

My boss offered me a raise in pay if I stayed. He said I was the best laboratory assistant they'd ever had.

The decision was taken out of my hands when I suddenly developed industrial acne as a result of being allergic to the chemicals I was using.

By the time I left the laboratory job. I had developed an interest in psychology. I had looked the word schizophrenic up in my dictionary and found out it was not a nationality after all.

I was more realistic about myself, now. I realised that the chances of me finding a job I was really happy in were remote. I needed to do further study. I decided to enroll in university for the following year, along with Jill who, having now completed her Leaving, was keen to study Law. . . .

I found university to my liking. I was amazed that none of the lecturers checked to see whether you turned up or not. Even missing tutorials wasn't a deadly sin. I spent many long afternoons in the library, reading books totally unrelated to my course. Then there were hours in the coffee shop, discussing the meaning of life, and days stretched out in the sun under the giant palms that dotted the campus, thinking about what a wonderful climate we had. . . .

By the time I'd been at university a term, I was finding it very difficult to study at home. Apart from the high noise level and general chaos, I had no desk to work at, and, being disorganised myself, I was always losing important notes and papers, which I had to replace by photocopying someone else's.

Then when the August holidays came around, it suddenly dawned on me that if I was to pass anything, I would have to actually do some work. The trouble was I'd missed out on so much I didn't know where to begin.

My first attempts at a concentrated effort were rather futile, because I had to keep interrupting my study to call out, 'Turn down that radio!' or, 'The TV's too loud!' or, 'Will you all shut up, I'm trying to study!'

After a week or so of constant yelling and arguing, I came to the realisation that it was impossible to change my environment. I decided to try and change myself instead. I found that if I tried really hard, I could work amidst the greatest mess and loudest noise level, with no bother whatsoever. I just switched off and pretended I was the only one in the house.

This was no mean feat, because our house was always full of people. Many of my brother David's friends would just doss down on the lounge-room floor, they loved staying overnight. David had just begun high school that year. It never occurred to any of us to tell Mum there'd be someone extra for tea. We just assumed that she'd make what she had go a little bit further. I have to admit I was one of the worst offenders, but Mum never complained. She always told us, 'Your friends are welcome in this house.'

My technique for passing my exams that first year was simple, I crammed. The knowledge I gained was of little use to me afterwards, because as soon as my exams were over, I deleted it from my memory. Why clog up my brain with unnecessary facts and figures? I passed that year with a B and three C's. Mum was pleased, but urged me to spend more time studying so I could score A's, like Jill. . . .

I decided that I would like to spend my second year at university living away from home. Mum was mortified by the idea. I would be the first to leave the family nest. She urged me to reconsider.

After weeks of tearful arguments, she relented and said that if the Repatriation Department agreed to pay my fees, I could go. Fortunately, they did agree, and I was soon esconced in my own little room in Currie Hall, a co-educational boarding-house just opposite the university.

Now for most of my teenage years, Mum had been concerned over my lack of interest in boys. I had had plenty of good friendships with the opposite sex, but never a real romance. She was worried I would end up an old maid, and she, an old lady with no grandchildren. But now that I was living in a co-ed college, she suddenly started worrying that I would develop an interest I couldn't control and join the permissive society.

It was difficult for Mum to let me grow up. She often visited me at Currie Hall, but she always left in tears. One night, we had a huge argument because I wouldn't kiss her goodbye. I thought she was expecting a bit much, wanting me to kiss her in front of ten male students gathered around the exit to my building. I had an image to maintain. Eventually, I asked Mum not to come and see me at all if she was going to break down. It was too exhausting.

I had great difficulty seeing through my second year. I had developed an intense dislike of the subject I was majoring in. I was dismayed when, at our first tutorial, I discovered that a good deal of our laboratory work involved training white rats. Rats were one of the few animals I disliked. . . .

I was sick of trying to master statistics. I had a mental block when it came to any form of mathematics. 'Rats and Stats', I complained to a fellow student one day, 'I came here to learn about people.' I wasn't the only student who was disgruntled. Many complained, but to no avail. I got to the stage where I was ready to pull out of university completely. However, I was going out with Paul, a schoolteacher, by then, and he persuaded me to stick it out. . . .

In a short period, Paul and I got to know each other well, spending a lot of time together. We discovered that we had a lot in common. I liked the artistic side of his nature and he seemed to find my wit amusing. Also, he fitted into our family well.

Paul had spent his childhood in the north-west, living mostly at Derby. His parents were missionaries, as were his grandparents and many of his relatives. When Paul was thirteen, his family moved to Perth, where his parents started a hostel for mission children who came to the city to attend high school. Paul found high school very difficult at first, because, apart from the normal adjustments all children have to make and the fact that he had come from such a vastly different environment, he had a language problem. He only spoke pidgin English.

By the end of the second term of my third year at university, we'd fallen in love and decided to get married. This came as a real shock to Mum, because I had always told her Paul was just another good friend. It kept her off my back. It took a few weeks before the fact that we meant what we said actually sank in. Then Mum reacted more normally: she panicked. . . .

My wedding day, the ninth of December, 1972, dawned bright and sunny. I nicked into town early that morning to buy a wedding dress. I found an Indian caftan that I liked, it was cream with gold embroidery down the front. I was pleased because it was lovely and cool. It was becoming obvious that the day was going to be a stinker. By the time I got home, the temperature was over the hundred-degree mark. . . .

The wedding ceremony was brief and to the point.

After the ceremony was over, I went in search of Nan. I'd been concerned that, with the yard full of people she considered strangers, she might pull one of her disappearing acts. Mum had already explained to her that it was important she be seen as she was the grandmother of the bride. It took me a while to locate her.

I finally found her behind our old garden shed, crying.

'Nan, what's wrong?'

'You kids don't need me any more,' she sobbed, 'you're all grown up now.'

'But we still need you', I replied, trying to reassure her. She shook her head and continued to cry.

'Would you like me to get Mum?' I asked anxiously.

She nodded.

So I patted her arm and went and explained to Mum about Nan and she went to comfort her. She persuaded Nan to go inside the house, where she settled her down with a cup of tea. I felt at a loss. It seemed it never mattered what I did, it was always the wrong thing.

The rest of the afternoon wasn't too traumatic. Little things like the chooks and dogs running wild and a few guests ending up drunk didn't seem to matter. Everyone enjoyed themselves immensely and quite a few people commented that it was the most unusual wedding they'd ever been to. Mum took this as a compliment.

It was close to midnight when the last guest finally left. No one had wanted to go home.

'I did all right, didn't I, Sally?' Mum asked smugly.

'Yeah', I replied, 'maybe you should go into the catering business.'

'I was thinking that myself!' I glanced at her in fear. We both laughed.

Shortly after my wedding, I found out that I had passed all my units at university except psychology. I wasn't surprised. I disliked the work I was doing so much that I hadn't bothered to study for my exams. I decided to change my major for the following year, but Paul talked me out of it. 'You'll have to repeat', he said.

'Repeat?' I was disgusted at the thought. Another year with the rats was almost too much to bear. However, when I looked at the alternatives, I realised that I could be jumping from the frying-pan into the fire. Also, I'd heard that there was some human content in third-year psychology. So I decided to persevere.

Towards the end of the summer vacation, Paul and I moved into a run-down old weatherboard house in South Perth. The toilet was miles down the back of the yard, only one gas burner worked on the stove, the hot water system wasn't even as decent as the old chip heater we'd had at home, and the place was infested with tiny sand fleas. After living in there a few weeks, we also discovered that there were rats residing underneath the floor-boards. For some reason, none of this seemed to bother us. We thought the place had character and it was adventurous being on our own. . . .

After a while, Jill moved in with us and then two other friends as well. We were a happy little group. Most of our evenings were filled with Bob Dylan music, poetry and long discussions about current world issues. It was a lovely time in my life.

The day the university year began, I had to force myself to attend. I was convinced I was going to fail again. Many times, I came near to giving up my course entirely, but Paul always talked me into continuing. He gave me the impression that some of my attitudes were very immature. That was quite a shock. I had never thought of myself as being immature before.

Now that Jill and I were once again living in the same house, we often had long talks about our childhood. And the subject of Nan's origins always came up.

'We'll never know for sure', Jill said one night. 'Mum will never tell us.'

'Hmmn, I might start pestering her again. We're older now, we've got a right to know.'

'What does Paul think?'

'When I asked him whether he thought Nan was Aboriginal, he just laughed and said, "Isn't it obvious? Of course she is."' Paul, of course, had been brought up with Aboriginal people.

'I don't think we can really decide until we hear Mum admit it from her own lips.' . . .

A few weeks later, Mum popped in for her usual visit, laden

with fattening cakes and eager to tell me about the latest bargain she'd bought at auction. . . .

We . . . settled down in the kitchen and I made a cup of tea. Mum was soon in a relaxed and talkative mood.

Then, after a while, there was a lull in the conversation, so I said very casually, 'We're Aboriginal, aren't we, Mum?'

'Yes, dear', she replied, without thinking.

'Do you realise what you just said?!' I grinned triumphantly. Mum put her cake back onto her plate and looked as though she was going to be sick.

'Don't you back down!' I said quickly. 'There's been too many skeletons in our family closet. It's time things came out in the open.' After a few minutes' strained silence, Mum said, 'Why shouldn't you kids know now? You're old enough, it's not as though you're little any more. Besides, it's different now.'

'All those years, Mum', I said, 'how could you have lied to us all those years?'

'It was only a little white lie', she replied sadly.

I couldn't help laughing at her unintentional humour. In no time at all, we were both giggling uncontrollably. It was as if a wall that had been between us suddenly crumbled away. I felt closer to Mum then than I had for years.

I was very excited by my new heritage. When I told Jill that evening what Mum had said, she replied, 'I don't know what you're making a fuss about. I told you years ago Nan was Aboriginal. The fact that Mum's owned up doesn't change anything.' Sometimes, Jill was so logical I wanted to hit her. . . .

When Mum popped in a week later with a large sponge cake filled with chocolate custard, I was ecstatic. Not because of the cake, but because I had a bombshell to drop, and I was anxious to get on with it. I made coffee for a change and I waited until Mum was half-way through a cumbling piece of sponge before I said, 'I've applied for an Aboriginal scholarship.'

'What?!' she choked as she slammed down her mug and spat out the sponge.

'There's an Aboriginal scholarship you can get, Mum. Anyone of Aboriginal descent is eligible to apply.' . . .

'Oh Sally, you're awful', Mum chuckled, and then she added

thoughtfully, 'Well, why shouldn't you apply? Nan's had a hard life. Why shouldn't her grandchildren get something out of it?' . . .

I don't think Mum realised how deep my feelings went. It wasn't the money I was after, I was still receiving the Repatriation scholarship. I desperately wanted to do something to identify with my new-found heritage and that was the only thing I could think of.

When I was granted an interview for my scholarship application, Mum was amazed. I think she expected them to ignore me. She was very worried about what I was going to tell them. Mum always worried about what to tell people. It was as if the truth was never adequate, or there was something to hide.

She had been inventing stories and making exaggerated claims since the day she was born. It was part of her personality. She found it difficult to imagine how anyone could get through life any other way, so consequently, when in response to her question about my interview, I answered, 'I'm going to tell them the truth', she was flabbergasted.

I was successful in my scholarship application, but for the next few months, I was the butt of many family jokes. We all felt shy and awkward about our new-found past. No one was sure what to do with it or about it, and none of the family could agree on whether I'd done the right thing or not. In keeping with my character, I had leapt in feet first. I wanted to do something positive. I wanted to say, 'My grandmother's Aboriginal and it's a part of me, too.' I wasn't sure where my actions would lead, and the fact that Nan remained singularly unimpressed with my efforts added only confusion to my already tenuous sense of identity.

'Did Mum tell you I got the scholarship, Nan?' I asked one day.

'Yes. What did you tell them?'

'I told them that our family was Aboriginal but that we'd been brought up to believe differently.'

'What did you tell them about me?'

'Nothing. So relax.'

'You won't ever tell them about me, will you, Sally? I don't like strangers knowing our business, especially government people. You never know what they might do.'

'Why are you so suspicious, Nan?' I asked gently. She ignored my question and shuffled outside to do the garden. A sense of sadness suddenly overwhelmed me. I wanted to cry. 'Get a grip on yourself, woman', I muttered. 'You don't even know what you want to cry about!'

Slowly, over that year, Mum and I began to notice a change in Nan. Not a miraculous change, but a change just the same. Her interests began to extend beyond who was in the telephone box opposite our house, to world affairs. Nan had always watched the news every night on each channel if she could, but now, instead of just noting world disasters, she began to take an interest in news about black people.

If the story was sad, she'd put her hand to her mouth and say, 'See, see what they do to black people'. On the other hand, if black people were doing well for themselves, she'd complain, 'Just look at them, showing off. Who do they think they are. They just black like me.' . . .

In a strange sort of way, my life had new purpose because of that. I wondered whether, because Jill and I had accepted that part of ourselves, perhaps Nan was coming to terms with it, too. I was anxious to learn as much as I could about the past. I made a habit of taking advantage of Mum's general good nature.

'Where was Nan born, Mum?' I asked her one day.

'Oh, I don't know. Up North somewhere.'

'Has she ever talked to you about her life?'

'You know she won't talk about the past. She says she can't remember.' . . .

Amazingly, I passed my psychology unit at the end of that year, I even scored a B. I was looking forward to my final year because there was quite a large slice about people in the course and that, after all, was what I'd come to learn about.

By now, both Jill and I had many friends at university. All our lives, people had asked us what nationality we were, most had assumed we were Greek or Italian, but we'd always replied, 'Indian'. Now, when we were asked, we said, 'Aboriginal.' . . .

Sometimes, people would say, 'But you're lucky, you'd never know you were that, you could pass for anything.' Many students reacted with an embarrassed silence. Perhaps that was the worst reaction of all. It was like we'd said a forbidden word. Others muttered, 'Oh, I'm sorry . . .' and when they realised what they were saying, they just sort of faded away.

Up until now, if we thought about it at all, we'd both thought

Australia was the least racist country in the world, now we knew better. I began to wonder what it was like for Aboriginal people with really dark skin and broad features, how did Australians react to them? How had white Australians reacted to my grandmother in the past, was that the cause of her bitterness?

About half-way through that year, 1973, I received a brief note from the Commonwealth Department of Education, asking me to come in for an interview with a senior officer of the department. I was scared stiff. . . .

'Mrs Morgan', the senior officer said as I sat down. 'We'll get straight to the point. We have received information, from what appears to be a very reliable source, that you have obtained the Aboriginal scholarship under false pretences. This person, who is a close friend of you and your sister, has told us that you have been bragging all over the university campus about how easy it is to obtain the scholarship without even being Aboriginal. Apparently, you've been saying that anyone can get it.' . . .

'Look', I said angrily, 'when I applied for this scholarship, I told your people everything I knew about my family, it was their decision to grant me a scholarship, so if there's any blame to be laid, it's your fault, not mine. How do you expect me to prove anything? What would you like me to do, bring my grandmother and mother in and parade them up and down so you can all have a look? There's no way I'll do that, even if you tell me to. I'd rather lose the allowance. It's my word against whoever complained, so it's up to you to decide, isn't it?'

My heart was pounding fiercely. It was very difficult for me to stand up for myself, I wasn't used to dealing with authority figures so directly. No wonder Mum and Nan didn't like dealing with government people, I thought. They don't give you a chance.

The senior officer looked at me silently for a few minutes and then said, 'Well, Mrs Morgan. You are either telling the truth, or you're a very good actress!'

I was amazed, still my innocence wasn't to be conceded.

'I'm telling the truth', I said crossly.

'Very well, you may go.' I was dismissed with a nod of the head. I was unable to move.

'I'm not sure I want this scholarship any more', I said. 'What if someone else makes a complaint? Will I be hauled in here for the same thing?'

The senior officer thought for a moment, then said, 'No. If someone else complains, we'll ignore it.'

Satisfied, I left and walked quickly to the elevator. I felt sick and I wasn't sure how much longer my legs would support me. It was just as well I'd lost my temper, I thought. Otherwise, I wouldn't have defended myself at all. It was the thought that somehow Mum and Nan might have to be involved that had angered me. It had seemed so demeaning. . . .

What if I had been too shy to defend myself, I thought. What would have happened then? I had no doubt they would have taken the scholarship away from me. Then I thought, maybe I'm doing the wrong thing. It hadn't been easy trying to identify with being Aboriginal. No one was sympathetic, so many people equated it with dollars and cents, no one understood why it was so important. I should chuck it all in, I thought. Paul was supporting me now, I could finish my studies without the scholarship. It wasn't worth it. . . .

The bus pulled in and I hopped on and paid my fare. Then I headed for the back of the bus. I just made it. My eyes were becoming clouded with unshed tears and if the bus had . . . been any longer, I would have probably fallen over in the aisle. I turned my face to the window and stared out at the passing bitumen. Had I been dishonest with myself? What did it really mean to be Aboriginal? I'd never lived off the land and been a hunter and a gatherer. I'd never participated in corroborees or heard stories of the Dreamtime. I'd lived all my life in suburbia and told everyone I was Indian. I hardly knew any Aboriginal people. What did it mean for someone like me?

Half-way home on the bus, I felt so weighed down with all my questions that I decided to give it all up. . . .

Just then, for some reason, I could see Nan. She was standing in front of me, looking at me. Her eyes were sad. 'Oh Nan', I sighed, 'why did you have to turn up now, of all times.' She vanished as quickly as she'd come. I knew then that, for some reason, it was very important I stay on the scholarship. If I denied my tentative identification with the past now, I'd be denying her as well. I had to hold on to the fact that, some day, it might all mean something. And if that turned out to be the belief of a fool, then I would just have to live with it. . . .

[M]y run-in with the Education Department did produce some

unexpected results. Mum suddenly became more sympathetic to my desire to learn about the past. One day, she said to me, 'Of course, you know Nan was born on Corunna Downs Station, don't you?'

'I've heard her mention that station', I replied, 'but whenever I've asked her about it, she clams up. Remember when David got that map of the north and showed her on the map where Corunna Downs was? She was quite excited that it was on a map, wasn't she? Yet, she still won't talk.'

'I know. It really upsets me, sometimes.'

'Mum, who owned Corunna Downs?'

'Judy's father.'

'I didn't know that. What was his name?'

'Alfred Howden Drake-Brockman.'

'Fancy that. I suppose that's why Judy and Nan are so close. That and the fact that Nan used to work for the family.'

'Yes. Nan was Judy's nursemaid when she was little.'

'Tell me the other things she used to do then, Mum.'

'I remember she used to work very hard. Very, very hard . . . Oh, I don't want to talk any more. Maybe some other time.'

For once, I accepted her decision without complaint. I knew now there would be other times. . . .

After I graduated from university, I continued post-graduate studies in psychology at the Western Australian Institute of Technology. . . .

Mum and I had many small conversations about the past, but they weren't really informative, because we tended to cover the same ground. Sometimes, Mum would try to get Nan to talk. One day, I heard Nan shout, 'You're always goin' on about the past these days, Glad. I'm sick of it. It makes me sick in here', she pointed to her chest. 'My brain's no good, Glad, I can't 'member!' . . .

'She's been like that all her life', she complained to me one day, 'she'll never change. When I was little, I used to ask about my father, but she wouldn't tell me anything. In the end, I gave up.'

'Who was your father?'

'Oh, I don't know', she replied sadly. 'Nan just said he was a white man who died when I was very small.'

I felt sad then. I promised myself that, one day, I would find out who her father was. She had a right to know.

In 1975, I gave birth to a daughter, Ambelin Star. . . .

By the time I'd had my second child, Blaze Jake, in 1978, a change was beginning to take place in our family. Nan's brother, Arthur, began making regular visits. He was keen to see more of Nan now that they were both getting older. And he was very fond of Mum.

'Who is he?' I asked, when I found him parked in front of the TV one day with a huge meal on his lap.

'You remember him. Arthur, Nan's brother. When you were little, he visited us a couple of times, remember?'

I cast my mind back and suddenly I saw him as he had been so many years before. Tall and dark, with a big smile. . . .

It took a while for me to get close to Arthur. He loved Mum, but he was wary of the rest of us. He wasn't quite sure what to make of us, and he wasn't quite sure what we made of him. If he had have known how insatiably curious we were about him and his past, he would probably have been scared off.

But on one of these early visits, he unexpectedly did provide us with a very vivid picture from the past. Some old photographs of Nan, taken in the nineteen twenties. Nan had always refused to allow any of us to take her photograph, so it was exciting to be able to see her as a young woman. . . .

[O]ne . . . afternoon, I wandered out to the backyard to find Nan and Arthur under a gum tree, jabbering away in what sounded to me like a foreign language. I sat down very quietly on the steps and listened. I prayed they wouldn't see me.

After a few minutes, Nan said, 'My eyes aren't that bad, Sally, I can see you there, spyin' on us.' . . .

'I'm going to write a book.' . . .

'A book about our family history.' . . .

Mum took me more seriously the following week when I bought a typewriter and started to type. . . .

'I went to Battye Library the other day, Mum.'

'What for?'

'It's a history library. Western Australian history. I wanted to read up about Aborigines.' . . .

'[W]hen Nan was younger, Aborigines were considered subnormal and not capable of being educated the way whites were. You know, the pastoral industry was built on the back of slave labour. Aboriginal people were forced to work, if they didn't, the station owners called the police in. I always thought Australia was different to America, Mum, but we had slavery here, too. The people might not have been sold on the blocks like the American Negroes were, but they were owned, just the same.'

'I know', Mum said. There were tears in her eyes. 'They were treated just awful. I know Nan . . .' She stopped. 'I better get going, Sal, I've got to go to work early tomorrow.'

'What were you going to say?' . . .

'I don't want to talk about it now. Maybe later. You'll have to give me time. If you want my help, you'll have to give me time.' . . .

'[F]or years, I've been telling people I'm Indian! I have a right to know my own history. Come to think of it, you've never gotten around to telling me why you lied to us about that. About being Indian.'

'Oh, let's not go into that, I've had enough for one night.' . . .

'I meant to tell you, I got a copy of your birth certificate the other day.'

Mum sat down just as quickly. 'How did you do that? I didn't know you could do that.'

'It's easy. You just apply to the Registrar General's Office. I said I wanted it for the purposes of family history. I tried to get Nan's and Arthur's, but they didn't have one. Hardly any Aboriginal people had birth certificates in those days.'

'Sally . . .' Mum said tentatively, 'who did they say my father was? Was that on the certificate?'

'There was just a blank there, Mum, I'm sorry.'

'Just a blank?' Mum muttered slowly. 'Just a blank. That's awful, like nobody owns me.'

I hadn't anticipated Mum being so cut up about it. I felt awful. She'd known all her life that Nan had never married.

'I'm really sorry, Mum', I said gently. 'I got your certificate because I thought it might give me some leads, but it didn't. Except that you were born in King Edward Memorial Hospital. That's unusual, because I wouldn't have thought they'd have let Aboriginal women in there in those days.'

'Is that where I was born?'

'Yep. You sure were.'

'Well, at least you've found out something, Sally.'

'You've asked Nan who your father was, haven't you?'

'Yes.'

'Maybe Judy would know.'

'She probably does', Mum sighed, 'but she won't tell. I asked her once and she just kept saying, "It's in the blood", whatever that means.'

'I bet you never asked her straight out. You beat round the bush too much. Why don't you corner her and say, "Judy, I want to know who my father is and I'm not leaving here till I find out." ' . . .

'I couldn't do that, I'm not brave enough. Anyway, he couldn't have cared less about me or he would have contacted me by now. And when Nan needed help, there was no one. He can't be much of a man.'

'You know, Mum, just on a logical basis, it must be someone who mixed with the mob at Ivanhoe in Claremont.' . . .

A few days later, I rang Aunty Judy. I explained that I was writing a book about Nan and Arthur and I thought she might be able to help me. We agreed that I would come down for lunch and she said she could tell me who Nan's father was. I was surprised. I had expected to encounter opposition. Perhaps I wanted to encounter opposition, it fired my sense of injustice. I felt really excited after our talk on the telephone. Would I really discover who my great-grandfather was? If I was lucky, I might even find out about my grandfather as well. . . .

During lunch . . . Aunty Judy said, 'You know, I think I have some old photos of your mother you might be interested in. I'll have to dig them out.'

'Oh great! I'd really appreciate that.'

'I'll tell you what I know about the station, but it's not a lot. You know, a relative of ours published a book a while ago and they got all their facts wrong, so you better make sure you get yours right.'

'That's why I'm here. I don't want to print anything that's not true.'

After lunch, we retired to the more comfortable chairs in the lounge-room.

'Now, dear', Aunty Judy said, 'what would you like to know?'

'Well, first of all, I'd like to know who Nan's father was and also a bit about what her life was like when she was at Ivanhoe.'

'Well, that's no problem. My mother told me that Nan's father was a mystery man. He was a chap they called Maltese Sam and he used to be cook on Corunna Downs. He was supposed to have come from a wealthy Maltese family, I think he could have been the younger son, a ne'er-do-well. My mother said that he always used to tell them that, one day, he was going back to Malta to claim his inheritance. The trouble was he was a drinker. He'd save money for the trip and then he'd go on a binge and have to start all over again. He used to talk to my father, Howden, a lot. He was proud Nanna was his little girl.'

'Did he ever come and visit Nan when she was at Ivanhoe?'

'Yes, I think he did, once. But he was drunk, apparently, and wanted to take Nanna away with him. Nan was frightened, she didn't want to go, so my mother said to him, you go back to Malta and put things right. When you've claimed your inheritance, you can have Daisy. We never saw him again. I don't know what happened to him. Nan didn't want to go with him, we were her family by then.'

'Did you meet Maltese Sam?'

'Oh, goodness, no. I was only a child. My mother told me the story.'

'How old was Nan when she came down to Perth?'

'About fifteen and sixteen.'

'And what were her duties at Ivanhoe?'

'She looked after us children.'

'Aunty Judy, do you know who Mum's father is?'

'Your mother knows who her father is.'

'No, she doesn't. She wants to know and Nan won't tell her.'

'I'm sure I told your mother at one time who her father was.'

'She doesn't know and she'd really like to. It's very important to her.'

'Well, I'm not sure I should tell you. You never know about these things.'

'Mum wanted me to ask you.'

Aunty Judy paused and looked at me silently for a few seconds. Then she said slowly, 'All right, everybody knows who her father was, it was Jack Grime. Everyone always said that Gladdie's the image of him.'

'Jack Grime? And Mum takes after him, does she?'

'Like two peas in a pod.'

'Who was Jack Grime?'

'He was an Englishman, an engineer, very, very clever. He lived with us at Ivanhoe, he was a friend of my father's. He was very fond of your mother. When she was working as a florist, he'd call in and see her. We could always tell when he'd been to see Gladdie, he'd have a certain look on his face. He'd say, "I've been to see Gladdie", and we'd just nod.'

'Did he ever marry and have other children?'

'No. He was a very handsome man, but he never married and, as far as I know, there were no other children. He spent the rest of his life living in Sydney, he was about eighty-six when he died.'

'Eighty-six? Well, that couldn't have been that long ago, then? If he was so fond of Mum, you'd think he'd have left her something in his will. Not necessarily money, just a token to say he owned her. After all, she was his only child.'

'No, there was nothing. He wasn't a wealthy man, there was no money to leave. You know Roberta?'

'Yes, Mum's been out to dinner with her a few times.'

'Well, she's the daughter of Jack's brother, Robert. She's Glad-die's first cousin.' . . .

'Can you tell me anything about Nan's mother?'

'Not a lot. Her name was Annie, she was a magnificent-looking woman. She was a good dressmaker, my father taught her how to sew. She could design anything.'

Our conversation continued for another half an hour or so. I kept thinking, had Mum lied? Did she really know who her father was? Was she really against me digging up the past, just like Nan? I had one last question.

'Aunty Judy, I was talking to Arthur, Nan's brother, the other day and he said that his father was the same as yours, Alfred How-den Drake-Brockman. Isn't it possible he could have been Nan's as well?'

'No. That's not what everyone said. I've told you what I know; who Nan's father is. I'm certain Arthur's father wasn't Howden, I don't know who his father was.'

'Arthur also told me about his half-brother Albert. He said Howden was his father, too.'

'Well, he went by the name of Brockman so I suppose it might be possible, but certainly not the other two.' . . .

I walked out to the front gate and, just as I opened it, Mum pulled up in the car. . . .

'Mum, are you sure you don't know who your father is? You've lied about things before.' It was a stupid thing to say, Mum was immediately on the defensive.

'Of course I don't know who my father is, Sally. Didn't you find out, after all?' She was disappointed. I felt ashamed of myself for doubting her.

'I found out. It was Jack Grime, and Roberta is your first cousin.'

'Oh God, I can't believe it!' She was stunned.

'Can you remember anything about him, Mum? You're supposed to look a lot like him.'

'No, I can't remember much, except he used to wear a big gold watch that chimed. I thought it was magical.' . . .

An overwhelming sadness struck me. My mother was fifty-five years of age and she'd only just discovered who her father was. It didn't seem fair. . . .

'Judy says Nan's father was a bloke called Maltese Sam. That he came from a wealthy family and wanted to take Nan away with him.' . . .

The following evening, Mum and I sat chatting to Arthur. After we'd finished tea, I said, 'I visited Judith Drake-Brockman the other day, Arthur. . . .

'I thought she might be able to tell me something about Corunna Downs and something about Nan.'

'You wanna know about Corunna, you come to me. I knew all the people there.'

'I know you did.' I paused. 'Can I ask you a question?'

'You ask what you like.'

'Judy told me Nan's father was a chap by the name of Maltese Sam, have you ever heard of him?'

'She said WHAT?'

Arthur was a bit hard of hearing sometimes, so I repeated my question.

'Don't you listen to her', he said when I'd asked again. 'She never lived on the station, how would she know?'

'Well, she got the story from her mother, Alice, who got the story from her husband, Howden, who said that Annie had confided in him.'

Arthur threw back his head and laughed. Then he thumped his fist on the arm of his chair and said, 'Now you listen to me, Daisy's

father is the same as mine. Daisy is my only full sister, Albert, he's
our half-brother, his father was Howden, too, but by a different
woman.'

'So you reckoned he fathered the both of you.'

'By jove he did! Are you gunna take the word of white people
against your own flesh and blood? I got no papers to prove what
I'm sayin'. Nobody cared how many blackfellas were born in those
days, nor how many died. I know because my mother, Annie, told
me. She said Daisy and I belonged to one another. Don't you go
takin' the word of white people against mine.'

Arthur had us both nearly completely convinced, except for
one thing, he avoided our eyes. Mum and I knew it wasn't a good
sign, there was something he wasn't telling us. So I said again,
'You're sure about this, Arthur?'

'Too right! Now, about this Maltese Sam, don't forget Alice
was Howden's second wife and they had the Victorian way of
thinking in those days. Before there were white women, our father
owned us, we went by his name, but later, after he married his first
wife, Nell, he changed our names. I'll tell you about that one day.
He didn't want to own us no more. They were real fuddy-duddies
in those days. No white man wants to have black kids runnin'
round the place with his name. And Howden's mother and father,
they were real religious types, I bet they didn't know about no black
kids that belonged to them.'

We all laughed then. Arthur was like Mum, it wasn't often he
failed to see the funny side of things.

When we'd all finally calmed down, he said, 'You know, if only
you could get Daisy to talk. She could tell you so much. I know
she's got her secrets, but there are things she could tell you without
tellin' those.'

'She won't talk, Arthur', I sighed. 'You know a lot about Nan,
can't you tell us?'

He was silent for a moment, thoughtful. Then he said, 'I'd like
to. I really would, but it'd be breakin' a trust. Some things 'bout her
I can't tell. It wouldn't be right. She could tell you everything you
want to know. You see, Howden was a lonely man. I know, one
night at Ivanhoe, we both got drunk together and he told me all his
troubles. He used to go down to Daisy's room at night and talk to
her. I can't say no more. You'll have to ask her.'

'But Arthur, what if she won't tell us?'

'Then I can't, either. There's some things Daisy's got to tell herself, or not at all. I can't say no more.'

After he left, Mum and I sat analysing everything for ages. We were very confused, we knew that the small pieces of information we now possessed weren't the complete truth.

'Sally', Mum said, breaking into my thoughts, 'do you remember when Arthur first started visiting us and he said Albert was his full brother?'

'Yeah, but that was before he knew us well.'

'Yes, but remember how he almost whispered when he told us the truth about Albert? He didn't want to hurt the feelings of any of Albert's family and he loved him so much I suppose he thought it didn't matter.'

'Yeah, I know. You think there might be more to Nan's parentage.'

'It's possible.'

'There's another possibility. Howden may have been her father, but there could be something else, some secret he wants to keep, that is somehow tied in with all of this. Perhaps that's why he didn't look us in the eye.'

'Yes, that's possible, too. And I can't see why he wouldn't tell us the truth, because he knows how much it means to us. I don't think we'll ever know the full story. I think we're going to have to be satisfied with guesses.'

'It makes me feel so sad to think no one wants to own our family.'

'I know, Mum, but look at it this way, just on a logical basis, it's possible he was her father. We know he was sleeping with Annie, and Arthur said that even after he married his first wife, he was still sleeping with Annie, so he could have sired her.'

'Yes, it's possible.'

'Well, that's all we can go on then, possibilities. Now, Judy said Jack Grime was your father, but maybe he wasn't. He was living at Ivanhoe at the time you were born, but that doesn't necessarily mean he fathered you, does it?'

'Oh God, Sally', Mum laughed, 'let's not get in any deeper. I've had enough for one night.' . . .

A few days later, I popped in to see Mum. Nan told me she'd

just gone up to the shops and would be back in a few minutes. I decided to wait. I wasn't intending to say anything to Nan about my trip to Judy's, I wasn't in the mood for an argument. Uncharacteristically, she began following me around the house, making conversation about whatever came into her head. I suddenly realised that she was anxious to hear what Judy had told me, but I decided to let her sweat it out and bring up the topic herself.

Finally, after half an hour of chatting about the weather, the cool-drink man and Curly's arthritis, she blurted out, 'Well, what did she tell you?'

'Who?' I asked innocently.

'You know, Judy. Mum told me you'd been to see her.' . . .

I said . . . 'She told me that you were the nursemaid at Ivanhoe.'

Nan grunted. 'Hmph, that and everything else.'

'You've always worked hard, haven't you, Nan?'

'Always, too hard.'

'Judy also said your father was a bloke called Maltese Sam.'

'What did she say?' Nan looked astonished.

'She said your father was called Maltese Sam, and that he visited you at Ivanhoe and wanted to take you away with him. Do you remember anyone visiting you there?'

'Only Arthur, and that wasn't till I was older.'

'There was no one else, you sure?'

'I'd know if I had visitors, wouldn't I? I'm not stupid, Sally, despite what you kids might think.'

'We don't think you're stupid.'

Nan pressed her lips together and stared hard at the red-brick fireplace directly opposite where we were sitting.

'Nan', I said gently, 'was your father Maltese Sam?'

She sighed, then murmured, 'Well, if Judy says he is, then I s'pose it's true.' I looked at her closely, there were tears in her eyes. I suddenly realised she was hurt, and I felt terrible, because I'd caused it. I decided to change the subject. I began to talk about my children and the latest naughty things they'd been up to. We had a chuckle, and then I said, 'Wouldn't you have liked to have had more children, Nan?' She shrugged her shoulders and looked away.

'Think I'll do some gardening now, Sal', she said. 'Those leaves need raking up.'

She left me sitting alone and confused in the lounge-room. What was she hiding? Why couldn't she just be honest with us? Surely she realised we didn't blame her for anything. Surely she realised we loved her? I swallowed the lump that was rising in my throat. One thing I was sure of: before this was over, Mum and I would have shed more than our fair share of tears. . . .

[T]hree evenings later, after they'd finished eating a big roast dinner, Mum said quietly, 'Don't go and watch television yet. Nan, I want to talk to you. Sit with me for a while.'

'I'm not talking about the past, Gladdie. It makes me sick to talk about the past.' . . .

'[Y]ou know Sally's trying to write a book about the family?'

'Yes. I don't know why she wants to tell everyone our business.'

'Why shouldn't she write a book?' Mum said firmly. 'There's been nothing written about people like us, all the history's about the white man. There's nothing about Aboriginal people and what they've been through.'

'All right', she muttered, 'what do you want to ask?'

'Well, you know when you write a book, it has to be the truth. You can't put lies in a book. You know that, don't you Nan?'

'I know that, Glad', Nan nodded.

'Good. Now, what I want to know is who you think your father was. I know Judy says it was Maltese Sam and Arthur says it was Howden. Well, I'm not interested in what they say. I want to know what you say. Can you tell me, Nan, who do you think he really was?'

Nan was quiet for a few seconds and then, pressing her lips together, she said very slowly, 'I . . . think . . . my father was . . . Howden Drake-Brockman.'

It was a small victory, but an important one. Not so much for the knowledge, but for the fact that Nan had finally found it possible to trust her family with a piece of information that was important to her.

Mum gave Nan a week to recover before tackling her about Jack Grime. She'd been trying to spend more time at home and, in a gentle way, talk about the past.

Finally one evening, she said, 'Nan, I know who my father was.' Nan was silent. 'It was Jack Grime, wasn't it, Nan?' Silence. 'Wasn't it, Nan?'

'Judy tell you that, did she?'

'Yes.'

'Well, if that's what she says.'

'But was he, Nan?'

'I did love Jack.'

'What happened then, Nan, tell me what happened. Why didn't it work out?'

'How could it? He was well-off, high society. He mixed with all the wealthy white people, I was just a black servant.'

Nan ignored Mum's pleas to tell her more and disappeared into her room, leaving Mum to cry on her own.

When Mum and I talked about this later, Mum said, 'You know, he probably was my father, Nan obviously had a relationship with him. If he was, I feel very bitter towards him. There's never been any acknowledgement or feeling of love from him. I was just one of the kids. Later, when he moved east with Judy's family, he never wrote, there were no goodbyes, I never saw or heard from him again. All I can remember is that he used to tell wonderful stories, he was like a childhood uncle, but definitely not a father.'

We hoped that Nan would tell us more about the past, especially about the people she had known on Corunna Downs. Mum was anxious to hear about her grandmother, Annie, and her great-grandmother, and I was keen to learn what life had been like for the people in those days. To our great disappointment, Nan would tell us nothing. She maintained that if we wanted to find out about the past, we had to do it without her help. 'I'm taking my secrets to the grave', she told Mum and I dramatically, one day.

Over the next few years, Arthur continued to visit regularly and to talk in snatches about Corunna. Sometimes, he'd say to Nan, 'Daisy, come and sit down. Tell your daughter and granddaughter about the past, tell them what they want to know.'

But Nan maintained a position of non-co-operation, insisting that the things she knew were secrets and not to be shared with others. Arthur always countered this statement with, 'It's history, that's what it is. We're talkin' history. You could be talkin' it, too, but then, I s'pose you don't know what it is.'

Nan hated Arthur hinting that she might be ignorant, so she replied vindictively, 'You always makin' out you're better than anyone else. Well, you're not! You're just a stupid old blackfella, that's you!'

Arthur was incensed. Raising his voice, he said, 'You're a great one to talk. Here I am in my nineties and I can read the paper and write my own name, too. I been educated! I'm not like you, you're just an ignorant blackfella!'

Nan was mortally offended. For a few seconds, she was lost for words, then she shouted, 'I don't know why I bother with you! You're always picking fights. You know they were s'posed to send me to school. It's not my fault I can't read or write. It hasn't done nothin' for you, anyway. I been listenin' to you, you can't even make up a good story!' . . .

'He shouldn't have said that to me . . . I can't help it if I can't read or write.' Nan looked sad and Mum was lost for words. It wasn't until then that anyone realised how deeply she felt about the whole thing.

'Lots of people can't read or write', Mum said gently, 'white people, too. It's not important. It doesn't make you any better than anyone else.'

'Yes, it does', Nan muttered. 'I always wanted to learn. Oh, go away, Gladdie, leave me in peace.' We all avoided mentioning anything to do with reading or writing after that, we didn't want Nan to think we were looking down on her.

The next time I saw Arthur, he asked me to tell him about the book I was writing.

'I want to write the history of my own family', I told him.

'What do you want to do that for?'

'Well, there's almost nothing written from a personal point of view about Aboriginal people. All our history is about the white man. No one knows what it was like for us. A lot of our history has been lost, people have been too frightened to say anything. There's a lot of our history we can't even get at, Arthur. There are all sorts of files about Aboriginals that go way back, and the government won't release them. You take the old police files, they're not even controlled by Battye Library, they're controlled by the police. And they don't like letting them out, because there are so many instances of police abusing their power when they were supposed to be Protectors of Aborigines that it's not funny! I mean, our own government had terrible policies for Aboriginal people. Thousands of families in Australia were destroyed by the government policy of taking children away. None of that happened to white people. I know Nan doesn't agree with what I'm doing. She thinks I'm trying to make trouble, but I'm not. I just want to try to tell a little bit of the other side of the story.'

Arthur was silent for a few seconds, then he said thoughtfully, 'Daisy doesn't agree, I know that. I think she's been brainwashed. I tell you how I look at it, it's part of our history, like. And everyone's interested in history. Do you think you could put my story in that book of yours?'

'Oh Arthur, I'd love to!'

'Then we got a deal. You got that tape recorder of yours? We'll use that. You just listen to what I got to say, if you want to ask questions, you stop me. Now, some things I might tell you, I don't want in the book, is that all right?' . . .

The following weeks, I flew to Sydney and then caught the bus to Wollongong. Aunty June, Judy's sister, and her husband, Angus, met me at the bus station. I felt very nervous. The last time I'd seen them, I was a child, now I was a woman with a mission.

I could not have had two kinder hosts. They did everything to make me feel at home. We swapped many funny yarns and stories about home.

Alice Drake-Brockman was in a nearby nursing home. She was ninety-three and in the best of health. Aunty June took me to the home and explained who I was and why I was there. . . .

'Can you tell me who Nan's father might have been, Alice?'

'Oh yes. Your great-grandfather was a Maltese, I think he came from a wealthy family, but was the younger son. He was always saying he must go back and right his affairs in the old country. He had good blood in him, but he never got past the nearest pub. One time, I think he managed to get as far as Carnarvon, but then he spent all his money and had to come back again.'

'Did you ever meet Nan's mother?'

'Oh yes! She was a born designer. On the hard ground, she'd cut out dresses, leg-o'-mutton sleeves and all. She could design anything. I didn't get to know her well, because I left the station, and, when I left, I took Daisy with me. Annie had said to me shortly before, "Take her with you, mistress, I don't want my daughter to grow up and marry a native, take her with you." It was at her request that I took Daisy. Of course, what I was doing was illegal, you weren't supposed to bring natives into Perth. . . . When I was prosecuted, they said, "How do you plead, guilty or not guilty?" My husband stood up and said, "Guilty, M'Lord." They asked us our reasons and I told them her own mother had said, "Don't leave my daughter here, take her with you." I brought other native girls in after that. I'd train them, then find friends who wanted one. I provided quite a few.'

'What was Corunna Downs Station like then?'

'Well, I can't tell you a lot about that, because I was only there once. . . . When I went to Corunna, there were about forty natives working for us. Every Sunday night, we'd roll the piano out onto the verandah, it'd be cold, so we'd have a big log fire out in the open. The natives would sit around and we'd have a church service and a sing-song. The natives just loved it. They lived for it. At nine o'clock, we'd stop. Then, they'd all be given cocoa and hot buns. That was their life. The natives never liked to work. You had to work with them if you wanted them to work. They always wanted to go walkabout. They couldn't stand the tedium of the same job. We used to change their jobs. Daisy always had that tendency. She'd get tired of one job, so I'd say, "Come on, let's chuck the housework", and we'd go shopping.'

'Did Nan ever see her mother again?'

'Yes. I sent her back for a holiday with Howden. I said, "Take her back for a holiday, let her see her mother." She went back by boat. She saw them and she was happy, but, by then, we'd become her family.' . . .

'Why did she leave Ivanhoe?'

'Why? The police came and took Daisy from me. She was man-powered during the war. No one could have any home-help, I wasn't allowed to have her. She was a wonderful cook. Later, she rented a little house near the Ocean Beach Hotel. I gave her quite a lot of furniture, brooms and things, that I could do without. That's how she supplied herself.'

'Can you tell me who my mother's father might have been?'

'No. I couldn't tell you. He must have been white, maybe a station hand. When Daisy was pregnant, I was absolutely ignorant. My husband said to me one night, "I think you'd better get up, Daisy seems to be in pain." She slept in a room just off ours, it was his dressing-room, we turned it into a room for Daisy. She was groaning and I said, "What's up, Daisy?" She said, "I don't know, mistress, but I think I'm going to have a baby." . . . So I went and packed a suitcase and took her to the hospital. The baby was born a few hours later, but who the father was, we never found out.

Gladys was always a beautiful girl. She went to Parkerville, we took her there. That was a home run by the Church of England sisters, it was a charity home for the ones that had no parents, we sent Gladys there. She grew up with just as nice manners as anybody could wish. Later, when she was grown up, I said to the florist in Claremont, "Will you take this girl?" They said, "No, we wouldn't. We couldn't take a native, because you know they're forbidden." I said, "Will you take her on trial for me, I just can't bear to think of her becoming a servant somewhere." So they took her on trial to please me, and they kept her as one of the family. She looked like a lovely Grecian girl. She never looked back. You see, she was so well brought up by those Church of England sisters. It was only through my being an old scholar that I was able to get her in. It was very hard to get her in.'

When Alice finished talking, I felt a little stunned. All my life, I'd been under the impression that Mum had lived with Nan at Ivanhoe. It was a shock to me to discover that she'd been placed in a children's home. Why hadn't she told us? I decided I would ask her as soon as I got back. . . .

In talking to Alice, it dawned on me how different Australian society must have been in those days. There would have been a strong English tradition amongst the upper classes. I could understand the effects these attitudes could have had on someone like Nan. She must have felt terribly out of place. At the same time, I was aware that it would be unfair of me to judge Alice's attitudes from my standpoint in the nineteen eighties. . . .

I decided to tackle Mum about Parkerville Children's Home. She had never told any of us she'd been brought up in a home. She'd always led us to believe that she'd spent all her childhood at Ivanhoe. It wasn't that she'd actually lied about it, it was a sin of omission more than anything else.

I popped the question over afternoon tea. Mum was shocked. But before she had time to gather her wits, I said, 'You deliberately misled us. All these years, I thought you were brought up at Ivanhoe with Judy and June. Why on earth didn't you tell us the truth?' It was yet another tactical error; if Mum hadn't been on the defensive before, she certainly was now.

'You're making a big deal out of nothing', she replied. 'I spent holidays at Ivanhoe. Anyway, there's nothing to tell.' . . .

It was difficult for me to decide how next to trace my family history. Nan and Mum had united. Now that Mum was feeling threatened, she suddenly found she had more in common with Nan than she'd ever imagined. . . .

After much thought, I decided that our best course was to return to Nan and Arthur's birthplace, Corunna Downs.

Paul thought this was a wonderful idea, he loved the North and he also could see no other way forward for us. He hoped we could persuade Nan to go with us.

When I told Mum about the idea, she wasn't very positive.

'You can't go up there. It's a silly idea, you don't know anyone. Nan won't want you to go.'

'Nan doesn't want me to do anything! All my leads have dried up, Mum, that's all there is left, now.'

When I approached Nan about the idea of going up North, she was disgusted.

'You're like your mother, you like to throw money away. All you'll be lookin' at is dirt. Dirt and scrub.' . . .

'You know', Mum said wistfully, 'I've always had a hankering to go North.'

'Who said anything about taking you? I mean, all you'd be doing is looking at dirt. You don't want to go two thousand kilometres for that.'

'You're not leaving me here?!'

'I don't want to be dragging a reluctant mother around', I said. 'No, it wouldn't work. You stay here with Nan. I'll go with Paul and the kids.'

'I'm coming and that's that!' she said.

Nan suddenly interrupted. 'You two, you're both nuts! You, Glad, you're like the wind, you blow here and you blow there. You got no mind of your own!'

'Well, Nan, maybe Mum'll chase the cyclones away!'

Over the following few weeks, I made arrangements for our trip. We decided to go in the May school holidays, that way the children could come and Paul, who was a teacher, could do most of the driving. As the weeks passed, Mum became more and more excited. . . .

By the time we arrived in Port Hedland, we were eager to begin our investigations. We'd been told to look up an older gentleman by the name of Jack, as he knew a lot of people in the area and might be able to help us.

As soon as we saw Jack, we liked him. He was very friendly. I explained who we were, why we'd come to see him and asked if he could tell us anything about the Brockman or Corunna families. We were amazed when he told us that Albert Brockman had been his good friend and that they'd worked together for many years.

'Jiggawarra, that's his Aboriginal name, that's what we all call him up here. Now, he had a brother and a sister that were taken away. They never came back. I think the brother was called Arthur.'

'That's right!' I added excitedly. 'And the sister was called Daisy, that's my grandmother.'

'Well, I'll be', he said, with tears in his eyes. 'So you've come back! There's not many come back. I don't think some of them are interested. Fancy, you comin' back after all these years.'

'Are we related to you, then?'

'Well, now, which way do you go by, the blackfella's way or the white man's way?'

'The blackfella's way.'

'Then I'm your grandfather', he said, 'and your mother would be my nuba,* that means I can marry her.' Mum laughed. We felt excited at discovering even that.

Jack went on to explain that he was, in fact, Nanna's cousin and that his mother's sister had been on Corunna in the very early days and had married one of the people from Corunna.

'I could have been there myself as a young baby', he added, 'but that's too far back to remember. I was born in 1903 and worked on Corunna from 1924 onwards. Foulkes-Taylor owned it then. They was a real good mob, that Corunna lot, but, slowly, they started drifting away. They didn't like the boss.'

'What about Lily?' Mum asked. 'Did you know her?' Lily was Nan and Arthur's half-sister.

'Lily? I'd forgotten about her. Oh yes, I knew Lily, she was a good mate of mine. So was her bloke, Big Eadie. He was a Corunna man, too. Aah, we used to have a lot of corroborees in those days. We'd all get together and have a good old corroboree. I can't explain to you how it made us feel inside. I loved the singing, sometimes we'd get a song and it'd last for days. Lily was a good singer,

---

* A person who is in the correct tribal relationship to another person for the purpose of marriage.

you could hear her voice singin' out high above the others. All those people are gone now. I suppose Arthur and Daisy are dead, too?'

'Arthur is, but my mother is still alive', replied Mum.

Jack was very moved. 'Why didn't you bring her with you?'

'We tried', I replied, 'but she reckoned she was too old to come North. Said her legs wouldn't hold her up.'

Jack laughed. 'That's one thing about mulbas',* he said, 'they can find an excuse for anything! She's one of the last old ones, you know. Gee, I'd like to meet her!'

'Maybe she'll come next time', I said hopefully. 'Did Lily have any children, Jack?'

'No. She wanted to. She was good with kids. Looked after plenty of kids in her time. She could turn her hand to anything, that woman. How many kids did Daisy have?'

'Only me', Mum said sadly. 'I'd love to have come from a big family.'

'Ooh, you ask around', Jack laughed, 'you'll soon have so many relatives you won't know what to do with them. You'd be related to a lot up here.'

'Really?'

'Too right. You might be sorry you come!'

'There was another sister', I interrupted, 'I think she was full blood, but died young, her name was Rosie.'

'That'd be right. A lot of full bloods died young in those days.'

'I can't believe we've met you', I sighed. 'All these people have just been names to us, talking to you makes them real. We didn't think anyone would remember.'

'Aah, mulbas have got long memories. Most around here remember the kids that were taken away. I should have been taken myself, only the policeman took me in after my mother died. Then he farmed me out to other people so I was able to stay in the area.'

'I suppose it wasn't often that happened.'

'No. I was one of the lucky ones.'

'Did you know a bloke called Maltese Sam?' Mum asked.

'Oh yeah, he's dead now.'

'Could he have been my mother's father?'

---

* The Aboriginal people of the Port Headland/Marble Bar area of Western Australia (derived from man or person).

'No, no, not him. I couldn't tell you who her father was. Maybe the station-owner. There's plenty of pastoralists got black kids runnin' around.'

I asked Jack if there was anyone else we should talk to.

'You fellas go and see Elsie Brockman, she's your relation, Albert's wife.'

'Are you sure?' Mum asked in astonishment. 'I thought they'd all be dead by now.'

'Oh, Albert's been gone a while, but Elsie's still here. Only be as young as you', he said to Mum. 'Then there's a big mob in Marble Bar you should see, and Tommy Stream in Nullagine. Any of you fellas speak the language?'

'No', I replied, 'but Arthur could and Daisy can. They wouldn't teach us.'

'Shame! There's mulbas here know their language and won't speak it. I'm not ashamed of my language. I speak it anywhere, even in front of white people.'

'Do you speak the same language as my mother?' Mum asked.

'I speak four languages. Light and heavy Naml, Balgoo and Nungamarda and Nybali. Your mother's language would be Balgoo, but she would speak Naml, too. All those old ones from Corunna spoke both. Those two languages are very similar.'

Mum and I exchanged glances. We were going to tackle Nan about that when we got home.

'You mob sure your granny never came back?'

'Not that we know of, why?'

'Well, I recall meeting a Daisy in '23. I was workin' between Hillside and Corunna at the time. Never seen her before. It was like she appeared outa nowhere. Took her from Hillside to stay at Corunna. She had family there she wanted to visit. Half-caste she was, pretty, too. She was pregnant, baby must have been near due.'

'I don't think it'd be her', I replied.

'Well, I just wondered.'

I was wondering, too.

It was all too much. Our heads were spinning, we seemed to be inundated with new information. The children were becoming restless, so Paul suggested that we go and have some lunch and talk over what to do. We said goodbye to Jack. It seemed awful, leaving him so soon. We'd only just met and we really liked him. We promised to call back in if we had the opportunity.

Over lunch, we talked about Elsie Brockman. Mum and I both felt it was probably a different person. We reasoned that, as Uncle Albert had been the oldest and quite a bit older than Nan, it would be unlikely for his wife to only be in her fifties. It would have made her, at the very least, thirty years younger than Albert. We decided to go to Marble Bar, instead.

Fortunately for us, we arrived in Marble Bar on pension day. This meant that most of the people were around town somewhere.

A group of old men were sitting patiently under a tall, shady tree in the main street, waiting for the mail to arrive. We parked nearby and walked over and introduced ourselves. Jack had told us to ask for Roy.

'We're looking for Roy', I said.

'I'm him', replied an elderly man with a snow-white beard, 'what do you want?'

'Gidday', I smiled and held out my hands. 'I'm Sally and this is Paul and my mother, Gladys.' We shook hands all round. 'We're trying to trace our relatives', I explained, 'they came from Corunna, went by the names of Brockman or Corunna. We heard you worked on Corunna.'

'Not me! I worked on Roy Hill and Hillside, but you'd be related to Jiggawarra, wouldn't you? I worked with him on Hillside, he built the homestead there, a good carpenter. A good man.'

Another older man interrupted. 'Who are these people?' he obviously asked in his own language.

'Brockman people', Roy replied.

'Oh yes', the other smiled, 'your mob's from Corunna. You'd be related to most of the people round here, one way or another.'

'You lookin' for your mob now?' another asked kindly.

'Yes', I replied. 'My grandmother was taken from here many years ago.'

'That's right', he agreed, 'hundreds of kids gone from here. Most never come back. We think maybe some of them don't want to come home. Some of those light ones, they don't want to own us dark ones.'

'I saw picture about you lot on TV', chipped in another. 'It was real sad. People like you, wanderin' around, not knowin' where you come from. Light coloured ones wanderin' around, not knowin' they black underneath. Good on you for comin' back, I wish you the best.'

'Thank you', I smiled, 'we are like those people on TV. We're up here trying to sort ourselves out.' Then, turning back to Roy, I said, 'Did you know Lily, Roy?'

'What do you want to know for?'

'She's my Aunty', Mum said proudly.

Roy was taken aback for a minute. 'That's right, I forgot about that.'

'Go on, Roy, tell them about Lily', the others teased.

Roy shook his head. 'I'm not sayin' nothin'. I'm not sayin' a word about Lily.' The other men chuckled. Lily was now a closed topic of conversation.

'What about Maltese Sam?' I asked.

'Maltese? He's finished with this world now.'

'I was told he was my grandmother's father, you know, the father of Jiggawarra's sister.'

'No, no, that's not right', said Roy.

'You got that wrong', others chorused, 'who told you that?'

'Oh, just someone I know in Perth.'

'How would they know, they not livin' here', replied another. 'We all knew Maltese, it's not him, be the wrong age.'

'Do any of you know who her father might have been?' I asked quietly.

There was silence while they all thought, then Roy said, 'Well, she was half-caste, wasn't she?'

'Yes.'

'Then it must have been a white man. Could have been the station-owner. Plenty of black kids belong to them, but they don't own them.'

Just then, we were interrupted by a lady in her fifties. 'Who are you people?' she asked as she walked up to our group.

'Brockman people', Roy said crossly, 'we're talkin' here!'

'You Christian people?' she asked Mum.

'Yes.'

'I knew it', she replied excitedly, 'I knew it in my heart. I was walkin' down the street when I saw you people here and I said to myself, Doris, they Christian people, they your people. Now, what Brockman mob do you come from?'

'My mother is sister to Albert Brockman', explained Mum.

'Oh, no! I can't believe it. You're my relations. My Aunty is married to Albert Brockman.'

'She's not still alive, is she?' I asked quickly.

'Yes, she's livin' in Hedland. She was a lot younger than him.' Mum and I looked at each other. We were stupid. We should have believed what Jack told us.

'Come home and have a cup of tea with me', urged Doris. 'I'll ring Elsie and tell her about you, she won't believe it!'

We thanked the men for their help and said goodbye.

As we walked down the main street, Doris said, 'You're lucky you didn't come lookin' for your relations any earlier, we've only all just been converted. Those Warbos* people came through and held meetings. It's made such a difference to this town, there's not many drunks, now.'

Doris made us a cup of tea when we got to her place and we encouraged her to talk about the old days. She said she could remember Annie, Nan's mother, from when she was a small child and that she thought she'd died somewhere in the thirties at Shaw River.

'All the old people had a little camp out there', she explained to us. 'There was nowhere else for them to go. All the old Corunna mob died out there.'

'Did Lily die out there, too?' Mum asked.

'Yes, she did.'

'Roy wouldn't tell us anything about Lily.'

Doris chuckled. 'That's because she was one of his old girl-friends. He doesn't like to talk about his old girlfriends.' We all laughed.

Just then, another lady popped in. She was introduced to us as Aunty Katy. She was Elsie's sister. We all shook hands and began to talk again.

'Lily was very popular around here', Aunty Katy told us. 'She could do anything. Everyone liked her, even the white people. She never said no to work.'

'How did she die?' Mum asked.

---

* Name used by Aboriginal people of the Port Hedland/Marble Bay area of Western Australia for the Aboriginal people of the Warburton Ranges area.

'Now, that's the funny thing', replied Aunty Katy, 'she came back from work one day and was doing something for one of the old people, when she dropped down dead, just like that! It was a big funeral, even some white people came. Poor old darling, we thought so much of her.'

'She married Big Eadie from Corunna Downs, but there were no children', added Doris.

'You know, if your grandmother was Daisy, then her grandmother must have been Old Fanny', said Aunty Katy. 'I'm in my seventies somewhere, but I can remember her, just faintly. She was short, with a very round face, and had a habit of wearing a large handkerchief on her head with knots tied all the way around.'

I smiled. Mum just sat there. It was all too much.

Just then, the rest of the family arrived. Trixie, Amy and May. We shook hands, then sat around and had a good yarn. In the process, we learnt that Nan's Aboriginal stepfather had been called Old Chinaman and that he had indeed been a tribal elder on Corunna and had maintained this position of power until the day he died. Also, Annie had had a sister called Dodger, who had married, but never had any children. We also learnt that Albert had been a real trickster, even in his old age.

We all laughed and laughed as funny stories about Albert's pranks kept coming, one after the other. By the end of the afternoon, we felt we knew Albert nearly as well as them.

Just as the sun was setting, Doris said, 'You fellas should go and see Happy Jack. He knew Lily well. She worked for his family for many years. He lives down near Marble Bar pool.'

We were anxious to learn as much as we could, so we took Doris' advice and headed off in search of Happy Jack.

One look at Jack's place and it was obvious that he was an excellent mechanic. His block was strewn with many mechanical bits and pieces, as well as half a dozen Land Rovers that he was in the process of fixing.

We explained who we were and showed him some old photos Arthur had given us of the early days. At first, he didn't seem to take in what we were saying, but when it finally dawned on him who we were, he was very moved.

'I just can't believe it', he exclaimed, 'after all these years.'

'I know you don't know us, Jack', I said, 'but it would mean so much to us if you could tell us about Lily, we know very little and we would like to be able to tell Daisy about her when we go home.'

'I'm happy to tell you anything I know', he said as we settled ourselves around his kitchen table. 'She was a wonderful woman. A wonderful, wonderful woman. She worked for my family for many years. You know, she's only been dead the better part of fifteen years, what a pity she couldn't have met you all.'

'We wish we'd come sooner', I replied, 'Doris told us so many of the old ones have died in recent years.'

'That's right. And that Corunna mob, there was some very good people amongst that mob. They were all what you'd call strong characters, and that's by anyone's standard, white or black. Now, my family, we started off most of the tin-mining in this area. We would go through and strip the country, and all that old Corunna mob would come behind and yandy* off the leftovers. I think they did well out of it. We were happy for them to have whatever they found, because they were the people tribally belonging to that area. It was like an unwritten agreement between them and us. Now and then, others would try and muscle in, but we wouldn't have any of that, it belonged to that mob only. We let them come in and carry on straight behind the bulldozers. It gave them a living. We were very careful about sacred sites and burial grounds, too, not like some others I could mention. The old men knew this. Sometimes, they would walk up to us and say, "One of our people is buried there." So we would bulldoze around it and leave the area intact.

'Now Lilla, that what a lot of us called her, not Lily, Lilla. She was a great friend of my mother's. She worked in the house and was a wonderful cook. Later when I married, she helped look after my kids, too. She had a fantastic sense of humour. You could have a joke with her and she'd laugh her head off. All the descendants of that mob are interlocked now, they're all related around here, I can't work it out. It's worse than my own family. What's Daisy like, is she fairly short?'

---

* A process of separating a mineral from alluvium by rocking in a shallow dish.

'Yes.'

'Yes, Lilla was like that.' . . .

'Is there anyone else we could talk to who might help us?' I asked after a few minutes' silence. I was amazed at how steady my voice seemed. All I wanted to do was cry, but my voice sounded so firm and steady, like it belonged to someone else.

'Yes', replied Jack thoughtfully. 'You should go to the Reserve and see Topsy and Old Nancy. Nancy is well into her nineties and Topsy well into her eighties, I think I remember them saying they were on Corunna very early in the piece, they might know your grandmother, they were great friends of Lilla's. The only thing is, they only speak the language, you'd have to get someone to interpret.'

'Thanks very much', I said. 'You don't know what this means to us.' We all had tears in our eyes then. While Jack had been speaking of Lilla, it was as though we'd all been transported back into the past. As though we'd seen her and talked to her. Lily was a real person to us now. Just like Albert was.

'Jack', I said as we left, 'would you mind if I put what you told me in a book?'

'You put in what you like. I'm very proud to have known her. I'm extremely proud to have known that woman. The way she conducted herself, the way she looked after her own people, was wonderful. Your family has missed knowing a wonderful woman.'

'Thanks', I whispered.

We drove back to the caravan park in silence. Even the children were quiet. We unpacked the van and set up our things for tea. Once again, tea came out of a tin. I don't think we'd have cared what we ate. We wouldn't have tasted it. Mum and I couldn't help thinking of all the things we'd learnt about our family. Our family was something to feel proud of. It made us feel good inside, and sad. Later that night, Mum and I sat under the stars, talking.

'I wish I'd known them', Mum sighed.

'Me, too.'

'You seem a bit depressed.'

'I am.'

'What about.'

'Dunno.' That wasn't true. I did know and Mum knew it. It

was just that I needed a few minutes to collect my thoughts so I could explain without breaking down. Finally, I said, 'It's Lilla. I feel very close to her in the spirit. I feel deprived.'

'How do you mean?'

'Deprived of being able to help her. We could have helped her with these old people. I feel all churned up that she did all that on her own. She never had children, we could have been her children. I mean, when you put together what everyone's said, she was obviously working hard all day and then going out to camp and looking after the old ones, feeding them . . .' My voice trailed off. Mum never said anything. . . .

By lunch-time, we'd pulled ourselves together sufficiently to be able to tackle the Reserve. We'd asked an Aboriginal woman called Gladys Lee if she would come and interpret for us. Jack had recommended her, as she worked with the old people through the recently established Pipunya centre. She was very happy to do so.

Armed with our old photos, we went from house to house on the Reserve, asking about Lilla. We drew a blank every time. I couldn't understand it.

Finally, we reached the last house. We stepped up onto the small verandah and Gladys showed the photos to two old ladies and then asked about Lilla. No, they didn't know her. Suddenly, I twigged from Gladys speaking that these two ladies were Topsy and Old Nancy. I asked Gladys to show them the photos again.

Topsy took a closer look. Suddenly, she smiled, pointed to a figure in the photo and said, 'Topsy Denmark'. Old Nancy took more of an interest then. After a few minutes, she pointed to the middle figure and said, 'Dr Gillespie.'

'That's right!' I said excitedly to Gladys. I pointed to the photo containing Nanna as a young girl and got them to look at it carefully. Suddenly, there was rapid talking in Balgoo. I couldn't understand a word, but I knew there was excitement in the air. Topsy and Nancy were now very anxious about the whole thing.

Finally, Gladys turned to me with tears in her eyes and said, 'If I had have known Daisy's sister was Wonguynon, there would have been no problem.'

'Who's Wonguynon?' I asked.

'That's Lilla's Aboriginal name. We only know her by Wonguynon. I loved her, she looked after me when I was very small. I used to run away to her and she'd give me lollies and look after me

until my parents came. She was related to my father. I am your relation, too.'

Topsy and Nancy began to cry. Soon, we were all hugging.
Gladys and I had tears in our eyes, but we managed not to break
down. Topsy and Nancy pored over all the photos I had, chuckling
and laughing and shaking their heads. They explained, through
Gladys, that they had been on Corunna when Nan had been taken.
They'd all cried then, because they were all very close.

'They lived as one family unit in those days', Gladys explained.
'They lived as a family group with Daisy and Lily and Annie. This
makes them very close to you. They are your family. Daisy was sister to them. They call her sister, they love her as a sister.' . . .

Later, we retraced our steps back down through the Reserve,
stopping at each house in turn and asking about Wonguynon. It
was totally different, now, open arms, and open hearts. By the time
we reached the other end of the Reserve, we'd been hugged and patted and cried over, and told not to forget and to come back.

An old full-blood lady whispered to me, 'You don't know what
it means, no one comes back. You don't know what it means that
you, with light skin, want to own us.'

We had lumps in our throats the size of tomatoes, then. I
wanted desperately to tell her how much it meant to us that they
would own us. My mouth wouldn't open. I just hugged her and
tried not to sob. . . .

The following day, we decided to go to Corunna Downs Station. Doris offered to come with us, as she knew the manager out
there. Also, she was worried we might take the wrong track and get
lost.

The track to Corunna was very rough. Apparently, it was the
worst it had been for years. After an hour of violently jerking up
and down, we rounded a bend and Doris said quickly, 'There's the
homestead.'

When we reached the main house, Trevor, the manager, welcomed us with a nice hot cup of tea and some biscuits. We explained why we were there and he happily showed us over the
house. To our surprise and delight, it was the same one Nan and
Arthur had known in their day. We saw where the old kitchen had
been, the date palm Nan had talked about, and, further over in one
of the back sheds, the tank machine in which Albert had lost his
fingers. I suppose these would be items of no interest to most

people, but to us, it was terribly important. It was concrete evidence that what Arthur had told us and what Nan had mentioned were all true. . . .

Yandeearra was a long drive away, so we set out as early as we could. We telephoned ahead to let the people know we were coming and also to ask permission to come. We didn't want to intrude. Peter Coppin, the manager, was pleased for us to visit and welcomed us all on our arrival.

Before we had met anyone else, an older lady came striding towards us.

'Who are you people?' she asked.

Mum explained who we were. The older lady suddenly broke into a big smile and hugged Mum.

'You're my relations', she cried, 'Lily was my Aunty, dear old thing. I knew you were my people. When I saw your car, I just knew. Something told me I was going to see some of my old people today. No one said anything to me, I just knew in my heart.' We were amazed. Dolly then pointed to Amber and Blaze and said, 'You see those kids, they got the Corunna stamp on them. Even if you hadn't told me, I could tell just by looking at those kids that you lot belong to that old mob on Corunna.'

Dolly introduced us to Billy and we sat and talked about the early days and who was related to who. . . .

'There are four groups', explained Peter, 'Panaka, Burungu, Cariema and Malinga. Now, these groups extend right through. I can go down as far as Wiluna and know who I am related to just by saying what group I'm from. We hear that further up north, they got eight groups. We don't know how they work it out, four is bad enough.' We all laughed.

Then Billy said, 'I think we got it now. You', he said as he pointed to me, 'must be Burungu, your mother is Panaka, and Paul, we would make him Malinga. Now, this is very important, you don't want to go forgetting this, because we've been trying to work it out ever since you arrived.'

Dolly and Peter agreed that those groups were the ones we belonged to. . . .

We were all sad when we left Yandeearra the following day. We'd been very impressed with Yandeearra and the way Peter managed the community. It was a lovely place.

Our next stop was Aunty Elsie's place in Hedland. She had a lovely home overlooking the ocean. . . .

We promised we would come to Hedland again and asked her to visit Perth so she could meet the rest of the family. We felt very full inside when we left. It was like all the little pieces of a huge jigsaw were finally fitted together.

The following day, it was time to head back to Perth, but there was one last stop to make. Billy and Dolly had told us to call in and visit Billy Moses at Twelve-mile, just out of Hedland. We were all exhausted by this stage, but we didn't want to miss out on anything, so we gathered together the last remnants of our energy and drove out to Twelve-mile.

When we arrived, we were told that Billy and Alma had gone shopping and no one knew when they'd be back, but we could wait near his house if we wanted to. Only five minutes had passed, when a taxi pulled in, bearing Billy and Alma.

They eyed us curiously, obviously wondering who we were and why we were waiting near their house. I felt embarrassed, what if Billy didn't know us after all? I decided to take the bull by the horns. I walked forward and held out my hand.

After introducing myself, I explained slowly who we were and why we had come. He listened seriously, trying to take in everything I said. Suddenly, his face lit up with a heart-warming smile and he said, 'You my relations! Yes, you've come to the right place. You my people. I am your Nanna's cousin.' There were tears in his eyes. I held his hand warmly. Alma smiled and said, 'You must be his relations.'

We walked back to his house and sat down for a chat. Billy said, 'I can't believe it. Some of my people coming all the way from Perth just to visit me. You always come here. You can come and live here, I'm the boss. This is your place, too, remember that.' We began to talk about the old times and Billy explained how he, too, was taken away at a young age.

'I was very lucky', he told us, 'I came back. I made it my business to come back and find out who I belonged to. It was funny, you know, when I first came back, no one round here would talk to me. You see, they weren't sure who I was. They were trying to work it out. I'd walk down the street and they'd just stare at me. Then one day, an old fella came into town, he saw me and recognised me.

He spoke up for me and said, that fella belong to us, I know who he is. I know his mother. After that, I never had any trouble. They all talk to me, now. I belong here. It's good to be with my people. I'm glad you've come back.' . . .

That afternoon, we reluctantly left for Perth. None of us wanted to go, Paul included. He'd been raised in the North and loved it. We were reluctant to return and pick up the threads of our old lives. We were different people, now. What had begun as a tentative search for knowledge had grown into a spiritual and emotional pilgrimage. We had an Aboriginal consciousness now, and were proud of it.

Mum, in particular, had been very deeply affected by the whole trip.

'To think I nearly missed all this. All my life. I've only been half a person. I don't think I really realised how much of me was missing until I came North. Thank God you're stubborn, Sally.'

We all laughed and then, settling back, retreated into our own thoughts. There was much to think about. Much to come to terms with. I knew Mum, like me, was thinking about Nan. We viewed her differently, now. We had more insight into her bitterness. And more than anything, we wanted her to change, to be proud of what she was. We'd seen so much of her and ourselves in the people we'd met. We belonged, now. We wanted her to belong, too.

When we arrived back in Perth, Nan was really pleased to see us. . . .

'I knew you'd all be safe', Nan said when she saw us. 'I been praying the cyclones wouldn't get you.'

We rounded up the rest of the family the following day and insisted on showing the video we had made of our trip. Much to our dismay, the film turned out to be pretty mediocre. It suffered from the faults common to most home movies. Lack of focus, zooming too quickly and panning too slowly.

Throughout the filming of Corunna, I watched Nan. She was taking a keen interest in the old buildings.

'There's the old date palm', she said. 'That used to be the garden down there. That's the old homestead, that part over there, that's where they had the kitchen.'

When it was all over, Nan said, 'Fancy, all those old buildings still being there, I didn't think there'd be anything left. What about the tank machine, Sally?'

'Yep! But the manager had tied it up so it couldn't be used. He was worried one of his kids might stick their fingers in it.'

'Ooh yes, it'd be dangerous.'

Mum told Nan what all the old boys had said about Lily. Nan laughed and laughed. 'Ooh yes', she chuckled, 'that was Lily, all right. She was the sort of person you couldn't help liking, she had a good heart, did Lily.' I was amazed, Nan had never talked about Lily like that before.

Over the next few days, Mum talked at length with Nan about the different people we had met. Nan feigned disinterest, but we knew it was just a bluff. She was desperately interested in everything we had to say, but she didn't want to let her feelings show. In many ways, she was a very private person.

One night when they were alone, Mum told her how Annie and a lot of other older ones from Corunna Downs had died at Shaw River. 'She and Lily', Mum said. 'She devoted herself to the old ones. Annie wasn't alone when she died, she had some of her people with her.' Nan nodded. There were tears in her eyes. Her lips were set.

'Do any of them remember me?' she asked wistfully.

'They all do', Mum said, 'they all remember you. Do you remember Topsy and another woman called Nancy? They said they lived with you and Annie on Corunna.'

Nan looked shocked. 'They still alive?' she asked in disbelief. 'Yes.'

Nan just shook her head. 'I'm going to bed', she muttered. Mum laid down and cried herself to sleep.

A few weeks later, I tackled Nan about being able to speak two languages, she was unwilling to discuss the subject. When I told her about the different skin groups, she said crossly, 'I know all that, I'm not stupid.' She wouldn't be drawn further. There'd been a slight change, a softening, but she was still unwilling to share the personal details of her life with us.

When Mum and I got together, we couldn't help reminiscing about our trip.

'Well, we found out one thing', said Mum, 'Maltese Sam definitely wasn't Nan's father.'

'That's right. Though it doesn't necessarily mean Howden was, either.'

'No, I know. Probably, we'll never really know who fathered her.'

'Do you reckon Jack Grime really is your father?'

'Oh, I don't know, Sally', Mum sighed. 'When I was little, I always thought Howden was my father, isn't that silly?'

'Howden? Why did you think that?'

'I suppose because he was Judy and June and Dick's father. I guess because I was little and didn't understand, I assumed he was my father, too. You know how it is when you're a kid.'

'Yeah, I could see how you might think that. You were all living there at Ivanhoe.'

'Yes.'

'Aunty Judy said you're the image of Jack Grime, though, that'd be some sort of proof, wouldn't it?'

'Oh, I don't know, people can look like one another, but it doesn't mean they're related.'

'Yeah. Hey, I know. I've got a photo of Jack, a big one, why don't we look at it, see if you do look alike?'

'I don't want to do that.'

'Go on! We'll hold it up to the big mirror in my room, you can put your head next to it and we'll see if you do look like him.'

'Oh, all right', Mum giggled, 'why not?'

Within minutes, Mum and I and the photo were all facing the large mirrors in the doors of my wardrobe.

'Well, that was a dead loss. You don't look anything like him, even taking into account the fact that you've put on weight. There's no resemblance there at all.'

'He doesn't look like any of you kids, either, does he?'

'Naah', I agreed. 'Hang on a tick and I'll get another picture.' I returned quickly. 'Okay', I said, 'face the mirror.'

Mum fronted up to the mirror and tried not to laugh. She felt silly.

Suddenly, I held up a photograph of Howden as a young man next to her face. We both fell into silence.

'My God', I whispered. 'Give him black, curly hair and a big bust and he's the spitting image of you!'

Mum was shocked. 'I can't believe it', she said. 'Why haven't I ever noticed this before, I've seen that picture hundreds of times.'

'I suppose it never occurred to you', I replied.

'You don't think it's possible he was my father?'

'Anything's possible. But he couldn't be yours as well as Nan's. You know, features can skip a generation. Say he was Nan's father, well you could have inherited those looks from that.'

'Oh, I don't know, Sally', Mum sighed. 'It's such a puzzle. You know, for nearly all my life, I've desperately wanted to know who my father was, now, I couldn't care less. Why should I bother with whoever it was, they never bothered with me.'

'But that's been the recent history of Aboriginal people all along, Mum. Kids running around, not knowing who fathered them. Those early pioneers, they've got a lot to answer for.'

'Yes, I know, I know, but I think now I'm better off without all that business. All those wonderful people up North, they all claimed me. Well, that's all I want. That's enough, you see. I don't want to belong to anyone else.'

'Me, either.'

We walked back to the lounge-room. After a few seconds' silence, Mum said, 'Sal . . . ?'

'What?'

'Aw . . . nothing. It doesn't matter.'

'I hate it when you do that. Come on, out with it.'

'We-ell . . . You know the Daisy that Jack said he'd met? You don't think that could have been Nanna?'

'Dunno. I asked her the other day if she'd ever been back North, but she just got mad with me.'

'It might have been her', Mum said tentatively. 'Alice did tell you she'd gone back once.'

'But if it was her, it was in 1923 and she would have been pregnant. Mum . . . do you think you might have a brother or sister somewhere?'

She nodded.

'But surely Nan would have told you?'

'Not if she wasn't allowed to keep it.'

'This is terrible.' I eyed her keenly. 'There's something you're not telling me, isn't there?'

Mum composed herself, then said, 'The other night when I was in bed, I had this sort of flashback to when I was little. I'd been pestering Nanna, asking her why I didn't have a brother or sister, when she put her arms around me and whispered quietly, "You have a sister." Then she held me really tight. When she let me go, I saw she was crying.'

I couldn't say anything. We both sat in silence. Finally, Mum said, 'I'm going to ask her.'

A few days later, Mum broached the subject with Nan, only to be met with anger and abuse. Nan locked herself in her room, saying 'Let the past be.'

'I'll never know, now', Mum told me later. 'If she won't tell me, I'll never know.'

'You mustn't give up! What does your gut feeling tell you?'

'Oh Sally, you and your gut feelings, you're like a bloody detective. How do I know my gut feeling isn't pure imagination?'

'What does it tell you?' I persisted.

She sighed. 'It tells me I've got a sister. I've had that feeling all my life, from when I was very small, that I had a sister somewhere. If only I could find her.'

'Then I believe what you feel is true.'

Mum laughed, 'You're a romantic.'

'Crap! Be logical, she could still be alive, if she was born in 1923, she'd be in her sixties, now. Also, if Nan had her up North, she could have been brought up by the people round there or a white family could have adopted her.'

'Sally, we don't even have a name. It's impossible! You talk like we'll find her one day, but it's impossible.'

'Nothing's impossible.'

'Could you talk to Nan?'

'Yeah, but she won't tell me anything. I'll let her cool down a bit first.'

'There's been so much sadness in my life', Mum said, 'I don't think I can take any more.'

'You want to talk about it?'

'You mean for that book?'

'Yes.'

'Well . . .' she hesitated for a moment. Then, with sudden determination, she said, 'Why shouldn't I? If I stay silent like Nanna, it's like saying everything's all right. People should know what it's been like for someone like me.'

I smiled at her.

'Perhaps my sister will read it.' . . .

It took several months to work through Mum's story and, during that time, many tears were shed. We became very close.

Although she'd finally shared her story with me, she still couldn't bring herself to tell my brothers and sisters. Consequently, I found myself communicating it to them in bits and pieces as it seemed appropriate. It was, and still is, upsetting for us all. We'd lived in a cocoon of sorts for so long that we all found it difficult to come to terms with the experiences Mum had been through.

By the beginning of June, 1983, Nan's health wasn't too good.

'You've got to take her to the doctor', I told Mum one day. 'She's not well.'

'You know how she hates doctors.'

'But what if it's something serious? You'll just have to force her to go.'

Mum took Nan to see our local doctor a few days later. They sent Nan for a chest X-ray, which revealed that one of her lungs had collapsed.

When Mum phoned through the news to me, I said gently, 'I think you should prepare yourself, Mum. I'm not trying to make a big deal out of this, but I think it will be serious.'

'You mean you think she might die?'

'Yes.'

'You don't know what you're talking about, Sally! It's only a collapsed lung, they can fix that!'

'But they have to find out what caused the collapse, don't they?'

'Well . . . yes. She has to go into hospital in two days' time for tests.'

The night before Nan was due to go into hospital, she stayed at my place. Mum had arranged weeks before to babysit some of her other grandchildren and it was an arrangement she couldn't break.

I made Nan a cup of tea and we sat in the lounge-room to talk.

'I'd like you to listen to a story, Nan, it's only a couple of pages. Is it okay if I read it to you?' . . .

'This is what I've been writing, Nan', I grinned. 'That's Arthur's story.'

'No! I can't believe it! That's Arthur's story?'

'Yep!'

'I didn't know he had a good story like that. You got to keep that story safe. Read me some more.'

I read a little more, and then we began to talk about the old days and life on Corunna Downs Station. For some reason, Nan was keen to talk. As she went on and on, her breath began to come in shorter and shorter gasps. Her words tumbled out one over the other, as if her tongue couldn't say them quickly enough. . . .

After I'd settled the children down, I walked quietly past Nan's bedroom door. I expected her to be asleep, but she wasn't.

'Sally', she called. 'Come here.'

'What is it?'

'I want to tell you more about the station', she smiled. I nearly stopped her, she could hardly breathe, but how could I tell her not to talk when it had taken a lifetime for her to get to this point?

I listened quietly as she spoke about wild ducks and birds, the blue hills and all the fruit that grew along the creek. Her eyes had a faraway look and her face was very soft. I kept smiling at her because she was smiling at me, but, inside, I wanted to cry. I'd seen that look before, on Arthur's face. I knew she was going to die. Nan finally settled down and closed her eyes. I tucked her in again.

'Hmmmn, this is a really good rug', she said sleepily. 'Where did you get such a rug?'

'Mum gave it to me', I muttered. And, turning off her light, I walked back into the kitchen. . . .

When Nan finished telling me her story, I was filled with conflicting emotions. I was happy for her because she felt she'd achieved something. It meant so much to be able to talk and to be believed. But I was sad for myself and my mother. Sad for all the things Nan felt she couldn't share.

Although, there was one thing I had learnt; that had quite surprised me. Nan's voice had changed as she reminisced. She could speak perfect English when she wanted to, and usually did, only occasionally dropping the beginning or ending of a word. But in talking about the past, her language had changed. It was like she was back there, reliving everything. It made me realise that at one stage in her life it must have been difficult for her to speak English, and therefore to express herself.

But this, too, only made me even more aware of how much we still didn't know. My mind went over and over her story; every word, every look. I knew there were great dark depths there, and I knew I would never plumb them.

I felt, for Mum's sake, I should make one last effort to find out about her sister. So a few nights later, when Nan and I were on our own, I said, 'There's something I want to ask you. I know you won't like it, but I have to ask. It's up to you whether you tell me anything or not.'

Nan grunted. 'Ooh, those questions, eh? Well, ask away.'

'Okay. Has Mum got a sister somewhere?'

She looked away quickly. There was silence, then, after a few seconds, a long, deep sigh.

When she finally turned to face me, her cheeks were wet. 'Don't you understand, yet', she said softly, 'there are some things I just can't talk 'bout.' Her hand touched her chest in that characteristic gesture that meant her heart was hurting. It wasn't her flesh and blood heart. It was the heart of her spirit. With that, she heaved herself up and went out to her room.

I went to bed with a face full of tears and a mind full of guilt. I was so insensitive, sometimes. I should have known better.

The early morning brought some peace. I would never ask her another thing about the past. And I had hope. She hadn't extinguished my small shred of hope. Why, she'd even admitted that she was pregnant before she had Mum. That was such a big thing. For the moment, it would have to be enough. I stretched and shouted towards the ceiling, 'I'm not giving up, God. Not in a million years. If she's alive, I'll find her, and I expect you to help!'

One night later that week, Nan called me out to her room.

'What on earth are you doing?' I laughed when I found her with both arms raised in the air and her head completely covered by the men's singlet she was wearing.

'I'm stuck', she muttered, 'get me out.' I pulled the singlet off and helped her undress. It had become a difficult task for her, lately. Her arthritis was worse and cataracts now almost completely obscured her vision.

'Can you give me a rub?' she asked. 'The Vaseline's over there.' I picked up the jar, dobbed a big, greasy lump of it onto her back and began to rub. Nan loved Vaseline. Good for keeping your body cool and moist, she always told me. She had a lot of theories like that. I continued to massage her in silence for a few minutes.

'Ooh, that's good, Sally', she murmured after a while. As I continued to rub, she let out a deep sigh and then said slowly. 'You know, Sal . . . all my life, I been treated rotten, real rotten. Nobody's cared if I've looked pretty. I been treated like a beast. Just like a beast of the field. And now, here I am . . . old. Just a dirty old blackfella.'

I don't know how long it was before I answered her. My heart felt cut in half. I could actually see a beast in a field. A work animal, nothing more.

'You're not to talk about yourself like that', I finally replied in a controlled voice. 'You're my grandmother and I won't have you talk like that. The whole family loves you. We'd do anything for you.'

There was no reply. How hollow my words sounded. How empty and limited. Would anything I said ever help? I hoped that she sensed how deeply I felt. Words were unnecessary for that.

When I finished rubbing, I helped her into her nightclothes. This was no mean feat, there were so many. It was well into winter, now, and Nan was anxious about the cold. I pulled a clean men's singlet over her head, then a fleecy nightgown and a bedjacket. While she pulled a South Fremantle football beanie down over her head, I covered her feet with two pairs of woollen socks. After that, she wound two long scarves around her neck.

'Are you sure you'll be warm enough?' I asked sarcastically.

'I think you better help me into that cardigan', she answered after a second's thought, 'better safe than sorry.'

Once that was on, I pulled back the rugs and she rolled in on top of her sheepskin. As I passed her a hot water bottle, she said, 'Do you know what I did? I put a wool rug under my sheet, it'll keep out the draught.' . . .

When Nan was getting ready to go home that weekend, she said, 'You'll keep what I told you safe, won't you?'

'Of course I will.'

'You liked it?' . . .

The weekend passed quickly. When Nan hadn't arrived at my place by ten o'clock Monday morning, I began to worry. The phone rang and I rushed to answer it.

'Sally?' It was Mum.

'What's wrong?'

'She's taken a sudden turn for the worse. The doctor says she can't be moved.'

'Is she conscious?'

'At the moment, she's slipping in and out.'

'I'm coming over.'

'Jill's coming, too.'

'Good.' I hung up. It'd come so suddenly. She'd been living with me for over six weeks. She hadn't seemed like someone who was dying. . . .

The Silver Chain sister visited that afternoon. As I saw her to the door, she said, 'Your grandmother's changed. I think she's decided to die.'

'She has', I agreed. 'It won't be long, now.'

She grasped my arm and looked at me with pity in her eyes. 'You're wrong, dear', she said, 'I've seen this happen before, many, many times. They give up the will to live, but they don't die, because their bodies just won't let them. She has a very strong heart and a good pulse. It could be weeks!'

'That won't happen with her', I replied confidently. 'She'll be gone soon.'

The sister shrugged her shoulders sympathetically. 'Don't count on it, dear, you'll only be disappointed. There'd be a chance if her pulse was weak, but it's not. I think you should face up to the fact that this could go on for quite a while.'

The following morning, my phone rang very early.

'Hello', I said as I lifted the receiver.

'I heard the bird call.' It was Jill's voice.

'What bird call?'

'This morning, about five o'clock. I heard it, Sally. It was a weird sound, like a bird call, only it wasn't. It was something spiritual, something out of this world. I think she'll be going soon.'

After breakfast, I hurried over. There was an air of excitement about the place. The heaviness that we'd all been living under seemed to have suddenly lifted.

Mum was mystified about the bird call. I think she felt a little left out. Jill couldn't understand why Mum hadn't heard it, it'd been so loud and gone on and on.

When I walked into Nan's room, I couldn't believe my eyes, she didn't look sick any more. Her face was bright and she was propped up in bed, smiling. Something had definitely happened, but none of us knew what. Even Mum and Jill were happier and bustling around like their old selves.

'Nan, you look really good', I said in surprise.

'Feel good, Sal.'

I just stood there, smiling. She seemed so contented. Almost like she had a secret. I was desperate to ask her about the call, but I didn't know where to begin. I sat by the bed and patted her hand.

Just then, Mum popped in. 'Doesn't she look well, Sally', she said happily. 'Look at her face, it looks different.'

'Sure does.'

'Get me some toast, Gladdie', Nan said cheekily, 'I'm hungry.' Mum rushed out with tears in her eyes.

'Nan', I said slowly as she looked at me, 'about that call, you weren't frightened when you heard it, were you?'

'Ooh, no', she scoffed, 'it was the Aboriginal bird, Sally. God sent him to tell me I'm going home soon. Home to my own land and my own people. I got a good spot up there, they all waitin' for me.'

A lump formed in my throat so big I couldn't speak, let alone swallow. Finally, I murmured, 'That's great, Nan. . . .'

Mum popped back in with tea and toast. ''Bout time', Nan chuckled. She ate a little and then lay back. 'Think I'll sleep, now', she sighed. We tiptoed out.

'Tell me about the call again', I said to Jill.

Jill's face was a mixture of fear, amazement and triumph as she described to Mum and I what happened.

'Wish I'd heard it', sighed Mum.

'Me, too', I said enviously.

Later, I whispered to Mum, 'You know, Jill must be very special to have heard that call.' Mum agreed. We both wondered what Jill's future held.

Nan had a very peaceful day that day. A happy day. The intense feeling that had surrounded our house for so long was gone, replaced by an overwhelming sense of calm.

At five-thirty the following morning, Ruth rang for an ambulance. Nan had insisted on it.

As they wheeled her out, she grasped Mum's hand one last

time. There was an unspoken message in her eyes as she whispered, 'Leave my light burning for a few days.'

They placed her in the ambulance and Ruth climbed in beside her. Mum stood silently watching, accepting Nan's choice. Knowing that this was her final sacrifice. She wanted our old family home free of death.

My phone rang at seven that same morning.

'Sally? It's Ruth. Nan died twenty minutes ago. It was very peaceful.'

'Thanks', I whispered.

I slowly replaced the receiver. I felt stiff. I couldn't move. Tears suddenly flooded my cheeks. For some reason, Jill's words from the previous day began echoing inside of me. I heard the bird call, I heard the bird call. Around and around.

'Oh, Nan', I cried with sudden certainty, 'I heard it, too. In my heart, I heard it.'

PART TWO
New Zealand

A home in this world

Robin Hyde

(1906–1939)

Robin Hyde (Iris Wilkinson) was born in Capetown, South Africa, the second child of an Anglo Indian father, Edward Wilkinson, and his Australian-born wife, Adelaide Butler. Edward Wilkinson had served in the Boer War, and remained in South Africa to work as an engineer in the construction of the post and telegraph system. Shortly after Hyde's birth the family moved to Wellington, New Zealand, where Edward Wilkinson worked on the establishment of the New Zealand post and telegraph system.

Hyde was educated at Wellington Girls College, where she began her career as a writer and saw her verse published in school publications and in the contemporary press. On graduating from high school she began her career as a journalist with the *Dominion,* where she became parliamentary reporter at the age of nineteen. An accident the year she turned twenty introduced her to morphine, upon which she became dependent for the remainder of her life.

While recuperating from her injuries Hyde learned that she had been abandoned by the lover she thought would be her life partner, and, on the rebound from this disappointment, she had a brief affair which left her pregnant and quite unable to tell her conventional family. She left for Sydney for her delivery, and returned to New Zealand after the child, whom she called Robin Hyde, died tragically.

Deeply depressed by her multiple losses, Hyde worked as a staff journalist for a number of Wellington newspapers, while writing her novel *The Godwits Fly,* an autobiographical treatment of her hopes and bereavement, and an early draft of *Journalese,* a set of reminiscences on the life of a journalist. While on leave from one journalistic job Hyde conceived a second child during a holiday trip, and entered one of the more desperate phases of her life as she struggled to conceal the child's arrival from family and employers. Her most stable employment was as an editor at the weekly Auckland magazine *New Zealand Observer,* where she wrote and edited stories on the life of the city. She published under several pseudonyms, and filled the magazine with many uncredited pieces. The combined stresses of overwork, anxiety about her child, and her sense of personal isolation began the spiral of a major breakdown, much of which was recounted in *Passport to Hell* (1936).

From 1933 to 1937, Hyde lived as a voluntary patient in Auckland Mental Hospital, where she sought treatment after attempted suicide. While there she kept a detailed autobiographical journal which formed the basis for *A Home in This World*. Unlike Janet Frame, Hyde was treated with compassion and encouragement during her stay in the mental institution, a time when psychiatric treatment allowed her the perspective on herself to write: ". . . I am caught in the hinge of a slowly-opening door, between one age and another. Between the tradition of respectability, which was very strong in my household and had cut me off from all real family love the moment I infringed it, and the new age, foretold by Nietzsche and some others."*

The benefit of this environment can be gauged by her extraordinary literary productivity during these four years. Her second volume of poetry, *The Conquerors,* was completed there in 1934, as was the second draft of *Journalese* (1934). A historical novel and *Passport to Hell* (1936) were written in 1935, and 1936 saw the revisions to *The Godwits Fly* (1938) and a further volume of poems, *Persephone in Winter* (1937).

In 1937, Hyde abruptly left the hospital and moved to a series of isolated beachside dwellings where she produced a further outpouring of verse and the manuscript of *A Home in This World* (1984). In 1938, Hyde left for her long-dreamed-of journey to England, the quest for culture and recognition which was such a deep part of the British Commonwealth writer's sensibility. She chose to depart on the eve of the 1939–45 war, arriving in Hong Kong as the Japanese incursion into China made travel perilous. She eventually reached England in September 1938, where her hopes for recognition were sadly disappointed. At thirty-three her short but richly productive literary career was ended by a third and successful attempt at suicide.

---

* Robin Hyde, *A Home in This World* (Auckland, New Zealand: Longman Paul, 1984), p. 28.

A HOME IN THIS WORLD

JUST NOW

If only there were a fire. I know other things are more important, such as making my peace with God and (if I can) with the medical superintendent of the asylum, for running away after I had been kindly treated. . . .

[M]y mind harks back again and again to the fire. The rain swishes past, a woman in a grey taffeta skirt—not a very kind woman, I think. If I took one of the little bach* rooms, down here in the bush where there's nobody, there couldn't be a fireplace. If I went up to the accommodation house, I couldn't lie doggo. Anyhow the fire there would be a sitting-room fire, and I don't believe that at present I could bear to walk into a sitting-room and hear people crackling newspapers, crackling the old dry aspidistra thoughts they reserve for accommodation house conversations. No, that isn't the kind of fire. I want the yellowest one you ever saw, canary-wing and yellow amber: and I want to make a confidante of it, to have it all to myself for at least an hour, lying face downwards on the rug where its little sparks hop off their twigs and burn black blisters, unless you brush them away. . . .

I like things to have their own voices always, but they have to be *little* voices, soft, pure and natural (odd when I shout so often myself). Water says things so clearly—I thought of a line for a poem once, 'Saying it over with little words of water'—and the slipping of heaped golden embers also speaks. There would be no trouble in this room, but no stinginess of soul either. No somebody inside and somebody, cut off, outside. One wouldn't stand isolated on a little island of safety, cut off from the rest of humanity. . . .

I would burn sweet herbs in the fire, called pardon and redemption and friendliness; only a very little of rue, to remind us of the day when we cried. . . .

There is no fire here. There wasn't one in the attic, either, where for three years I worked, a shut door and a flight of steep stairs below, and up with me spiders and an occasional starling—the lat-

---

* Unheated holiday shack, modeled on a Maori cabin. Ed.

ter, like idiots, insisted on flying in through the windows, and then expected me to catch and release them. They trembled so; violet gleams streaked their foolish young trembling breasts. There was a fire in the big Lodge sitting-room, where nobody must disarrange the cushions and the carpets were carefully rolled up every night, but I never went into it. There the loudspeaker lived, and I am sorry, it is somebody I can't get used to. . . .

I'm afraid of the man in the loudspeaker, in case one day he should turn round and show his face—little bristling military moustache, flamboyant cheeks, full lips (wet, because his favourite instruments are women and the saxophone), but *no eyes.* . . .

At this point an explanation is necessary. Although with the instincts of a reactionary (curious, the discredit into which that word has fallen, when its literal meaning should simply be the derivative adjective from 'response to things'), I am a socialist, and would sooner be shot with the communists any day, if it came to the point, than call myself a conservative. For the name of conservation has been disgraced by a pack of damned scrimping cheat-at-cards scoundrels, Alice in Wonderland's pack of cards, but with faces I do not like. I don't want to live in those flat-faced houses so self-consciously designed for newness that hidden in them even Marxian professors look fairly natural—taking on ground colour, like Arctic foxes. Neither do I want to live in the old sullen house, the haunted house, of English conservatism. . . .

Now the lights of Auckland are all out, wonderful from this distance, wonderful as old-time pantomime jewels, as the great sparkling misty jewels that never were, and never will be. Over the city they sparkle and tremble. There is tenderness in them as in the beating breasts of the foolish young starlings who got trapped in my attic. And something heartbreaking, as if the stars had alighted chanting on the earth, and taken the town, and strolled about friendly in silver helmets, but no man knew it, because we were all too blind. About our nightly business we went, swearing, sweating, fornicating without desire, or with desire that died out on a whimper, grunting, walking rapidly up mean streets, streaming out of the cinemas with eyes half-shut from sleep, a blurred vision of great enigmatic unreal faces on our pupils, and no consciousness of the people going by. The lights are something which should mean an irresistible beckoning, a promise of humanity come true: and they are this only from my distance of nearly twenty miles. . . .

I know now what I am looking for. It is a home in this world. I don't mean four walls and a roof on top, though even these I have never had, the attic at the asylum and the stilt-legged Maori cabin where I spent three weeks at Whangaroa constituting my nearest approach to habitations. As often as not, though, four walls and a roof get in the way, are the very point where one is fatally side-tracked from ever having a home in this world.

I want a sort of natural order and containment, a centre of equipoise, an idea—not a cell into which one can retreat, but a place from which one can advance: a place from which I can stretch out giant shadowy hands, and make a road between two obscure villages in China, teach the Arab and the Jew how to live together in Palestine, tidy up the shack dwellings and shack destinies of our own thin Maoris in the north (but not to such an extent that the smell of soap and socialism would wreck their faith in human nature for ever, poor gay dears. Well said some philosopher whose name I forget, 'Whatever is good, laughs.' And they laugh).

And when I say I, I don't mean, either, this self, this runagate, half-frozen, half-dazed and almost completely incoherent, sitting on a bed in a bach room: but all the people whose love and power runs out between their two hands, the people who are a broken cup, never full of either kinsman or stranger to pick them up and be refreshed. I have known many of such people, and they are not the worst in the world. They're better than the cups of cold poison, and God knows you have enough of those. . . .

[W]e need our homes in this world, without them we have no power to create an order. Those whose creeds fly like kites in a wild wind, and like kites are hauled back and broken . . . those who feel their sharp new nationalism like a boy just past puberty feeling his manhood . . . that Bishop stinting earth for a Heaven in which he does not believe (else why are his earthly symbols so potent, and so relaxing to the mortal senses?), that great army swinging by, hoping to find in death the justification for the fact that it carries maiming and murder, that it has kept the road open through the centuries to the place of skulls . . . we are all of us seeking for our homes in this earth. I say, may the very need of earth, which we have wronged but which also we have loved, and which, therefore, must forgive us (like the woman earth is), strengthen all the homeless on their dark journey tonight. . . .

And you a poet? A bit out of the swim. Got to stand them on

their heads and pretend they were born that way, like the Spender-Auden-Lewis gang. Should exempt Lewis, nice boy, wrote some pretty verses. 'The Ecstatic' much better than Shelley's 'Ode to a Skylark'. . . . All the same, you go to Shelley for real inspiration—that thing they can't get, and so despise, like most impotents—in between his banks of moss, wild rose and eglantine. I like his quality of moss and vendure tempered by thorns. 'The Masque of Anarchy.' I get my politics direct from Shelley and Shakespeare, with an occasional hint from the Holy Ghost. . . .

There is a memory, casual and small, yet strange, with that indwelling quality of strangeness which means, 'I will never forget you never.' . . . Once, long ago (I can't remember either the exact circumstances or the place), I missed a train. It must have been a fair-sized station, for there were long dark ugly faithful-snouted trains hulking up, one against the other, and one drank water in sizzling gasps. Gloaming came down, and the flat white discs of light went on. There were some hours to wait. Somehow, I don't recall the way of it, I was sitting in a little house belonging to strange people, sitting in their kitchen and talking to them. Of course I must have asked them if I could come in. Probably I gave them sixpence, but I don't remember. I had tea, and talked for a while. The mother wore a blue apron, and there were young children playing about.

I remember them now, as if unawares I had tasted there the Holy Grail. Their memory has never been entirely absent, only covered up. Very ordinary creatures, they must have been, and stared and asked questions, and had a brown teapot. I think of them, too, as I think of the homeless seeking homes. . . .

My life has been all ciphers and codes for the past several years. I showed the illustration to Dr. Geranty, who smiled at it, but I don't know whether or not he saw how beautiful it was. I couldn't often get him to talk. I shall never forget how once, while I still hated him, he looked at the frontispiece of a book on the mysteries of ancient Egypt; it showed the head of an Egyptian priest. 'These savage people all had those pointed heads,' he said. I stared at him, too engulfed in fury to get a word out. My beautiful Egyptian priest. . . . I could only repeat loudly, 'Now I know I'm in a madhouse,' which was untrue as well as being bad form; it was horribly bad form to call the Lodge a madhouse, as it was a convalescent ward. Even 'mental hospital' didn't go so well, though the medical superintendent, Dr. Salys, preferred 'asylum' and said so, in his jolly

Scotch voice. . . . Once you got to know him, it was Dr. Geranty who understood. . . . He was a code-and-cipher person, too, a doctor of dreams. You had to give him time, his mind always had to be pulled back from something else. . . .

[I]t was the sudden clash of dream against a person incompetent to dream that made me run away, that and the fact that all the glow had gone out of the attic. I called out after a retreating back, 'You're most unjust,' and was choking with words to say, but apart from going to the head of those too-much-polished stairs, those unforgettable scarlet stairs which, off and on, were polished from six-thirty in the morning till nine at night, those stairs which were a duty and a ritual, how could I say them? . . . Then I had to decide what I could take without attracting attention. My typewriter: a manuscript that had to be posted: pyjamas, tooth-brush, comb, Shakespeare, and for return to the Library all my subscription books. . . .

By giving in notice, I could have left anyhow in a week's time. But I couldn't, for which I will pay hereafter, either in conscience or in convenience. The retreating back had belonged to a person with no sense of privacy, who said his unpleasantnesses where people can hear them. . . . I went in the clothes I stood up in, and, as the luck of the day would have it, these were unsuitable, consisting of my best frock (turquoise-green), a lettuce-coloured flannel coat, which clashed abominably, a large black floppy hat with roses in front (I now find that they run in wet weather), and navy-blue shoes. Under normal circumstances I would have stayed and changed my frock, reasoned about it: this just seemed impossible, for the same reason that giving in my notice and going after a week's gossip seemed impossible. After four years, mainly happy until Dr. Geranty went away, I couldn't. . . .

[W]hen you're bottled up for months and for years, sane but scared of insanity, faintly or utterly discredited with relatives (according to their outlook), and above all, given no real outlet except this polish-and-mop business, you'll talk about *anything*. Polish-and-mop, dreaming and scandalmongering are the three occupations. . . .

I went down into my garden, which was dug out for me at Dr. Geranty's instructions, and which is most of the time a shocking mess, but occasionally bright with ill-constructed colours all happy together, and picked there three pieces from the rosemary tree. I

planted one rosemary, one lassiandra, one breath-of-Heaven, one
scarlet kowhai, two daphnes (but one died), one scented boronia
(also deceased), one little azalea, which turned out to be done up in
a rag, with no roots at all (though a mass of apricot flowers when I
got it), two cherry trees, now guarding the broken asphalt steps,
one Japanese maple, one scented verbena, which had grown very
well. Most of the daffodils I had put in a week before, but still the
place looked desolate, and I knew I had neglected it, and it cried out
in my heart. I had been so happy, so unreasoningly dream-happy,
after years when the veriest sap of a psychologist could tell you it
would be impossible for a woman ever to be happy again. . . .

After I had picked the rosemary there was nothing more to do;
so I went, and didn't look backwards at the attic windows, though
there, unless they burn the place down or blow it up, a face will
dwell for ever, my own face looking out. Unless, strangely and
unexpectedly, I should find any freedom. I drove in a taxi to Rosalie's and Gloria's, and Gloria had done the third chapter of
Madame Turehu. Ordinarily she would have shown it to me, she
had probably been working hard, like an elf turned navvy, all morning long, but as soon as Rosalie came into the room, I said, 'Well,
I've run away,' and then, of course, Gloria's Madame Turehu (a
turehu is a redheaded Maori fairy, full of dirty tricks) had to quirk
its mouth, shake its head and slip away into the background. . . .

I went down to the Tourist Office and got a little satisfaction out
of asking the officer, 'Have you any trains this afternoon or evening
for anywhere?' He repeated, 'Where to, Madam?' and I, 'Anywhere.' He had only Wellington, Rotorua or Hamilton, and I had
reasons of my own for keeping out of all those places. Before going
back to Rosalie's I bought Nurse O'Donoghue a necklace of opal
beads with diamond clasp—and they were Kohn's, too, not Wool-
worth's, as I hope she will realise but am afraid she won't—and for
my garden ten shillings' worth of ixias, for my old room half a
crown's worth of flowers—all to be delivered on the morrow. The
thought of errand boys arriving in a continuous stream with boxes
from their runaway didn't make me laugh at the time—there was
too much not to laugh about—but now, even if only God and I see
it, it was funny. I also got some medinal* and a huge packet of typ-

---

* A hypnotic. Ed.

ing paper, some ink, some envelopes, some stamps, some soap. Without these things I am miserable. I did think of 'longs' and a shirt—lovely and warm—but the shops were closing. I went back to Rosalie's and wrote two letters, one to the retreating back which had been so unjust to me, the other (tried not to make it longer or more apologetic than I could help) to Dr. Salys, the medical superintendent, who was away on leave, caravanning happy as a lark or a lad. . . . Only Rosalie and Gloria knew where I was going. That was to this bach room. Suddenly I had remembered the old boarding-house in the mountains; one Christmas I had Mother there for a weekend, it rained all the time, we sat up till two listening for a King George V broadcast which turned out to be ecstatic static, and Mother complained there wasn't enough to eat. But I had noticed these little rooms tucked away in the bush, and guessed they'd be empty at this cold time of the year. . . .

At Rosalie's I began to cry, since all else was done (except the brandy, which I hated as much as ever). She was lovely: she has the warmest, queerest heart, and at rock-bottom is almost completely detached and unsentimental, though capable of fury against injustices. . . . Gloria has a central calm, much more than mine: an active, radiating calm. Rosalie has not merely an imagination, but *the* imagination, and rock-bottom beneath it. If nerves don't trip her up, she and Gloria may conquer the world, which would be better than Alexander's botching and boggling. She hid her eyes under fluttering hands while I gulped more brandy. . . . There were sticks of asparagus hot on toast for tea, and I ate the sticks but left the toast, feeling this struck a decent medium between desire to perish of starvation, desire to show I appreciated Rosalie's asparagus. . . . If only I could be sure that this night's half-laughter won't leak out of my boots, leaving me going in circles, abject, half-fainting from hunger, and from sorrow, along the flat grey pointless sands. It is not fair to be one moment in such a condition that the huge surfs at Piha are as meaningless as a child's rattle: the next inclined to laugh at everything. Well then, the Irish have a reputation for insincerity. Poor luckless devils, they're only being true to their schizophrenia.

A taxi brought me here, swooping like a great bird through the night away from city, into sky towering over the beautiful heart-breaking lights. . . . It was raining. I found this little place, and they took me down, and told me not to be afraid of the possums. I was not, but I was afraid when my mind started making idiotic funny sentences which ran into one another, which slipped round and round, tired of holding up one another's tails. I was very much afraid, and thought, So steady on. I took a medinal tablet, went out and watched the lights for a while, then came back again. Wept bitterly, but in the morning I opened to Shakespeare, as if he were the Bible, for the best of a pointered sentence, as dear old ladies used to do in the long ago, so that their elastic-sided steps might be quicker through the day. . . .

I was angry inside, a few weeks ago, coldly angry and impatient, when a married woman who did not love her husband, but was attached to her children and to her fairly comfortable way of living, told me that if anything happened to her marriage, her life would be at an end. It seemed to me her life was an unreal thing, which could never have had a beginning. Now I am in the same predicament. I never had much, except dreams: I was desperately unhappy sometimes, and I hated the loudspeaker, the mop-and-polish laws, the way the beds creaked, the sluggish world mentality *behind* the huddle into which women patients went— . . . I hated that so much I often thought an earthquake or a thunderbolt would be excellent. Yet I don't know that I can bear it if the dance is done. If there were a smile, a backward look, a last sequin of gold light from the empty ballroom, it would be so different. However, one can't bet on it. . . .

I am opening a drawer with a curled wooden knob, and it sticks a bit. Pull hard . . . jerk it. Inside, right on top of the things I was curious about, is the horrifying decrepit tail of a rat. No rat attached, tail pure and simple. Grown-ups: explanations. It is the tail of a muskrat, nothing else will give clean hankies and linen quite the desired odour. Yes, but why think of it now, now, now? . . .

[T]here is a moment in the life of most people when all their associations—once happy, once tragic, once annoying—stand up around them, like the hosts of dead silvery trees one sees in the New Zealand bush. Whole hillsides belong to these silvery trees. Sometimes fire has been through them, or one way or another their life has been lopped; sometimes they have just died, en masse. . . . They are silent and terrible, the most substantial shapes I have ever seen death take. Well, so the past can be; the people you loved, the people you lived with, the people you quarrelled with, the people

whose business throats you would have cut, given an opportunity—
all standing around you, skeleton silvery trees. . . .

I had a past moderately scarlet, but not cut-throat (by cut-
throat I mean either mercenary or vindictive). It lacked, I am afraid,
in any sense of humour, and I took my sins with a diabolical seriousness—real plum-pudding sins. 'I must confess . . . hold this
baby.' Squalling sin dumped, wet-napkined, on the knee of a surprised young man. Or much more often, I confessed nothing at all
by words, but everything by action.

It seems to me now that I am caught in the hinge of a slowly-
opening door, between one age and another. Between the tradition
of respectability, which was very strong in my household and had
cut me off from all real family love the moment I infringed it, and
the new age, foretold by Nietzsche and some others. Just as Presby-
terians who now get up in congress and heatedly discuss the effects
of dancing, and of one glass of claret-cup on the bloodstream and
subsequent purity of the race, seem to most of us a little droll, so
in time will an Iris Wilkinson, knocking her head on the ground
and her bleeding knuckles on the door, seem extremely queer to
those who have learned to be happy without self-consciousness. To
minimise my own agony would be to slander and make a joke of
thousands upon thousands of women and girls who have shut
themselves up in iron cages, thrown themselves into rivers (or into
the arms of complete bounders, who have felt justified in dropping
them hard 'when the dance was done'), and also to lie about the
education we received in our childhood and girlhood. No mercy,
only a thin soupy trickle of 'charity' was ever preached to us. . . .

I will carry my skinned knuckles and sometimes abject countenance through life, and so will a good many other women. If
another generation is allowed to do the same thing, I say, more
fools men: for a woman can be a pretty thing when she is happy,
and a soul, like a cloth, becomes heavy to carry when it is sodden
through with tears.

Because one man had been somewhat unfair to me, almost in
my childhood . . . I had, in honour, to hang out a sort of notice:
'Not a Virgin. Unfairness Invited, Apply Within.' It tainted friendship and spoiled the possibilities of love, though physically and
mentally I was fairly well adapted for both. . . . Of course there
were the lazy, jolly, come-and-get-it-boys women, as well as the

others. And I suppose somewhere in the world there was also the safe, happy protected community of constitutional virgins. . . . For a time . . . I took the happier road. I became less than a woman again, a figure attached to white trees and crackling brown leaves; to sitting with knees drawn up staring and staring at the beads of ice frozen upon crystal reeds beneath a waterfall; to the madder rose suddenly streaking unbudded willows as the first flush of the year came round again. I was happy then, and companionless. For a body I had something that walked, and ate as little as possible, and consorted with furry things, with bright-black wings and a throat flung back sipping honey from flax, in the forest. The incredible deep eastern blue of the sky at dusk, over snow-mountains, amazed me, and I loved the way the heavy fir-branches dragged to earth under a fall of snow. But then the question of money arose. I had to get a job and keep a job. . . .

. . . ([A]s work on my newspaper was really hard, drudgery which earned my £4 10s 0d a week and would have earned twice as much if I had been a man) I ate a considerable amount of steak and onions at Joe's, got fat and coarse-looking, with misty eyes, went to champagne parties given by Trixie's unending string of boy-friends, interviewed people, and occasionally struck on a really beautiful thing.

I wonder if those are worth mentioning? Small rainy wild chrysanthemums in one leather-coloured women's garden . . . in another, fantastic cacti, and a sunporch where Simla moths hatched out from pupae as big as walnuts. I actually saw the liquid pulsating through the now-transparent brown pupae become solid; crawl out to the exterior of its cracked shell, hang limp and draggled, then begin to swell with life. I saw the veins take pattern, as along them this liquor of life spread itself. Then the thing, the moth, was whole and flew. It sensed its purpose was to fly, it knew what to do with these new veined instruments which had been liquid two hours before. Ah, God, and what of us? To come by a harder road into this world, to be bedraggled indeed, and then to be taught, not what we must do that shall make us whole and complete, but such tawdry lies that every evil face you see in the streets accuses you of them. It was an ill day, God, a very ill day, when you set up Man for your interpreter. And of course the modernist will say I have the proposition the wrong way round; it was an ill day when Man allowed the access of God on his punishments. But that perfected man, innocent and clean, *is* my God, what else? And he wears Christ's sandal and has Shelley's eyes. . . .

Lonnie was in looks a little like one of the silvery trees himself. He was young, but thin and grey-haired. . . .

Lonnie became my lover without premeditation, almost by accident. One moment I was wearing a scarlet and gold net frock (which Trixie had sold me on commission) and telling teacup fortunes in a hotel lounge, the next—that was that. He didn't regret it, but soon made an opportunity to tell me about his wife and family, who did not seem to me to matter one way or the other. I had no intention of hanging on to Lonnie, distracting his attention; I hadn't wanted him in the first place. . . .

Lonnie's first comment (by letter) was, 'Do you think you could find your share of £20?' The £20 was for an abortion. Well, I thought, you can't say we haven't got sex equality all right. I wrote back and said I didn't want that. . . .

It was finally arranged with Lonnie. I was to remain his friend—and a discreet one—he was to help me with medical and nursing expenses, I was to retreat to some obscure country spot for a time, then take up my lucrative job again. The retreat was arranged rather well. I paid a visit to a doctor, who gave me a certificate for six months' leave of absence, on grounds of dicky heart. My lucrative job would let Lonnie out of the necessity for financial transactions thereafter. The office, which liked my work, not only gave me that six months' leave, but also thirty shillings' worth per week of free-lancing, which provided admirably (though they didn't know it) for the months in the obscure country retreat. . . .

On an afternoon a few days before I left Wanganui, I walked round Virginia Lake—an artificial pond, but a pretty one, in those autumns of burning gold leafage. A cricket threaded the air with its incessant little stitch of song. I went slowly and heavily, and so did the leaves, which in their ripeness fell to earth, and pressed there their damp cheeks, as if they had at last found comfort and satisfaction. Outside the park there was a chapel of roughcast white concrete, alone and empty, but open, and more wet gold of leaves pressed against it. I walked in, and put my forehead against the wood of one of the benches in front. There were no candles, but the white lilies, that could not burn, shone steadily. The touch of wood was like an old friend's hand, an old humble brown friend: Joseph's hand, I dare say. I have always loved many of the people in the

Bible, whether with oddly-distorted snivelling stained-glass faces they stare out over my head, in robes of deep scarlet and blue, or whether they are merely an old remembered phrase, a comforting hand of wood. But I am not a Christian. It is the four seasons that wax and wane in me, it is autumn that hangs so heavily golden-ripe, spring that is pallid and fretful and full of a strangeness of cherry flowers. Nevertheless, now people trample over their heads, the saints would not mind perhaps, that I should make use of their drinking cups. I knelt and with my head against the bench of wood repeated what I had learned in childhood. 'My soul doth magnify the Lord, and my spirit rejoiceth in God my Saviour. For, behold, from henceforth, all generations shall call me blessed. For he that is mighty has magnified me, and holy is his name.'

Working by what strange auguries? But the liquid of moth pulsating into the vein and solid of moth, is that less sacred than the conception of Christ? . . .

[W]hat I chiefly wanted was to find the right place in the country.

I discovered it through thinking of our school friends who had become teachers, and gone off to the most remote bits of island imaginable, bits where nobody ever visited them, for there would be no tourist attractions, few roads, nothing but a handful of snotty-nosed brats who had to be educated that they might then help in their fathers' cowsheds. I thought of Eve, who had gone to Brindle Pass, a white channel of whirlpools a day's launch-trip from the head of the Sounds. Dumont Island, almost completely uninhabited, lay near it, accessible by sea. I wrote to Eve, and she was sure that a family on Dumont Island would take me as a boarder. . . .

I was lonely because I was an alien: there and in many other places. In France they call an asylum 'maison d'aliénés'. It is my own fault, I make my own bars: too cold a selfishness, too much sporadic desire to do good—whatever 'good' may be—too much of the defensive, learned in childhood, too easy a gift of making other people seem in the wrong. And insisting on going through life in quietude is rather like travelling on pneumatic tyres; but what else can I do? . . .

When I became, to look at, 'conspicuous', Mrs. Snape [Hyde's landlady] asked me to leave. . . .

The inconvenient, unwanted, rather hateful move . . . turned out amazingly well. . . .

I loved the Maoris in Picton. Their pa* was some distance away, in a neglected bay of flaring wild gorse. But the whole of that little town took mercy on me. The sunshine was a light, plumy gold, laughing at winter, the landlocked harbour was so still that with very little effort I taught myself to row, and was soon admiring the cliffs and starlings of Mabel's Island, three miles from shore, and the streets were so quiet and secluded that I felt much less an object of notice than when on my rock. I stayed in an unfrequented old boarding-house, with meals upstairs, before the glow of salt-steeped driftwood fires. There was a tiny library in wild disorder (the librarian warned me *not* to take out the works of Margot Asquith, as Margot was not a respectable woman), and all the days were wandering, dreaming, drifting days, healthy with salt, tall with trees. . . .

Picton had the littlest and the biggest and the clearest everything. The littlest grey birds and littlest fishes; the most towering bluegum trees, which when they burst out in white bolls of blossom contained a bird to every flower-tuft; the biggest flames, too, shed on the worn carpet, and the funniest little library, and when spring came the most dancing little white kids, with bud horns, and lambs with eyelashes; and the clearest of mellow sunlight, a German hock sunlight, and the clearest sense of ease. Even the little churchyard slumbered and slept, hill-sheltered, without a trace of remorse or apology. . . .

I couldn't write—wrote nothing all the time except the free-lancing thirty shillings' worth for the Wanganui paper, which kept me, and one poem to a dead man whom I had loved a number of years before—but I was not unhappy. That earth was too quiescent, its skin was like my own; brown skin against white skin, and the high-stalked bracken watching. I thought it would not be bad for my child. From the beginning I had made up my mind, since I was going to have this infant, to want it. . . .

Lonnie had sent nearly all the money for nursing home and doctor, and a good deal it was. There was a green room with white lace curtains, and kindliness, and cleanliness. I was going to have

* Camp. Ed.

those. Lonnie wrote, with fitful cheeriness or fitful grief, saying how he had lost or won at the races, and this fiver would be a bit of a hurdle. I let him take his hurdles. . . .

Then a note from my paper in Wanganui. They were sorry, but . . . well, there was no lucrative job to go back to, no job of any kind at all. They made no allegations, but I guessed one of Trixie's girl-friends or boy-friends had gossiped a little. I wrote and asked them for a month's notice money. Got it. . . .

The baby, making no bones about the matter, was keeping its promise to arrive in the world in about a fortnight's time. . . .

I was glad to be in hospital. White and green and clean. Curtains and quiet, babies like funny little milk-full puppies. You're being so wonderful, Mrs. Challis. Then, rather to everybody's distress and astonishment, Mrs. Challis was not being at all so wonderful; but the doctor coped with that.

Then there was this red-visaged little creature, with solemn blind slate-blue eyes, done up in white clothes, and streaks of sovereign-coloured hair all over its head. I was rather proud of that. . . .

What I was going to do with him next I hadn't the faintest idea, except that we must immediately leave for a city, and there I must immediately find a job. The first stop was Wellington. Certainly I couldn't take Derek to my home and family. I had written informing them that I hadn't a job any more, and already they were furious. Derek would be a different thing, an act of violent cruelty, not on their part but on mine. They were not caught in the jamb of the door, they were on the other side: all their associations, love, friendship, building-up of sound life from life of poverty, were on that other side. To disturb them with a baby would have been a crime: and besides, I'd been enough of a trouble to them already.

Derek was to be smuggled. I had bought him, for cradle, a dress-basket, wherein he lay quite complacently, sleeping most of the time. He was a baby with character. He had an elf face, at first faintly like his father's, and that red-gold hair, and large unblinking eyes. Inopportunely he had developed a rash. The Sister told me it was only red gum, and that nearly all babies take it, but it did not improve his appearance. Where he was not slate-blue eyes and red-gold hair, he was large pink spots. The smuggling was arranged in Wellington by a doctor whom I had told about his coming with joy and pride (pompous words); a doctor who had known me as a sick and nerve-torn child, years ago, and who was quite pleased, though vaguely harassed, that I should take to myself some sort of happiness, unorthodox or not. . . .

Dress-basket, Derek and I went aboard the *Tamahine* in fair weather, and the sunshine was steeping the no-less-gold of the laburnums, which had touched my hands every day I walked down from the hospital beneath their dripping fringes, trying to find my feet again. This, to the day, was three weeks after Derek was born. . . .

Strolling on the deck I saw the creamy-haired, black-sticked figure of a Wellington artist, old 'Dolla' Richmond, who knew me moderately well, though my family not at all. Still, to have explained to her that she mustn't mention to anyone I was travelling with a new baby and a dress-basket seemed to me, at the time, an undertaking of which I was quite incapable. I fled down to Derek, and looked at him in his basket. He was wide awake. I had a bottle handy, ready to shove into his mouth and say, 'Here, take this.' He gave me a rather dirty look; I suppose he blamed me for the pink blotches all over his face and neck, and the way the *Tamahine* rolled.

'Don't cry,' I implored him, 'please don't cry.'

It was not a mother's imagination. The steady slate-blue look was replaced by one of elfish understanding. Derek, all the voyage, lay staring at the cabin ceiling like a Buddhist at his navel. He sucked steadily at his bottle when I administered it, hiccuped, but did not cry. . . .

The nursing home where, owing to Dr. Sidney's intervention, they were able to take Derek as a boarder at two guineas a week, was a good place but not to be counted on for long, because mostly it took straight-out maternity cases. Of Lonnie's money and mine I had about £20 left. There should have been more—the hospital gave me a discount for cash, which I hadn't reckoned on—but I mentioned I was a bad spender, and it had gone on a mail-order-trousseau for Derek, gone unaccountably, just leaded away. I suppose I should have felt apologetic towards him: but whenever his slate-blue eyes stared at me, they seemed perfectly wise and understanding. . . .

The first thing I had to do, on getting to Wellington from Picton, was to smuggle Derek (Derry) to the Harris Nursing Home, where Dr. Sidney had warned them to expect him. That meant I couldn't let my people know when I was arriving. I had to drop out of the blue and say, 'Well, Mother, what's for tea?' I waited until all the people had disembarked from the *Tamahine*. Then the dress-basket, Derry and I grandly loaded ourselves in a taxi, and went to the Harris Nursing Home. I was, of course, Mrs. Challis, and wore Lonnie's wedding ring, which he had given me with his slight silvery smile and the words, 'You've no idea how much these things cost.' At the Home they arranged Derry in a white stoutly-tucked crib alongside rows of other babies, mostly newer than he was—the boys on one side, under blue labels, the girls under pink ones: seg-regation of the sexes begun rather early in life. He was as stout-hearted as ever, but his red gum rash decidedly did not improve his appearance. He looked as spotty as a Dalmatian, only pink. Out of this gazed the big unwinking eyes God, Lonnie or I had given him; he still had the elfish expression, dependent mainly, I think, on his pointed chin. . . .

Then I went home, and was Iris again, and the garden was lovely, with all the heavy brooms in flower. I had a special name for Mother's garden. I called it 'Companionable Garden'. It hadn't just occurred or been planted, you see, it had grown against the heavi-est odds imaginable—stiff clay soil and no money to buy the roses that would have suited it, sweeping, howling, cataracts of gales, my Father's extreme reluctance to cut the hedge, his habit of cutting down to the bare quick and leaving the whole place exposed if Mother drove him to it, lack of fertiliser, banks, couch-grass that wouldn't grow into a lawn, a thick, stubbly, grumbling old holly hedge, like an unshaven tramp, that should have been rooted out years before but was now too deep for my mother's strength. . . .

Companionable garden . . . All the roots had got to know one another, they were a thick fibrous talkative mat under the earth, they had conquered even the clay. Delicate things wouldn't grow, though there was a dear little buttonhole rose, and in spring the snowdrops pushed up heavy and thick, and sent the green-pointed hailstone showers all over the upper beds. . . .

Like the thick roots under the earth, so were woven my mother's and sisters' very hard-purchased associations with a few friends, a few pleasures, that wouldn't cost too much. I had been out of it for years, ever since my first illness: no, really, for long years before that, when I had discovered I wanted love above all things else, and hadn't discovered I was caught in the door. . . .

In the house, then, I found myself hated: there is no other word.

I had deliberately lost a good, profitable job, playing about for six months round about islands and channels. I didn't even look appealing. 'You look about thirty. Fat and coarse. I can hardly believe you're my daughter.' . . .

That cursed house . . . that house I used to love . . . that money-haunted, money-worried house, with the death-watch beetle in its deadly walls, with old loves, old cleanliness, old jokes and hopes, all compressed into six rooms, lavatory-and-bathroom, the bath not even painted. And companionable garden outside. . . .

I couldn't stay in that house any longer. Gwen sent me the money to come to her and bring Derry. She was living now in Hawke's Bay, at a tiny place called Hatuma. Her own baby was nearly ten months old, and had at first been delicate. Now she said he was big, with a lovely complexion.

I smuggled Derry on to the train—more excuses so that nobody at home should have a remorseful spasm and want to see me off, but one gets quite clever at lying—I said I was getting a lift in a private car. So the soldier of fortune and I started off, he in his dress-basket, possible a little over-heated and wondering what had become of his cobbers, but most gentlemanly quiet so long as I filled him up with bottle whenever he showed the least sign of puckering his face. . . .

I was growing slimmer again, looked more like a human being, the person Gwen had been prepared to like, less like some queer lumbering figure out of a Norman Lindsay drawing. . . .

Percy and Gwen were going away. I had to find somewhere for Derry, and Gwen thought of an aunt of hers in Palmerston North, whose next-door neighbour, an old Irishwoman named Mrs. Rattan, had sometimes boarded babies. I couldn't take him back to Wellington and the Harris Nursing Home. So little of the money I had was left that I was afraid of their two guineas a week; more afraid of having him close to me if I couldn't find a job. So the aunt wrote that Mrs. Rattan would take a baby boarder, and I prepared his last feed before the journey—lime juice, then milk, not orange juice yet, but very soon. . . .

I was reasonable size again, and rejoiced in it. Absence hadn't made Mother's heart grow so very much fonder, but seemingly the less volume there was of me, the easier she could bear it, with a sort of grudging, coming-round affection. (But do you see? She hated *us,* or the sake of the brilliant, laughing, courageous children we should have been; she prodded *us*, unsuccessfully, to make us tread in the paths they would have taken—the little University Scholarship brats, the famous-woman-scientist brats, the Better-than-Jean-Batten-brats; not that Jean Batten had ever been heard of at the time. She had worked and sacrificed and slaved, gone hungry, gone lonely, to make us that, and we remained soft. I, the only one she didn't think soft, was a deal worse—dangerous. I am not quite sure whether I love or hate those little brats, but I know that they haunt our money-haunted house. Mother slicing and slicing away at the Golden Pear, rubbing and rubbing away at the Silver Nutmeg, and still we couldn't get them down our throttles. It was pitiable, as pitiable as the fact that girls are young and that women grow old). . . .

And then, one day, in our letter-box, there was a telegram for me.

I went up the path with the telegram hidden behind my back, like an idiot child. I suppose the story was written on my face.

'You can't guess what news I had today.'

Mother said quickly, 'You're going to get married.'

'Oh, no I'm not. Nothing about marriage. But I've got a job, a decent job. Look at that. I'm going to Auckland.'

Mother read the unfolded telegram. She was glad enough. It was a weekly paper job; I was to start in February, about a month's time. From then onwards, I was somebody in the house. . . .

It was that year (1932) when men started shouting at one another down in Wellington, in the House of Representatives, with its carved wooden plaques, each inscribed with the name of an engagement in which the New Zealand forces had taken part during the war. The word 'Depression', like an untimely child, grew big and swelled the belly of the world, leapt out to devour. What was a drop in England's bucket, in the way of expenditure, debts, unemployment figures, threatened to swamp New Zealand altogether. There was nothing for the Government in power to do but sit tight and twist its lips; it had done its spending. . . .

In the first Auckland year public distress wasn't nearly so evident as later. The Napier and Hastings earthquake stood out; it started in Auckland, where we had felt not a tremor, as rumour, a flickering whisper. I was at Devonport, reporting some affair. The light dry rumour flicked cheek after cheek. The *Veronica* (one of our cruisers) has sailed full steam for Napier. . . . Napier and Hastings have been destroyed, wiped out. . . . Nobody believed it. . . .

[T]hen plain news came through, in pieces. There was martial law in both cities. All roads were blocked, people were being dragged out from under blazing ruins. One of the beautiful Travis girls was dead . . . most of the girls in the Nurses' Home . . . Gwen, from Hatuma, wrote a god-send of a letter, which we published. Her chimneys had come through her roof, and her floor split in two. I thought of the big unblown pines lying all along those droughty roads. Frank Sturt flew down and got the first pictures. It wasn't an earthquake, it was a sensation, the story of a lifetime. . . .

To our office the quake was terribly important, life or death. Our real boss, with almost all his capital investments, lived in Napier. This weekly paper in Auckland was a little show, a sideline, revived after decrepit years when it had kicked about in barbers' shops and dentists' waiting-rooms. The question was, how much had he lost? We weren't paying yet, or anything like it. Would he pull out his capital? There were other partners, few-hundreds men, but he was the man with the few thousands, and crucial. We heard he had lost £100,000 in the quake. 'Of course if he gets out, I go?' I said to the editor, who was only a few years older than myself. He nodded. . . . Then the Napier boss flew up and announced that he had decided to keep going. He was a small man with light red hair. If he had liked, he could have walked between cheering ranks of linotypists, compositors and printers. The editorial cheer would have been small though hearty, as there were only the two of us, excepting the cartoonist, a white-moustached old-timer who had been there for ever and was uncommonly proud of his hobnailed liver. . . . [W]e were faintly snobbish, playing for the sporting fraternity on the one hand, for the social set on the other . . . but headlines strong if not too hot, and above all, topical. . . .

I knew nobody, male or female, child or adult. On arrival I had beached myself at a boarding-house, which smelt dank, and played very quarrelsome bridge (and the old man in the next room sniffed all night long), but somehow I had to discover all about Auckland. . . .

Always once a week Mrs. Rattan wrote me illiterate, sprawling, friendly little letters, sometimes with snapshots. My salary was £3

16s 0d, the odd shillings from £4 going to the Government's new unemployment tax of a shilling in the pound—from which reserve, by the way, no provision was made for unemployed women, only for the men. I paid Mrs. Rattan £1 a week for Derek, and sent him what clothes he needed. . . . When our paper got its wish, and became social, well-supplied with news by the bright young things and, often enough, by their fathers, I went to Government House functions in long black mittens. Gloves I could not afford. I had replaced Trixie's scarlet and gold net, which was falling to bits, with something quite classical in black satin, and a furrier who stayed in the same boarding-house used to lend me a white rabbit coat. The mittens seemed a chaste Victorian compromise.

Reporters at dances . . . You are growing old, old, old, you are decidedly not a virgin, very tired, very busy, and watching youth. . . . Scraping and scraping away at your mind, frittering it away in paragraphs . . . never a woman or a dog passed in an alley but she or it mightn't be a paragraph . . . never a chance word dropped, but it mightn't come in handy as a paragraph. Also film pages, book page, special articles (the ones that made the banner headlines and the billboards), personal paragraphs, comic rhymes, one-line digs at civic memorials and dignitaries, and later editorials. Fun. But not for years and years, only as oakum-picking might be if you did it for a lark, one afternoon making a tour of the gaol with a smiling and indulgent warder. . . .

I became a Douglas Creditor: or at least drifted into a meeting, got up and spoke as everybody else was speaking on the shameful-ness of throwing food away while people of the world were starv-ing, and was pleased and flattered when a man rose to his feet. 'I think we ought to vote this lady on to the committee.' The lady was voted on to the committee, and from thence onwards spent some time in the evenings making speeches, mostly impromptu; also fir-ing off 'paper pellets' at orthodox economists, of whom I can only say, their own works are the best possible illustration of that old Frenchman's snarl, 'Oh, that mine enemy had written a book.' . . .

Major Douglas ultimately came to New Zealand (at New Zealand's expense, or rather, at the shilling-collection expense of that portion of the populace who held by his doctrines). Of his visit, the less said the better. Nevertheless from the Waikato straight down through the North and South Islands, the meetings started in the cheaply-rented wooden halls, where the lantern-jawed idiot always would get up with his, 'Yes, but in Russia . . .' had New Zealand farmers reading, writing and talking economics, probably for the first time since the 1913 strike had filled them with the idea that if they were to survive, the cockies would have to come to town and thrash the city strikers. The Douglas Credit organisation was a chief factor in displacing the Coalition Government, and putting the Labour Government into power. The small farmers were convinced they were going to get something for nothing, the Labour candidates talked the Douglas Credit vernacular (and dropped it soon after the election), and the farmer's invincible reluctance to vote for a Labour man melted away. . . .

Once I brought Mrs. Rattan and Derek up from Palmerston North. She stayed placidly at a boarding-house, her bosom immense as ever in her dirty black dress, her cigarette twisted down from the end of her mouth, her serene kindness unflawed. Derry had grown queerly beautiful. She had Little Lord Fauntleroy locks on him, but his intensely blue eyes dominated the rest of his face, which had lost its peaky look. He was doing all the wrong things, it seemed, living on condensed milk and biscuits, having his meals whenever he pleased, learning no good tricks . . . except to be Derry . . . we were left alone in the bedroom, he crying loudly, one shoe off, kicking on the strange bed, which apparently didn't please him. I said to him, 'Hullo, Derek . . . hullo . . .' as if he were a grown-up, or Anna the possum. He stopped crying and stared at me. Blue eyes, the deepest blue I had ever seen. . . .

She and I—the big, careless, affectionate Irishwoman, possibly with a streak of Maori blood to account for her still-black hair and her passion for children—didn't hate one another. I think she is one of the most beautiful people I ever met, the only one connected with Derek who made me feel at home. . . .

She loved him; but she was bringing him up on unholy foods and customs, that wouldn't do. I'd have to bring him to Auckland. She was quite unconcerned about his behaviour. 'Oh,' she said, with her big laugh, 'Tommy allus wets the bed, don't you, Tommy?' Tommy didn't mind, she didn't mind. (She liked calling him Tommy, it came more naturally to her than my bit of fancy dress). . . .

At the quarrelsome-bridge boarding-house (I had never had time or energy to drag myself out of it, I was going, going, going, doing twice a man's work in a day, sandwiching Douglas Credit meetings between the reporting of dances, thinking of Derry and of other things at odd moments) one night I dropped into the sitting-room to beg a couple of aspirins. My head was bad, the shops were shut. . . . The street was a good street—no traffic except smooth-running cars, great old English trees shimmering down their golden-green light and in autumn their rusty pools of leaves, and Albert Park, which I loved in spite of its name, not far away. But the furniture of this place was bursting and decrepit. . . . There was a hopeless quiet dejection about it, it hadn't even been allowed to die decently.

When I said, 'Can anyone let me have a couple of aspirins?' . . . [L]ittle quiet grey man got up and said he'd fetch me the aspirins. After the bridge game he knocked and asked me if my headache had gone. He had a slow, soft, drawling voice, an odd voice, as of an adult trying to talk baby-talk for a child. . . . I said, no, it hadn't gone, and went back to the sitting-room to smoke a cigarette. . . . Little grey man took a folded paper out of his pocket.

'You wouldn't take what's in *this*.' Talking to a child again, as much as to say, 'You wouldn't believe me if I said this was a sherbet sucker.'

He unfolded the paper slowly; fine white powder.

'Well, what is it?'

He said in his slow little soothing voice, 'Morphia.' . . .

'You wouldn't take that . . .'

'Wouldn't I?'

Sort of a game. Now I'll fold up the paper and put it back in my pocket and smile. Now I'll edge a tiny bit of the white powder into a corner, and say. 'You can have that much.' (Did he say 'That much,' or 'Dat much'? I think it was 'Dat much'.) Then, slither the whole of the powder into the spill of paper and give it over. A glass of water. Then the little paper burned in the slow-eating flames of the boarding-house fire.

Little flames, wandering desolately about on inadequate shoddy coal, all dressed up and no place to go. But that also was true of everybody now. Frightened little people . . . frightened of the great steel winds pouring over the world, of being evicted, of having to pay one shilling in the pound unemployment tax, of having the banks close down on them (the banks were now the real mortgage-holders over almost all the cracking farms), of being found out for having illegitimate babies, of finding themselves out, in dark of the early morning, finding themselves out and thinking, 'I don't come up to much.' . . .

After a short space, the white powder did make a sort of tingling feeling creep over me . . . not sleepiness, nothing much to write home about; nothing of the same effect as when, in hospital, they inject it. Still, it was probably morphia after all, which I hadn't quite believed. . . .

Customs change in the world. It seems to me that if I am anything at all, I am a poet, a dreamer and a lover, and at one time or another none of these was an occupation to be despised. I have stayed a long time, but now I am gone, as you wished: and perhaps I came to this asylum of yours not because I was made, but because I needed madness if I were to survive—which is not an impossible state of affairs. . . .

This afternoon I thought, 'I can't go on with this, no, certainly I can't go on.' And then, 'The wise write only in shards and fragments, in little intricate pieces of filigree, so delicately wrought, so finely polished that they never cease tempting the eye.' Then I thought of some of those great ones who have tried to handle the stuff of the world, much less careful about the effects they achieve than about the heavy, bulky, cumbersome substance of what they have to say. . . .

I was sick, and cold, and miserable: the mood when one clasps hands about one's knees and spends hours staring at nothing, dreaming. Then I thought, 'Get up,' and went to the house, which is empty today except for Peggy, Betty and June, the only guests having gone last night. And I got my fire, without asking for it. I think Peggy likes me, after all. She built a fire in the brick hearth, and the little flames crisped and crackled. I've been sitting there for hours, reading and dreaming, but always with the one thing at the back of my mind. . . .

I remember how, when I left the boarding-house nearly two years after coming to Auckland, and got myself what was called a flat—a room with a folding-up bed, a tin-roofed verandah divided into kitchenette and bathroom, but plenty of clean hot water, which I loved—the light cut into the heavy purple flesh of the gladioli in the vase. I had always liked flowers beyond reason, and bought them extravagantly, but these purple flowers, some kind of botanist's emperor, were more than liking. Gathered up in their petals

they seemed to have all the soft weight, dignity and beauty of creatures in a fairy-tale. Then letting down the folding bed, I sat up and
read Swinburne, who is efficacious in a tearful way, beyond what
some of the moderns can do if you only want music and an emotional relaxation of your senses; and took morphia tablets, and lay
still, but was not asleep; catching sight of the purple gladioli from
time to time.

Derek was in Auckland. . . .

At last I found a house with a lawn, pleasant enough people,
the husband unemployed. He was there, and learned to do back
somersaults in the garden, and I saw him once a week, never alone.

Only once, really. That was when the little grey man at the
boarding-house took the entire family down to Titirangi for a bush
picnic. Derek was nearly two, his curls cut short, and he wore a
sun-helmet. We came to a place where a waterfall splashed down,
white and thin into its stony pool, and I fastened on his little blue
bathing-suit. He went in . . . smiling back, half-frightened because
it was cold, half-proud because everybody cried what a clever boy
he was. Then he was under the waterfall, splashed all over. Laughing, not crying, laughing in gasps. . . .

That day, we were alone somehow, going along a trail in the
bush, where the yellow leaves had been trodden into the ground.
We found a small bach cottage where an old woman lived alone,
but not, apparently, very lonely, and she invited Derek in for a cup
of milk. In a wire cage, quite a big cage, she kept tiny flickering
grass-green and grey lizards, uncanny twigs come alive. Derek was
enchanted with their tops and tails. He drank his milk in gulps,
staring at them. 'And there's possums, too,' said the old woman,
quite delighted, 'big possums, that come down and clamber on my
roof.' He looked up at the ceiling as if he expected the Holy Ghost
to descend in the form of a possum. . . .

In between his second birthday and his fifth, I never saw him. I
think I am glad.

Money affairs weren't so desperate as when I had first come to
Auckland, but I was almost obsessed by them . . . obsessed by the
certainty that I was going to be ill, and had to do something about
Derek. You are taking drugs, eating cold poison. . . . Yes: I started,
in a weary, half-broken body, job hunting three weeks after childbirth, racked with anxiety and with exile, horribly overworked,
horribly overtired, ever since. And I think my heart is, not broken,

but frozen . . . Which came first, taking drugs, or being so deadly tired and knowing a crash is straight ahead? It didn't seem to affect my work. Lonnie and I were fighting a kind of shadow fight with the gloves off. I had promised, it was my nice high-headed Wanganui promise, that we would always be friends, he would pay the hospital and the doctor, and after that I wouldn't ask him for money. Now I wanted to get out of my promise, make him agree to look after Derry when I crashed. . . . I was determined now (frightened) that he should stabilise Derry; he was equally determined that unless forced to it, he wouldn't. Was it Lonnie's fault that I had a baby instead of an abortion, lost a job, hunted about like a vixen whose earths have been stopped up, got another job, found the work too much, would like to throw the social pages in the women's silly red faces, tell them to tear them to pieces with their silly red talons, took morphia, read Swinburne, wanted love more than anything else on earth and spent money on deep velvety purple gladioli instead of devoting it, decently, to sensible purposes? . . .

Once I went down to Lonnie's city. I meant to be like the letters. I met him in front of the Post Office wearing his shabby leather coat; his hair was silvery, his eyes enquiring, and his elf-face peaked. He was wondering, 'Will she be in good temper or not?' All the war oozed out of me. Curious, that; since the day when Derry began to be, Lonnie and I never were lovers, never had kissed, but when I met him in the flesh—and so little of it—I never wanted to hit him. We passed that day a thread of a river, silvery like some old Hollandish etching, and great trees. . . . We should never have been lovers, we should have been friends—we *are* friends, in our manner—but most of all we shouldn't have been in business together. A drug-taking Irishwoman, a dream-ridden horse-racing silver man with a nose distinctly Semitic . . . Hell, no. Lonnie promised to see a lawyer and find out if he couldn't make some arrangement for adopting Derek if I were really ill, or died. He came back and told me that the lawyer said it was impossible without his wife's consent. So that was ruled out, and yet I wasn't unhappy. . . .

It was that year that my mother came up to Auckland for a holiday, and here, to this green place where the countless umbrellas of tree-ferns give the hillside a sombre, almost a hypnotic stare, a stare of old eyes sleepy and heavy-lidded. Tane's eyes. She had known about Derek for some time. I hadn't told her; gossip was so obliging. 'If I had known at the time, I think it would have killed me,' she said. 'Now it doesn't seem to matter so much.' She didn't want to see Derek, but knitted him a blue cardigan. She hadn't told the others in the house, that went without saying. We never told one another anything, unless driven to it by circumstances, delirium or helpless rage . . . and even in delirium or helpless rage we had always had the art of saying many things, while keeping the vital ones unsaid. . . . She had written, and shown me, two poems; one had been especially for me, written long ago when I was ill at Hanmer Springs. I kept it locked up in a little leather writing-case, whose gold key I eventually lost.

Janet Frame

(1924–   )

Janet Frame, the third daughter of a family whose life was shaped by the railroads of New Zealand's North Island, shares a childhood of daunting poverty with her Australian counterpart, Patsy Adam-Smith. Unlike Adam-Smith, Frame was one of a large family, although the supporting circle of sisters and brother contracted during her childhood as two sisters died of heart failure, and her brother was disabled by severe epilepsy.

Certainly New Zealand's most distinguished contemporary novelist, Frame explores the visionary capacity of madness in her fiction, using the alienation and loneliness of the seemingly insane to highlight the contradictions and soul-destroying uniformity of the modern welfare state, of which New Zealand is often regarded as a shining exemplar. Using the central figure of the mad person, Frame is able to explore, not merely the routine dullness of a bureaucratic world, but the smallness and insecurity of colonial societies, an insecurity which she sees as the cause of their savage rejection of anyone who is "different."

Frame's opening novel, *Owls Do Cry* (1960), was considered the first fiction by a New Zealander to carry universal significance, and thereby to claim a place in the canon of modern English fiction. In this respect she resembles her Australian contemporary, the Nobel laureate Patrick White, whose fiction examines an Australian society which scorns and fears the creative and imaginative individual as profoundly as does Frame's New Zealand.

Frame's literary genius enables her to write compellingly believable stories about the discontinuity of the personality, the seemingly insuperable problems of human communication, and the impoverishment of the imagination which accompany the standardization of modern societies. In *Owls Do Cry, Faces in the Water, The Edge of the Alphabet, Scented Gardens for the Blind,* and *The Adaptable Man* we see the hand of a master forging gripping and coherent narrative out of stories of discontinuity, madness, and fantasy.

Frame's *Autobiography* is written in three parts; the middle part, "An Angel at My Table," has become familiar to millions of movie viewers through the 1990 Australian film version. Seen as a whole the three-part memoir is a quest narrative in which the author seeks to escape confining and inflexible family bonds only to succumb to an even more confining and judgmental larger society. We see her perpetually on the train, in a vain quest for a sustaining niche within a hostile New Zealand environment, finding it in her thirties in the shelter of other outcasts, her homosexual writer mentor, and his circle of literary and artistic friends.

Volume One lays out the dimensions of Frame's bloodchilling family dilemma. Volume Two shows us the narrator retreating into fantasy and mental illness to shelter in institutions which are even more authoritarian and without human sympathy than her family, while Volume Three shows us the final journey into freedom, and the discovery of an authentic voice.

In the first two sections Frame outlines the dilemma of the colonial intellectual of her generation, more alive to Wordsworth and Keats than to the cadences of her own world, or to the imagery of her Southern Pacific island home. In the last this predicament is resolved through the vivid experience of other cultures, found through affinity rather than taught through authority, and with that resolution comes the final dismissal of the idea that she is anything other than normal and gifted with a powerful drive to write. In the process of writing about this transformation during her years in England Frame writes powerfully about the problems of the colonial writer long before postmodern literary theory fastened attention upon postcolonial literature and its supposedly hybrid creators.

AN AUTOBIOGRAPHY

I recall that Grandma Frame began working in a Paisley cotton mill when she was eight years old; that her daughters Polly, Isy, Maggie spent their working lives as dressmakers and in their leisure produced exquisite embroidery, knitting, tatting, crochet; and that her son George Samuel, my father, had a range of skills that included embroidery (or 'fancy-work', as it was known), rug making, leatherwork, painting in oils on canvas and on velvet. The Frames had a passion for making things. Like his father, our Grandad Frame, a blacksmith who made our fire pokers, the boot-last, and even the wooden spurtle smoothed with stirring the morning porridge, my father survives as a presence in such objects as a leather workbag, a pair of ribbed butter pats, a handful of salmon spoons. . . .

Mother's family, the Godfreys, had long been established in Wairau and Blenheim and Picton, where Mother, Lottie Clarice, was born and brought up. . . . Mother, a rememberer and talker, partly exiled from her family through her marriage out of the Christadelphian faith and her distance from Marlborough, remembering her past as an exile remembers her homeland. . . . When Mother talked of the present, however, bringing her sense of wondrous contemplation to the ordinary world we knew, we listened, feeling the mystery and the magic. . . .

Mum and Dad (Mother was known as 'Mum' until I considered myself grown up enough to acknowledge her as a separate personality) were married at the Registry Office in Picton three weeks before Dad sailed to the Great War. . . . [O]n 28 August 1924 I was born, named Janet Paterson Frame, with ready-made parents and a sister and brother who had already begun their store of experience, inaccessible to me except through their language and the record. . . .

[W]e were railway people. And when I was three, we shifted house to Glenham in Southland. . . .

My memory is once again of the colours and spaces and natural features of the outside world. On our first week in our Glenham house on the hill, I discovered a place, *my place*. Exploring by myself, I found a secret place among the old, fallen trees by a tiny creek, with a moss-covered log to sit on while the new-leaved branches of the silver birch tree formed a roof shutting out the sky except for the patterned holes of sunlight. The ground was covered with masses of old, used leaves, squelchy, slippery, wet. I sat on the log and looked around myself. I was overcome by a delicious feeling of discovery, of gratitude, of possession. I knew that this place was entirely *mine*; mine the moss, the creek, the log, the secrecy. . . .

This passion for the outside world was strengthened by the many journeys we made in Dad's grey Lizzie Ford to rivers and seas in the south, for Dad was a keen fisherman, and while he fished, we played and picnicked and told stories, following the example of Mother, who also composed poems and stories while we waited for the billy to boil over the manuka fire. . . .

When I was two months from my fourth birthday, our youngest sister, June (Phyllis Mary Eveline), was born. That winter . . . is remembered as miserable yet with the misery shared and banished by the way in which, instead of acting as my teasing enemies, Myrtle and Bruddie became allies against the terrible Miss Low—Miss Low, the sister of one of Dad's fishing mates, who came to look after us while the baby was born and during the first few weeks. . . .

Wyndham was the time of cabbages in the garden, of pump water, of candles and kerosene lamps at night with 'real' darkness and night shadows, the people in the twilight seen as if striding across the surface of the world, and at noon, standing in small people-clumps. I learned to think of everything as sharing its life and its place with a shadow; and when the candles were lit at night, Mother used to say, 'I have a little shadow that goes in and out with me.' . . .

And Wyndham was the time of the dentist and starting school and Grandma Frame's dying: all three memorably unhappy, although Grandma Frame's death was different in being world-sad with everyone sharing—the cows, the hens, the pet rabbit, even the stinky ferret as well as the family and relations—while going to the dentist and starting school were miseries that belonged only to me. . . .

As soon as we arrived at Fifty-six Eden Street, Oamaru, we children began crawling and climbing everywhere, over every inch of the red-painted iron roof, along every earthy space between the piles under the house. We noted the inhabitants with whom we were to share our life: the insects, bees, mason bees, night bees, butterflies, grandfather moths, spiders, red spiders, furry spiders, trapdoor spiders; the birds, flocks of goldfinches, waxeyes, blackbirds, sparrows, starlings. We found cat skeletons under the house and sheep and cattle skeletons in the long grass of the bull paddock, where there was no longer a bull, only, from time to time, a group of young, skittering steers. We discovered every climbable place in the hedge and trees and on the summerhouse, accumulating our treasure of new experiences, which soon included the neighbours on each side and across the road, and beyond the bull paddock to the hill with its caves and fossilised shells, the zigzag with its native plants, and the seat at the top with the plaque 'Donated by the Oamaru Beautifying Society'; and the pine plantations, to be known as the 'plannies': the first one harmless, where you could look through to daylight beyond, the second frightening with the trees so densely packed that halfway through it you found yourself in a brown pine-needle darkness and knew there was no turning back, the third planny, small and full of daylight, the fourth, of stripling gums leading into pines extending down the hill at the end of Glen Street Gully, near the 'orchard', which, because it appeared to stand alone, independent of any house or person, we believed to be ownerless and therefore, in the 'finds keeps' tradition, belonging to us.

We soon learned to know the creek, too, in its every change of flow regulated by the water in the reservoir. We knew the plants on its banks and in the creek the rocks, cockabullies, eels, and the old weighted shredded sacks of drowned kittens and cats. Each morning we set out foraging for experience and in the afternoon returned to share with one another, while our parents, apart from us now, went about their endless adult work, which might better have been known as 'toil' in all its meanings—trap or snare, battle, strife, a spell of severe, fatiguing labour—meanings of which we were unaware. Dad worked all day, and sometimes, on night shift, all night, sleeping during the day, while we, the railway children, vanished into the pine plannies or along Glen Street Gully to our orchard or crept stealthily about the summerhouse, 'Sh-sh, Dad's asleep.' . . .

Our lives changed suddenly. Our brother had epilepsy, the doctor said, prescribing large doses of bromide which, combined with Bruddie's now frequent attacks, or fits, as everyone called them, only increased his confusion and fear until each day at home there were episodes of violent rage when he attacked us or threw whatever was at hand to throw. There had usually been somewhere within the family to find a 'place' however cramped; now there seemed to be no place; a cloud of unreality and disbelief filled our home, and some of the resulting penetrating rain had the composition of real tears. Bruddie became stupefied by drugs and fits; he was either half asleep, recovering, crying, from the last fit, or in a rage of confusion that no one could understand or help. He still went to school, where some of the bigger boys began to bully him, while we girls, perhaps prompted by the same feeling of fear, tried to avoid him, for although we knew what to do should he fall in a fit at school or outside at home, we could not cope with the horror of it. Mother, resisting fiercely the advice of the doctor to put Bruddie in an institution, nursed him while we girls tried to survive on our own with the occasional help of Dad, who now combed the tangles out of my frizzy hair each morning and supervised our cleaning of our bedroom. . . .

Anyone observing me during those days would have seen an anxious child full of twitches and tics, standing alone in the playground at school, wearing day after day the same hand-me-down tartan skirt that was almost stiff with constant wear, for it was all I had to wear: a freckle-faced, frizzy-haired little girl who was somehow 'dirty' because the lady doctor chose her with the other known 'dirty and poor' children for a special examination in that narrow room next to the teacher's room. I had tide marks of dirt behind my knees and on my inner arms, and when I saw them, I felt a wave of shock to know they were there when I had been sure I had washed thoroughly. . . .

One day I found a friend, Poppy. . . .

Each day we'd arrive at school and home with armsful of flowers, the names of all of which Poppy knew and taught me. We were studying grasses and weeds at school, and we were both drunk with the glory of the new names—shepherd's purse, fat hen (what a giggle!), ragwort, where the black and white caterpillars lived, though we preferred the woolly ones that turned into *Red Admirals*. . . .

Then one day Poppy asked me if I would like to borrow her special book that she kept in her washhouse among a clutter of treasures in an old beer barrel. 'It's *Grimm's Fairy Tales*,' she said. I had never heard of such a book, but I said I'd like to borrow it. And that night I took *Grimm's Fairy Tales* to bed and began to read, and suddenly the world of living and the world of reading became linked in a way I had not noticed before. 'Listen to this,' I said to Myrtle and Dots and Chicks. They listened while I read 'The Twelve Dancing Princesses', and as I read and they listened, I knew and they knew, gloriously, that *we* were the Dancing Princesses— not twelve but four; and as I read, I saw in my mind the place in the coat cupboard in the corner of the bedroom where we could vanish to the underground world and the orchard that was 'our' orchard along the gully where the boughs of the trees honked and cried out when they were broken, silver and gold trees; and in the end it was Myrtle who married the old soldier who, in my mind, looked like Vincent, the man of twenty-two, to us, shrivelled and old, who had fallen in love with Myrtle, who was barely twelve when she went for a holiday to the Wyndham Walkers.

And the shoes, danced each morning to shreds, we knew about these, with our own shoe soles flapping away from the uppers, and Dad sitting carefully marking and cutting the leather, and with the tacks in his mouth, bending over the bootlast while he half-soled and heeled our shoes, complaining, like the king in the story, 'Where have you been that your toes are scuffed and your soles are worn through?' Where indeed!

What a wonderful story it was—orchards hung with silver and golden apples, boughs that spoke and sang and cried out, underground seas and rivers and splash splash through the dark caverns, then suddenly the lit palace and the ballroom.

All the stories had a similar measure of delight and excitement—'The Blue Light', 'The Juniper Tree', the old favourites from the primer reading books—'Hansel and Gretel', 'Snow White', all the tales of Mother, Father, Sister, Brother, Aunt, Uncle, none of whom were more or less than we were, for all the list of extraordinary gifts, miracles, transformations, cruelties, and the many long years of wandering and searching, full of hope and expectation. *Grimm's Fairy Tales* was everybody's story seen in a special way with something new added to the ordinary rules of observation. Even the insects and animals in the stories had speech; I'd always felt as if they had; I'd known when the sheep looked at me that it was talking to me. And when the flies from the sticky flypapers were caught in my frizzy hair and buzzed and zoomed in my ear, there was no mistaking their frantic speech. . . .

I felt desolate at school. I longed for impossible presents, a doll's house, a sleeping doll, birthday parties, pretty dresses, button-up shoes, patent leather, instead of lace-up leather shoes with their heavy soles and heel and toe plates, hair that fell over my face so I could brush it away, saying, 'My hair's always getting in my eyes . . .', instead of frizzy red hair 'up like a bush' with everyone remarking on it. . . .

Suddenly, in the midst of my discontent and longing, I was promoted to Standard Four, to Gussy (or Reuben) Dimmock's class where I became, inexplicably, the teacher's 'pet'. It had always been other children who were the teacher's pets—pretty little girls with clean hair ribbons—and hair that accepted a hair ribbon as natural—and nice clothes and well-mannered little boys with clean shirts who confidently played their role unperturbed by the certain number of envious and unkind remarks it attracted. . . .

Under Gussy's care I blossomed then both as a scholar and as an athlete, for Gussy believed that because every child had a special talent he, as a teacher, had to give everyone a chance to discover the talent. Gussy was known as something of a fanatic in the classroom and on the sports field, and being in Gussy's class meant that when you were running in a race you were training to find out if you would qualify for the Olympic team. The slow, awkward children who couldn't read aloud in those excruciating reading lessons discovered they might be future Olympic champions or they might be 'good at' gardening or handwork, which, Gussy stressed, were of equal importance, and with such encouragement, some, their confidence returning, even learned to read aloud and recite their arithmetic tables. In spite of Gussy's teaching that all were equal and special, I did have the joy of being his pet, and as I lacked the customary qualifications for such a post, I never discovered the reason for his choice, unless it was that he thought it was the only way to deal with me and my tics and terrors. . . .

As that year was ending, I was told that I was Dux of the School, equal with another girl from another Standard Four. Some said it was because I was Gussy's 'pet', and it may have been so in that he encouraged me in my lessons. . . .

I knew that in being Dux I had pleased my father, and this pleased me, for day by day as I brought home tales of life in Standard Four, Dad had begun to say, 'Well, are you going to be Dux, then?'

When all the excitement was over, I remembered that the envelope presented to me with the Dux medal contained a year's subscription to the Oamaru Public Library, known as the Oamaru Athenaeum and Mechanics' Institute. 'I can go to the Athenaeum free,' I said, not quite sure what *Athenaeum* meant. And in the holidays, when one day I went to the loco foreman's office with a hot pie for Dad's lunch, I heard Dad say, 'My daughter goes to the Athenaeum.' . . .

My new library subscription was a family affair. I brought home for Bruddie a 'William' book, which we all read. I found *Grimm's Fairy Tales,* the same kind of red-covered book with the thin pages packed with black print that I'd borrowed from Poppy. I found a Western for Dad and a Dickens for Mum, who had no time to read it but who touched it and opened it and flipped the pages and read out striking descriptions, saying, 'How wonderful, kiddies, Charles

Dickens, born in poverty, growing up to be a great writer.' Then, after a prolonged season with the Brothers Grimm I became bold enough to read other books—The Bumper Books for Girls and Boys, Boarding School books, while I continued, on the side, as it were, with Myrtle's *True Confessions* and *True Romances*. . . .

Of that junior year I remember little apart from . . . the delight of learning French words and songs and the names of science apparatus (Bunsen burner, litmus paper); the cooking lessons, lemon sago, puff pastry, cream crackers; how to scrub a wooden table; the sewing, embroidery with the eternal *crewel* needles and the Clarks stranded cotton, all of which had to be bought and therefore asked for at home and the reply endured, 'You'd be better off working at the mill', and the final consent received under the weight of that Dux medal and the new parental dream, 'She's going to be a teacher like Cousin Peg, who emigrated to Canada.'

There might have been a time when the supply of crewel needles and stranded cotton, the pens, pencils, nibs, blotters, compasses, set squares, protractors, rulers, exercise books 'ruled faint with margin' (at which Dad made his joke, 'Faint all right, at the cost of all this'), journal covers, journal pins . . . all might have ceased had not that year, 1935, become the year of the first Labour Government with its promise of Social Security, free medical treatment, free hospital treatment for all. Our debts to the doctor and the hospitals were then so enormous that we had given up hope of paying them, and Dad, with his skill as a fisherman, was still making peace offerings of salmon, trout, whitebait, and crayfish. The election of the Labour Government was almost like a Second Coming, so great was the joy in our household, and so revered the new prime minister, 'Mickey' Savage, whose poster-size photograph was now pinned to our kitchen wall, where it stayed for the rest of the time we lived at Fifty-six Eden Street, and even when the Second World War was declared, Mickey Savage was moved only slightly to make way for the map of the world with the tiny pinned flags, 'Flag the Movements of the Allied Forces from Day to Day'. . . .

It was in my second year at Waitaki Junior High School that, making up my mind to be a 'poet' when I 'grew up', I began to write poems regularly in my small railway notebook. This renewed interest was prompted no doubt by our teacher's interest in poetry: . . . Miss Lindsay used to read for hours from Tennyson's *Idylls of the King,* as if it were her personal poem, and it was partly her absorption in it that compelled me to listen and wonder. I can still see her as she gazed toward the classroom door, as if toward a lake, saying, 'an arm rose up . . . clothed in white samite, mystic, wonderful . . .' as if she had experienced it, as if the jewelled sword Excalibur 'all the haft twinkled with diamond sparks, / Myriads of topaz-lights, the jacinth-work / Of subtlest jewellery . . . ' had been part of her life that she, like Sir Bedevere, was reluctant to give up. She mourned, too, the passing of Arthur, in a way quite unsuited to *our* Miss Lindsay with her ordinary brown clothes and patchy face. . . .

This other land revealed to me by Miss Lindsay, whom we laughed at because her face was like a cow's face, with a dewlap, and she wore funny shoes with pointy toes, could contain all the unspoken feeling that moved alive beneath the surface of each day and night and came above the surface only in the way earthworms came, when there was too much rain; and these feelings were secrets that this new land could receive without shock or horror or the need for revenge or punishment; it was yet a private place, even described by Miss Lindsay when she read the lines:

> A place
> where no one comes
> or hath come since the
> making of the world. . . .

I wrote poems about everything around me. I wrote a poem about the sand, the sky, the leaves, a rainbow (taking care to list the exact colours—'orange, yellow, red, and heliotrope, a lovely green and blue'). I wrote about Marie Antoinette and the Palace of Fontainebleau. . . .

The year ended. I received two small leather-bound books for a prize and a bursary for five pounds to help me 'go on' to senior high school, where there were three courses—professional or academic, commercial, or domestic, with no mixture of subjects as in the junior high school. My parents, now taking it for granted that I would become a teacher, decided to allow me to continue at school, although Dad warned me that if times were hard, I might have to leave school or change to 'commercial' and work in an office. . . .

My father concentrated his attention more and more on the 'abilities' of his daughters. Each day, when I came home from school, he'd say slightly in jest, mostly in earnest, 'Were you top of the class today? Who did you beat today?' He learned the names of our 'rivals' at school and would ask, 'Well, did you beat M. or S. or T. today?' . . .

At the end of the year I was given a prize, *Boys and Girls Who Became Famous,* which I and my sisters and brother read eagerly during the holidays. We came to know and love the story of the Brontës—the bleak setting of the Yorkshire Moors, the parsonage, the churchyard. We felt close to the self-contained family with the 'wild' brother, the far-off parents going about their daily tasks, the Brontës with their moors, us with our hill and gully and pine plantations. They knew death in their family, as we had, and their lives were so much more tragic than our life which, in spite of everything, was predominantly joyful, that we could give them, thankfully, the sad feelings which sometimes overcame us. . . .

I remained part of the small group of 'scholars', who compared their answers to problems and often worked ahead of the others on extra mathematics. The brightest of our group was usually W. (her father, the manager of the woollen mills), who lived beside the school and had a large doll's house on her front lawn. W. was advanced in reading, too, having read all the children's classics— *Alice in Wonderland,* Kipling's *Jungle Books, Toad of Toad Hall,* and she knew the answers to questions that we thought obscure and unanswerable, such as quotes from poems we had not read or heard of. She was the girl to whom my father referred when he said to me, 'Well, did you beat W. today?'

I longed to be close to my father. Sometimes he still asked me, 'How did the sheep look at you?' and dutifully, after all those years, I'd hide my face and put on my 'sheep look' as a way of sharing painlessly with my father. I shared the crosswords, too, and the quiz sessions and the detective stories that he had begun to bring home—small square books, in appearance like the 'love' and the 'boarding school' and the 'Westerns' that we girls read now and again. These were the *Sexton Blake Library.* I despised the way they were written; yet I kept my criticism to myself, dutifully reading each new volume.

'I read the latest Sexton Blake,' I'd say to Dad. 'It's pretty good.'

Dad would answer (the gratitude in his eyes made me pity him), 'Well, it was so-so. I'll bring home some more in the weekend.' I felt, now, that I could see through my father's feelings, and the tragedy I thought I perceived filled me with sadness. When Mum happened to say, 'Both Jean and her father like reading those detective books', I felt an inordinate pride and gratitude. . . .

That year, also, I discovered the Ancient Mariner. One morning Miss Gibson came into the classroom and without any preliminary discussion sat at her table, opened a book, said in her 'announcing' voice, ' "The Rhyme of the Ancient Mariner" by Samuel Taylor Coleridge' and began to read. She read the entire poem and said, 'Write an essay on the Ancient Mariner for next week', then left the room. The lesson was over.

I had not known of the Ancient Mariner, and while Miss Gibson was reading, I listened, only half understanding, to the story of the grim journey; and all else vanishing, I, too, was alone on the sea, living the living death, feeling the nearness of a seascape that was part of Oamaru. The sighting of the albatross was at the same time a farewell to the nightingales, for although I had never seen an albatross, Mother had talked of them and in our days at Fortrose and Waipapa she had sometimes pointed to distant seabirds and murmured, 'They may be albatrosses, kiddies.'

I did not comprehend the curse and the blessing of the mariner, only the journey and the suffering, and when in the last stanza Miss Gibson adopted her familiar preaching tone to read, 'He prayeth best who loveth best', I resented her intrusion and the intrusion of the land and the landscape and the reduction of the mariner, seen through land-focusing eyes, from a man of mysterious grandeur even in guilt to a 'grey-beard loon'.

All that day I lived within the dream of the Ancient Mariner, a massive, inescapable dream that Miss Gibson had thrust upon us without explanation or apology, a 'pure' dream of that time on the sea in the embrace of weather that existed of itself without reference to people or creatures and their everyday lives of church, wedding guests, long-drawn-out tales. And of school, studying, playing basketball, swimming, writing poetry. And of milking cows. . . .

My life centred on my schoolwork and my walks on the hill and reading and trying to write poetry. I was beginning to find that when I answered a question in school, the reaction of the class and the teacher was one of surprise, often of amusement. 'Jean's so original', the teacher said one day, causing me once again to feel trapped by the opinion of others. I did not think of myself as original: I merely said what I thought. Yet an acknowledgement of an apparent 'difference' in my thinking seemed to fit in with the 'difference', as I thought it to be, of my life at home with the dramatic terrifying continuing episodes of my brother's illness, the misunderstanding of it, the confusion of our parents trying to 'face' it, our brother's loneliness, my father's subdued withdrawal of 'control' over his daughters, our fervent promises not to 'stay out late, go with boys, drink, smoke', with the supposition that such an innocuous way of life would cure all. . . .

Therefore in an adolescent homelessness of self, in a time where I did not quite know my direction, I entered eagerly a nest of difference which others found for me but which I lined with my own furnishings; for, after all, during the past two years I had tried many aspects of 'being'—a giggling schoolgirl who made everyone laugh with comic recitations, mimicry, puzzles, mathematical tricks, such as 'Think of a number, double it', attempts at ventriloquism; and now I was at home, with some prestige and fairly comfortable.

And while I struggled, enjoying my ambitions and my supposed 'difference', out in the 'world', far from New Zealand, the Nazi Party was in power in Germany with speeches by Adolf Hitler being broadcast over the wireless. We mimicked his raving delivery, the Nazi salute, and the goose-stepping armies. . . .

Another year at school with our class, the Lower Fifth, even smaller than our Fourth Form. . . .

Our class teacher, Miss Farnie, was small, ugly in the accepted sense, with her nose and chin too big, her face a blotchy red, her hair dark and scraggy. Her voice was soft yet clear, her eyes a calm grey, and her manner of teaching generally thought of as inspired with her passion both for English literature and for mathematics, which, she explained to us, converting me entirely to the cause of mathematics, was a form of *poetry*. I believed her and therefore flourished in maths.

It was she, too, who 'converted' me to Shakespeare, who I'd previously thought was a bore. . . .

It is strange to think of my life being lived as I then lived my 'real' life, so much within and influenced by English and French literature, with my daily adventures a discovery of a paragraph or a poem and my own attempts to write. It was not an escape in the sense of a removal from the unhappiness I felt over the sickness at home or from my own feeling of nowhereness in not having ordinary clothes to wear even to prove that I was a human being and there was a peopled world beyond home and school; there was no removal of myself and my life to another world; there was simply the other world's arrival into my world, the literature streaming through it like an array of beautiful ribbons through the branches of a green, growing tree, touching the leaves with unexpected light that was unlike the expected deserved habitual light of the sun and the seasons. It was the arrival, as of neighbours or relatives or anyone who belonged there and was at home, of the poets and the prose writers and their work at Fifty-six Eden Street, Oamaru, 'the kingdom by the sea', bringing their hosts of words and characters and their special vision. . . .

I have often wondered in which world I might have lived my 'real' life had not the world of literature been given to me by my mother and by the school syllabus, and even by the death of Myrtle. It was my insistence on bringing this world home, rather than vanishing within it, that increased my desire to write, for how else could I anchor that world within this everyday world where I hadn't the slightest doubt that it belonged? Oamaru, the kingdom by the sea. Did I not already know people in Oamaru who had been 'trodden down' by the 'hungry generations'? And did we not have the natural ingredients for literature—a moon, stars ('Pale star, would I were steadfast as thou art'), sea, people, animals, sheep and shepherds ('Go, for they call you, shepherd, from the hill'). We had skylarks dipping and rising above the hill ('Hail to thee, blithe spirit!') and pigeons and goldfinches and wax-eyes clamouring to have their say above the nightingales. . . .

In early September of that year, in the midst of a concentration of characters from fiction and poetry . . . that storm and that lightning which I had defied by standing near the light of the dining-room window, with the sky beyond, struck not only our house but also all the houses in Eden Street, in Oamaru, New Zealand, the world, in the outbreak of the Second World War. . . .

I think of the remaining years at school as part of the nightmare of the war, the daily casualty lists, the hymns and Bible readings in school assembly:

> Eternal Father strong to save
> whose arm hath bound the restless wave . . .
> O hear us when we cry to thee
> for those in peril on the sea . . .

and

> Fight the good fight with all thy might . . .
> Christ is thy strength and Christ thy right.

and

> Peace perfect peace in this dark world of sin
> the blood of Jesus whispers peace within.

I recall the seriousness and fervour of my singing, the (then innocently) sexual languor of the many hymns steeped in blood, such hymns being favourites with the girls, most of whom in the past year or two had acquired a new relationship to blood, made strange by the repeated reference to the spilling of blood in wartime, and the everlasting preoccupation with blood in a country that based its economy on the killing and eating of farm animals. . . .

With the concentration on the coming exams and their very name—*University Entrance*—there was talk among the girls about their future university courses and of life at university, which some even dared (to my alarm at their familiar tone) to call *varsity*. . . .

Our parents had receded from our lives. We discussed school affairs with them, asked them for money for this and that, and either were given it or not. We were impatient with their ignorance of school subjects. Aware now that Mother had turned increasingly to poetry for shelter, as I was doing, I, with an unfeelingness based on misery of feeling, challenged the worth of some of her beloved poets, aware that my criticism left her flushed and unhappy while I felt a savage joy at her distress. I had begun to hate her habit of waiting hand and foot, martyrlike, upon her family. When I was eager to do things for myself, Mother was always there, anxious to serve. I now felt the guilt of it, and I hated her for being the instrument of that guilt. . . .

[A]t school the University Entrance exam came and went, and I passed, remembering the exam now chiefly for the two guineas which it cost to enter and which I struggled to get, with my father insisting that I should leave school. A few years later my first published story in the *Listener*, 'University Entrance', earned me that sum, confirming for me once again the closeness, the harmony, and not the separation of literature (well, a simple story!) and life. . . .

The year of the Upper Sixth was a cruel year, the cruellest I had known. My school tunic was now so tightly fitting that it pressed on all parts of my body; it was torn and patched and patched again, but obviously it was no use having a new one, for I was leaving school at the end of the year. Also, I knew that my homemade sanitary towels showed their bulk, and the blood leaked through, and when I stood up in class, I'd glance furtively at the desk seat to see whether it was bloody, and when I stood in morning assembly, I placed my hymn book in one hand and shielded either my back or front, whichever was bulkier, with my other hand. Because I was now a house captain, I stood in front of Gibson House, unable to hide but thankful that my years of standing almost always alone in assembly would soon be over. I could never understand why no one 'formed twos' with me in assembly or physical education, when the command was given, 'Form Twos'. My shame was extreme; I concluded that I stank. . . .

The next event was the interview conducted by Mr Partridge, the principal of Dunedin Training College, where I tried to appear bright and teacherly, making sure that he knew I was a house captain, captain of the B basketball team, conductor of the house choir, leader of the sixth-form jazz band, a good student . . . I think he was impressed, probably seeing the bouncy, sporting, uncomplicated schoolgirl which I was not (I the shy, poetic, timid, obedient). . . .

[A] few weeks later word came that I had been accepted for teachers' training college. . . .

There were many . . . end-of-term functions that I had no part in—dances, socials, afternoon teas, bike rides. I knew no boys except those next door (too old, and one dead in the war), over the road (too young or too old); my social recreation was the 'pictures' now and again and walks on the hill and along the gully. Although we girls often felt our life had a tragedy and difference compared with the apparent life of others of our age, toward the end of my years at school I emerged from a shocked concentration on the turmoil of being in Oamaru, the state which received so much blame for so much that had happened to us, to a realisation that many other girls had not even reached high school because their parents had not been able to afford it or made the sacrifices to afford it as our parents undoubtedly did. I thought of the family of seven children up Eden Street who went barefoot, not always by choice, and of how I'd seen them running to school on a frosty morning, their feet mottled blue with cold; and of the family in Chelmer Street who lived only on soup made from pork bones from the bacon factory. And nearer home, as I seemed to awaken from a long, troubled family sleep, I was suddenly aware of other girls with 'funny' uniforms that were flared without the regulation pleats. I was astonished to discover that apparently K., who was in the sixth form first year and had been accepted for training college, showed no embarrassment over her peculiar dress and that of her sister in a lower form. We became friends. . . .

When I stopped wearing my school tunic after six years of almost daily wear, I felt naked, like a skinned rabbit; and the letter written by the warden of the teachers' college, listing the essential clothing of a training college student, was the cause of our panic. . . .

And so the future, which had been talked of and dreamed of for so long, toward which our teachers had directed their urging, threats, even their own long-lost ambitions, had begun as the present once again, the Is-Land from which there is no escape, and I was equipped to face it as a shy young woman most at home and experienced with 'creatures' such as cows, sheep, dogs, cats, insects, anything living that was not human; with the natural world of sea, earth, sky, and the plants, trees, and flowers; and with written and printed language with its themes and thoughts and its alphabet with the bowers of A's and O's and U's and D's large enough to hide in. . . .

I took little part in college social life. I yearned for the time when I could buy a crumpled gaberdine raincoat (the student uniform). In complete ignorance of the ways of love and sex, I watched with envious wonder the lives of those women who, finding their 'man', fulfilled not only their own expectations but those of their family and friends and thus added a bloom of certainty to their being. My only romance was with poetry and literature. . . .

Many of my student days and experiences are now sealed from me by that substance released with the life of each moment, of each moment's capture of our life. I remember and can relive my feelings but there is now a thirst for reason in what had seemed to be so inevitable. I did not realise the extent of my loneliness. I clung to works of literature as a child clings to its mother. I remember how *Measure for Measure,* the deeply reasoned play crammed with violations of innocence, with sexual struggle and comment, with long discussions on life, death, and immortality, won my heart and persisted in my memory, *accompanied* me in my daily life. . . .

My visits home became fewer. I'd buy a privilege ticket to travel on the Friday night train, arriving at Oamaru between one and two in the morning, returning to Dunedin by the Sunday slow train. On the way home I'd imagine that all would be peaceful, different, at Fifty-six Eden Street, but as soon as I arrived I wished I had not come. Isabel and June were busy with their own lives, the antagonism between my father and my brother had increased, while Mother, self-effacing, maintained her role of provider of food, peacemaker, poet, with a new dream to add to 'publication' and the Second Coming of Christ—a dream that set her among the characters in fairy tales—that each of her daughters, now grown, should have a white fox fur on her twenty-first birthday. Her dream for Bruddie, for health or fame in spite of ill-health, was unchanged.

My dissatisfaction with my home and family was intense. The ignorance of my parents infuriated me. They knew nothing of Sigmund Freud, of *The Golden Bough*, T. S. Eliot. (I forgot, conveniently, that at the beginning of the year my knowledge of Freud, *The Golden Bough*, T. S. Eliot, was limited. . . .)

I hated being home, for I felt that I had left home forever, and except for occasional visits, I would never return. I could see the family so clearly enveloped in doom that it frightened me. I felt that my mother lived in a world which in no way corresponded with the 'real' world, and it seemed that her every word was a concealment, a lie, a desperate refusal to acknowledge 'reality'. I was not even aware that I, in my turn, had joined the world of pretense which I so condemned in others.

I could see my father as a helpless character struggling against the buffeting winds of a cruel world. . . .

I knew the family was desperate to find somewhere to live. Dad, who handled all the money, took shares in a newly formed building society with the hope of getting a loan from the monthly ballot, while Mother, who never had personal money, contributed her faith, 'God knows what you have need of even before you ask', and, miraculously, the following ballot produced a loan of three hundred pounds, just enough to buy a ramshackle rat-ridden old cottage set in three and a half acres of land on the outskirts of Oamaru. . . .

Seeing the earth floor and the 'nowhereness' of the interior of the house, I felt depressed and lonely and I knew the Willowglen house would never be my home; it was too small, everyone was too close to everyone else; in the front bedroom you could hear the wireless from the kitchen as if you were in the kitchen. You could hear the arguments, too, the raised voices, and the soft murmur of pleading that you knew to be, 'Don't raise your voices to each other', from Mother. . . .

Word came in January that I was to teach standard two at Arthur Street School, Dunedin. I had applied for a class of that age living in what we had learned was 'the latent period', when children were thought to be malleable—oh how thoroughly we thought we knew that mythical 'child'!

And in response to my advertisement in the *Otago Daily Times,* 'Quiet student seeks board near Arthur Street School', I heard from a Mrs T. in Drivers Road, Maori Hill, offering me 'full board'. . . .

I arrived with my growing self in Dunedin. This was to be the year of my twenty-first birthday at the end of August. 'Twenty-firsts', as they were known, were part of the continuing ritual of growing up, when one became 'of age', a legal citizen able to vote, to make a will, or, as the song said,

> I'm twenty-one today.
> I've got the key of the door,
> I've never been twenty-one before.
> I'm twenty-one today.

At the end of the year, also, I hoped I would gain my certificate as a teacher, after my probationary year at Arthur Street School. I hoped also to add another unit to my arts degree course, and as I felt that English III would prove to be too engulfing of my interest, I decided upon Philosophy I, a first year of psychology.

My secret desire to be a poet, fed by the publication in the College Magazine of my two poems ('Now they'll find out that I'm really a poet!'), occupied much of my planning. . . .

I boarded with Mrs T., a widow with a married daughter, Kathleen, living in the new government housing estate at Waikari, where Mrs T. spent most of her days, taking the bus after breakfast. . . .

For the sake of appearances, I sometimes had meals with Mrs T. instead of taking them to my room 'as I have study to catch up with and lessons to mark and prepare . . . ' and then I would sit opposite her and listen, fascinated, while she described the day 'over at Kathleen's'—how they'd done the washing together and tidied the house, how Kathleen and Bob were hoping some day to get carpet 'edge to edge' in every room. 'There are quite a few carpeted now edge to edge.' I, the 'quiet shy teacher, no trouble, no trouble at all', spent most of my free time in my room, marking, preparing lessons, and cutting out paper stars in different colours to reward the children's efforts; and studying my textbook of psychology; and writing and reading poems. . . .

I delighted in the children at school and in teaching. I was full of ideas for encouraging individual development. I revelled in the children's art and in their poetry, for they wrote poetry and stories almost every day, and these, with the paintings, I pinned around the walls for everyone to enjoy. I took pains, too, in teaching other subjects. My failure was as a member of the staff, for my timidity among people, especially among those who might be asked to judge and comment on my performance as a teacher, led to my spending my free time alone. Too timid to go to morning and afternoon tea with a room full of other teachers, I made excuses about 'having work to do in the classroom', aware that I was going against all the instructions about the need to 'mix in adult company, take part in social events and discussions with other teachers and parents', and that 'morning tea in the teachers' room' was an almost sacred ritual. My fear of being 'inspected' by the headmaster or inspector inspired me to devise a means of postponing the day of reckoning, by inventing a serial story which I could continue whenever I heard the steps of authority approaching along the corridor, so that a visit by the headmaster to a class sitting rapt with attention (the content of the story ensured a rapt audience), might 'prove' my ability as a teacher with the result that I could 'pass' my 'C' Certificate at the end of the year.

My escape from teaching was the psychology class and the psychology laboratory, where we performed a range of interesting experiments and tests supervised by two fresh young lecturers. . . .

In spite of the worries about teaching and my future, I found the year mostly pleasurable. At school and University I gave little thought to my home and family, and when I spent one of my few weekends at home, I tried to detach myself from the place and the people. My family appeared like tired ghosts trying to come to life for the occasion. . . . The attentive habits of my parents saddened, pleased and infuriated me, leaving me with a feeling of helplessness—what could I do for them? I could see the pattern of their past lives slowly emerging, like a script written with invisible ink and now being made visible to me, warmed by the fire kindled simply by my growing up. I could see, too, an illumination produced by that same fire, the shadows emerging as recognised shapes of a language full of meaning for me: the language of the love and loss and joy and torture of having a place fast within a family when all my awakening longing was directed towards being uprooted, quickly, without leaving behind a cluster of nerve endings, broken threads in danger of being renewed.

On 28 August I 'came of age' without a party but with some special presents given to me by my family—'things' showing that I was a part of the world, after all: I had a new wristlet watch, and a new pair of plaid pom-pommed slippers with fleecy lining.

That month, as a kind of surface skimming of all the feeling set to boil away until old age, I wrote and published my first story, 'University Entrance', for which the *Listener* paid two guineas.

And now the year was passing quickly with the school inspector's crucial final visit soon to be faced. Inevitably, one bright morning of daffodils and flowering currant and a shine on the leaves of the bush along Queen's Drive, where I walked to school each morning, of a hint of warm gold in the sharp lemon-coloured sunlight, I arrived at school to find that it was the Day of Inspection, and at midmorning the inspector and the headmaster came to my classroom. I greeted them amiably in my practised teacherly fashion, standing at the side of the room near the display of paintings while the inspector talked to the class before he settled down to watch my performance as a teacher. I waited. Then I said to the inspector, 'Will you excuse me a moment please?'

'Certainly, Miss Frame.'

I walked out of the room and out of the school, knowing I would never return. . . .

Writing an autobiography, usually thought of as a looking back, can just as well be a looking *across* or *through,* with the passing of time giving an X-ray quality to the eye. Also, time past is not time gone, it is time accumulated, with the host resembling the character in the fairy tale who was joined along the route by more and more characters, none of whom could be separated from one another or from the host, with some stuck so fast that their presence caused physical pain. Add to the characters all the events, thoughts, feelings, and there is a mass of time, now a sticky mess, now a jewel bigger than the planets and the stars.

If I look through 1945 I see the skeleton of the year and shadowing it with both the shadow of death and of life, the atom bomb, the homely crocuses surviving in the late spring snow, birthdays and deathdays, and two or three other events bring those dreamed-of planets and stars within the personal world of myself and many others in New Zealand. . . .

Time confers privileges of arrangement and rearrangement undreamed of until it becomes Time Past. I have been writing of the memory of publication of stories and poems. In actual memory I am sitting talking to two Borstal girls, on the way to Seacliff hospital, where I shall be a committed patient.

The six weeks I spent at Seacliff hospital in a world I'd never known among people whose existences I never thought possible, became for me a concentrated course in the horrors of insanity and the dwelling-place of those judged insane, separating me for ever from the former acceptable realities and assurances of everyday life. From my first moment there I knew that I could not turn back to my usual life or forget what I saw at Seacliff. I felt as if my life were overturned by this sudden division of people into 'ordinary' people in the street, and these 'secret' people whom few had seen or talked to but whom many spoke of with derision, laughter, fear. . . .

When I left Seacliff in December 1945, for a six-month probationary period, to return to a Willowglen summer, the shiningest time at Willowglen, I felt that I carried within me a momentous change brought about by my experience of being in a mental hospital. I looked at my family and I knew that they did not know what I had seen. . . .

My visit to the Seacliff doctor at the Oamaru hospital brought its own bewilderment, for the medical certificate stated: Nature of Illness: *Schizophrenia.*

At home I announced, half with pride, half with fear, 'I've got *Schizophrenia.*'

I searched through my psychology book, the chapter on Abnormal Psychology, where I found no reference to *Schizophrenia,* only to a mental illness apparently afflicting only young people like myself—*dementia praecox,* described as a gradual deterioration of mind, with no cure. In the notes at the end of the chapter there was an explanation that *dementia praecox* was now known as *schizophrenia. Shizzophreenier.* A gradual deterioration of mind. Of mind and behaviour. I suffered from *shizzophreenier.* It seemed to spell my doom, as if I had emerged from a chrysalis, the natural human state, into another kind of creature, and even if there were parts of me that were familiar to human beings, my gradual deterioration would lead me further and further away, and in the end not even my family would know me. . . .

My life away from the boardinghouse consisted of evening lectures on logic and ethics, and weekly 'talks' with John Forrest in a small room on the top storey of the University building known as the Professors' House. I also spent time in the Dunedin Public Library, where I read case histories of patients suffering from schizophrenia, with my alarm and sense of doom increasing as I tried to imagine what would happen to me. That the idea of my suffering from schizophrenia seemed to me so unreal, only increased my confusion when I learned that one of the symptoms was 'things seeming unreal'. There was no escape. . . .

I was on the usual adolescent path of worry and wondering how to 'cope' with everyday living; yet, strangely, in order to lessen my anxiety, I found myself forced to choose a more distinctly signposted path, where my journey drew attention and so, I found, drew more practical help. I don't think it occurred to me that people might be willing to help me if I maintained my ordinary timid smiling self. My life so far had trained me to perform, to gain approval by answering questions in examinations, solving problems, exhibiting flashes of 'cleverness' and 'difference'. I was usually ashamed of my clothing. I was baffled by my fuzzy hair and the attention it drew, and the urgency with which people advised that I have it 'straightened', as if it was an ordinary grey-feathered bird that spent its life flashing one or two crimson feathers at the world, adapting the feathers to suit the time in life. In my childhood I had displayed number riddles, memorising long passages of verse and prose, mathematical answers; now, to *suit* the occasion, I wore my schizophrenic fancy dress. . . .

After a few weeks in Christchurch I arranged an appointment with Mrs R., John Forrest's friend, with the intention of asking her to help me with arrangements for having my teeth extracted and come with me to the dental department of the public hospital, but when I presented myself at her house in an exclusive suburb and she, a tall angular woman dressed in fawn and brown, opened the door, I, sensing the impossibility of being able to explain my plight, I, standing there (mouth closed), a blooming young woman of twenty-two with no obvious disabilities, again turned on my 'schizophrenia' at full flow: it had become my only way of arousing interest in those whose help I believed that I needed. Nevertheless, it was several weeks before I could say that my urgent problem was my decaying teeth. Mrs R. kindly arranged for me to have my top teeth extracted at the hospital; she would come with me, she said, and might it not be a good idea for me to admit myself as a voluntary boarder to Sunnyside Mental Hospital, where there was a new electric treatment, which, in her opinion, would help me. I therefore signed the necessary papers.

I woke toothless and was admitted to Sunnyside Hospital and I was given the new electric treatment, and suddenly my life was thrown out of focus. I could not remember. I was terrified. I behaved as others around me behaved. I who had learned the language, spoke and acted that language. I felt utterly alone. There was no one to talk to. As in other mental hospitals, you were locked up, you did as you were told or else, and that was that.

And when I had been in hospital several months beyond the voluntary period and was declared a committed patient, that was the beginning of the years in hospital which I have already described. . . .

The years that followed, until 1954, when I was finally discharged from hospital, were full of fear and unhappiness, mostly caused by my confinement and treatment in hospital. Early in my stay there were two or three periods of several weeks when I was allowed to leave hospital and each time I needed to return as there was nowhere else for me to live; I was fearful always, like a condemned person returning to the executioner. . . .

[M]y writing saved me. I had seen in the ward office the list of those 'down for a leucotomy', with my name on the list, and other names being crossed off as the operation was performed. My 'turn' must have been very close when one evening the superintendent of the hospital, Dr Blake Palmer, made an unusual visit to the ward. He spoke to me—to the amazement of everyone.

As it was my first chance to discuss with anyone, apart from those who had persuaded me, the prospect of my operation, I said urgently, 'Dr Blake Palmer, what do you think?'

He pointed to the newspaper in his hand.

'About the prize?'

I was bewildered. What prize? 'No,' I said, 'about the leucotomy.'

He looked stern, 'I've decided that you should stay as you are. I don't want you changed.' He unfolded his newspaper. 'Have you seen the Stop Press in tonight's *Star*?'

A ridiculous question to ask in a back ward where there was no reading matter; surely he knew?

'You've won the Hubert Church Award for the best prose. Your book, *The Lagoon*.'

I knew nothing about the Hubert Church Award. Winning it was obviously something to be pleased about.

I smiled. 'Have I?'

'Yes. And we're moving you out of this ward. And no leucotomy.'

The winning of the prize and the attention of a new doctor from Scotland who accepted me as I appeared to him and not as he learned about me from my 'history' or reports of me, and the move by Dr Blake Palmer to have me spend less time in the hospital ward by using me as a 'tea lady' in the front office and allowing me to have occupational therapy, where I learned to make baskets, to fill toothpaste tubes with toothpaste, and, from a book written in French, to weave French lace, and to weave on large and small looms, all enabled me to be prepared for discharge from hospital. Instead of being treated by leucotomy, I was treated as a person of some worth, a human being. . . .

I was discharged from hospital 'on probation'. After having received over two hundred applications of unmodified E.C.T., each the equivalent, in degree of fear, to an execution, and in the process having my memory shredded and in some aspects weakened permanently or destroyed, and after having been subjected to proposals to have myself changed by physical operation, into a more acceptable, amenable, normal person, I arrived home at Willowglen, outwardly smiling and calm, but inwardly with all confidence gone, with the conviction at last that I was officially a non-person. . . .

I joined the new town library and discovered William Faulkner and Franz Kafka, and I rediscovered the few books left on my own bookshelf. I began to write stories and poems and to think of a future without being overcome by fear that I would be seized and 'treated' without being able to escape. Even so, the nightmares of my time in hospital persist in sleep and often I wake in dread, having dreamed that the nurses are coming to 'take me for treatment'. . . .

I felt the train arriving at Auckland station, and suddenly there was 'up north' again, the blue paradisal air and light.

And there were June, Wilson, and their three children to meet me and drive me to their newly built house in Northcote. . . .

I spent the next week getting to know my sister and her husband and the three children. June told me that Frank Sargeson, the writer, had visited her one day, as he had heard that I was her sister. He had said that he would like to meet me if I ever came to Auckland.

'Would you like to see him?' they asked.

'Oh no. I don't know him.'

'We can take you. He lives in an old bach at Takapuna.'

Why should I visit Frank Sargeson? I knew *Speaking for Ourselves,* and I had read some of his stories in New Zealand and English *New Writing.* I hesitated about meeting him.

Our visit was short. What could I say? I was self-conscious, the 'funny' sister being taken for a drive. Mr Sargeson, a bearded old man in a shabby grey shirt and grey pants tied with string, smiled kindly and asked how I was, and I said nothing. He had an army hut vacant in his garden, he said. I was welcome to live and work there. I neither accepted nor refused, I was so overcome by my 'mental' status, and by seeing in person the famous writer whose anthology of New Zealand writing, *Speaking for Ourselves,* was a treasured book; the famous writer for whose fiftieth birthday I had signed a letter of good wishes, not knowing him and knowing nothing of the other signatories of the letter. Frank Sargeson. Mr Sargeson.

He suggested that I come to see him one day, by myself.

'How about this Friday?'

'Yes,' I said shyly. . . .

And so on Friday I set out from Northcote towards Mr Sargeson's place in Takapuna, walking along the largely unformed road with paddocks of scrub and toetoe on either side, past swamps of mangroves—mangroves!—and stands of native bush. It was late spring of 1954, and I'd had my thirtieth birthday, an occasion for a photograph and, in poetic tradition, for a poem. . . .

Mr Sargeson then began to talk of *The Lagoon and Other Stories* while I listened uneasily. I had not approved his choice of 'The Day of the Sheep' for the Oxford anthology.

'Do you have a copy of the Oxford anthology?' he asked. I had not. He promptly found his copy and gave it to me, signing it.

He then asked about future work.

'I don't know,' I said guardedly.

'Have you thought about coming to live and work in the hut? You'd be free to write. It's no good your living in suburbia among the nappies and bourgeois life.'

I hadn't heard anyone say the word 'bourgeois' since history lessons on the French Revolution, and I wasn't sure if I knew its modern meaning.

'I have to find a job, though,' I said.

'Why? You're a writer.'

I smiled with wonder. 'Am I? They've refused to give me sickness benefit.'

Mr Sargeson looked angry. 'After all those years in hospital? Look, I've a good friend, a doctor who's understanding and who will probably arrange a benefit for you while you work at your writing.'

'Really?'

I felt overwhelmed and shy, and protected. I accepted his offer of living and working in the hut, if he would allow me to pay him each week for my board. Although he objected at first, he finally agreed to take one pound a week. His own income was low. The first flush of publication and attention given to his work was over and he had reached the stage when he most needed money, for his books were out of print. . . .

I arrived at Mr Sargeson's place with my 'things', including my rust-coloured skirt, my dull green twinset, and the dull green overcoat I had finally bought from Mademoiselle Modes in Dunedin. I felt bound by the rules dictated by the colour wheel and the art teaching at training college and by the colour of my hair to choose dull greens and browns and yellows. Primary colours, bold bright colours, were 'bad', I had been taught, while the ones I chose were supposedly 'good'. There had long been an overflow of moral judgement upon articles of clothing, colours, shapes, with the 'good' linked to 'taste' and fastened with notions of superiority.

I was sure, then, that my clothes were in 'good taste'. In my state of extreme compliance as a yes-woman, a Simon Says woman, go there, come here, of course, I had even bought myself—at last—a corset or girdle, because the women at the Grand Hotel, and my sister in Auckland, had told me that my behind showed through my skirt, and in those days your behind was not at liberty to show. My only freedom was within, in my thoughts and language, most of which I kept carefully concealed, except in my writing. For conversation I reserved a harmless chatter which—surely—no one would label as 'peculiar' or 'mad'.

Once I arrived at Mr Sargeson's, however, with the prospect of living as a writer, with a place to work, to be alone, with no worry over money, and sharing meals and company with someone who actually *believed* I was a writer, the worry over colours, 'good' colours and 'bad' colours, the continued advice about my frizzy hair and the complaint that my behind showed through my skirt all became insignificant and far away. I had an army hut containing a bed, a built-in desk with a kerosene lamp, a rush mat on the floor, a small wardrobe with an old curtain strung in front, and a small window by the head of the bed. Mr Sargeson (I was not yet bold enough to call him Frank) had already arranged for a medical certificate and a benefit of three pounds a week, which was also the amount of his income. I thus had everything I desired and needed, as well as the regret of wondering why I had taken so many years to find it. . . .

The time was ripe. I bought an exercise book, typing paper (green, Frank said, was easiest on the eyes), typing ribbon, and began to write my novel. . . .

Each day after breakfast I went to the hut to work on my novel. I had not, as Frank suggested, written a list of characters, but I had set out in my exercise book a few ideas and themes, and the names of the parts of the book which I saw as a whole before I began typing. In my exercise book I ruled lines to make a timetable with day, date, number of pages I hoped to write, number of pages written, and a space headed *Excuses*. Each day I marked the number of pages written in red pencil. . . .

I finished *Talk of Treasure* two weeks before my thirty-first birthday, and taking my typescript, newly bound with tape in the way Frank had shown me . . . I travelled home for two weeks to Oamaru and Willowglen. . . .

Two weeks later I heard that Pegasus Press had accepted my book. They enclosed a contract to be signed. I was bewildered, pleased, and scared, while Frank, having learned the routine of writing and publishing, and knowing the *etiquette,* said, 'We must celebrate.' Spending more than he could afford, he bought a bottle of Vat 69 whisky, which we drank that evening. . . .

[M]y next 'move' . . . according to Frank, was for me to 'travel overseas' to 'broaden my experience', a convenient way, both he and I realised, of saying that I was 'better out of New Zealand before someone decided I should be in a mental hospital'. We both knew that in a conformist society there are a surprising number of 'deciders' upon the lives and fate of others. . . .

[W]e planned a letter to the Literary Fund applying for a grant for me to 'travel overseas and broaden my experience'. . . .

[T]he telegram came from Frank.

'Privately informed. Three hundred pounds granted. Congratulations.'

So my journey away from New Zealand was to be a reality. I had so little notion of the value of money that I could not judge whether three hundred pounds, which to me seemed like a fortune, was much or little, or how it would provide me with fare and expenses, and for how long. . . .

The cheque arrived. I gazed unbelievingly at it. I showed it to Frank.

'What shall I do with it?' I asked. I had never had a bank account, for, like so many other facilities, bank accounts were thought to be for 'other people'. . . .

That afternoon, instead of taking his usual rest, Frank went with me and the cheque to the Bank of New South Wales, where he introduced me to the manager. I was a highly recommended client, he said, praising me as a writer.

My next move was to pay seventy-eight pounds for a berth in a six-berth cabin in the *Ruahine* sailing from Wellington to Southampton at the end of July. I then applied for a passport and arranged for a primary vaccination for smallpox. I was on my way overseas. . . .

Frank's friends, returned from Spain, also gave advice.

'If you want to make your money last,' they said, 'Ibiza is the place.'

'Ibiza?'

'It's spelt with a "z" but you say it the Spanish way, "th".'

'Oh.'

'You can live on the island of Ibiza for three or four pounds a month.'

Frank reminded me that Greville now lived at Tossa, with a flat in Barcelona, and he would write to her, and they'd meet me at Barcelona and see me on to that boat to Ibiza.

'I suppose Ibiza would be the place to stay, then, as I shan't have much money.'

'See, here it is on the map, just below Majorca and Minorca. Majorca where *Robert Graves* lives.'

'Robert Graves!'

We'd been reading his prose and poetry. Frank's friends told how friends of theirs had visited Majorca and called on Robert Graves! . . . .

My passport arrived. I had my ticket (with return travel guaranteed by the anonymous donor of the fifty pounds for clothes), and I'd booked my sleeping berth on the night express to Wellington.

Then I became ill, very ill, with the effects of the smallpox vaccination. I felt as if I were dying. I lay only half conscious in the hut while Frank spoon-fed me with *Farex* mixed with milk, the kind of food given to babies and kittens separated early from their mother. And just when I was recovering from the vaccination I was stricken with the influenza, called the '1918 flu', that spread over Auckland that year. My recovery was slow as I was now dreading the prospect of travelling anywhere. Frank, very kind and patient, tried to cheer me as one would cheer a sick child, bringing items to distract and please—a glass globe enclosing a snowstorm, a Japanese paper flower that opened in water. He hung Chinese wind chimes at the open door of the hut, where they played a tinkling tune as the breeze passed through the window and out into the space of garden by the pawpaw tree. . . .

Albion Wright of the Pegasus Press disliking my title, *Talk of Treasure,* suggested I choose another. I thought of *Within Sound of the Sea* but he said no, there had recently been a book *Within*

Sound of the Bell (by a school teacher). What about *When Owls Do Cry?* I said. No, *Owls Do Cry,* he said.

In the evenings now I sat listening to the latest topic of conversation. 'Janet is going to Ibiza to live until her money runs out. . . .' 'Janet plans to go to London first, then take the train south . . . she will probably stay overnight in Paris . . . then to Barcelona . . . then take the boat to the Balearic Islands. . . . Janet is . . . Janet will be . . . Janet has . . .'

Beneath my gloom was a rising sense of adventure. I knew that Frank's gloom concealed a feeling of relief that he would be free to continue more peacefully with his writing. I could not even remember how it had been decided that I would leave the country; I knew only that there was no way back, that if my path did lead back there would be no second chance for my survival, that it was best for me to escape from a country where, since my student days, a difference which was only myself, and even my ambition to write, had been looked on as evidence of abnormality. . . .

Far from the New Zealand coast the *Ruahine* pitched and rolled through the wintry July seas. . . .

After three days of continuing seasickness and a return of a recent attack of 'flu, I was taken to the ship's hospital where, in a state of great weakness familiar to those who ever have suffered from motion sickness, I lay almost helpless for nearly two weeks until as the ship began to slow down preparing to enter the Panama Canal, I was able to sit in a chair and watch the theatre of the Panamanian jungle with its basking crocodiles; the gaudy parrots flitting among the trees that leaned, burdened with blossoming vines, to touch the water; to the accompaniment of the American guide announcing the dollar worth of everything within sight. . . .

And as I watched and listened I comforted myself by trying to feel superior as I said to myself, 'Little do they know that I'm recording everything in my mind, that I can see through them, beneath their masks, right to the bottom of their heart, for if I'm to be and stay a writer I must follow all the signs in everything they say and do, and in the silence and inactivity, reading their faces and the faces and the eyes that are mapped with their private isobars and isotherms above the fertile lands, the swamps secret with marsh birds, the remote mountains sharp with rock formations, softened with snow. I must forever watch and listen.' . . .

After thirty-two days at sea, on the day after my thirty-second birthday, the *Ruahine* berthed at Southampton where the passengers boarded the waiting train to Waterloo Station, London.

Waterloo Station. I am standing with my two suitcases, my green haversack containing my typewriter, and I'm holding fast to my *Traveller's Joy* handbag as I propel my luggage towards the street and the row of taxis. Repeating almost dutifully to myself, 'so this is London', I watch as the other passengers are swept away by welcoming groups of friends and relatives. . . .

That first day in London was dreary and uncomfortable. Already, in late August, London was drawing down the blinds for a darkening winter. The YWCA where I found a room for two nights reminded me of a mental hospital without the noise. . . .

On Hampstead Heath I did not know whether to thank or curse John Keats and others for having planted their sedge, basil, woodbine, and nodding violets, and arranged their perennial nightingales to sing in my mind. Misgivings (mis-givings) could not detract entirely from my first literary experience of London. That evening in my Garden Room I read and recited Keats and others (I having followed the advice of Jess Whitworth and joined the local Clapham Library and greedily accepted the rule—'as many books as you wish').

Already, in practical pursuit of my literary aim I had bought copies of the *New Statesman,* the *Times Literary Supplement, John O'London's Weekly,* the *London Magazine,* the *Poetry Review.* (One wet day I visited the rooms of the Poetry Society where I gazed and gazed but did not enter.) I read exciting new poetry and prose by writers from the West Indies, some written in literary English, others with a West Indian version of English but all charged with a morning vision of London and the United Kingdom. I was much influenced by the West Indian writers and, feeling inadequate in my New Zealand-ness (for did I not come from a land then described as 'more English than England'?), I wrote a group of poems from the point of view of a West Indian new arrival and, repeating the experiment that Frank Sargeson and I had made with the *London Magazine* when I pretended to be a Pacific Island origin, I sent the poems to the *London Magazine* with a covering letter explaining my recent arrival from the West Indies. The poems were returned with the comment that they were 'fresh, original' and the editor would like to see more of my work. The poems submitted did not quite come up to the standard of English required. I did realise that such literary pretences were a safeguard against the discovery by others that my 'real' poetry was worthless. They were also a reflection then of a New Zealander's search for identity beyond her own country where being thought 'more English than the English' was felt to be more insulting than praiseworthy. In a sense my literary lie was an escape from a national lie that left a colonial New Zealander overseas without any real identity.

Other practical matters, however, interrupted my poetic dreams. I had booked on the ferry to Dieppe, the train to Paris, a night in a Paris hotel, the train to Barcelona, the ferry across the Mediterranean to Ibiza—the journey was simple and done with if I said it quickly! . . .

Frank Sargeson had written to his friend, the writer Greville Texidor, who lived in Spain, telling her of my visit. I was met at Barcelona by Greville's daughter, Christina, who with her husband, the painter Paterson, took me to lunch at La Plaza Roma, remembered as an old square lined with grey eucalyptus—or were they olive?—trees with the surrounding buildings standing like ancient earthforms, earth coloured, with their roots deep in the red soil. There appeared to be a dust of sun fallen over everything, with the square enclosed in quiet, like a private pathway to other times. Unburdened by ridiculously beleaguering luggage,* I felt my being untethered, my senses sharpened by my night of waking. I was aware not of the noise and traffic of Barcelona but of this background of overflowing quiet that enveloped me with a feeling of being at home, in place at last, like a piece of human furniture that has been shifted and reshifted and rearranged, never before exactly right, in all corners of the world. I did not know yet whether this was the common experience of travellers, in response to foreignness, difference, an abrupt removal of all tethering and bonds to a native land.

Later I met Greville and her husband and their twelve-year-old daughter at their city apartment where I sat smiling, empty headed and shy. I met also Colin, introduced as an English poet, who was returning to Ibiza on the same boat and who had kindly offered to make sure I found somewhere to stay.

---

* Frame's luggage was mistakenly checked rather than booked on her train. Ed.

'A room for a few nights,' he said. '*Una habitación.*'

'*Una habitación,*' I repeated nervously, aware that I knew nothing of Spanish.

That evening I saw Colin, briefly, as I boarded the ferry. The boat seemed frail, a cockleshell, the Spanish night was dark, *obscure,* the sea was dark, calm with small clumps of waves rocking and glinting white like a rooted bed of flowers, asters, or Queen Anne's lace. I hurried to my sleeping berth and waited, sleeping most of the night until morning. . . .

I stood in my room smelling the pervasive Ibicencan smell that I could not yet identify, feeling tired, anxious about finding a *permanent* place to stay, inferior because I was not a poet, but, overturning all these feelings, was my eagerness to begin my new life in a foreign land.

First, I needed a phrase book that was not directed entirely at the rich buying, skiing, photographing, share-accumulating traveller likely to be a paratrooper going bankrupt, being measured for a new suit, who is struck by a thunderbolt while suffering from a fractured skull at the railway station.

And so, joyously, because I had no luggage to take care of, I went in search of a bookshop where I bought a tissue-paper-thin edition of the *Daily Telegraph,* several Spanish newspapers, Paris newspapers, and a phrase book of Catalan, *Learn Spanish With Me,* which I then used to buy bread, butter, cheese, an apple, and a banana. I bought also a cake of chocolate costing more than the sum of the other foods. It had creatures inside it, waving their tiny heads from their tiny nests.

When night came I discovered that the one small ceiling light in my room was so dim that I could barely see the outline of the furniture, and when I looked into the street below, I saw that the shops were candle-lit, with all lights dim. I slept then, and woke full of anticipation for my first 'pure' morning in Ibiza. I would walk, I decided, in search of a place to stay.

I walked towards the old city on the hill, along the narrow cobbled streets to the remains of the Roman wall with its stone figure of a Roman warrior at the entrance to the tunnel leading to the upper city. Walking carefully to avoid the piles of dog and human mess in every corner, I came into the daylight of the hill where I looked down on the harbour and the buildings across the harbour, perfectly mirrored in the clear tideless ocean. At the top of the hill I could see the other side of the island beyond the fields and olive groves to the transparent Mediterranean. I sat leaning against a grey rock that was massed like an accumulation of layers of ancient olive leaves. I shared the solitude with a small herd of wild goats, and the silence with the distant sound of the fishing boats. The grey-leaved olive trees with their twisted branches and trunks turned in defence against the sea wind, and the white-grey stones like long-fallen snow that had refused to melt, on the red soil beneath the trees, drew from me a feeling of tenderness as if this land were mine and I had known it long ago. It was, of course, Shelley's world, and I had known it in poetry, and they were Shelley's phrases that came first to mind allowing me the—parasitic—indulgence of reunion with 'Ode to the West Wind'.

> Thou who didst waken from his summer dreams
>   The blue Mediterranean, where he lay,
> Lulled by the coil of his crystalline streams,
>   Beside the pumice isle in Baiae's bay,
> And saw in sleep dim palaces and towers
> Quivering within the wave's intenser day . . .

before clearing the space where I wanted my 'own' thoughts to be. It was tempting, however, to sit remembering my first ice-clean exposure to poetry, like the first spring of all time, and for the moment I was happy just to *be* where I had always felt most at home—outside, under the sky, on a hilltop overlooking the ocean; and I might have sat there, as I used to sit for hours had I not remembered the purpose of my walk—to find a place to stay.

I followed the narrow path along the bowed ridge of the hill where the storms had struck more harshly and the bowed vegetation showed its agonised struggle to grow in the face of the wind with little roothold except in the crevices in the snow-grey rock.

As I walked I saw two figures in black shawls, stockings, and shoes, bending to gather twigs and branches to heap into their large woven baskets, and again I recognised them because I had known them before—in paintings depicting the toil of peasants or as casual onlookers in the midst of a miracle, or in descriptions by Victor Hugo and Pierre Loti and Daudet. The two women furnished the landscape as if it were an interior long ago formed, decorated, occupied with no prospect of change.

Consulting my new phrase book, I murmured, 'Buenos dias.'

'Buenos tardes,' one replied, pointing to the sun.

I spoke hesitatingly, 'Jo soy de Nueva Zealanda. Janet. Quiero habitación.' I placed the palms of my hands together and rested them against my cheek.

The two women began to talk excitedly together. They turned to me.

'El Patrón,' they said. 'El Patrón.'

I gradually understood that they were *Catalina* and *Francesca* and I was *Janetta,* and they would take me to their *patrón* who would rent his house to me. I dissolved any suspicions they might have had when I explained that I was not a *tourist*—'No soy turista,' I said firmly. 'Soy *escritora.*'

Grasping me lightly by the arm, Catalina led me down the hillside through the narrow cobbled streets to *Ignacio Riquer* where, they said, the house was next to theirs. El Patrón was in charge of the Museum and his brother *Fermin* was in charge of the house where I might be able to stay. At Number Six Ignacio Riquer they pushed open a heavy unlocked front door. A starved-looking cat sitting on the wooden table in the kitchen lashed at us with its claws as it vanished in a streak of grey.

'Los gatos,' Francesca said angrily, explaining that they were wild cats who would attack me if I left the door open. Would I wait, Catalina asked, while they fetched El Patrón?

Within five minutes they had returned with El Patrón's brother, Fermin, slightly built and in his mid-forties, who appeared to be agreeable to my staying in the house and who named a rent comparable to that mentioned by Frank's friends in New Zealand who had stayed on Ibiza, and after Fermin had shown me the room where I could sleep, and the lavatory at the end of the terrace, and the kitchen (there was no bathroom), I said I'd return to my hotel to pick up my shopping bag. I understood that I was renting the entire house. Later when I arrived with my shopping bag and my Traveller's Joy, Fermin was in the sitting room overlooking the terrace, playing a violin. He stopped playing as I entered. He looked surprised by my lack of luggage. I hastily turned the pages of my phrase book.

'No hay equipages,' I said. 'A Paris.'

At last I was able to explain that my luggage had been deposited at the Paris railway station and I'd be sending for it and if all was well it should arrive within two weeks. I explained that I was an *escritora* and my typewriter was in my luggage. . . .

For me, that marvel was the light, the sky, the colour of the olive trees and of the buildings thumbed and worn like old stone pages, with none of the restlessness of New Zealand buildings, none of the sensed fear of sudden extinction by earthquake or volcano. These rose like opened books on a lectern of earth and were turned perhaps once in a hundred years, their certainty lying in their age and their openness. And crowning the marvel was the receptiveness of the tideless ocean admitting to its depths the entire world standing on its shores, creating a mirror city that I looked upon each day.

Without my typewriter I felt limbless, and it was good news when I heard that my luggage was on its way to Ibiza. I happened that day to be walking past a café when I saw Colin, the English poet, sitting with friends at one of the tables on the footpath, and I did not realise until I saw him how miserably lonely I'd been feeling without my typewriter and my luggage and with my several hundred worthless pesetas. Mildly self-conscious but trying to hide it, I strolled past his table and looked towards him. 'Oh,' I said, in a tone of surprise. 'Hello again.' Then in a burst of excitement, I said rather more loudly than I had meant to, 'My luggage is coming soon! And I've found a place to stay.'

His friends stopped in their eating and drinking to stare. At first Colin did not seem to recognise me. Then he said coolly, dismissively, 'Oh, hello.'

He simply stared, showing no delighted response at my news.

I may have exaggerated his coolness; I certainly remember it. I felt a chill current swirling about me and I wished I had said nothing. He and his friends were so much in place there, drinking at the kerbside café table, just as Maurice Duggan, sophisticated and clever, had described, and as Frank Sargeson had recalled to me, saying, 'It's the continental way.'

I hurried away from Colin, the English poet, and his friends, and after my rebuff I made no attempt to mix with or meet the English-speaking colony. I therefore spoke only in Spanish and French, coached by Catalina, originally from Algeria, who also spoke French, and by Francesca, Fermin, and José, the twenty-year-old son of El Patrón, a law student, who came each week to the house to bathe in the tin tub in the kitchen and who, after his bath, came to my room to try to teach me Spanish.

Each morning when Fermin finished practising his violin he also taught me a few words and phrases of Spanish, and sometimes he reminisced about his past. He unlocked one day a large cupboard, drawing out the double doors to reveal a lit interior with carvings of the crucified Christ, on shelves, and pinned to the inside of the door, a poster of a young handsome General Franco, El Caudillo.

'He saved us from the Communists,' Fermin said. 'He was younger then. And I was young.'

He shrugged and looked ashamed.

'Things are different now. It was long ago. Mirra.'

He led me to the window that like my bedroom window overlooked the city and the sea and, nearer, the road leading from the Roman tunnel to the church on the hill. He pointed to the stone wall bordering the road.

'The Stations of the Cross,' he said. 'El Caudillo lined up all the Communists there and shot them. I saw it. But I was a young man. It's different now. And El Caudillo . . . '

Fermin shrugged and went to the cupboard. I thought he was about to spit on the poster. Instead, he ripped El Caudillo from the wall and thrust the crumpled poster on the lowest shelf of the cupboard. Then he shut the door and locked it.

'Those are my carvings in there,' he said. 'I'm an artist, too. But it's different now.'

As each day passed and I occupied myself with writing poems and letters and stories, telling myself that when my luggage arrived with my typewriter I'd begin work on my book, Fermin would bring news of my luggage, for each morning he inquired at the wharf. My luggage and his secret cupboard locking away the dreams of a younger man became our bond. And one day he came to me with a small box closely packed with small religious pictures.

'This is another treasure,' he said. 'Which Saint would you like, Janetta?'

I hesitated.

'Oh. St Francis.'

He found the picture of St Francis and gave it to me.

'These are long ago, too,' he said. . . .

So what have I seen in memory? Memory is not history. The passing of time does not flow like a ribbon held in the hand while the dancer remains momentarily still. Memory becomes scenes only until the past is not even yesterday, it is a series of retained moments released at random. I am remembering Fermin's face as he spoke of his once-passionate hate of the Communists, how in showing me the Stations of the Cross where the executions had taken place, he talked not of distant enemies with a vaguely fearful ideology but of friends and neighbours, even relatives, and how he had approved the killing because the orders came from his beloved Caudillo. Now he was shocked, saddened, and unsure whether the killing had been necessary.

He could not even tell of his doubts through the medium of his violin. He may have known that his family laughed at his violin playing, or smiled tolerantly when they happened to hear him. I smiled politely, murmuring a phrase that might have been 'Bueno, bueno.'

I still see Fermin's troubled face as he stares from the window at the Stations of the Cross. . . .

It was near Christmas when my luggage arrived by sea. When Fermin brought the news there was great excitement and when the truck delivered the two suitcases and the green canvas haversack. . . .

When later in the privacy of my room I opened the suitcases, I looked distastefully at everything I had packed. Then, as I saw again my books, the small stove, the Girl Guide cutlery, the army pots and pans, I felt more kindly towards my outcast luggage. Ah, there was the blue 'tube' dress I had sewn from a length of jersey silk, the material that 'everyone' in New Zealand was wearing. Now the colour appeared too bright and out of place in a land where clothes were black. . . .

In the days that followed I sat wrapped in my rug, nursing my filled hot-water bottle while I typed my novel, *Uncle Pylades*. I looked out of the window at the children playing hopscotch under the eucalyptus trees, the markings for the game drawn with a stick in the white dust. I listened to the chanting

> Tengo tengo tengo
> tu ne tiene nada
> tengo mantequilla . . .

and I watched the elder sisters sitting in the doorways, their lace pillows propped on their knee, working their lace bobbins, hands swiftly passing one bobbin over the other, and I thought of that time in hospital when I had made French lace, gathering from the French instructions a feeling that although I was being denied books and writing and ordinary human conversation, new life was being channelled to me through those instructions in the *Manual of Lacemaking: Plantez un épingle au point Deux . . . jetez trois fois . . .* Language that had betrayed, changed, influenced, could still befriend the isolated, could help when human beings had withdrawn their help.

Thunderstorms came crashing above the house. Lightning played vividly in the room, and winds wailed, cried, screamed as I'd never heard winds, reminding me of the ancient gods, creatures born of thunder, lightning, storm, raging up and down the windowpanes as if trying to get in, clawing the glass, mouthing it as if it were an instrument of music. Often, in the midst of the storm, I'd walk outside, up the street to the other side of the island and I'd sit on the grey rock among the battered silver-grey plants and trees, and I'd think that I had never felt so much at home. I rejoiced that I was alone on a Mediterranean island, speaking no English, with my Spanish welcomed as my English had never been, for my struggle to express my thoughts was attended by the kindness of those who were proud that I was trying to speak their language and who were eager to explain, suggest, help, and teach, whereas in speaking one's native language to others who also speak it one is alone, struggling to meet the expectations of the listener.

As I sat at my table typing, I looked each day at the city mirrored in the sea, and one day I walked around the harbour road to the opposite shore where the *real* city lay that I knew only as the city in the sea, but I felt as if I were trying to walk behind a mirror, and I knew that whatever the outward phenomenon of light, city, and sea, the real mirror city lay within as the city of the imagination. . . .

I had been told that spring came early in Las Baleares. Even so, its outbreak of blossom in early January encircled the island with a new bond of sweetness so excessive that it forced dark pleats of pain to be folded within the pleasure.

With the black-and-white beanflower filling acres of fields, the orchards pink and white with colours, never reproduced in paintings, that remain locked within certain flowers, with the spring wind warm, full of the scent of the wild flowers, the almond and avocado blossom, and the beanflowers, I prepared to tolerate the poetry I knew I would try to write in the midst of writing my novel. Often I remembered with a feeling of strangeness that I hadn't spoken English for three months, although I was aware of my English speech tucked away in a corner of my mouth with the key turned in the lock, but I did not realise how rusty with disuse were the key, the lock, and the speech until, arriving home from my walk one afternoon, I met Francesca who repeated excitedly, 'El Americano, el Americano,' while I listened mystified until I saw a tall brown-haired young man coming down the stairs into the sitting room.

He was equally startled to see me.

'Hi,' he said. 'I'm Edwin Mather. I've rented the studio upstairs. I'm a painter.'

I had to search for my English words. (*My* words indeed!)

'I live in the front room,' I said. 'I'm a writer.'

'I guess we share the kitchen and the john outside?' . . .

On this first meeting Edwin and I, like candidates for a post which both had to accept (for he, too, may have thought he had rented the entire house) explained our presence in Ibiza—his funds were from a scholarship which he collected from Andorra where the money market was 'free'. . . .

[Frame has a passionate affair, her first physical awakening, the ending of which propels her departure from Ibiza. Ed.]

I was beginning to suspect that I might be pregnant. I was over-taken by an alarm that did not quite match my image of perfect love. Also, my money would not last for ever. Edwin, whom I did not tell of my possible plight but who knew my funds were low, suggested I might try living in Andorra, the 'free' money market he had spoken of before. He sensed that Ibiza had become an intoler-able place for me—Ibiza, my island now in its warm balm of blos-som with the interior and the gentle hills shining with the forests of light-green pine trees, their branches tipped a glossier lighter green with new growth—Ibiza was suddenly changed, steeped in my own feelings, destroyed by my glance. Where before my surroundings (I supposed) had existed in their own right, the sky and the sea and the weather and the Mirror City, and I, too, had existed in my own right, with the island and its features as my companions, now all suffered an effect, not the Midas touch but the touch of ash: I could almost see the trees decaying, the olive blossoms withering; also, I was invaded by knowing others on the island, I was no longer alone, creator and preserver of my world, in harmony with other worlds because I could interpret them as I wished: I was tasting the sour and bitter of absence and lost pleasure, bound to a magnet of reality.

(When autumn is over and the leaves have fallen from the trees with only the dark evergreens retaining their bulk which is at once a shelter and an obstacle to the passage of light, we see that we have never been alone in the forest. Shapes of houses emerge, people going about their daily lives; there's a new perspective of distance, a discovery of horizons one could never see during spring and summer and guess at only, throughout autumn. Look at those tall chimneys rising from fires we never knew were lit but that still burn, fuelled in secret! Look at the newly revealed paths! Now I, more clearly looking through this and that world and its seasons, become also more clearly looked at. My own surroundings lose their camouflage; I myself lose my camouflage. There is even the possibility of nests, new or abandoned, in my own tree!) . . .

[Frame's pregnancy ends in miscarriage and she returns to England to take up the writing of her novel. Ed.]

For twenty-seven shillings a week I rented a large front room on the second floor in the home of Ted and Joan Morgan in Grove Hill Road, Camberwell. The Morgans' daughter, Myra, and a middle-aged boarder, Tilly, slept on the third floor, while my room was next to the main bedroom, with a small kitchen (to be shared with Tilly) and a bathroom and lavatory (to be shared with all) on the same floor. My room, overlooking the street, had a large mirrored wardrobe, a dressing table, a large dining table covered with a green and white checked oilcloth that I remember affectionately as I spent most of my time writing at one end, eating at the other: two chairs, one a fat armchair with outsize padded arms and floral covering, an old stretcher bed dipping in the middle beneath a mattress full of hard unevenly distributed parcels of kapok. There was a disused fireplace and a small kerosene heater. . . .

I began to write the story of my experiences in hospitals in New Zealand, recording faithfully every happening and the patients and the staff I had known, but borrowing from what I had observed among the patients to build a more credibly 'mad' central character, Istina Mavet, the narrator. Also planning a subdued rather than a sensational record, I omitted much, aiming more for credibility than a challenge to me by those who might disbelieve my record.

The book was written quickly. . . .

I . . . continued the method I had adopted of buying a new school exercise book, carefully writing my name in the space provided on the cover, with the word 'novel' in a juvenile, laborious hand beside the *subject*, then ruling various columns to record timetable, progress, with spaces for *Excuses*, now called *Wasted Days* as I did not need to identify the known excuses to myself. I had already made, in my mind, an entire book from which I chose chapter headings to remind me of the whole. . . .

I finished *Faces in the Water*. . . .

A. M. Heath suggested I not sign the Pegasus contract which again removed most of my rights to the book. My advance for *Owls Do Cry* was 75 pounds divided with Pegasus after a deduction of ten per cent for the agent. My advance for *Faces in the Water* was 100 pounds similarly divided. George Braziller of New York gave similar advances, in dollars.

After writing *Faces in the Water* and existing through the inevitable few weeks of 'Wasted Days', I began to write *The Edge of the Alphabet*. . . .

Faces in the Water was a success with reviewers and sold more copies than *Owls Do Cry*. There were foreign translations with advances less commission divided equally between myself and Pegasus Press in New Zealand, but for *The Edge of the Alphabet* the agents at last persuaded me to sign separate contracts with each publisher. *The Edge of the Alphabet* before publication was among those from which 'Book of the Month' was chosen and therefore, published, was entitled to wear a gaudy yellow sash. The sudden attention to my work (not personally as the agent protected me, the supposed character of *Faces in the Water*) brought new lessons for me. When the agent and publisher received the typescript of *The Edge of the Alphabet*, the agents suggested I omit one chapter, the publishers that I enlarge the same chapter; there were other conflicting suggestions some of which I diffidently tried to follow. When the book was published, some reviews said of the now diminished chapter, 'It could have been longer,' while others praised parts criticised adversely by the agent and publisher but which I had not changed, while yet others criticised parts that had been praised. This confusing experience reminded me of what I already knew and strengthened my resolution never to forget that a writer must stand on the rock of her self and her judgement or be swept away by the tide or sink in the quaking earth: there must be an inviolate place where the choices and decisions, however imperfect, are the writer's own, where the decision must be as individual and solitary as birth or death. What was the use of my having survived as a person if I could not maintain my own judgement? Only then could I have the confidence to try to shape a novel or story or poem the way I desired and needed it to be, with both the imperfections and the felicities bearing my own signature.

Another lesson was as personal: reading praise of me and my writing, I could feel within myself an inflation of self-esteem similar to my feelings as a child when I won school prizes or had poems published in the newspapers, and I thought as I walked along Thames Street, Oamaru, North Otago, New Zealand, the South Pacific, the Earth, the World, the Universe, 'Everyone everywhere will know how clever I am!'

Now as I walked along Charing Cross Road I thought to myself, 'I wonder if these people know it is I whose photo was in the paper today, it is my writing they were praising, my book described in headlines?' I'd glance at the literary types in Charing Cross Road and I'd think, 'If only they knew! I know I don't dine in fancy restaurants nor am I mentioned in the "About Town" notes of the *Evening News* and the *Evening Standard* ("promising novelist seen . . . etc"), but I'm in London, I'm here, I'm secret, and I'm in the reviews and some have compared me to Virginia Woolf!'

This self-inflation lasted until, reading the inevitable adverse criticism that hurt, that seemed not to 'understand' what I had written, that seemed 'unfair', and that sometimes described me as 'a woman who had been insane', I experienced the anguish of wondering who I thought I was that I could aspire to be a writer; I, with little talent, few words. I knew I had feelings and I could see inside people without having learned about them, but these were too few qualifications: I should never have begun writing.

Once *Owls Do Cry, Faces in the Water, The Edge of the Alphabet* were published I'd had enough experience of opposing reactions to make a deliberate effort to smooth my feelings about all reviews, to allow myself to believe neither the praise nor the adverse criticism, become neither overjoyed nor depressed, and if possible not to read reviews unless it was obvious that the writers had read the book and not just the blurb and a few biographical notes (not provided by me) that referred to 'insanity', and who, understanding or not understanding the book, made intelligent comments about it.

These early lessons remained with me and helped to simplify the complex mechanism of publication where the author is in danger of being trapped and even disabled.

During the snowbound quiet of the London winter I wrote two volumes of stories from which the *New Yorker* and other magazines that I learned were known as 'glossies' chose stories. When my cheque arrived from the *New Yorker* I was amazed and guilty that what had seemed an enjoyable exercise had been rewarded with so much money. I now had over six hundred pounds in my bank account—the magic number for those on National Assistance; soon, with fragments of advances being paid, I knew I would no longer be eligible. I planned to try to move to a quieter room. . . .

Miss Wilson and a Miss Collins . . . were enthusiastic about the Suffolk cottage. . . . Their problem was that they were unable to use the cottage until they retired and it needed a tenant, the right tenant to care for it all year. There was also a dog to be walked and fed. . . .

They'd installed hot water, with the Raeburn stove, a flush lavatory, and a bath. Coll, with her special feeling for roses, had planted the rose garden while Will had cleared the paths and repaired the front gate and searched until she found the heavy oak door to replace the too modern glass-panelled door with its frosted picture of a stag beside a mountain. East Suffolk had been the most wonderful discovery of their lives. . . .

Later the next day Will and Coll drove back to London, leaving me alone with Minnie the mongrel bitch, my typewriter, the country quiet, and my plans for my next book.

I now thought of myself as living the life of a writer, for my two books of stories had been published and *Scented Gardens for the Blind* was about to be published, and during my time at Grove Hill Road I had been aware of a subtle shifting of my life into a world of fiction where I spread before me everything I saw and heard, people I met in buses, streets, railway stations, and where I lived, choosing from the displayed treasure fragments and moments that combined to make a shape of a novel or poem or story. Nothing was without its use. I had learned to be a citizen of the Mirror City. My only qualification for continuing this autobiography is that although I have used, invented, mixed, remodelled, changed, added, subtracted from all experiences I have never written directly of my own life and feelings. Undoubtedly I have mixed myself with other characters who themselves are a product of known and unknown, real and imagined; I have created 'selves'; but I have never written of 'me'. Why? Because if I make that hazardous journey to the Mirror City where everything I have known or seen or dreamed of is bathed in the light of another world, what use is there in returning only with a mirrorful of me? Or, indeed, of others who exist very well by the ordinary light of day? The self must be the container of the treasures of Mirror City, the Envoy as it were, and when the time comes to arrange and list those treasures for shaping into words, the self must be the worker, the bearer of the burden, the chooser, placer, and polisher. And when the work is finished and the nothingness must be endured, the self may take a holiday, if only to reweave the used container that awaits the next visit to Mirror City. These are the processes of fiction. . . .

My experiences and impressions of East Suffolk, the inhabitants, the countryside, were absorbed to emerge later when I returned to New Zealand and wrote *The Adaptable Man*. And because my life had shifted, as I have described, to Mirror City, I now watch the story of myself receding also to Mirror City, for under the light of the ordinary sun and the ordinary day, the 'real' experiences hold diminishing interest for me, for these are the scraps only of the ultimate feast. The more I lived as a writer, the less interesting to outward eyes my life became, ruled by routine, and even in Braiseworth near Eye, with my writing crowded out by domestic duties of *garden, clean, walk the dog, shop,* the Mirror City stayed in my mind as the true desirable dwelling place. . . .

Lauris Edmond

(1924–   )

Lauris Edmond was born in New Zealand, the eldest child of Fanny and Lewis Scott, unconventional utopians devoted to the political ideas of Social Credit. At twenty-one she married Trevor Edmond, giving up her own education to support his training as a teacher, and his aspirations to rise to the top of the teaching profession.

The Edmonds embodied the values of the 1950s in their marriage and the six children (five daughters and a son) who made up the family. Thus Edmond was forty-four before she completed her B.A. and forty-eight when she earned her M.A. Betty Friedan's *Feminine Mystique* (1963) helped prompt Edmond's determination to rediscover the intellect and creativity she had put on hold as a young woman to become the ideal mother and the helpmate wife whose own intellectual interests were not taken seriously.

Although she had been a supply teacher briefly before her first child was born, Edmond's serious teaching career began in 1968 when she started teaching English at Huntly College; she then moved on to edit the New Zealand Post-Primary Teachers *Journal* when she was forty-nine. By the time her writing career was fully launched in her mid-fifties and she had escaped the deadening constraints of an empty marriage, Edmond became Tutor and Lecturer at Massey University in Palmerston North, taking stints away as Writer-in-Residence at Deakin University in Melbourne in 1985 and Victoria University, Wellington, in 1987.

Edmond made up for the frustration of a long-postponed writing career by a burst of extraordinary creativity in her fifties and sixties, publishing six volumes of verse between 1975 and 1985,* and seeing two volumes of selected verse published to great critical acclaim in 1984 and 1991. This achievement won her a New Zealand P.E.N. Award in 1975, a Commonwealth Poetry Prize in 1985, and the Order of the British Empire in 1986.

---

* *In Middle Air* (1975), *The Pear Tree* (1977), *Salt from the North* (1980), *Seven* (1987), *Wellington Letter* (1980), *Catching It* (1983), *Selected Poems* (1984), *New and Selected Poems* (1991).

Her achievement as a memoirist is also remarkable. *Hot October* (1989), *Bonfires in the Rain* (1991), and *The Quick World* (1992) constitute a three-volume autobiography which is one of the richest and most compelling recent accounts of the stages of a woman's life. Edmond's prose benefits from the poet's eye, and her gift for images makes even the recurring routines of an unhappy marriage command the reader's attention.

BONFIRES IN THE RAIN

There were bonfires on the hillsides in those days . . .
—'Ohakune Fires,'
from *In Middle Air,* 1975

AUTHOR'S NOTE
. . . This account of my life in the years from 1946 to 1975 is as true as I can make it. In other words it is again my version of events and my interpretation of their significance. Others would tell the story differently.

Our landlady in Dunedin was a bit of a floosie. . . .
We rented the two front rooms, both large and square with sash windows facing the street across a few bushes and a small front lawn. In one was an enormous feather bed with four brass knobs. It had no apparent base or foundation: getting into it was a dive into limbo, a formless enveloping softness with an occasional feather floating above your head or into your nose. There, in the central hollow of the bed, we made love gleefully—and actively, since beating off the enclosing advances of the mattress was always necessary. . . .

If the bed was unusually large, the fireplace in our sitting room was so small and narrow that in cold weather we sat in front of it with our coats on. . . .

For all that, we rather enjoyed the cold climate, our austere circumstances and that sense of living in a superior outpost that Dunedin seems to confer on its citizens. The severe spire of Knox Church in George Street, the Gothic archways of the university and the old-fashioned stylishness of many of the public buildings combined with the thin cold Leith and its stone bridges to shed an atmosphere of dignity and permanence. . . . Being married made me feel proud, excited, safe. A grand romantic momentum propelled both of us, in fact, through this early part of our marriage—and so easily, so strongly, that it would have demolished much greater difficulties than ours. We were cold, uncomfortable, occasionally lonely; I was secretly bored by Trevor's preoccupation with sport, he was visibly uninterested at my disappointment in relieving teaching—but none of this really mattered. We could have lived waterless in the Sahara and still found it fun to be together. . . .

Married and grown-up we might be, but of course we still behaved like students. Trevor and the others were genuinely studying, but for me too everything was an experiment, and I relished the sense of playing a new part in the unfolding drama of my life. . . . Every time I served a meal, or opened the door to a visitor, or slid into bed with my husband, I acted as one self while another stood by and marvelled at such extraordinarily convincing proofs of maturity. . . .

We had moved to Dunedin for Trevor to take up his third-year Physical Education course; I expected to find work as a relieving teacher and hoped it would be in a speech clinic. Sure enough, there was a clinic, and in the first few months of the year a vacancy on the staff. I confidently wrote out an application, and was highly disconcerted when a local teacher, untrained in speech-therapy, got the job instead—and all the more when despite my furious protests the Education Board refused to change its mind. . . .

Speech therapy was my passion, it was unthinkable to give it up without further struggle—and yet, I did. Did marriage weaken all other resolves? Perhaps so; I continued to be a relieving teacher in whatever school asked for my service. . . .

[I]f anyone had asked me what I expected from marriage, I would probably have replied 'everything'. Yet even I could see that happiness didn't just fall into your hands like a ripe plum from its tree. . . .

However, if the world had taught me (through a thousand stories in books and plays, and especially in films) that marriage meant happy-ever-after . . . You had to understand the other person's point of view, put yourself in their place, shift your ground. . . .

The day came when living in Dunedin was suddenly at an end. . . .

We told each other it had been a good year and we were sorry

it was over, but I was privately surprised at my own detachment. . . . Perhaps marriage was a small shell, the house I now took
with me, wriggling more and more closely into it, unable any longer
to imagine myself uncovered and alone.

For all that, I had an occasional sense of being invisible to
Trevor when he didn't approve of what I did. And sometimes when
I spoke or acted with particular passion and abandonment I had a
curious feeling that he was nervous, embarrassed: such bursts of
exhilaration (which he called my 'silliness') could not be shared
between us because he mistrusted them. I was disappointed, but
thought that no great matter, no more than a grain of dust caught
inside the enclosing marital shell. . . .

Wellington. February. Blazing hot by day, the smell of the heat
all night in small rooms built of old timbers; a small street in Kil-
birnie. The morning tram came down the open valley of Island Bay
and clanked to a stop at the terminus at 8.30 each day. From there
I set out to walk along the beach and up into the next break in the
hills, known as Happy Valley; this, in 1947, was the only way to get
to the little sole-charge Ohiro Bay school before 9 A.M. when classes
were supposed to begin. By the time I, their teacher for the first
term, arrived at the door it had been unlocked by the caretaker,
though the children—all twelve of them—had to play outside till I
rang the first bell at five to nine.

From then on the day was a tight knot of planning, like a piece
of knitting in which I did not dare to drop a single stitch. . . .

At four o'clock a bus on its way from Brooklyn and back came
past the school gate and I locked the door and left this shadowy
place. There was often mist in the hollows, and even on clear days
the little settlement seemed to crouch between close dark hills on
either side, within sound of the sea and the forlorn crying of the
gulls. . . .

However that may be, I was happy there. I worked hard, rather
pleased at the odd location which relieving teaching in Wellington
had found for me, wanting to keep this small buzzing enterprise
running well if I could. In March we decided to try and have a baby,
studied the facts about fertile and 'safe' phases in the menstrual
cycle and acted in accordance with them. Nothing happened. I went
to the doctor and asked for a check-up. While she was talking on
the phone I leaned over and read her pad; the note said 'sterile?' I
went home checked-up but depressed. The next month we mixed

up the dates by mistake but pregnancy ensued anyway, so for most of the time I was at my little country school I felt sick and easily tired. For all that, I was secretly in my glory; my view of the whole world changed with the knowledge that I carried a miraculous second life with me wherever I went. . . .

We didn't think much about money, being apparently sustained, like others before us, by love in a cottage. Moreover there was a convention, acknowledged by both our mothers, that they should provide many of the basic items of baby equipment. . . .

I went to antenatal classes, practised my exercises, read Grantly Dick Read on natural childbirth and was convinced that it could be painless. . . .

What had actually happened the night of my baby's arrival I didn't tell . . . anyone. . . . My labour had in fact shocked and horrified me all the time it was going on; it was an interminable nightmare, with myself at the center roaring and shrieking to an array of busy yet impassive spectres who acted upon me as though I was a joint of meat, to be turned this way and that and carved to the bone.

The puerile idea that if I relaxed all would be well lasted no time at all. Once the pains became strong and frequent, I could do nothing. I would try to relax as each began, but quite soon it would grow larger, deeper, more gripping, more savage and mountainous, till I lost all vestiges of sense or control and yelled and yelled. I'd never done such a thing before, or ever imagined doing it, but equally odd, the nurses seemed not at all surprised—as far as I could think about them, which wasn't much.

Then I opened my eyes, realised I'd been asleep, and was given, to lie beside me, the most beautiful baby in the world, dressed in one of the new gowns, and also asleep. 'It's a girl,' they said, 'isn't she a prize?' Then the doctor arrived and said, 'You did very well.' What on earth were people like who did badly? . . .

There was no limit to my child's perfections. She had a wide beautiful mouth, big dark blue eyes, curly black hair, ears like the best of our family . . . small and close to the head, infinitesimally tiny feet which I could find underneath her blankets and hold in my hand, opening and closing it as though to convince myself again and again of their microcosmic wholeness. . . .

Fanny [Edmond's mother] was still a huge figure on my landscape. Her conflicts remained my own, in particular a profound ambivalence about truth-telling, 'plain speaking', being honest—whatever you called it. This was an article of faith. But I had come to see that unadmitted lies lay beneath this creditable surface. We had learnt long ago to take extreme care of Fanny's sensitivities—her touchiness, in fact—and this had induced in me too a kind of deviousness that fitted very well with the broader lessons that all women unconsciously absorbed. Be nice, not rude or angry. If there are faults and misunderstandings, blame yourself . . . or appear to do so.

In other words, I had brought with me as part of my family inheritance a habit of concealing 'unsuitable' behaviour, often even from myself. The disease of noble dishonesty. I think I had it in quite an advanced form.

Ours became a famous baby. . . .

But the changes were immense. Each came as a discovery, and was upon us before we knew how to be ready for it. . . . I had been a heavy sleeper; suddenly I woke if there was the lightest sigh or sniff from the next room. Through the previous nine months I had come to see my body as capable of plurality, but now I was really separate from someone who nevertheless was somehow more to me than I was to myself. . . .

Still, one morning when Virginia was several months old I woke up early—even earlier than she did—and was suddenly appalled at the casual way I had come into the stunning and terrifying inheritance. I looked back and saw that something like this had happened quite often before. Experience arrived like a train stopping at my personal station; again and again I'd thought, 'No, I'm not ready, I don't know enough', yet each time I'd felt the excitement of trying, and so after only a small hesitation I jumped aboard and it carried me on to places I had never known existed. . . .

At the end of the holidays Trevor took a relieving job at South Wellington Intermediate, then at Te Aro School; if there weren't visitors I spent evenings working as hard as he did, helping to prepare work for his next day's classes. Only during the day, after the washing was done and Virginia was sleeping, could there be small islands of time for me. Then I got out the old green notebook and wrote and wrote. When I ran out of time I squeezed it into the bottom compartment of a chest of drawers where I kept paper and envelopes and unanswered letters. It would no more have occurred to me to tell Trevor about it than to describe how I'd cleaned my teeth, or washed my face. It was a completely private act. . . .

On my now rare visits to town I occasionally called in to Modern Books, intensely aware of its poignant associations. . . . My center of concentration had shifted entirely; I had only the interval between baby feeds, perhaps on a Friday night when Trevor was at home, and there was no time to linger. . . . My secret desire to be a writer mostly concerned the act of writing, catching experience and pinning it down. But clearly there was something else—a tiny, barely awake worm in the brain that dreamed about being read, known, recognised. The ambition factor. Well, it had better stay asleep; its time had certainly not arrived. . . .

Trevor applied for a job in the high school section of Ohakune District High School, and got it.

Ohakune? Somewhere in the middle of the island, wasn't it? High country . . . wasn't there a mountain? We peered at the atlas. Our conversations became all wild surmise, we looked at everything in a newly dramatic way. We had become a family with a future; we too had plans, a destiny waiting to take us up like a magic carpet and whirl us into a shimmering distance. Yes, well . . . Trevor hesitated. But there was an all-electric three-bedroomed house. And high school teaching—it might be rather interesting. . . .

I began to sort and pack.

Quite soon I came to the drawer of letters, my writing notebook, a few scraps of poems; next, the sewing drawer with carefully folded-up pieces of spare material and used patterns. Then the bookshelf made of lengths of wood supported by bricks that held our collection of red-covered Left Book Club books, favourite poets, my old copies of *The Mill on the Floss* and *The Cloister and the Hearth,* together with Marie Stopes and *Birth Control of Modern Couples.* . . .

'Ohakune lies on the south-west edge of the central or volcanic plateau of the North Island. . . . Its latitude is 39 37' and its longitude 175. By road the center of the area is 191 miles from Wellington, 240 miles from Auckland, 187 from Napier and 167 from New Plymouth. Ohakune is a "Main Trunk Town". A few miles to the north lies Horopito, half way crossing place for the night trains from Auckland and Wellington.' . . . This was part of the opening paragraph of Trevor's MA thesis, which he eventually conceived and wrote as a 'participant-observer survey.' . . .

I wrote Trevor's for him because by that time I was quite as desperate as he was to get the thing finished and sent away. It was 1962, thirteen years later; it had been with us in one form or another for the whole time we lived in Ohakune. It was a good piece of work, but there were many times when I thought we would all die of it.

I saw the town first, as we'd agreed, coming from Hamilton by car. It was early September, a perfect spring day, clear and sunny; everything was lit by a vivid, powerful light of a kind I'd never seen before. The mountain was enormous, so close you could almost reach out and touch it, a vast glistening presence, white to the very bottom, where the dark blue-greens of the bush banked against it. The air was so sharp and cold I had to breathe in a new way to take it in. . . . We stood about in the road—small and stony, rather like Osier Road in Greenmeadows—and gazed at the house where I would live. A neat, undistinguished, three-bedroomed wooden bungalow, probably built to an Education Department plan, and much the same as thousands of other school houses. Flat oblong section, a few straggly bushes, no trees. But as I could see at once, the open spaces of the country, houses here and there widely dispersed among the fenced paddocks, made a kind of privacy in themselves. If the air had to be taken in heady gasps, so did the whole sense of being out in the open, surrounded only by endless green distances, the overshadowing bulk of Ruapehu, and a new kind of silence.

Once our daily lives there had begun, it was this silence that struck me with the greatest force. It was a new element, almost as unlike the apparent quiet of a city suburb as if we'd moved from air to water. . . .

[T]hough I was much occupied by the lively social networks that obviously held the town together, I found I had sudden attacks of forlornness. The space about us was wide and silent enough to make me shiver, however busily its other occupants filled it with friendly reverberations. Besides, there were patches of strange living that I was not invited to approach. Maori kids made up about a third of the school population, but I met none of their parents, nor did I find out where they lived, though there was a conglomeration of shacks far back from the road a few streets—or roads—from our house, and from these untidy brown urchins emerged each morning. There was a pa* on the other side of town and a flourishing Maori community at Makaranui on the way to Raetihi; many of these people became Trevor's friends when he taught their kids, but they were always shy with me—and I, equally, with them. . . .

In my first few months in Ohakune I had a miscarriage. . . .

A few months later, when I was successfully pregnant . . . in our second year in Ohakune . . . it became more and more obvious . . . that the other teachers were our natural companions, mine as well as Trevor's. Some invisible barrier lay between the 'locals' and the 'itinerants'—the farmers, timber workers, market gardeners, shopkeepers whose town it really was, and people like us who, with varying degrees of surprise, found ourselves in what still felt like a frontier town. . . .

As we had found in Dunedin, people who live in institutions in a cold climate are glad of friends with houses and fireplaces. Most of our wood was slab from one of the mills, delivered at the gate in truck loads, but we could also buy (or be given) 'real' wood from one of the outlying farms. This meant matai or better still maire, a dense grey timber that burnt like coal. Sometimes on a clear night in those first winters I would go to the front door, stand for a moment on the front porch and look at the mountain, standing there beside me like a great menacing presence beneath a sky brilliant with stars. I almost believed it waited only for my back to be turned to move in and devour me. I would shudder and go inside, tempted, absurdly, to lock the door. The only predator was winter itself. . . .

My second baby was a girl. Raetihi Hospital was a very different proposition from the systematic Bethany, geared to the naming of days, almost of hours, according to their place in a faultless routine. This was a country hospital, small but comprehensive; all but the most serious cases (which were sent to Wanganui) it dealt with in its operating theatre, its 'general end' or its 'maternity end', so named because of the long thin shape of the building. . . . When I lumbered in about nine o'clock on a hot Saturday night in February I found that the nurse who was to admit me was a plump and smiling Maori girl who'd turned fifteen and left school in December to

---

* Village. Ed.

do 'nurse-aiding'. Shy but firm, she told Trevor he need not stay, took me into the office and began to fill in my admission form. In the space for *occupation* she wrote 'housemaid'.

Reading it upside down, I took a moment to prepare a protest, and in that interval the grip of a labour pain put everything else out of my mind. I agreed readily to the bath and pubic shave that came next; indeed, I felt so knowledgeable about the whole process after one experience of it that I was hardly even frightened, at least at first. As the pains grew in ferocity, however, it was impossible not to panic, and the night nurse's examination of 'dilation'—a word which sounded like ecstasy but was not—threw me into despair. How could any baby hope to emerge through an exit described as 'sixpence', or after hours of effort, 'a shilling'? To make matters worse, I knew Dr. Jordon was away on holiday, and that there were alarming rumours about the Raetihi man; it was said he was some-times so drunk that the Sister on duty had to put him to bed for a few hours before he could perform an operation. I imagined my baby imprisoned for ever in its dark and slithery tunnel with the merest dot of light at the end, while I groaned and shrieked and the doctor snored on in the Day Room next door.

Instead, the Sister on duty reprimanded me for making a noise and knocked me into silence with an ether mask, after which the doctor—a young locum*—successfully delivered my baby. I woke up to a fine early Sunday morning and a little girl with a red face, an enormous mouth, beautifully shaped, and a loud and assertive cry. . . .

The world outside the hospital, even after one week, looked startlingly fresh and alive, the mountain blue and bare for summer, except for the white streaks of its glaciers; the farms along the Raetihi road were a good green, their rows of stumps like streets of small dark buildings across them. Even the grey unpainted shacks of the Pakahi mill looked picturesque that fine morning. . . .

The pattern of our lives came vividly into my mind as we drove towards it down our quiet, shingly road. There was Trevor who concentrated on the History and English he taught to everyone from Form 3 to 6A; he had several units of English in his degree and no History, but it was History he liked. Most of his evenings were

---

* A substitute. Ed.

spent marking or planning or 'reading round' the subject. On Friday afternoon he and Murray went to the Pioneer Club for what they called a few end-of-the-week beers. No one was used to drinking, and there was a good deal of fuss about this ritual; Murray made self-conscious jokes. Trevor pretended he didn't really want to go but thought it good for 'colleague relations'. I considered this a laughable lie and said so. However, fuss or not, they continued to go with unshakable regularity, and gradually attracted Colin and Leo and some others to what I crossly called their boys' party.

My days were spent in the washing, cleaning, ironing, sewing, cooking that my household demanded. . . .

Sometimes I went to meetings. I learnt from Kay, who was Plunket and district nurse all in one, of the frustration of visiting families who knew nothing of child health and nutrition and cared less, and were resistant to all advice. She told me hair-raising tales of babies nourished by (or at least fed on) beer and fish and chips, kept up in smoky rooms till parents went to bed, sharing food with dogs and cats and even sheep. The more money her committee of parents raised, the more books, pamphlets and pictures for teaching parents she could provide. I joined the Plunket committee, and while Trevor marked essays and Virginia slept I went to the Plunket Rooms, five minutes' walk away, for serious and even momentous deliberations. Policy, salaries, care for frail babies, worried mothers. I found instead that almost the entire evening was spent in loving concentration upon the question of sandwich fillings for the jumble sale on an approaching Saturday. Back and forth the urgent assertions snapped and rattled. Cucumber . . . too slippery . . . egg . . . smelly if hard boiled . . . ham, too tame . . . what about mincing? . . . It couldn't stop, I gradually realised, because a night out is a Night Out when Dad minds the kids, and these end (as Dad had often proved) around midnight.

I went home and wrote a story about small-town life; the next day I typed it on a borrowed school typewriter and sent it to the *Listener*, which published it a few weeks later. In one swoop my vague and uncertain literary ambitions cohered, became a solid, accomplished fact. Yet this was not somehow good enough; was the story too close to reality to count as genuine fiction? Or was it that it was funny? Did funniness not count? There was something unrealised about this first success which prevented my exulting as I might have expected.

But in any case there it was, our Ohakune life. . . . In the afternoons when both children slept I brought out my folder of untidy pages and wrote bits of poems or stories; sometimes I too fell asleep in the middle. Then friends would call in and I'd make tea, answer the phone. At night I sewed, making clothes for all four of us, though I didn't get beyond shirts and pyjamas for Trevor. . . .

At the end of 1951 the wayward and abstracted Mr. Cook decided to leave Ohakune and take a job in a larger Auckland school. . . .

The chief consequence for us was that the new man wanted the school house rather than George McCullough's farmhouse, which we would now have to move into. In some ways this was tempting. It stood on a hill far back from the Miro Hill road, and connected to it by a long curving track. It was close to the Junction, within sound of its noisy night trains, and had a wide view of the surrounding country. It was the 'real country' aspect I liked—all those hills to wander about on, the whole recovered world of grassy places and high quiet sky which had slipped away from me with my childhood.

The reality was, of course, not at all like that. The drive, as we euphemistically called it, was made of rough metal, some stones almost boulder size, and pushing my pram with its double load through the loose piles of stones and patches of puddly mud, always uphill (it managed to have hills at both ends, with a dip in the middle), was a grunting, shoving struggle. Once out the gate I had a mile to walk to town. . . . The hills rising about the house, fenced in on a section of flat land to keep the stock out, were indeed grassy and pleasant, but this wasn't a rustic idyll either—our lavatory, a tin can in a little outhouse, emptied by the night-cart man, was a hundred yards from the house round the shoulder of a spur. . . .

As for parenthood, that pungent experience, it seemed I couldn't have enough of it. For most of Frances's second year I was pregnant again. There were other events too, new friends, changed habits. The farmhouse was much further away from the school, not so many people dropped in, there were afternoons when I could write, even for short spells. I always put my papers away when the children reappeared after a sleep or rest, and I did not of course consider talking to Trevor about an urge that felt even to me like a secret vice. . . . [W]hat was there to say? 'I want to become a real writer and these snatches are a kind of practise. . . .' Oh? Harbouring a secret ambition? He would have been pleasant, and missed the point. . . .

And ambition? Nobody would or could disagree that my main occupation was fully formed; I liked it, the career ambitions in the family were Trevor's entirely. If I had suggested these left me out—which I didn't for a moment think of doing—he would have been shocked. *Of course* it was all for me too, for us all, the long hours spent talking to teachers, the weekends coaching sports teams and taking them on trips, the evenings of marking. And the work was valuable. For his own pleasure? No no, not that; for everyone's, the family's. . . .

Where was my marriage in all this? I didn't know. The adult solitude and small-child companionship that made up the main part of my days I usually found no fault with. My little girls were a delicious pair, my pregnancy burdensome but bearable; I had some time to do my precious writing, though this was small, and diminished as Virginia and even Frances outgrew a daytime sleep. Trevor and I continued to be partners, lovers, parental colleagues; we were, as our friends said, a happy couple.

But there were undoubtedly shifts and alterations, subterranean changes of emphasis in our shared lives that showed so little on the surface that it was easy not to recognise them. I had occasional spells of deep melancholy that seemed to have no cause. . . . Trevor's unwritten thesis hung over us, a vague malaise. . . . I talked to Trevor who tried as always to be helpful and kind: I should do more, join the newly revived Drama Club, the Parent Teacher Association, better still the Community Arts Service. . . . It's true we were both willing to take part in the ubiquitous club and committee life of the town, and I wasn't against such advice, indeed I took it. But the dark spells recurred all the same. Sometimes at night I cried long and silently, without relief.

Was there a kind of loneliness in spending almost all one's time with small children, delightful as they were? Or, underneath my eagerness to belong, did I actually find Ohakune an isolated, dull, cramping place? Was my marriage doing what good marriages should do—whatever that was? Who could tell. . . . I did know there was something I obscurely wanted and could not expect from my school-obsessed husband, with his cheerfully unsubtle distinctions about the good and bad in the way human creatures behaved.

Even our physical intimacy, enjoyable though it was, sometimes left me feeling stranded and alone. At the same time, he was wonderfully interesting and well informed when it came to more public affairs. My knowledge of political events, their history and significance, was always vague; his was precise, packed with revealing facts, authoritative. He was becoming a specially admired History teacher, and I could see why.

Contradictions. Mixtures. A room full of ill-matched furniture, but drawn together, for me, as if through fine muslin at its window by my lifelong training in 'positive thinking'. I admitted nothing. On the contrary, I was always keen to defend the domestic vocation. . . .

Another summer came, Christmas, January, long hot days to carry my fat body through. Then in the middle of that quiet month, when all duty and obligation was in abeyance and everyone we knew was away at the beach, I had my baby, and it was a boy. Enormous (over nine pounds), healthy, beautiful—and a boy, a boy! So Trevor greeted him—I had had no idea he so distinguished between fatherhood of daughters and sons, and was dismayed by it, though I too was exuberant at having achieved both sexes in the same family. . . .

Coming back to Ohakune after holidays . . . I was struck by the comparative primitiveness of our mountain village circumstances. The weather was always colder (it could snow even in summer, and rain could gather and fall round the mountain when the whole of the rest of the country was having a heat wave), the farmhouse was old and small, our furniture cheap and in some cases rudimentary. Some of the cupboards were forty-pound apple boxes which Trevor had nailed together and I had covered with gingham, including a gathered curtain to provide a door. But of course it was home, and I was glad to be there.

Money. Ah, money, that pervasive pest. Ours was like a pallid and lugubrious guest, always hanging about the house looking miserable, chronically hungry but never strong enough to do anything useful. We kept making plans to liven it up, and some of them worked. The *Wanganui Chronicle* for instance, Trevor knew several borough councillors, and indeed was interested in practical politics at that level himself; one had told him that the *Chronicle* wanted more coverage of events in Ohakune and asked if one or both of us might like to write for them. We would, by God we

would. We could hardly wait to start. A pound a column represented riches indeed. Bad for literary style, I told Trevor, because
the more we puffed up our reports with useless words the more we
earned. As it turned out I, who cared more about this hazard,
proved the better puffer-up; I was sometimes ashamed of my over-
decorated effusions about the Tennis Club's annual meeting, or the
Council Works Committee meeting, each extending satisfyingly far
down its column and rich in pointless and irrelevant speculation.
The *Chronicle* car delivered the papers at the corner dairy at the
Junction every morning about six o'clock, and the driver then
picked up our copy, which at some time during the night one of us
had delivered. You had to slip it into the crack where a metal plate
advertising AMP Insurance didn't quite connect with the verandah
post at the corner of the pavement. Finishing a report late at night
and then walking over the hill in the quiet dark, lights out in the few
houses and the only sound a muffled shunting from the station, was
one of my pleasures. I always wanted to be the one to go. . . .

[My fourth baby's] advent went smoothly. I was weeding the
garden one afternoon, judged there was time to cook the family
dinner (so nonchalant had I become), we installed a friendly Sixth
Former as babysitter—teachers being away in January—and as
darkness fell on a warm summer evening Trevor and I drove to
Raetihi, slowing down when I writhed and groaned, as at regular
intervals I did. . . .

I had several times tried to persuade Trevor we had spent long
enough in Ohakune, but I now argued in favor of buying our own
house, and for once he agreed. Reluctantly, dubiously and with
maddening slowness—but still, he agreed. It was a fine house, big
and plain and solid and set in a quite wonderful long-cultivated garden, a section of nearly an acre running down to the Mangawhero
River at the back. . . .

The question of what life is for or, more exactly perhaps, how
something beautiful, or even sound, can be built out of it when one
is given such disappointing materials . . . is urgent at some times,
quite forgotten at others. One of the best ways to forget—though
you don't realise it at the time—is to hand your life over to others
who seem to need it more than you do. Your life, I say; well, your
energy, concentration, purpose, time—most of all, time—and imagination, intellectual struggle, the bouquet of yourself called personality . . . I'm thinking of course of parents and children, and myself

in particular: four children, a house in the country, a time when women's most sensitive pleasure was to serve. . . . Natural obsessiveness made me the most thorough parent alive (the soaking of barley for nourishing soups, the endless seams on dresses and shorts and crawlers and jackets, the sewing of hems and plackets long after midnight, the nightly story reading, no matter how sleep-numbed my voice and brain).

There was little else to demand my full attention. Trevor's absorption with his work continued to intensify; Ohakune had long since defined its limits. Friends were precious, but friendship itself had become an aspect of child management, since all the women I knew well were mothers too. . . .

[T]here were changes in the subterranean forces that shaped our lives. The buying of the house, for instance, oddly confirmed a growing separateness in what concerned each of us most closely. I became more confidently established on my territory of house and garden, friends and children, Trevor more secure in his authority as a strong and popular teacher with a passion for sport. Ownership itself turned out to be an intermittently compelling occupation. It worried Trevor because it meant a mortgage, problems with paying bills, the need to attend to gutterings and drainpipes, paintwork and rust in the tanks. I, being of a more optimistic temperament, thought the immense amount of gardening I had to do, and the fairly regular painting of rooms, not to mention the general upkeep of my vast and sprawling establishment, all worthwhile because it was so beautiful. However, I too was depressed by the monthly bill-paying (or bill-postponing) during glum evenings at the kitchen table. . . .

But we had made a gesture of belonging. We weren't 'doing country service' nor even 'having the country experience'—we *lived* in Ohakune. . . .

Taking to the road in our car was natural and frequent; I made occasional trips to Taihape or Wanganui, once or twice we drove to Taupo and back, a distance of seventy miles, to spend the day by the lake, and every January we chose a beach to camp beside for ten days or a fortnight. . . .

Some of our journeys were to make connection with the other Scott families—to Wairoa, for instance, where we camped on the lawn beside Lindsay and Doug's house and spent all day cavorting with our children in the swimming baths or by the river. In the evenings, after a certain amount of swapping children between house and tent, the four parents settled down to talk their heads off, till we were so drugged by exhaustion that there was nothing for it but to stagger off to bed. . . .

Nothing like this would have been remotely possible with Trevor's family. For one thing their holiday trips to lakes or beaches were to rented houses, where they seemed to live rather as they did at home; and they would no more have thought of squeezing double the number of children and parents into those than we would have thought of going. . . .

It occurred to me at some time in those years that there was a strange irony in my having linked my fate and future with a clan so alien in its outlook and habits to my own. The very conservatism of the Edmond household, the quality I'd thought of as 'essential bourgeois', had been what I liked best, because it appeared to offer me a certainty and confidence that my own shy and cranky family could not give. Yet as time passed it became more and more obvious that the Scott family model produced far more affection, vitality and action—a lively humanity which could and did grow by shared experience. Observing these contrasts I had a first inkling that my choice of conventional security had been part of twenty-one-year-old immaturity, and something I would leave behind as I grew older. The developing life of the families, expressed in letters, gifts and shared expeditions, was part of that process.

But every holiday ended with the beginning of school, and 'Trevor's school' could still encroach largely on life at home, detached though the Burns Street locality might be. In 1954 it ceased its existence as a district high school and became Ruapehu College. There was much ceremony about the opening. Buildings, teachers and children were all the same, yet each acquired a new lustre by recognising a motto, a crest, a principal (more august than a headmaster) and most of all the status of 'college'. . . .

Trevor . . . began to spend more time on his thesis, and to talk of the need to make his mark as a teacher and organizer, because he didn't have 'subject qualifications', only Education as theory—and practise. . . .

I had a good many headaches, in fact, but though each one temporarily crippled me, I did not see how I could live differently and so perhaps prevent their onset. On the contrary, the charge that drove my daily life, and dictated its speed, seemed to grow stronger and fiercer all the time. I no longer had time to write—or only very occasionally, late at night when everyone was in bed, the lunches cut, clothes ironed and set out for the morning, and Trevor at a meeting or away on a school trip. In those spells of brief and confined solitude I didn't write stories but poems, or parts of poems, fragments, lines that rushed urgently down the page. . . . I stuffed these scraps into folders, and shoved them into drawers where letters and telegrams, old speech therapy notes, other scribbled writings lay jumbled together. There was never time to look at them again or revise. My daylight self was altogether more active and external, my head full of planning, conversations tense with news and stories. . . .

In 1957 I had another baby, and two years after that yet another, two more girls. Catholics traditionally had big families, so did our Maori and Chinese neighbors, but we just seemed to go on as though we couldn't think how to stop. . . .

I had once said that with my first child I took on 'the life of coping'. Now it was a decade later—Virginia was almost ten when Stephanie was born. Ten years of a life of action and planning, of management, watchfulness, the organising of systems that constantly loosened, expanded, teetered, finally fell and then had to be re-formed, differently. . . .

I lived richly and fully in those years, and scarcely even noticed the absence of any separate adult life I might have had up till then—I was thirty-two when Stephanie was born. Nor did I observe that marriage itself, the adult relationship that after all formed a major part of the family system (and financed it), was not now a particularly vital enterprise. It no longer had the inner momentum of the first few years; instead we put almost all of ourselves into our separate occupations.

The children of course were indisputably Trevor's as well as mine, and I was conscious that his work provided us all with house, car, clothes, everything we had; also that it was his ambitions that could change our course. However, the sharing of a family began gradually to show different facets to each of us. After a week or ten days of our summer holidays Trevor would become restless, want a newspaper to see the School Certificate results, to talk about school. It was the beginning of a new tension, or the deepening of an old one, which cast me in the role of suppliant, for time and attention he was often reluctant to give.

As if to confirm the decision that underlay my lack of decision about the size of my family, the birth of my fifth baby was spectacularly more satisfying than any of the others. It was a hospital error, oddly enough, that made the difference. I lay in bed in the 'maternity end' trying to read, interrupted by increasingly ferocious labour pains and, occasionally, one of the monstrous intrusions of an examination for cervical dilation. On the last of these the nurse dismissed my case quite peremptorily. 'Nothing doing here,' she announced, and went off to attend to more important matters in the 'general end'. It was about nine o'clock in the evening. Left to themselves, my as yet invisible baby and my experienced and businesslike muscular system went quickly through the pains that expand and began the pains that expel. There were three or four cataclysmic seizures. I had never before been conscious when they occurred and was amazed—they went beyond pain; they had become irrelevant. They were instead a huge natural surge of the force of life itself. It took over my whole body, shook and contorted it, split it open, and my baby burst out onto the bed and lay there, half curled up still, grey with sticky vernix, taking seconds (hours, I thought) to gasp and cry. I held up an edge of blanket to protect her from the cold air at the open window. I hung on the bell. And a nurse did appear at the door, gazed horrified at the pair of us and rushed out again shouting, 'My God! My God!' . . .

I called my daughter Katherine,* spelt like Katherine Mansfield, and Lindsay after my cherished sister, and we pleasurably occupied our little island of protected time in the hospital making friends with each other. Then I took her home to my truly vast household. . . .

I was myself developing an apparently unruffled style which I used to keep a kind of control of the burgeoning complexities of my household. The process began in a strange sickness that beset me when Katherine was a few months old. I had a choking sensation, a

* Edmond's sixth child. Ed.

sense of suffocating constriction as though I had too tight a collar round my throat; I developed an anxious habit of loosening something that wasn't there. 'Strain,' said Bill briefly, 'you have to go away for a while, take a break.' So carrying my baby in the carry cot I'd made for the purpose, I caught a train to Wairoa to spend a week with Lindsay. It was a long time to be away, but my sister was welcoming and sensible, insisted that I not spend the time worrying about those I'd left behind. Naturally restless and excitable, I had been threatened with obliteration by the force of my devouring days, and now had to devise a weapon of self-protection. I tried to practise calmness. I succeeded too, with my new accomplishment; I returned home to enter a period of high activity, more dense and sustained than any I had known, and survived it. I did not for some years realise how superficial this managerial equilibrium really was, nor how damaging, in that it induced a kind of internal paralysis from which eventually I must consciously recover.

In the mean time, it served me well. In these years, the last of the fifties (though nobody thought in decades; time was continuous then), everything in my daily life intensified, became more so. More children, all growing bigger minute by minute, larger platefuls at meals, bigger shoes to buy, more questions to answer (and more still to push aside as unanswerable), more school lunches to cut, teachers to get to know, homework to watch over; more panic at high temperatures or sudden falls (subdue it how I might) and relief at peaceful bed times, at safe returns from a swim, a long ride, bush or mountain expeditions; more laughter, labour, terror, exhaustion. . . . We bought a wallowing old station wagon, filled it with kids and camping gear and saddles and sheet music, gumboots and garbage . . . sometimes when I gathered my children and their friends from the school gate I counted wrongly and had to go back for one forlorn straggler. I fell asleep in the middle of reading a story and woke to hear the valiant listener continuing the tale by heart. . . .

And then everything stopped. Trevor suddenly got a job, as first assistant at Kuranui College in Greytown. Dismayed, we stared at one another, trying to take it in. 'We can't *shift*,' cried Frances, 'this is where we live.' Even I agreed, though of course I'd known of the application, and indeed helped to write it. Now it could not be reversed; Ohakune was suddenly not for ever, it was a phase. . . .

We had six weeks of summer holidays to gather ourselves

together, and after the frantic whirl of those hot days I sometimes went and sat on the cool steps of the front verandah and looked up into the shifting shadows of the beech tree, as I had done a hundred times in the years this house had been home. . . .

My own family now filled almost every part of me; like a full tide it had come in, spread over and through me, widened me into shapes I had not known I could take. Sitting there in the cool summer dark I thought with a sudden flash of knowledge: my children will grow up with the memory of this house in their bones. All their lives it will be these cabbage trees rattling in the wind, this hill where the old nags browse and knock over the fences, this hot little winter room where we've so often huddled in the smell of coal smoke to dress and undress, read the nightly stories, cram in homework and sewing and books and even saddles and bridles being oiled for a ride the next morning. When they have grown old and feel their way back to the unconscious residue of sensations and shapes in their minds, the deeply laid layers of childhood experience, this will be what they find. . . .

I had a conviction too that more than ever before, at this moment of leaving, my home was something I took with me wherever I went. I had become so intimately and profoundly connected with my children, and Trevor, their father (which was how I now most often thought of him), that I existed more significantly with them than by myself. . . .

Thirteen years I'd lived in this little mountain town, all my children but one had been born here; I was moving into the middle of my life—soon I would be forty. And I was not, so far, a writer of poems or stories, a known recorder of New Zealand experience; instead I was a mother of six children, a woman who had taken up the familiar pattern of my generation. Certainly I had expanded it—no family I knew had so many children (except Clive, with seven)—but I hadn't otherwise changed or challenged the conventions I'd inherited. I didn't think of this regretfully, I simply observed it with a small, detached surprise, and went back to reflections about what it was we were leaving.

'Aren't you ever coming in?' Trevor demanded from the front door. Oh yes, I would come soon. . . .

I'd had no choice in where or when, indeed *if* we moved—I'd badly wanted to, and we'd stayed; now I didn't care and we were going. But I *could* sit on in that caressing dark alone, and think

about it. The residue of the years, what I would take with me—
some shadow, colour, whiff of sound or smell that would always
bring this place back—what was there? . . .

Greytown was about the same size as Ohakune but worlds
away from it: a self-conscious, educated village, filled not with civic
defensiveness but civic pride (not to say complacency), in touch
with city people, some of whom lived there and worked in Wellington. A charming, tree-shaded township where the old buildings
were carefully preserved and even old trees defended by public
protest if threatened by someone's axe. A small town tingling with
committee activity, but this time the Beautifying Society, the Settlers' Museum, the mobile library were the aristocratic centres, not
footballing and drinking. The Wairarapa, unlike the King Country,
was 'wet' and the pubs were substantial old wooden piles, quite
grand in their way, and entirely fitting the wooden shop fronts with
upstairs quarters where families still lived. Their high sash windows
looked out over their verandahs as they had for a hundred years in
a settlement begun in 1860 and named after Governor Grey.
Ohakune was raw, tough, sketchy in its communal life, Greytown
old and proud and conservative; a few of its larger houses were
mansions, its orchards and farms had 'homesteads' (the name, in
fact of one apple orchard), there was a life of refinement and
sophistication there, of cocktail parties and soirees. As well, and in
some ways associated with this local grandeur, there were artists—
potters, weavers chose to live there for the ambience, painters liked
the light on the hills, the old buildings, the trees; parties of friends
drove over the Rimutakas to concerts and exhibitions in Wellington, others sang in choirs in Masterton. 'Take care on the roads,'
Noeline Bruning had advised, 'there's a lot of money in the
Wairarapa, and long straight roads for fast cars to get up speed.'

Greytown had been the natural choice for a secondary school
to serve the small Wairarapa towns, and busloads of students came
from Martinborough, Carterton and Featherston to Kuranui College which stood, still self-consciously new, at the southern end of
the town. Its first principal, Sam Meads, had learnt his craft in the
old-fashioned boys' school tradition of Wellington College. He was
intensely chauvinistic, proud, competitive, a fomenter of that
ancient institutional virtue *esprit de corps,* though by 1962 when
we arrived this was simply called 'school spirit'. He had invited
Trevor to be his first assistant because he knew him—a highly

respectable way of choosing staff. He was bluff and hearty, with a footballer's physique (and a family name made famous by football), an old-style Kiwi joker's suspicion of women, and a good heart. A grown-up schoolboy and a small-scale imperialist. 'His' teachers lived in a cluster of new houses near the school and locally known as 'Meadsville', but there was not a place there (or perhaps a house large enough) for us, so Sam had arranged for us to live above the chemist's shop in the middle of the main street. In the four years we were there I continually tried to persuade Trevor to move to one of the houses I was always finding for us, but had no more success than I'd had when I wanted to leave Ohakune.

Trevor had a capacity for passive resistance ('inertia' was my word) at which I sometimes marvelled, occasionally I laughed, often—and more as time passed—I raged. None of these reactions made the slightest difference. He agreed to make changes if forced to, and every year we lived together made it more obvious that there was only one power that could do this—the school, its expectations of him, its rewards in better jobs and the honourable gratitude of parents and other teachers. I saw him, in rare moments of detachment, as a deeply conservative man, caught in the grip of an all-but-consuming ambition.

I detested that house. It was cramped and ugly and dark and noisy, and its back yard was abominable, a patch of concrete and grass bounded by a wire fence and an alleyway, a carpark and the wall of Wright Stephansons' liquor store. The back door took you into this open cage, the front door on to the street at the side of the shop. The windows of our bedroom looked over the shop-verandah roof and on to the passing traffic and the butcher's opposite. My first visitor was the teacher's wife who'd lived there before me and had hated it as much as I now did . . . in Sam's mind (and he was all-powerful), teachers' wives were poor creatures, necessary servants of the great enterprise of the college, but of no interest in themselves—unless they spoke up, in which case they were queer, unsuitable, perhaps radical, rather frightening. . . . I had only one ambition regarding Sam; it was to have a conversation with him in which one sentence, just one, was spoken by me and listened to and answered by him. It never happened. . . .

The pattern of life in Greytown came into focus. For all that it was a small village, to live right in its main street was to live 'in town'. I felt less private, less free to think my own thoughts and considerably less independent than I ever had before. This sense of being at the mercy of my community, almost possessed by it, was strongly reinforced by my membership (unwanted as it might be) of Sam's patriarchy: he was the headman, and teachers and their families the tribe. . . .

In the heady atmosphere of his new authority, Trevor seemed to take on some of the colour of Sam's view of the world—that is, of the school and the insufficient creatures—the wives of teachers—who nourished and supported the front line. He spent longer times than ever at school and when, quite soon, he began to produce Gilbert and Sullivan operas, the whole location, the very base of his existence, seemed to move from home to school. . . .

The effects of all this I felt most strongly at teachers' parties. These had quite a different character anyway from the more homely gatherings I'd known in Ohakune; they were larger, smarter, more glittering, more tense. They had an undercurrent of competitiveness that I found menacing, as though this was a social courtroom in which everyone knew and obeyed the law, and I alone was condemned for ignorance or inferiority. . . .

I supposed my awkwardness made for them a particular sharp contrast with Trevor's popularity and ease. Whether this was so or not, Trevor himself thought me exasperating, recalcitrant: why couldn't I enjoy these do's? . . .

Impossible to explain that I had become wracked with jealousies about school, the other teachers, the whole enterprise that so stunningly enclosed him and left me out—in fact I hardly realised myself that jealousy was the name for the horrible dread that took hold of me when he went off to dance, laugh, joke, flirt with Mona or Doreen or Stella. I only knew that my smile became stiffer than ever, my conversation more jerky and irrelevant, my urge to go home (which began almost from the moment of arrival) more insistent. Later in our Greytown years one of the other men began to make a great fuss of me, and this I had to admit I enjoyed, but by then I was beyond the hope of safety or comfort on the risky carousel of aging marriages. . . .

Trevor too began to apply for jobs. He brought the *Gazette* home and we scanned it, then the map, for towns we didn't know, before filling in the elaborate form which we hoped would produce a summons to an interview. . . .

He was called next to Opunake, a small town in Taranaki, and

I went with him to the interview in the Education Board office in New Plymouth. On the journey we had great fun; it was exciting to be away for a whole day and a night without any children, and we were both exhilarated by the knowledge that the success so longed for was on its way. After dinner at the little Opunake pub (a night at a hotel was like an orgy), we walked about the town and made up stories about its inhabitants, including the triumphant new arrivals, ourselves.

The next afternoon I waited in the car for the conquering hero to emerge from the dull but portentous portals of the Board office. When he came out and walked across the road I scarcely recognised him. His face was grey and set; as he approached the car he looked at me but could not smile—indeed he could hardly speak. When he did, his voice was a dry croak: 'I've got it.' I set about offering him congratulations and assuring him that success at last would be a wonderful thing, it was terrific news. Nothing made any impression. We drove home almost in silence; when we got there he did not want to see anyone, least of all Sam or the other teachers, though the phone kept ringing with their congratulations.

It was a strange time. For several weeks he behaved as if he had moved into a kind of darkness where nobody could follow. He would go to school, and appeared to perform there much as usual—except that he smoked far more heavily and came home earlier. Then he would simply sit upstairs in our room in a state of black terror, and I would talk to him, on and on, trying to make the new job and all that went with it seem easy and manageable. . . . As pressure mounted for him to talk to the new school board, make decisions about the house we were offered, plan courses for the next term, it slowly became clear that he had no real intention of going. . . . Finally I could not support the inexplicably slippery situation alone any more: I rang Sam.

About the same time Noeline Bruning visited us; after only a few minutes of talking to Trevor and observing the lost look on his face, she said, 'He must see a psychiatrist—I know the right person.' A psychiatrist? 'This is a breakdown,' said Noeline briefly. She knew an elderly Jungian therapist, a Mrs. Christeller, who was no longer in practise but would take occasional cases for friends. Trevor must go to her—and in due course he did. . . .

Sam, Doug Banks, the local GP, and I . . . explained his withdrawal from the new job on medical grounds and agreed in advance that he would not apply for another for two years. We began to make regular visits to Wellington. Trevor would go to Mrs. Christeller . . . [who] saw him as a scholarly, thoughtful person who would be better to stay away from the urgent pressures of institutional authority. . . .

He turned to teachers' union politics instead. The Post-Primary Teachers Association offered expansion without danger, and he took to it as though born for committees, negotiations, meetings, chairmanship. He moved upwards quickly and before long was spending a good many weekends at regional or national meetings, staying in hotels in various towns with other teachers, discussing policy, convincing the indolent or ignorant of the importance of political action. . . .

I detested PPTA parties, when I had to go to them, almost more than the local staff jollifications. Here, I thought nastily, was another closed circle, ripe with complacency. . . . [A]t the same time a sort of slow indignation began to take shape in my mind. Not merely that Trevor now spent almost all his time, and certainly his best energies, on projects that kept him away from our big busy household, which I thus managed alone. As well, I had a growing sense that I had spent a great deal of my time and thought on helping him regain his peace of mind (or trying to), and each time he emerged encouraged and cheerful from a black spell he redoubled his efforts at school, in the ubiquitous operas, with rugby and cricket teams, or for PPTA. None of the benefit, I savagely—though silently—observed, came my way.

I did not in the least understand why such a morass of rage and pain should roll about inside me like slowly heating lava. I admonished myself: Trevor had suffered a kind of hidden terror I had never known, he must have whatever experience restored his balance, his forward momentum. . . .

Only very gradually did I come to suspect that my own eager helpfulness might have been part of the cause of this dislocation. . . . My response to Trevor's trouble had been simple, childlike, naive: I loved him, I must do everything I could for him in his distress. In those years I learnt a whole new knowledge, a new vocabulary, a new cynicism. In dealing with depressive illness, helpfulness was often a delusion, loving observation misplaced egotism, generosity a trap. Everything had the wrong names, an evil underside; to give was to lose, hope bred despair, love came back as cruelty, and was perhaps half cruelty itself. They were bad days and, when I woke up and couldn't go back to sleep, black and fearful nights.

I came to think of illness as a predatory monster. . . . Had I not learnt in childhood, and practised ever since, the habit of sustaining my own family, feeling their woes as mine? Had I not gloried in my prowess as supporter, sympathetic listener, patient friend? The extreme thanklessness of Trevor's response felt at first like an undeserved punishment; I slowly learnt that this is the character of this kind of illness, greedy and heartless monster that it is, and that if I didn't learn to put myself at a distance I would remain part of its inexorable cycle of despair, recovery, relapse.

Through all this my children, and apparently the rest of the world, ate, slept, played, lived what are called normal lives, had pleasures and adventures, grew older, changed. . . .

As for their awareness of the difficulties that beset their parents, this seemed not to matter too much, at least on the surface of things. We were used to carrying on through lesser crises—having no money to pay half the bills, month after month postponing buying new shoes, raincoats, suitcases, camping gear, blankets . . . my frequent eruptions of hatred for our narrow boxed-in living quarters; sporadic tears and quarrels, which of course were kept for late at night. . . .

The summer before the Opunake crisis something else had occurred which was hardly recognisable as a major event, yet as time passed proved to have been the beginning of a profound and enduring change. It happened, however, only to me, and affected me most deeply. We were in Napier for our summer camping holiday, installed in our big tent in the grassy expanse of Kennedy Park. It was the last year of the full-scale family holidays, and everyone was there.

One afternoon I sat in the tent alone and watched the family out on the grass playing cricket with their father. I often elected to stay in or about the tent instead of romping about with bats and balls because it was a chance to feed, even temporarily, my permanently unsatisfied craving to read; it was also the only time in the year when Trevor, a natural sportsman, was completely at his children's disposal. All was well. I turned my pages peacefully, then at a sudden shout looked up, and as I watched a kind of somersault took place in my mind. The figures moving about on that green background suddenly changed, took on a new angle, almost a new dimension. I saw them as I never had before—they were my dearest people in all the world, almost everything I thought and did was directed towards their welfare, their happiness and fulfilment. And I saw with blinding clarity that not one of them thought there was a single thing to be done for me, in my turn. I didn't *have* a turn. I didn't exist, except as I helped them to exist. Without them I was nothing, and so they perceived me—theirs, useful, indeed necessary, loved, of course, depended upon; but as a person with possible separate requirements of my own, not there. And nobody, not even I, thought this unbalanced or wrong. I shook all over, that moment in a hot afternoon, I was so struck by the momentousness of the discovery. It must have happened gradually—was that why I had seen nothing of it till this instant? It was not even as though a major cathartic event had shed light on it; this was a peaceful day with everything in order. Perhaps it was an idea, a little nub of knowledge, that had been waiting just outside consciousness for a very long time and, catching me off guard, quickly and quietly entered.

Trevor, when I talked to him . . . made the quite sensible suggestion that as I'd always regretted not finishing my degree I should enrol as an extramural student at Massey University. I was interested at once, and keen to begin. English was the obvious first choice, related as it was to my twin passions of writing and reading; and I was tempted to complete the Education II course I'd begun as part of speech therapy training. . . .

Another project appeared too—the teaching of Play Centre mothers in the Wairarapa. I would drive to Martinborough in the evening, once a week, and for two hours discuss child rearing with young mothers less experienced than I. The course was based on a series of printed lectures . . . [and] I was now a paid tutor. I hadn't earned any money to speak of . . . since I'd taught at Worser Bay School the year my first baby was born. . . . The tiny tutor's fee was absurdly pleasing. . . .

We had a visit from another tutor, who happened to ask me if I'd read *The Feminine Mystique* by Betty Friedan, and lent me her copy. At once I was in the middle of a whole series of mental somersaults, a carnival of sudden new views and changed ideas . . . a revolution. I could hardly believe it. Thousands of women all over America were saying in interviews again and again that their families were well, happy, busy fulfilling their ambitions, their husbands likewise, and yet beneath this apparently perfect facade they themselves suffered a profound and inexplicable malaise. . . .

[B]ecoming a student again was so enormously interesting that I didn't have time to think of what other changes might be possible. Then Trevor's illness engulfed me, and with it the urgent desire to maintain family equilibrium and reduce shocks and uncertainties to a minimum. . . .

I went to vacation courses, alone, wonderfully alone. Trevor agreed to stay home, friends helped; it seemed hardly possible that everyone would survive my absence, but they did, quite easily. The lectures were like bombs going off in my head. By the end of the afternoons my head hurt, not with a headache, rather a feeling that the brain was expanding so fast that its stiff joints hurt as they were rushed into action. Every word was an illumination. A writer's shaping of fictional characters, as these dazzlingly perceptive lectures described it, was so filled with currents and eddies of the real life and real people I knew that I felt constant little stabs of recognition; my whole body tingled with them. . . .

The next year I took French. . . . But French had changed too. You had to speak the wretched language, not just recite verbs. . . . Plays were performed (at the vacation course) without introduction or explanation in English—like Sartre's 'Huis Clos'. I was fascinated and appalled at the idea of hell being a cycle of constant small cruelties inflicted by one person on another and repeated through all eternity. This was part of another revolution in my mind and outlook, prompted not by reflection on my own experience (or not that alone), but by my first encounter with one of the great intellectual philosophical movements of the century—existentialism. . . .

'L'absurde', I discovered, was a name for the anguish of modern man who wants to live for ever but can no longer believe he will go to heaven when he dies. From there I followed them to 'moi, c'est mon projet': my life is my own, it is all I have; mine—since God will no longer take it for me—is the responsibility to find its meaning, to become (as they put it) 'authentic'. . . .

Reading and learning, constructing essays, took over from the writing of stories and poems as my secret life, to be cherished but not talked about. . . .

I turned forty, and though I hadn't taken much account of such landmarks—even twenty-one had not seemed especially significant—I did find, in the years of the early forties, that again and again I looked at my life more consciously and critically. For the first time it occurred to me that I would not after all do everything—become the good pianist I'd not managed to be, compose piano music, take up drawing, neglected since my teens, be a scholar instead of the dilettante I felt I was, even become a brilliant conversationalist, not someone seized by vagueness and confusion at crucial moments. And, of course, be a writer. Write poems. Even that had slipped away, and I'd never done it so it mattered anyway. I had not in fact published a single poem, ever.

I talked to Trevor about some of these realisations, and found he had them too, though the details were different. We did still, though less often now, have peaceful, engrossed conversations that weren't about school or headmastering or PPTA or problems. . . .

Trevor and I could still occasionally find a shared point of view, but there were more and more currents and fluctuations in my mind, and undoubtedly in Trevor's, which we kept to ourselves. For one thing the deep discontent I had felt during his recovery from his illness remained unresolved. Probably more significantly, the Greytown years represented for me some loss of ground: if marriage is a bargain, a tension, a constructive mechanism to contain the 'battle of the sexes', ours had begun to shift its axis. The two poles between which we moved in orbit were 'home' and 'school' as separate enterprises. In the four years we'd lived above the chemist's shop, 'school' had captured a good deal of territory, which I had been powerless to hold. Partly of course this was because the older children actually joined that camp, if camp it was. . . .

At the same time, whether anyone knew it or not, I was making intellectual journeys of my own. In those years I entered a larger world, though I wouldn't have claimed I had any sort of foothold in it. I went on reading feminist writers, so knew that my lowly status in the family was one that millions of women shared with me. My literature study in both English and French had opened up new philosophical vistas, and in an odd way I felt at home with these discoveries. . . .

In January, having for two years avoided applying for headmasters' jobs, Trevor returned to the race and was appointed principal of Huntly College in the Waikato. I had tried hard to persuade him to consider other possibilities, especially lectureships at teachers colleges. . . . I remained much more wary than he about the warning inherent in the Opunake crisis. We left Greytown in the May holidays.

Evidence of the elevated status we were to enjoy in Huntly came as soon as we arrived. We were installed in the town's chief hotel while our house was being freshly painted. . . . We laughed a lot, we fancied ourselves; apparently there was advantage for everyone in this dreaded headmastering. . . .

[I]t was an ugly town, with a crabbed and ill-tempered image of itself; mining villages surrounded it and provided some of its money—it was quite a wealthy place—but it had failed to develop the civic pride we had grown used to in Greytown. There we had been received with congratulations for having chosen our location so well; here, characteristically, people we met began with, 'Did you have to come?' or 'We're only here for a while' or, more concisely, 'The money's good.' . . .

After our move to Greytown I'd taken six months or more to establish even the most rudimentary sense that I belonged. Every new person, every occasion or event, seemed to have nothing to do with me, even if I was publicly welcomed and officially included. . . . [M]y spirit, my real self, wasn't there. It floated in a forlorn limbo between some lost region and a landing not yet made. In Huntly I found the same dissociation—a greater one, in fact, because this community was much less coherent than Greytown and therefore colder, less spontaneous. . . .

I had been so engrossed in my extramural studies I was in no mind to wait a whole year, or even part of one, to make my approaches to the new university at Waikato. . . . I hastened to address myself to the university officials; the first term was over, I had the remaining two to cover a full year's work. I was sure I could manage this easily and begged to be admitted, Stage III English my particular goal.

'Professor Sewell is not here today,' I was told. . . .

Eagerly I drove the twenty miles from Huntly the following afternoon; it would not do to keep the Professor of English—the first in the new university—waiting a single moment. Alas, I didn't. Professor Sewell wasn't there. I made another appointment, again dashed across the farmlands of the rural end of River Road . . . but once more he hadn't appeared. The expressionless secretary gave me his home address.

I knocked at the door of a small prefab in a settlement of such places, gathered together for new university staff. It was a fine morning. The ground was bare, the whole suburb (as it was called) was like a refugee camp; it could have been put down by helicopter the day before. The person who opened the door was a slight, elderly man with the most enormous luminous eyes I had ever seen. Intelligence, prescience floated in their blue depths. He drew me in and began to talk of philosophers. . . .

As for courses at Waikato, yes yes, naturally I must be enrolled; he would tell the Board of Studies to waive the late fee. The question of getting the work done—no, I must not be tiresome, he could see I'd be able to do the work in two terms . . . the only thing was, it was clearly difficult to come to lectures from Huntly: I must attend only his. No others. He would arrange it. Eventually we had to have lunch. But we had drunk several glasses of gin and, according to the bottle, tonic water; something must be found to eat. I opened a cupboard. Empty bottles. Another, the same. Finally I found a tin of toheroa soup and heated it in a small saucepan; there was no bread or anything, we just ate the soup. . . .

I did go to Arthur's* lectures, racing into town in the afternoons (they were held late to accommodate teachers who were finishing 'old' degrees). They were thrilling in the way some at Massey had been, but there was a new ingredient, an emotional undertow that I'd never encountered before, yet which matched perfectly my own response to what I read. Great writing didn't merely send the horizons of your mind shooting off into the distance, it could break your heart as well. When Professor Sewell lectured on John Donne's poetry I wept, and, incredibly, so did he, at the vastness of the tremulous new world opened by the Elizabethan giant. And also, he told me later, at his own eloquence. I'd never met anyone the least like this before; he brought a cultivated European sensibility to his scholarship, but there was a quick tenderness in him too; and with all this he was a show-off, a clown, a rogue. An unholy delight of a man.

I would go and talk to him in his room before and after the lectures; I could not get enough of his delectable, fastidious talk, extraordinarily funny but deeply serious at the same time. . . .

---

* Arthur Sewell. Ed.

When I graduated—the English and French courses were the final pieces in the mosaic of my BA—I went to dress, in the robes one hired from the Federation of University Women, in the newly established Founders Theatre. (The year before, Waikato graduation had been held on the campus in a tent.) Arthur came downstairs, wearing his own august regalia, pressed through the crowd in the women's dressing room and kissed me. My first congratulations, too precious to speak of to anyone. Others behaved correctly and waited till the degrees were actually conferred.

Alcohol played part in our taking increasingly separate directions, Trevor and I, in the short, sharply eventful time we spent in Huntly. It was a businessman's town, and its prominent citizens—those who controlled such bodies as the college board of governors—were commercially thrusting; they lived well, some of them drank heavily and in their company so did he. . . .

Hamilton itself was said to be a centre of commerce rather than culture— 'the fastest growing commercial centre in the Southern Hemisphere'. However—and this was my special luck—there *was* the university. There I began to explore the possibilities of a life that I might choose for myself, independently of my family; there too I made the only friends who mattered in the time I lived in the Waikato. . . .

[T]his recovering of a separate self, particularly in a student environment, did often seem like going right back to where I'd left off being 'just a kid' and responsible only for myself. Of course my family experience was vital and central, I had grown up in it, and was still responsible for a widening circle of others beyond myself. And yet, curiously, some part of me had got left behind. Here it was, the childish creature still alive in me, doubled up with laughter, barely able to stand, on the pavement outside Barbara's Hamilton house, because her dog had bitten the seat out of Robert's trousers and quite a piece out of his bottom too. Robert (pronounced Robair in the French manner) was a young friend who on better days joined in our rather adolescent pleasures and the ludicrous enactments of our conversation exercises. . . .

The disturbances that wracked Trevor and me affected everyone.

What had happened was no less remarkable than the transformation in him that day in New Plymouth when he got the job in Opunake. The illness that took hold of him with such extraordinary suddenness had remained with me as an evil ghost, though on one level his acceptance of a new job seemed to mark its final demise. . . . If I'd thought that the predatory monster of illness had reached out to grab me before, it was nothing to what it did now. It—whatever 'it' meant—now took over Trevor's whole personality, at least when he was not at school. Instead of the gentle, affectionate (if preoccupied) person I'd known, the man who came home in the evening was angry, peremptory, abusive. At the dinner table he talked insistently, scoffing at what I produced as opinions . . . as though I was too stupid to be answered at all. This was inconceivable—and, I found, unmanageable. I raged at myself as much as at him, but nothing seemed to dislodge the alien creature that had taken possession of his personality, nor give me any authority to counter it.

Everywhere I turned hurt and disappointment seemed to lie in wait. . . . What was happening, of course, was that both of us were changing, and neither could forgive the betrayal implicit in the change. Nor could we understand the process. Trevor's presence at home was more often than not an incomprehensible punishment; I irritated and disappointed him at every turn. Some such puzzlement and pain must have been enacted in a thousand other households, at a time when women were looking for opportunities and occupations they had never been allowed to have, or even to hope for. There must have been men everywhere who, like Trevor, expected in their most successful years an unquestioning and increasingly deferential loyalty from their wives and found instead that even what they had was slipping away from them.

It wasn't merely the question of whether women worked at jobs that took them away from home. The tensions lay far deeper, in the very bones of the shared body of marriage—and ours, like many others no doubt, was stiff with old habits. Changes hurt. When I said I wanted to look for achievements of my own, Trevor's reply was probably typical: 'Your satisfaction is in what I do.' Yet when I did begin my paid work as a teacher, he was pleased with the results; he didn't particularly oppose my university work nor the trips to Hamilton. In fact, had we been able to see it, our separate lives, of action and experiment and challenge, worked for us both. It was what we shared that had gone badly astray, and neither of us could understand why. . . .

I seemed to have lost a whole person, one I'd loved and

depended on for almost all my adult life; home itself, the place where I'd always so intensely belonged, was no longer the haven that kept me safe, nor the adventure that gave me my direction. It had become hostile, even dangerous, a place where I was abused for wrongs I had no idea I'd committed. . . .

I reflected on the wider question of how people decided the direction of their lives when (in their forties, as we'd said) it became entirely their own affair. I remembered the phase 'reverting to type' that I'd learnt at training college: in the middle of your life you tended to become the person you most fundamentally were, however this had been disguised or overlaid in your youth. I began to think of myself as not naturally submissive: the habit of wifely accommodation which I had taken for granted seemed after all to be a thing of the times; history now encouraged me to throw it off. Perhaps—a stunning idea—we had *both* been betrayed by the old conventions, Trevor into a kind of authority he didn't like or want, I into a humility that didn't fit my inclinations. . . .

I saw an entirely different way of looking at the world, freer, more truthful, more demanding, but also more pleasurable. It came with knowing Arthur and others at the university, and through my explorations in English and French literature, and the glimpses they gave me of a humane European tradition. . . .

Occasionally I saw with painful clarity how much I had helped to construct the system of beliefs which now imprisoned Trevor, and from which I could escape. Then I'd lose that quick glimpse and think: now is now. If I fitted that mould, I fit this one too.

I joined some women's groups. I gave talks about self-determination, harnessed my knowledge of existentialism, the philosophy of personal responsibility, I held forth. . . .

There were few enough occasions when the privileges given to people like me, wives of public figures, could be said to be a pleasure. I presented prizes, of course; I attended official afternoon teas at school and parties given by board members; I organised staff parties myself. I made conversation, I dressed decently in suits and pleated skirts . . . but my heart was not in it. The place where I was saying what I really thought was quite different, and known to nobody, not even my new friends at the university.

In the early afternoons, with Mungo the dog in the car, I drove down to a place by the lake where there was quiet water, trees, no people. Mungo ran about and snuffled in the grass, and I, for the first time with absolute seriousness, wrote poems. On and on, a great many of them. It was as though some voice in me said at last: 'To hell with it all, this is what I want to do'—and I did it. Many of them had careful rhyme schemes, formal structures, all were dense, tightly packed, full of meanings. They were not in the least 'confessional' (not that I knew the word), but I was aware that my very real unhappiness had a good deal to do with the urgency with which I wrote.

I bought an ancient typewriter, tiered like a grandstand, and typed them out. Some I sent to Pat Lawn who was by now the secretary of the English Department at Victoria University in Wellington, and asked her to type them decently. Perhaps I secretly hoped she would do more than that; anyway, without asking, she did show them to Don McKenzie, a lecturer on the staff. I was overwhelmed, and ecstatic, to get the poems back with detailed comments written in that august hand. If he praised poems—and he did—I saw them thereafter in letters of gold; if he criticised (and he did so intelligently—'echoes of Eliot . . .') I was at once prepared to read an entire literature to understand my flaw. This was the first time . . . that I'd admitted my secret occupation. It was a mark of my new seriousness. . . .

For me the political movements of the time were beginning to coalesce into a general perception that personal freedom was always at the heart of political action. I had embraced principles all my life—Social Credit, diet reform, the labour movement—but only now, when the onset of my own middle age coincided, miraculously enough, with some sort of growing up of the world at large, did I realize that liberal theory was to do with how you actually *lived*. It was a matter of choosing for yourself, as the teaching of the women's movement was telling me I could, and I must.

The conference, every speech, every paper, was riveting. I had especially wanted to go because Jean-Paul Sartre, whose writings had shaped so much of my personal revolution, was to be there. Alas, he was not, but I eventually read his paper, 'On Genocide', and I did listen to Conor Cruise O'Brien, Felix Greene and the New Zealander John Male; I saw in a way I never had that important ideas needed knowledge as well as humanity, industry as much as vision. These were men of action; the utopian dreams I'd shared with my father long ago seemed now the merest preparation for this comprehensiveness.

I, of course, could have nothing to do with the Vietnam War, beyond marching in the street (which, tingling with the adventure of it, I did). But there were other things I could do. Another noisy public argument was about abortion, and women's 'right to choose'. In Huntly I was asked to take part in a debate on the subject; Professor Liley of the Auckland Medical School was to lead the team advocating the foetus's 'right to life'; I and a local lawyer spoke on the other side. This too seemed to take me back to an earlier, younger time; I had last debated when I was a training college student more than twenty years before. Virginia by this time was engaged to a young Wellington lawyer and they were home for the holidays; Fraser gave me useful legal facts to support my case. The next day the *Waikato Times* ran a headline. 'Mother of Six Favours Abortion', which made me shudder. A woman in town rang me and said, 'Even if nobody else will speak to you, I will still be your friend.' Politics, it seemed, had come home. . . .

Trevor's professional advancement followed the proper course. He had made a success of a difficult country school, stood well with teachers and inspectors; when Heretaunga College, one of the big city schools in the Hutt Valley, advertised for a new principal, he applied and was appointed. When he rang to tell us after the interview he sounded resigned rather than triumphant; unlike me, he would have liked to stay in small towns. . . .

The first thing we had to do in Upper Hutt was find our own house. Despite the turmoil of the last couple of years, I didn't consider living anywhere but at home. Even at the worst of times it hadn't occurred to me that I could go elsewhere. *Leave? Leave home?* Where would I live? And on what? We looked at houses.

Upper Hutt was a city; Trevor would be head of one of several large secondary schools; he would have money and position (land agents were deferential). Otherwise we could fend for ourselves. We had left behind the affectionate, inquisitive concern country people feel for their public figures; here nobody took much interest in us, which suited me because it released me from public duties as the headmaster's wife. We were better able to establish ourselves too because we had some money from Trevor's parents' estate and we could look for a presentable house. In fact it was more than that, it was elegant, spacious, shapely, by far the most beautiful house we'd ever occupied. . . .

[I]n a diary that by now I consistently kept, I grieved endlessly at the limitations of my life, acknowledged the ruin of my marriage. . . .

> All power has left me. Any good mental ferment acting on the words, faces, ideas that float in the pool of daily living has vanished. My interior life is thick and sluggish, composed of futile arguments about the hopelessness of fitting both myself and Trevor into the mean little territory our marriage has become. We dwindle in each other's company till we are like two wary little dogs circling around each other waiting for the moment of attack. The dust lies under our feet and the gay and beautiful world round us fades into a dull blur beyond the ends of vision. We stare and growl and tremble with fear and dislike. If only we could stand up to full height and be good, calm and compassionate people, as once we seemed to be. . . .

I . . . decided to go back to universtiy—Victoria this time—to do an MA. The excitement, the expansion, of my experience at Waikato were all repeated—but without Arthur. Not that Arthur himself disappeared, or my friendship with him; on the contrary, both flourished. . . .

Some months after our move to Heretaunga, Barbara Green, my friend of the French classes at Waikato, invited me to spend a weekend with her in Hamilton. . . . I accepted and went.

Barbara and I did indeed luxuriate in our theorising. 'Right action . . . is determined by her by a regard for absolute values as laid down by God' (I wrote in my diary), 'for me it's to do with human dignity, that's the basic value. . . .' We talked and talked. Then I went to visit Arthur. He was alone, very pleased to see me; he opened a bottle of wine. It was a clear evening in late October and the light beautifully faded as we sat near a window and talked, laughed, not in theories but using the stylish and profound nonsense I so enjoyed in his company. Nothing could have been a greater contrast with the harshness I'd left behind. I did not want it to end.

Then suddenly events took a new turn. Arthur too wanted me to stay, and for the first time I realised he wanted us to make love—a possibility which I saw had been with us ever since our first meeting, but which I'd been too naive, or too inexperienced, or too conventional to recognise or admit. And too married? That too. I had never seriously considered that such a thing could happen to me; now it had, and I was filled with excitement and dread. Most of all, I was simply frightened out of my wits. I insisted I must leave, I struggled to go; and in the end, foolishly and ingloriously, I ran out.

That evening Barbara took me to Frankton station to catch the night express. Arthur was there standing on the platform and proposed coming too, travelling through the night and returning to Hamilton in the morning. Again I panicked and rushed on to the train alone—then spent the entire journey restless and awake in an agony of doubt and confusion. For several weeks I wrestled with the question, looked at it in every way I could; and slowly, in a state of shocked, yet profoundly serious resolution, I decided to accept Arthur's poignant proposition.

He began to come and stay, a few days at a time, in the Heretaunga house, and was affectionately received by everyone. The long times I spent with him alone after the others had gone to school (on days when I didn't have to) had a particularly luminous quality. He was no ordinary friend and family visitor, nor did he pretend to be. What he could do was have natural friendships with everyone else in the family; he told me he liked them, his warmth wasn't policy. One evening he took me, Virginia and Michael, a friend of hers, to dinner in town. In the exceedingly decorous atmosphere of a superior restaurant he caused mild havoc—not at all by breaking any of the social codes, his manners were faultless. What he did was to engage the entire company—waiters, other guests, ourselves—in a mesmerising performance of wit and absurdity, a brilliant monologue, in which he drew each person by turn, as a high-class comedian invites the front row on to the stage. At the door when we left, he tapped Michael on the chest: 'You're a very nice young man,' he said, 'but next time we meet, please don't monopolise the entire conversation.'

He died a year or so later, after a crushingly painful cancer illness. I stayed a few days with him not long before his death, a time for quiet, searching conversations in what seemed, all day, to be a glow of evening light. Afterwards I missed him greatly. He was the first person to show me that the real truth about the world contained its most disgraceful parts as well as its most beautiful; he taught me not to be afraid of folly and egotism and greed, even cruelty—he himself could be cruel—because these taught you the courage without which love, the ultimate good, cannot survive. . . .

After my work at the university came to an end, I didn't really want to stay at school. I was sick of schools, I'd seen too much competitiveness, too much artificial authority, heard too many hours of dull, spiteful, claustrophobic staff room conversation. . . .

A job was advertised in the *Education Gazette* for the editorship for the Post-Primary Teachers *Journal;* I applied, prepared for the interview as for an exam, and got it. I realised that because it was part-time, most promising male English teachers would not apply, and that was a bit of luck. . . .

For the next six months I had so much energy I hardly knew what to do with it. This new job made me feel as I'd felt as a child when we stood in a doorway and pressed the backs of our hands outwards. We'd step out, and our hands would rise right above our heads entirely by themselves. My hands, my whole self, did that. If I was tired of teachers, I *loved* journalists; they were real, ordinary, direct; I as editor needed them, they equally needed me for the typesetting and processing I gave them, or to publish their articles. . . . I liked the way they talked too; many of them were openly left-wing and often very knowledgeable about politics. Nobody had to prepare a subject for classroom consumption or please educators who might fuss about the effect on the family, the school. . . . We said what we liked.

I was writing a good deal myself, and was also for the first time in touch with New Zealand writing, partly because writers sent poems and stories to the *Journal.* I encouraged them; I wanted the magazine to be read by others outside the teaching profession, even though the PPTA general secretary grumbled that I was making it into 'another *Landfall*'. I found a brilliant illustrator called Jim Gorman who worked in School Publications and had a quirky, original style. With him I published a poem a month (one per person, no more) for years. I also met Denis Glover.* The previous editor of the *Journal* had been Alister Taylor, a journalist with a marvellous rascally flair . . . he'd established a new journal called *Affairs*. It was for sale in schools, it gave a voice to the 'counter-culture' that arose out of the sixties revolution. Of special interest to me was a series of articles about New Zealand writers, which he invited me to write. I seemed to think if I couldn't be one, at least I could talk about them, and I accepted.

Some time after the article about Denis Glover was published,

---

* A New Zealand author. Ed.

I met the old gentleman at a party at Alister Taylor's house, and he decided, apparently, to 'take me up'. What that meant was that he invited me to edit the letters of A.R.D. Fairburn, having waited, he claimed, seventeen years for the right person to turn up. He was Fairburn's literary executor. . . .

I gave one of my finished pieces to Denis. It was a half-nonsensical address to 'Mister Dog', my reliable companion during forays to Trentham Park, the secret place in which I now did most of my writing. Working with him on the Fairburn letters entailed listening to many hours of tales about the two poets' shared past; we spent a great deal of time together. Sometimes he visited me at home, made friends with my family, and had once remarked that he loved each one, but Mungo most. This was the poem:

Mister Dog

He does not need to speak.
Words would be in any case too crude
too simple, plain, incompetent indeed
to give the least idea of his pride
his arrogance, his placid certitude
that he is not as foolish men are made.
He does not need to speak.

He would not want to speak.
For with conceit a certain kindness comes
for silly, fussy us who wave our arms
and shout and contradict, tell lies, make storms
in teacups; life's few simple aims
the body's eloquence expressly names.
He would not want to speak.

Thank God he'll never speak.
We love him for his inability;
our antics he approves, apparently.
But if he said with sudden honesty
our snarls and whines are all futility—
he'd have to go. We require servility.
Thank God he'll never speak.

Denis's response was yet another surprise. He said that if I had others like this he would help me to publish a volume of poems.

I could hardly wait. I took my battered manila folders to the office and as soon as the day's work was done I fell upon them, sifting, criticising, re-writing, trying various combinations of phrases and words, wondering what shaping idea might make thirty or forty poems into a collection. Sometimes I took the train from Upper Hutt and used the hour's journey morning and afternoon in the same way. . . .

But every day ended with going home. The miseries of my conflict there continued, though as time went on its character changed. For one thing Trevor began to feel more acutely the effects of my withdrawal from the support and scapegoat role we had together somehow shaped for me. One day when the house was full of young holiday visitors he asked me to go to his room and talk to him alone. I saw then that behind the bursts of rage he was himself badly shaken, and as miserable as I. He had come to hate going to school, he said. We talked a little of his family history.

The conventional bourgeois confidence of his family, which I had once so admired, had contained within it, as all families do, a particular psychological and social structure. A fiercely dominating father, a kindly mother sharing her weakness with a sensitive young son. We had talked of this before, but had not seen that it was likely to create for him an insoluble conflict about authority itself—that he could become a person who was driven towards authority and at the same time longed to be protected from it. This moment of rational speculation didn't really help us; rather it induced, in me at any rate, a forlorn sense that there was no way back to that good time, now irretrievably lost before we had begun to damage everything we touched together, as we now did.

As for my children, I had no such illuminations. Because my love for them did not diminish, I could easily imagine that all was well, that they wanted my life to expand, and were pleased to take a lesser place. Not so. There were disturbances I had never known before and could not explain, but in the end had to see as expressions of a deep disquiet, a sense of betrayal, of loss. The two youngest girls joined in escapades with rebellious kids who at their worst stole a car and drove it about Upper Hutt; it belonged to the mother of one of the boys and on the scale of teenage delinquent acts this was quite minor. Nevertheless, it did highlight a new rootlessness in the family, a dislocation in once stable loyalties. So tightly knit together had we been, my children and I, that it took them a very long time to recognise my unaccustomed eagerness for myself, my new ambitions, and still longer to accept them. Some did not manage to do it at all, but preserved a sense of grievance and betrayal which I in turn failed to recognise as the complex distress which the disintegration of a family causes. . . .

I loved my editor's job and the time given to work and friends of my own choosing. I must at times have seemed to Trevor and the children, at home and away, like Nero fiddling while the city burned. Nobody thought about the larger questions raised by Trevor's (and now my) devotion to work, though the new science of sociology was beginning to associate our generation with something called 'the work ethic'. We were puritans, we held to the secular morality of hard work and tangible success. In our children we had failed to allow for differences, other values, room for individual happiness without overt achievement. . . .

I did not seriously apply the new theories to my own case, or to the family that Trevor and I had created without knowing our rules would become discredited. I didn't see that 'the drive to achieve' (as one now knew to call it) had run right through the shaping of our family—nor that we had denied our children the chance to be ordinary, different, 'non-achieving'. . . .

Women's ambitions, I (and others) believed, were different from the old destructive drives that had so controlled the lives of men; we were broader, more humane, more likely to include family and personal claims in our schemes and policies. This was partly true too, but undeniably I was competitive myself in some of the old ways. I wanted my new self, but could not bear to leave the old, and neither I nor anyone else in the family could see the faintest glimmer of where we might be going. Or if, in fact, the lifelong 'we' of ourselves, so deeply embedded in our consciousness, would survive at all. . . .

I no longer wanted to be the kind of wife I'd been. I certainly couldn't be the same kind of parent; my children were leaving home, one every two years (as they'd arrived). By the time I went to Victoria as an MA student, only Stephanie and Katherine were still at school. . . .

As children grew away from home some parents did of course find they still 'had each other', but it was clear that we had not made the common life that would survive the end of the family years. The quarrels we now had were a way of saying, 'You've turned into someone I didn't expect, and I don't like', as though strangers (our real selves perhaps) had all the time been lying in wait to take us over when our children stopped holding us together. 'Who were the guardians . . .' (I asked in a poem I called 'The Reckoning') 'and who . . . the guarded?' While we were taking care of our children, how much were they protecting us from the selves we would eventually have to become? . . .

There are times in people's lives when the distance between visible surfaces and tumultuous realities within grows so wide that a break has to occur, and for us this happened with unexpected and appalling suddenness. Rachel had been at university for a year and a half, having chosen Auckland because it offered Art History. She'd taken a strictly academic course at school but was very interested in art and did small elegant drawings of her own. She lived there in a variety of flats with groups that formed, changed, dissolved, moved on; she appeared to spend a good deal of time with the older members of the Edmond family, all living in Auckland. The only time I felt any particular concern about her was when friends of Virginia's said on a holiday visit that Rachel was moving too quickly, taking shallow root in the more sophisticated milieu of older students, could lose touch with herself.

And this, apparently, she did. One night Virginia rang to say that Rachel had taken an overdose of sleeping pills and been taken to hospital. I was so unprepared for such an event that at first I could make no sense of it, and when with the help of friends and family she seemed restored, I wondered if it had actually taken place. . . .

Rachel had another crisis, and it was with Frances that I stood in the intensive care unit in Auckland Hospital as she came back to consciousness after another overdose. It was a terrible moment. She opened her eyes, looked at us and realised what had happened, turned away; her eyes filled with tears. She murmured, 'I don't want to be here.'

She was by then established in a fairly stable household in a pleasant old house in Ponsonby, and several times I stayed with her there. She came home too, she brought friends—Gerard, with whom she'd had a passionate love affair, and on whom she'd come to depend a good deal; Max, who also lived in the Jervois Road house and was the partner in a new relationship. Indeed she was surrounded by friends, but as I stood among a group of them round her bed as she recovered in hospital, I had a troubling glimpse of her not quite concentrating, of being adrift at the heart of her own networks, however affectionate they were. . . .

And then it happened again. She had a cold, spent a day at home, and when I came in from my day in the *Journal* office (which of course I wished I hadn't gone to) she was pale and silent, and had again the terrible hollow look in her eyes. 'I have to tell you it's come back, I can't help it,' she whispered. The next day I did stay home; we talked—unbelievably, and terrifyingly—of her wish to die. . . .

At the end of that day of desperate struggle she slipped out and bought some lethal stuff and took it; then she wandered, cold and distracted, about the park where we'd so often walked. . . . She died slowly in hospital over the next day and night. A young house surgeon, a friend of Frances's, talked to her after any of us, and said, 'I think you have really done it this time—are you sorry?' and Rachel had said no, she was glad.

By the time I knew that, I also knew that suicide attempts made after an apparent recovery almost always succeed. The patient has greater strength and uses it to follow the dictates of the inner voice that Rachel had heard, and wanted to obey, so many times before. . . .

This was a greater loss than any I had known, and a greater defeat. It had the effect, in some way permanently, of detaching me from all other experience; as though I said—and I did—that if something so precious could be swept away in a moment, what value could anything have? Every person, every moment, carried within itself its own temporariness, and the source of its own destruction.

Grief was work, I found, the hardest work I had ever done. Rules emerged, and once I understood each one I had to keep it. One was that I must never say, 'Why us? Why me?' because that led on to self-pity and turned me aside from the truth of this terrible event, and from Rachel herself. I came to believe that what I had to do, working from day to day, was to *learn* the truth, take it into myself, possess it, live with it, keep it in me. I thought of it some-times as a large, black, sharp-edged rock that would never change and never move. It stood between me and everything that was living and hopeful and happy; somehow I had to change, enlarge my understanding of the world to make room for it, so that living could go on with me in it, and Rachel, and her death. . . .

The reasoning, the thinking and shaping of these ideas—and of course my constant writing about it—was my occupation in the most central way. Every time I finished a poem about Rachel, or the experience of her death (and I wrote an enormous number), this had the effect of briefly—but only briefly—ordering the chaos in my mind. . . .

[T]here were times of absolute blackness, waves of unimaginable misery when I simply did not know what to do. The first and perhaps the worst of these came in the first few weeks; I woke up one morning with the full realisation burning right through me; I stood up, and it was as though my whole body was a sheet of pain; I stumbled into Trevor's room in some sort of reaching for someone to touch or tell. But he could do nothing. Of course he could do nothing, as I, now, could do nothing for him when he was in extremity; we had moved too far away from each other for there to be more than a generalised kindness for each to give. I was truly on my own—and came eventually to be surprised that I could have lived so long without fully knowing this before. . . .

[M]y own writing and reading gave me a sense of wider networks in which I could have some place. More and more I could at least come within sight of a new knowledge, that my loss was part of something much greater than myself. The more I felt the reality of this greater milieu, the better able I was to understand the impaired life I now had. At times I felt there was something miraculous about this realisation, as if I stood in a vast chamber filled with echoes of every human experience; there I was nothing, or close to nothing, and greatly at risk—and yet somehow in the right place, and at home. . . .

In Middle Air came out towards the end of the year. Fiona Kidman, a new and already important friend, had a first book too and we launched them together. At a party afterwards, at her house, the heightened emotions of the moment plunged me into hopeless tears, nevertheless I knew that however damaged, however incomplete I felt myself to be, this new work, my own writing, was the beginning of my next journey.

PART THREE

Canada

When life itself is the journey,
what use is a compass

Dorothy Kathleen Livesay

(1909–)

Dorothy Kathleen Livesay was born in Winnipeg, the only daughter of two Canadian journalists who moved to Toronto when Livesay was eleven, when her father became manager of the Canadian Press.

Educated at private girls' schools and the University of Toronto, where she received a B.A. in 1931, Livesay was influenced there by Shaw, Ibsen, and the feminist writings of Emma Goldman. Conscious of a deep attraction for a close woman school and college friend, Livesay had already thrown over most bourgeois standards during her undergraduate years. Reading French and Italian literature at Trinity College led her to Continental rather than British literary models. Leaving Toronto for Aix-en-Provence and Paris, where she earned a Diplôme d'études supérieures in 1932, Livesay's British radicalism was strengthened by her experience of Paris and French modernist culture, and by her first serious liaison with a fellow male student.

On her return to Toronto and the depths of the great Depression, Livesay, whose strongest interests were aesthetic and literary, nonetheless took a degree in Social Work at the University of Toronto, and spent several years working with the urban poor in Montreal and New Jersey, connecting in both settings with committed Communist organizers of the working class. With them she accepted the demands of socialist realism, a dogma that was to defer her serious creative career until the late 1930s.

In 1937, after a move to Vancouver, Livesay married Duncan Cameron McNair, entering a marriage in which her career aspirations were always in tension with the needs of her husband and two children. Her mature style as a poet emerged during the early forties, when a congenial circle of literary friends provided the links she needed to contemporary Canadian poetry. Deeply personal and lyrical in mood, her poetry broke free of conventional Canadian subjects, which struggled to adapt inherited British Romantic and Augustan modes to the Canadian experience. Livesay's concerns were social, announced with her striking "Call My People Home," a poem about the wartime treatment of Japanese Canadians. The work which followed mingled documentary realism, imagist fantasy, political polemic, and confessional styles, interweaving poetry and politics in a manner reminiscent of W. H. Auden and Stephen Spender.

Livesay's four volumes of verse led to the publication of her *Collected Poems* (1957) and a further expanded collection in 1972. A collection of short stories, *A Winnipeg Childhood*, followed in 1973. Fresh volumes of poetry appeared in 1975 and 1984, testimony to Livesay's prolific muse. Her poetry has earned two Governor General's awards for contributions to Canadian literature, and her total oeuvre of twenty-five published volumes has been recognized by numerous honorary degrees, and in 1987 by the Order of Canada.

Her memoirs reflect the many styles of the woman, shifting from personal conversation with the beloved woman student who was the focus of her emotional life during and after college, to brisk exposition about the experience of a social worker in Montreal in the 1930s, to inner monologue about her experience of abortion. The sections which deal with her years teaching in Zambia (1960–63) as a UNESCO worker mix lyrical responses to the natural environment with astringent political commentary, and wry observations about the exhilaration of her midlife experience of widowhood and freedom.

JOURNEY WITH MY SELVES:
A Memoir
1909–1963

Sometimes one's life, looked back upon, appears to be enclosed in a series of Chinese boxes. Each one taken by itself seems to have no significance; but when fitted, each within the next size, a pattern is visualized, there is a sense of completion. So it has been with my desire to live fully, overflowing into friendships of all kinds, and at the same time to put it down. Out of experience to create something new.

Recently I visited Erindale College and nearby St. Peter's Cemetery where my parents are buried. . . . I passed the spot where Mazo de la Roche had her studio cottage and had left her mark on a street sign: Jalna. Next to this, at 1219, I stopped and saw that my father's house, Woodlot, was still standing.

The house had not changed much from how I remembered it. All the original characteristics were in good repair. The clapboard was painted brown as it had been, though maybe a little darker, and the Georgian door with fan window above and glass panels either side was still trimmed with white. On the grounds I could see blooming the rare red trilliums, their common cousins the white, then the small violets, the bloodroot and the hepaticas, all of which my father had transplanted from the woods in Erindale. Forty, fifty years ago, my sister, Sophie, and I had helped my father do this by carrying slabs of shale from the cold creek to his parked car and then from his car to deposit them where he indicated so they could be used as the basis for his rose garden. Beyond were the trees that Sophie and I, former prairie children aged nine and eleven, had discovered and plunged into in the month of May, with its breathtaking cherry and apple blossoms. For us, then, the trees came to be almost as real as people; the maple, oak and cedar were as distant friends, but the slim silver birches were embraceable. On moonlit nights I used to walk closer to them and place my cheek against the bark to listen to the pulsing sap. It was after such nights of listening to the birches, now frail and tottering, and to the flutelike song of the whippoorwill that as a young girl I was ready to imagine stories and find the words for poems. . . .

Woodlot is where I had spent my weekends, away from Glen Mawr School and, later, Trinity College. Here I escaped from study to have free time to write or read at will. I had no household chores to do, no dishes to wash or beds to make, as there was always a housekeeper in charge. While I wrote or read, my father disappeared to his log cabin in the woods, away from the telephone and "the wimmin"; my mother sat in the sunroom writing poems or translating Ukrainian folk songs or working on a piece of freelance journalism, and my sister went sketching, taking the dog with her. Next door, in summer, Mazo de la Roche was writing the Jalna novels. It seemed to be an ideal country life, but the prim Ontario farming community looking rather askance at us, regarding us as "the mad Livesays." . . .

[A]utobiography, or memoirs, are not written to satisfy a secret personal urge. They are written by an actor who performs behind a mask. The aim must be to attract an audience. A formidable task; and one much akin to that of the novelist.

My perspective on events and people is undoubtedly lopsided, slanted, with many unavoidable gaps, tempered by my own early view of my parents, brought up as I was with so many inhibitions implanted by my mother and so many ideas of freedom urged by my father. It is small wonder I have found it hard to disclose my inner life to the public. But I am the sum of all these perspectives; what I hope to present, therefore, throughout these pages, is a series of selves, views of myself. . . .

I was born in Winnipeg on October 12, 1909, during the first snowstorm of the year. After my sister, Sophie, arrived three years later, we moved to Lipton Street, where we lived in a small two-storey white clapboard house in a lower-middle-class neighbourhood. The wooden sidewalks had been down long enough to require new boards sometimes, fresh-scented golden boards from the sawmill. Grass grew with difficulty on the narrow boulevard between the sidewalk and the paved road, and timid, spindly young elms had been planted at intervals, just near enough to the curb for the Eatons' horse to reach, stretching his neck to nibble the tender leaves. On this unprepossessing street my father had chosen a corner lot, which gave him some scope for his passion for fence building. Kitty-corner across the street was the west-end firehall, which housed those great grey stallions, ever ready, when the huge red doors sprung open, to do their daily rehearsal. In summertime I would sit safely on our front porch steps surrounded by flower beds. Inside this domain there were dazzling arrangements of poppy, bachelor's-button, sweet william; masses of portulaca and nasturtium, purple pools of pansy and the whole of this punctuated by the scent of mignonette. . . .

Father's flowers, however, left my sister and me with almost nowhere to play. . . . Only in one cool corner, next to the back porch, did we have any play space. Father made us a sandpile there, and later a slide built of heavy planks; a wide winter slide this, onto which pails of water were poured, only to freeze instantly into a glassy mirror. On frosty days, seated on tin trays, we were the envy of the neighbourhood, as we banged our way up and down this homemade rollercoaster. . . .

At a very early age I saw my words in print. My mother, who

wrote a column for the *Winnipeg Free Press,* occasionally quoted "Dorothy's Sayings." These ranged from the word plays I made, saying *wintersaults* instead of *somersaults*. . . .

Later, at five or six probably, I felt that my mother was sharing her work with me, getting me interested in what she was writing on the typewriter. When schoolchildren, especially those from Indian reserves and residential schools, began writing letters to her as a columnist, my mother urged them to write their stories, just as she had urged me to tell her some. These stories, too, were published, and when printed were cut out and kept in a scrapbook. . . .

I saw my parents busy at writing every day, and I was sometimes taken down by streetcar to the Free Press building where my father's office, the Western Associated Press, was installed. The pressroom, thundering away with typewriters and reporters wearing green eyeshades, gave me a feeling of identification with the outside world of adults. Especially when the ruddy-headed, gruff editor, John Dafoe, would pass by and pat me on the head. . . .

I do not remember the beginning of World War I, but my emotions were early affected by the feverish excitement. Perhaps that was the last time in our century when people approached war as a glamorous event. . . .

So it was, at long last, in 1918, that my father finally attained his heart's desire: he had been accepted as a war correspondent. By listening hard to grown-up conversations (without seeming to), one thing was clear to me: Father wasn't going to shoot with a gun; he would be safe enough; he was only going to write, not to fight. . . .

When we came from Winnipeg to Toronto in 1921, I was a naive twelve-year-old, alternately spoiled and neglected, living in my own imaginative retreat. Because I was supposed to be high-strung, I had had little formal education. . . .

When we settled in Toronto our parents made the decision to send us to a private school. Immediately, one had to be dressed properly, books had to be bought, school lunches were put on the bill. Every month when that school account arrived, my mother would go over it groaning, saying that we'd have to cut out the extras. . . .

In consequence, I think, I felt deprived, mean, drably dressed; the word *poor* became a real word. We were poor. And yet we lived in a middle-class neighbourhood and were supposed to be comfortably off. Although I continued to accept funds for my education, I felt "kept," and longed to earn my own living. . . .

It was small wonder that my parents sent me to a private girls' school rather than to the stream that would head for Harbord Collegiate. I would have an opportunity, they must have reasoned, to participate in the arts, and to get personal encouragement with writing. Besides, both my parents had been educated in private schools; their children must have the same opportunities. . . .

Undoubtedly it was the freedom to enjoy rural life, which my parents accepted as a human right, that developed in me a love of solitude and induced a poetic sensibility. Soon after our settling in Toronto, my father purchased nine acres of woodland in Clarkson. . . .

[M]y sister and I were free to explore the woods on our own, and the dog went along joyfully, chasing rabbits. The treasured place in Clarkson for us was Hammond's Wood, a valley below Erindale, where a small creek wound its way over stones. There might have been snake fences then, or barbed-wire fences for the cows, but we climbed over or crawled under these; there were no signs, as there are today, of "Trespassers Will Be Prosecuted" or "Private Property." We walked along the Credit River, or the shores of Lake Ontario, unimpeded. Mother, as I recall, never went for any real walks; she sauntered about over the grounds at Woodlot, looking for wildflowers, mushrooms and the birds that had been a part of her childhood in Compton, Quebec. In March, when the snow still lay on the ground, she instituted a miniature sugaring-off by boiling maple syrup and letting snow stiffen it until we could twist it around a fork. The early search for the first crocus on the Winnipeg prairie was transferred to the search for hepaticas and trilliums in the Ontario woods. . . .

[JFB*] implied that there was far too much fuss made about virginity; "It's so unrealistic," he said. Ironically, to prove his point, he gave me *Tess of the D'Urbervilles* to read. In such ways he cleared away my inhibitions long before I was ready to act on them.

My mother was an influence of the opposite kind. Once, looking through a volume of Michelangelo's prints my father had found in a secondhand store, she asked disgustedly: "What is so beautiful

* John Frederick Bligh Livesay, the author's father. Ed.

about nakedness? The human body is ugly, ugly!" As if to emphasize the fact, she wore shapeless clothes, her petticoat showed and
her stockings seemed always to have runs. Slovenly, my father
called her, to her face, and in front of us children.

A sense of family and individual conflicts dominated my teenage years in Toronto. It was only with my best friend, Gina, that I
felt at ease, free to speak out my real feelings concerning the institutions of family, religion and capitalism, from all of which I longed
to break free. My dream was to combine the childish belief in a
fairy-tale Prince Charming who would rescue me, Cinderella, from
the shackles of my life, with the mature desire for a purposeful feminist career as a novelist. . . .

During that first year of marriage, before I appeared on the
scene, FRL* kept up her freelance writing and her guided reading
program. Both she and JFB were extremely interested in the Canadian poetry of Roberts, Lampman and D. C. Scott. It is clear that in
the early years of their marriage, when my sister, Sophie, and I were
toddlers, there was an intellectual exchange of ideas between my
parents that was more important to them than the difficulties lying
dormant: her Victorian prudery and his sophisticated European
romanticism, which ran counter to his own strict Plymouth Breth-
ren upbringing.

At that time—the second decade of the century—Winnipeg was
a stimulating town and newspaper reporters were in the centre of it,
having access to all the cultural entertainments, the travelling
actors, singers and distinguished lecturers who came for one-night
stands. In addition, for my mother there was the Winnipeg
Women's Press Club where she met some fascinating feminist
friends—Cora Hind, Kennethe Haig, Valance Patriarche, Ruth
Cohen—and where Nellie McClung and Emily Murphy (Janey
Canuck) were already legendary. . . .

In the 1920s the stresses between my parents became more
marked. Mother often considered divorce, but in those days if a
woman left home she had no recourse. She might take the children,
but she would have no income. Legally, she was nowhere; so
divorce was out. I think it would have been very traumatic for me,
and probably for my younger sister, too, had FRL divorced my

---

* Florence Randal Livesay, the author's mother. Ed.

father. Nonetheless, it might have cleared up the growing antagonism between them if they had been separated. Sophie and I might have had a better chance to know each parent in their own realm, rather than in the household with all the bickering. . . .

The concept of wife as helpmeet was strong in the days at the beginning of the century. Yet my mother had refused to say the word "obey" in the Anglican marriage service. She would love and honour but not obey her husband. As a student, I admired her for having taken this stand, but I saw, all too clearly, that every day she was obliged to subscribe to her husband's needs.

My mother was torn between her very traditional, conservative, provincial, Protestant upbringing and her desire to become a person in her own right; my father was an emigrant drifter who rejected the old world and sought a new start in a democratic society where women would be the equal of men and where there was no shame in being called a radical, one who goes to the root of things. Life's frustrations developed from the conflict between his idealism and the raw individualism, the jockeying for power in the Canadian newspaper world. . . .

"Never trust a person with brown eyes," my father pronounced. Yet later he was charmed by my young friend Gina and her brown eyes. . . .

Ah, Gina, is it only after seventy years of living that I begin to understand you? We met when we were about twelve, in the spring of 1921. The place was Clarkson, Ontario, a small village on the highway between Toronto and Hamilton. Both your parents and mine were using the Blue Dragon Inn at Clarkson as a place to stay pending househunting in Toronto. . . .

I was a timid, lonely child, somewhat at a loss because of the uprooting from Winnipeg where I had had one close friend, or chum, as we called her. Here in an Ontario village I knew no one, did not know how to make friends, and at the one-roomed country school the older children scared me. . . .

And then, for two or three weekends, there you were! Tall, thin, boyishly built with silver-blonde short hair: a gamine, your fair and rosy skin contrasting with your brown eyes, soft as velvet and deep as a woodland stream. But what a tomboy you were! I had never met a girl like you, so rough, forcing me to wrestle with you as you seized hold of my arms. Only two years later, when we ended up in the same girls' school, did I discover the other side of your nature: sylphlike, darting through woodlands, leaping over streams, delighting to find rare wildflowers and birds. And reading poetry all the time, as I was. . . .

We must have been an incongruous pair, you so tall and slim and I broader and shorter but with disproportionately long legs and arms. By the time we were in the upper fifth, we were very conscious of our bodies and uncomfortable with them. No matter how much the healthy and hearty gym teacher told us that menstruation was normal—"it proves you have entered into womanhood, not a time for misery"—we knew differently. Some girls suffered more than others and I was one of those. You were, as always, stoical.

During this period of late adolescence I was probably only aware of delight in your companionship. But you have tape-recorded what you experienced through participating in the Livesay household games. I remember how your own home life was strictly Victorian, with hours laid down for housework, study, shopping, piano practice, whereas my life must have seemed wildly bohemian. . . .

I recollect my shock when you went so far as to wear only boys' striped cotton shorts instead of rayon panties. Of course we had to wear skirts, well below the knee; but we would have revelled in the blue-jean era! Whatever clothes you wore, Gina, you always looked striking. Perhaps you don't remember how, by the time we were in the sixth form and reading Michael Arlen's *The Green Hat* (read aloud to us, of all things, by our English teacher, Mary Jennison) you took on the role of femme fatale, wearing flared skirts, orange sweaters and, of course, a dashing green felt hat with a feather in it! At one point you even persuaded your parents to give you a white Russian wolfhound with which, on leash, you sauntered along Bloor Street between Markham and Spadina (such dizzying delights!). . . .

Soon afterwards you led a movement to have the school adopt uniforms, as did other private schools such as Havergal or Bishop Strachan. This involved wearing a white tailored blouse, a short navy-blue serge tunic and long black stockings. My mother objected to the expense involved but my father, the Englishman, emerged from his usual detachment in such matters to state that I should conform to the school pattern. This solution left me free from worry about my clothes. My hair, however, was still long, drawn back with a barrette, whereas the other girls went along with the trend and were bobbed. But my hair was the only part of my physical being that afforded me any satisfaction. It was fine and wavy, nut brown in colour, with golden lights when I dried it in the sun. My eyes did not please me, being neither dark blue nor grey but something in between. In the summertime my face and arms were heavily freckled. Fine gold hairs had begun to show above my upper lip. So on a frosty winter day as we walked home up Spadina, you cried out in glee, "Dee, you should see yourself—you've got a white moustache!" You were often disposed to put me down in this way, and loudly; but I developed a defence—laughter. . . .

We both loved the woods and the Ontario countryside—that was the great bond between us. Whereas our schoolmates would spend their Saturday afternoons skating or "going to the show," which was, in those days, the stock company theatre, you and I would take the streetcar to the top of Yonge Street and go walking in Hog's Hollow, or saunter in the spring rain over the Rosedale Bridge. The trees waving below in the ravine seemed themselves to be weeping green rain. Then, after my father had built Woodlot, the first half of a house-to-be in the Clarkson woods, you would manage to get permission from your very strict parents to spend some weekends with me, especially in spring or fall. . . .

[I]t was the shared poetry that meant the most to us emotionally. We memorized some of Shakespeare's songs and sonnets, Robert Herrick, Andrew Marvell and the poetry of the Georgians: Walter de la Mare, Humbert Wolfe, Edward Thomas (my favourite). Then we discovered the women: Elinor Wylie, Katherine Mansfield, Emily Dickinson. . . .

[T]here were only two of us who were mavericks in that sixth-form class of a dozen girls, we formed a solid and indestructible minority—an "underground" if you like—in a small girls' school that had always been stamped with gentility. . . .

It was an accepted part of life in a girls' school—even in Toronto—that one developed crushes on older girls or young teachers. . . . I still remember the sense of utter shattering of one's privacy, yet the exaltation derived therefrom, when we admitted to each other that we were in love with a fellow student. . . . [I]t was Julie, a new girl who came to Glen Mawr in our last, sixth year, who really aroused our awakening sexuality.

This was the year in which I had to study for honours matriculation, doing senior courses in English, French, Latin, German and modern history, as well as the horrors of algebra and geometry, for which both you and I had to take remedial coaching. So the tension of looming examinations was ever with us. . . .

The way out of this tension was to indulge in an infatuation or crush. It was quite natural that the nearest object was a girl, perhaps a year older than we were, and very sophisticated. Julie belonged to one of Toronto's old families living in Rosedale. She told us that her parents had broken up, that she had had a mysterious illness, and that she had been sent to this boarding school for her finishing off before she would become a deb and enter the exclusive rounds of Toronto society. All this of course added to Julie's fascination. . . .

That summer, when we were both getting prepared to attend university, marked the beginning of the end of our intense friendship. When I went to Trinity College, my courses, classmates and professors were so differently orientated from scientific ones at the pre-med level that we would only see each other perhaps on a Saturday afternoon, going for a walk in the ravine or sitting in your rooming-house digs listening to Beethoven's Fifth on your portable gramophone. Once a week at Convocation Hall there was an organ recital where we went together to listen to Bach, Haydn and Mozart. . . .

By our second university year something else was happening to your emotional life that distressed me deeply. You were in love with a camp counsellor and had been on the verge of a lesbian relationship that summer. I hated to think of it. And now, on campus, you were going around with a known lesbian crowd. True, they were not regarded with the sense of taboo associated with "fairies"—our name for homosexuals. It was a peculiarity of women's state that there were no laws prohibiting them from cohabiting. Perhaps this was because women did not pervert children, as it was believed men did? In any case, *The Well of Loneliness* was *the* book, yet it did not help me to accept your new role. This caused a rift. . . .

By my fourth year we were friends again, but on a different level. You had left home and were living in rooms at the Old Elm on Harbord Street. This was a "tearoom" frequented by the students of Trinity College—the red-brick men's residence across the street. In this curious way you and I, Gina, moved for the first time with the same crowd. Literary and political discussions, Chianti parties, sleigh-riding on moonlit snowy nights when we sang to the jingling of the horses' bells—these were some of the delights. By now you had broken with your lesbian circle and were ready to take on the men. Alas for Dee! For as soon as there seemed to be a young man interested in me, the time came to introduce him to you. And there was no way I could be your rival. You were like a rocket among candles: lithe, sinuous, graceful. Your pale silver-gold hair worn longer than a bob, your brown eyes the colour of a river in sunlight, your rose-petal skin: how do I find the words to describe the young woman you had become? You were avid for love and sex and you thought of me as a sister in whom you could always confide. . . .

[Livesay spent her junior year at the Sorbonne, and began living with a fellow student of modern languages.]

[W]e came to set up housekeeping together on boulevard Saint-Germain, in a sixth-floor two-roomed flat. In between lovemaking and eating in cheap restaurants on the Boul Mich (remember the automats?) we started in seriously to work at our *diplômes,* researching every day at the Bibliothèque Nationale or the Ste-Geneviève, a wonderfully happy and stimulating time, isolated though it was from friends and colleagues. . . .

It is true that I blossomed but it was also true that my sexual needs were stronger than those of my partner. So the tensions grew if we were together too long—as on weekends. But we did begin to take a great interest in the French political scene. Tony was reading Marx and Engels and applying their theories to the current collapse of the capitalist system: unemployment, strikes and the buildup towards war, Hitler's goose-stepping youth. We read *L'Humanité* daily and began to go to rallies of the left where we witnessed police brutality against the organized and unemployed workers. On the five-mile parade commemorating the Paris Commune I heard for the first time the voices of young *blouses bleues* chanting their Brechtian slogans, songs and skits. Although I was writing love poems at the time (published years later as *The Garden of Love*) my social conscience was roused. I felt that a poem must speak more about the times. My first longer effort was entitled "Père-Lachaise" (the name of the great Paris cemetery where the 1871 martyrs are buried). But in between these emotional "highs" we were both working doggedly at our Sorbonne theses.

Before the winter was over we decided to live separately again. Tony, I discovered, did not want an adoring, mothering love-mate.

He thought I should learn to "stand on my own pins." I know he was right, but at the time I could not accept an independent feminist role. . . . But then he had to take off for Italy. . . . When Tony returned from the south, he was not a little disconcerted by my new milieu, my growing independence and my socializing with friends of the Levys, mostly Canadian artists and graduate students like Leon Edel. However, for our last month in Paris, May to June 1932, Tony persuaded me to return to him. This time we found a suite far from the student world, on the east side, the working-class area of Ménilmontant. At home, writing our theses, we saw no one but each other. For that short time it was blissful rather than claustrophobic. I had a scare about being pregnant. . . . We were still deeply devoted when we set sail for Canada, bearing high marks from the Sorbonne (indeed, Professor Cazamian wanted me to stay on and do a *Doctorat d'état*). But at home in Canada, as you, Gina, were finding out, the Depression had struck and there were no more funds available from our parents for student travel. We had made it, just by the skin of our teeth!

That was a stormy summer, back living with my parents at Woodlot, or staying alone part of the week in their Toronto house, 20 Rosemount, near St. Clair. . . . We became members of the Progressive Arts Club. . . . There I learned how to write agitprop for the magazine *Masses*. We were by now firmly attached to the party line and adamantly rebellious against our parents and their conservative views. . . . But before Christmas I had to face the fact that Tony had definitely broken off our relationship. . . . For I was still desperately trying to see and talk with Tony—only to discover that he was having an affair with you. . . . [I]n the autumn of 1933, I left Toronto and went with Maysie to Montreal to work in a Protestant family welfare bureau as an apprentice caseworker.

There we were thrust into the depths of the Depression under the most repressive regime in Canada. Montreal's unemployed were in daily confrontation with Taschereau and the laws of R. B. Bennett's Section 98. This experience was the most traumatic of my life up until then. . . . That . . . year . . . I was promoted from the Young Communist League to membership in the Communist Party, one of many like-minded young people who wanted to build the movement against war and fascism. The policy in 1934–35 was still that of a United Front of workers and progressives from the middle class. Being one of the latter I was chosen to contact organizations such as the YMCA, YMHA, church groups and welfare groups with a view to setting up a youth peace movement in Canada. . . .

I spent the summer months engaged in the same activist directions as before, but with an added sort of experience as organizer-secretary for an office and shoe salesman's union. . . .

. . . 1935–36, with Spain being murdered by Franco, working for that magazine gave me my first real opportunity to see myself in print, speaking out on the ills of the Depression. I travelled west, through Manitoba, Saskatchewan and Alberta to British Columbia, writing documentary reports about strikes, lockouts, demonstrations by the unemployed. All during those years I was in the main writing prose, documentary realism. . . .

I never returned east to live. As a government-employed social worker in Vancouver I married an unemployed Scot, Duncan Macnair, who had been helping me sell subscriptions to *New Frontier*. He was thirteen years older than I. Eventually he got a job and I lost mine.

Nineteen thirty-eight must have been the watershed of our youth. What we had worked for and dreamed it could lead into was a decade without war, without dictatorship, when man's urge for power and destruction might be curbed for good. Instead, the scene was dominated by Mussolini, Franco, Hitler and Stalin. . . . [W]hen the phony war ended, when Stalin and Churchill formed their united front, when in Canada our friends and comrades were released from jail, we were all in favour of stopping Hitler. . . .

I stayed at home, with a son born in 1940 and a daughter in 1942. . . .

By the time I was twelve, I had begun to find it a dizzying experience to write a verse and have it rhyme. But I did not want my mother to see it. Somehow the experience was my own, hidden in the back of my bureau drawer and not to be shared. However, one day when I was about thirteen, I came home from school to find FRL flourishing scraps of paper. "Why, Dorothy, these are real poems!" . . .

By the time I was sixteen, I had become ambitious enough to send out poems myself, to the *Canadian Magazine, Saturday Night,* the *Canadian Forum* and to the Canadian Authors' Association. It must be said on FRL's behalf that she did not change the sense or the imagery of my poems, she only sought to emphasize the requirements of metre and the delights of repetitive verse forms. She herself loved Robert Herrick's poetry and the French forms: rondeau, rondel and triolet. I tried them out to please her, but I was not good at them. Instead, since Mother subscribed to *Poetry: Chicago* (which had published her poems and her Ukrainian translations), I became more interested in free verse and the imagist movement. I remember being particularly attracted to Richard Aldington, H.D., Ezra Pound and Amy Lowell's renditions from the Chinese. . . .

All my knowledge of love came from books. In this sense my father had not failed me. Indeed, he was probably the only parent in the city of Toronto in the twenties who combined a passion for Henry James with a passion for women novelists: Jane Austen, Charlotte Brontë rather than Emily, Virginia Woolf and Katherine Mansfield. It was a somewhat precious, specialized reading. The social frustrations women faced in the nineteenth century were no less galling than the social freedoms of the twentieth; in neither case could a woman be wholly a human being. For an Englishman, my father was unusually sensitive to this problem. . . .

Charlotte Brontë's life filled me with the greatest curiosity. The isolated world surrounded by illness and death paralleled her passionate desire to live, to love and to be loved. What she underwent at the hands of the Belgian schoolmaster who was not great enough to give in return; or at the hands of her father, so adamant against her marriage to anyone; and, finally, in her fortieth year, as wife for a few months: all this pain burdened and yet enriched the novels: they set me on fire. . . .

From the lyric period of my youth, undoubtedly my best, most finished poems were in *Signpost*, my second book, published in 1932. These poems came from the intensity of unrequited love; it was an infatuation rather than a realistic affair. It is evident from his correspondence that my father pushed for the publication of this book, also. *Signpost* did not appear, however, until I was away from Canada for a second time in France.

E. J. Pratt was probably the Canadian poet I most admired when I was a fledgling. At Victoria College, University of Toronto, he had been given a teaching position in the English department, under Professor Pelham Edgar. The congenial atmosphere in the late 1920s must have afforded him more leisure time for writing, no longer in the style of his first book, *Newfoundland Poems*, but in mock-epic style. . . .

It would seem that there are two kinds of sexual love a woman experiences. One is physical, the electric shock of touch; the other is mental, "the idea of the person." When these two forces are joined, when a woman can respond to both, in one man, then the experience is one of great wonder. But so often the problem is: "Either this, or that." Or else, given that the woman marries a man who provides full completion, familiarity tends to breed contempt. The "idea of the person" becomes somewhat worn out, threadbare: in daily living a new "person" emerges and what was simply the man's shadow takes on flesh, becomes his twin, his *doppelgänger*. This creature hangs around her neck! Perhaps therefore the happiest marriages may be those of the sailor or the fisherman, for absence revives the pristine image and when the man returns from his voyaging he is greeted as when he first came into her arms.

In my own experience of love this problem has been paramount. Too often I have been forced to choose between "either-or"; too often I have yearned for wholeness. Physical satisfaction without real love is the least to be desired. Invariably if a situation has started with the physical I begin to "fall in love," to seek the other as a person. And so, though there was a time when free love was much in fashion and marriage was too expensive, I have since found it wiser to forgo having a relationship merely for the sake of sexual pleasure. When circumstances force a woman to live alone, the "ideal" love is the better. For absence and abstinence, as Emily Dickinson and Charlotte Brontë could verify, are stimulants to passion. A woman *feels* beloved. Although she may be frustrated physically, she moves in happiness. Under such circumstances I believe she can be truly creative as an artist. . . .

[W]hen I was thirteen or fourteen and again when I was nineteen, I had a fleeting experience with "touch." The first one was not with a boy my own age, but with a small child. There was a family of cousins with young children whom I used to look after sometimes. I remember that young Bobbie, about five years old, had elected to take me on a walk back of a farm in that farming country I loved, around Cooksville. I don't know why we two were the only ones going for a walk, but it must have been a fine spring day because I remember the dazzling new green leaves on the poplars, and the wind shaking them, and clouds running races up the sky. We ran, too, Bobbie and I; and when I had stopped chasing him, he came to walk beside me and put his hand into mine. It was then that the shock came. An electric current, it seemed, passed from the pressure of his fingers against my palm, up through my arm, shaking my whole being. That sense of communication with another gave me a glimpse of what might come, sometime. I did not know how.

The next experience was equally unexpected, and more strange. I had come from France, in the spring of 1930, to visit my father's boyhood home on the Isle of Wight. We visited not only Ventnor . . . but also the environs, hiking all day long across the Downs, or along the cliffs to Shanklin via Sandrock Spring, where his aunt, the painter, had lived. And on most of these walks a relative, Pam, a year younger than I, came along with us. She was outdoorish, lean and sturdily built, dark-eyed and vivacious with that wonderful rose complexion that English girls possess. We had never met before but she looked up to me with some admiration, I suspect, because I was a Canadian and because I had been away from home and to a French university. Her enthusiasm for the family history and her love of the sea and the cliffs were as intense as my father's. On one of our excursions we ended up at a comfortable old inn set on a lonely headland. We stayed there the night. My father had a room to himself whilst Pam and I shared an upper bedroom, looking out to sea. After a British "tea" we were tired from the long day's hike and crawled into the double bed early. But we were no sooner in bed than we grew awake, alert, laughing and chattering as girls do. When finally there was a lull, Pam said softly: "I'm so glad you came, Dee." And she laid her hand on my belly.

Tremors seized me. Then they seized her. And before I knew it I was also stroking and caressing her limbs, her breasts; kissing her and leaning to hold her close, body to body. For me it was an utterly new sensation. I cannot speak for her, and I rather suspect that since she had come from an English boarding school she already knew something of these pleasures. But for me, heaven opened. I became aware that my body had always longed for another's body; that it experienced completion when touching the other. That was all: just a most delicate touching, pressing, caressing. Then it was over; we must, finally, have slept. In the morning we made no reference to it. . . .

As I reread these passages I ask: is that the whole truth? And I am bound to say, no! For I do remember a short conversation with Pam the next day, in which she expressed her devotion to me and in which I (feeling older and wiser) advised her that we should forget about the night we had spent together: it was not a good thing. In saying this, I hurt her; I felt myself to be cruel. Yet I believe I took this stand from lack of understanding, lack of knowledge. Love is wisdom; and I had not enough love in me, then, to be wise. . . .

Throughout my last year I had been meeting some of the young men who had graduated from the *Varsity* staff and had gone into newspaper work, some with Canadian Press, others on local news-papers. Such were Nathaniel Benson, Paddy Ryan and others. This was a much "tougher" crowd than the university people I had known. Their main interest, weekends, was drinking and having parties. They each had a girl, more or less permanent, and I drifted somehow into being the girl who went with one I shall call Hugh. He was a very different sort from the students I had known: older, from the prairies, he had known the rough-and-tumble of making his own way. Yet he was very interested in politics, as I was begin-ning to be, and had studied some of the theories of the United Farmers, the OBU (One Big Union) and finally of the CCF. Hugh's problem was that he was inarticulate; rather clumsy, ungainly, he was often tongue-tied. He was twenty-eight or twenty-nine when I knew him, just a reporter on a country-town paper who had drifted aimlessly, wanted to settle down with a girl perhaps, but had no "dash." Rather, his virtues were the hidden ones of solidarity and loyalty. He was a man of silences, yet there was poetry in those silences. I sensed something of this, but though I liked Hugh very much as a friend, I felt no infatuation, no physical pull towards him. It was therefore a surprise to me (as well, I think, to him) that we began to spend those early summer weekends together; he took me to supper dances and canoeing on the Humber River. He was deferential to anything I took it into my head to do. And so eventu-ally, one night in our empty Toronto house, I took it into my head that I wanted to explore sex, deeply, and for the first time, and he was the one who could best guide me. He was surprised, taken aback, and I was completely unaware that a deflowering presented dangers to the male.

Strangely, it was a kind of pre-wedding night. "May I come up?" he asked. As in the initiations where the shaman is assigned to deflower the virgin, I went upstairs and undressed, lay on the only available double bed and covered myself with a sheet. Then he fol-lowed and slipped in beside me. I was trembling, but he soon quieted that. Then he pressed into me. After that we hardly slept at all. It was the opening for me of a whole new world of sensation and wonder, which I recorded much later in the poem "Comrade." At one point, I remember he was hungry. We ran downstairs naked, only to find oranges in the icebox but nothing else. No steaks! However, he contented himself with the oranges. Then, as we looked outside at the soft grey dawn coming, we saw that it was beginning to rain. "Let's go out in the rain!" I don't know who said it; it could have been either one of us; we were moving so harmoniously together that whatever happened it was one rhythmic movement. So we ran out naked into the arms of the sleeping city, into the back garden under the elm trees and stood there laughing, letting a mist of rain fall on us. Then he laid his hands on my flank, and we turned as one person and ran up to bed again.

That was how I "lost my virginity." I was twenty.

I didn't see Hugh after that, until he came with the Charlotte's crowd to the train station to see me off to Paris. . . . He must have guessed that I was not in love with him. What he did not know was the debt I owed him, for I never lost the knowledge that ecstasy was possible in the communion created by the union of two bodies. I came to realize that for some human beings these bodies could be of the same sex: but for me at that time they had to be male and female, each one taking turns at domination and passivity, each one searching how to become human. . . .

In the Montreal of 1933–34 Maysie Roger and I were plunged into a world of stress and confusion. We were apprentices with a Protestant family agency that delivered welfare vouchers to unemployed families. Applicants would go to the front office for an initial interview. Then, if the need was felt to be legitimate, cases would be assigned to area workers. That meant a house visit, and interview with questionnaire in hand, an attempt to sympathize with the clients' problems, social and emotional as well as immediate and realistic: a week's supply of coal gone too soon, electricity cut off, rent overdue with threats of eviction, hungry children, no carfare. For Maysie and me, young WASPs, it was not only a physical shock to see poverty face to face, it was a psychic shock. . . .

To Maysie's credit, she . . . never object[ed] to me having political meetings in our small sitting room cum kitchenette, where I had a cot for sleeping. She seemed content to have the refuge of a bedroom-study where she could retreat. I am afraid, though, that my comrades from the communist underground never thought of lowering their voices. So Maysie joined a group of music lovers, recorder players, who met on the same nights as did my political unit.

Actually, my real interest was in the theatre. In Paris I had been fascinated by Brecht's influence on guerrilla theatre. . . .

I was still timid about participating in public places. I particularly remember getting up at 5:00 A.M. one wintry day so as to be part of a strikers' picket line beside a steel mill. Back and forth, back and forth we walked, brandishing slogans and talking *en français* with the workers. After doing my stint (quite nervously) I caught a bus back to the welfare office. Not arrested! Montreal, that winter, was seething with political upheavals, but the only section of the city that I knew was the Jewish and Protestant enclave between St-Denis and St-Laurent. The French-Canadian unemployed came under a different welfare administration. . . .

My particular comrades were young men and women of European descent working in the needle trades. Their heroes would have been Sam Carr and Fred Rose, rather than Ontario's Leslie Morris and Tim Buck. I remember that in our unit, Joe, the son of a Jewish tailor, pleaded that he would have to drop out of the party because his wife was going to have a baby. She was becoming very nervous about his underground activities. I sympathized with him, but the other members, mostly solid married couples, were scornful. They put the party first. *They* had no babies.

No babies. That was the general rule we had to face up to. If we were to do useful political work—preparing and distributing pamphlets, picketing, organizing unions, rallying at meetings—we could not be tied down to nurturing children. Moreover, on the seven dollars a week that a party organizer earned, how could he or she afford to be a parent? The rest of us had precarious jobs.

While I had always thought of myself as a lover of children and a potential mother, that role would have to be reserved for the future. In the meantime: how to find a mate, yet prevent conception? In our student days Gina and I had learned a good deal about birth control from the lectures of Emma Goldman and the books of Marie Stopes. In Paris, with Tony, I had successfully used the chemical cone. But now, in Montreal, the French safe was the only easily available contraceptive method. We knew nothing of the rhythm method practised by some Catholics, nor of withdrawal, which I consider a cruel experience for women. Indeed, for me, so wonderful was the act of becoming as one, body to body, that I tended to ignore mechanical techniques. The year before I had been near despair at losing Tony. I was still empty, missing him. So when a young comrade in my unit, Don, began walking me home through the snowy streets of the inner city, I found it natural and inevitable to invite him to my warm flat for "a cup of tea and a bun." Maysie would be fast asleep in her room. We talked in whispers and were soon comforting each other, body to body, all sadness dissolved. . . .

I was not in love with him, but his gentleness and kindness made him a true friend. When the inevitable happened that spring, and I found myself pregnant, both of us were dumbfounded. "You mean I could be a daddy?" he queried. "You can't be," I said. "It can't happen. You have no job, or hope of jobs."

I set about finding a friend who could advise me what to do. . . .

I guess it was a sign of mutual maturity in our relationship that I was able to tell JFB of my predicament and he was able to offer help: "But we won't tell your mother." That summer my parents were living at Woodlot. I told my father the date of my appointment. It was to be in the evening, a time when the small medical building would be closed. Of course the doctor had his keys. He would let me in, then drive me home to Rosemount Avenue.

I was alone; neither Gina nor Lon was allowed to come with me to the appointment. I had qualms, of course, and the surgeon's manner was not too reassuring. But, having got this far, I had to go through with it. After examining me he said, "This will hurt." He could not give me any anaesthetic or shots so it did hurt—to the point of my screams. I had never known such pain. He put a towel in my mouth, saying, "Nearly over now." Soon he was helping me get off the bench. I was trembling, fumbling with my clothes. He turned to the basin to wash his hands, his gloves, then took the crook of my arm and walked me down the office stairs. By then it was dark outside. His car was parked in a back lane. In silence he drove me home. "Wear a napkin," he instructed. "Stay in bed tomorrow."

Alone upstairs I panicked. I telephoned my father. "It's done," I said. "But I'm scared. Can you come?"

"Right away."

"Good. Tell Mother I have a fever." And so they came. In the morning Gina and Lon visited, closed my bedroom door and helped with the bedpans. They had to tell my mother that I was having a hemorrhage and should stay absolutely quiet. Inevitably, she insisted on calling our family physician. In those days people didn't rush to hospital, for which I was thankful, and I knew this doctor well enough from childhood to tell him the truth. Such a small, fussy man, I thought.

"Why didn't you come to me directly—weeks ago?"

"I didn't think you'd approve. I had to do this."

"I respect my patients' trust," he said, then added, cunningly, "Who is this abortionist fellow?" Of course I would not tell him. I would not give him a clue. "Well, it's all over for you now. Lie low. See me next week."

A month or so later the family allowed me to have a weekend party at Woodlot. The invited were all young communists—university students, artists, writers. We had a potluck supper, then sat on the floor in the many-windowed living room, a fire glowing in the large stone fireplace. Led by a comrade just returned from Russia, we sang Russian folk songs, with a few IWW—Industrial Workers of the World—rousers thrown in. In the morning my friends packed their sleeping bags and set off through the woods for the railway station. The tallest, best-looking, most sophisticated comrade stopped a moment to thank the Livesays for their hospitality. My father shook his hand, but as they disappeared down the path he asked me, sotto voce, "Was he the one?"

"No," I smiled sadly. "That one lives in Montreal." . . .

I came to British Columbia because I wanted to get to the literary scene in San Francisco. I had been on the editorial board of *New Frontier,* and I was devoted to the magazine and to its aims: namely to document the spirit of the times through reportage, fiction, poetry and literary criticism. The editor, my friend Lon Lawson, suggested that if I went west I could popularize the journal and interview people who might subscribe or write for it across Canada.

My trip by train across the prairies was the best learning experience anyone could have had. I stopped off in Regina and Calgary. With my credentials as a reporter for *NF,* I was able to meet labour leaders who had witnessed the riot of 1935 in Regina when the RCMP attacked a peaceful meeting of the On To Ottawa Trek; leaders of the single unemployed had been explaining their plight to sympathetic people of the city when shots rang out. In Alberta, I talked with the miners of Corbin, on strike for months, then crossed the border into B.C. at Fernie, a ghost company town. The provincial police scanned my identification and believed my story that I was only visiting a relative in that town. Vancouver lay ahead. . . .

I wanted to know about writers, journalists and poets who might like to submit work to us. But also, I needed to find someone who could sell subscriptions. "Well," said A.M., "I think I have just the man for you. He is a Scot from Glasgow—veteran of the Great War who first came to Vancouver around 1920 and fell in love with this young city. He met Dr. Ernest Fewster and other members of the Poetry Society and the theosophical group. Then he went off to Australia. Next we met him returning from China in 1927; and here he is again, having spent the lean thirties in northern Ontario in the gold-mining camps. He is an accountant."

After such an introduction to Duncan Macnair, my curiosity was aroused. It was arranged that we would meet that week on Granville Street near the Birks clock and go to the Honey Dew Café. What I saw was a tall, upright, smiling man in his midthirties, with fine dark hair springing upwards and olive green eyes, who spoke "the Doric," a slight Scottish burr.

"Are you Florence Livesay?" he asked. I burst out laughing, as my mother was well into her middle age; obviously Duncan had never heard of *me*. . . .

For me, Duncan's outstanding credential was his enthusiastic response to poets and philosophers. He knew something of politics also, for he had lived and worked in China at the time of its upheavals in the 1920s. He told me at the outset, as we drank an orange drink, that the reason he admired poets like Charlie [G. D. Roberts] was because they toured the inner country, the north and west, meeting Canada's working people. "Poetry should not be shut up in an ivory tower," quoth he.

Well, I could not have agreed more. I showed him copies of *New Frontier* and asked him if he would care to help me sell subscriptions. A.M. would give us a list of contacts. Duncan admitted that since he quit the Ontario mining jobs—from sheer depression at the isolation: "seven years of bondage"—he had been unemployed. He had had a few months as a labourer, digging in the

Toronto tunnel, but he yearned for the climate and the spaces of sea and mountain. Any little he could earn would help towards room and board.

Since I had the promise of a social work job with a family welfare agency, it would be possible to meet again at noon hour or after five, with Saturday afternoon free for canvassing. On a bright blue and gold May afternoon we set out to walk to the University of British Columbia, calling on the way on a list of progressive professors. Among them were G. G. Sedgewick, the Shakespeare scholar, Hunter Lewis, A.F.B. Clark and the schoolteacher Madge Portsmouth. We walked all the way to UBC and back, talking our heads off. It was then Duncan told me that his favourite novel was *Diana of the Crossways* by George Meredith. This convinced me that he was a supporter of women's rights and of women artists, just as my father had been. Not that Duncan in any way resembled JFB in appearance or speech, but he was also an iconoclast, a challenger of received opinion. He was ripe for the philosophy that informed *New Frontier* and he was down-and-out, one of the thousands of unemployed single men who were lining up in the soup kitchens of Vancouver's East End. I guess the first gesture I made, as a good comrade, was to invite him for supper at my flat on Haro Street.

We were married in August 1937. Our day would soon be darkened by signs of defeat for the Spanish Republicans, through lack of English and European sanctions against Hitler's tanks and Mussolini's planes.

Our first home was an upstairs apartment on Pendrell Street, a block from the lovely curve of English Bay and backed by the tall cathedral-like forest of Stanley Park. As winter approached I was forced to give up my social work job with the B.C. Welfare Field Service. At that time no married woman could be legally employed in the professions of teaching, nursing or social work. Duncan, however, nearly forty, was eligible for employment as a family man. It was through his left-wing activities and contacts that he acquired an accounting job at Forst's, a Vancouver firm whose management was liberal-minded and progressive. But I grew despondent from lack of work. . . .

By midwinter my association with *New Frontier* magazine as western correspondent began to provide some interest. *New Frontier* was a United Front magazine set up in contradistinction to another, more radically communist magazine, *Masses*. It was to rally the middle-class intellectuals and artists to the cause of the international working class against war and fascism. . . .

The real challenge to artists in those days was the unemployed struggle. May 1938 found the jobless single men on a sit-down in the federal post office at the foot of Granville Street, as well as in the city's art gallery. . . . In the post office there were young men lying down, standing up, talking, taking sandwiches brought them each day by women sympathizers. After one month the men were met, at 5:00 A.M., June 19, by the RCMP and ousted by means of hoses and tear gas. . . .

Many were the reasons why I stayed on in Vancouver. The loss of my government job, after marriage, was a depressing blow, but it did give me time for writing and for community volunteer work. Also, at about this time, 1938, I met lifetime friends, Alan and Jean Crawley, who stimulated my literary interests and encouraged me to broaden my perspectives by writing for radio.

It was in the days at the English Bay bathhouse in Vancouver that the group of mostly young writers stimulated me, but failed to give me what I most needed: serious literary criticism. I had in a sense quelled and submerged any beliefs I might have had concerning the importance of poetry in my life and my own worth as a poet. I was drawn to help create the writers' group at the West End Community Centre, but the acclaim I had been used to in the east, writing documentaries for *Masses* and *New Frontier* and lyrics for the *Canadian Forum,* did not sit well with the preponderantly male members of the group. Poetry was not their main concern. . . . I felt crushed, intimidated. What I most needed was serious literary criticism. Duncan loyally defended me, but he was a nineteenth-century man. What I needed was a lover of contemporary poetry. Alan Crawley was such.

By 1938, Alan and his wife, Jean, had moved to Vancouver from Victoria and were living in the Sylvia Court in an apartment overlooking our bathhouse centre. I learned from poet friends that Alan would like to meet me. They explained that Alan was a Winnipeg corporate lawyer who had been stricken with a virus at the age of 40; he had completely lost his sight. As a diversion he took to memorizing poems that he liked, modern British and American. By the fall of 1934, when the Crawleys moved to Victoria, Alan already had a repertoire of modern poetry that he recited aloud to friends. In January 1935, the ex-lawyer was invited to attend a meeting at the Empress Hotel where modern American poetry was to be recited. At the conclusion, Mr. Crawley rose to his feet. "I cannot see," he remarked in his incisive yet persuasive way, "that the poetry we have just heard is either typically American or typically modern. How about" . . . and here he went on to mention the names of contemporary British poets, knowing less, he apologized, of Canadian ones. After the meeting, Doris Fern introduced herself to Alan and asked if he would come to a gathering to meet some local Canadian poets. She mentioned Floris McLaren and Anne Marriott. So it turned out that as soon as Alan met these young Victoria poets he began to make a study of other contemporary Canadians.

In Vancouver, where he moved the following year, he met Anne Angus, who was doing reviews and criticism for the Vancouver press. She was so enchanted by his way of saying poetry that she arranged for readings at the Georgian Club and other Vancouver gatherings.

At the time when we met, that late summer of 1939, my own life was changing. Earlier, in June, I had travelled east to Woodlot to visit my parents. I was in a somewhat rundown state, physically, so it seemed a good time to have a medical checkup. The doctors recommended an appendectomy. Father, ever generous, offered to underwrite the cost of operation and hospital. Some two weeks later I was well and eager to go back to Duncan, who had been writing daily letters of appeal. It was summertime, wasn't it? We should have his one week's holiday together. We could go northwest, explore the coast, board at a camp on Nelson Island, far from the madding crowd. We had never had a honeymoon. We had never gone boating, swimming, fishing. Now was the time to enjoy and to forget politics. Of course I agreed. Once we were there, we decided, in spite of the world crisis, to have a child.

So it was that at the time I met the Crawleys I was already pregnant and anxious to do my stint of good walking. Alan and his spaniel, Roddy, needed a guiding hand. Stanley Park with its seashore and giant firs opened its arms to us. Sometimes, Jean would put Alan on a bus that I would meet, and we would enjoy the whole summer afternoon sitting out under the cherry tree in my backyard until Jean or Michael, their younger son, called by for drinks and social laughter. Often I made notes at night about our conversations, some of which eventually appeared in articles or radio talks.

There was never any lull in our conversation. We talked of politics in Canada, of the Spanish Civil War, of social conditions and of being born in Manitoba, as both of us had been. Alan was greatly interested in my Paris year, when I was studying the French symbolists and their influence on Eliot, the Sitwells, Huxley and Pound. . . .

Although Alan was twenty years older than I, his enthusiasms were those of a boy seeing the world for the first time. . . .

That was why he was able to respond favourably when I was sent by Floris McLaren and the other women poets in Victoria to ask him to be the editor of a poetry journal. . . .

A few days later, I was able to telephone the good news to Floris McLaren: "He will do it." It was decided to set up an editorial committee in Victoria with Floris as managing editor, second in command.

From that day forward I was part of Alan's editorial committee, for he usually liked to read selections aloud to a listener before making his final decision. In that way we both discovered new poetry by Earle Birney, Anne Marriott, Jay Macpherson, Miriam Waddington, P. K. Page. . . .

By 1951 . . . it was time for the magazine to fold: "It has done its job. There are now *Northern Review* and *Fiddlehead* which have taken up the cause for poetry." I felt crushed, realizing how much I myself owed to the experience of being on the editorial committee, and now dawningly aware that I would see less and less of my dearest friend. . . .

Although my friendship with Alan Crawley always remained platonic, in the time of my need I was truly in love with this man. He, in his old age, and in his cups, confided that he had also been in love with me. We sustained each other through some dark years, yet remained loyal to our enjoined commitments.

It has been one hundred years and more since Alan Crawley was born in late August 1887. Now, some dozen years since he died, I feel he has never left me. During the last week of his life in the Victoria nursing home, he was not only blind, but deaf. All I could do was squeeze his hand which responded, quick with life. I don't know whether he knew if the bedside person was Dorothy or

Pat or Jean, but he uttered stumbling words of love. For in spite of all his handicaps he loved life. I believe he thought of life as a gift, a gift to be grateful for and to make the most of. This view is what I have clung to over my stormy years. Not my father, not my husband, but Alan is the one I think of as Virgil, guiding me always. . . .

"I will marry you for the coming years, but I cannot promise you that I will stay married when I am fifty. I might want to start another life." How vividly I remember saying that to Duncan before our marriage, August 14, 1937. And now, looking back, how strangely true that prophecy became.

The twenty years between 1938 and 1958 were years of consolidation for me. When war broke out in 1939 we had to give up, or at least lay aside for the future, the idea that our generation could change the world. The fruits of that struggle in the thirties only began to ripen in the seventies; for now, as I write, half the world is socialist or communist. But there was no withering away of the state, as Marx promised; and we must seriously wonder whether the men in charge of the nuclear age are going to destroy our world. . . .

Day and Night, though published in 1944, contains poems written in the latter years of the thirties. It won the Governor General's medal, an honour only—as in those days no money was attached. Of course there were fewer books of poetry being published, so it was not surprising that I won the award again with *Poems for People* in 1947. This certainly established me as a significant poet in Canada. From then on there were requests to read and speak and teach creative writing. For radio I wrote the documentary drama about the evacuation of the Japanese Canadians from the coast, *Call My People Home,* and after two different CBC performances the Ryerson Press published it in 1952. But another twenty years went by before the Canadian public began to realize what had happened; my play had failed in its aim to rouse the wrath of the people. It was ahead of its time. . . .

Duncan had been educated not as a Presbyterian Scot but as a free thinker, an admirer of Thomas Huxley and of the Scottish militant labour leaders such as Keir Hardy. He shared George Meredith's liberal view of women and his adherence to theosophy led him to be an advocate of women as creative human beings. All this I am sure of, until there were children, household duties and a very small income. When, after World War II, I sought to remedy the situation to free myself for more writing time, friends laughingly told him, "We know who wears the pants." So Duncan set about taming his shrew, in good Elizabethan style. A real crisis came when he beat me up and I took the children and ran with them, by bus, to Horseshoe Bay and across Howe Sound to the safety of Roberts Creek. A retired nurse, whom we had dubbed Aunt Ruth because she was a foster mother to difficult or sick children, lived there. Marcie, aged three, had stayed with her for two months with great benefit. Alan Crawley lent me the fare, and it was he who gave Duncan some stringent advice. Our marriage, like most, had its stormy periods. We did love each other. But Duncan was thirteen years older and as time passed he took on the role of adamant father who demanded his comforts. To this I reacted rebelliously, as I had done with my own father. Moreover, our sex life was not happy for either of us. All this was the source of much frustration for us, as many of my dreams and poems reveal. In the poem "Wedlock" I wrote, "We are each one bereft / and weeping inwardly," and "a thousand ancestors have won." . . .

The war and having children changed all my perspectives: from being a participant in the struggle for a better world I became an observer. All community efforts narrowed down to that of the home.

Yes, I was still writing poems, time snatched in the basement supervising an old washing machine with hand wringer, or waiting until everyone was asleep to put on a record and write to music. . . .

A year or so after my father's death I did receive a kind of message from him. I had a dream in which JFB told me to write to Mr. Hindmarsh of the *Toronto Star,* for whom I had worked in the thirties. The message was: *Offer to go to England to describe the postwar rehabilitation in progress.* To my considerable astonishment and apprehension, a telegram came back forthwith, offering me two or three months in England, my fare there and back, and very good pay on the basis of three articles a week.

This was my first real opportunity to go it alone, although I had been east with small Peter during the war. But this time I would have to leave the children and arrange for their care. Today, I wonder how I managed it. My only close family relative in Canada was my mother, and she agreed to come from Toronto to stay in our New Westminster home, apparently without any qualms. Neither she nor Duncan realized that she wasn't resilient enough to cope with small children. I knew she couldn't keep house or cook to any extent, but a cleaning woman would be assisting her. By October 1946, FRL was installed and I was on my way, flying to London.

About two weeks later, Duncan threw in the sponge and told his mother-in-law to leave. He sent the children to boarding care in the country at Roberts Creek. Peter was six, just starting school. Marcia, in particular, flourished in the quiet, relaxed and loving atmosphere of "Aunt Ruth's." When I returned home some two months later, our family was most happily reunited.

But while I was away I had enough experiences to give me a new lease on life, new vistas. . . . [A] very good friend was back in London from British Columbia, where she and two children had been refugees. She was Celia Strachey, wife of John Strachey, the journalist. He was now minister of food in the British postwar government. I was happy to be invited for a weekend at their country home, with time to walk and talk with the minister. One of our stops was at the village store, where John collected his family ration of oranges—golden oranges from Greece, no doubt. I could see that this detail would make a neat headline for the *Toronto Star*. My meeting with Strachey also led to introductions to the planners of new-style housing developments and new school programs.

Hindmarsh must have approved of all this, for instead of beckoning me back to Canada he sent me to Ruhr, to do a survey of rehabilitation programs in areas of Cologne and Düsseldorf. . . .

By the time I returned to Canada I had enough material to write the novella *Give My Love to London,* which was never published, and poems for the book *Poems for People.* I continued to write articles on social and living conditions, this time about B.C., for the *Star* and the *Star Weekly.* I was also given a generous helping hand by CBC Radio in Vancouver. They produced *Momatcum,* a poetic documentary on the plight of B.C. native people. A few years later, in 1952, the same people produced *Call My People Home.* . . .

By the early fifties I began to see that I would have to plan for a life of my own after the children were educated. I had so much enjoyed teaching creative writing at UBC's Extension Department, and then working at the YMCA for two years as a young adult supervisor, that I decided I would like to qualify as an adult education teacher. Unfortunately, there were no such courses at UBC.

Instead, the education faculty advised that I would have to enroll for a year's course to get a high-school teaching diploma.

I quail now as I think what this meant for me, physically and emotionally, and what it meant by way of change for Duncan and family. Today, many young married women pursue such courses without a qualm, but I was considered quite mad for doing so, especially by my husband's Scottish friends. . . .

When we moved to North Vancouver from UBC in the summer of 1956, it was to a new house on Grand Boulevard. We had bought this at quite a risk, as houses were scarce and house prices were soaring. But I had the assurance of a teaching position at Magee High School in Vancouver. I would be near the bus to town and the children would be only a block away from Sutherland Junior High. Duncan's job as accountant at Denby Brothers was shaky, but he got into something he liked much better, as accountant for the Grouse Mountain ski lift and resort. We all liked the modern bungalow facing the park on Grand Boulevard, and the mountains beyond. It seemed that all would be well. Alas, I put in two of the worst years of my life, trying to teach teenagers. I had loved teaching adults and had, I think, a good rapport, especially with women. . . . The iron hand, I learned to my deep grief, was the only way to handle high-school students, even in grade twelve. . . .

I was advised to resign from the school board that spring of 1958, presumably instead of being fired, and I applied for a new grant that was being made available by the Humanities Council for teachers who would like a refresher year in a country where they could observe and study their own discipline. I knew from educational reading that the British method of teaching English as a creative subject was greatly to be preferred to the rigid and old-fashioned British Columbia program. So I applied for the bursary and I was awarded a grant of $2000, through the intervention of a poet friend, Dr. Roy Daniells of the English department at UBC. My joy may be surmised, and also the complications that this offer presented. How to persuade Duncan to let me leave the family for six months? . . .

The decision was made by both of us that Duncan would stay on in our house facing the park on Grand Boulevard, with our devoted Scottish dog, Sukey. A young couple we knew, presented with their first baby, were desperate to find a place to live; they agreed to board Duncan and look after the housekeeping. And so it was, with scarcely any forebodings, and no regrets, that I set off on my first real march towards freedom. It was September 1958. Ahead lay the third year of my life in which I could live abroad.

It was a breathless time, that autumn. . . . The London stimulus was such that I felt as young as if I were just a graduate student returning for a year's refresher course. More importantly, I was enjoying the freedom to speak out on the subject so dear to my heart, teaching creative English, and with a chance to sit in on different school classes at every level of British education. . . .

And where was that Christmas spent? In Paris? Belfast, with my sister? I only remember being back in London by January and February, again attending the institute classes and visiting schools. On a Friday afternoon in February I went to a university concert where *Dido and Aeneas* was being performed, an opera I had never heard before. It took my breath away. As I walked to the Penn Club in the gathering dusk my mind was still harmonizing, tethered to that music of Purcell's in which Dido dies and Aeneas goes off to found Rome.

In the narrow hallway of the club was a rack for letters and a bulletin board. I barely glanced there when I noticed a thin blue envelope with my name on it. Tearing it open, I read, "Father passed away last night, February 12. Love, Peter."

I stood in the hall, shaking. Instead of going upstairs to my room, I went outside again, stumbling along into the twilight street. The only words that would come to me were, "I'm free. I'm free."

On my return to the house, I met the club secretary, brusque and British. "When did this telegram come?" I asked her. "Oh, around noon," was the response.

"My husband has died," I told her.

"Indeed!" she replied. Nothing more.

That's when I came to my senses and telephoned family friend Gladys Downes, who was then studying in London. From her flat we spent several hours trying to get through to North Vancouver by telephone. Finally, there was an answer from Jimmy Campbell, a close family friend; he gave me the details. A massive stroke. Duncan had been taken to emergency in a coma. Peter was with him throughout the night. My son was arranging for the funeral and wanted to know when I would be coming home.

It took another two or three hours that night before I could confirm a flight to Vancouver. Marcia had to fly home also, from Colorado. The memorial service was held at the Vancouver Unitarian Church, where a passage was read from Duncan's favourite essayist, Edward Carpenter—a recluse, a gentle theosophical essayist—and from Dylan Thomas's wonderful elegy for his father, "Do not go gentle into that good night." As he would have wished it, Duncan the theosophist was cremated. His close friend, Arthur Peacey, and our son, Peter, aged eighteen, were my strong supports.

In one week's time we sold the house on Grand Boulevard. I flew back, into the arms of London. There, at the end of 1959, I was heading for my fiftieth birthday. What lay ahead was a new life in Paris, with UNESCO. Then Lusaka.

I had worn four hoods: childhood, girlhood, womanhood and motherhood. Now there were two more waiting: widowhood and selfhood. . . .

Gabrielle Roy

(1909–1983)

Gabrielle Roy was born to an impoverished French Canadian family in St. Boniface, Manitoba, and educated at St. Joseph's Academy and Winnipeg Normal School. As a young woman her earnings from teaching supplied the cash income that kept the Roy family financially afloat, while her success provided the psychological fulfillment her heroic mother needed to sustain the loss of her husband and the defeat of her dreams for her other children.

The power of Roy's memoir comes from her capacity to evoke the dimensions of "Maman's" need for her gifted daughter, while at the same time involving the reader in her growing resolve to leave. Thus, when she sets out for Europe in 1937, with a vague plan to study drama, we know she will not return.

Roy's narrative, which truly does blend "enchantment" and "sorrow," manages to convey both external and inner life with equal vividness, alternating between poetic, philosophic, and historical modes. She, being a doubly colonized person, must, on her travels, come to terms with both French and British metropolitan culture, something she conveys with a lightness of touch unrivaled by any other writer in her generation. Thus we see her comforted by a vision of her native prairie sunshine, while feeling alone in a crowd on a bus traversing the Place de la Concorde. And we find her happily discussing with a busload of Londoners where she should look for the quiet and refreshment of nature on a trip to Epping Forest.

When, during her last months in England, as the country is bracing for war with Germany, Roy dismisses her fanatical fascist lover and refuses to become embroiled in his political world, we must ask ourselves what it was in Roy's background that kept her from the political dead end which silenced so many of her contemporaries, like Livesay, or Dorothy Hewett. As Roy begins to write stories and articles for journals like *Le Jour, La Revue Moderne,* and *Le Canada,* it is not her British or French experience which feeds her imagination but her life on the prairies, and her sense of French Canadian life, a sense she can convey uninfluenced by political stereotypes.

One of the first French Canadian novelists to explore the life of city-dwelling workers, Roy was the first Canadian writer to win a major French literary award when she received the Prix Femina for her first novel, *The Tin Flute* (1945). *Where Nests the Water Hen* (1950) was her earliest effort to treat life on the prairies in fictional form, to be followed by a series of acclaimed novels treating the lives of ordinary Canadians, both rural and urban.

Awarded the Order of Canada in the nation's centennial year, Roy was also the recipient of two Governor General's Awards for contributions to Canadian literature. Married to Dr. Marcelle Carbotte, Roy lived the last half of her life in Quebec City, although in her prairie childhood remained the fertile ground of her imagination.

Hers was a literary genius which could subsume the full range of human experience within the closely examined world of a prairie farm and neighboring village, or within the gritty setting of working-class Montreal. Readers around the world found her view of the human predicament compelling, and were transported into the lives of Canadians by her prose. Although *Enchantment and Sorrow* was originally written in French, the translation of *La Détresse et l'enchantement* was undertaken with the assistance of the translator of Roy's novels into English, and the guidance of her literary executor, so that Patricia Claxton's translation has won wide acclaim for its capacity to capture the spirit of the original.

ENCHANTMENT AND SORROW:
The Autobiography of Gabrielle Roy

When did it first dawn on me that I was one of those people destined to be treated as inferiors in their own country? I don't think it was during any of the frequent forays that Maman and I made to Winnipeg, leaving our little French city of St-Boniface and crossing the Red River by the Provencher Bridge. It would be easy to suppose so, since our capital city never really received us otherwise than as foreigners, but when I was a child I rather liked the feeling of crossing a border and being in a strange place, light years away but right next door to home. I think it opened my eyes, trained me to observe things and stimulated my imagination. . . .

We almost always set off in high spirits and full of expectation. Maman would have read in the paper or heard from a neighbour that Eaton's was having a sale of curtain-lace, or printed cottons suitable for making aprons or house-dresses, or maybe children's shoes. Always, as we began these shopping expeditions, we were drawn by the hope that so warms the hearts of poor people, that of turning up a real find at the bargain counter. It occurs to me now that we hardly ever ventured into the rich metropolis next door except on buying trips. This was where a good portion of our hard-earned money went—and it was pennies from the pockets of poor people like us that made the city such an arrogant and intimidating neighbour. . . .

[W]hen we crossed the bridge, we were rich, with all our possible acquisitions still intact in our heads.

But as soon as we were on the other side, we'd undergo a kind of transformation that made us draw together, as though solidarity would help us face a kind of shadow that had fallen over us. It was partly because we were now on dismal Water Street beside the railway sorting yards, undoubtedly the most woebegone part of Winnipeg, full of drunkards, the wails of crying children and the hiss of escaping steam; the hideous face which the haughty city couldn't hide, a mere stone's throw from its broad airy avenues. But there was more to it than that; our discomfort came partly from inside us too. We'd suddenly be less sure of ourselves, the money we were going to spend wouldn't seem so inexhaustible, and our plans for it would have come back down to earth.

We'd arrive at Portage Avenue, which was so inordinately broad it could swallow a throng of thousands without showing it. We'd still be speaking French, of course, but perhaps less audibly, particularly after two or three passersby turned around and stared at us. . . .

Only when we arrived at Eaton's was it decided whether or not there would be a confrontation. It all depended on Maman's frame of mind. Sometimes she'd begin by calling for a saleswoman who spoke our language to serve us. . . .

So if Maman was having one of her good days, if her confidence was up and her tongue felt nimble, she'd take the offensive and demand one of our compatriots to wait on us. The more forceful she was, I'd observed, the more accommodating the floorwalker would be. . . .

On days like that we probably bought more than we should have, being so grateful to be doing it in our own language that the money slipped through our fingers even faster than usual.

But there were also times when Maman felt beaten before she began, weary of a struggle that had to be taken up again and again and was never won for good and all; at such times she found it simpler and less taxing to "bring out" her English, as she used to say.

We'd move from counter to counter. Using her hands and facial expressions to help, she really managed pretty well, though some times a real problem arose, like the time she wanted some chamois ("shammy" to the English) to line a coat, and asked for "a yard or two of Chinese skin to put under the coat." . . .

We came home from our expeditions to Winnipeg dog-tired and, in truth, almost always depressed. Either we'd been sane and sensible and had bought only what was essential (and whoever reaped joy from sticking to essentials?), or else we'd done something idiotic (like buying the hat that suited me so well but cost the earth), and then we felt guilty; we'd have to make it up somewhere else, Maman would say, and besides, she would hint, not let Papa know what we'd paid. Being so strapped for money all the time meant that sooner or later we'd overspend and then we'd be more strapped than ever.

In any event, though we crossed the bridge on the way out with our heads full of plans as if we were rich, we never recrossed it feeling anything but poor, three-quarters of our money having slipped through our fingers, very often without our being able to say where it had gone. . . .

Now Maman and I would be speaking our own language with all the confidence in the world, neither in whispers nor too loudly as we would in Winnipeg, where our behaviour was governed by our self-consciousness, or by the shame of it. And we'd be hearing the sound of other French voices in harmony with ours. In our relief at being back in our natural surroundings we'd find ourselves greeting almost everyone we met, though it's true that between us we knew practically everyone in the city, at least by name. The farther we went, the more people Maman would recognize as friends, exchanging greetings and snatches of personal news with this one and that. . . .

At last we'd arrive at Deschambault Street. We must have felt it was something like a miracle to find our house still intact and standing guard over our French way of life, protecting it from the hurly-burly and disparity of the Canadian West, for in the last minute we'd hurry towards it, as though we might arrive to find it had been snatched away from us.

It was a pleasing but unpretentious house, with dormers in the attic, lots of big windows on the second floor, and a wide veranda with a row of white columns around the front and west sides. We always came back to it as though returning from a harrowing expedition. . . .

Why is it that we who were so often unhappy could also be so happy? That's what astonishes me most, even today. Just as I also find the coming of happiness more surprising than the coming of sorrow, not because it's more unusual but perhaps because it's less easily explained.

Happiness came to us like the wind, from nothing and from everything. Summer was a festival in itself for us. When I was a child I didn't know anyone who cherished summer as we did. Whatever worries or sorrows Maman had, as soon as summer came she'd drop everything to gather up the geraniums and fuchsias that had spent the winter on the windowsills and plant them in the earth around the house. We'd soon see the pale, sickly things return to health. Papa used to plant a big vacant lot not far from our house, having obtained permission from the municipal council to cultivate it until it was sold, which couldn't have happened for a long time because I seem to remember our always having that big, beautiful vegetable garden. And summer repaid our efforts. Our fruit trees gave us sweet-smelling flowers and then tart little apples from which Maman made an exquisite jelly, and also cherries and small blue plums. Our yard behind the house was surrounded by a wooden fence and was always full of robins and sparrows, which sang so loudly and cheerfully we couldn't help hearing them, even when our troubles were many. It wasn't a very big yard but it bordered a lane which in turn bordered an unsubdivided meadow, so that all the open space behind the house looked just like a glimpse of green prairie. My father would sit in the half-darkness by the open door of the little summer kitchen and contemplate it endlessly. And sometimes you could see a red glow in the sky between two street corners beyond, mysteriously deepening the narrow cleft between the houses and making it seem to reach into a kind of limitless space, right in the middle of the city. If we ever went to talk to

Papa at that hour as he sat at his observation post, there was a strange and surprising peacefulness in his voice. It was as if we'd brought him back from some infinite distance, from his youthful excursions in the wilds, perhaps. . . .

[W]e used to spend the summer holidays with my uncle Excide, the youngest of the Landry sons.

We used to take the train at the domed CN station, which we called *le dépôt,* though I don't know why. In no time we'd reach the flat land around Winnipeg. From above, the train must have looked like some black caterpillar crawling into eternity beneath the immense prairie sky. I loved the open prairie; I've always been fascinated by it. For all its reticence, it's always had more to say to me than any other landscape. But on these train trips to the settlement area called Pembina Mountain, the centre of attraction to which all our thoughts turned was the mountain itself. About an hour out of Winnipeg, shadowy hills would begin to show against the pale blue sky. A little later the train would enter those hills so gradually that we wouldn't notice it. Only when we were in the middle of them would we realize we were in broken and even mountainous country, or so it seemed to us, who were so used to flatness. We'd come to a place of no importance called Babcock. The train would stop for a minute or two, and I still wonder why, for as I recall there was nothing there except a shack and an abandoned quarry. But also the mountain. Just an elevation really, crowded against the railway line, its flank forming rocky escarpments. To see its summit, Maman and I would crouch till we were almost kneeling, our eyes level with the bottom of the window. That way we could see all of it. It took our breath away. Such altitude! Such soaring height! On the way there, we'd talk about nothing else, Maman and I. We'd be watching for it from the moment the train left the station. Afterwards it so dominated what we remembered of the ride that it banished all other recollection. On a visit to Manitoba a few years ago, I felt an intense desire to see the mountain that had stirred my soul more, I'm sure, than the Rocky Mountains did later, or even perhaps the Alps. I found myself in a tiny out-of-the-way place closed in by heaps of quarried stone left lying about and hiding the skyline. But I could see absolutely no mountain! Finally, among the piles of stone, I did distinguish a more or less natural butte.

I'm still not sure who had the better vision, the impassioned child with her nose pressed against the train window, or the sea-

soned traveller who had to have a real mountain before her eyes to
believe in it. . . .

My uncle Excide with his big black moustache would be waiting for us, pacing up and down the wooden platform, as high-
strung as he'd always been. He'd drive us to the farm, which wasn't
much more than two miles from the village, in his little high Ford
with mica windows in its canvas doors. But our hearts lightened
because we were really going much, much farther than two miles,
back into time past, through the generations, almost to the begin-
nings of our family. We were finding something from the old days
still alive in the brisker air of the plateaux, here in the third of the
homes our forebears had built since they began their wanderings.

This third home in fact began near the village of St-Léon, six
or seven miles beyond the farm. It was there that Grandfather
obtained his concession and built his house, which was exactly like
the one at St-Alphonse-de-Rodriguez, with a wing of the same
shape but smaller and lower. Those people were amazing. I must
say; they'd leave everything behind, then begin all over again to
make everything just the way it had been at the other end of the
earth. I've always been touched by this. It reminds me of the birds,
who always build the same nest wherever they go in the vast
expanses open to them. . . .

At the time I myself remember best, we found the spirit of my
pioneer grandparents still almost intact in Uncle Excide. For all
that, he'd given up the much-loved paternal house and built one to
his own liking on a new farm just a few miles from Somerset. And
so we began to oscillate between Somerset for reasons of business,
which was done mostly in English, and St-Léon for the good of our
souls. Sometimes we'd go to one and sometimes to the other, and
finally we went to Somerset almost always; it was closer and really
more convenient.

My uncle, who'd become a widower at a very young age, was
always happy to see Maman arrive. She'd at once take the running
of the house in hand, much to the relief of my cousin Léa, who at
the age of fourteen had found that weighty responsibility on her
shoulders. The house was spacious, pleasant, and very comfortable
for the time, with a hand pump which brought water inside from a
well under the summer kitchen, and central heating too. It was in
the middle of a little wood, which my uncle had long sought, he'd
so missed having trees over his head as at St-Alphonse. Though he'd

left there when very young, only five, he'd apparently been longing
ever since to have at least a grove of trees around him.

In truth, the little wood around my uncle's house played almost
as important a role in my life as did the mountain at Babcock. It
was probably rather sparse as woods go, composed mostly of
poplars and small oaks, but for years it was the archetypal forest to
me, embodying all the shadowy and magical things I used to imagine about a forest. I loved it, but I think most of all I loved the contrast it provided, always renewing the feeling of space you'd get
from the open prairie beyond. When you came out of that little
wood at the end of the farm road, you'd instantly feel you were
entering infinity. From there the prairie stretched away as far as you
could see; in one immense, rolling plain it unfolded in a series of
long, fluid waves sweeping unendingly to the horizon. I've seen
nothing more harmonious anywhere, except perhaps where the
downs of Dorset flow down to the sea.

In that permanence in constant motion, in that tranquil yet
beckoning immensity, there was a beauty that tugged at my heart
like a magnet, even when I was still very young. I kept returning to
that vista as if it might get away from me if I left it alone too long.
I'd arrive at the end of the farm road, reach the place where the
trees parted, and the vast, magnetic expanse would appear, and
each time it was the world laid at my feet again. But really much
more than the world, I know that now. . . .

One evening during the year I was a teacher in the neighbour-
ing village of Cardinal, I arrived [at my uncle's house] when I probably wasn't expected. It was mild and snowing abundantly, one of
those tranquil, silent snowfalls that come straight down, unde-
flected by any wind, and as steadily as if to smother all traces of
uncleanliness. There must have been some happy gathering, because all the lamps were lit and the house was resplendent, and
through this same window I could see silhouettes bustling about
cheerfully. But the most beguiling part of the scene was outside,
where a delicate stream of light from the brightly lit windows was
falling on five or six horsedrawn sleighs lined up by the door. Since
there was no real cold in the air, no one had bothered to take the
horses to the stable. They'd been left hitched to their sleighs, with
blankets thrown over their backs, and more blankets had been
spread over the sleighs to keep the snow off the seats. Ever so gently, the snow was piling up like an additional warm, fluffy blanket

over the covered seats and over the animals standing there with their heads drooping, asleep on their feet, you'd swear, if you hadn't spied their eyelids blinking now and then.

Just as I'd stood at the end of the little dirt road from where I could see all that boundless space and been certain I'd find happiness some day, when I witnessed the scene on the night I describe my heart was flooded with longing for something still more wonderful, which was peace of mind. . . .

As much as I'd let myself go during the holidays, with my endless rides on the prairie and the airy castle building they lent themselves to, as soon as school began I'd fling myself into my schoolwork with equal abandon. Having wandered to my heart's content all summer, I now stayed riveted every evening to my little desk in my secluded room, reading and getting as much of the material into my head as possible. I learned by heart with extraordinary ease. Very often I'd read a paragraph attentively but effortlessly and then realize that that was all I'd had to do to remember it word for word. However, I soon forgot a text I'd learned without a lot of effort.

I'd promised Maman I'd apply myself so totally to studying that I'd always come first in future, having resolved to make it up to her that way for all her sacrifices for my benefit. . . . [M]ost of all, I think, I had to realize that my mother was driving herself mercilessly, trying to run the house.

How did she do it? I think it was mostly by taking lodgers and sometimes boarders. It seems to me we always had strangers living with us. Sometimes they were well mannered and pleasant. That kind we treated like family, and some we made friends of and missed long after they left. Others we disliked, finding them coarse or loud, and those we had the greatest difficulty enduring under our roof. . . .

I must have been about fourteen when I began to immerse myself in my schoolwork the way one enters a cloister. I'd been beating around the bush, telling myself over and over that I'd get down to business next month. Then there came a day when I began to suspect that Maman was losing ground, and that she wouldn't be able to hold on if she didn't get some encouragement to brace her. The year-end examinations were approaching. I began reviewing my schoolwork in earnest. I'd get up well before the rest of the household and come down to study in the peace and quiet of the kitchen while I had it to myself for an hour or two. When Maman came to put the morning porridge on the stove, she'd find me at the big kitchen table with my books spread around me. So as not to disturb me she'd greet me simply with a nod, as she might one of our boarders, and a look of approval and commendation. Then she'd set to work with as little noise as possible.

At the end of that year I came first in my class for the first time in my life. I even won a medal for some subject or other. But what I'll never forget in Maman's face when I brought home the first instalment of her reward. It was immediately as though I'd lifted the weight of years past from her, and her anxiety about the years to come as well. She didn't pay me any lavish compliments, but she was radiant. Though she didn't know it, two or three times I heard her boasting about me to neighbours, artfully finding an appropriate opening in the conversation for the disclosure that "my daughter won the Bishop's medal this year." Once I appeared on the scene just as she was dropping a reference to that ordinary everyday medal, and I was struck by the expression in her eyes. They were shining as I'd rarely seen them do, like two deep pools of tender radiance from which all the dark, bitter waters of hardship seemed to have been drained.

That was the support I was able to give her. How could I not have wanted to keep on giving it? She'd spared nothing in her support of me. It made me giddy to see myself able to lighten her step at so little cost. Coming first made me giddy, too. I even wonder if this wasn't the beginning of a habit that wasn't altogether good, because I took it very badly when I came second one year, uncovering a weakness in needing to come first that I had to learn to fight. . . .

Evan Maman came to think I was overdoing it. To make me leave my books and get to bed at a reasonable hour she'd sometimes cut off my electricity by taking out the fuse for the circuit my room was on. This way she could retire in peace, knowing I wouldn't be putting on my light again that night.

But at last I was keeping the promise I'd made her some years earlier in the hospital; year after year I was bringing home the medal awarded by the Manitoba French Canadian Association for the highest marks in French. Then I won the most coveted of all, the one given by the Quebec Department of Education to the student with the highest year-end marks in French in all Manitoba. If I remember correctly, it bore in effigy the rather Roman head of

Cyrille Delage, the noted Quebec writer on wines and gastronomy. My collection of medals was impressive by now, almost filling a drawer. Maman kept them carefully there, where they wouldn't get covered with dust. She who'd attended only a humble little village school and never won anything more than a fifty-cent book, which she still cherished, was quite dazzled by my drawerful of big fat medals; I suspect that when she was alone she often opened that drawer so she could admire them at her leisure. . . .

In grades eleven and twelve, the Manitoba French Canadian Association prizes were fifty and one hundred dollars respectively. These were handsome sums in those days, almost comparable to today's Canada Council and Cultural Affairs grants, and you didn't have to apply for them, which was especially nice. I won both of them, which covered my enrolment at normal school and the purchase of the necessary books, so that I cost my parents practically nothing after I finished school, and that was essential, since by then they'd come to the end of their meagre resources.

When we were so far from Quebec, for those of us who finished school the achievement wasn't so much to have done so but to have done it in French as well as in English. And despite the law that allowed only an hour a day for the teaching of French in public schools in French-speaking neighbourhoods, it seems to me that the French we spoke was every bit as good as in Quebec, in the same period and for similar social strata. . . .

[O]ur schoolteachers, mostly nuns but also some lay teachers . . . used to give extra, unpaid time to the teaching of French despite already onerous schedules. A few used to take quite brazen liberties with the law; passionate and defiant, some of them drew the ire of the school board; they may have done us more harm than good. . . .

Sometimes I wonder if the opposition we were subjected to wasn't a service rather than a disservice to us. There were so few of us that if we'd been left alone the easy route would have been the fastest one to perdition, it seems to me. We were certainly spared the easy route. And we managed to learn and preserve the French language in all its beauty and elegance, but to tell the truth it was for the pride of it, the dignity; it couldn't equip us for everyday life.

In any event, if we were going to pass our exams and get our degrees or certificates, we had to comply with the program laid down by the Department of Education, which meant learning most subjects in English: chemistry, physics, mathematics, and most history. So we were more or less English in algebra, geometry, the sciences, and Canadian history, but French in Quebec history, French literature, and particularly history of religion. This gave us an odd turn of mind, constantly alert to readjusting our focus. It was like being a juggler with all those plates to keep in the air.

Sometimes this was a blessing. I remember the keen interest I took in English literature as soon as I had access to it. And for good reason. Our French textbooks acquainted us with Veuillot and Montalembert, pages and pages of them, and very little else; practically nothing of Zola, Flaubert, Maupassant, even Balzac. And what idea could we have of French poetry when it was reduced almost exclusively to François Coppée, Sully Prudhomme, and Lamartine's "Le Lac", which we parroted so many times that today, by some curious reaction—mental block perhaps—I couldn't recite a single line of it. And yet I remember getting 99% for my essay on that poem in a competition sponsored by the Manitoba French Canadian Association.

The doors to English literature, however, were open wide and gave us access to its greatest minds. I'd soon read Thomas Hardy, George Eliot, the Brontë sisters, Jane Austen. I knew Keats, Shelley, Byron, and the Lake poets, and adored them. Fortunately for French literature, our program of study did include the sparkling Alphonse Daudet. At fifteen I fell upon his *Lettres de mon moulin* (*Letters from My Mill*) and learned it by heart from beginning to end. Sometimes I wonder if the soft spot in my heart for Provence, which had taken me to every corner of it, isn't partly owing to my enchantment at my first encounter with graceful French prose when I was fifteen. Without this, French prose would have seemed very dreary beside the English. If, at that age, I'd been able to read Rimbaud, Verlaine, Baudelaire, and Radiguet, I can only imagine what it would have done to me.

My first literary encounter was with Shakespeare. He profoundly repelled my classmates and, it seems to me, hardly enthused the nun who was our literature teacher either. But I was enthralled by his passionate earthiness, joined sometimes to such sensitivity it would melt your heart, the expression of the soul's upwelling, with all its tenderness and turmoil.

I had the good fortune to attend a performance of *The Merchant of Venice,* presented by a London company that was touring

Canada. The magic began for me at the Walker Theatre in Winnipeg—which in itself predisposed me to the sorcery of the stage, with its rows and rows of ornate balconies, its immense chandeliers, and its heavy crimson velvet curtain. All question of French or English or forbidden or imposed language disappeared. There was only a language that transcended languages, like that of music. In the highest balcony, leaning over the rail towards the actors—who from that height looked very small—I could barely catch the words, which for me were pretty obscure anyway, yet I was spellbound. I've never really been able to fathom the fascination of my very first evening of Shakespeare, a fascination which is as much a mystery to me today as it ever was. . . .

That was in my last year at the Académie Saint-Joseph, grade twelve. . . .

Then there came the long-awaited day of what we called *la graduation.* There were twelve or fifteen of us graduating, I think, a fairly big group in those days when not many girls of our milieu went that far in school, often by choice but mostly for lack of means. The principal, who loved an excuse for holding celebrations and receptions, decided she couldn't let the occasion pass without making a big splash that "would for ever be remembered in the annals of the school."

A large number of both French and English dignitaries were to be invited. The commencement ceremony was to take place in the auditorium, with parents and guests seated in the audience and we, *les graduées,* sitting or standing on the stage where everyone could see us, with all the ferns from the convent arranged behind and around us. It must have given us a sylvan setting indeed, since the big backdrop behind us, I think I recall, was painted with tall interlacing trees as well. We were to be dressed all in white, including our shoes. In the crook of the left arm, near the heart, we were to hold identical bouquets of red roses, bought all together at a small discount and costing us five dollars each. And we were to be photographed up there on the stage in all our glory, holding our bouquets, and it was all to be so beautiful that some of our teachers were already close to tears as they coached us in the bows we were to make, "bending from the waist, but never looking down. . . ."

And so for the day that should have been one of pure delight for her, Maman was obliged to eke even more than usual out of nothing. How she did it I'd rather not know, but I had my two dollars for the photograph. "Smile, you pretty liddel ladies," beseeched the Armenian photographer, for there was always one of us drifting wistfully off as the shutter snapped. He never did get us all smiling together at "the beautiful life waiting for you, just think, liddel ladies, like a morning in June." I had my white shoes. I had my bouquet of roses, the first bought flowers I'd ever held. A florist's delivery still makes my heart skip a beat, and it's probably because of those roses.

And the dress. Where could Maman's thoughts have been when she sat down to make it? I think I recall that Papa's condition worsened about that time, although I myself didn't really notice, I was in such a turmoil over pleasing him by coming first. Increasingly, everything was falling on Maman's shoulders and on hers alone.

From up there on the stage, I searched and searched through the faces in the crowd. Finally I caught sight of her, and she remains for ever in my memory as I saw her then. Her poor face was grey with fatigue—she may have finished my dress only late the night before—but was lifted, straining towards me, smiling at me across the distance. For all its sunken eyelids and drawn cheeks, it shone with pride, and that hurt more than anything I'd seen before because suddenly I knew how much all this had cost. The wave of cruel realization swept over me, gripped me in vice-like anguish, robbed me of all my joy in the day, then faded, leaving me with my insouciant youth up there in my place of honour. . . .

I entered the Winnipeg Normal Institute that autumn. It was a big building in barracks or firehall style, on Logan Street as I recall. . . . [W]e now passed into an institution which was strictly English. Well, no; we did have one French-speaking instructor. She came a number of times to pronounce three or four laborious sentences reminiscent of Ionesco's comically mechanical verbalizations in *The Bald Soprano*. Perhaps they even originated in the same textbook. Having by mistake posed questions to one or other of our little French-speaking contingent and got real answers in real French, she ceased thenceforth to call on us at all, and the lessons proceeded as previously, between people talking at cross-purposes without understanding a word of what they were saying.

But we weren't just passing from one language to another. We were passing from one climate to another. We were leaving a little world in which the nuns overprotected us perhaps, sheltered us too much from reality, and venturing into the lion's mouth, one might say. . . .

For a time I saw the school as the scene of a battle to be waged, and nothing else. Hitherto, the tactics we'd been taught to use against our English adversaries had been tact, diplomacy, cunning strategy, and polite disobedience. In my imagination, the time had now come to cross swords. I was soon presented with my opportunity.

After perhaps a week of classes, the school's principal, the kindly old Dr. Mackintyre whom I became so fond of later, came to give us his principal's word of welcome. He was a teacher of psychology, and he delivered an hour-long, rambling peroration consisting merely, to me at that time, of an old duffer's well-intentioned maunderings. In fact, long before the notion of self-fulfilment came to be common currency, this man was talking of nothing else, using terms like "an opening out" and "a blossoming of self." . . .

He had a strong Scottish brogue, a fine head of white hair, and, I was soon to learn, a warm, kind heart.

As he spoke, I was waiting for an opening. Suddenly, there it was. I put up my hand, asking to speak.

Agreeably surprised at such interest in the midst of the prevailing somnolence, he adjusted his spectacles and turned to the seating chart showing each student's name and place in the room.

"Miss Roy" (pronounced the English way in that milieu), "you have a question to ask?"

I stood up. My knees were shaking, only barely holding me up. But there was no turning back. It was now or never for my profession of faith. My voice sounded very weak, as if rising into a vast acoustical void and coming back from afar distorted and quite unrecognizable.

"I agree with you, sir," I said, "that a child's education must first take account of his own personality."

"Well," said he, all smiles, "I see you've been closely following what I've been saying. Have you something to add?"

"Yes, that I see a terrible contradiction between theory and practice. For example, take the case of a little French-speaking child coming to school for the first time in his life, and it's an English school. From the minute he arrives he'll have to be put in the mould designed for little English Canadians. What chance will there ever be for his personality to blossom?"

A deathly silence fell around me. I'd touched the forbidden subject. Woe to the one who lets scandal through the door. I had the impression the whole class was turning away from me. Dr. Mackintyre studied me with a look of surprise, but one in which there was neither animosity nor disapproval.

"Quite so! Quite so!" he said. Then he invited me to consider that the subject hardly lent itself to class discussion and suggested that I stop by his office after four o'clock; we'd talk about it then. . . .

At four o'clock I went to the principal's office. The stoop-shouldered old man with the shock of white hair gave me a weary smile as he waved me to the chair on the other side of the huge desk.

"Brave girl!" he muttered. In my surprise I didn't realize at first that he was speaking of me.

Then he confided that when he was a young man in Scotland he'd experienced the same racial and linguistic injustices suffered by the French community of Manitoba. And that he'd often been laughed at for his burr, too.

"Language is the vehicle of communication," he observed, "but it's created more misunderstanding in the world than anything else, except perhaps faith."

He then pointed out that since our French contingent was not a large one, it would probably be better not to waken the sleeping hounds of fanaticism on either side; that he could see only one course for us to follow, which was to excel in everything, always to be better than others.

"Work at your French," he said. "Always be faithful to it. Teach it when you get the chance and as much as you can . . . without getting caught. But don't forget you'll have to excel in English too. The tragic thing about minorities is that they have to be better, or disappear. . . . Can you yourself, dear child, see another way out for you?"

I shook my head. . . .

My father's health was declining day by day. This had been going on so long that I hadn't yet realized how fast his condition was deteriorating now. . . . I was working hardest on my English accent, having made the class laugh several times at my expense. I finally threw myself totally into my work and lost sight of my father's suffering image.

That's the way it's been too often in my life. In my haste to accomplish and thus bring support, comfort, or reason for pride to those I love, I haven't been attentive enough to see that they couldn't wait.

During the second term we were sent out into various schools of the Winnipeg School Commission, where each of us was to take charge of a class under the supervision of the regular teacher, who would evaluate our teaching prowess and ability to keep order. The marks we'd get from the teacher were to count heavily in our final marks for the year. Most of us were terrified by the prospect, because if we happened to get a harpy for a teacher it could be disastrous. Which is what happened to me. . . .

[S]he told me to carry on with the lesson where she'd left off; I don't remember what the subject was, geography, perhaps. All I recall of that class is the horror of it. The pupils were from a district known to be a rough one. They were fairly big, aged twelve to fourteen, and half boys, half girls. They quickly saw how shy and frightened I was, and went wild. I've never heard such an uproar in a classroom. . . . Beyond my despair of the moment, another still more devastating was rearing its head: if I have to cope with this to be a teacher I'll never make it, I was telling myself, I'll never be able to stand it. And I saw the door to the only occupation I'd been prepared for closing before me. . . .

But most devastating of all was the haunting image of my ailing father. His pulmonary edema had suddenly worsened and he'd been hospitalized for several days. . . . Before leaving the house that morning I'd gone to look at him as he slept, still under the sedation given him during the night. I'd been struck by the change in his face and had asked Maman if I hadn't better stay at home that day, but knowing what a hard day was awaiting me and how nerve-racking it would be to put it off, she took it on herself to reassure me, not realizing herself, perhaps, how close the end really was.

"Go and do your best," she'd told me. "When this day's behind you you'll be happier and in better shape to help me.". . .

[A]t the point where I could take no more and was perhaps about to break down in tears, throw in the sponge, turn tail and run, the door opened a crack. The school principal beckoned to the teacher, who went to join him in the hall. She returned with a very different face. First in surprise and then in fright, I thought I saw sympathy for me in her expression now. She bent forward and said softly in my ear:

"Go now. Go quickly. They've just telephoned to say your father . . . is . . . very ill. . . ."

I'd be at a loss to recall exactly who was there, for I had eyes only for the head on the pillow. I have never seen such an avowal of pain on a human face. Not physical pain; from that, at least, he'd been delivered by a strong sedative, which was no doubt also affecting the thinking realms of his being since he appeared unconscious, though from time to time he'd still give a little moan as if in recollection of suffering more than from its present effects. But what his face expressed now that all defences were down, was the incredible accumulation of suffering in a single human life. I was fascinated by that defenceless face; as I looked at it, I was hearing a soul's long, soundless lamentation for the first time in my life. So that's what life is, I said to myself, a torment so frightful one's face can no longer mask it when the end comes. And I think it was that extraordinary, otherworldly openness which must at last have made me see death as something majestic and beautiful. . . .

I began to cry in great sobs, I was so distraught that life should be such a tissue of misunderstanding. Thinking perhaps that my misery came from feeling my father hadn't loved me, Maman now tried to persuade me otherwise. Still kneeling beside me and rocking me as she held me to her, she whispered that two nights ago when he'd begun to suffer so much he'd told her she could depend on me because I was really a brave, hard-working child; that two or three weeks ago, when I was running a bit of a fever but had gone to the school as usual, he'd been very upset, saying, "She's got my delicate health, poor child. I'm afraid she's going to have a hard life." And so on, not suspecting she was wringing my heart, because my grief lay in seeing no possibility of making amends. My relationship to my father would remain for ever as it was when death separated us. Nothing could ever be added, taken back, corrected, or wiped away.

If only I'd had just one visit with him in the hospital. "One little visit," I told myself pleadingly as if it just might be possible, as if the lost opportunity might miraculously be recaptured. Or perhaps I resented his not waiting, not giving me a little more time to bring him my teacher's certificate. So I wept as I thought about the joy we could have had together.

Now there was no going back. All I had to console me was my memory of that wheelbarrow ride with my old father holding the handles high and me in the box, lifting to him what I really believe was a beaming face. . . .

Almost as soon as the funeral was over I had to get back to my studies to prepare for the approaching examinations. To my great surprise, I passed them without difficulty. Perhaps the dragon-teacher had repented at the last minute and given me a good mark. Or perhaps Dr. Mackintyre had intervened. I'll never know, but I finished not far from the top of the class.

If the news had come in time it would have brightened my father's last days, but now I didn't know what to do with it. I longed to be able to bring him back to life so I could tell him. What was so great about it if it was just for me? Later it was Maman I longed to bring back, so I could tell her about all the wonderful things that were happening with *The Tin Flute*. In my imagination she wouldn't believe me as I told her, and I'd be saying, "Come on now, Maman, I'm almost rich, so you can rest in peace now." And she, back there in the shadows, would be shaking her head sadly, not believing I wasn't still poor and defenceless. . . .

Just before the school year finished at the end of May, Dr. Mackintyre called me to his office. . . .

At that time of the year, he told me, a school board without enough substitute teachers sometimes asked the Normal Institute to send them one of its graduating students. He'd just had such a request and had thought of me. The school was in a little village about fifty miles from the city. The trip wouldn't cost much. I'd earn five dollars for each school-day. But the best part of it was that when I applied for a permanent teaching job, which would be soon, I'd be able to show I'd had a little experience, without, he observed artfully, having to specify that it had only been for a month. . . .

I came bounding into the kitchen.

"Maman! Maman! Guess what!"

I wonder how many times I'd burst in on her that way, all youth, verve, and excitement, when she was coping with her worries and grief. . . . I was rather ashamed of my euphoria but I really couldn't contain it.

"Guess what! A school, Maman! My first school!"

"Stop your babbling about a school!" she retorted, losing patience. "We're still a long way from September. And you're just out of school yourself."

"That's what's so wonderful! I've got one already. For the month of June. I start the day after tomorrow. *My* school, Maman!" And I tried to throw my arms around her, tried to spin her round with me.

It was too much. She shoved me away almost roughly.

"A school? Where?"

"At Marchand."

"Marchand!"

All of a sudden she was bristling and hostile. I was bewildered. Hadn't her life been focused on seeing me get a school at last so I could stand on my own feet? . . .

In the end she came and sat down at the kitchen table. She folded her hands and stared in front of her, not believing what was happening, hurting with the pain for which she herself had laid the groundwork. And finding distress when I thought I was bringing her pleasure, I reminded her of this, not thinking I was rubbing salt in her wounds.

"You're the one who's wanted me to be a teacher all your life."

She was weakening, about to give in.

"When is it?" she asked in a small, resigned voice.

"Well, I really have to leave tomorrow."

"Tomorrow!"

A shower of exhortations began to fall on me. With all those uncouth people out there I'd have to be careful to keep my distance. Be polite, yes, but never familiar. Make sure I didn't get put upon, either. "Oh dear," she sighed, "you're too young to start off surrounded by tough, bad-mannered hicks."

"Maman, so what if I have to learn fast?"

In the end she mustered up a smile for me and left everything she'd been doing to come and help me pack.

By the next day she'd found an acquaintance who was going to be driving in the direction of Marchand and had agreed to take me.

Such was her distress over seeing me leave the house that I think she forgot to kiss me. All that mattered was that I should look out for myself, keep my place, stand on my rights, and, if the going got too tough out there, come home. . . .

[T]hat day when I set foot in Marchand, terrified and homesick already, how far I was from having any sense of the aptitude I had—or would have, like a seed lying dormant in the ground long before germinating—for turning moments of my life into stories that would create a bridge between me and other people. And those moments that have made me feel the most alone have often won me the most hearts among strangers. One knows less about one's own destiny than about anything else on earth.

Not until I was halfway up the precipitous stairs on the way to my room, behind the hefty figure of the lady hotel-keeper, who was lugging up my two suitcases, did I suddenly remember one of Maman's most specific enjoinders.

"Before you take a room find out the price," she'd said. "Be very careful they don't take advantage of your inexperience. Considering what you're going to earn, don't let yourself in for more than twenty-five dollars a month, room and board."

Behind the ample back I heard myself pipe up with the question in a voice so faint and shy that scorn was the only reaction it could draw from a person so unmistakably sure of herself.

"Madame, the rent . . . what will it be? How much will you be asking?"

Perhaps irritated that I should bring it up in the middle of the staircase, and to her back, and in any case being of a nature to want to take me down a peg, she plonked the bags down right there.

"First off you can do yer own fetchin' and carryin'."

Several steps farther up, when it was my turn to be out of breath, she deigned rudely to tell me what I wanted to know.

"Anyway, young miss, you needn't think I'm gonna feed you and give you a bed and light and . . . and . . . for less than twenty-five dollars a month."

I heaved a sigh of relief despite her offensive manner. That was the limit Maman had fixed. I could accept it without argument, and Lord knows I had no heart to haggle with that awful woman. . . .

I went outside. I took the path leading to the schoolhouse, which was not far from the houses and, like them, built right on the sandy ground. I went in. I sat down at a desk that was up two steps on a dais if I remember correctly, unless I'm confusing it with the school at the Little Water Hen. The silence around me was oppressive. It weighed heavily on my stomach. It even invaded my thoughts, frightening them and preventing them from taking shape.

Through the row of windows in the south wall of the schoolhouse I could see a straggly troop of those puny spruce trees standing as motionless as one could imagine, stuck in their woebegone poses. And sitting there I peered into the obscurity ahead of me, trying to catch a glimpse of the life awaiting me.

The following September I began teaching at Cardinal, a larger and less indigent village but no livelier, located on the opposite side of the province. I was dreadfully homesick there and uncomfortable besides, for I was boarding in a flimsily built house with the barest suggestion of heating, even when winter set in and its winds blew through the thin walls. If I didn't freeze to death it was because my landlady took pity on me and made me a voluminous feather comforter. Pulled up over me in bed, it felt like a light and marvellously soft mountain. After that I wasn't cold any more, not at night anyway, even when the water in the pitcher beside my bed froze hard. . . .

[T]he year I spent there was one of the most important in my life. That year turned a spoiled child into an industrious young teacher, perhaps even a first rate one, since the inspector's report must have had something to do with my getting a position the following year at the Académie Provencher in St-Boniface, just a stone's throw from our house. Now Maman could stop worrying about my living in the boondocks. . . .

The high marks I'd got from the inspector at Cardinal combined with the principal's recommendation were enough: at twenty, there I was on the teaching staff of our city's major school for boys, which must have had nearly a thousand pupils at the time. . . .

So I began adulthood already launched on a career, seemingly for life, in conditions that looked almost unbelievably good to Maman after our years of hardship. In fact, because of the Depression, my starting salary at Cardinal, a hundred and ten dollars a month, was reduced to only ninety-six in St. Boniface. Nevertheless, to Maman the life we led was easy and pleasant in comparison to the way it had been before.

"It's almost too good to be true," she'd say from time to time. "Do you think it'll last?"

She had such confidence that things had finally begun to go

right for us that she even thought we might manage to "save" the house, as she used to put it. Yet we'd always known that we'd have to resign ourselves to parting with it one day. . . .

I have to admit that after we'd been talking about selling it, the house had a way of seeming more attractive than ever before, with its row of white pillars, its crabapple trees in flower, and the elms my father had planted, now as high as the window of my attic room, where I'd spun so many dreams of marvellous accomplishments as a child. That house was part of us as only a house can be whose inhabitants have experienced everything from birth to death within its walls.

With the house sold and Maman dead, we did get together a few times more, Adèle, Clémence, Dédette, Anna, and I, at Anna's lovely property in St-Vital, with its house and little outbuildings all white with blue trim, nestled along a lazy loop of the winding Red River. Our old Bell piano had come to rest there. I used to let my fingers wander over its yellowed keys, trying to bring back a tune my father had been particularly fond of. I'd feel a wave of sadness rise up in me, as much for what I sensed I was going to lose as for what I'd already lost. I'd reached an age where one begins to lose much, and being the youngest in the family, I sometimes glimpsed a period in which I'd see all my remaining family depart before my own turn came. . . .

So now when I go to Winnipeg for my visits to Clémence, who is in a home, I take a room in a hotel. It's a very curious feeling to be in an air-conditioned room a step away from the city where I was born, grew up, went to school, and earned my living, and suddenly to realize that I'm waiting at least for the phone to ring, though I haven't yet told anyone I've arrived. . . .

There's no longer really anything to make me feel at home in Manitoba, except the little section roads that stretch away beneath the endless sky, if only I can get to them, and if when I do my friends will just leave me alone for an hour or so to commune with that utterly silent horizon. There are some who understand, who'll take me to the edge of the open prairie and release me as you'd release a bird, then go away pretending they have things to do elsewhere. They know they won't lose me, though many's the time I've longed to go and lose myself for ever out there—that's just a childish fancy; one doesn't put oneself away like that, however strong the urge may be at times.

So I set off, feeling buoyed nevertheless, walking towards the red glow low down in the sky where the prairie ends, because for the magic to work I need not only an illusion of infinite space but also the gentle time of day just before nightfall. Then, for a few moments, my heart may soar once again.

Maman was happy during the last years we spent together, though less on her own account than because she felt I was content with my lot. . . .

So it was no wonder she took new heart, began to hope again, with me and for me. I could be gay and entertaining, I did wicked parodies of local characters, I often made her laugh till she gasped for breath, and as for love, though I seemed to inspire it then as naturally as I breathed, I wasn't yet letting myself be caught. . . .

Lively, exuberant, mischievous though I appeared to be, and probably still was at the time, the worm was already in the apple so to speak; or at least, something was eating away at my merry, carefree nature. Hardly a day went by without the strange thought entering my head that I wasn't really at home here, that I had a life to make for myself elsewhere. I'd been brought up to be French, but what would I find here to nourish and sustain me? . . . So I'd hurry to Winnipeg to hear concerts, or to watch entranced as the great dramatic characters I'd discovered in my teen years came to life before my eyes: Lear, Richard, and poor Lady Macbeth forever sniffing her hand, from which all the perfumes of Araby would not wash away the smell of blood. It was always the same hateful dichotomy: in French we'd play Labiche, Brieux, Bernard, even Molière, all rather clumsily, but it was nice, pleasant; in English I'd hear great words that remained in the heart of the listener indefinitely.

It didn't escape me that our life was an inward-looking one, which led almost inescapably to a kind of withering. The watchword was survival, and the principal standing order, though it was never formally pronounced, was not to fraternize with the outside world. I seemed to feel a little more of my lifeblood escaping every day.

I can still recall bits and pieces of the almost constantly carping and negative preachings of those days: the beach was an accursèd place, dancing was an abomination (especially the popular slow waltz of my twenties), going steady was a mortal peril, particularly between "us" and "them" because it led to mixed marriages, the direst of calamities. . . .

With an eye to a possible departure, I'd begun to put aside a sum of money each year, a minute one, since the circumstances Maman and I were coping with were as difficult as ever. Where would I go? To Quebec? The previous summer, friends had driven me there during the holidays. . . .

What was I expecting? That everything would suddenly be different? That the language I'd been told was the most beautiful and charming would flow from every mouth? That friendship would beam at me from all eyes? . . .

Instead of which I found I was that curiosity, a little Franco-Manitoban who still spoke French, bully for her! Or sometimes "the little cousin from the West." In vain I'd explain that both my parents were born in Quebec and that I was returning to my roots. Nobody treated me as though I'd come home. I remained pretty much an outsider in fact. "Very nice, speaks just like us, but not exactly family." I realized then that we French Canadians don't really have a sense of common blood. Of nationality, yes, but not from the heart like the Jews or other scattered people. Our own, once out of sight, are no longer really our own. . . .

So the next time I left I wouldn't be returning to Quebec. Why not Europe? Yes, that was it, I'd go to France. Perhaps France would recognize me as her own.

I must have been mad! Yes, raving mad in my frenzy to be loved, wanted, to feel at home somewhere at last. I must have been really dreaming to imagine I'd be more warmly received in France than in Quebec. The astonishing part is that in fact I did get that warm reception, but much later; such an unbelievably warm reception that I very nearly fainted with emotion. Which goes to show that I may have been mad, but not insane. . . .

Deep inside me was something I was carefully hiding from myself, I was so frightened of the stern face it would show me. This was my urge to write, when I still hadn't the least idea how to express myself in a personal or engaging manner. I think it was the Quebec writer Paul Toupin who said that discovering the sound of one's own voice is in itself a very difficult experience. Nothing could be more true. Furthermore, I kept longing for a home and not knowing where it was; perhaps even then I was hoping it was the whole world and all mankind. I'd long for a past, and it would slip away from me. I'd long for a future, and see none on the horizon. . . .

It took me seven years—eight counting Cardinal—to scrape together, penny by penny, the sum of money I felt I had to have to contemplate leaving. I had about eight hundred dollars in the bank. I raised this to almost nine hundred by adding the modest proceeds of selling my bicycle, my fur coat, and a few other objects. Maman was alarmed to see me disposing of things she knew I treasured. It didn't help to tell her I was only going for a year, which I earnestly believed; to her I was behaving like someone burning her bridges, or turning a page in her life.

Precisely how my plan to go to Europe developed and why it took over and ruled my life so utterly, I'd still find it difficult to say. So at the time, I suppose, I didn't understand it at all. It was, it must have been, one of the mysterious calls one hears and obeys blindly, half confident, half confused. . . .

But I had a feeling my urge to leave hadn't begun with me alone. Often I thought it must have come from previous genera-tions, whose yearning for fulfilment had been sapped by unde-servedly obscure lives, an urge reborn in me, inspiring me to strive for their ultimate liberation. Perhaps I was still gripped by my old childhood dream of making it up to my people with my own suc-cess. I liked to keep telling myself so during these months of tor-ment, for I was often terrified by the uncharted future towards which I kept driving myself. I suddenly grasped how big, how impenetrable my future was, seen from my peaceful, countrified lit-tle Deschambault Street: a misty vastness in the distance, pierced but not dispersed by brilliant lights. I wanted to turn back but it was too late. I had put the inevitable between myself and my fear, as I was learning to do to protect myself from perpetual indecision.

It must have been my last year of teaching, or possibly the next to last. I still had my first-grade class. I was comfortable with my lit-tle immigrants and they seemed comfortable with me; we were drawn together by a subtle feeling that we were all strangers—at least, strangers to an absurd element in life that was ruining it for humankind.

Surprisingly, after a tenacious fight to keep me at home, Maman suddenly gave in. I told how her resistance ended in *The Road Past Altamont*, partly fictionalized, or transcended rather, but containing the essential truth, and I don't want to return ever again to that old wound.

She resigned herself more readily than I expected to selling the house. From lack of experience, I didn't understand at the time that she was tired out from struggling, but only where material possessions were concerned. Later, although more tired than ever, she found enough energy to come and visit me in Montreal. And if her children were unhappy or in danger, she'd run to them still, even just before she died. . . .

Maman finally found a buyer and the transaction was quickly concluded, almost without hesitation. All my life, or at least since I'd been able to understand such things, I'd been hearing that selling the house was inevitable. Many times the prospect had come close enough to touch us with its clammy wing, then gone away again and left us in peace a while. Then suddenly it was done and there was no turning back. When Maman told me, pretty calmly, "I've sold the house . . ." the shock I felt was something I've never really recovered from. For me it's still as though she told me she'd sold a living, breathing part of us that day.

From that point on, Maman seemed to accept the fact with surprising composure. Once liberated from much that she had accumulated in her life, furniture, objects of one kind or another, she perhaps felt for the first time that she could turn to many of the things that she'd been wanting to do. It may have been like casting off a weight. In any event, she seemed to undergo a mysterious and sudden rejuvenation, ready, one might say, for a new, more carefree, airy existence, with no ties but those of the heart.

We didn't get much for the house: once the debts were paid, barely enough to provide Maman with a very small allowance for a year or two—until I came back from Europe, I thought. But we were pleased with an agreement we had made with the new owner. For a modest sum he would rent us three rooms upstairs, made into a convenient little apartment. . . .

That year, Maman went as usual to spend the summer with her brother Excide. . . .

The wonderful summer holidays came to an end. I went back to my class at the Académie Provencher. This would definitely be my last year of teaching.

By the end of September, Maman had still not come home. That year the threshing had been much delayed by torrential rains. She was no doubt loath to leave her brother before the heavy work was finished. But I imagined that she was also finding consolation for the loss of her house in the permanence there, things that never let her down: the farm, the high, clear sky of Pembina Mountain, the seasonal farmwork which never changed from one year to the next.

When October came I began to feel she was overdoing it. Her brother was so much younger than she, I didn't like to think of her, at sixty-nine, working her fingers to the bone for him. I suspected that before coming home she was putting the house in order, inspecting the curtains, mending the ones that were still holding together, making new ones to replace those beyond saving, filling cupboard shelves with jams, jellies, and vegetable preserves of all kinds. I suppose I was a little jealous, but I resented the fact that she should put herself out so much for a brother who at times, I felt, had taken rather too much advantage of her.

At last she came home. It was a late October evening. There was frost already. The first snow was about to fall. She arrived with a fat suitcase bulging with jams, pembina jelly, sweet butter, fresh cream—to us, priceless presents from the farm, which Maman intended to share with others. Some of these good things had been sent with Maman for Rosalie, her only sister living in Winnipeg, whom Uncle Excide hadn't wanted to forget.

The next morning, with a cold coming on and extremely tired, I thought, she was determined to go that very day to take Rosalie her share of presents. I'd found her looking poorly when she returned from the farm. She'd lost weight and seemed to have worked beyond her strength, as if on purpose, to escape some kind of punishment, perhaps. I tried to keep her from going, telling her that the day was cold, the sidewalks icy, and that my aunt could certainly wait another day for her share of the gifts from the farm. To which she replied that she had brought some homemade bread that Rosalie was particularly fond of, and she wouldn't dream of not letting her enjoy it right away, poor soul, after all she'd spent the summer glued to her sewing machine. At that I lost my temper and told her it really was ridiculous, a woman of her age slaving all summer at Uncle's, then when she'd barely set foot inside the door going out in the streets again like a beggar woman. . . . I stopped short. . . .

I was uneasy all that day, though I couldn't put my finger on the reason why.

"Maman hasn't phoned?" I asked when I came home.

"No," Clémence said, "she must be on her way. Or else Aunt Rosalie has kept her for supper."

At six o'clock I called my aunt. She told me Maman had left two hours before, presumably by streetcar.

It was seven o'clock when a policeman rang at the door. He was bringing me the news that Maman had had an accident in the street and had been taken to Misericordia Hospital, which was not far from my aunt's. She had been crossing the icy pavement to reach her streetcar and had fallen and broken her hip. The driver of a car had picked her up.

I left immediately for the hospital, which was at the other end of the city, in an English neighbourhood, of course. . . .

Riding home on the streetcar through the darkness, heaven forgive me, I foresaw that Maman might remain a permanent invalid, or at the very best considerably handicapped, that at best her accident would consume most of the money left from the sale of the house, that I wouldn't be able to leave her under the circumstances, meaning I wouldn't be leaving at all. I saw my dream being snuffed out, like the dreams of many of my forebears no doubt, the curious dreams that had driven me for years to achieve something I couldn't identify, that would allow me to be myself. And I grieved for the part of me that now would never come to life, would remain hidden from me. But I also felt a cowardly kind of relief at being spared that lonely, hazy, difficult road, at being allowed to walk down the comfortable beaten path where I'd have company and support on every side. In the darkened window of the streetcar, I could see myself far in the future, gazing out a window, docile and resigned, contemplating what I imagined I might have been. . . .

I arrived late at Dr. Mackinnon's office, having made the wrong transfer on the way. I was taken aback to see a man who was old and ill-looking, with a crimson face and great bags under his eyes. In fact, he was to die before Maman. I've rarely seen a man so unmindful of his own ills, thinking only of those of others. I'd hardly sat down facing him in the light of a heavy-shaded lamp when he leaned his big white head towards me.

"Don't worry. Your mother's not in danger."

"Oh! Good! What needs to be done, then?"

"Operate. Reduce the fracture. Then immobilize her in a body cast that will cover her trunk, both arms and one leg."

"Oh, how awful!"

"It is indeed. Especially for an energetic woman like your mother. She's wonderful," he volunteered. "I've met two or three people in my life, not many more, who've given me the impression of loving life as passionately as she does.". . . .

"How much will it be for the operation?" I remembered to ask at last. . . .

"Ordinarily," said Dr. Mackinnon, "it's two hundred and fifty dollars, but I see little signs I recognize because my people weren't rich and I can tell you aren't either. How about a hundred dollars?"

I shuddered, not because of the sum but because the past was so vivid in my mind I'd lost sight of where I was for a moment.

"A hundred dollars!"

And suddenly, buoyed by the confidence the doctor had inspired in me, I found myself opening my heart to him as I'd never done to anyone before. I told him I had enough money in the bank to pay for everything if necessary, the hospital, the anaesthesia, the operation too, but it was money I'd scraped together bit by bit over eight years so I could go and spend a year in Europe, I couldn't really say why, even to myself. Perhaps it was to test myself, to see if I had the stuff to become someone or something, though I had only a muddled idea what, and it wasn't certain I even had any talent, but that was the way it was and I couldn't help it, it was like a mania driving me to find a place for myself. And it was now or never because soon I wouldn't have the strength to leave, I had only just enough now; I could feel the bonds of routine, security—and love—closing tighter around me every day, the better to hold me back.

He'd pushed aside the desk lamp a little, in case it was bothering me no doubt, and the soft half-light encouraged me as I talked.

Suddenly he stood up, and with feeling and determination that took me by surprise told me:

"Go! Go before life swallows you the way it's swallowed so many of your people. Mine too," he added sadly. Then his tone brightened as he continued. "Do we have a bargain? I'll cure your mother. I'll put her back on her feet. And you'll leave. . . . Sometime in the future, if you can and if I'm still in this world, you can repay me whatever you think's right. I'll leave that to your conscience.". . .

I found Maman less dispirited than the night before, almost cheerful in fact. . . .

As soon as I began to tell her about my visit to the doctor and the decision to immobilize her in a cast, her cheerfulness vanished. For a moment she was dumbfounded, then she rebelled.

"Never! Never!"

At her age, she argued, it would be madness to let herself be shut up that way. She'd never live through it. Better she accept being crippled and in time be able to move around a bit, and, who knows, perhaps it wouldn't turn out to be so serious as all that.

"And make sure you keep me shut up with you," I said cruelly. I'd suddenly realized that this was the only weapon I had against that iron will of hers.

She blanched. The wound in her eyes told me how surely the blow had struck. She looked down.

"Well, if you think I should go through with it . . ." she said.

But next morning the principal came to my classroom door to tell me Dr. Mackinnon wanted me on the telephone.

"Your mother refuses to have the operation," the kind, gravelly voice told me.

"Oh, dear heaven! Can it wait? Long enough for me to . . . ?"

"One or two days, not much more. I'm afraid of infection. And her heart's showing some signs of fatigue."

"I'll go to the hospital as soon as possible." . . .

Maman looked away. . . .

"I've been told bones sometimes mend very well on their own," she said, "that they join by themselves when they're broken and after a month or two you can start walking again, even with a break like mine. A woman in the next room who had it happen came and told me. And it won't cost as much. . . ."

"And supposing what your woman says is true," I retorted derisively, "what are you going to look like when you walk?"

Thereupon, calling up all my powers of mimicry, I turned myself into an old relic; with one hip protruding, my neck twisted, my face contorted, and one leg dragging pathetically, I staggered across the room, clutching, leaning on anything within reach, moaning, and making enough heavy weather to melt the hardest heart. . . . [F]inally Maman laughed.

"All right," she said, giving in as easily as a child, "but . . ."

I knew at once what she wanted. I should have thought of it before. We had a friend who was a nurse, who was very dear to Maman.

"Clérina's free," I said. "I'll go and see her tonight. I'll ask her to be with you tomorrow when they put you to sleep and when you wake up.". . .

Summer came. Maman had always greeted it with a delightful array of flowers attractively planted around the white-columned veranda and in borders and circular beds in the lawn. This year we didn't have even a square foot of ground in which to plant the few bright red geraniums from the apartment, but Maman didn't seem to miss the garden as much as I'd expected. As her possessions dwindled, she had more love and attention to give to those she had left. She took to her freedom far better than I thought she would, in fact; it allowed her to concentrate on inalienable possessions. I only came to understand this when I myself stopped wanting possessions of any other kind.

Maman was to spend the summer at her brother Excide's again. Suspecting she'd be so grateful to be cured she'd fling herself more ardently than ever into serving others, I lectured her about her tendency to overdo whatever she undertook.

"At least," I said to her, "when they're shorthanded don't go and offer to milk the cows."

She gave me that too-ready smile of assent which generally meant she'd do exactly as she liked. . . .

At the beginning of September . . . I had a room with board at the Misses Mullers' for a few days while I waited for Maman, who was to join me there. This, of course, was when I fully realized how badly I missed our house and formed some idea of how much Maman must feel its loss.

I didn't go back to see Deschambault Street, thinking it would be too painful. Nowadays when I go to Manitoba, thoughtful friends will drive me there. We slow down, then stop in front of the house that was ours. It's changed somewhat but it's been kept in good condition and I always feel grateful to its buyer, who has obviously taken great care of it. I look up in silence at the little third-floor window, at which I used to listen on spring evenings to the mating songs of frogs from the ponds at the bottom of the street. And I feel compassion, not for the adult I've become, knowing well that the future is only really glorious long before you reach it, but for the child up there who was so dazzled by its glory.

Maman arrived from Somerset. She was to return there after I'd gone and would come back to St-Boniface with Clémence in the autumn, when they would take an apartment in town. Again I found her thinner, her face drawn, as though a little shrunk. I was annoyed to find her looking so tired and chastised her, no doubt rather bitterly, for tending to overdo things at her brother's. . . .

[T]he big brass bed.

It was the only one in the room. I was going to sleep in the same bed as Maman for the first time in my life, I think, unless I'd done so when I was very young, which is likely, though if I did I don't remember. I'd always been an independent child, insisting on keeping rather to myself, my own bed, my own little place to study, away from everyone else. Maman had understood this need and respected it, perhaps having wanted privacy for herself.

Lying side by side, neither of us could sleep. Fears for the future; sorrows of the past; insecurity, life's constant companion. Being side by side and defenceless in the dark made these things weigh all the more heavily on us, perhaps. Ever since that night I've felt that unless you've lain in the same bed beside someone, even one of those closest to you, you can't know much about that person, and you'll probably know even less about yourself.

I sensed Maman near me, tense, not allowing herself to move for fear she'd keep me awake. I was doing the same for her.

"You're not asleep yet?" I said finally. . . .

We both pretended to be on the verge of sleep a few seconds longer, then abruptly I put an end to the silliness and spoke up about what was bothering me.

"These two little rooms you've taken for yourself and Clémence—it seems to me you'll be cramped and have no view. I'm afraid it's going to be very depressing for you."

No, she assured me, and tried to convince me that once the house had been sold, the sacrifice made, she'd felt liberated, and perhaps this was true. She didn't much mind now where she lived. There was a lot to be said for getting rid of things. When you can lose nothing more, you can finally relax. She'd taken far too long, she said, to realize that furniture, rugs, and that kind of thing just tied you down as you aged.

I listened, almost more grieved at this detachment than I'd been at her still recent determination to cling to every reminder of the past. . . .

A few minutes later, wearily, and sadly, she asked me to forgive her for letting herself talk about this just before I was to go away. It was just that she was so worried about Clémence.

"Who'll take care of her when I'm gone?" she said. "Sometimes I'm afraid, very afraid, there won't be a soul in the world who'll look after her." . . .

"I'm not going," I said. "There are too many obstacles."

Maman sat bolt upright. She reached over my head to turn on the light. It was dim, but her eyes, though still weary and sad with worry over Clémence, burned with renewed energy.

"That's all we need!" she declared. "Your ticket's bought, your passport's ready, everyone's been told, your replacement at school's been found, and now you go and change your mind. You'll have everybody laughing at you, and so they should!"

"Have everybody laughing at me? I'm used to that!"

"You're going," she said emphatically. "Otherwise you'll never forgive yourself, and you'll have me never forgiving myself either." . . .

"You're the only one I kept. Till now." Maman's voice was firmer. "Do you think I could forget you've stayed with me till the age of twenty-eight?"

I didn't tell her it wasn't just because of her that I'd stayed, though she probably knew this as well as I did. It was good I didn't say it. From that night of whisperings we needed to be left with a feeling of lasting closeness, unshakeable tenderness towards each other.

"Go to sleep now," I told her.

"You too," she replied.

Neither of us went right to sleep even then, each still hearing echoes of the things that had passed between us that night, echoes we'd hear ever after. What a little thing it takes sometimes to unite people, or estrange them! If we hadn't lain in that big strange bed together, Maman and I, we might never have known many things about one another. . . .

[W]hen the evening of my departure came and I arrived with Maman at the old Canadian Pacific station, to my surprise there were friends in every corner of the concourse. I was positively jumping with joy, running from one group to another, suddenly overcome with dizzying tenderness for these young men and women of my own age who I hadn't believed were so close to me, but who suddenly were. . . .

My friends crowded around for a goodbye hug, some bearing little ribboned packages, others slipping into my coat pocket or handbag an envelope in which I'd find a bank note with a few words like "For a pair of stockings . . ." or "For a square meal some hungry day. . . ." Dear, kind friends. . . .

The conductor shouted his "All aboard!" I jumped onto the step of the train. . . . Then, in the midst of my euphoria, beyond the sea of young, smiling faces, my mother's distraught little countenance caught my eye, suddenly old and creased with the grief she could no longer hide. I'd been so carried away by the affection being shown me I'd forgotten to kiss her goodbye, and with the look in her tired eyes she was allowing herself just barely to remind me of this. I remembered the look we'd exchanged on the day of my graduation, when I searched for her from the stage and our eyes met, hers shining with so much pride that they lit up my whole being. Today the light seemed on the point of going out. I jumped off the train. I ran to her. I put my arms around her. . . .

It was she who first loosened our embrace, saying, "Your train . . . your train!" because it had slowly begun to move. I jumped back onto the step of my car. I clung to the handrail. I looked at but didn't see the young faces, the smiling faces. I could see nothing but the lonely little figure in the midst of happy people. I watched her pull her rather skimpy coat around her, something I realized only now I'd seen her do at least a hundred times. It revealed so well the way she was, proud and diffident at once. Her sorrowful eyes were fixed on me as though they'd never lose me wherever I went. It became unbearable. I saw too well that she knew I wouldn't be coming back, that destiny was taking me away to another life. My courage failed. It was clear now that I wasn't leaving so I could make good for her, as it had pleased me to believe. Dear heaven, it was really so I'd be free of her, wasn't it? Free of her and the family woes clustered about her, in her keeping. . . .

Next I think I shed some tears. Of shame? Compassion? I'll never know. Perhaps it was the bitter taste of desertion that made me cry. . . .

Of all the foreigners who stream into Paris every day there was surely never one more bewildered than I in the autumn of 1937. I knew absolutely no one. However, a letter had been sent from my faraway Manitoba to prepare the way for me. . . . [T]oday I can't remember the name of the young woman with the book whom I sought so frantically, and who helped me so much when I finally found her.

I stepped out into the terrifying horde that gets off a train arriving at the Gare Saint-Lazare from the coast. In the sea of constantly changing faces, I kept trying to recognize one I'd never seen before. . . .

Then suddenly the crowd began to thin. It happened so quickly that I was surprised and even more distraught. Soon there were only a dozen or so lost-looking souls still wandering about, making the huge space look ten times bigger than before. Finally there were only two little figures left at opposite ends of all that emptiness. Each of us began a hesitant approach towards the other. I didn't have my magazine and she didn't have her book. She'd left it on the Métro, I learned later. We exchanged beseeching looks. She was the first to speak.

"Are you Gabrielle?"

I flung my arms around her neck as if she were suddenly the dearest soul in the world. Yet I'm still trying to find her name. I seem to have had it on the tip of my tongue for years. Perfidious memory! Will it ever give me back that precious name? . . .

As we drove into the City of Light at last, along street after street I saw nothing but tall façades severely shrouded in darkness. Even the streetlamps yielded no more than a paltry glow.

"I've found you a suitable *pension*, Madame Jouve's," my compatriot told me, "one they'd say here is *tout ce qu'il y a de bien*, all you could ask for. But tonight for sure Madame Jouve will come down on you like a ton of bricks for arriving so late. After midnight, everything's barricaded like a mediaeval fortress there. Have you seen Carcassone?" she asked, then returned to my landlady. "If she attacks, you counterattack. If she snarls, snarl louder. That's the way to get along in Paris."

"How awful!"

"No, because then you're respected." . . .

Madame Jean-Pierre Jouve opened the door, wearing a dressing gown, her eyes heavy with sleep and a reproach on her lips, although a polite one.

"This is some hour to be arriving! You could at least have let me know you'd be late, sent me a wire . . . telephoned. . . ."

At last I was safe and sound in the sixth-floor apartment. . . .

Exhausted, I finally fell asleep. But not restfully. I dreamed I was trudging across Paris with my trunk on my back, having become a street porter, one of those poor wretches of days long past whose picture had sprung from the memory of books I'd read. Next I was tripping on the king's cobblestones at Versailles, fleeing from ruffians who'd been set at my heels. Then I was Jean Valjean of Hugo's *Les Misérables* in the sewers of Paris, clinging to my trunk and being swept along on the evil-smelling waters. The flushing water, the basement at Madame Jouve's, and memories of books from my childhood had joined forces to produce one of the most vivid dreams I've ever had. Suddenly I was attending a *bal musette* with accordions playing and my trunk in my arms, trying to make it dance to a rollicking air. I opened my eyes. It was broad daylight. . . .

For the moment I'd have given anything for another hour of sleep . . . [but] my compatriot was arriving.

"What!" I heard her say in a loud voice as soon as she was inside the door, "Gabrielle's not up and ready yet? We've got a lot to do today."

To my surprise, when Charlotte paused briefly I heard Madame Jouve rise to my defence. . . .

"Marie," she called towards the kitchen, "Mademoiselle's breakfast. And good and hot, eh!"

I lifted the steaming bowl, half fragrant coffee and half scalded milk, and found its taste exquisite. Then I took a croissant still hot from the oven and, since my compatriot had been served coffee too, followed her example and dipped it in my coffee. It was delicious. A warming sun flooded through the window from which I'd seen the moon as if it were rising over battlements. The anemones I've loved so much ever since kept drawing my eye and I longed to touch them. Though my throat was burning, which meant I was probably in for a cold, this morning I felt myself timidly beginning to find my feet in Paris, like a bruised plant in a protective layer of compost. I would willingly have stayed a while at this table; later I would realize that in a way breakfast in Paris is the pleasantest moment of the day, a time of peace and serenity, a time for reverie almost, a pause at the start of the day before you're caught up in the hustle and bustle of life. Many is the time it would help me to take new heart, set me back on my feet when I thought I couldn't cope with Paris any longer. . . .

I never knew where I stood with Paris, the cat-city, as Ionesco so aptly called it. One day for no reason at all it would bare its claws and scratch me, and the next it would touch me with a kittenish paw, equally without reason, just because summer was lingering or the sky was kind. . . .

Even so, I can't ever forget that I made my first important discovery about myself in Paris; I've never totally lost sight of this. . . .

I was coming home joylessly in a crowded bus. It was rush hour. . . . I followed my compatriot's advice and took a number from the machine. I still don't know if the right it gave was "priority" or "precedence," but "precedence" fits the situation so well I can't help liking it better. I'd no sooner taken my ticket than I realized I was on the wrong side of the street—my bus was just then drawing up on the opposite side. A dense crowd milled about, the conductor standing on the bus platform shouting "Number?" and everybody shouting a number in answer. Each time I saw this incredible scene replayed I was stupefied, but also filled with a kind of admiration to think that every day in Paris little courts of justice held sway in hundreds of places at once, the conductor filling the role of referee. . . .

Without a second thought I bounded across the street and joined the harassed little crowd. The conductor called, "Sixty-eight. . . . Is there anyone before that?" To which a weak voice replied, straining to be heard from the back, "Sixty-five." "Sixty-five . . ." bawled the conductor. Then came my call, triumphant in the certainty that for once I was a winner: "Seventeen!" "Seventeen!" exclaimed the conductor. "Make way, *m'sieurs-dames*. Come forward, seventeen." The crowd, suitably impressed, parted as it might have for the maimed and halt. Mine was the last available place, standing shoulder to shoulder with others on the bus platform. The conductor fastened a light rope across the rear entrance, which I imagine was supposed to keep us from tipping off at corners. Suddenly intrigued, he held out his hand and took my number. . . .

"You deserve to be put off, little lady. If you ever do that again you won't get off so lightly, make sure you get that into your head!" I did my best to shrink out of sight in the mass of humanity, but he kept his eyes on me and persisted, "They begin one day by taking a place from some poor mother who's hurrying home to put on the soup, then the next. . . ." As I raised my eyes to him in supplication, to my astonishment he winked at me and carried right on in the same indignant tone. . . .

From the moment I ran across the street the entire little scene had taken perhaps three or four minutes, but to me it had seemed interminable and it had left my nerves tied in a large knot. Little by little, however, I began to feel better, lulled by the rocking of the bus. . . .

We were arriving at the Place de la Concorde. I craned my neck, trying to catch at least a glimpse between the close-packed heads and shoulders. The stately square had come to represent what I valued most about Paris. It was like a piece of my native prairie, for which my soul yearned deeply here. Its broad expanse in the heart of the cramped city always brought me peace. I would suddenly have a feeling of relief. And the stone statuary enclosing the space perhaps made it seem even bigger and more open. I had never crossed it without beginning to picture what it would be like in a driving, swirling Canadian snowstorm. I used to imagine how beautiful it would be to watch the progress of the white furor.

Peering between the close-packed heads, I'd caught my glimpse of this marvellous space. Then while the bus took a sharp turn which would have flung us on top of each other if we hadn't been packed so tightly, I had a fleeting view of the Tuileries Gardens. As brief as it was, it showed me the pond with children playing around it, the impeccable rows of round-headed chestnut trees, and down at the far, far end, a fiery red sky, extending the space to infinity. It was just like the flaming sunsets at the end of the lane behind the house on Deschambault Street when I was a child, which opened a path I was sure must reach the edge of the world. An incandescent ray from the far horizon even touched my face. It moved me so deeply I turned to see its reflection on the faces around me, forgetting I'd been an object of scorn in their midst only minutes before. Weariness and gloom were all I saw, preoccupation with cares or the bad news in an open newspaper. Apparently no one else had seen the glorious display of sunset at its most intense. In that instant the city had revealed itself to me, the eager stranger, not to its own with their jaded eyes. And I, marvel as I might, didn't know what to do with it. I would need to marvel many more times yet, uselessly one could say, before learning how to share my wonder with others.

What I can't forget is that seeing the beautiful garden of Paris illuminated by a sun straight from my prairies made me realize I had a faculty for observation I hadn't really been aware of before, together with an infinite longing to know what to do with it. . . .

In November when it was cold, wet, and gloomy, as no doubt my whole life was going to be through my own fault, I embarked on the Calais-to-Dover ferry. The sky was thick with cloud and fog. As the small ship's propeller churned the dark water, gulls cried overhead, close but invisible, expressing so well the pain of departures, and of arrivals. In no time I lost sight of the coast of France. I thought I'd never return and it made me infinitely sadder than I could have imagined.

I would in fact return to France many times. Some of these occasions were the happiest in my life outside Canada; one, probably the best of all, has left me with a glowing memory—of receiving the major literary prize awarded less than ten years later for my first novel. . . .

I journeyed for a long time without a compass, but when life itself is the journey, what use is a compass? . . .

My new life began, with a scattering of classes here and there over the week. This time I went at it with a stout heart and persistence, though never with enthusiasm. I forced myself. . . .

This was the pattern of my life during these months in London. I would be lonely and depressed, pushing myself to do things that seemed to be taking me nowhere; then suddenly my youth and the cheerful side of my nature would take over and I'd be finding the humour in things, laughing and making people around me laugh as in the days of our touring shows in Manitoba, as later too when I was in Provence. . . .

Was it this magical springtime that brought love to my life? Perhaps. Although the sudden burgeoning of life exhilarated me beyond words . . . it also made me aware of how alone I was in London . . . so the intensity of my exhilaration had a bitter side too, for it showed me how desolate it was to be far from home without anyone to love or give me love. Again I was asking myself some hard questions: why I had come to London, what I was doing here, why I was studying drama, and where it was going to lead me. Again everything I'd undertaken seemed worthless and futile beside what I ought to be undertaking. There was also a listlessness, persistent, corrosive, that prevented me from taking an interest in any effort I made to escape from the mood I was in. . . .

This was my state of mind when I set out one day to meet, if you will, my destiny. For all my inactivity I hadn't stopped going once a week, more or less, to Lady Frances Ryder's on Cadogan

Gardens in South Kensington. This generous lady used to open her London apartment every day at tea-time to students, regardless of colour, from every corner of the Empire. . . .

The copious fare served us at tea was for many students by far the best meal of the week, and many would tuck away quantities of butter-soaked crumpets, cheese petits fours, and little tarts smothered in Devonshire cream. The spacious drawing rooms also featured a luxury that most of us had learned to do without: warmth, maintained by central heating. So we'd shed the heavy sweaters we wore almost constantly in winter and move around more at ease, both minds and bodies less constrained, ready for friendly conversation. . . .

The great dream of unity among brothers within the Empire was so deeply instilled, on the eve of its disappearance, that we only needed to be students from South Africa, New Zealand, Canada, Australia for the doors of noble residences and simple cottages alike to open wide for us.

In the group called, I think, Overseas British Empire Students, I was the only French Canadian. As such, though I don't know why, I received particular consideration. . . . In the end . . . I did accept an invitation to spend a week in Monmouthshire near the marvellous ruins of the old Cistercian abbey celebrated by Wordsworth. Perhaps it was my desire to see these ruins that overcame my hesitation. As Lady Curre's guest I was introduced to fox hunting, black-tie dinners, and some famous personalities. . . .

A Lady Wells, who was often our hostess in place of Lady Frances . . . crossed the room . . . holding my hand and . . . said simply, "Stephen, this is Gabrielle whom I told you about . . ." and probably something else which I didn't register. . . .

I don't remember anything about the next hour except that soon almost everyone around was looking at us in surprise to see us just sit and gaze at each other endlessly, as if magnetized.

We left together, having agreed with no more than a glance towards the door. . . .

[Roy and her young lover next attended the opera together. Ed.]

When he took me home he said at the foot of the stairs, "Don't let's ever stay two days again without seeing each other. It's like an eternity. Promise me we'll see each other every day."

I wanted nothing less myself. At this point I barely glimpsed to what a submissive, dependent state I was being led by my feeling for this young man I hardly knew. . . .

I remember very little about going with him to the National Gallery. My most lasting memories of a visit there are of a time when I went alone during my second trip to England. I remember particularly, though I don't know why, the portrait of "Giovanni Arnolfini and His Bride" by Jan van Eyck, which comes to my mind almost every day of my life. When I was there with Stephen I didn't see the works of art very well; we were holding hands all the time, that electric current kept passing between us, Stephen was whispering tender things to me, and all I really heard, all my ears retained, was the tumult of my emotion. . . .

Were we happy? I don't think so. Our love was too feverish, too tumultuous, too possessive to allow us any rest, and when there are no islands of calm at which to pause, love soon reaches a point of exhaustion. My feeling for Stephen destroyed almost all power of reflection in me. He made me think I was living with great intensity, but in reality he was keeping me away from practically everything beyond his control. I was no longer seeing anything but brief glimpses of the world around us, which seemed more and more distant, strange, and out of reach, though it was we who were cut off, wrapped up in our passion, isolated as if for ever. Later, when I tried to analyse what had happened to us, it seemed to me that Stephen and I had been like butterflies or night-flying moths, those myriad creatures of the air drawn helplessly by some ruse of Nature like wavelengths or a certain smell. I wonder if the electrifying attraction we were subject to isn't one of the cruelest of all life's pitfalls and misconceptions. Because of him, once free of this subjugation I was long in mortal fear of the thing called love; perhaps I always shall be. . . .

Our happiest days were in the next few weeks perhaps; we were unaware that they were the last we'd be granted of this period of confidence. Stephen rented two bicycles so we could explore large sections of London together. I'd never ventured anywhere more daunting than country paths or peaceful little side streets in St-Boniface on a bicycle, and the thought of braving the heavy traffic of London filled me with terror. . . .

In stages, stopping fairly often to give me a chance to rest, we rode to Richmond Park in less than two hours. It was a weekday and there weren't many people there. We had the whole magnificent park almost to ourselves, we and the free-roaming deer, hinds, and fawns. We fed them pieces of bread, which several came and ate out of Stephen's hand. . . .

We pushed our bicycles up a grassy slope. There was a huge tree at the top whose spreading branches were like an umbrella, blocking the heat of the sun. We leaned the bicycles against its sturdy trunk and stretched out on the grass, half in the sun and half in the shade. We lay on our backs with Stephen's head in my lap, forming a kind of cross.

He gazed up at the sky. It was clean and pure above the great island of verdure formed by Richmond Park in the London of those days.

We stayed this way for a quarter of an hour, perhaps more. For the moment we didn't need to look at each other or caress. We were content to lie in a cross and gaze at the tranquil sky, finding such happiness in this that we needed nothing else.

With his eyes still fixed on the clear blue sky, as if the admission were extracted by a kind of infinite goodness in everything around us, or perhaps his own staggering realization, he said:

"I think I love you." . . .

He left me at the bottom of the stairs that night. I was so tired I could hardly stand. He seemed very weary also, and still had to return the two bicycles. . . .

The next day I didn't hear from him, though ordinarily not a day went by without Geoffrey calling up the stairs, "Your friend's on the phone. . . ."

He was away nearly a month. Then one night Geoffrey called up the stairs, "Your friend's on the phone. . . ."

Little by little he revealed fragments of his other life. I learned that he belonged to a group of Ukrainian militants financed by Ukrainian-American patriots, and its cause was nothing less than the overthrow of Soviet power in the Ukraine and the restoration of the independence it had enjoyed for a single day during the First World War.

I had already had a premonition that his dreams, aspirations, and secretiveness made Stephen profoundly alien to me. That night, sitting on the bench in the little square, I was convinced that in all essentials we had nothing in common. . . .

[S]itting on the bench with the leaves rustling softly overhead as in Richmond Park not so long before . . . my love had died. There was no mistake; I knew it instantly. What I didn't know was how long after the mortal blow love keeps trying to come back to life, begging to be allowed to live. . . .

In the end I came to hate the little room I'd thought was so calming at a time when I was more or less calm already. In July under a white-hot roof, it was stifling. It's strange how often I've had little rooms that are made unbearable by the summer sun at times when I've been most alone. . . .

I fell into the habit of slipping away to Trafalgar Square, where I'd spend whole days. The water from the fountains filled the pools beneath and the pools overflowed, keeping the huge square relatively cool. . . .

[O]ne day when my mind could focus a little better on my surroundings, I noticed small forest-green buses arriving every half-hour from one direction or another. . . .

This Green Line went close to forty miles into the country, so you could go out and come back in a day, perhaps even half a day. I learned this from an old cockney who came and sat on the bench beside me. . . .

Moments later, one of the sprightly little forest-green buses appeared and drew up at the Green Line sign. From where I sat I could easily read the tall letters on the front that announced its destination. "Epping Forest", they read. . . . All I remember of this moment which had such a momentous repercussion on my life is an irresistible urge to drive away in that bus. It gave a gentle roar. It would be leaving any minute. Suddenly I raced across the square. The bus was already in motion when I jumped onto its step. The driver took one hand from the wheel, held it out to me, and drew me inside. As he manoeuvred into a free lane, he chided me gently for giving him such a turn, nearly running under his wheels like that.

"This isn't the forest yet, so you can't go running round like a hare without looking right or left."

We left the noisy square behind. Without realizing, I was on my way to one of those blessed havens to which life has steered me over the years, each a place in which to pause and gather strength and momentum before moving on.

"Where to, Ma'am?" asked the driver-cum-conductor with the affable manner so many Londoners used to have with foreigners, as though sensing their vulnerability better than anyone. . . .

"I don't know the forest," I said. "Could you show me a pretty place where I could walk a while without getting too far from the bus route, so I can catch the bus back after a few hours?" . . .

We passed King's Cross and my fellow passengers still hadn't decided where they should send me. The driver finally settled the matter in favour of Wake Arms.

"There's only an inn," he told me, "but it's a friendly place. You can stay there if you like till I come back in two hours' time, or you can go for a walk. On the left there's a quiet path mostly in the forest but not too lonely. Sometimes it comes out in the open and there are farms in the distance now and again . . . oh yes, and a beautiful moor full of red heather. It's a lovely little path that I'm going to come and explore some more soon myself when I've got a day off." . . .

The driver must have recognized my delight as he watched me watching the forest through his rearview mirror, for when I glanced in it I saw him smile with the genuine pleasure you feel when you find someone enjoying what you enjoy yourself.

"Marvellous, isn't it?" he commented when I turned my eyes gratefully back to the great, serene archway overhead, all my weariness and heartache banished for the moment.

The bus slowed.

"Wake Arms," announced the driver.

The inn was all alone in a small forest clearing by the road. For the time being, with its pub closed and the upstairs windows shuttered, it looked either deserted for the day or abandoned to a deep torpor. It had a very beautiful sign, as did all English inns in those days, which hung well out from the front of the building on a wrought-iron frame. What was on it? I must have known but, alas, I can't remember. . . .

It never even crossed my mind to disturb the sleepy inn for information or any other reason. I set off at once down the narrow track leading from the bus stop into the forest. It was just a cycle and walking path, in fact, and I didn't meet a soul. At first I enjoyed being completely surrounded by nothing but Nature. I kept seeing swarms of bees, wasps, and butterflies pass by. I walked on and on, loath to turn back, drawn farther and farther down what I would call a trail, at least around the next curve, for it kept bending one way or the other, always in full sunlight, however, since at this hour the sun was directly overhead and the shadows no longer reached me. Soon I felt very tired from the heat and fresh air, and probably from relaxation of nerves long under tension. I was also thinking that I was foolish to venture so far into the deserted forest and that soon I wouldn't have the strength to return to the bus stop in case this path didn't really lead anywhere, as I was beginning to suspect.

But I couldn't resist walking a little farther, then a little farther still, driven by the excitement, the anticipation of happy surprise that I've always experienced on unknown roads. . . .

Eventually, however, frightened by the persistent silence and near the end of my strength, I was about to turn back when I saw signs of habitation just ahead, half hidden in the trees. . . .

The Little House was very low to the ground and surrounded by trees and flowers, the hollyhocks and tall, pale blue delphiniums reaching almost to its thatched roof. It couldn't be made for living in, I thought, just for playing at living in; the humble little Tudor cottage of Old England on the tins of fine biscuits my mother used to buy when I was a child, mostly for the tin I'm sure, because we treasured those tins and kept them for years to hold batch after batch of other, less expensive biscuits.

The minute I saw it I felt as if I'd returned to the safety and peace of my early childhood. There was a sign nailed to a tree, which I can see in every detail, though I've forgotten many more important things. In crude, hand-painted letters it read, "Fresh-cut flowers, tea, scones, crumpets . . . 1 s." Under an arbour at one side there was a rustic wood table with chairs to match. All around, the air was full of the ecstatic humming of bees, wasps, and hornets, drawn undoubtedly by the flower garden from miles around. Perhaps the swarms I'd seen go by were coming here and had arrived not long before me.

I knocked at the squat little door under the low-hanging eaves. It was opened by a young hunchback with the pleading eyes one often sees in the disabled. I asked her if it was too early for tea and she said no, she was just about to put the kettle on, in fact. Barely fifteen minutes later she re-emerged bearing such a heavy tray for her frail arms that I hurried to help her. . . .

In no time I'd devoured just about everything on the tray, including a little pot of black-currant jam that the wasps descended upon, competing frantically with me until I thought of putting a spoonful aside for them, which they went to and ate delicately, leaving the pot for me. Since then I've known that wasps and humans can eat together peacefully in a garden if one is generous enough to provide a little share just for the wasps. . . .

I felt as though no harm could reach me here; the peace of this place would be mine as long as I stayed. I called the young woman back.

"I walked much too far getting here to go all the way back today," I said. "Couldn't you make some room for me for the night?"

"I would with pleasure, but it's a wee place as you can see," she said with a sad little gesture towards the house. "There's hardly room already for my father and my mother, been paralysed for years, she has, and it's me as does for her. . . .

"If you think you can walk a bit more, not far, scarcely a mile by this same path, you'll come to a wee village called Upshire. . . . Look for Century Cottage. . . ."

For someone approaching from the south as I did, the village was set on a gentle upward slope tapering away into a beautiful clear sky. Behind, the forest pressed close, a constant companion, but the vista ahead was boundless and the unexpected sight of so much space was probably what made me take an instant liking to Upshire. . . .

I found Century Cottage without difficulty. Though with its second floor it stood much taller than Felicity's little house, it seemed to be no less buried in a tangled profusion of flowers. . . .

I came to a door of dark wood. I reached out for the knocker, but as if I'd had enough strength only to bring me as far as this doorstep, I suddenly drooped against the door frame. I think I was so tired that tears came to my eyes, so exhausted I felt I was arriving not just from Wake Arms or Fulham, or from a love that had left me more alone than it found me, or from the agonizing uncertainties I'd been living with so long, or from a thousand mistakes on my part, not just from these but from much farther, the very beginning of my life perhaps. This was my last thought before letting my head fall against the door, no longer able to keep my eyes open. This was how Esther must have found me, almost asleep on her doorstep. . . .

A very few minutes later, as if I were a guest she'd been expecting, she said, "Would you like to see your room?"

I followed her up a rather steep staircase. She opened a door. The most inviting country bedroom met my eyes, with a big brass bed, a washstand complete with water jug and soap dish, and a fireplace with a mantel holding a cluster of small old photographs in frames, and other keepsakes. . . .

Esther pulled down the counterpane, folded it, and draped it over the foot of the bed.

"To look at you I'd say you'd run all the way from your faraway Canada without a single stop for breath," she said. "Come on then, lie down. Rest a while. I'll come and tell you when tea's ready." . . .

I didn't argue much longer. . . . [I]t seemed I'd only just gone under when I was being wakened again.

"Gabrielle dear, tea's ready. It's nice out still so we'll have it in the garden." . . .

At last we went in. Esther wouldn't hear of my helping her. . . .

One behind the other, we climbed the stairs. . . .

Esther handed me the candle.

"There's a lamp all ready by your bed, and matches and some books in case you'd like to read a while. But do get to sleep as soon as you can. I'd like to see you looking better in the morning, and specially to see less unhappiness in your eyes." . . .

When I woke I was perhaps more at peace than I had been since the days of summer holidays at the farm when I'd wake on my first morning in my uncle's house not knowing where I was; then I'd recognize the inside and outside smells and know for certain I was happy again in the house I loved so much, where I'd known only peace and happiness.

From the big brass bed I could follow the sweep of the downs. In the soft morning light they had a green, silky sheen that made them even lovelier than the day before. . . .

With the return of this peaceful feeling so long absent from my life, I discovered just as suddenly a burning urge to write. This had happened before. I would wake up happy to be alive, in a tranquil, receptive mood, and there in my head would be a story, ready and waiting, which I was eager to write. . . .

I hurried to a small table under one of the big windows where there was something to write on. Carefully I detached a few pages from the middle of a school copy-book so as not to damage it in case Esther was using it for keeping accounts. . . .

The story I began with such enthusiasm that morning doesn't count for much today. If I dwell on it at all it's because it was at least better than anything I'd written before. It flowed well and, most important, it was irresistibly absorbing, restoring me to a state of contentment I hadn't known for a long time. As I recount this, it occurs to me how curious it is that one can only be happy when one is pleased with oneself. I'm sure it must be the same for everyone.

The story I found waiting when I woke and which flowed so well was coming in my mother tongue, in French. For a time I had thought it might be a good thing to write in English; I had tried with some success and I was torn. Then suddenly there could no longer be any hesitation. The words coming to my lips and from the point of my pen were French, from my lineage, my ancestral bonds. They rose to my soul like the pure waters of a spring filtering through layers of rock and hidden obstacles. . . .

The reason for what happened that morning was crystal clear, a miracle in a way, though the miracle would occur many times in my life. When I arrived the previous afternoon I had found myself with people who loved me instinctively. Where I've felt loved and have loved in return I've felt safe, and where I've felt safe I've found courage. Only affection can bring me such confidence that life no longer frightens me, I've known this for a long time now. Then I'm brave enough to throw myself into the work of writing, which never ends and has no real goal, an ocean without shores. . . .

I finished the long story I'd begun soon after I arrived at Esther's and at once began another. There seemed to be no end to the material coming to my mind and I expected to keep on living in this heady state of excitement. I tackled a series of short articles on Canada, an idea that had occurred to me when I was answering questions from Esther about what it was like, how we did things, what winter was like, and summer, and the people and so forth. I had barely finished three of these without a pause when on an impulse I put them in an envelope addressed to the editor of a Paris weekly I knew only through having bought an occasional issue in London. Then I ran at once to post them for fear I might change my mind if I hesitated even for an hour.

Sometimes I still shudder to think of my nerve at the time. I had no one to advise me or edit me and I hardly even reread anything myself, so my writing must have read like what I consider today to be a first draft and wouldn't dare show to anyone. But on reflection, the path I chose almost unconsciously is an exacting one, and perhaps one ought to set foot on it with a measure of thoughtlessness. Otherwise who would ever take this endless road? . . .

Time kept going by with life so sweet I found myself thinking this couldn't be real everyday life but some likeness of things as I'd subconsciously willed them. And yet I'd still sometimes feel a stab from the memory of the days of happiness and torment I'd known with Stephen. The days of happiness perhaps hurt the most. So happiness prepares the way for sorrow, I told myself rather naïvely. But now I was spared the steady ache I'd thought so unbearable for a time, because I was rediscovering the excitement and pleasure of telling a story. . . .

One day Mrs. Stone the postmistress called to me from her house next door to Century Cottage, "A letter from Canada for you, dearie!" and came and handed it to me over the picket fence between the properties.

It was from my mother. I began to tremble as soon as I recognized the writing. I always trembled when her letters came, not because I was afraid of reading reproaches or complaints—there never were any—but because seeing her writing was enough to open the door to memories of all the suffering culminating in me. Surely I shouldn't be the only one to escape, I would think, and I'd feel condemned to suffer, as if it were a duty.

I tore open the letter. This time Maman hadn't really been able to hide her anxiety. Why had I come to this insignificant little village, she wanted to know. Was I discouraged? Had I completely run out of money? If only she had a little to send me! . . .

When I'd read and reread her letter I looked up at nothing in particular and saw—I imagine by one of those miracles of normal life which happen more often than we think—I truly saw my mother, on the other side of the earth, sitting at a wooden table writing to me, a bottle of ink nearby, her glasses slipping down her nose, her face showing anxiety at being unable to help me and determination at least not to upset me. At this, I was so ashamed of having been happy when she was so sad that I was really upset. Dragging my feet, I went where only yesterday the trees had watched me recite and gesticulate, this time to weep in silence.

How long it took me to accept my mercurial nature! Or life itself perhaps. One day all song and freedom from care, the next all torment and distress!

Not long after, the postmistress called across the picket fence. "Another letter for you, dearie! This time from Paris. My, but you're popular!"

What this letter contained was enough to make me jump out of my skin: a cheque and a few electrifying lines. The first of my articles was accepted—for an upcoming issue—and the two others would be published shortly. I thought I would die of excitement. I don't think I've ever felt as truly like a real, honest-to-goodness writer as I did that day in the little yard among the dandelions. I ran and waved the cheque under Esther's nose and I think was piqued that she didn't go as wild with excitement as I was. The sum wasn't large, about five dollars, but none I would ever receive later would seem as fabulous, or arrive more opportunely. For want of human company to appreciate the magnitude of my glory, I went to the forest to dance and sing and perhaps even try a leap or two among the stern trees. I think I really learned then that of all that comes our way, the hardest to bear in solitude is triumph. . . .

Nothing happened to break the spell for several weeks. Then from my window one morning, whom should I see approaching, already close, but Stephen. . . .

When lunch was over . . . I had an idea of my own. The moment had come to show Stephen my first finished story, I thought, and especially the cheque from Paris. . . .

When I put the cheque before him the delight he showed almost outdid my own. . . .

Then I told him I had something better to show him, and produced my manuscript. I wanted so badly to get an opinion on my work at last that I think I was trembling with trepidation and hope.

Stephen took the manuscript from me, scanned a few lines, and at once expressed even greater enthusiasm than he had over the cheque. . . .

He read aloud with a pencil in his hand, correcting typing errors as he went, and soon, with my permission, grammatical and careless mistakes. I had known he had an admirable command of French, but not to the point of being able to pick up all kinds of little errors at first reading, even awkward expressions for which he proposed substitutes that suited my text so well I was as pleased as if I'd found them myself.

Eventually he observed that I was inclined to use far too many adjectives. The noun, according to him, being the strong element in the sentence, could do without qualifiers if it was an adequate one. It didn't occur to me at the time that when writing his tracts with their abrupt, incisive style he had developed a manner of writing totally opposed to mine. That day, however, I was so subservient to his views that for a long time I strove to purge almost all adjectives from anything I wrote. That is, until I realized I was making my writing dry and parched, for a well-used adjective makes a phrase live, makes it touch a chord inside a person.

But Stephen wasn't only interrupting his reading to propose corrections. Much more often he'd exclaim, "That's good! That's very good!" with a pride that lifted me as if on the crest of a wave. . . .

Later, however, I saw that what he had praised most highly was perhaps not the best in my writing but the facile, the provocative but shallow, the playful, a tendency to caricature, all things I would try to rid myself of later. Still, this hour of work in the little old-fashioned parlour, a cricket singing intermittently outside among tall flowers which seemed almost to be coming in through the window, had a major effect on my life thereafter. In this little room I discovered what a delight it is for two to work side by side at something both truly enjoy. There is no greater delight, in fact. The caresses bestowed by eyes and hands, which are pretty much the same for all lovers, are so banal beside the encounter of two minds, the part of us we keep most ferociously to ourselves most of the time. I think also I was vastly relieved to feel that however solitary the way ahead of me might be, having companionship at least for a while on occasion wasn't out of the question after all. . . .

Several times I'd seen Stephen glance at his watch. Now he jumped up and announced he'd have to leave immediately if he wasn't to miss the last bus back to London. . . .

Esther then looked at me and asked if I didn't think it would be a good idea to go with him to the end of the village to show him the short cut; it would take him less than fifteen minutes to reach Wake Arms if he took this path rather than the long way past Felicity's, which was all in the forest and would soon be dark and worrisome. I think she had a feeling we had something important to settle between us and wanted to give us a chance to be alone a few minutes more. . . .

As we passed beneath one of the streetlamps, Stephen turned to me in the wan light and took hold of my wrists. His face was grim.

"Go!" he said. "Leave England. Go back to Canada. I didn't want to talk about it seriously in front of Esther and the old man, he's so emotional, but I don't see how we're going to avoid war. It's almost certain, and it will be very soon."

"But how about you?"

"Oh, me. . . . I'm still a Canadian citizen and there's a good chance I'll find myself in the Canadian army to fight the Germans sooner or later. I'll leave before that if I have to because one of these days you'll find it's Stalin more than Hitler who'll be the enemy we have to destroy. The two of them may go through the motions of a pact but it won't last, and while I'm no friend of the Nazis I'm even less a friend of the Bolsheviks. So if there's war between them I won't be for the Soviets, I'll be for Hitler, because in order to get the Ukraine on his side he'll give guarantees of freedom for my poor country." . . .

I listened, overcome by the same horror and revulsion I'd felt sitting beside him on the bench in the faintly lit little square when he first revealed his militancy. . . .

But he wanted me as well. He begged me to keep trusting him . . . until the day when, if the bloody mêlée didn't end in apocalypse, he'd move heaven and earth to find me, because then he'd have no other thought than to live happily ever after with me.

My only reply was to point out that if he didn't leave soon he'd miss his bus, and perhaps his rendezvous with his Nazi allies tomorrow too. . . .

I walked with him a little farther without speaking. In these minutes I really thought I hated him and would never stop hating him. I pointed briefly to the path beside the wall bounding the manor house grounds.

He started down it. Several times he turned around and raised a hand. I stood motionless, watching him go out of my life. . . .

I knew I would never see him again. . . .

I boarded ship in Liverpool. . . .

Long before we reached the estuary, the waters of the Mersey were tossing us about abominably. The weather was atrocious;

rain, fog, howling wind. Almost every minute you could hear the chilling, mournful toll of a bell-buoy, no doubt marking the channel between reefs. On this apocalyptic note I left the shores of England. . . .

There had probably been other times when I wished I could die. Perhaps everyone has wished this at least once, even in the course of a happy life and especially in one of perpetual adversity or discouragement. But this time it was not a vague wish. I kept looking at the choppy waves buffeting one another, the leaden clouds gathering on the pale horizon; my eyes blurred with tears, I wanted so much to leave this life. Where was it taking me? Nowhere, of this I was certain now. I had left my teaching, hurt my mother unbearably, given up all I had, crossed the ocean, squandered the money I'd so painfully saved, tried all manner of new things, and today was I any further ahead? I felt I had failed in everything, love, drama, writing. Yes, in everything. Why continue the struggle? What would I gain? All I could do now was to go back where I had come from and dig myself in, stay quiet, and consider myself lucky in my lot, as most people must in the end. Or I could sink in the waves and let them carry away my grief, remorse, regrets—perhaps also good things to come, which now I would never know. I think my mind was set on this for several days. But would I have had the courage. . . .

The sea was still very rough. We were going to sail up the St. Lawrence, and despite my mood I was looking forward to rediscovering the route in the steps of Cartier, Champlain, and Maisonneuve. I would be seeing the country from the river again, in reverse order this time, renewing my pleasure in the sight of villages along the shore with their brightly flashing church roofs, which were almost always galvanized in those days. From a distance you'd have thought they were sending friendly signals.

Shortly before the estuary, however, the ship entered a huge field of icebergs and was forced to reduce speed to a crawl. This was the month of April, early April admittedly, yet the Strait of Belle Isle was still icebound. The captain was ordered to go to Saint John, from where a special CPR train would take us to Montreal. So in the end I returned by one of the country's dreariest gateways. . . .

[W]hen I first arrived I lived in the most horrid little room imaginable except in a prison. It was so cramped I had to turn sideways to pass between the grey metal bookshelf and the iron bedstead. The window overlooked the yard behind the principal bus station in Montreal, which was then on Dorchester Street. There dozens of buses were drawn up, always some with motors idling noisily, sending clouds of stifling fumes straight through my window. The loudspeaker never stopped announcing departures and arrivals. "Leaving for Rawdon, *traque numéro sept,* track number seven . . . leaving for Terrebonne, *traque numéro onze,* track number eleven. . . ." Sometimes I used to repeat in my sleep, "*Traque numéro douze,* track number twelve. . . ."

The atmosphere of wayfaring, confusion of tongues, and dizzy whirl of activity wasn't unpleasant. It suited my state of mind and was certainly more congenial, more friendly than some tranquil little street inhabited by equally tranquil people who have lived there for years. I always seem to have had the right place to stay at the right time.

Two letters arrived at the post office general delivery which I didn't dare open until I was back in the safety of my room, fragile haven though it was. One as from the St. Boniface School Board reminding me that I had been allowed a second year's leave of absence without pay and the privilege couldn't be renewed. I must therefore either return to work or resign. The second was from my mother. I can see myself reading her letter, holding it on my knees as I sat at the foot of my little iron cot.

"*Mon enfant,*" it read, "so you're back in Montreal, not so far from home now. Home isn't a house any more, of course, but with the bit of money I have left and what you'll be earning we'll be able to live pretty well, you'll see. And with you so independent and me probably too possessive, I'll try to get used to letting you lead your own life. I imagine I can expect you home soon. . . ."

I looked up and inches away, in the mirror on the little chest of drawers, I saw my distorted face. The flaws in the mirror? My own emotion? The old knot was in my throat again, just as in our days of greatest hardship, perpetual fears, and all that futile courage.

I looked at myself and knew that the time had come to make a decision from which, good or bad, there would be no turning back. I couldn't avoid it any longer.

I left the letter on the chest of drawers, the pages filled with the rather untidy writing which alone always told me better than anything else how strained and bruised Maman's nerves had been.

I went out. . . . I didn't know a soul in the city. I wandered the streets though I don't remember which. I must have walked some distance on St. Catherine Street, then up to Sherbrooke, for behind my agitated thoughts I remember the clanging of streetcar bells, then, as had happened once in London, a sudden intrusion which at first I didn't recognize, the rustling of early spring leaves. And as I had in London and Paris, I kept searching the indifferent faces in the crowd, hoping someone would at least glance at me. At last I walked downhill to where the lights were less bright, St. Antoine or Craig Street perhaps. Down here there was less traffic and less bustle on the sidewalks, and instead something like the murmur of a more private, friendlier sort of life. I wonder why I've always felt less lonely among ordinary people than in drawing rooms and society gatherings, however fondly I'm regarded by others present.

What shall I do? What shall I do? I kept asking myself as I walked. The question hammered at my mind, tormented me much as had the Song of Destiny and the mournful sound of the bell-buoy at Liverpool. What shall I do? Stay or go back?

I had no means of support nor assurance of even the most humble employment here, not even a friendly hand to reach out to me now and then. But could I live in Manitoba's suffocating French climate, its suffocating climate altogether, now that I knew there was something better? For it was misfortune enough to have been born French in Quebec, but infinitely worse, I now perceived, to have been born French outside Quebec in our little colonies of the Canadian West. Though I was lonely here, around me as I walked I heard French being spoken with what seemed a very heavy accent after that of Paris, but with the words and expressions of my people, of my mother and grandmother, and I found this comforting.

Without knowing the way, I somehow reached the banks of the old Lachine Canal. I stopped short, intrigued. Barges were gliding slowly by, their sides scraping against the old timbers lining the canal. Their horns, requesting the opening of the lock gates, raised strange, repeated cries, like lamentations. I think I stayed for hours, dreaming of nothing in particular, as if abandoned by my own thoughts but not distressed by this. The night was rather mild as I recall, far from the miraculous spring of London but with the kindly feel of our Canadian spring. In the little streets of wooden houses and wide-spaced streetlamps where I went to walk, still aimlessly, I heard sounds of water trickling along the gutters, and here and there saw puddles of melting snow.

The bleatings of barge horns were not all I had for company.

This district of St-Henri, whose name I had yet to learn, was constantly shaken by passing trains. First you heard a thin warning bell announcing the approach of a train towards each level crossing, then the long black-and-white-striped arms of the safety gates lowered and the crossing lights began to flash. The great trains bound for east and west came thundering down the track, shaking the ground, the windows of the houses, and perhaps something in the soul that remained quivered, in suspense, after the din had ceased. . . .

Sitting on my bed and leaning against the wall with the writing paper on my knees, I wrote first to the school board thanking them for keeping my position open for me and herewith resigning. Then I wrote to my mother. What did I tell her? Probably to be patient, to expect me back in a year or two. She would soon be seventy-two. . . .

When I had written my letters I counted the money I had left. Fifteen dollars and a few cents. Enough to pay my rent for a week. . . .

On the advice of a journalist at *The Gazette* to whom I had a letter of recommendation from a colleague posted in London, I made the rounds of a number of magazines and weekly papers. All I had to show a modicum of talent was the small collection of articles published here and there over the previous couple of years. At *Le Jour* I was given to understand that they might, when there was room, publish a short column on a subject of my choice, for a fee of three dollars per column. At *La Revue moderne* they would pay up to ten dollars for a longish story if I could write it in the style the readers liked.

I went back to my room. I sat on the bed leaning against the wall with my typewriter on my knees, my thoughts invaded by relentless announcements—"*Traque numéro huit,* track number eight . . ."—terror-stricken to realize that now there was really no turning back; to earn my living, I would henceforth have to write and keep on writing. I suddenly saw how ill equipped I was.

I began with anecdotal accounts of my adventures in England and France. Alas, in my downcast state of mind, no longer stimulated by elation, I could bring forth only platitudes. It took close to a year before I began to write articles with some substance, given the opportunity by a farmers' publication, the *Bulletin des agriculteurs,* to write on subjects involving fact, reality, close observation.

It was even longer before I began to build on the reveries germinated beside the old canal that April evening, coming by stages to the major task whose prospect filled me with even greater terror than I had felt on Stanley Street when I began to write for a living. But now at least I was totally absorbed in my subject, helped and sustained by all the experience of human nature and other resources I'd acquired, as well as by my feeling of having come home, of oneness with my people, whom my mother had taught me to know and love in my childhood.

But back in my room on Stanley Street, I could only write insipid little pieces in which one would probably have searched in vain for traces of the torment and delight that have been with me since I was born, and no doubt will leave me only when I die.

Yet a bird, almost the minute it's hatched, I'm told, already knows its song.

Rosemary Brown

(1930–)

Rosemary Brown was born in Kingston, Jamaica. Educated at private schools, and raised in a female-led family presided over by her formidable grandmother, Brown was encouraged to aspire to leadership, encouraged to excel in debating and drama, and expected to have a distinguished career.

At twenty Brown left Jamaica to attend McGill University, where she met the American black undergraduate William Brown, whom she married after her graduation in 1955. Brown's encounters with racial discrimination in Montreal and in Vancouver, where her husband was completing a medical degree at the University of British Columbia, raised her political consciousness and set her on a career of activism after she and Bill Brown became Canadian citizens in 1959.

Joining the British Columbia Association for the Advancement of Coloured People, and enrolling in social work at the University of British Columbia, Brown became active in fighting discrimination and in efforts to improve child health and welfare while juggling a professional career and raising her two daughters and son.

Her appearance on a popular television show of the early 1960s, concerned with counseling troubled families, brought her public attention, while her lobbying efforts to ensure implementation of the recommendations of Canada's 1970 Royal Commission on the Status of Women brought her to the attention of provincial leaders of the rapidly burgeoning women's movement.

Encouraged by feminist colleagues to run as a New Democratic Party candidate for the Provincial Legislature in 1972, Brown became the first black woman to be elected to a provincial parliament in an election that carried the New Democratic Party into office as British Columbia's ruling party. When the N.D.P. government was defeated in 1975, Brown retained her seat despite a massive voter swing to the right, and thus began to be a figure in national N.D.P. politics.

When the longtime national leader of the N.D.P. announced his retirement in 1975, a loose coalition of feminist supporters of the Party encouraged Brown to contest the national N.D.P. leadership, using the campaign to highlight feminist issues and to hold the Party leadership to account for its neglect of women's concerns. Brown's campaign, under the slogan 'Brown is beautiful,' succeeded in its objective, and resulted in an extraordinary show of support for a western Canadian in a Party always led from central Canada's industrial provinces.

After returning to British Columbia politics, Brown served with distinction, until her retirement from political life in her mid-fifties, to take up a career teaching women's studies at Simon Fraser University.

BEING BROWN:
A Very Public Life

I was born on June 17, 1930, in the house of my mother's mother in Jamaica, delivered by a midwife. Family legend has it that I was my father's favourite child—that he doted on me. My memory of him is a hazy mixture of riding high on the shoulders of a tall man who smelled nice, laughed a lot and filled the whole world with happiness.

That is the good memory—the other one is of running around the living room and verandah one afternoon trying to make the grown-ups laugh and play with me—puzzled and frustrated because they wouldn't. The grown-ups were sad and there was nothing that I could do to stop my mother and my grandmother from crying.

I never saw the big happy man again after that—I was never taken on anyone's shoulders for walks, never thrown up in the air and caught, never felt quite so secure nor ever again smelled anyone like that. For years, I never knew what I had done to make him angry enough to leave me—but I always thought that it had to do with my running around and laughing while the grown-ups were crying, and I wished that I could tell him that I was sorry.

Years later my nurse told me that I had behaved badly at my father's funeral, that I had run around laughing while the father who had doted on me was lying in a coffin in my grandmother's living room.

———

I grew up in my grandmother's house on Portland Road. It was a large place that was filled with the noise of women and children, with their laughter, their joy, their anger, their conflict, their jealousies and their love—but it was a safe place. The men who came and went—uncles, brother, cousins—did so quietly and with respect.

My grandmother's house was big and old and had many rooms. It seemed to be elasticized, because as the number of people who came to live with us increased, rooms would be added on, and bathrooms would be added on, and the kitchen would grow, and the number of small, one-room semi-detached houses where maids and garden boys lived would increase and shrink depending on the need. It was surrounded by a big yard with lots of trees and bushes, ideal for playing hide and seek, cricket or doctor with the neighbourhood kids and visiting cousins. My Aunt Leila and Uncle Tommy built and lived in a two-bedroom bungalow at the back of the yard. There was a large garage, big enough to house two cars. And attached to one side of it, under the mango tree, was a large completely furnished one-room dollhouse that was transformed into a house for one of the yard boys when we outgrew it.

A large verandah ran around three sides of the house, and on rainy days we would spend hours racing back and forth around it playing 'catch' or some other noisy, touching, running game. It was also the stage on which we performed for visitors, because the large doors opening onto it from the living room meant that not only could the guests seated on the sofas and armchairs in the living room be entertained by us, but so also could the maids and other helpers, who would sit on the outside steps during our performance. . . .

I loved entertaining visitors; I loved reciting and acting out dramatic poems; I loved the applause, and the way that grown-ups used to predict great things for my future. "That one is going to be a great courtroom lawyer," some would say to my grandmother. The more religious ones would predict a future as a great preacher or teacher. No one mentioned politics until many years later, which is not surprising: although our history records acts of greatness by women during slave and maroon rebellions, in Jamaica in the 1930s politics was not regarded as a traditional arena for women except as helpers and workers. . . .

I competed in elocution and debating contests always with outstanding success and, in time, I fell in love with words. I was a voracious reader. I was excited by unusual words or the unusual use of words. I used to like to play with words, using them in unusual and outrageous ways. . . . I loved the poetry of the spoken word and of sentences and phrases skilfully and carefully crafted—I used to spend hours listening to the BBC broadcasts on shortwave radio just to learn new words and new ways of using familiar words.

I loved listening to preachers, politicians, teachers and lawyers—anyone who was eloquent—and I used to lock myself in my bedroom and give brilliant speeches to the mirror, debate against myself and dream of being a great courtroom lawyer, destroying my opponents, not necessarily with logic but certainly with words. Yes, there is no doubt about it, as the saying goes, I was 'full of myself'—the only thing that saved me from being obnoxious was my self-deprecating humour; I laughed at myself and pretended not to take myself too seriously. . . .

There were no stories of abuse, kidnapping or murder and no hint of the violence that was to wrack the island in later years. I never learnt of incest until I was an adult, never saw a man strike a woman member of his own family until I came to this country and never learnt of rape until then, either. In retrospect, I now realize that my sister, my brother and I were shielded from ugliness, pain, poverty and all things evil by a doting grandmother, nurse, aunts and mother. It was an unreal world, filled with people who went to great pains to let us know that they thought we were clever, bright and beautiful. . . .

The most important concern in our life was to get a good education. . . .

My school day started at 6 A.M. with a short walk from my grandmother's house where I lived to the beach (Bournemouth) for a quick swim. When I returned home I would have a shower and dress for school. Combing my hair was a real problem and quite painful because it was, in Jamaican terms, 'knotty'—to distract me my nurse developed a routine. Hair combing time was used to study the collect in the Anglican prayer book or some long passage from the Bible, and everything had to be committed to memory. My hair, which was thick and independent, was tamed by being oiled and braided into three plaits or sometimes two with a large bow attached to the end of the braids. . . .

Soon after beginning high school, I discovered the wonder of boys and was promptly sent to Westwood, a girls' private boarding school, 'for my own good'; my family believed that prevention of contact was the best form of sex education. I loved boarding school. It proved, like my grandmother's house, to be a safe place filled with the energy and sound of women. My teen years seemed to speed by in a blur of books, boys, dancing and an increasing addiction to politics. I returned to Kingston to attend Wolmer's High for Girls for my last two years of high school, so that I could graduate from the same private school that my mother and aunts had attended.

One day during my very early school years in 1938, the whole school was called into assembly at lunch time. . . .

When we were all quiet, Miss Wilson, the principal, told us to return to our classrooms quickly, collect our books and go straight home. She said that there was an 'insurrection' in Kingston so we were to get home as quickly as possible and to stay inside listening to reports on the radio until it was safe for us to leave our house— there would be no more school, she told us, "until the insurrection was over." . . .

When I ran into my house still shouting "insurrection, insurrection," my grandmother told me very sternly that insurrection was no laughing matter, that there was a riot downtown, that some people could get killed and that I was to sit quietly by the radio and listen to the news.

That was the first time that I learnt that people in real life really did kill and did die because of their beliefs. This was not stuff in the history books like the War of the Roses, these were people like us who were angry that they were deprived of the right to vote because they were not property owners as the law decreed. They were looting, burning and even killing each other in the hope that the 'mother country,' as England was called by all of us, would introduce fair labour practices and enfranchise them. . . .

[M]y grandmother . . . sat with us and talked very quietly about the injustices of the system, about why universal suffrage was a right worth dying for . . . that sometimes the only language that the mother country understood was violence. And how, although she did not condone uprisings, she certainly understood why they occurred and hoped that the army would not be too hard on the rioters. . . .

I became very angry with the mother country that day and remained angry until Jamaica gained independence in 1962. . . .

I grew up thinking that everybody discussed politics every day—certainly in my Jamaica they did. . . . Not even the Second World War, although it consumed our interest for a while, succeeded in distracting us from the words and deeds of our politicians. . . .

I cannot actually tell when I decided to become a politician or when I fell in love with politics Jamaica-style. I just know that one day I decided not to become a brilliant lawyer after all, but a brilliant politician involved in my island's destiny instead, and I began to prepare myself. . . .

J.A.G. Smith and Norman Manley, who were the founders of the People's National Party (PNP), based on the British Labour Party model, were giants among the political thinkers of the day. Sir Alexander Bustamante, founder of the Jamaica Labour Party (JLP), although he was their ideological opponent, was no less magnificent in intellect and stature. The heroes and heroines of my youth were not athletes nor even entertainers, they were politicians and political activists. . . .

In those days words were the weapons and outrageous promises the battleground—and the women were as tough, as scathing, as bright and eloquent as the men and it was wonderful to be caught up in the excitement of it all.

My grandmother was the first—and most—political person I have ever known. She was a social democrat. Why or how she became one was never clear to me. I doubt that she ever thought of herself in terms of ideologies—her doctrinal system was quite simple and straightforward. She was a member of the People's National Party—she believed in the basic decency of people; she believed that those who had, shared with those who didn't have, and that if a government was run by people who practised these principles, that government would ensure that everyone had shelter, food, employment, health care and the basic necessities needed to cope with and to enjoy life in dignity. She was a profound Christian who experienced politics as an extension of her religious beliefs and always explained it to us in Christian terms—based on the firm moral difference between right and wrong, good and evil. . . .

I am telling you this much about my family because I am so

much a product of their collective moulding, shaping and crafting. . . .

To Aunt Lil fell the task of trying to translate my genetic acceptance of social democracy into an ideological framework. She described herself as a Fabian socialist; although my grandmother gave the impression that she did not think that God played as important a role in Aunt Lil's politics as He should, she nonetheless gave it her grudging approval and was always proud when Aunt Lil could clarify some political act or decision that baffled us. Because of her, I began to read politics and history, trying to make some real sense of all the political talk around me. She encouraged the use of the word 'why.' "Always question," she would exhort me, "always seek to know why." . . .

My uncle, as the surviving male child of my grandmother, assumed the duties of father and became the male to whom we all looked as head of the family. The result of this was that although my mother married a number of times after my father's death (five times, to be exact) there were no major adjustments or trauma accompanying the entry and exit of these men through our lives; they remained my mother's husbands—they were never our stepfathers. . . .

I was both excited and terrified by my female elders. To me they seemed overpowering, independent, self-assured and strong. I was convinced that I would never be able to measure up to their standards nor carry on in their footsteps. On the other hand, they were very convinced that I could. They had great expectations of me and a very high opinion of my abilities and talents, and like John Donne's God, they encouraged and hounded me, and hound me even now. . . .

Today my friends, observing my tendency to be a workaholic, are amused when I say that happiness for me is leading a life of idleness and sloth. . . . I suspect that unconsciously I am so overwhelmed by the debt that I owe my foremothers and so fearful of my inability to repay that debt in some tangible way, or even to live up to their expectations of me, that my striving will never end. . . .

I find it difficult to imagine a time when I will ever be able to turn my back on any struggle for dignity and human rights anywhere. I guess in time I have rolled all my role models into one person who is represented by my grandmother—my nurse, my aunts, my mother, Sojourner Truth, Mary McLeod Bethune, Angela Davis . . . all those tough, strong, independent women who opened doors for me to walk through, and who by their lives set standards for me to live up to. Those women have given meaning to my struggle and reason to my life—and they are the strength that I always reach back to when I feel myself 'going down for the third time.'

There were two significant males in my childhood after my father died. One was Uncle Karl. Dr. Karl Wilson-James was not the slightest bit intimidated by being the only male in a family of high-powered women. He was himself a high achiever who won a medical scholarship to the University of Edinburgh and went on to become one of Jamaica's leading surgeons. . . .

He was one of the driving forces behind the development of the University of the West Indies and was one of the members of its first Board of Governors. He firmly believed that a good education made all things possible and his primary concern was to ensure that the children received the best education the family could afford for them. . . .

The Aunts inspired me to explore the universe—Uncle Karl inspired me to hit the books! His favourite advice was "It will still be there when you are through studying." "It" being whatever thing, matter or person seemed to me to need my attention more urgently than studying at any given instant. . . .

Roy, the other significant male of my adolescent years, sort of snuck up on me and remained my first true love. He was one of my brother's friends—the wonderful thing about older brothers is that they have so many friends. In later years my brother confessed that the reason he had so many friends was that he had two sisters and his friends found him to be the best conduit to them. . . .

Roy became my 'steady' from then until I left for university in the fall of 1950; in truth he was one of the reasons why I left Jamaica to attend university elsewhere.

The debate began the year before I completed high school. As the time grew closer for a decision it became more intense and more family members became involved. There was never any question about 'whether,' only about 'where.' Until then, members of our family had always attended university in Great Britain. It was sort of a family tradition and it had always been assumed that it would continue to be so. After all, all of Jamaica's outstanding public and professional figures had been educated in the mother country—

some had returned with accents so British that they were unintelligible, except to other refugees from British institutions of higher learning; this marked them as 'cultured.'

Two things coinciding with my day of decision created the debate. One was my open and outspoken dislike of England's treatment of Jamaica, a situation that led family members to say over and over again that "my mouth would surely get me into trouble" in England. . . . The polite racism to which early West Indian immigrants had been subjected was fast disappearing, and whereas that early type, though painful, could be ignored, the violence could not.

Second, the University of the West Indies was in its early and formative stage and some family members thought that my attendance there would be the best solution to the problem. . . .

If not Great Britain, then where? The United States was out of the question because Americans were considered to be uncouth and uncultured, and their educational standards questionable. In any event, because of 'my mouth,' I would surely not be safe in such an openly racist country as the USA.

Just when all seemed lost, Dr. Cyril James came to the rescue. I did not know Dr. James, none of us did. We only knew that he was the President of McGill University in Canada and that he had been very helpful in getting the University of the West Indies started. We knew that Canada as a part of the Commonwealth would have high educational standards. The family had heard no wild tales about the treatment of Black people in Canada, so despite 'my mouth' they felt that I should be relatively safe there. . . .

On August 10, 1950, dressed from head to toe in new clothes and accompanied by every living relative in Jamaica, I arrived at the Kingston airport one hour ahead of my scheduled time of departure. As well as relatives, many friends, some of whom had taken time off work, were there to see me off. The night before had been one long send-off party and it carried on until it was time for me to board the plane. I kissed everyone good-bye, leaving Roy for last. As I left, I promised myself that I would return to Jamaica in four years with a Bachelor of Arts degree, then marry Roy and enter the political arena. My future was clear and simple.

I entered the plane, got into my seat, buckled my seat belt and plunged into the most severe case of homesickness that I have ever experienced.

————

Living in Montreal, even in the relative seclusion of Royal Victoria College, the women's residence at McGill University, brought me my first contact with racism, Canadian-style. I had been raised on a diet of poems and stories about the oppression of being Black in the United States, but always there was the rider that Canada was different. Indeed, my family thought that by sending me to university in Canada they were guaranteeing that I would not have to deal with what they referred to as the 'ugliness' of prejudice while receiving a reasonably good education (not as good as I would have received in England, but certainly superior to anything offered in the United States).

I must confess that the graduates of McGill, Dalhousie and the University of Toronto I met before leaving Jamaica fed the myth of a discrimination-free Canada by never mentioning prejudice. They spoke glowingly of their Canadian friends, indulgently of their Canadian professors and lovingly of their Canadian social experience. There are many jokes about the weather, some feeble attempts to include French phrases in their conversation and great bragging about the superiority of the academic standards. . . .

I was happy with the prospect of my studying in Canada; so was Roy. We both assumed that I would not have any interest whatsoever in Canadian men, that I would not be distracted by a glittering social life; I would study, complete my four years and return to Jamaica, probably to attend the law school that was in its infancy at the University of the West Indies. In any event it was obvious to both of us that we were destined to marry and grow old together, and the four years apart would only serve to strengthen our attachment to each other.

Canada was not what I expected. Three weeks after I had settled into a double room in Royal Victoria College, the assistant warden of women called me into her office and explained that I was being given a single room, because the College had been unable to find a roommate to share the double with me. She tried to break the news to me gently, pointing out how lucky I was to secure a single room and how much more private and quiet that would be for studying. I was moved into a single room at the same rate as the double—and two white women students were immediately moved into the double room.

I was stunned! I could not believe that not one of the other students in residence had been willing to share a room with me. Other

West Indian women who had been at Royal Victoria College before me shrugged the matter off as not being surprising; having had similar experiences themselves they had known all along that no roommate would be found to share my room. Every year, West Indian women, given the option, requested the cheaper double room, moved in and were later moved into the more expensive single rooms at the lower double room rate. . . . It eventually became clear that the experience would be typical of the prejudice I ran into during my years in residence—polite, denied and accepted.

The dining room behaviour was another example of the peculiar brand of racism practised in Royal Victoria College at that time. Whenever I entered the dining room at mealtime I would anxiously scan the tables, hoping to find a seat at a table with another Black student. If there was none available, I would look for a seat with one of the two or three white friends I had managed to make (I had made some, including Sue Curtis, whose father was the Attorney General of Newfoundland at the time). If that failed, I just sat anywhere, knowing that I would probably complete my entire meal without anyone speaking to me or including me in their conversation.

I was neither lonely nor unhappy during my stay at McGill. The West Indian community was large, vibrant and close-knit. My closest women friends were two other Jamaicans, Patsy Chen and Merle Darby, who had attended Wolmer's, the same private school that I had, and whom I knew well. In addition, because the ratio of male to female West Indian students was almost three to one there was never a shortage of dates. Many of the older male students were dating white Canadians but in the early 1950s interracial dating was not as acceptable as it is today and many more of the male students either refrained from doing it or did it clandestinely.

Interracial dating was absolutely taboo for West Indian women. We were all very conscious of the sexual stereotypes that we were told inhabited the fantasy world of white males, and at that time it was still very important to West Indian men that the women they married be perceived to be pure and virginal. The tragedy, of course, was that the West Indian male students internalized and accepted the white criteria of beauty and since the 'only life' Black women had to live could not 'be lived as a blonde,' as a popular TV commercial of the time exhorted, the Black men assumed that white men saw no beauty in us, and therefore their only interest would be in our sexual availability.

Even more tragic was the fact that we Black women students (unlike our counterparts of today) shared this perception of our unattractiveness and consequently closed ourselves off from the world of white males. Tragic because the decision to do so was not based on our assessment of our worth, but on our acceptance of our male colleagues' assessment of our lack of worth.

The real excitement of my academic life at McGill was discovering Hugh MacLennan and Canadian literature. During my voracious reading years as an adolescent and teenager, I had discovered and come to love Mazo de la Roche and Lucy Maude Montgomery, and for me that was all there was to Canadian literature. . . .

It was with a sort of bemused inquisitiveness that in my second year I registered for the course in Canadian Literature taught jointly by Hugh MacLennan, the author, and Louis Dudek, the poet. As the works of Gabrielle Roy, Morley Callaghan, Earle Birney and Hugh MacLennan entered my life, they opened up such a rich and exciting world to me that I came to see Canada through new eyes and to develop an addiction to Canadian authors that I have never lost.

In addition, I fell in love with Hugh MacLennan. . . .

Although the women who shared the residence at Royal Victoria College were content just to treat us as though we did not exist, never acknowledging our presence except when necessary and then only with the minimum of courtesy, the landladies and landlords who lived in the neighbourhoods near McGill had no such inhibitions. There was nothing subtle about the racism of the landlords and ladies of Montreal. . . . [M]y first summer in Canada, I hastened home to Jamaica and remained there until it was time to return to school. I needed desperately to be free of prejudice and discrimination, to see my family, and to reassure myself that I was still a whole and valued human being; and to assess my feelings for Roy. But by the following year, I was in love with one of the male students and wanted to spend the vacation in Montreal to be near him.

Job hunting in Montreal that summer proved to be a nightmare. My Chinese-Jamaican friend Patsy Chen secured a job imme-

diately as a waitress at a golf and country club. Although I applied
to the same club that she did, and to others as well, I was never
accepted. The employment counsellor kept recommending that I
accept childcare jobs or light housework jobs, despite the fact that
I explained I was not interested in doing housework or caring for
children. She finally explained that although she had personally recommended me for a number of different jobs, only the people seeking domestic servants were interested in hiring me.

The older, wiser, senior West Indian women students, experienced in these matters, had never bothered to seek employment in
Montreal. As soon as the academic semester ended, they headed for
New York, where they were able to secure any type of work they
wanted.

Discouraged by my job hunt, I reported to Gretchen Weston,
the assistant warden in residence who was also the designated
counsellor for foreign students, that I would be returning to
Jamaica for the summer since I had been unable to find employment. Gretchen, who happened to be the daughter of one of the
Westons of Weston's financial empire and was herself a student at
McGill, was clearly upset by my report; she asked me to allow her
to make some enquiries and report back to me in a couple of days.
The following day she called to tell me to report to the Weston's
plant in Longueil for work the following Monday. . . .

Once I had secured a job, thanks to the influence of Gretchen
Weston, I had to find an apartment, and that's when I ran into the
open, hostile and impolite racism of the landlords and landladies I
spoke of earlier. These men and women made no secret of their dislike and distaste for Black people. They were rude, obscene and
straightforward about refusing to rent us accommodation, often
slamming the doors in our faces to emphasize their rejection of our
request. . . .

The mild anger and frustration I had felt for the students in
Royal Victoria College turned to hatred for the landladies and landlords of Montreal. I fell into a common, irrational habit of including all members of that group in my rage and outrage, rather than
just the specific ones who had hurt me. . . .

Ten years after graduation, when we returned to Montreal so
that Bill could compete his residency at the Allan Memorial Hospital, I found that little had changed. . . . By then, although the hatred
had evaporated, the anger and hurt remained; we were the parents

of two small children and the prospect that they would have to face similar treatment because of our decision to make Canada our home added guilt to my feelings of rage.

After that experience, I escalated my efforts to get Bill to decide to leave Canada . . . but always he returned to the conclusion that this was a country whose benefits outweighed the liabilities of racism, and that raising our children with self-esteem despite the experience of prejudice was a challenge we just had to face. I disagreed strongly; I wanted my children to experience my safe, loving and positive childhood, but I was not prepared to take them and return to Jamaica without Bill. So, to my rage about racism was added my anger at being powerless to control my family's choice of country of residence. . . .

Every year at the end of the spring semester West Indian students had to go to the immigration office to ask for an extension of our student visas over the summer. We had to lie through our teeth about not working during this time, saying that we would just be lazing about enjoying the Montreal humidity until time to resume classes in September; as students we had been issued special visas that very clearly forbade us working. Before being accepted as students we had to prove that we were financially able to attend university without needing to work or receive any financial assistance from Canada, and at the beginning of the academic year we had to show a balance of $1,000 in our bank accounts to cover the year's tuition fees and living expenses. The immigration officers suspected that we were lying about not working but they had no proof, and the frustration drove them into a frenzy. We had to show up at the immigration office with a passport, bank book and letter of acceptance to the fall semester at McGill. We also had to have an address and a phone number, as well as a letter of reference from a respectable member of the community, the Dean of Women for the women, one of the lay preachers from the Student Christian Movement for the men. The officers desperately wanted to find reasons to deport us, and as we sat across from them, watching the rage struggling to erupt as they cross-examined us, we would begin to sweat. For emotional support we would go down to the immigration office in groups. . . .

I used to think that nothing in my childhood had prepared me to deal with this nightmare phenomenon. I was angry at my family for raising me as though racism were a foreign unpleasantness, which I would be spared; I felt that they should have either protected me or prepared me better for this degradation.

I envied Black Americans their access to violent struggle—they could fight back. As Black students in Canada, we seemed to have no options but to rail against our treatment in private and keep our heads down in public, trying to get through the four years to graduation without incident, determined to leave this country without a backward glance or kind thought. Racism seemed to pit me against everyone, including myself—my powerlessness sent *me* into a frenzy.

I was wrong, of course. . . . Unlike Black Americans and Black Canadians, I did not become a member of a racial minority group until I was an adult with a formed sense of myself. By then, it was too late to imprint on me the term 'inferior.' I knew that all the things we were told Blacks could not do, all the jobs that were closed to us in this country, were in fact being done ably, competently and sometimes in a superior way by Blacks at home and in other parts of the world. . . .

Even as I write this, I also recall how each incident would send me racing to the West Indian community in search of succor and to drown the violence exploding in my mind in the laughter and the humour, the music, the dance and the camaraderie that I found there. Anything to forget the glares of hate, the obscene epithets or the look that just went through me as though I wasn't there—and my own unbearable powerlessness. . . .

[I]n those years I changed in profound and basic ways—for I was never the same after my encounter with racial discrimination, Canadian-style. With the passage of time, the hatred faded and disappeared. But I never lost the rage at the injustice, stupidity and blind cruelty of prejudice.

Before I left home, Uncle Karl decided it was necessary to warn me about some of the pitfalls that awaited me in the larger world outside Jamaica. His sharpest admonition concerned the West Indian Society at McGill, which he had been told was a hotbed of communism. . . .

So on registration day when I was approached by a Black male student with a non-Caribbean accent inviting me to join the West Indian Society, I declined, telling him that I was not a communist and had no desire to be involved with a communist organization.

Many years later, after we had been married, when Bill would recount our first meeting he liked to say my response made it clear to him that I was 'in sore need of an education.' It was the challenge this presented, rather than romance, that triggered his initial interest in me. We both chuckle at that explanation since we recall that although there were at least three other West Indian girls present in the registration line that day, I was the only one he approached and invited to join the Society.

As it turned out another student, Noel Edwards, the nephew of a friend of one of my aunts, who I had met in New York while en route to McGill, happened to be president of the West Indian Society. . . . Since I was fascinated by him, I threw my Uncle Karl's admonition to the wind and joined the Society forthwith. . . .

Members of the McGill Student Christian Movement did not fit the stereotype of Canadians that I had developed. They were humane, compassionate, worldly, political and treated me as though I were a person, rather than a Black person. The SCM house was a place for political and sociological discussion and debate, where much of my Canadian left-wing attitude and commitment was bred, fashioned and expanded.

I deliberately closed my mind to the Canadian experience. I was a West Indian student who cared only about West Indian politics, and although I could not ignore the reality of Duplessis's Quebec, I went to great pains to demonstrate that I could not care less what the people of this racist country did to themselves or to each other.

By the time I graduated with a B.A., Bill Brown and I had decided that we would get married. He had graduated with a doctorate in biochemistry a year ahead of me and had left for British Columbia to attend medical school there. Before he left we had discussed our relationship, and although we had some doubts as to whether our love was made in heaven, we decided that I would remain at McGill to complete my course to graduation. If at the end of that time we still wanted to make a life together, I would join him in British Columbia, where we would get married. After that, I would work and support us through his years of medical school, then it would be his turn to support me in the graduate program of my choice. . . .

I considered myself to be in love. Although he was different from Roy in many ways and I realized that I felt differently about him than I did about Roy, I just assumed that I was experiencing the more mature form of love that comes with age. I have always been attracted to exceptionally intelligent and intellectual men who challenged me and forced me to think, and from whom I could learn. Psychologists tell us that girls seek their fathers in their husbands. I guess I unconsciously sought my Uncle Karl, who remained for me one of the brightest, most intelligent and interesting men I had ever known. . . .

When he left for British Columbia, neither of us was sure that our commitment would survive a year's separation, although we hoped that it would. As it happened, the separation created a fantasy world in which we both lived, writing long romantic letters to each other, running up budget-breaking phone bills and building up expectations for love ever after that it would have been well nigh impossible to sustain. . . .

I knew that his childhood, though happy, had been 'segregated' and that his ambition had been to be a railroad engineer. . . .

I also knew that his bright, carefree manner masked anger at a world that would permit him to be a doctor but prevent him from being a railroad engineer, that would make the colour of his skin a prison to limit his options, proscribe his movements and direct his choices. . . .

I knew that I loved him as a kindred spirit who shared my love of dance, music, books and laughter, as well as my hatred of injustice, my reverence for life and, alas, my hopeless addiction to flirtation! . . .

In retrospect I am appalled that all the life options that I considered on graduation revolved around my relationship with the men in my life. . . .

[T]here I was, an adult in my final year at university who was willing to go anywhere, study anything, depending on which man I thought I was in love with at the time. . . .

[W]hen I speak to women students today, I am struck at what a difference feminism has wrought in their thinking and their attitude. I am always pleased and relieved to meet these students who are planning their lives according to their own goals and their aspirations, rather than the goals and plans of the men with whom they are involved. . . .

In the end I chose to follow Bill to Vancouver. . . .

I arrived in Vancouver on the evening of August 7, 1955. I was so nervous that I sat frozen in my seat and was the last person to leave the plane. Bill was so happy to see me that my fears immediately vanished. The following morning we went to the B.C. vital statistics office on West 10th Avenue, picked up a marriage licence and submitted to a venereal disease test. The law in B.C. at that time was that if either of us proved positive on the VD test we could not marry each other. Bill seemed sure that his Wassermann would be negative so I decided not to worry about it. . . .

Our marriage exposed me to another face of Canada. One of our witnesses was Bill's landlady, Mrs. Olive Reid. I was surprised to meet a Canadian landlady who was nice, decent and appeared to be completely non-racist. She certainly challenged my stereotype and over the years she and her husband, children and grandchildren all became our very close friends. . . .

Because my initial contact was such a surprisingly happy one, I fell in love with British Columbia and its people, and I thanked heaven that the memory of Canada I had been carrying around in my head was being changed and widened to include decent landlords and landladies, friendly fraternity brothers and sisters and people who cared enough about others to share happy and special moments with them, regardless of race. . . .

Over the years, throughout my relationships with boys or men there had always existed two Rosemarys. There was the cool, sure, sophisticated woman on the outside and the insecure, old-fashioned little girl on the inside. There was clearly a great deal of confusion about my sexual identity, and the submissive, dependent Rosemary I secretly believed to be the real me was always struggling to remain hidden behind the assertively smart, independent Rosemary, true to the role the women in my family had created for me. And though I admired my mother for never staying in a marriage that oppressed her, I envied my friends and relatives who lived in stable, traditional families, and secretly dreamed of such a family for myself.

Much of the ambivalence and anxiety I had about getting married was rooted in the determination that for me there would be only one marriage and that it had to work. . . .

Immediately on our return to Vancouver, I began job hunting. It soon became clear that the reluctance of employers to hire Black people was even more entrenched here than in Montreal. Indeed, the front-page story of the day was of a teacher at an exclusive private school who had married a Jamaican woman who was Black, and the consternation that this caused despite her protestations that she was only one-fifth Black and therefore more white than Black. The Black population here was small and scattered, and the unwritten rule seemed to be that, aside from entertainment, the special jobs open to them were domestic work for women, and portering on the trains for men. There were, as with all things, a handful of exceptions, but for the most part when I showed up for job interviews at banks or offices, personnel managers seemed very surprised that I had responded to their advertisements.

I explored every avenue in my job search. I used the services of employment agencies as well as the newspapers. An employee at one of the employment agencies finally confessed that she wished she could return my fee, because she was sure that she would never be able to find me a job except as a domestic. . . .

We were not destitute, of course. We had savings from our summer jobs plus $1,000 that my family had given us as a wedding present; as well, Bill received a small monthly cheque from his parents. So by 1955 standards there was really more rage than panic in our situation.

Since I spent all my time job-hunting, Bill decided to take responsibility for finding us an apartment. Moreover he had been in Vancouver for a year and knew exactly where he wanted to live. He wished to be near the university since most of his classmates lived there; it was cheaper to be able to walk to classes rather than use the bus and it was convenient to the library and labs. Again, it soon became very obvious that like the Montreal landlords and landladies, those in Point Grey were unwilling to rent us even a basement suite. . . .

[B]ecause we had not anticipated a problem . . . we were too late for university housing that semester, so our name went on a waiting list and Bill kept searching. . . .

Despite the efforts of white friends and classmates who themselves had no difficulty finding housing, since there was actually a glut of apartments on the market, we found that we were not welcome in the West End, nor in the neighbourhood around Vancouver General Hospital. We finally managed to rent a bachelor suite in an old converted house at the corner of 6th Avenue and Spruce overlooking a dirty and sluggish False Creek, which at that time gave no hint of its trendy, fashionable future. The rent was $40 a month and accommodation consisted of one room with cooking facilities and a bathroom down the hall that we shared with two other tenants on the same floor. . . .

A week after we moved into our apartment I answered an ad placed by the Registered Nurses Association of B.C. for a clerical worker. When I arrived for my interview, I was introduced to Miss Alice Wright, the president, who spoke happily of her visits to Jamaica and of the friends she had made among the nursing community there. She asked why I was applying for such a junior position despite my clerical experience and university degree. I explained about the difficulty I was having in securing employment. She was genuinely upset by my story and offered me the job although she felt that I was overqualified for it; she insisted that I treat it as a temporary placement until something better came along.

I worked at the Registered Nurses Association office on Cypress Street for one year at $130 per month, until I was hired to work as a library assistant at UBC for $181 monthly. I remained in that job until a month before the birth of our first child and only daughter, Cleta. . . .

Over the years I developed the 'one person' theory, on the basis that no matter how many people in a situation are willing to discriminate against you for racial, religious or other reasons, there is always 'the one person' who will refuse to go along with the pack. So the secret to living with discrimination is to hang on and keep fighting until 'the one person' in any given situation is found— because that person always exists. Certainly the story of my life in Canada is the history of these 'one persons' who always marched to a different drum when prejudice and discrimination surfaced. . . .

Everyone knew of and spoke openly and at great lengths about racism in the United States; everyone spoke openly and at great length of our sense of betrayal at finding racism in the mother country—England—but for some strange reason we did not discuss racism in Canada.

Part of the reason, I guess, is because of the subtle and polite nature of Canada's particular brand of racism. We often found it difficult to describe to each other racist experiences because, except in the case of housing and employment, their form was so nebulous—a hostile glance—silence—being left to occupy two seats on the bus while people stood because no one wanted to sit beside you—being stopped and questioned about your movements by the police in daytime in your own neighbourhood—the assumption of every salesperson who rang your doorbell that you were the maid. How do you protect yourself against such practices? How do you tell someone to beware? How do you explain that sometimes you feel ashamed to be the recipient of such treatment and that the reluctance to acknowledge its existence is somehow linked to lowered self-esteem and self-worth? . . .

After two years in our bachelor pad, my pregnancy precipitated the need for us to seek larger accommodation, and once again we were faced with the tedious reality of anti-Black and anti-children landlords and landladies. Pregnancy compounded our dilemma: now we could be refused housing, not because we were Black but on the ground that we were about to have a child. . . .

In any event, once again just when it seemed that there was no hope, 'the only person' in all of Vancouver willing to look beyond our colour and my pregnancy and rent us accommodation appeared. In this case, it was Margot Ney, a school teacher who had given birth to her daughter in July, one month before Cleta, our daughter, was born, and her husband, Phil, a medical student in the year behind Bill. They described themselves as Christians, who believed that because all people are created in God's image, no one person or group of persons was inferior to any other person or group, and that to hold a prejudice against anyone would be to hold a prejudice against God. . . .

Although we occasionally saw other Black people in the city and would always smile and say hello, it was not until Bill's third year in medicine that we actually became acquainted with any members of the British Columbia Black community. During a hospital rotation at the Vancouver General Hospital, Bill met a patient named Dolores Collins. He was so excited that he phoned me on his lunch break that day to tell me of this first meeting with a real live Black Canadian in Vancouver. Mrs. Collins seemed genuinely pleased to know him, and they chatted every day that she remained in the hospital. On her discharge we were invited to her home for dinner and there we met Frank, her husband, and their children, and learnt about the B.C. Association for the Advancement of Coloured People, which was just in its formative year—Frank was the president. . . .

We joined the BCAACP immediately and became very involved

in its struggle against racism in British Columbia. In the process we learnt much about what it was like to grow up as a true visible minority person in this province. . . .

There was no highly visible Black ghetto as in Montreal and in many American cities, but with one exception all of the Black families lived and owned homes in the east end of Vancouver. The exception was Mrs. Ruby Sneed, who lived with her husband and two daughters on West 8th Avenue near Alma and taught piano lessons.

The BCAACP . . . was an active and aggressive organization. It established a few priorities for itself and pursued them vigorously. It was determined to open up housing and employment to Black people and to ensure that young Black people pursued education and professions as one means of fighting discrimination. . . .

[B]oth Bill and I worked with it in its efforts to force the provincial government to introduce human rights legislation and a human rights commission. Neither of these goals was achieved until after the election of a New Democratic Party government in 1972, an election in which Emery Barnes and I became the first Black people to be elected to any provincial parliament in Canada's history.

By the time Bill graduated in 1958 either our painful memories were fading or Vancouver was changing. In any event we were expecting our second child and planning to purchase a house and put down roots in Vancouver. I still longed to return to Jamaica, and especially so that my children could grow up in a warm and loving Black environment, and Bill had nostalgic longings for the stimulation and excitement of Montreal.

Bill's career plans ruled out both options. At a time when internships were becoming difficult to secure he was fortunate to have been accepted at the Vancouver General Hospital. By that time, also, he had decided not to return to research but to pursue the specialty of psychiatry. When in addition he had been assured of a position in the UBC residency program . . . we accepted that we would be living in Vancouver for a long time.

Before marriage, Bill and I had spent hours exploring the options of where we would settle down. We desperately wanted to live and raise our children in a Black environment, I because my experience had been such a positive one and he because growing up a Black child in the southern United States had been so fraught with anxiety and tension. Despite this, wherever we looked, it seemed that political instability, economic underdevelopment and lack of social resources were the lot of the English-speaking Black countries of the world. . . .

[B]ecause I came in contact with racism later in life I knew that there was a qualitative difference to life for a Black person in a white community. Because that Black person is always 'on guard.' A seventh sense is developed that is always alert, a radar scanning for hostile signals. I remember reading somewhere that Black women in North America never let their babies out of their sight when away from home—not in a shopping buggy or on a playground swing—not because they were afraid their children would fall, wander off or get into mischief, but because they feared that someone would hurt them. . . .

The discussions about a place to live escalated to arguments, but Bill was adamant. He believed that it was important for our children to live and survive and excel in this country. . . . Eventually, the compromise we worked out was that at the completion of his medical training, we would return to Montreal. He would complete his residency and establish a practice there, and I would return to McGill to study law. We would be close to Jamaica and to his family in Georgia and our children would have easy access to both these Black communities. . . .

The subtle magic and beauty of British Columbia, combined with the FLQ* uprising in Quebec, convinced us that British Columbia was home and that we should put down our roots right here.

With each passing year Bill had contributed less and less to responsibilities around the home since his studies were so demanding, and I began to doubt my ability to juggle parenting, homemaking and studying. So I decided that I would have to pursue a program that was shorter and less demanding than law, but I had no idea what it would be. Bill repeated his commitment to support me during my course of study in return for the four years I would have to work while he pursued his psychiatric residency, plus the four years he had studied medicine and interned. I found myself

---

* French nationalist organization—the Front Libération de Québec. Ed.

negotiating for eight years of educational support, even as I was deciding that I would have to restrict to less than four years the time of study I could pursue.

We accepted that B.C. was home—in 1959 we applied for and received our Canadian citizenship. For better or for worse this was our country now. We were Canadian and what happened to this country was part of our responsibility since we now had the right to become actively involved in its workings. . . .

On the surface, our life was uneventful, but the birth of children mobilized us into wanting to change the community and world in which we lived. All around us Canadians were organizing to protest the worldwide testing of nuclear weapons; women across Canada linked their forces in the powerful Voice of Women organization, which called on Canadians to raise our voices against the threat to our children and our world that was inherent in the fallout from the continued testing of nuclear weapons.

A small branch of the Voice of Women was formed in our neighbourhood. We used to meet regularly in our homes for the exchange of ideas and information and to develop lobbying action directed at the federal government. We collected our babies' teeth and sent them off to be part of research about the presence of strontium-90 in breast milk and cows' milk. We prepared briefs, participated in marches, signed petitions, wrote letters to newspapers and politicians—all with the one goal of bringing an end to nuclear testing. . . .

It was . . . our first involvement in Canadian politics. Because we were now Canadian citizens, we were not afraid of deportation; and because we were parents, we were prepared to take any risks to ensure that the world was safe and secure for our children. . . . On two occasions eggs were thrown at our front door; this time, however, the attack was not because we were Black but because we were working for peace. . . .

As our second baby grew older the time approached for me to return to work. . . .

[B]ecause of my relationship with Aunt Leila, the idea of social work intrigued me. I had always admired the way she had mobilized people to change their lives in positive ways; in some ways social work did not seem too different from the profession of law, since it was a way of helping the defenceless to defend themselves.

I explored all these ideas with Bill. This was a period of great closeness between us. He sensed my growing frustration with home-making, and he really wanted to help me to become more involved in interesting pursuits. He had always been unusual in that respect. Because his mother and all the women in his family had professions and worked outside the home, he seemed to accept that this was the norm for women. He did not believe that homemaking offered sufficient intellectual stimulation and reward for a woman, any more than it did for a man, and he never expected or encouraged me to make motherhood and homemaking a full-time job. He believed that all women were like his mother, and he assumed that it was natural for those women who wanted to work outside the home to do so. I later learned that his view of the world through his mother's experiences skewed his appreciation of feminism in strange and subtle ways. Because he had never lived in an equal relationship with a feminist—and because what is acceptable in a mother is not necessarily so in a spouse—the difference between the intellectual acceptance of women's equality and the reality proved problematic for him in many ways. . . .

[A]t the Children's Aid Society . . . I learnt much about the suffering of children. Foster parents who were in the business because they loved children were a rarity. More often fostering was perceived to be a way to make a few extra dollars while a woman was at home rearing her own children. However, because government, then as now, computed the accurate cost of raising a child and paid the foster parents considerably less, expecting them to subsidize the cost of that child's care, foster parents found that caring for these children was an economic liability rather than an asset, and the drop-out rate was high. . . .

I developed migraine headaches and stomach problems, both as a result of my frustration of being unable to do anything to help the children and because of my anger at what I considered the neglect of the children by both of these communities.

I had grown up in an environment where people who could always took care of children in need. My grandmother, mother and all of my aunts adopted children—not legally, they just took them into their homes and assumed responsibility for them. . . .

At the end of my two years at the Vancouver Children's Aid Society I applied to and was accepted into the Bachelor of Social Work program at UBC. That was a very difficult year for me. All my fears about juggling parenting, homemaking and studying proved well grounded. Bill was giving less assistance at home and spending less time with the family. As he became more engrossed in his work, tension developed between us. I was always tired, over-worked and fighting a cold.

On one occasion when I had an important school deadline to meet and felt yet another cold coming on, I took two penicillin tablets and headed for my desk. Bill had gone to the movies after putting Cleta and Gary to bed, so that I could have absolute quiet in which to work. In a few minutes my heart began to race, my throat began to close and I was gasping for breath. I thought I was dying. I staggered upstairs to kiss my babies good-bye and headed back downstairs to telephone the neighbours. I must have passed out on my way down, because when I opened my eyes I was in Emergency at the Vancouver General Hospital.

Bill tells me that he had been standing in line at the Dunbar movie theatre waiting to purchase his ticket when he suddenly decided that he didn't want to see that particular film after all. He immediately returned home and found me unconscious at the foot of the stairs. He had no idea what had happened to me except that I had a very slow pulse, so he gave me a shot of Adrenalin, called in the neighbours and asked them to keep an eye on the kids, and rushed me off to the hospital Emergency ward.

The doctors there, concluding that I had had a massive allergic reaction to something, did what they could and waited for me to wake up. That was the first inkling I had that I was allergic to peni-cillin. I remained weak, with swollen feet and fingers, for some time, but the swelling in my throat receded and I returned to school to complete my year. At the end of the academic year, when we moved to Montreal for Bill's final year of psychiatry residency at the Allan Memorial Hospital, I went to the allergy clinic for tests and learnt that I was allergic not only to penicillin, but to all forms of local anaesthetics and to anything with any derivative of cocaine in it.

I really hated the year we spent in Montreal while Bill com-pleted his residency in psychiatry. Once again I was working, this time at the Montreal Children's Hospital. Because of the prejudice of apartment managers and owners we were forced to settle for substandard housing in Notre Dame de Grace, and while Bill blos-somed at his work and his social life grew in this, his favourite city,

I was trapped between work and the care of two small children. After life in Vancouver with its parks, free libraries, beaches and beautiful surroundings, Montreal proved to be a nightmare. . . .

Bill controlled the use of the car because his working hours were unpredictable, which meant that I was often caught in the worst weather, having to depend on public transit. In general our relationship deteriorated at an alarming rate. I felt old, fat, ugly and desperate.

I survived because I made friends at work and found my job challenging and interesting. I worked with the families of children who were brain-damaged. The condition of many of these children was the result of encephalitis, but more often it was caused by automobile accidents. . . .

Although we tried to ignore them, the unexpected racial incidents kept gnawing away at me. And in Montreal, as was not the case in Vancouver, I seemed absolutely powerless to insulate either myself or my children from them.

On one occasion when I was having a particularly severe toothache, Agnes Sunderland, who used to be a neighbour in Vancouver before moving to Montreal, suggested that I see her dentist. She phoned and asked him to see me as it was an emergency and he agreed. I waited in his office until he had completed his day's appointments. Then he called me in to his work area: he launched immediately into a tirade, shouting at me about waiting until I had severe pain before telling my employer of my dental problem, forcing her to call him. He accused me of taking advantage of the fact that since she was one of his regular patients he would be forced to work beyond his already long work day to see me so as not to jeopardize his relationship with her.

As he continued to shout and rant at me, I sat there stunned. I realized that he thought I was Agnes's maid and that that gave him the right to abuse me. When he finally finished his hysterical harangue, I apologized for the intrusion and explained that I would have to seek the services of another dentist. Of course, by then my toothache had disappeared—I was growing aware that my sanity was about to snap and that in the process I would kill the dentist. As he launched into yet another tirade, I removed myself from his chair and went in search of my coat.

His nurse, who had been embarrassed and terrified by his behaviour, suggested to him that I be referred to another colleague.

She explained that she had already called another dentist; he had agreed to see me immediately. She had in addition called a cab to take me to his office. The dentist calmed down and agreed that that was a good idea. As he began to explain to me about the referral, I interrupted to inform him that he had not heard the end of the incident and that Mrs. Sunderland would certainly be given a graphic recounting of his behaviour. I was shaking as I left.

When I arrived at the office of the other dentist, I told him that my toothache had stopped and that I did not need his services. I described my encounter with his colleague and told him that in my present state of mind it would be better that we not proceed with the appointment. He was stunned, apologized profusely on behalf of his colleague and assured me that he would pursue the matter with him.

He no doubt did, because early the following morning I received a phone call from a very chastened dentist apologizing for having mistaken me for a maid. Despite my explanation, he never understood that my rage was not at being assumed to be a maid because I was Black and female, but at the fact that he dared to speak to me with such rudeness just because he believed the colour of my skin and my economic status gave him the right to do so. . . .

Bill received his certificate in psychiatry, and one August morning in 1964 we set out in our brand-new Buick Wildcat to drive back to British Columbia. I was very happy to leave Montreal, but not just because it had been such an unhappy year: a year earlier, before leaving Vancouver, we had used $5,000 of Bill's inheritance from his mother to put a down payment on a home at 3863 West 11th Avenue, and I was eager to move into our first house. . . . Although we had run into some racism in the purchase of the house, there had also been an unexpected act of wonder. Oliver Kuys, the realtor, an immigrant from South Africa, had responded to the vendors' concerns about our race by explaining to them that he had left South Africa to escape racism, so he was not going to tolerate it in Canada. He added that if they were going to refuse to sell their property to us because of racial considerations, he would not continue to be their realtor. The vendors backed down. . . .

The return to Vancouver and moving into our home proved to be wonderful. To our children's delight there were twenty other children living on our block, at least six of them within their age group. . . .

I became pregnant with our third child just before leaving Montreal to return to Vancouver. I welcomed the pregnancy as an opportunity to get a break from working. I seemed to be exhausted all the time. Working, homemaking and even taking that year out to attend university were taking their toll.

Bill plunged into building up his practice, and I lost myself in fixing our home and awaiting the birth of our third child. Before long I was back working with the B.C. Association for the Advancement of Coloured People and the peace movement. . . .

We decided that the time had come for me to take our two children for their first trip to Jamaica, because they were old enough and it would be cheaper and easier than travelling with three children later on. . . .

Cleta and Gary loved Jamaica. I could actually see them relax —the tension, the 'on guard,' dropping away and the mounting of joy at being surrounded by friends, relatives and even strangers who were Black. I too relaxed and wished that I never had to return to Canada—I was home, and for the first time in years I felt safe! . . .

About a week after we arrived in Jamaica, as I was putting the children to bed one night, Cleta confessed that she had always thought the stories her dad and I used to tell her, about places in the world where most people were Black, were really fairy tales. She thought we had made those stories up, and that in fact everyone in the world was white except our family and some of our friends.

One morning about a week before the baby was due to be born I was sitting in the rocking chair I always had in my kitchen, relaxed and planning the day ahead. . . . I was tired, as always at that time of day, after preparing breakfast and getting two children and one spouse off to school and work, carrying around a nearly full-grown, about-to-be-delivered baby. But I knew that for a few minutes at least I could sit and rock, looking at the mountains in the distance, before beginning my round of bed-making and housework. Suddenly the baby within me heaved and a searing pain shot through my body, then all went still. My heart was racing and an immense sense of doom settled over me. I knew that something had happened. I didn't know what, and I was immediately gripped with panic. . . .

Two days later I delivered a beautiful, full-grown, stillborn daughter, with the umbilical cord tightly wound around her neck. . . .

I will never forget returning home from the hospital, getting out of the car, my heart breaking because my hands were empty. I stood rooted to the spot, whimpering that my hands were empty and that I couldn't walk because my hands were empty, because there was no baby in my arms. Bill, sensing my desperation, tried to encourage me to move, but I was paralyzed. My legs would not move. Finally, on a gamble, he handed me one of the pots of mums we had brought home from the hospital and said, "Here, carry that." With tears streaming down my face I walked into the house clinging to that pot of flowers.

The loss of my baby gave me my first encounter with 'sisterhood,' even though that word was not in common use then. I was almost never alone. Women I hardly knew, but whose children attended school or played with my kids, women in the neighbourhood, with whom I had not exchanged more than a polite greeting, showed up at my home. They brought baked goods, home-cooked meals, casseroles and sherry, and stayed to visit. Many of them spoke of their own losses—of miscarriage, stillbirth, death of a small child or other loved one. . . .

A friend, Joyce Lockhart, heard her friend Gordon Bryenton speak of looking for a back-up social worker for a CTV panel show, *People in Conflict,* on which he was a panelist. Joyce suggested that such a job would cheer me up and pull me out of my depression. When Gordon approached me with the offer, I wanted to decline, but Bill encouraged me to accept. He pointed out that I would only be working one day each month, since the station filmed one week's programs in a day, and that it would be fun to work with Gordon, whom I knew and liked; and of course I would be earning a lot more money than I would as a social worker. . . .

I loved being on the show and remained with it almost until the birth of our son Jonathan two years later. *People in Conflict* was a national show. . . .

The format was very simple. It consisted of a panel of three professionals: a lawyer, the flamboyant H.A.D. Oliver, who was always running off the set to check with his broker; a psychologist, my friend Gordon Bryenton, who was also a marriage and family counsellor; and a social worker, the position I occupied one week each month. Our job was to respond in a helpful and positive way to people who appeared before us with problems. . . . People off the street volunteered for the show. They were told the problem they were to present to the panel, and they were left to act out and present their stories in their own way. Before the show the panelists would be briefed as to the nature of the problems, but we were never sure what twist or turn a story line would take. . . .

Bill and my friends proved to be correct, and *People in Conflict* did help me survive one of the down periods of my life. I soon became pregnant again and, with the birth of Jonathan on November 13, 1965, we decided that our family was complete. . . .

It was time once again to go job-hunting. I now had a Master's degree in social work and I was confident that finding employment would not be difficult. Over the years we had insulated ourselves more and more against racial discrimination. Our children had the occasional taunt to deal with, but for the most part they were making friends and seemed happy enough. . . .

We spoke to them about Black people in positive terms and kept reinforcing that being born Black they had much to be proud of. Our task was made easier since the civil rights movement in the United States was receiving a lot of media coverage, and they could see bright, articulate young Black leaders fighting against the barriers to their advancement.

Cleta, as the eldest child, had always had a more difficult time than the others, because in every case she was the first Black child in her school and remained the only Black child until her brother joined her two years later. She was a very serious, sensitive child who asked searching questions and spent long periods of time just quietly observing the activities going on around her. Nonetheless, she always had friends and never seemed lonely. I am convinced that she suffered most of all the family from having to grow up not just in a country steeped in racism, but in the bizarre situation of being in an environment where she was the only person of her race. . . . I stand in awe of her strength and power. I have never envied her and know that I could not have survived her ordeal as well as she has.

I have a different kind of relationship with each of my children. With Cleta I have shared the unspoken fears of being a Black woman living in a white country. I worried that, surrounded by all the messages of beauty being white, blond and blue-eyed, she would internalize those criteria and come to see herself as being ugly and unlovely. . . . Bill and I told her constantly how beautiful we thought she was, but our words were continually contradicted, by TV, comic books, movies and other images in her environment.

We worried that as she grew older her feelings of being unlovely would be exacerbated by difficulty in having dates, and by seeing her brothers, and other Black men in the community, dating and marrying white women. We explored the possibility of sending her to school and university in either the West Indies or the United States, and we prepared to build an elaborate shield around her until she was mature enough to recognize that she was beautiful, bright and very, very nice. Time proved that our worries were exaggerated; Cleta has always dated, had lovers and enjoyed a social life. Nonetheless my antenna remains tuned for the slightest sign of dysfunction in her life. . . .

While I was thinking about returning to work, I was approached by Bea Lipinski, from Simon Fraser University, and told about plans to develop a suicide prevention and crisis centre in Vancouver. The idea intrigued me and I assured her that I would be happy to become involved. I offered to help design the volunteer training program and to train the first batch of volunteers. . . .

Before my volunteer stint with the suicide prevention centre was complete, Bea asked whether I would be interested in joining the counselling service at Simon Fraser. She was the director; the service was large and growing, with a psychiatrist and a number of psychologists on staff. She found that a number of students were coming to the service because of problems with the provincial Department of Social Service and thought that it might be a good idea to have a social worker on staff part-time, to whom she could refer these cases. She also wanted me to be involved with some of the group counselling programs.

I was excited at the prospect, especially since she agreed to allow me to develop a volunteer outreach program that would encourage students to volunteer for community work. Little did I know that once again my life was about to change and that this job was literally the first step of a fourteen-year adventure.

The day that Malcolm X was assassinated in 1965, Jonathan was conceived. Bill and I clung to each other, stunned that one of our own could have pulled the trigger to end the life of someone who spoke so clearly to us of our condition and our oppression. We had anticipated that someone from the white community would snuff out his life prematurely, but in our naiveté we assumed that the Black community would have been a haven of safety for someone so important to us as a people. We were immobilized by a mixture of rage, despair and a sense of betrayal, by the realization that our prophets and our revolutionaries—even those who dwelt among us—would never be protected or safe from their enemies. We wanted desperately to do something about the situation, because, although we did not endorse Malcolm's call to arms, we certainly identified with his appeal to us as a people to reject oppression and discrimination and to believe in our value, our talents and our rights. Many years later, a political acquaintance visiting our home noticed the large framed portrait of Malcolm on the wall of Bill's library and commented that he had not realized that we were 'the sort of people' who would have liked Malcolm X, thus revealing once again the ignorance about the relationship of Black people to Black people that survives and pervades even the political community.

It was the year 1967. The Black Panther party was achieving greater visibility in the United States, and Eldridge Cleaver was emerging as one of its most articulate spokesmen. In Canada a small group of us was beginning to meet from time to time to discuss the formation of a national Black coalition, and the Royal Commission on the Status of Women was established by an Act of Parliament.

Bill's practice was thriving. Our children were healthy and happy. I was depressed. . . . I had a very clear sense that the Black Panther movement was pushing the United States into a bloody racial conflagration. Ever since the assassination of Malcolm X two years earlier, I had concluded that white America would never permit or tolerate justice or equality for its Black citizens. I believed that the Civil Rights Movement was doomed, and I was being crushed by the realization that my children and grandchildren would face a life of prejudice and discrimination.

I gave up all hope and began to question the point of living. I was not really suicidal, however—I knew that I dared not face my dead grandmother and aunts on the other side with the excuse that I had killed myself because I had been defeated by life. . . .

Someone, I can't remember who, loaned me a copy of *The Feminine Mystique,* by Betty Friedan. Suddenly, it was all there, the story of my life—as I read the book, I became more and more agitated; I realized that I was not unique, that there were women all over North America, women of all colours, who were experiencing the same sense of being unfulfilled in their personal lives. Learning this fact should have depressed me further, but it didn't. The effect was the opposite. The fact that I was not alone reassured and mobilized me.

The Feminine Mystique, with its simple examination and revelation of the lives of women in North America, was one of the three 'jolts' that have hardened my commitment to feminism; the other two were Marilyn French's *The Women's Room,* a book about the sometimes brutal relationship between men and women, and a strange little TV drama called *The Stepford Wives,* which depicted the ideal wife as a robot programmed to respond with unquestioning obedience to her husband's wishes. Once the programming of the robot is completed the real-life wife is murdered. I know that none of these are profound analytical works of great import—but for me, each in its own way shocked me and reminded me that the dislike and distrust of men for women touches every aspect of our life, even the most petty and superficial. In later years Alice Walker, through her poems and writings on the experience and condition of Black women, was to put it all into perspective and remind me of the legacy of strength and resilience with which my ancestors had inoculated me. . . .

I am grateful to those women in the Civil Rights Movement in the United States who spotted the discrepancy between the principle they were fighting for and the way they were being treated by their male comrades, and who began to speak about the sexism within that movement. Their writings triggered the conflict in me that had been heightened by the growing hostility of both Black men and women in the Civil Rights Movement in Canada to the involvement of Black women in the feminist struggle. Black Canadians insisted that feminism was a white ideology and the women's movement a white, middle-class movement. They saw it as yet another attempt to drain the energies of the Black struggle, and to siphon off the commitment and weaken the determination of the small band of activists working against prejudice.

I agonized over this conflict. As a Black person, I believed that every criticism they leveled at the women's movement was correct. Indeed, I realized that they had not gone far enough in their censure. Yet as a woman, I knew that much of my exploitation and oppression would continue even if the colour of my skin turned white, so long as I remained a woman. I could not turn my back on the women's struggle, yet I did not enjoy being perceived as a traitor to my race when I spoke out about the sexism of the Black male. . . .

If either the struggle against racism or that against sexism was won, the victory for me would be a fifty percent solution. To achieve one hundred percent success both struggles had to be successful. And so, quite frankly, I could not afford to turn my back on either one. The challenge that faced me was how to articulate my position in a positive and convincing way to the Black community. . . .

I was not . . . concerned or surprised by the racism that I knew existed in the women's movement. I knew that I could extract enough from the analysis and ideology to strengthen me, and my contact with some women in the consciousness-raising groups had taught me that sisterhood was possible between Black and white women. . . .

I was . . . very deeply concerned about my Black Canadian sisters and wanted urgently to convince them that feminism could be a liberating experience for us. I knew that I needed to get beyond their appraisal of the movement as a white women's movement, and beyond their fear that the struggle for equality could damage the tenuous and fragile relationship they had with Black men.

North American Black women have been indoctrinated with the belief that our salvation was tied to the liberation of the Black male—that his ego, his rights, his needs were paramount; and that it would be up to him, once he had improved his position in society, to raise that of his women and children. They were brainwashed into accepting that their role was to support and work for the rights of their fathers, husbands and sons, and that they should not compete with them because the struggle for racial justice would be weakened by such an act. . . .

What I had learnt from feminism was that women's place had as much to do with the social and economic system as it had to do with race. I believed that Black women had to take control of their lives, establish their priorities and pursue their goals. I also believed that an independent, secure woman had more to contribute to any struggle than an insecure, dependent one, and that the battle against racism would be fought more effectively by women and men standing side by side as equals, rather than by an unbalanced, lopsided team of unequal partners. . . .

[I]t was not until I was invited to deliver the keynote address at the Annual Banquet of the Negro Women's Association of Ontario in 1973 that the opportunity I longed for occurred. The Association suggested that I speak on any topic of my choice, so I prepared myself carefully and extensively to deliver what remains for me the most important speech of my lifetime, entitled "Black Women and Women's Liberation."

In preparation I developed a rationalization I have used whenever I have been faced with controversial speaking engagements since, namely to assume that such a speaking engagement offers a once-in-a-lifetime opportunity. Hence, I cannot waste it by speaking to the audience of what it wants to hear, but instead I have to use the opportunity to speak of truths that have to be told. That way, if a second invitation is not forthcoming, there are no regrets, since I have said it all the first time anyway.

This was definitely such an occasion. On the night of the banquet there were nearly 300 people in an audience that included the Governor General of Ontario, the Mayor of the City of Toronto and a large number of white Canadians. Although the topic was one of which I would have preferred to speak to an exclusively Black audience, because once again I feared being accused of betraying private family secrets to the other side, I decided that this opportunity to speak out could not be ignored.

My anxiety and nervousness about the occasion shut my stomach down and I was unable to eat anything at the banquet. My heart raced, my mind went blank and sweat oozed out of my pores. Despite this I tried to smile and chat throughout the meal, appearing to all the world relaxed and confident. Nonetheless, I was a shaking, nervous wreck as I walked towards the podium, anticipating the hostility that my words would generate.

However, as I began to deliver the speech, I became caught up in the urgency of the content and the force of my conviction; I heard

my voice move out and across the room and capture the attention
of the audience, I saw the intentness in the faces before me, and I
knew that they were not just listening but were actually hearing
what I had come to say:

> ... Whenever anyone—male, female, Black or white—asks me
> why I am part of the women's liberation movement, I always re-
> ply 'because I am a woman.' Then I wait for the significance of
> their question to dawn on them—for in reality, what they have
> said to me is that since I am a Black person, Black oppression is
> the only oppression with which they expect me to concern myself.
>
> But for me not to participate in the women's liberation move-
> ment would be to deny my womanhood—for indeed I am twice
> blessed. I am Black and I am a woman—and to be Black and
> female in a society which is both racist and sexist is to be in
> the unique position of having nowhere to go but up! And to be in
> the unique situation of learning about survival from being able
> to observe at very close range the Achilles' heel of a very great
> nation.
>
> Indeed, my Black friends who congratulate me for speaking
> out on racial issues chastise me for being a feminist. And my sis-
> ters who love me for speaking out on issues of the movement
> chastise me for being preoccupied with my race. Add to all of this
> the fact that I am a socialist living in a capitalist country and you
> will wonder what worlds are left for me to conquer or be con-
> quered by.
>
> Yet I enjoy a strange kind of freedom—because in order to
> survive I have had to learn and learn well about racists and about
> sexists and about capitalists. And the wisdom that I have gleaned
> from these studies is that all people depend on all people, and that
> unless all of us are free—none of us will be free, and that indeed
> when I fight for your freedom, I am also fighting for my own and
> when I am fighting for my freedom I am also fighting for my sis-
> ters and brothers and for all of our children.
>
> I learnt also that this country, this Canada, is beautiful and
> strong only because of the people of both sexes, and of all races
> and political persuasions who have lived in it and contributed to
> its culture and its soul and its growth. And that its strength and
> its beauty will increase only to the extent that it is able to accept
> and respect all of its people equally.
>
> But what did I learn of us? Of you and me—the Black
> women who through choice, or luck or by birth make this our
> home? Where do we fit into this space and into the changes and
> developments that are taking place about us? ...
>
> [U]nless the women's liberation movement identifies with
> and locks into the liberation movement of all oppressed groups it

will never achieve its goals . . . unless it identifies with and supports the struggles of the poor, of oppressed races, of the old and of other disadvantaged groups in society it will never achieve its goals. Because not to do so would be to isolate itself from the masses of women—since women make up a large segment of all of these groups. . . .

At the end they very graciously accorded me a standing ovation, but I was so exhausted and wrung out that I barely made it back to my seat. The applause was sustained long after I sat down, and in the back of my mind, as the thumping in my heart, which had been drowning out the applause, subsided, I heard my grandmother and the aunts saying "Not bad, not bad at all, girl."

One of the perks of working at Simon Fraser University was that staff members sometimes had their way paid to attend conferences at other universities and educational institutions. . . . Bea Lipinski, my boss, approached me and asked whether I would be interested in attending the conference to discuss the recommendations of the Royal Commission on the Status of Women that was being sponsored by the UBC Department of Continuing Education and the University Women's Club.

I was ecstatic. I wanted to attend the conference anyway as the representative of the B.C. Council of Black Women, a very small and impoverished group of which I was the president, and of the National Black Coalition, of which I was the western representative. Bea's offer to send me meant that SFU would pay the registration fee and I could represent all three groups at the same time. . . .

The Vancouver Status of Women Council was born that evening, and Anita Morris was chosen its first president. The goal of the organization was to ensure that the 167 recommendations included in the final report, which had been tabled in the House of Commons on September 28, 1970, not be ignored. We knew that during its tour across the country, the Commission, headed by Florence Bird, had received 468 briefs and more than 1,000 letters. We believed that the recommendations reflected accurately the wishes of most Canadian women, but we also knew that Royal Commission reports had a history of languishing on shelves collecting dust and generating little or no action. . . .

Soon after that initial meeting I was approached by Anita Morris and asked to design and develop an advocacy structure for women, along the lines of the Ombudsman concept. I was delighted and excited to do so. . . .

The Ombudservice was the challenge I had been preparing for all my life. A small grant from the Department of the Secretary of State paid for a post office box and the purchase of an old typewriter. The media gave the service generous and free coverage, and soon women in Vancouver knew that there existed a place to which they could bring complaints against government, the law, unfair labour practices or whatever, and that every effort would be made to work for a positive resolution of their problems.

Like all other positions in the Status of Women Council, mine was a volunteer one; I worked on those days when I was not at Simon Fraser University. There was a committee that worked with me. We were the first Ombudswoman's service in Canada, and the committee felt like freedom fighters—determined not only to protest bad laws or the absence of good laws, but also to tender recommendations for the introduction of 'equality' legislation. . . .

The efforts of the Ombudservice on behalf of married women in the province led us to oppose a particularly flawed amendment to an Act regarding wives' and children's maintenance in 1971. It was introduced by Grace McCarthy, Minister without Portfolio in W.A.C. Bennett's Social Credit government. Mrs. McCarthy was infuriated by our actions, but we were adamant that what women needed was a completely new bill that reflected their equal status with their husbands within the marriage and their right to fifty percent of all the family assets. A delegation of us appeared before the standing committee of the legislature on health and welfare to formally present our arguments in opposition to this Act, and our alternative recommendation.

The Bill was eventually defeated; but I remember the day of our presentation for another reason. At the conclusion of the meeting Dennis Cocke, the NDP member for New Westminster and a member of the Legislative Committee, approached me. He said that he wanted me to meet Dave Barrett, his leader, and he wanted me to run as a candidate for the NDP in the next provincial election. I thanked him for his suggestion and assured him that seeking political office was not part of my life plan. I thought that was the end of the matter. However, as our delegation was leaving the legislature to catch the ferry and return to Vancouver, we ran into Dennis at the door with Dave in tow. Dave said he was impressed with what he had heard about me, and wanted to encourage me to seek an NDP nomination for the next provincial election.

Bill and I had a good chuckle over that at home that evening, because we knew that no Vancouver riding* would choose a person who was Black, female and an immigrant to be its elected representative. . . .

Right from the beginning the Council members decided that we would not be satisfied to have the concerns of women remain in the hands of male politicians. We wanted to elect politicians of our own. We agreed that to continue to focus solely on lobbying, supporting, even educating male politicians to translate our issues into public policy would be a waste of our time and energy. Our focus, therefore, was to find women of all political parties who had even the faintest desire to run for public office and to build the support and infrastructure that would translate that desire into reality.

Our only requirement was that these women support the findings and recommendations of the Royal Commission Report on the Status of Women. Women who shared that goal needed only to seek our endorsement and support to be assured of the willing and full cooperation of the Council members. Many of the ideas, techniques and strategies being used by 'Winning Women' groups across Canada today in their thrust to get women elected to public office by 1994 were pioneered by the political committee of the Vancouver Status of Women Council.

Because of the open and aggressive political thrust of the Council, for many years the women of B.C. were perceived by feminist groups across Canada as being in the forefront of political action and awareness in the women's movement. Long after groups in the rest of Canada were saying "Let's keep politics out of the women's movement," we were saying "Politics is what the women's movement is all about."

So the education committee proceeded to study, research and expand on the rationale behind the Royal Commission recommendations. The speakers bureau continued to groom its members to carry the message of the Report and its recommendations to organizations, schools, institutions and any group in the community

---

* Electoral district. Ed.

willing to listen or curious enough to learn of it. The media committee was mandated to keep our activities in the public eye, and
the finance committee, which was really the fundraising arm of the
organization, launched an appeal to convince both government and
community that the funding of our activities was in the best interest
of women throughout the province. . . .

Meantime, the search for women candidates continued. By the
time Premier W.A.C. Bennett called a provincial election for August
30, 1972, the Vancouver Status of Women Council was ready.
Three members of the Council had won the nomination of their
parties as well as the endorsement of the Council. All Council members were exhorted to become actively involved in the campaign for
the woman candidate of their choice; fundraising was accelerated,
and the money was distributed equally among the three members
who were running. A major all-candidates meeting for female candidates was sponsored and organized at the downtown YWCA.
The Vancouver Status of Women newsletter carried full reports on
the three candidates and urged that all members give them their
support. The three publicly declared their membership in the Status
of Women Council and their support for the Royal Commission
Report and commitment to its implementation.

The Council was seen as a force to be reckoned with by three
of the four political parties, and commitments of support were
given by all except the Social Credit Party. Since one of the women
candidates supported by the Council was running for the Liberal
Party, and the other two were New Democrats, the Council was
confident of some success in achieving its goal as long as the Social
Credit government was defeated. Since all the membership shared
the common goal of defeating the Social Credit government, there
was much sharing of workers and materials between the Liberal
and NDP women's campaigns. . . .

The 1972 election was the first time since the disintegration of
the Voice of Women that the women of urban areas of B.C. had
united and mobilized against a government. Although the opposition parties treated the efforts of the women seriously, the Social
Credit people, with the particular arrogance that is their trademark,
underestimated both the commitment and the determination of
B.C. women. . . .

[The] two successful NDP candidates were Phylis Young of

Vancouver-Little Mountain riding, and Rosemary Brown of Vancouver-Burrard.

The 1972 NDP government became the first provincial government in Canada to fund rape relief centres, transition houses and women's health collectives. The government also expanded childcare services, from 2,500 spaces in 1971 to 18,603 by 1975, and introduced the Women's Economic Rights Branch in the Ministry of Economic Development. It created the committee to eliminate sexism in textbooks and curriculum in the Ministry of Education. . . .

Many of the women appointed to new commissions, boards and directorates had been active members of the Status of Women Council; the irony of the Council's successful sortie into electoral politics was that it decimated its leadership ranks. . . .

However, its spirit was captured by the women of Canada when, as Penney Kome described it, "a political earthquake occurred . . . in 1981." They mobilized to force a recalcitrant group of male political leaders to rewrite Canada's Charter of Rights and Freedoms. Gathered in a kitchen in the Ottawa Convention Centre, in a last-ditch attempt to finalize the bargains that would result in the nation's Constitution, those gentlemen forgot the fifty-two percent of the population that is female, and failed to protect their equality. At that point, women and women's groups of all political ideologies united to create the powerful force that convinced them to include the equality sections, number 15 and number 28, thus enshrining the equality of all of Canada's women before and under the law.

The first time my friend Marianne Gilbert spoke to me about seeking public office I was pleased but dismissed the suggestion with a touch of humour. Coming as it did just a week after Dennis Cocke had made a similar suggestion, it seemed that the fates were teasing me. At the time, I desperately wanted to be elected to the federal House of Commons. Most of the Royal Commission recommendations dealt with the federal level of politics and my involvement in the Black movement and the women's movement convinced me that both struggles had to be fought and won on the national level if they were to benefit all Canadian women equally. . . .

Despite my Canadian citizenship and the fact that I had spent more years living in Canada than I had in my place of birth, Jamaica, I still felt obligated to make my work serve and benefit Jamaicans and other Black people in some way. In retrospect I realize that working for OXFAM or CUSO or some other development organization would have brought me closer to my goal. But in 1970 I believed that when I worked for peace in Canada, or for women's rights, or against racism, or for the elimination of poverty, Canada as a positive force in international politics would convert these benefits into advantages for the developing world, too. : . .

My part-time job in the counselling service at SFU pitted me directly and continually against Phil Gaglardi, the Social Credit minister responsible for welfare, and the frustration of my position and my anger at the government combined with Marianne's suggestion. In time, I began to 'wonder if. . . .'

Just a word of explanation about my job. The government of British Columbia had a policy that forbade welfare recipients to attend university. They were encouraged to take short-term training courses and programs, although such training inevitably led to low-paying jobs that often left them no better off than when they were on welfare. Recipients were actively discouraged from pursuing any career that required an extensive time of study, as this was seen to be an abuse of the system.

From time to time people would defy this regulation and secretly enrol in university. They were inevitably discovered, and it was my responsibility as a social worker to plead their case with the Ministry of Rehabilitation and Social Improvement, as it was called despite the fact that it crushed all attempts at either rehabilitation or self-improvement. The method I used was to develop a financial statement that forecast the cost of the government of continuing to support the student for the four-year course of study in university, and to include the almost certain tax-paying employment the student could secure upon graduation. I would compare this with the long-term cost of continued support for the student without university study, or on a short-term training program. Since there was never any additional cost for a recipient attending university, it was simply a matter of comparing the cost of support for the recipient to attend university with the cost of years of welfare dependency. Since a person without skills would remain on welfare until her children were grown, the duration of support could be eight, ten or twelve years. As a social worker, I also knew that extended support could mean that in time the children too would become dispirited, defeated welfare recipients.

In every instance, I was able to prove that the dollar return to the government in taxes, human labour and productivity for a student in university far outweighed the other two options. The government would invariably permit the student to continue and complete her course of study—with the understanding that a special exception had been made in her particular case and that its action was not to be considered a precedent. . . .

My work as Ombudswoman brought me into constant contact with the law and with lawyers. Many young female lawyers . . . were active members of the Council and volunteered their services generously for the Ombudservice. My own latent interest in law began to resurface, so I jumped with enthusiasm at the suggestion of Michael Jackson, a young activist professor of law at UBC and a VSWC volunteer, that I should apply for entry into UBC law school. . . .

Along with my application to the UBC Faculty of Law, I was asked to submit transcripts going back to the beginning of time; and when I asked for an interview with the admissions professor, he expressed the opinion that my age would be a liability in meeting the admission requirements of the school, and added that in any event the deciding factor would be my score on the LSAT. In the end my score on the LSAT was so mediocre that UBC had no problem rejecting my application.

Professor Michael Jackson was furious, and suggested that I should have been accepted under a special category reserved for students who had made an unusual contribution to the community, and for whom the study of law would result in further benefit to society. The year I was rejected, two businessmen, both older and with fewer academic qualifications than I, had been accepted without being required to sit the LSAT.

The rejection of UBC law school plunged me into a depression. . . .

Nineteen seventy-one began as a down year for me; I felt stymied and blocked in every direction. Jonathan was almost ready for kindergarten, Cleta and Gary were settled in school, Bill was enjoying his profession and it was once again time for me to seek full-time employment. . . . My depression didn't last for long, however, because Bea Lipinski, my boss, became involved in the possibility of having women's studies introduced at Simon Fraser; and the NDP was increasing the pressure on me to consider a nomination in an election it knew would not be long in coming.

When Marianne Gilbert approached me to join the NDP and run for public office, that was the first inkling I had of her party affiliation. She had been a member of the VSWC political committee since its inception, and had always seemed very knowledgeable about the workings of government and the various political parties. I made the mistake then (as I had on other occasions) of assuming that, like many other members of the Council, her interest in politics had developed as a direct result of her contact with the Royal Commission and its report on the status of women.

I had come to learn over the years that British Columbians kept their party affiliation a closely guarded secret; this created the impression that, although people voted in an election and some people even worked for political parties during an election, politics, like religion and sex, was a clandestine activity and not a topic for casual discussion or explanation.

Often in my early years in B.C. I used to make the mistake of assuming that British Columbians were really not very interested in politics. . . .

I was baffled by this phenomenon; it was important to me to know people's political affiliation. My emotional and social connectedness with people was influenced by their political and ideological commitment; indeed one of the problems Bill and I had in developing friendships while settling down in B.C. was the superficial nature of the friendship that many of our acquaintances seemed to want to maintain. Politics was so much a part of our life that we found it difficult to develop deep and sustaining friendships where political bonding was absent—in time we learned how.

I was relieved to learn that Marianne was an NDP supporter, because I really liked her and hoped that we could be friends beyond our VSWC contact. On one of her visits to me at SFU, Marianne brought an NDP membership card with her. She explained that, whether I ran in the next election or not, I should join the party. I agreed without hesitation, filled out the card, wrote a cheque for my dues and became a party member. The year was 1971.

"I have spoken to some people in the Vancouver-Burrard constituency and they are interested in meeting you," Marianne said afterwards. "They will know whether you can win an election in that riding or not. The last NDP members were Tom Berger and Dr. Ray Parkinson. Tom, as you know, is no longer interested in running for public office. Ray Parkinson is, but we are not supporting him. Please agree to meet with them."

I blanched (to the extent that I'm able) at the information. Ray Parkinson was a partner in Bill's medical office. He and his wife were friends of ours. We once sublet their cottage in the Gulf Islands when they were away in the summer, and we had supported him financially and otherwise in the 1969 election. I explained all this to Marianne, saying that to challenge him for the nomination would jeopardize his partnership with Bill and the friendship of the two families. I categorically refused to consider running in Vancouver-Burrard. Marianne was disappointed but told me to think about it.

Once again Bill and I had one of our long discussions. He assured me that my political plans and Ray's should have nothing to do with their medical partnership, and that if I wanted the nomination, then I should go after it. . . .

Bill and I decided that my running would increase the profile of the Ombudservice and the Vancouver Status of Women, *and* get the election urge out of my system, but that was all. He was adamant that I should not expect to win, nor go into a depression if I lost.

Marianne again asked me to meet with the small group from the Vancouver-Burrard constituency that she had mentioned earlier, just to give them the opportunity to meet me. I agreed. When the Saturday arrived for the meeting, I was so nervous I felt physically ill; I knew that this was not a simple social gathering, that I was going to be probed and examined and analyzed for my worth as a candidate and a spokesperson for the NDP. Despite my protest about not wanting to run, I certainly dreaded being told that I was not electable. I wanted to cancel the meeting. And I wanted to attend it. In the end, as I knew I would, I presented myself to them.

I learnt afterwards that the seven people who met and grilled me in Astrid Davidson's apartment that Saturday morning were considered the left-wing radicals of Vancouver-Burrard; this meant that they were extreme indeed, since Vancouver-Burrard, despite having elected such luminaries as Grace MacInnis and Tom Berger, was considered a part of the radical wing that kept the party on its toes. . . .

To me the group members appeared to be very intense, very

serious, totally humourless political analysts in search of the 'perfect' candidate. Although I could sense Marianne's nervousness, she concentrated on reassuring me that nothing was at stake and that I should relax. Bill's attitude had been exactly the same. "If they find you imperfect," he reassured me, "that means they don't know a winner when they meet one." . . .

The meeting lasted three hours. I was tense, alert and on guard throughout. Marianne told me afterwards that everyone had been impressed by my relaxed and assured manner. I left the meeting not knowing whether I had made a favourable impression or not but very relieved that I had survived. Later that evening Marianne phoned to say that the group wanted me to run for the nomination on a ticket with a young man named Pat Dodge, and was ready to go to work on my behalf.

The Vancouver-Burrard Dodge-Brown nominating machine was a flawless, precision-built, accurate, energy-powered, politically sophisticated and astute organization, which was truly impressive to behold! It was absolutely state-of-the-art.

However, before accepting their invitation and endorsement, more agonizing, soul searching and discussion ensued between Bill and me about the conflict and trials that we knew awaited us. My friend Gene Errington, who was also a social worker and succeeded me as Ombudswoman at the Council, was especially enthusiastic; she pledged to sign up every friend and relative living in the constituency to support my nomination. The executive of the Vancouver Status of Women Council was ecstatic. The hierarchy of the New Democratic Party was furious.

I received phone calls suggesting that a decision to run in Vancouver-Burrard would be divisive, that Ray Parkinson had 'paid his dues' and deserved the right to the nomination, that he had chosen Norm Levi as his running mate, that Burrard was a swing seat that had been lost to the party in the last election and could be lost again unless the 'right' candidates were nominated. Some of the same party people who had telephoned to encourage me to run now telephoned to exhort me not to run. Emery Barnes, the other Black hopeful in the party, phoned to offer me his place on the ballot in Vancouver Centre. Gary Lauk, his running mate, phoned to withdraw the offer on the ground that 'a woman' could not win that riding. Norm Levi, the other hopeful in Burrard, phoned to suggest that he and I should run in Vancouver South so that Ray Parkinson could choose another person to win with him in Burrard.

My phone was ringing continually; for every person who phoned to tell me not to run in Burrard, there was one who would exhort me to do so. I was torn by all the conflict swirling around me. I had not yet decided whether to seek the nomination in any riding, yet Bill was beginning to feel tension growing between him and Ray Parkinson in the office. There was tension developing between the party hierarchy and me, and once again Burrard was at war, both internally with its membership and externally with the party brass.

While I was being buffeted by this turmoil, the Dodge-Brown machine was quietly making lists, signing up new members, lobbying old members and preparing for the nominating fight of its life.

I must confess that the excitement set my adrenaline soaring, and I was probably off and running before I knew it. The act that confirmed my decision was almost anticlimactic when it occurred. One evening Ray Parkinson telephoned me. I remember very little of the conversation except that it was tense and it was brief. He explained why he thought I was not electable and he asked me not to run since I would surely lose the seat for the party. I pointed out to him that he had already done that in 1969. When I hung up the phone, Bill explained that he had had a similar conversation with him, that Ray had asked him to 'tell' me not to run, that he had explained to Ray that he was unable to compel me to do anything and wouldn't even if he could, so Ray had told him that he would phone me himself.

Bill added that none of that mattered now that I had decided to run. When I told him that I had still not made a decision, he told me that in my conversation with Ray I had made it quite clear that I would not be influenced or deterred by his assessment of my electability, thus leaving the clear impression that I was seeking the nomination.

I was stunned to realize that without being aware of it I had formed the intent and declared my entry in the race. . . .

That night Bill and I had yet another of our long discussions; and once again he assured me of his full support and repeated that his partnership with Ray Parkinson should be of no concern to me.

However, he also repeated that he did not want me to build up any false hopes since, with the party establishment against me, I could surely well lose.

I spent about two seconds worrying . . . [that] the loss of the nomination would follow on the heels of the law school rejection and the Board of Governors defeat, and decided that despite the possibility of a loss this was a once-in-a-lifetime opportunity. I decided that it was the chance that my grandmother had never had, that it was the opening every Black person in Canada dreamed of. It was the goal of feminists who supported the Royal Commission report, and it was the possibility that Bill and I had worked to bring within reach of our children. It was unthinkable that I should turn my back on it.

For the next two months my schedule never varied. Every day I would get home from work by 3:30 P.M. I would spend some time with the children, prepare and eat dinner with the family, then leave to visit NDP members in Burrard; Bill supervised the older children's homework and prepared Jonathan for bed. The routine never changed except on Saturday and Sunday. On Saturday during the day I would sometimes do visits. I would often take Jonathan and Gary with me; Cleta was usually too busy and too 'cool' to want to tag along.

It was a slow, time-consuming process, but well worth it, because I had the opportunity not only to knock on doors, but to actually sit and visit with the membership. I learnt a lot of the NDP history of Burrard and made some good friends. . . .

The preparation for nomination night was the worst part. Vancouver-Burrard was a double-member riding; that meant that each delegate voted for two people. The first two candidates to gain fifty percent plus one of the votes cast would be the winners. Everyone wanted to win on the first ballot for a number of reasons. First, at least ten percent of members who promise support will fail to attend the meeting for one reason or another. Then, of the ones who do attend, another ten percent or more will leave after casting their ballots without waiting to hear the results or to vote in the event of a second ballot call. There is also the fear that people may change their minds between the time they give their commitment and the time they vote. Strange things happen on second ballots; they are a wild card and totally unpredictable, and no politician cares for them unless they have been carefully factored into the strategy. . . .

In April 1972, the Burrard nomination was held in the old Indian Centre on Yew Street. The press, smelling blood, were out in full force. They had been excited about the idea that an ex-MLA might be defeated, curious to see whether the Status of Women Committee endorsement would be a liability or an asset to me and intrigued by the prospect of a Black woman being nominated for the first time in Canada to run in a provincial election. They were not alone—half the provincial New Democratic Party membership also turned up to view the spectacle.

I was a nervous wreck. I could not eat for days and I could not sleep. Two weeks earlier I had decided that I needed a buffer against the depression that I knew would surely engulf me after the loss of the nomination, so I went to visit my friend Toni Cavelti, the jeweller. He had always admired my hands and would tell me that I should model rings. I asked him to design for me an inexpensive ring of gold that would lift me out of my impending melancholy. That April morning I picked up the very simple ring of bold design that he had crafted for me, and its classic modesty lifted my spirits immediately. . . .

The building was packed to overflowing, mostly with spectators. Every NDPer in the Lower Mainland was there, including the 'heavies': the future attorney general, . . . future minister of finance. . . .

I had determined not to read my speech, so I fell back on an old technique that I still use occasionally. After writing the speech, I practised its delivery over and over until I was satisfied that I had the accents in the right places and the tone and timbre of voice correct; then I recorded it, and recorded it, and recorded it until I had a perfect version. The cassette of the perfect version accompanied my every move, and I played it until the words and the tone and the sound of it were seared into my brain. . . .

Despite my preparedness my legs were trembling so hard that when my nominator announced my name, I was afraid to stand in case I might fall. The applause that greeted my ascent to the platform, however, was deafening and sustained. That proved to be all I needed. I began to speak, got caught up in the words, the memory drive kicked in and I never missed a beat. When I was through, I could tell from the applause and grins on the faces of my committee that, although I might not have converted any opponents, I had held my supporters and picked up the uncommitted vote. The results proved me correct.

That night, on the first ballot, Norm Levi and I were nominated to represent the riding of Vancouver-Burrard in the upcoming provincial election. Six months later Bill and Ray Parkinson severed their medical partnership.

I suspect that each of us carries inside a memory that is so startling, so vivid, that it remains alive long after all our other recollections fade. . . .

August 30, 1972, was my miracle. That was the day when Canadians living in the area of Vancouver bounded by 16th Avenue, Fraser Street, Waterloo and the Pacific Ocean elected me to represent them in the British Columbia legislature. Because it made very little sense to me that people who had for years refused to rent me accommodation or hire me for employment would entrust me with the responsibility of representing them in the place of power, where laws governing their lives were drafted and enforced, I had run in the election with my intellect but not with my heart. . . . I had run hard, run to win, but deep inside I had known that racism—that faceless coward that dogs the endeavours of all non-white people in North America—would strike at some time, barring the way and putting an end to the dream.

So in this election, as on so many other occasions, I had prepared myself for defeat. Together with Bill I had constructed the defensive shield, part rationalization, part extrapolation, that would protect me against despondency and self-blame. . . .

The decision of the Vancouver-Burrard voters stunned me. Not since 1858, when Mifflin Wistar Gibbs sat as a councillor in the City of Victoria, had a Black person held public office in British Columbia. So, on August 30, 1972, when the voters overturned that tradition and included Emery Barnes and me with the thirty-six other New Democrats chosen to form the first social democratic government in B.C., they were not just making political history but writing Black history as well.

I do not believe that our election resulted from any revolutionary decision on the part of the voters to strike a blow for racial equality. Rather, their discontent with the existing government and their determination to turf it out of office overrode their prejudices, and resulted in the temporary colour and political blindness that allowed them to support us despite the fact that we were both New Democrats and Black.

My miracle encompassed a triumph not just over racism but over sexism as well. Despite the fears expressed by the more traditional elements in the party that my outspoken support for the women's movement would cost me votes, I had held fast to my decision that women were my constituency and would receive my outspoken support. . . .

My victory signalled in some small measure the potential power of those groups, made me a national curiosity and confirmed British Columbia's reputation for eccentric politics. For me, victory was also a vindication of my decision to reject the Uncle Tom role that is often touted as the best route to success in society for Blacks and women.

When I awoke on August 31, my stomach was queasy and waves of nausea washed over me. . . . I was sure that I lacked the ability to live up to the expectations of the electorate and I felt like a fraud, as though somehow I had managed to fool everyone into thinking that I could be a politician. The voters had called my bluff and now I was about to be unmasked! . . .

[T]he phone calls and telegrams promptly came pouring in. It seemed that every Black person in Canada had been following the campaign and had had a personal stake in Emery and in me. They were celebrating right across Canada. Like Lincoln Alexander's before us, our victory gave them hope that the individual could rise above racism, and their outpouring of love, pride and awe added to my torture.

Feminists were ecstatic. . . .

I lay in bed in a near catatonic state while Bill and the kids, boisterous and ebullient, handled the phone calls and raced around—happy, stunned and amazed. From time to time Cleta or Gary would come into the bedroom just to stare at me. Then they would give me a hug and with a wild whoop race out of the room, adding their noise to the increasing din in the house. Jonathan had no idea what the excitement was all about, but he was enjoying every minute of it. Lying there, I could hear Gary and Cleta asking Bill what it would mean to have a politician for a mother and spec-

ulating on how this would change our lives. . . . I was terrified and
tried to escape thoughts of the future by reliving the campaign from
the night of my nomination to the present. . . .

The only hostile questions directed at me concerned the hypo-
critical fear that my children would suffer as a result of my political
activities, and accusations of their impending neglect. At first the
question made me defensive because I shared those concerns
myself. I felt guilty about spending a lot of time away from the children, aged fourteen, twelve and five, so I handled the question
badly. In time it became clear that the Socreds realized they had
found my Achilles' heel. I was not fooled. I knew that the questioners cared not one whit about my children, but they saw that their
questions wounded me and so, smelling blood, they kept tearing
away, heckling, questioning and accusing me every chance they got.

My committee became alarmed and I became concerned about
my obvious vulnerability and about the ease with which my opposition were using my guilt to undermine me. Norman and the committee offered me extensive advice on how to handle the matter,
primarily that I should resort to humour as a means of diffusing the
discomfort. But guilt and fear curled up tight in the secret recesses
of my mind and I knew as I tried to dislodge them that in this
instance, humour was impossible; I was no equal to the demons
that whispered to me that I was placing my selfish ambition ahead
of my children.

I raged against my guilty feelings, roared silent curses about the
unfairness of the fact that in a similar situation Bill would not be
plagued by any such emotions or considerations. I knew my feelings
were irrational; that, far from being neglected, the children were
thriving in the care of their father, a housekeeper and me. I knew, in
addition, that they loved the excitement of the campaign and revelled in all the attention they were getting from their peers and
mine. I argued and fought with myself in an attempt to destroy
the assumption that somehow my physical presence protected my
children and stamped me as a good mother, while my absence
automatically branded me bad and placed them at risk. Finally,
exhausted and enlightened by the struggle, I came to accept that I
would not lose the feelings of guilt, and that I had a choice: either
quit the campaign or accommodate and adjust to reality.

I forced myself to mock my fears and to incorporate my guilt
into the humour that then came easily. I began my speeches by first

thanking all the Socreds in the audience concerned about my children for their caring, and reported that the children were asking for their assistance in sending me to Victoria. After a few more throw-away lines, I would launch into the body of my presentation, from time to time referring to my experience as a mother and a wife and to the added dimension those two roles gave to my perception of the world, emphasizing this as one more asset that I would bring to the political sphere. Questions about my parenting responsibility and abilities soon disappeared.

I learnt a lesson from that experience that I used throughout my fourteen years in public office—namely to be the first person to identify my own weakness, my own Achilles' heel, and then to deal with that weakness before it becomes a public issue. Doing so is a task that calls for clearsighted and brutal honesty, but it is essential, not only because the opposition always seems to have an instinctive knack for ferreting out a politician's weakness, but more importantly because the fear of the public exposure of a hidden fear, or concern about the fear itself, is a problem that is better prevented than cured. . . .

I am a very private person, even a little shy; contact with racial hostility has left me wary and hypersensitive to the point that I found political canvassing excruciatingly painful and repugnant. In NDP politics, however, canvassing is mandatory so I had to do it, and do it with a smile on my face and a bounce in my step. To achieve this I had to use the process of displacement: I thought of myself and often spoke of myself in the third person, speaking of Rosemary Brown as a person I respected, loved and knew to be honest and dependable and to have integrity. I also used heavy doses of denial, so that the hostile response was always rationalized as being directed at the party, the ideology or the policy, but never at me personally. . . .

[A]s I lay in bed on the morning of August 31, I realized that I had been so totally wrapped up in the fate of my own riding and oblivious to the province as a whole that I was unprepared for the defeat of the Social Credit government; and my panic returned as the knowledge dawned that much as I had wished it, I had not prepared myself for victory and consequently was at a loss as to how to handle it. . . .

[T]wo weeks passed before I heard from the premier. When word came it was in the form of a memo announcing a caucus meeting in Victoria and requesting my attendance. By that time he had named his cabinet and the caucus meeting was really just a chance for the socialist hordes to preen and indulge in the inevitable photo opportunity.

Neither Emery Barnes nor I was named to that first cabinet, which consisted only of those elected members who had served in the legislature prior to 1972. . . . Although I was disappointed by my exclusion, I was not really surprised. The response in the Black community, however, was immediate and negative. . . .

Liberal and Conservative feminists greeted my exclusion from cabinet with a mixture of disappointment and relief; relief because for them my exclusion was proof that sexism was as alive and well in the New Democratic Party as it was in their own parties, a fact that gave them comfort. Most other women who had worked for the election of the NDP saw my exclusion as an ominous sign. They believed that they had been used by the party to gain power, and that their issues would be ignored now that the election was over. . . .

I knew that inside the caucus women's most stubborn enemy was not misogyny but paternalism. The premier, as well as a number of male colleagues, held fast to the belief that they knew better than women themselves what our needs were and how best to meet them. . . .

An example of the most glaring paternalism centered on the introduction of a women's ministry. The Women's Rights Committee of the NDP had embarked on a very long and analytical search for a way to implement and monitor policies to attack the systemic inequalities in women's lives. After many hours of research, consciousness-raising, exploration and debate on this issue, it was decided that the solution lay in the careful crafting of a ministry designed to do this job. The debate was not confined to B.C. All across Canada, feminists were searching for the best structure through which to address their political goals.

A women's ministry had the unanimous support of the B.C. feminist community. The hope was that such a structure would serve as a pilot that could be copied by the federal government and other provincial governments. . . . After the election Dave Barrett, the new premier, publicly rejected the policy of the women's ministry on the ground that he did not believe in giving any group special status. He did at the same time, of course, appoint a minister of Indian Affairs. . . .

The depth of his ignorance about women's condition was profound and equalled only by his belief that the women's movement was a temporary aberration, a blip in history supported only by a few discontented women. . . .

The disillusionment and the speedy demise of our high expectations of the government, coupled with the knowledge that the Socreds were an even more regressive option, was the cruel and bitter trap in which we found ourselves. . . . [E]ven after the NDP provincial convention of 1973 reaffirmed its overwhelming support for the establishment of a women's ministry, Dave immediately informed the press that the resolution was not a priority and would not receive his support. Many of the tired, exhausted and angry women delegates dissolved into tears as a retreat from the violence that raged through our heads and battered our brains. . . . We were determined that he had not heard the last of us; it was left to women outside the party, however, to respond by working for his defeat in 1975. . . .

I . . . concluded that being excluded from cabinet could be interpreted as a compliment to me—it meant that my outspoken feminism and my close ties with the radical wing of the party placed me in a position of being thought too independent to be relied upon for total allegiance to the leader at all times. . . .

How do I really feel? There is power, prestige, influence and money attached to a cabinet appointment. In cabinet I could have done more for women, visible minorities and other disadvantaged groups who made up my constituency. The Black community would have been proud and it would have been a clear and positive message to feminists about the NDP's support for women's rights. On the other hand, I have often wondered whether the post of cabinet minister, with its heavy workload, would have deterred me from grabbing the once-in-a-lifetime challenge to seek the federal leadership of the party in 1975, with the opportunity that particular experience gave women to make feminism the topic of political debate on a national scale. On balance, would a provincial cabinet post have been more important than that? Who knows? I only know that given the choice, I would not have traded the experience of seeking the federal leadership for a cabinet appointment. . . .

Once I had overcome the initial shock of being elected part of an NDP government, I plunged into political life with impatience and anticipation. I believed in the power of governments to create change and I believed in the commitment of the NDP to improve the quality of life of all British Columbians. . . .

[M]y goals and tasks seemed very straightforward and uncomplicated. I had two major items as well as a number of lesser ones on my agenda. First and foremost, because of my personal experience with discrimination, I wanted tough, ironclad human rights legislation, legislation to plug every loophole through which any individual or organization had ever been able to discriminate against a person because of her or his race, gender, religion, disability or marital or economic status. I wanted to be sure that all persons, regardless of those factors, would be free to live, work, eat and worship wherever they desired or could afford to.

Again because of personal experience, I was concerned about the discrimination in housing that was aimed at people with children. I was prepared to explore the possibility of legislating against such practices, without infringing on the right of senior citizens to exclusive and separate accommodation if they so wished. . . .

My theory . . . was that people should be empowered to pursue their own liberation, and one step on the road to such empowerment, one external service we politicians could provide, was to remove the hurdles and open the doors to opportunities. . . .

People wrestle with internal and personal demons born of years of negative socialization; these cannot be defeated by provincial legislation alone, although it can remove the practices on which much of that socialization rests. Provincial legislation can state quite clearly 'thou shalt not discriminate,' and introduce special measures to right the historical imbalance that has victimized any one group in a profession, trade or other type of employment. . . . [E]mpowered women and men working for their own equality was my dream; political process was the route through which I hoped to make it happen. . . .

The task of formulating perfect, loophole-proof human rights legislation involves political risk-taking in its more dangerous form, a fact that often terrifies politicians. . . . [T]he courageous and brilliant Deputy Attorney General of the day, was, however, equal to the task. He earned my respect and gratitude as he hammered out a Human Rights Act that was too strong for the more timid members

of the caucus; nonetheless, with the navigational skills of . . .
the . . . Attorney General, it survived to become the best piece of
human rights legislation ever introduced in this country. . . .

For the three years that we were the government I existed as a
multi-personality. I endeavoured to be a full-time mother and wife,
an active feminist and outspoken advocate, a public figure and the
fun-loving member of a small clique in the caucus. Needless to say,
my immune system was thrown into turmoil and before the three
years were over, I experienced a series of eccentric and grotesque
ailments. During that period I developed symptoms of brain
tumour, gall bladder ailments, angina and hemorrhoids. I had problems with my teeth, my eyes, my skin and my bladder. I nearly doubled my weight in the first year, lost the added weight in the second
and gained it back in the third.

Much of the time in Victoria I was desperately lonely; I began
eating and drinking too much. Despite this, I continued to overwork and over-extend myself on behalf of my constituents, women,
visible minorities and my family. It was a nightmare, relieved only
by my return to Bill and the children in Vancouver each weekend. . . .

I survived those three years in part because . . . the women's
community remained supportive and nurturing, and because my
family remained a haven and a secure oasis. But, unrecognized by
me, a shift was taking place in my life. Imperceptibly and in subtle
ways, I was becoming less dependent on my family, and more
dependent on my political and feminist friends—almost stealthily
they began to replace my family as my source of guidance, advice
and succor. Despite my determination to prevent it, the erosion of
my family life had begun. . . .

Soon after August 30, Robin Geary volunteered to help me
handle the massive flow of mail that resulted from my election.
When I learnt that she was a better spinner and weaver than she
was a typist, I struck a bargain with her to supply me with spun
wool for my weaving and crocheting, in exchange for which I
would do the typing. She remained to become the politically astute
constituency representative who organized and administered my
constituency office in Vancouver throughout the seven years that I
represented Vancouver-Burrard. . . . She was there through the bat-
tles of the NDP government years, and in 1975 almost single-
handedly forced many feminists who planned to boycott the

election campaign to rethink their position and to work for my re-election.

Primarily, she was the buffer between me and the disappointed and disillusioned constituents who felt betrayed by the government's failure to deliver on their expectations. At the same time she insistently focused their attention on the positive aspects and actions of the government. Her efforts contributed greatly to my re-election in 1975, the election that saw twenty-six New Democrats go down to defeat—including the premier himself.

Despite my own disillusionment with the government I was saddened by the defeat in 1975. I was proud of the government's achievements on women's rights. . . .

[W]e were the first provincial government to fund rape relief centres, women's health collectives and shelters for battered women. Publicly funded daycare spaces were increased. A guaranteed minimum income as well as extended medical benefits that included the cost of prescription drugs for seniors were introduced. . . .

The human rights legislation introduced by the Attorney General prohibited discrimination based on sex or marital status, and a Royal Commission . . . examined the dual area of children and the family. Its report included many sweeping and fair recommendations in the area of division of property in the event of a divorce. . . .

All these positive acts proved unable to reverse the early sense of betrayal experienced by labour, anti-poverty groups, women's groups and other of the traditional supporters of the NDP. . . .

Whenever anyone asks me what I achieved during my years in politics, I think of two things, one an obsession—namely the introduction of legislation for mandatory use of seatbelts for children in a moving vehicle, which was passed in October 1983—and the other a sobriquet. . . . I was an irritant who kept the attention of both government and opposition members focused on the concerns of women and disadvantaged groups. . . .

One of my proudest moments was being called upon to second the Speech from the Throne on January 26, 1973, at the beginning of the first full parliament of the first NDP government in British Columbia. . . .

[A]s I looked about the magnificent legislative chamber with its intricate carvings, domed ceilings and red carpeting . . . I began to speak of my history and my hopes, and to plead with the gov-

ernment to live up to our expectations of it. As I spoke I could feel
the presence of women, Black women, Native women, slaves,
immigrant women, poor women, old women and young women—
I could feel their support, encouragement and hope envelop me,
sending a surge of energy through me, empowering my words and
my voice. I tried to convey their sense of urgency and their struggle,
and I hoped fervently that the premier and his cabinet were hearing
my words.

. . . I remain totally dedicated to the goal of increasing the number of women who enter the political life of this country.

I have some feelings of guilt about this pursuit, knowing the
hurt that could await these women; nonetheless because I see the
political arena as one of the important theatres in which the struggle against our inequality takes place, I persevere in the task of
enlisting women to seek public office. . . .

In 1972 when I entered the B.C. legislature, I discovered that all
the washrooms in the building meant for the use of elected members had been built with urinals in them. In the particular wash-
room being used by female politicians and staff, the urinal had been
concealed behind a temporary box-like wood structure—a clear
indication that our legislative forefathers had not conceived the
possibility of women one day serving as elected members in that
building, and that our presence there is still accompanied by the
hope that our sojourn will be temporary. . . .

[M]any male politicians still view the entry of women into politics as an unwelcome intrusion and invasion of their privacy. Many
of them are annoyed at the prospect of being expected to clean up
their language and their jokes in the presence of female colleagues;
they are threatened by having their prejudice and distorted beliefs
about women challenged by female colleagues, and dislike having
to defend or justify the bizarre or sexist positions they take on matters affecting women. . . .

[M]ale politicians remain defensive and embarrassed by having
to participate in public debate on such issues as family violence and
child abuse. . . . [O]thers barely conceal their belief that there is
something obscene, repulsive and illegitimate about women with
power. . . .

I was aware at all times of the impact that my assertiveness and
radical demands were having on my colleagues both in caucus and

in opposition. As with other New Democrat members, there was a sense of urgency about me; like theirs, my election had raised expectations; and, like them, I wanted to get on with the business of delivering on my promises. . . .

While the women's movement in B.C. was battling the indifference of government, the movement in the parts of Canada, faced with similar roadblocks, began to explore other avenues of pursuing the goal of equality. Guided and encouraged by the Report of the Royal Commission on the Status of Women, there began an explosion of activity by feminists in the academic, business, religious and cultural communities. Many non-profit organizations that sponsored shelters for battered women, rape relief centres, women's centres, health collectives and status of women groups began to network and link up into national organizations. . . .

[A]lmost concurrently the National Action Committee on the Status of Women (NAC) was born, as was the federal government's Advisory Council on the Status of Women, with its regional political appointments, the federal women's office in the public service and the Canadian Research Institute on the Advancement of Women. . . .

To have been a woman in Canada during the late '60s and early '70s was to have had the great fortune of witnessing and participating in one of the important struggles for personhood. Not the most important, of course, because that had been won for us by the early feminists of the women's suffrage movement. But after the interregnum that followed the Second World War, the '60s marked an awakening. Those were heady, exciting and challenging times for Canadian women who chose to view them as an opportunity to be independent and equal persons.

Those were my double-life years, when I straddled the feminist revolution and political demands at the same time and burnt my candle at both ends. . . .

"Why did you work so hard to defeat my bid for the leadership?" I asked David Lewis.

"Because you were a genuinely dangerous threat to the party," he replied. . . .

For the first time, David Lewis and I were completely relaxed with each other, so I felt free to put to him the question that had bothered me throughout the federal leadership race to replace him. I had never understood why he worked so hard against my candidacy because before my challenge, he . . . and most of the establishment of the federal party had treated me with affection and respect. The passion of their opposition to my attempt to win the party leadership was intense and forceful; and as the campaign progressed and my strength grew, their efforts seemed to take on panic proportions. Because this was so contrary to what was happening in the party as a whole, where my support was growing, it confused and puzzled me. . . .

[H]is perception of my threat sprang from his observation that my leadership campaign attracted the support of party members who wanted to change the direction of the party in profound ways. . . .

[H]e and many others of the party leadership credited my almost spectacular level of support to the fact that, like a magic wand, I awakened every dormant discontent in the party; I appealed to people who saw in me hope for their cause and so flocked to my side. I attracted people who presented new challenges to the party based on a determination to expand its ideological parameters, people who demanded that it address the specific concerns of those new and emerging groups for whom democratic socialism was the means to the end of their oppression. . . .

I did feel that the party was not living up to its potential for women, visible minorities and some of the commitments. . . . So in the age-old debate about whether the NDP should be a 'movement' or an electoral machine I invariably came down on the side of movement, although I did not see the two sides as mutually exclusive. It must have been clear to David Lewis and others of the party leadership that in the event that a choice became inevitable, I would have chosen to see the party remain a social movement rather than sacrifice any commitment in order to achieve political power.

It was the cause of women, however, that catapulted me into the leadership race, and it was the cause of women that seemed to engender the most hostility to my candidacy. The decision to place a feminist candidate with a feminist agenda in the leadership exercise was seen as divisive and a public embarrassment and betrayal of the party. It was described as a slap in the face to all those women who had toiled in the party over the years, confident in the assumption of their equality, and of all those men who had always affirmed and reaffirmed the truth of that assumption.

My decision to support the Women's Committee and to be its

candidate resulted in a marked change in my relationship with certain party members. . . .

Although the hostility to my running hurt, it never at any time threatened my decision to stay in the race. I was sure that running a feminist for the leadership of the party was necessary at that time and that such an endeavour would in the long run strengthen and benefit the party.

So, when David Lewis announced his retirement and the members of the Women's Committee realized that a new federal leader would have to be chosen in 1975, International Women's Year, the opportunity for rebellion blew our minds. Once we identified the leadership race as an opportunity, the coincidences seemed to tumble into our laps.

The first of these was a national NDP women's conference scheduled for Winnipeg in July 1974. . . . The B.C. NDP Women's Committee decided to send as large a delegation as possible, to continue the debate on the relationship between feminism and socialism that we had begun and carried forward since earlier conventions.

The second coincidence was that I was scheduled to be one of the keynote speakers at the conference and so would be able to probe gently and canvass the question of a feminist challenging the leadership.

Robin Geary first raised with me the suggestion of a woman leader to replace David Lewis, and added in the same breath that I should seek to be the Women's Committee choice as the candidate for that position. . . . [W]henver I had thought of NDP leaders, it had always been with amazement that anyone would want to compete for the job of leading a group of people I perceived to be fractious and cantankerous, albeit dedicated and committed to very strongly held views. The challenge of holding the multiple and diverse parts of this group together through a shared vision of justice for all seemed to me nothing short of herculean. I had always admired the leaders, but never envied them. . . .

[W]e allowed ourselves the luxury of imagining what the government of B.C. would have been like if instead of Dave Barrett we had had a feminist premier in our province. . . .

Stimulated by this flight of fantasy, we went on to imagine the federal party with a feminist at the helm, and the wonderful policies and programs that a truly egalitarian social democratic party would spawn. We were not deterred by the thought of those few women who, having achieved leadership in other parts of the world, had not exercised their power to terminate the abuses of women and children but instead had ignored or continued to perpetrate them. . . .

I held firmly to the belief that there was and is a clearly qualitative difference between the way men and women wield power. . . .

[W]e had come to the conclusion that although men and women share the same world, due to a combination of genetics, history and socialization women do inhabit the world and experience it differently from men. Personal experience, as well as study and observation, had led us to conclude that the world community of men and that of women are different; consequently the priorities of the two are different, and this difference is reflected in their political agendas. . . .

Although a feminist leader would be a welcome gift to any party, the job of deciding the direction and goals of the NDP rested not with the leader but with the membership. So for the Women's Committee, the primary purpose of participation in the leadership race would be to use the national debate around feminism and socialism in the party as a consciousness-raising catalyst to our definition of true democratic socialism.

Our priority therefore would be to find a strong feminist who was also a gifted teacher and communicator to take on the task of making this debate happen. . . . I came pretty close to fitting the description. . . . The youth of my children, the stress that such a job would place on my marriage and my inability to speak French all seemed to add up to 'insurmountable barriers.' In addition, we recognized that if my bid were successful, the questions of my race and sex could prove to be so distracting that I could become the issue in future campaigns, rather than the party's message of equality, justice and peace. These all clinched the decision to sit this opportunity out.

Robin, a New Zealander by birth, agreed with me, a Jamaican, that the Canadian attitude to democratic socialism was truly disheartening. Although we were at a loss to explain why, we were fully aware that the ideology was so loaded with negative and threatening connotations, and so shrouded in fears, myths and distortions, that it would take the safest, most acceptable and bland of communicators to be its messenger to the Canadian voter. With a chuckle, we decided to change the criteria for a candidate: instead of a feminist teacher-communicator, it should be a person who combined the safe qualities needed to win with the qualities of a radical left-wing feminist who would take risks on behalf of women. Relieved that we had clarified our leadership prototype, we decided to go in search of such a creature. . . .

One day in the late fall of 1974, Merran Acaster, who had been a tireless worker in my election campaign, came to visit me in my Victoria office. She explained that the Victoria Socialist NDP Women's Caucus wanted to support my bid for the federal leadership. I trotted out all the arguments as to why I was unable to entertain the idea of seeking the leadership and, as I did with Robin, spent some time describing the profile of the person best suited to be our candidate. . . . She believed that my primary role was not to win the leadership but to be the catalyst for the debate around feminist issues. In the unlikely event of a win, however, she thought we could confront my concerns about family, race and sex at that time. . . .

I learnt that the search committee had done an unofficial, superficial poll across the country and had unearthed surprisingly strong support for my candidacy among groups other than women's committees in the party. The women felt that there was a real possibility that I could win, so that added another dimension to the debate. Most of the evening was spent, however, reiterating that the importance of my campaign was the message and the process, not my candidacy.

The message was that since feminism embodied justice for women, socialism was not possible where sexism in any form existed. The process would place women in positions to develop the skills in planning and running all facets of a campaign, and would be invaluable to all those women whose only previous experience in campaigns had been following instructions.

It became increasingly difficult for me to deny the committee and myself the opportunity that seeking the leadership presented at that time. Family and personal considerations remained as barriers, however, and I was not prepared to allow the committee to decide on those matters for me.

After a very long and exhausting evening I agreed that, if a successful resolution to my personal and family concerns was possible, I would allow my name to stand in candidacy for the leadership.

Robin and I returned to my apartment on Dallas Road; she planned to spend the night, then return to Vancouver with me on the following day. We heard the phone ringing as we approached the apartment and ran to open the door; it was Bill, he had been phoning since midnight to find out the results of the marathon. I gave him as detailed a report as possible, then asked him to think about us and about the children and about what a leadership race, even a losing one, would do to our family.

His immediate response was that the family would support my decision whatever it was, but that he would indeed give the matter serious thought. Neither Robin nor I slept that night—we argued, debated, agreed, disagreed, decided and undecided till daybreak.

AT 6 A.M. Bill called again. He had not been able to sleep either. Fortunately, since it was Friday, I would be returning to Vancouver that afternoon for the weekend, but we agreed that he should tell the two older children what the possibilities were so that we could all discuss the pros and cons over the weekend. The women with whom I had met the night before had extracted from me a promise of a speedy response, so I hoped there would be a resolution one way or the other before I returned to Victoria on Monday.

I was totally ambivalent about the leadership. Although I welcomed the opportunity that it would give us as women to rearrange the policy priorities and direction of the party, I was terrified of the responsibilities inherent in the job; I disliked the competition of the campaign and hated the idea of placing more space and time between my family and myself.

Serious thinking led me to acknowledge my secret feeling of always being underqualified for any task that confronted me. Whether it was the decision to seek public office, to apply for a job or to enter graduate school, there was always self-doubt. Because I realized that these feelings of inadequacy were in my head, and that they persisted despite the fact that from childhood I had always been told that I could do anything that I set my mind to, I was forced to conclude that negative messages had somehow infiltrated my socialization, and that these resulted in very deeply buried feelings of inadequacy. . . .

Some of them no doubt stemmed from growing up under colonialism and learning at a very early age of the existence of barriers, often invisible to the naked eye, but real nonetheless; learning that one had to be careful and test the future before moving beyond a given point, because these barriers had a recoil mechanism that caused pain and shame when bumped into. How could I have developed feelings of inadequacy as a woman despite the strong role models and positive reinforcement I had known long before the advent of TV, and before billboards and magazines with sexist images penetrated my awareness? Why did doubts about my ability to achieve linger in my head and increase as I grew older and more observant of the world around me?

Part of the terror I felt about the strong women in my family was the fear that they would discover that I was not as bright, as smart or as capable as they kept reassuring me I was. Part of the conspiracy we shared and the secret I carried through adolescence was that I never admitted to them that I recognized that there were barriers around them too, and that they could not always do anything that they set their minds to. And even though I had always signalled agreement when they assured me that I could be whatever I aimed to be, deep inside my consciousness somewhere I had always doubted the veracity of those protestations and had always sensed that they knew of the existence of my doubts.

Over the years I had developed a 'swimming plunge' technique to deal with challenging situations. I would first imagine the worst possible thing that could happen to me if in fact I had reached beyond my grasp: I would live through the embarrassment, humiliation or pain in my imagination. Then I would hold my nose, back up, take a run and, with eyes closed, leap. I must confess that each time that I survived the leap, my confidence soared, and in time fewer and fewer challenges triggered my 'sense of inadequacy' mechanism.

The idea of being the federal leader of the third largest political party in Canada sent my entire sense of inadequacy mechanism into convulsions. When I tried to visualize the worst possible scenario in that situation, it was so terrifying that I terminated it and came up gasping for air.

Once the debate, the analysis and the intellectualizing were over, only the terror remained. How could I possibly explain to anyone that I was simply afraid of the job? . . .

In the end I did face up to the nasty little toad in my head who kept reminding me of my inadequacy, and decided to discuss my fears first with Bill, then with Robin. In a nutshell, I confessed that I was just not fit to be leader of Her Majesty's Loyal Opposition, nor was I prime ministerial material. I believed that I could lead a movement, or even the third largest political party in Canada, but if there was the slightest chance that the status of the party would change, then I would be out of my depth.

Bill was very pragmatic. He pointed out that leadership was not a tenured position and I could resign at any time, that if I felt I could handle the job as it was presently constituted, that was good enough.

Robin's position was different. She was absolutely certain that I would not win the leadership—but that if I did win, the status of the party would change and we could find ourselves in the position of official opposition. Despite this she saw no necessity to worry, however, because her reading of the party hierarchy was that they would force David Lewis out of retirement and back as leader if there appeared to be the slightest chance of my victory. So she gave her personal guarantee that my campaign would be successful in every respect except making me leader. . . .

As soon as I notified the women's committee of my intention to seek the leadership, I felt as though a load had been lifted from my shoulders. I knew that I had done the right thing and that my grandmother would have been pleased.

A campaign committee was constituted immediately to begin the very important task of designing the campaign. . . .

The committee decided that I should make a formal declaration as soon as possible—they wanted me to be the first in the race so that our platform could be placed before the party for discussion and debate before the hype and hoopla began. . . .

Our strategy worked; since I was the only declared candidate until Lorne Nystrom and Ed Broadbent entered the race, on March 24 and in early April respectively, I had nearly six clear weeks during which the press divided its time between covering my status, speculating on which other candidates would challenge me, and discussing various aspects of the platform. Party members also had that much time to read and digest the policy papers and organizational material emanating from my campaign. . . .

[B]ecause we wished it to be our opportunity to test as well as illustrate the viability of our feminist beliefs concerning leadership and power, we built into it much that we had learnt through our involvement in the women's movement.

We established five rules:

1. The campaign was not going to be star-personality oriented.
2. I was going to stay in until dropped from the ballot, and not be the stalking horse for anyone.
3. There would be no deals, such as first ballot support.
4. All decisions were to be arrived at collectively.
5. The campaign would be run on the issues of feminism and socialism.

Our campaign issues were developed collectively by a group of feminists headed by Hilda Thomas. They were presented in a paper called "Feminism and Socialism" that I delivered to the Learned Societies meeting held in Edmonton on June 4, 1975. In it, I referred to the 1910 statement of August Bebel that "there can be no liberation of mankind without social independence and equality of the sexes." The argument was then developed that both socialist commitment and feminism were rooted in the struggle for "social independence and equality." The conclusion of the rather lengthy presentation contained two observations that clearly stated the rationale for the campaign:

1. If we accept socialism as a philosophy which is committed to the removal of all barriers that make one human being dependent on another, and further if we accept that the oppression of women is based on social dependence as well as on economic dependence, on social exploitation as well as on economic exploitation, then we see that socialism, although quite capable of dealing with economic dependence, has so far not really been successful in dealing with social dependence.
2. It is becoming increasingly evident that socialism, feminism and anti-racism, because they share a common enemy, would be short-sighted indeed not to pool their resources and experiences in a common struggle, and that when the collective goal is achieved what we will have is a more ideologically socialist society than presently exists anywhere in the world. . . .

Children were encouraged to play an active part in the process, from donating their art work for a fundraising poster, to working the Gestetner, stuffing envelopes, stapling material and staffing the information booths at both provincial and federal conventions, to adding their ideas and suggestions to fundraising plans. Indeed

Vanessa Geary, Robin's nine-year-old daughter, an inveterate and experienced political worker, on one occasion single-handedly ran off 1,000 copies of the discussion paper on women's rights for mailing; with no one around to consult, she decided to do so on pale pink paper, throwing her mother into a state of apoplexy about whether pink was the politically correct colour for a paper on feminism!

The campaign was also intended to be the laboratory where women could experiment with ideas and learn from experience about preparing policy statements, designing leaflets, making speeches, dealing with the media and organizing meetings, tours and fundraising events.

Anyone who has ever worked in a collective knows of the time, frustration, aggravation, turmoil and joy that go into hammering out each and every decision. On the other hand, she or he also knows how supportive such a structure can be, because although all responsibility is shared, so are all victories and all losses.

In the B.C. collective I can remember only one incident of serious tension, and it occurred at the very beginning of the campaign. It concerned the time that I would spend away from the legislature. It consumed hours and days of discussion, and actually threatened the solidarity of our committee. In a nutshell, the problem was that in the B.C. legislature there is a rule governing attendance. It states that any elected member who is absent from the precinct for more than ten days during a session, except in the event of illness or other disaster, will be fined $100 per day. Presumably the intent of the rule was to assure that the level of absenteeism condoned in the federal Senate not occur in the provincial legislature, and presumably the rule had been made necessary by the election of large numbers of men with competing business and professional interests.

Obviously one cannot seriously run for the leadership of a large political party in ten days. A few of the committee members suggested that I should absorb the cost of the fines for the days that I was absent from the legislature. I refused. I argued that the fines were a legitimate campaign expense and as such should be part of the campaign budget.

Feelings ran high, relations became strained, but I held my ground and by so doing received the support of the majority of the committee members. However, since we were a collective, majority opinion was not good enough. We had to stay with the issue until the whole committee arrived at a consensus, which they did, and $1,100 was added to the campaign budget to cover an additional eleven days' absence from the legislature. Furthermore the committee agreed that it would move heaven and earth to schedule my travel so that my total absence would not exceed twenty-one days, which my ten days permitted and eleven days covered by the campaign would allow. . . .

Between February and July of that year, I visited all ten provinces and the Yukon, covering nearly fifty towns and cities. On many occasions I would arrive at an airport unsure about what to expect, only to find a large welcoming committee, a packed meeting and an active and high-spirited 'Brown' committee, which had tied up the support of many of the delegates in that riding.

The travel across the country was exhilarating. The flight attendants all knew me and were concerned that I be very comfortable— the airport porters refused to allow me even to pick my baggage off carousels; cab drivers, hotel workers, in short, every working person with whom I came into contact tried to make my travel as easy and stress-free as possible.

Conservative and Liberal women turned up at my meetings just to wish me luck and to make financial donations to the campaign. Parents brought their children out to see me. I was invited to visit schools, daycare centres, seniors' homes. From coast to coast my travel was one great high! It just did not tally with my earlier perception of a country of people with cold faces, slammed doors and hate in their hearts—between February and July 1975, it seemed that with the exception of the NDP hierarchy, everybody loved me. . . .

In 1975 the proposed budget for the campaign was $7,283. And although we actually spent $13,147.04, because we had raised nearly $15,000 we had probably the only leadership campaign in living memory to finish with a surplus.

The raising of that much money was a major accomplishment and imbued the women in the party with an incredible sense of achievement, because . . . we did not have the support of the party's traditional large donors.

What we did have was the imaginative and innovative fundraising ability of women in the party. They designed activities that were a combination of fun and politics built on and emphasizing traditional female events such as craft sales, raffles, auctions, music, a festival and the sale of a poster designed by our children, their friends and Leni Hoover, one of our very talented artists who also happened to be a member of the committee. To this was added the financial donations of many women and visible minority people, most of whom were not known to me, and were not members of the party, but who desperately wanted to see my campaign succeed. These donors were many and far-flung, including an elderly Black gentleman in a nursing home in Alberta who donated a lottery ticket, and women in the United States, England and the Caribbean who had read about the campaign in their newspapers.

The campaign touched and excited women everywhere in Canada, and donations poured in in denominations of five, ten and twenty dollars. Many two-dollar bills were received from seniors, some of whom identified themselves as old suffragists, who promised to send two dollars each month until the campaign was over. Larger donations were received from those women who could afford to give more. There were never any strings attached, just a confession of excitement at the prospect of a woman leader and a desire to lend support. There were so many donations that in time they added up to more than we needed and gave the lie to the myth that women in politics are unable to generate financial support.

The role played by the press in my campaign was an interesting one. . . .

Their response was immediate, and it took the form of disbelief mingled with amusement. However, they were intrigued by the gall of my ambitious move to shoot for the top job in the party after only two and a half years of electoral employment. . . .

As the campaign continued and it became obvious that I was not a stalking horse for any other candidate and that my support was sufficiently alarming to the party leadership for them to pressure a reluctant Ed Broadbent back into the race, the press found that they could neither ignore me nor continue to trivialize my campaign. There was a subtle shift away from superficial discussions of my 'elegance,' 'private school education' and 'home in the fashionable Point Grey district of Vancouver' to more thoughtful and serious speculation as to the potential effect of my candidacy on the New Democratic Party and on Canada. . . .

When the convention opened in Winnipeg, the members of the press corps found to their delight and surprise that, because our

campaign continued our practice of open meetings, they were free
to sit in on all but the most private strategy sessions. They were horrified by what they considered to be the political naiveté of some of
our decisions. However, because we refused to fudge or play games,
they were impressed by the integrity, honesty and forthright manner
in which we conducted our business with them, and they trusted us.

The result of including them in many of our deliberations was
that their coverage of our activities was accurate, clear and unbi-
ased. Some of them even ventured to offer advice from time to time,
especially when they thought that we were going overboard with
our purity—such as when we returned unopened the bottles of rye
and scotch that arrived at our committee room as a gift from a local
distiller.

The tour was very exhilarating for me. It was obvious that
many undecided votes were swinging to my campaign and that I
was picking up momentum as we progressed. I was meeting a number of the members for the first time and some who attended out of
curiosity became supporters and committed workers. Gradually I
became less tense, and by the time the tour rolled into Vancouver I
was having fun. . . .

By the end of the tour my campaign committee was almost
euphoric. The level of committed support had increased dramatically; campaign expenses were expanding to keep up with donations. The media were beginning to sit up and reassess their earlier
pronouncements. . . .

By the time the campaign committee arrived in Winnipeg two
days prior to the convention, I was no longer intimidated by the job
of leader. I had grown so much during the campaign and been so
impressed by the talent within the party that I had become confident that no matter who the delegates chose as leader, the NDP
would remain a force and influence in Canadian politics.

I was completely caught up in the excitement and enthusiasm
of the committee and hung between a state of exhaustion and exhilaration most of the time. By then I had stopped eating and had lost
twenty-three pounds.

We knew that we would be arriving at the convention with me
sitting in second place. The goal of all the provincial committees was
to lock their support in tight, and then to work on picking up additional delegates as other candidates were dropped from the ballot. . . .

Just for one second as the plane touched down in Winnipeg, Robin, Hilda and I looked at each other in a moment of silent panic—this was it. All the months and hours of hard work would end in three days. The party would have a new leader, and no matter who was chosen, we knew that we had achieved at least one of our stated goals: the national debate on feminism had occurred, the consciousness-raising had happened, the shift towards full equality was taking place. The battle we faced over the coming days was for socialism. This was going to be a tough one. . . .

The hierarchy had interpreted our feminist position as just a cleverly constructed mask to hide our true left-wing intent. Grudging as they had been in espousing many of our feminist demands, they had done so in the hope that, satisfied, the women would abandon 'the Left,' split the coalition and allow the Brown campaign to die after a brave showing on the first ballot.

We were determined that this would not happen. We had come to our feminism through socialism and to us the two remained indivisible. We quickly shifted into overdrive and hit the tarmac running. . . .

The 'Brown is Beautiful' slogan, a modification of the phrase coined by the Black movement in the United States, was first introduced by Clare Powell into the Saskatchewan campaign. It proved so successful that it was adopted by all the other committees and became our official slogan. No one seemed to be concerned about its links to the Black Panthers or Malcolm X; all welcomed it as a symbol that we were radicals without being extremists in the American way.

As a symbol, for me it went beyond a play on my name. It linked me to the American Black struggle and gave me an opportunity to be identified with it. I was really pleased with the committee's decision and with the use of the colour brown (with its root and earth connection) in the design of the logo. . . .

My experience of the convention in reality was limited by the very small role that I played as a candidate. Experience in subsequent leadership races in which I have been involved as a worker taught me that the real work in such campaigns is done far away from the limelight and from the candidate. . . .

I was assigned four tasks by the campaign committee. I was to meet and talk with the delegates, participate in the floor debates, deport myself well in the 'bearpit' session (the public forum in which questions are hurled at the candidates, as TV lights glare and the audience surrounds you in a circle so close that you can almost feel the warmth of their breath) and excel in the final candidate's speech. . . .

I felt the weight of my supporters' expectations and I was terrified of failing them. Everyone was on a high. Our support continued to grow, and, although our second place position never changed, we were widening the gap between ourselves and Nystrom and closing the gap ever so slightly with Broadbent.

The bearpit, when it arrived, proved to be easier than I had feared. I lost no supporters, gained a few more and the consensus of the committee was that I had conducted myself well.

The next hurdle was the final speech; however, the committee insisted that some time had to be spent participating in the policy debates on the floor. They believed that my involvement in that aspect of the convention was more important than any more media events or delegates' meetings. They were determined that my position as a thoughtful participant in the debate and discussion of party policy should be emphasized, and that I should not be seen to be the kind of leader who would only turn up at conventions to deliver the keynote address and socialize with delegates. . . .

Saturday morning I arrived at the convention relatively rested, but tense. I was anxious to be with the speechwriting committee; however, since I agreed with the committee's decision about my participation in the floor debates, we consulted and agreed that two interventions would be sufficient. . . .

I recognized that the talent of this particular group of speechwriters was so formidable and this speech so crucial that I dared not even dream of tampering in any way with their creation. Since it was a collective and I was a part of it, I was able to have enough input so that I hoped I could be comfortable with the style, but I was not sure. I was desperate, therefore, for the speech to be completed so that I could go off to a quiet corner and rehearse it. Time, alas, did not permit this, and as the time for delivery approached, my anxiety level rose almost to the point of immobilizing me. I suddenly remembered how much I hated public speaking and I just wanted to chuck the whole thing and disappear.

At 5:30 P.M. Robin came to collect me. It was time to dress, to be in the committee room relaxed and smiling to give a boost to the workers and to reassure them that I was ready for the fray. There was no time to return to my hotel, so I dressed in the committee room behind a sheet held up by two workers. I calmly applied my makeup while Hilda read the speech to me. At that point, true to form, my stomach shut down and I could neither eat nor drink. However, I forced myself to give a brief pep talk to the workers and to look to all the world cool, calm and relaxed. Only Bill and Robin knew that my heart was pounding, that my hands were freezing, my breathing laboured and my mind a blank, and that my legs would soon begin to tremble.

After my little pep talk, Bill led me to a corner behind the stage. He held both my hands in his very tightly and said in a calm voice, "Breathe in, breathe out, breathe in, breathe out, breathe in. . . ."

The loud, long and sustained applause, the bright lights . . . lifted me and carried me through my first words, "I'm here today to ask you to select me to be the new leader for our party, a party whose traditions we love . . . and whose future we trust. . . ." As I continued to weave the vision we had for the NDP of the future, the number of interruptions by applause continued to grow.

And as I spoke of ending poverty and creating equality, I was emboldened and strengthened by the hopes and dreams we had for this country; my voice was clear and my words firm, and I knew that I was doing as good a job as my supporters would have wished and a good job as well for all the women, Black people, poor and voiceless who had inspired me to champion causes and enter public life in the first place. . . .

> To all of you I make this pledge: That I will never forget that our party has its roots in the Prairie soil, where it grew in spite of dust and Depression, fed by sweat and tears and the passionate hatred of injustice; that I will never forget that we are the party of the working people, and that our task and our duty is to bring them legal and moral justice in the face of attacks from power and privilege; that I will be unbending in my stand against every form of oppression which deforms and crushes people and prevents them from the fulfillment of their lives; and that as leader of our New Democratic Party, I will be answerable to the members of this party as we go forward to become the government that will build a truly socialist, truly humane society—here in Canada.

I did not hear the applause at the end of my speech because by then my brain and my hearing had collapsed under the combination of exhaustion, tension, anxiety and relief, but I have been told that it was deafening. My task was over; I wanted to go home and go to bed.

Because of the time constraints on all candidates' speeches, I had to delete parts of the complete speech, so it was decided that I would give it in its entirety in the committee room at the end of the evening. When I arrived there, the room was packed. All the committee members were spinning with excitement. . . . My speech had picked up support, votes were shifting our way, the delegate count was rising.

When I looked around the convention floor on Monday, my workers seemed to be everywhere, huddling, speaking to delegates, conferring. I had no task to perform, no role to play. I sat beside Bill and across from my brother at our constituency table and worried.

What if we had been able to pull it off? What if, after the votes came in, I was indeed leader of this party? What would it really mean to the chances of the party ever forming the government in Canada? What if the pundits were right and I was the 'kiss of death' to this party, which for so long had acted as Canada's conscience? . . . My brother reached across the table and touched me. "Smile," he said, "you're on 'Candid Camera.'" I looked up and sure enough there was the camera trained on me. Just then someone walked up and delivered a rose, which had been sent by an anonymous admirer in Vancouver. . . .

Tension on the floor mounted as we awaited the results of the first ballot. When it was reported, our committee breathed a sigh of relief. Their count had been accurate, I was in second place, 413 votes to Broadbent's 536 total. . . .

We began the day with 395 ironclad committed votes that we hoped to build on, and clearly they were all there on the first ballot. Before the beginning of the second ballot, Svend Robinson came to visit me. He pointed out that, if I delivered my 413 supporters to John Harney, he would then have 726 and the surprise move would stun both Broadbent and Nystrom into immediate defeat.

I told him that this would be a bold move, which would work even better the other way around since I was sitting in second place and John was down in fourth. "In any event," I added, "even to contemplate such an action would violate two of our ground rules concerning making no deals, and not dropping out until defeated." Svend decided that as the candidate I had very little say anyway and went off in search of Robin or some other committee member. He never returned and John Harney was defeated on the second ballot.

The third ballot plunged our committee into a momentary state of gloom, for although I was still in second place, Ed was widening the gap between us, and some of the unexpected votes we had received on the first ballot had deserted us. We were now down to our core vote of 397, Ed had 586, Nystrom was still in third place with 342. As I looked around I noticed that the Broadbent workers were beginning to look less anxious. Panic hit them, however, when Nystrom was dropped after the third ballot, leaving a clear two-way fight between Ed and me. Although Ed had a comfortable lead with 694 ballots to my 494, Nystrom's exit meant that 413 ballots were up for grabs.

The gloves were off. . . . [A]ll the big guns were running around the convention floor twisting arms, calling in chips, working at an energy level hitherto unheard of. My committee was doing the same. It was fascinating to behold. A life-and-death struggle for the party seemed to be taking place there on the convention floor that Monday morning.

I sat detached and watched it all. Bill, as a psychiatrist, was enthralled. He had never seen or experienced anything like that before. My brother concentrated on his responsibility, that of maintaining my smile for the benefit of the TV cameras that now encircled me, and which I'm sure also encircled Ed. The camera people wanted to catch the instant reaction, the immediate response to the results of the final vote.

Marilyn Roycroft, chairperson of the Brown Campaign balloting committee, came and knelt beside my chair. "Keep smiling," she whispered, "but listen carefully." Something in her voice forewarned me, so I found my smile, beamed into the cameras and listened. She explained that we needed seventy-five percent or 307 of Lorne Nystrom's support to win. Everyone had worked the Saskatchewan delegates, but Blakeney, Nystrom and the powers that be had a tight rein on them. "We are just not going to make it," she said. We smiled at each other one more time for the benefit of the camera and she stood up and left. Bob Beardsley came over, patted my shoulder and slipped a note into my hand. "Move that it be unanimous," it read, and I knew that Robin was off somewhere weeping. The press was very generous. "Brown Last To Be Defeated—Leadership Race Tight To The End," headlined the *Win-*

nipeg Free Press. "Brown wins believers in defeat," read *The Province. . . .*

In the end Ed had garnered the support of 948 delegates; I had 658.

I waited for the predicted letdown, anticipated the inevitable depression that must follow such a long and sustained level of activity and anxiety—but it never came; instead, there was only bone-deep weariness.

Bill had greeted me with an embarrassed smile after my speech on Saturday night and a query as to where I thought he had planned to take me as a gift and a treat when the campaign was over. I suddenly remembered that his dream had always been of one day being able to afford to have us stay at the Banff Springs Hotel. . . .

I felt sick at the possibility that I might have ruined his gift by my attack on the CPR owners of the hotel in my speech at the convention. . . .

We boarded the train in Winnipeg later that night and, not surprisingly, the Black attendants all came to greet me and congratulate me on what they felt was a successful and proud moment for the Black community. . . .

It has been thirteen years since that convention. It is now clear that the choice of the party was a sensible one. Ed Broadbent has been a solid and reliable leader who went into the federal election of 1988 ahead of both the Conservative and Liberal leaders (according to the polls) as the person the Canadian people would most like to be their prime minister. . . .

The 1988 election results left us where past elections have left us, in third place, except that we won more seats than ever before. Who knows, maybe that is the way a federal NDP government will come in Canada, inch by inch, one election at a time.

The leadership convention of 1975 remains a political milestone in my life. It opened up the country and showed me another, more friendly and caring face of Canada. It caused me to travel farther, dig more deeply and learn more about this country of my adoption than if I had been born here; and for that I'm truly grateful.

I'm grateful also that the campaign came and went before

Canada began to measure the success of political campaigns by the extent to which they ape and resemble the American model. It was good to know that the primary concern, of the media as well as all other Canadians, was about the quality of service I would give to the country rather than about any aspect of my or my family's personal and private lives. Politically I was pleased that the New Democratic Party reinstituted a tradition, older than the party itself, and even predating suffrage, of national political debates on women's issues, a tradition which had disappeared in modern times, and I am grateful to have been the conduit through which the first trickle flowed.

The one aspect of the experience that gives me my greatest joy, however, is knowing that on July 7, 1975, all over this country, Black people, children as well as adults, eyes and ears fixed on TV and radio, waited for the results of that final ballot, and for that short while, dared to dream of the impossible. . . .

[O]n December 11, 1975, the first NDP government of British Columbia went down to devastating defeat, losing all but twelve of its sitting members. Norm Levi and I survived the battering. The premier did not.

The close vote in Vancouver-Burrard necessitated a recount. As soon as my re-election was confirmed, I flew to Jamaica, where for two weeks I tried to erase all memory of the nightmare campaign. . . .

The only ray of light in that whole experience was that Robin, who had been a scrutineer at the recount, reported that a consistently large number of voters had jumped party lines and voted for the two women candidates in the riding, and that it was this very clearly biased 'women's' vote that had assured my victory. Sisterhood *is* powerful—the gender gap was emerging. . . .

The first day that I returned to the legislative sitting I thought would surely be the worst day of my political career, but I was wrong. The humiliation and insults hurled across the floor at us by government members never let up, so that in time we became inured to them and began to respond in kind. . . .

In time, Dave won his by-election and returned to the Assembly. He immediately began to plan for the next election. He filled us with hope and enthusiasm, and convinced us to hold on to our seats so that we could be the foundation on which a new, wiser NDP government would be built. He was evangelical in this zeal, and so open and cooperative that I was seduced by his dream. And so when the opportunity I had always wanted presented itself to me, I rejected it.

Bill and I were relaxing one Sunday morning, listening to the CBC, when the phone rang. It was Ed Broadbent. He asked me to run in the anticipated federal election. He explained that NDP polling had shown that with the right candidate they could beat . . . the sitting Liberal member in Vancouver-Kingsway. . . .

Bill's immediate response was that it was a gift and I should grab it. He was particularly impressed that Broadbent, whom I had challenged for the leadership less than a year before, now wanted me in his caucus. Bill had assumed that, as in other political parties, NDP leadership races leave irreparable hurts.

I was sorely tempted. I wanted to be a federal member more than I wanted any other job, with the possible exception of High Commissioner to Jamaica. . . .

In the end, Dave convinced me, when I discussed the offer with him as a courtesy and indicated that I wanted to accept it, not to do so. He was convinced that we had a chance of forming the government provincially after the next election, but only if we all held on to our seats. He asked me to give the provincial party this one more chance to return to power, after which I would be free to stay and be a part of the government or leave to seek a federal seat. He was certain that there would be other federal opportunities for me, but that there would be no other opportunity for us provincially, if we lost the next election. . . .

So in the end I had to phone Ed and decline the offer of his support in securing the nomination. He was disappointed, but I was so much more so that I wouldn't allow myself to reopen the idea once it was closed.

Two years later, a government gerrymander eliminated my provincial seat of Vancouver-Burrard. The next time that an opportunity beckoned me to a federal seat, I had retired from politics and was too busy and too weary to heed its call. . . .

After ten years in opposition against an undemocratic, intransigent government, which continued to erode the rights of parliament and the opposition, I began to falter, so that when Dave Barrett announced to the caucus his intention not to continue as leader, my thoughts too turned to retirement. . . .

I was awakened by the sun filtering through the sheer curtains; the sound of children's voices and the sounds of birds slowly penetrated my consciousness. I stretched and rolled, closed my eyes and pretended to sleep. For the first time in fourteen years, I was free to be abed, fritter my life away, do as I would.

The day before I had publicly announced my intention to retire and I felt wonderful. Barb, my constituency assistant, had been angry at my decision to leave; the executive of the constituency felt cheated that I had changed my mind and decided so close to an impending election not to run. I was sorry and apologetic, but suddenly I knew that the time had come for me to go, so I was leaving. . . .

The round of farewell and testimonial dinners organized by the women's community highlighted for me the source of strength that the women had always been to me. From the very beginning of my political career, my goal had been to change the status of women, racial minorities and other disadvantaged groups in society; but I realized that I would not have been able to do any of the public things or participate in the political arena except that women identified me as their spokesperson and worked to get me into the position where I could place their issues on the public agenda. The Black and other racial minority communities in B.C. lacked the clout to do so. Much as they would have liked to elect a candidate of their choosing, they could muster neither the numbers nor the resources to do so. They had had to be content with supporting Emery Barnes and me, the person whom the women in the New Democratic Party worked to insert on the party ticket. . . .

On October 22, 1986, the Socreds won yet another election, and the NDP in Burnaby-Edmonds very sadly were defeated. Two days later Bill and I moved out of our Burnaby house and I received notice that I had been appointed to the Ruth Wyn Woodward endowed chair in Women's Studies at Simon Fraser University. . . .

I was free at last to explore the interests and opportunities opening up to me in education, international development and peace; free at last to stomp the country encouraging women to enter the political arena. I would have time somehow in some way to place the experience and skills I had developed in Canada at the service of the women of my roots.

After fourteen years, I had time, too, to garden, enjoy my

granddaughters and pursue even more intensively the passionate commitments that are the legacy left me by those older, stronger women in the family who continue to be my driving force. . . .

My interest in power had always stemmed from a belief in its potential as an instrument of change. As far back as I can remember, I have wanted to change the world, and I always knew that the use of power was essential to that goal. I was interested in entering the profession of law in order to change unjust and unfair laws. I entered social work because, as a young woman in Jamaica, I had seen it help people change their lives and empower them to fight the system. I entered politics convinced that it was indeed the root of and enforcer of all wrongdoing, and that any real change, to be effective, had to begin at and go to that root. I believed that politics could be a revolution without guns. I believed in it and in its potential to be a power in a positive and good context. I stand before you wiser and sadder about the limits of politics as mould breaker or architect of a new social structure. . . .

The fact that my efforts resulted in failure many more times than they did in success reinforced my sense of powerlessness. I felt cheated; somehow the power that seemed to be promised by the position of 'legislator' was denied me, as though an open door slammed shut upon my approach, leaving me frustrated and bewildered outside. Conversations with other women politicians have helped me see that this too is a shared experience, rather than a personal one.

Throughout my time in office, I was able to observe the ease with which the men twisted each other's arms, to see that even when they opposed each other's views there was an underlying respect, a feeling of family, between them. My approach, on the other hand, even to those members I considered friends, was met with wariness. It was as though they were positioning themselves to defend against attack. A smile would always greet me, but it would only reach as far as the lips. Their eyes would be veiled—and on guard. I'm not sure whether this was a phenomenon peculiar to their relationship with feminists, or all women, or whether I was witnessing the way men would invariably respond to a woman they considered their equal.

On the other hand power, or the perception of having power, created a whole curiosity and myth about what kind of person I really was. On more than one occasion people would comment with surprise on my physical size. One day while I waited for the light to change, a woman approached me at a street intersection. "I thought you were six feet tall," she commented, "but you are just average." She viewed me with a mixture of amazement and disappointment. I have often heard this comment made about other public figures, "he was shorter than I thought," "she was smaller than I expected," as though as a society we endow people who hold power with height also, as though we expect them to be giants. . . .

I found that for some men the idea of a woman with power was tantalizing. They were clearly curious about my susceptibility to seduction. I remember an occasion when I was at a party, and a well-known roué decided to monopolize my time, to my delight and pleasure because he was a wonderful dancer and I love to dance. We were having a great time indulging in fancy footwork and light flirtatious repartee; it was fun!

"Who are you?" he asked. "How is it that our paths have never crossed before?"

"I'm Rosemary Brown," I replied. He was convulsed with laughter.

"Don't be silly! You couldn't be that man-hating battle axe— you are wonderful," and with that he twirled me around the room, laughing about my having tried to put one over on him.

For women in power, sexuality presents a dilemma concerning dress and behaviour. The struggle is to be true to one's wishes to be attractive and charming without being perceived to be seductive. Some women unconsciously place a layer of fat between themselves and this world, as an unspoken message that they are to be seen simply as powerful persons, rather than as women, as an attempt to hide their femaleness and blend into the grey anonymity of the male world. Clearly these women have come to believe that being female places them at a decided disadvantage in the power arena, and they would like to eliminate that factor. Other women try with varying degrees of success to maintain a balance between their femininity and their public life. . . .

Throughout fourteen years in public office, I was constantly running into the mythical Rosemary Brown, the creation of other people's minds, and invariably she was taller, tougher, smarter, sexier and more powerful than I was—but she always was and remains even today the person that I wanted to be. . . .

I believed then and still do that elected politicians do have some power. This is why, despite my discontent with not having sufficient 'traditional' power during my term of office, I continue to encourage women to enter the world of politics. . . .

As a 'role model,' I soon picked up that the message of feminism is doomed as far as young women are concerned, unless it is possible to prove that it is compatible with the traditional male/female relationship. I learnt that like me, young women want it all, the husband, the children, the profession; and they fear that feminism might be unable to deliver that package.

The result is that a large percentage of women continue to deny themselves the opportunity of pursuing public and professional goals; many others retire from public and professional life prematurely. Others persevere and accept the disintegration and termination of their marriages, and the lucky few manage to maintain both successfully. In my own case, when a crisis directly or indirectly created as a result of my political career, and certainly exacerbated by it, threatened our marriage, both Bill and I were forced to make some major compromises in order to ensure the marriage's survival. Whether we succeeded, only time will tell.

I am willing to assign seventy percent credit to husbands when marriage survives a woman's acquisition of power and ninety percent blame to them when there is failure. Because in the final analysis the success or failure of the marriage has less to do with how the woman behaves than with the man's ability to deal with the reversal of their roles.

Men have not been socialized to be equal partners in marriage nor to accept a status secondary to that of their wives. Women who place these demands on men are asking them to break the pattern in which they were moulded. Men either have to see some benefit to themselves or have to have a genuine commitment to equality between the sexes before they will willingly embark on such a course.

In any event, many of the women to whom I spoke stated that their spouses genuinely believed that they were being supportive of their endeavours, and denied that their sniping, critical observations, promiscuous behaviour or any other hostile act was in any way an attempt to sabotage their wives' careers. These men maintained that they were not affected by the teasing of other men, nor by the subtle and unconscious ways society demonstrates its anger at their acceptance of the role reversal.

On a more personal note, I would like to add that regardless of gender, marriage to a politician can be very stressful. I remember Yvonne Cocke being asked by a student at a panel on women and politics held at UBC to speak about the benefits that accrued to her as the wife of a cabinet minister; she replied she could not recall "one single redeeming feature" in being in such a position. Politics, if practised properly, is a demanding full-time occupation that can take over all of one's thoughts, ideas and attention. It is difficult for anyone to compete successfully against such an abductor.

In retrospect, I now realize that retirement did not just free up my time, it released my mind, interests and preoccupations from fourteen years of being deaf, blind and unaware of anything outside of its political context.

So in reality for me even the word 'retire' is a misnomer. As I teach, lecture and speak to groups across the country, I now know that I carry on the same struggles—only the place and the date have changed. I haven't retired, I have simply expanded my modus operandi. . . .

PART FOUR

The United States

Somehow I would tell the world
how things were as I saw them

Lillian Hellman

(1906–1984)

Lillian Hellman was the daughter of American Jewish parents, and spent the first five years of her life within the family's affluent circle in New Orleans. When her father's business failed in 1911, she and her parents moved to New York, where their circumstances approximated genteel poverty, and where Lillian longed every year for the date when they would return to New Orleans.

A not very serious student at New York University, Hellman took her first job at eighteen working for the New York publishing house of Boni and Liveright. A year later she married Arthur Kober, and moved with him to Hollywood in 1930. Here Kober became a scriptwriter and Hellman began to work on scripts for Samuel Goldwyn.

Her marriage to Kober was already fading when she met Dashiell Hammett in Hollywood during her first year on the West Coast. Shortly after their first meeting the relationship which was to last until Hammett's death thirty years later began.

During the thirties Hellman made several trips to Europe, journeys which alerted her to the rise of fascism and the increasing virulence of anti-Semitism. This awareness is reflected in her early plays, now worked on seriously and systematically following Hammett's model of the working writer. *The Children's Hour* (1934) shocked contemporaries for its open examination of prejudice against lesbianism. *The Days to Come* and *The Little Foxes* continued to examine the themes of social oppression and prejudice. During the 1939–45 war Hellman wrote her widely acclaimed *Watch on the Rhine,* a passionate alert about the hazards of fascism, and a number of pro-Soviet plays, most notably *The North Star* (1943). These led to her blacklisting as a fellow traveler in 1948, and to her summons to appear before the House Un-American Activities Committee in 1952, a summons with which she refused to comply.

Her emotional resources were severely depleted when Hammett died in 1961, and her writing took on an elegiac tone, as she undertook a series of memoirs—*An Unfinished Woman* (1969), *Pentimento* (1973), and *Scoundrel Time* (1976). While these have won praise for the elegance of their style and the originality of their construction, their description of Hellman's political role in the 1950s and 1960s has been bitterly disputed by her contemporaries. Hellman reacted with equal emotion to her questioners, so that, at the time of her death in 1984, she was engaged in litigation to protect her reputation.

Her drama, prose, and social commentary always focused on the moral questions individuals face in the events of everyday life, in the manner of Ibsen or Chekhov. She was also a moralist of pragmatism, concerned with the nature of truth in its relation to action, and she manifested the typical American reformer's concern with the role of money and greed for money in American life.

Although concerned about anti-Semitism and other forms of prejudice, Hellman had almost no interest in her Jewishness, her roots, or in feminism, though she lived the life of an independent, liberated woman.

She is a master of scene and character so that her story unfolds in a strongly flowing series of scenes, almost movielike in their fast-paced procession of images. The most fully developed characters in her story of early life are not her white Jewish family but the black women to whom she looked up, and whom she saw as the real sources of maternal affection in her life.

AN UNFINISHED WOMAN:
A Memoir

I was born in New Orleans to Julia Newhouse from Demopolis, Alabama, who had fallen in love and stayed in love with Max Hellman, whose parents had come to New Orleans in the German 1845–1848 immigration to give birth to him and his two sisters. My mother's family, long before I was born, had moved from Demopolis to Cincinnati and then to New Orleans, both desirable cities, I guess, for three marriageable girls. . . .

[T]hat New York apartment* where we visited several times a week, the summer cottage where we went for a visit each year as the poor daughter and granddaughter, made me into an angry child and forever caused in me a wild extravagance mixed with respect for

---

* It belonged to Hellman's mother's family. Ed.

money and those who have it. The respectful periods were full of self-hatred and during them I always made my worst mistakes. But after *The Little Foxes* was written and put away, this conflict was to grow less important, as indeed, the picture of my mother's family was to grow dim and almost fade away. . . .

I made my father's family too remarkable, and then turned both extreme judgments against my mother.

In fact, she was a sweet eccentric, the only middle-class woman I have ever known who had not rejected the middle class—that would have been an act of will—but had skipped it altogether. She liked a simple life and simple people, and would have been happier, I think, if she had stayed in the backlands of Alabama riding wild on the horses she so often talked about, not so lifelong lonely for the black men and women who had taught her the only religion she ever knew. . . .

My mother's childbearing had been dangerously botched by a fashionable doctor in New Orleans, and forever after she stood in fear of going through it again, and so I was an only child. . . . I had always known about the powers of an only child. I was not meaner or more ungenerous or more unkind than other children, but I was off balance in a world where I knew my grand importance to two other people who certainly loved me for myself, but who also liked to use me against each other. I don't think they knew they did that, because most of it was affectionate teasing between them, but somehow I knew early that my father's jokes about how much my mother's family liked money, how her mother had crippled her own children, my grandmother's desire to think of him—and me—as strange vagabonds of no property value, was more than teasing. He wished to win me to his side, and he did. He was a handsome man, witty, high-tempered, proud, and—although I guessed very young I was not to be certain until much later—with a number of other women in his life. Thus his attacks on Mama's family were not always for the reasons claimed.

When I was about six years old, my father lost my mother's large dowry. We moved to New York and were shabby poor until my father finally settled for a life as a successful traveling salesman. It was in those years that we went back to New Orleans to stay with my father's sisters for six months each year. I was thus moved from school in New York to school in New Orleans without care for the season or the quality of the school. This constant need for adjustment into very different worlds made formal education into a kind of frantic tennis game, sometimes played with children whose strokes had force and brilliance, sometimes with those who could barely hold the racket. Possibly it is the reason I never did well in school or in college, and why I wanted to be left alone to read by myself. I had found, very early, that any other test found me bounding with ease and grace over one fence to fall on my face as I ran toward the next.

There was a heavy fig tree on the lawn where the house turned the corner into the side street, and to the front and sides of the fig tree were three live oaks that hid the fig from my aunts' boarding-house. . . .

I learned early, in our strange life of living half in New York and half in New Orleans, that I made my New Orleans teachers uncomfortable because I was too far ahead of my schoolmates, and my New York teachers irritable because I was too far behind. But in New Orleans, I found a solution: I skipped school at least once a week and often twice, knowing that nobody cared or would report my absence. On those days I would set out for school done up in polished strapped shoes and a prim hat against what was known as "the climate," carrying my books and a little basket filled with delicious stuff my Aunt Jenny and Carrie, the cook, had made for my school lunch. I would round the corner of the side street, move on toward St. Charles Avenue, and sit on a bench as if I were waiting for a streetcar until the boarders and the neighbors had gone to work or settled down for the post-breakfast rest that all Southern ladies thought necessary. Then I would run back to the fig tree, dodging in and out of bushes to make sure the house had no dangers for me. The fig tree was heavy, solid, comfortable, and I had, through time, convinced myself that it wanted me, missed me when I was absent, and approved all the rigging I had done for the happy days I spent in its arms: I had made a sling to hold the school books, a pulley rope for my lunch basket, a hole for the bottle of afternoon cream-soda pop, a fishing pole and a smelly little bag of elderly bait, a pillow embroidered with a picture of Henry Clay on a horse that I had stolen from Mrs. Stillman, one of my aunts' boarders, and a proper nail to hold my dress and shoes to keep them neat for the return to the house.

It was in that tree that I learned to read, filled with the passions that can only come to the bookish, grasping, very young, bewildered by almost all of what I read, sweating in the attempt to understand a world of adults I fled from in real life but desperately wanted to join in books. (I did not connect the grown men and women in literature with the grown men and women I saw around me. They were, to me, another species.) . . .

[I]t was in the fig tree, a few years later, that I was first puzzled by the conflict which would haunt me, harm me, and benefit me the rest of my life: simply, the stubborn, relentless, driving desire to be alone as it came into conflict with the desire not to be alone when I wanted not to be. I already guessed that other people wouldn't allow that, although, as an only child, I pretended for the rest of my life that they would and must allow it to me.

I liked my time in New Orleans much better than I liked our six months' apartment life in New York. The life in my aunts' boardinghouse seemed remarkably rich. And what a strange lot my own family was. My aunts Jenny and Hannah were both tall, large women, funny and generous, who coming from a German, cultivated, genteel tradition had found they had to earn a living and earned it without complaint, although Jenny, the prettier and more complex, had frequent outbursts of interesting temper. . . .

I think both Hannah and Jenny were virgins, but if they were, there were no signs of spinsterhood. They were nice about married people, they were generous to children, and sex was something to have fun about. Jenny had been the consultant to many neighborhood young ladies before their marriage night, or the night of their first lover. One of these girls, a rich ninny, Jenny found irritating and unpleasant. When I was sixteen I came across the two of them in earnest conference on the lawn, and later Jenny told me that the girl had come to consult her about how to avoid pregnancy.

"What did you tell her?"

"I told her to have a glass of ice water before the sacred act and three sips during it."

When we had finished laughing, I said, "But she'll get pregnant."

"He's marrying her for money, he'll leave her when he gets it. This way at least maybe she'll have a few babies for herself."

And four years later, when I wrote my aunts that I was going to be married, I had back a telegram: FORGET ABOUT THE GLASS OF ICE WATER TIMES HAVE CHANGED.

I think I learned to laugh in that house and to knit and embroider and sew a straight seam and to cook. Each Sunday it was my job to clean the crayfish for the wonderful bisque, and it was Jenny and Carrie, the cook, who taught me to make turtle soup, and how to kill a chicken without ladylike complaints about the horror of dealing death, and how to pluck and cook the wild ducks that were hawked on our street every Sunday morning. . . .

I was now spending most of my time with a group from an orphanage down the block. I guess the orphan group was no more attractive than any other, but to be an orphan seemed to me desirable and a self-made piece of independence. In any case, the orphans were more interesting to me than my schoolmates, and if they played rougher they complained less. . . . It was Louis Calda who took Pancho and me to a Catholic Mass that could have made me a fourteen-year-old convert. But Louis explained that he did not think me worthy, and Pancho, to stop my tears, cut off a piece of his hair with a knife, gave it to me as a gift from royalty, and then shoved me into the gutter. I don't know why I thought this an act of affection, but I did, and went home to open the back of a new wristwatch my father had given me for my birthday and to put the lock of hair in the back. A day later when the watch stopped, my father insisted I give it to him immediately, declaring that the jeweler was unreliable.

It was that night that I disappeared, and that night that Fizzy said I was disgusting mean, and Mr. Stillman said I would forever pain my mother and father, and my father turned on both of them and said he would handle his family affairs himself without comments from strangers. But he said it too late. He had come home very angry with me: the jeweler, after my father's complaints about his unreliability, had found the lock of hair in the back of the watch. What started out to be a mild reproof on my father's part soon turned angry when I wouldn't explain about the hair. . . . My mother left the room when my father grew angry with me. Hannah, passing through, put up her hand as if to stop my father and then, frightened of the look he gave her, went out to the porch. I sat on the couch, astonished at the pain in my head. I tried to get up from the couch, but one ankle turned and I sat down again, knowing for the first time the rampage that could be caused in me by anger. The room began to have other forms, the people were no longer men and women, my head was not my own. I told myself that my head had gone somewhere and I have little memory of anything after my Aunt Jenny came into the room and said to my father, "Don't you remember?" I have never known what she meant, but I knew that soon after I was moving up the staircase, that I slipped and fell a few steps, that when I woke up hours later in my bed, I found a piece of angel cake—an old love, an old custom—left by my mother on my pillow. The headache was worse and I vomited out of the window. Then I dressed, took my red purse, and walked a long way down St. Charles Avenue. A St. Charles Avenue mansion had on its back lawn a famous doll's-house, an elaborate copy of the mansion itself, built years before for the small daughter of the house. As I passed this showpiece, I saw a policeman and moved swiftly back to the doll palace and crawled inside. If I had known about the fantasies of the frightened, that ridiculous small house would not have been so terrible for me. I was surrounded by ornate, carved reproductions of the mansion furniture, scaled for children, bisque figurines in miniature, a working toilet seat of gold leaf in suitable size, small draperies of damask with a sign that said "From the damask of Marie Antoinette," a miniature samovar with small bronze cups, and a tiny Madame Récamier couch on which I spent the night, my legs on the floor. I must have slept, because I woke from a nightmare and knocked over a bisque figurine. The noise frightened me, and since it was now almost light, in one of those lovely mist mornings of late spring when every flower in New Orleans seems to melt and mix with the air, I crawled out. Most of that day I spent walking, although I had a long session in the ladies' room of the railroad station. I had four dollars and two bits, but that wasn't much when you meant it to last forever and when you knew it would not be easy for a fourteen-year-old girl to find work in a city where too many people knew her. . . .

I bought a few Tootsie Rolls and a half loaf of bread and went to the St. Louis Cathedral in Jackson Square. (It was that night that I composed the prayer that was to become, in the next five years, an obsession, mumbled over and over through the days and nights: "God forgive me, Papa forgive me, Mama forgive me, Sophronia, Jenny, Hannah, and all others, through this time and that time, in life and in death." When I was nineteen, my father, who had made several attempts through the years to find out what my lip movements meant as I repeated the prayer, said, "How much would you take to stop that? Name it and you've got it." I suppose I was sick of the nonsense by that time because I said, "A leather coat and a feather fan," and the next day he bought them for me.) After my loaf of bread, I went looking for a bottle of soda pop and discovered, for the first time, the whorehouse section around Bourbon Street. . . . [T]he second or third time I circled the block, one of the girls called out to me. I couldn't understand the words, but the voice was angry enough to make me run toward the French Market. . . .

I flew across the street into the coffee stand, forgetting that the owner had known me since I was a small child when my Aunt Jenny would rest from her marketing tour with a cup of fine, strong coffee.

He said, in the patois, *"Que faites, ma 'fant? Je suis fermé."*

I said, *"Rien. My tante attend*—Could I have a doughnut?"

He brought me two doughnuts, saying one was *lagniappe*, but I took my doughnuts outside when he said, *"Mais où est vo' tante à c' heure?"*

I fell asleep with my doughnuts behind a shrub in Jackson Square. The night was damp and hot and through the sleep there were many voices and, much later, there was music from somewhere near the river. When all sounds had ended, I woke, turned my head, and knew I was being watched. Two rats were sitting a few feet from me. I urinated on my dress, crawled backwards to stand up, screamed as I ran up the steps of St. Louis Cathedral and pounded on the doors. I don't know when I stopped screaming or how I got to the railroad station, but I stood against the wall trying to tear off my dress and only knew I was doing it when two women stopped to stare at me. I began to have cramps in my stomach of a kind I had never known before. I went into the ladies' room and sat bent in a chair, whimpering with pain. After a while the cramps stopped, but I had an intimation, when I looked into the mirror, of something happening to me. . . .

Sometime during that early morning I half washed my dress, threw away my pants, put cold water on my hair. Later in the morning a cleaning woman appeared, and after a while began to ask questions that frightened me. . . . I ran out of the station. I walked, I guess, for many hours, but when I saw a man on Canal Street who worked in Hannah's office, I realized that the sections of New Orleans that were known to me were dangerous for me.

Years before, when I was a small child, Sophronia and I would go to pick up, or try on, pretty embroidered dresses that were made for me by a colored dressmaker called Bibettera. A block up from Bibettera's there had been a large ruin of a house with a sign, ROOMS — CLEAN — CHEAP, and cheerful people seemed always to be moving in and out of the house. The door of the house was painted a bright pink. I liked that and would discuss with Sophronia why we didn't live in a house with a pink door.

Bibettera was long since dead, so I knew I was safe in this Negro neighborhood. I went up and down the block several times, praying that things would work and I could take my cramps to bed. I knocked on the pink door. It was answered immediately by a small young man.

I said, "Hello." He said nothing.

I said, "I would like to rent a room, please."

He closed the door but I waited, thinking he had gone to get the lady of the house. After a long time, a middle-aged woman put her head out of a second-floor window and said, "What you at?"

I said, "I would like to rent a room, please. My mama is a widow and has gone to work across the river. She gave me money and said to come here until she called for me."

"Who your mama?"

"Er. My mama."

"What you at? Speak out."

"I told you. I have money . . ." But as I tried to open my purse, the voice grew angry.

"This is a nigger house. Get you off. *Vite*."

I said, in a whisper, "I know. I'm part nigger."

The small young man opened the front door. He was laughing. "You part mischief. Get the hell out of here."

I said, "Please"—and then, "I'm related to Sophronia Mason. She told me to come. Ask her."

Sophronia and her family were respected figures in New Orleans Negro circles, and because I had some vague memory of her stately bow to somebody as she passed this house, I believed they knew her. If they told her about me I would be in trouble, but phones were not usual then in poor neighborhoods, and I had no other place to go.

The woman opened the door. Slowly I went into the hall.

I said, "I won't stay long. I have four dollars and Sophronia will give more if . . ."

The woman pointed up the stairs. She opened the door of a small room. "Washbasin place down the hall. Toilet place behind the kitchen. Two-fifty and no fuss, no bother."

I said, "Yes ma'am, yes ma'am," but as she started to close the door, the young man appeared.

"Where your bag?"

"Bag?"

"Nobody put up here without no bag."

"Oh. You mean the bag with my clothes? It's at the station. I'll go and get it later. . . ." I stopped because I knew I was about to say I'm sick, I'm in pain, I'm frightened.

He said, "I say you lie. I say you trouble. I say you get out."

I said, "And I say you shut up."

Years later, I was to understand why the command worked, and to be sorry that it did, but that day I was very happy when he turned and closed the door. I was asleep within minutes. . . .

I woke to a high, hot sun and my father standing at the foot of the bed. . . . He said, "Get up now and get dressed."

I was crying as I said, "Thank you, Papa, but I can't."

From the hall, Sophronia said, "Get along up now. *Vite.* The morning is late."

My father left the room. I dressed and came into the hall. . . . Sophronia was standing at the head of the stairs. She pointed out, meaning my father was on the street.

I said, "He humiliated me. He did. I won't . . ."

She said, "Get you going or I will never see you whenever again."

I ran past her to the street. I stood with my father until Sophronia joined us, and then we walked slowly, without speaking, to the streetcar line. Sophronia bowed to us, but she refused my father's hand when he attempted to help her into the car. I ran to the car meaning to ask her to take me with her, but the car moved and she raised her hand as if to stop me. My father and I walked again for a long time. . . .

At Vanalli's restaurant, he took my arm. "Hungry?"

I said, "No, thank you, Papa."

But we went through the door. It was, in those days, a New Orleans custom to have an early black coffee, go to the office, and after a few hours have a large breakfast at a restaurant. Vanalli's was crowded, the headwaiter was so sorry, but after my father took him aside, a very small table was put up for us—too small for my large father, who was accommodating himself to it in a manner most unlike him.

He said, "Jack, my rumpled daughter would like cold crayfish, a nice piece of pompano, a separate bowl of Béarnaise sauce, don't ask me why, French fried potatoes . . ."

I said, "Thank you, Papa, but I am not hungry. I don't want to be here."

My father waved the waiter away and we sat in silence until the crayfish came. My hand reached out instinctively and then drew back.

My father said, "Your mother and I have had an awful time."

I said, "I'm sorry about that. But I don't want to go home, Papa."

He said, angrily, "Yes, you do. But you want me to apologize first. I do apologize but you should not have made me say it."

After a while I mumbled, "God forgive me, Papa forgive me, Mama forgive me, Sophronia, Jenny, Hannah . . ."

"Eat your crayfish."

I ate everything he had ordered and then a small steak. I suppose I had been mumbling throughout my breakfast.

My father said, "You're talking to yourself. I can't hear you. What are you saying?"

"God, forgive me, Papa forgive me, Mama forgive me, Sophronia, Jenny . . ."

My father said, "Where do we start your training as the first Jewish nun on Prytania Street?"

When I finished laughing, I liked him again. I said, "Papa, I'll tell you a secret. I've had very bad cramps and I am beginning to bleed. I'm changing life."

He stared at me for a while. Then he said, "Well, it's not the way it's usually described, but it's accurate, I guess. Let's go home now to your mother."

We were never, as long as my mother and father lived, to mention that time again. But it was of great importance to them and I've thought about it all my life. From that day on I knew my power over my parents. That was not to be too important: I was ashamed of it and did not abuse it too much. But I found out something more useful and more dangerous: if you are willing to take the punishment, you are halfway through the battle. That the issue may be trivial, the battle ugly, is another point. . . .

New York University had started its Washington Square branch only a few years before, with an excellent small faculty and high requirements for the students it could put into one unattractive building. I was, of course, not where I wanted to be and I envied those of my friends who were. And yet I knew that in another place I might have been lost, because the old story was still true: I was sometimes more advanced but often less educated than other students and I had little desire to be shown up. And by seventeen, I was openly rebellious against almost everything. I knew that the seeds of the rebellion were scattered and aimless in a nature that was wild to be finished with something-or-other and to find something-else-or-other, and I had sense enough to know that I was overproud, oversensitive, overdaring because I was shy and frightened. Ah, what a case can be made for vanity in the shy. (And what a losing game is self-description in the long ago.)

It was thus in the cards that college would mean very little to me, although one professor opened up a slit into another kind of literature: I began an exciting period of Kant and Hegel, a little, very little, of Karl Marx and Engels. . . .

A good deal of the college day I spent in a Greenwich Village restaurant called Lee Chumley's curled up on a dark bench with a book, or arguing with a brilliant girl called Marie-Louise and her extraordinary, foppish brother, up very often from Princeton, carrying a Paris copy of *Ulysses* when he wasn't carrying Verlaine. . . .

In my junior year, I knew I was wasting time. My mother took me on a long tour to the Midwest and the South, almost as a reward for leaving college. We returned to New York for my nineteenth birthday and the day after I began what was then called an "affair." It was an accident: the young man pressed me into it partly because it satisfied the tinkering malice that had gone through the rest of his life, mostly because it pained his best friend. The few months it lasted did not mean much to me, but I have often asked myself whether I underestimated the damage that so loveless an arrangement made on my future. But my generation did not often deal with the idea of love—we were ashamed of the word, and scornful of the misuse that had been made of it—and I suppose that the cool currency of the time carried me past the pain of finding nastiness in what I had hoped would be a moving adventure.

In the autumn, feeling pleasantly aimless, but knowing that I deeply wanted to work at something, I went to a party and met Julian Messner, the vice-president of Horace Liveright. I had never met a publisher before, never before had a conversation with a serious man much older than myself, and I mistook what was an automatic flirtatious interest for a belief that Julian thought I was intelligent. In any case, by the time the party was over, I had a job.

A job with any publishing house was a plum, but a job with Horace Liveright was a bag of plums. Never before, and possibly never since, has an American publishing house had so great a record. Liveright, Julian, T. R. Smith, Manuel Komroff, and a few even younger men had made a new and brilliant world for books. In the years before I went to work, and in the few years after I left, they discovered, or persuaded over, Faulkner, Freud, Hemingway, O'Neill, Hart Crane, Sherwood Anderson, Dreiser, E. E. Cummings, and many other less talented but remarkable people, all of them attracted by the vivid, impetuous, high-living men who were the editors. It didn't hurt that Horace was handsome and daring, Julian serious and kind, Tom Smith almost erudite with his famous collection of erotica and odd pieces of knowledge that meant nothing but seemed to; that the advances they gave were large and the parties they gave even larger, full of lush girls and good liquor. . . .

They were not truly serious men, I guess, nor men of the caliber of Max Perkins, but they had respect for serious writing. Their personal capers, which started out as outrageous and dashing in the fusty world of older publishing houses, became comic and, in time, dangerous and destructive. In the case of Horace himself, the end was sad, broken, undignified. But I was there at a good time and had a good time while I was there.

By the time I grew up the fight for the emancipation of women, their rights under the law, in the office, in bed, was stale stuff. My generation didn't think much about the place or the problems of women, were not conscious that the designs we saw around us had so recently been formed that we were still part of the formation. (Five or ten years' difference in age was a greater separation between people in the 1920's, perhaps because the older generation had gone through the war.) The shock of Fitzgerald's flappers was not for us: by the time we were nineteen or twenty we had either slept with a man or pretended that we had. And we were suspicious of the words of love. It was rather taken for granted that you liked one man better than the other and hoped he would marry you, but if that didn't happen you did the best you could and didn't talk about it much. We were, I suppose, pretend cool, and paid for it later on, but our revolt against sentimentality had come, at least, out of distaste for pretense. . . .

I was not, therefore, attracted by the lady intellectuals I met at Liveright's. They puzzled me. They talked so much about so little, they were weepy about life and men, and I was too young to be grateful for how much I owed them in the battle of something-or-other in the war for equality. They came through the office door as novelists or poets or artists and, there, I caught only glimpses and heard only gossip. But at parties I saw them in action and felt envy for their worldiness, their talent, their clothes, their age—and bewilderment at their foreign, half-glimpsed problems. . . .

[T]he office was a wacky joint in a brownstone house on 48th Street. Certain jobs were more clearly defined than others, but even the stenographers and shipping clerks often wandered about reading manuscripts, offering opinions about how to advertise or sell a book, and there was seldom a day without excitement. Some days a "great" new book was found; some days no corner could be found for work because too many writers were in town or had just dropped by; sometimes one of the editors had been in mysterious trouble the night before and everybody went around to his house or hospital to call upon him; on no day could you ever be sure what you would see through a half-open office door, or how long lunch hour would be for Horace and the editors, or who was taking a long nap afterwards. All the men in the office made routine passes at the girls who worked there—one would have had to be hunch-backed to be an exception—and one of the more pleasant memories of my life is the fast sprinting I would do up and down the long staircases to keep from being idly pinched or thrown by a clutching hand on a leg. . . .

I knew there was talk of firing me—I had misplaced an important manuscript, I didn't know how to file, my typing was erratic, my manuscript reports were severe. I would have been fired if I hadn't that very week discovered that I was pregnant by the man who, a half year later, I would marry.

A young man called Donald Friede had just been made a partner because Horace needed the money Donald brought into the firm. (He always needed money and often found it by selling part of the business to rich young men.) Donald seemed friendly, more my age, and I was so desperate to find an abortionist that, foolishly, I asked if he knew such a doctor. He found one immediately, swore himself to secrecy, and I made an appointment with the doctor for the following week. The morning following Donald's vow of secrecy, every member of the firm called me into his office to offer money, to ask the name of my child's father, to guess that it was one of them, to make plans and plots for help I didn't want. I was suddenly a kind of showcase. I was angry about that and so, throughout the good-natured questionings, I sat sullen, staring into space, refusing answers, trying not to think about the vicarious, excited snoopiness I knew was mixed with the kindness.

The operation, done without an anesthetic in a Coney Island half-house, with the doctor's mother as assistant, was completed on a Monday evening. I went home, weak and more frightened than I had ever been about anything, and so ignorant that I was awake all night worried that my parents could tell what had happened by just looking at me. On Tuesday morning, feeling sick, but sure that my mother would call a doctor if I said that, I went back to work. Horace called me in to ask how I was and to give me a glass of mid-morning champagne; Friede stopped by my desk to ask if I had now decided to reveal the name of the father; Julian Messner asked me out to lunch and bought me a drink that was called a pink-un, and stared at me throughout lunch as if I were a recent arrival from a distant land. We didn't talk much at lunch, but as we walked back to the office he said, gently, "I don't understand what you're about."

I said, "That's all right, Julian," and knew he didn't like the answer.

As we climbed the steps of the brownstone, T. R. Smith yelled, "Julian, tell that ninny to go home to bed. She shouldn't have come to work today. Tell her to get out of here."

I was sure this was his way of firing me, so on my way past his office, I stopped in. I said, "I know I've lost the manuscript, Tom, but I've been nervous and tomorrow I'll find it—"

He said, "What are you made of, Lilly?"

I said, "Pickling spice and nothing nice."

He said, "That kind of talk. I don't understand you kids. Go home."

I said I couldn't, that if I went home too early my mother would be nervous and make a fuss, so I'd go to the movies.

He said, "You look awful. Lie down on the couch. I'll send you in some supper. When you feel better, go home, or go wherever you go." . . .

I had left my job at Liveright's to marry Arthur Kober, who was a charming young man working as a theatre press agent and just beginning to write about his friends in the emerging Jewish-American lower-middle-class world.

We didn't have much money, but we had enough for a pleasant life of reading, afternoon bridge for me, and nice, aimless evenings. I found that I liked to do the good New Orleans cooking of my childhood and wanted to learn more about the excellent backwoods cooking of my mother's Alabama. I went back to writing short stories in fits of long hours of secret work. But I knew the stories were not very good and so I always put them aside. . . .

I think we were younger in our twenties than people are now because the times allowed us to be and because we were not very concerned with position or the future or money. (That came to most of us a few years later.) And I was even younger than my friends. . . .

The time came when my idle life didn't suit Arthur and didn't suit me. I wasn't any good at finding jobs or keeping them, and so Arthur found them for me in the theatre. I worked as a press agent for an arty little group who didn't pay me after the second week. I worked as a play reader for Anne Nichols, the author of *Abie's Irish Rose,* who wanted to become a producer. I had a good time for four months in Rochester, New York, working for a stock company and gambling every night for money to spend in Europe that summer. Once, for a few weeks, I went back to the short stories, but I convinced myself that I was not meant to be a writer. I was rather relieved by that discovery—it gave me more time to listen to a gangster who ran Rochester's underworld, more time to win money at bridge from Rochester society, more time to read and drink. . . .

I know only that I was ignorant pretending to be wise, lazy pretending to work hard, so oversensitive to a breath of reservation that I called it unfriendliness and swept by it with harsh intolerance. It was the fashion then to like the witty insult behind the back, the goose-grease compliment before the face. (That fashion has now returned and we like only those we consider "pleasant.") But I did not want that form of human exchange. I respected only those I thought told the "truth," without fear for themselves, independent of popular opinion. And thus, like so many lady extremists, I began a history of remarkable men, often difficult, sometimes even dangerous.

I did win enough money in those scrubby Rochester days to go to Europe that summer of 1929. I went to Germany, liked Bonn, and decided to study there for a year. I lived in a university boardinghouse waiting for the day of enrollment and went on nice picnics with large healthy blondes. I thought I was listening to a kind of socialism, I liked it, and agreed with it. But one day on an autobus, riding out to the picnic grounds, two of them gave me a cheesy-looking pamphlet about their organization—I cannot remember its name, but it was, of course, a youth group publication of Hitler's National Socialism—and asked if I wouldn't like to become a member, no dues for foreigners if they had no Jewish connections. I said I had no other connections that I knew of, although a second cousin in Mobile had married the owner of a whorehouse, non-Jewish. But nobody paid attention to what I said, because Hellman in Germany is often not a Jewish name. I left Bonn the next day and came back to New York.

It has been forgotten that for many people the depression years were the good years. True, my father, like so many of his generation, took a beating from which he did not recover, but Arthur was offered a job as a scenario writer for Paramount Pictures at more money than we had ever seen. We had been living in a beat-up old house on Long Island and I was reluctant to leave it. So Arthur went ahead of me to Hollywood and I fooled and fiddled with excuses until the day when I did go, knowing even then, I think, that I would not stay. . . .

A short time later Arthur and I separated without ill feeling and I went back to New York.

[Shortly thereafter, Hellman began her relationship with Hammett. Ed.]

[I]n the late summer of 1937, I had been invited to a theatre festival in Moscow. I showed the cable to Dash and suggested he might like to make his first trip to Europe. I pointed to four handsome volumes he had just bought on the art of the Hermitage. "You could see the pictures for yourself." . . .

I said I had never been to Russia, that I wanted to see the Russian theatre.

Dash said, "No, you don't."

"Why do you think I don't?"

He shrugged. "I'll write it down for you some day soon." . . .

About the third week I was in Paris, in reply to two letters asking him to tell me why he was so certain I didn't want to see the Russian theatre, Hammett wrote: "I think, I don't know, of course, but I think that you would not betray anybody for any reason about anything—and I am not a man who thinks in such terms—unless somebody offered you a free subway ride to Jersey City and then we'd all be in danger. That's one reason you made this trip, and always will. So have a good wasted time but stop telling yourself you want to see the theatre. You don't. You'll see three plays and I'll bet you'll leave all of them by intermission. Then somebody'll give you a party and if the guests include an electrician or a property man, you'll find him and not want to talk to anybody else. . . ."

Although I have long ago lost the diary of that trip, Dash was right: I did not enjoy the Moscow Theatre Festival, except for a production of *Hamlet* with the Prince played as a fat young man in a torpor. I went to one official party and saw no other Russians. (I had sent off a few letters of introduction, but when they weren't answered I put it down to the Slav habit of postponement.) I did not even know I was there in the middle of the ugliest purge period, and I have often asked myself how that could be. I saw a number of diplomats and journalists but they talked such gobbledygook, with the exception of Walter Duranty and Joseph Barnes, that one couldn't pick the true charges from the wild hatred. . . .

In 1939, soon after *The Little Foxes,* I bought a Westchester estate, so called—large properties were cheaper in those days than small ones—and turned it into a farm. Hammett, who disliked cities even more than I did, came to spend most of his time there, and maybe the best of our life together were the years on the farm. At night, good-tired from writing, or spring planting, or cleaning chicken houses, or autumn hunting, I would test my reading on Dash, who had years before, in his usual thorough fashion, read all the books I was reading, and a great many more. They must have been dull and often irritating questions I threw at him—my father had once said that I lived within a question mark—but Hammett used to say he didn't mind the ragging tone I always fall into when I am trying to learn, because it was the first time in our life together I had been willing to stay awake past ten o'clock.

But this time the ragging, argumentative tone came for a reason I was not to know about for another ten years: a woman who was never to be committed was facing a man who already was. For Hammett, as he was to prove years later, Socialist belief had become a way of life, and although he was highly critical of many Marxist doctrines and their past and present practitioners, he shrugged them off. I was trying, without knowing it, to crack his faith, sensed I couldn't do it, and was, all at one time, respectful, envious, and angry. He was patient, evidently in the hope I would come his way, amused as he always was by my pseudo-rages, cold to any influence. I do not mean there were unpleasant words between us. None, that is, except once, in 1953, after he had been in jail and gone back to teaching at the Jefferson School. I was frightened that his official connection with the school would send him back to jail and was saying that as we walked down 52nd Street. When we were a few steps from Sixth Avenue, he stopped and said, "Lilly, when we reach the corner you are going to have to make up your mind that I must go my way. You've been more than, more than, well, more than something-or-other good to me, but now I'm trouble and a nuisance to you. I won't ever blame you if you say goodbye to me now. But if you don't, then we must never have this conversation again." When we got to the corner, I began to cry and he looked as if he might. I was not able to speak, so he touched my shoulder and turned downtown. I stood on the corner until I couldn't see him anymore and then I began to run. When I caught up with him, he said, "I haven't thought about a drink in years. But I'd like one. Anyway, let's go buy one for you."

A few years after I bought the farm, the United States declared war. It was useless now to say yes, many of us knew it was coming; during the war in Spain, Hitler and Mussolini could have been stopped, the bumblers and the villains led us into this. (I had tried to write some of that in *Watch on the Rhine*.)

When the war came I thrashed around trying to find something useful to do, but all the jobs offered were official, tame, bound to high-sounding titles enclosed by office doors. Then Hammett disappeared for a few days and reappeared having enlisted as a private, although he'd had a tough time convincing the doctor who found the old First World War tubercular scars on the X-rays.

After he left Pleasantville, I felt lonely and useless, jealous of his ability to take a modest road to what he wanted. I spent the next year or so doing what I knew to be idle lady stuff: I wrote a few speeches for people in Washington, I planted a granite field that broke two plows, I made speeches at rallies for this or that bundles for something-or-other, I watched other people go to a war I needed to be part of. And then, suddenly, I was invited to go on a cultural mission to the Soviet Union.

I was invited because a month after we declared war William Wyler, the movie director, and I, both under contract to Samuel Goldwyn, had agreed to make a documentary film of the war in Russia. (Wyler and I had made a number of pictures together by that time and were old friends.) I no longer remember exactly how the plan started because its origins were kept from us, but Harry Hopkins, without involving President Roosevelt, had set it in motion. The Russian news was very bad that winter of 1942, but all of America was moved and bewildered by the courage of a people who had been presented to two generations of Americans as passive slaves. . . .

Twenty-two years later, the same week in October when I had arrived during the war, the plane lowered for the Moscow airport. I put out my cigarette, took off my glasses, closed my book, and was shocked to find that I was crying. All women say they do not cry very much, but I don't because I learned long ago that I do it at the wrong time and in front of the wrong people. The two young English commercial travelers opposite me stared and then turned their heads away, but the German in the next seat made no secret of his interest, and a Russian across the aisle shook his head at me. I shut my eyes on all of them. What fragment at the bottom of the pot was the kettle-spoon scraping that it had not reached before?

I told myself that maybe I was worried about seeing my old friend Raya: it is not easy to see an old friend after so many years, and certainly not women because they change more than men. But I knew the tears were not for Raya: they were for the me who had, twenty-two years before, been able to fly across Siberia for fourteen days in an unheated plane, lying in a sleeping bag on top of crates, knowing the plane had few instruments even for those days, starting to be sick in Yakutsk, unable to explain in a language I didn't know, not caring, thinking that whatever happened the trip was worth it, although when the pneumonia did come, I changed my mind about that. The tears had to do with age and the woman who could survive hardships then and knew she couldn't anymore. I was sorry I had come back to Moscow. . . .

I had no need to worry about seeing Raya again. She was twenty-four or twenty-five when I last saw her, a girl with a sweet, gentle face, a small girl, now a small woman, but very little changed. Her first husband had been killed, before I met her, in the famous student defense of Moscow when raw boys with guns that had to be shared marched out to the airport to hold back the Germans. By the time I met Raya the daughter of that marriage was four years old. (The daughter is twenty-six now and has a baby of her own.) But neither Raya nor I talked about the past for five whole days except in an occasional, shy sentence, but when the memories did come, they came pell-mell strong.

In the immediate postwar years after I left Moscow in 1945, we had written many letters, but after a while I no longer heard from Raya and put some of it down to Slavic putting-off-until-tomorrow, but knew, also, that some other wall had gone up for both of us. Now, in wanting to explain, she was shy, stumbling, finally saying that she did not know how to write about herself or her country in the postwar Stalin years, and so had postponed the letters until it seemed too late to take them up again. I felt my own kind of pain in this mishmash summary of the years that had passed: I was also shy and stumbling when I tried to talk about the McCarthy period which had changed my life, and when Raya asked me about the farm in Pleasantville, I had a hard time telling her that I had sold it in 1952, guessing what the future would be for Hammett and myself. I tried to explain why Hammett had gone to jail and why I, who offered to testify about myself but not about other people, had not gone to jail, but that was tough going with a foreigner, the legal complications, and the personal—Hammett and I had not shared the same convictions—and so I gave up, saying finally that I guessed you could survive if you felt like it, but you only knew that after you had survived.

We were in a restaurant, Raya and I, when we talked of those years. Neither of us said any more than was necessary, both of us soon fell silent. When I got back to my hotel through the cold November rain, I fell asleep, and for the first time in many years dreamed of the farm in Pleasantville: a dream of the walnut trees and the weeping beech, of November pig killing, of spring scilla, and pickerelweed and skunk cabbage when it is purple, and the lovely mush that was spring. I woke before curtain time for the Bolshoi and canceled the tickets because I didn't want to move from the room. The dreams had brought back a time of me and I needed to spend the evening with it, knowing now that the tears from the day on the plane would come back again if I continued to bury this period of my life. I would not have chosen the gloomy National Hotel in Moscow for the digging up of frozen roots, but there I was.

The night was confused. I felt as if I had a fever, and it is possible that I was half drunk during the night because sometime that evening a waitress brought me bread, caviar, and a small bottle of vodka, and there was no vodka left the next morning. The sessions of sweet, silent thought were not always silent: that night in the hall, somewhere near my door, a man and a woman were having an argument in French about Intourist food tickets; and downstairs somewhere somebody was playing the piano and singing in German; and my bathroom pipes clunked as the heat faded; and during the night I knocked over a large china figure of a Greek athlete and crawled around the floor trying to find his hand; and after that I washed my hair and fell against the tub and bruised my arm.

The memories mounted with the cigarettes and, I guess, with the vodka. They were not bad memories, most of them, and I was not disturbed by them, or so I thought, but I knew that I had taken a whole period of my life and thrown it somewhere, always intending to call for it again, but now that it came time to call, I couldn't remember where I had left it. Did other people do this, drop the past in a used car lot and leave it for so long that one couldn't even remember the name of the road?

The road had to be to the lake in Pleasantville. But at first, I could only remember the last day I had ever walked it. After the moving vans had left the house, I had gone down to the lake remembering that we had left two turtle traps tied to a tree. I climbed up and around to bring in the traps, and then wondered what to do with them, how to ask the storage people to keep turtle traps safe for the future. Then the memory of the turtle traps brought back the first snapping turtles Hammett and I had caught, the nights spent reading about how to make the traps, how to kill the turtles, how to clean them, how to make the soup; and the soup brought back the sausage making and the ham curing, and the planting of a thousand twelve-inch pines that must now be a small forest; and the discovery of the beaver dam, and the boiled skunk cabbage and pickerelweed for dinner, in imitation of American Indians, that had made everybody sick but me; and working late into the night—I had written four plays at the farm and four or five movies—and then running, always with a dog and sometimes four, in the early summer light to the lake for a swim, pretending I was somebody else in some other land, some other century. And then back again to that last day: I had carried the turtle traps back to the house, forgetting, until I got to the tree nursery along the lake road, that I didn't own the house anymore. I stopped there to look at the hundred French lilac trees in the nursery, the rosebushes waiting for the transplant place they would never get, the two extravagant acres of blanched asparagus, and standing there by the road that May afternoon of 1952, I finally realized that I would never have any of this beautiful, hardscrabble land again. Now, in the Moscow room, I was glad it was gone, but sorry that the days of Joseph McCarthy, the persecution of Hammett, my own appearance before the House Un-American Activities Committee, the Hollywood blacklist, had caused it to be gone. There could never be any place like it again because I could never again be that woman who worked from seven in the morning until two or three the next morning and woke rested and hungry for each new day. . . .

Is it age, or was it always my nature, to take a bad time, block out the good times, until any success became an accident and failure seemed the only truth? I can't sleep, I have had a headache for three days, I lie on the bed telling myself that nothing has ever gone right, doubting even Hammett and myself, remembering how hard the early years sometimes were for us when he didn't care what he did or spoiled, and I didn't think I wanted to stay long with anybody, asking myself why, after the first failure, I had been so frightened of marriage, who the hell did I think I was alone in a world where women don't have much safety, and, finally, on the third night, falling asleep with a lighted cigarette and waking to a burn on my chest. Staring at the burn, I thought: That's what you deserve for wasting time on stuff proper for the head of a young girl.

Edmund Wilson's friends are nice people. Mrs. S is a bluestocking but handsome and with good manners. Her husband, much older than she, is an art expert. Bluestockings are the same the world over, but the European variety has learned a few graces: Mrs. S, of course, chose the table in the restaurant and ordered the dinner, but she pretended that her husband did and he was pleased. When I got back to the hotel I felt cheerful, for the first time in a week. I sat on the balcony outside my room and looked at the old church across the square. . . . But Dash . . . used his age to make the rules.

One day, a few months after we met, he said, "Can you stop juggling oranges?"

I said I didn't know what he meant.

He said, "Yes, you do. So stop it or I won't be around to watch."

A week later, I said, "You mean I haven't made up my mind about you and have been juggling you and other people. I'm sorry. Maybe it will take time for me to cure myself, but I'll try."

He said, "Maybe it will take time for *you*. But for me it will take no longer than tomorrow morning."

And so I did stop for long periods, although several times through the years he said, "Don't start that juggling again."

Many years later, unhappy about his drinking, his ladies, my life with him, I remember an angry speech I made one night: it had to do with injustice, his carelessness, his insistence that he get his way, his sharpness with me but not with himself. I was drunk, but he was drunker, and when my strides around the room carried me close to the chair where he was sitting, I stared in disbelief at what I saw. He was grinding a burning cigarette into his cheek.

I said, "What are you doing?"

"Keeping myself from doing it to you," he said.

The mark on his cheek was ugly for a few weeks, but in time it faded into the scar that remained for the rest of his life. We never again spoke of that night because, I think, he was ashamed of the angry gesture that made him once again the winner in the game that men and women play against each other, and I was ashamed that I caused myself to lose so often. . . .

[T]wo months ago when, poking about the beach, a long distance from the house Helen and I had lived in, I found a mangled watch, wondered where I had seen it, and knew a few hours later that it was the watch I had bought in the Zurich airport and that had disappeared a short time after I gave it to Helen. The answer now was easy. She never walked much because her legs hurt. Sam had brought it down to the beach and she didn't want to tell me that my dog, who loved her but didn't love me, could have done anything for which he could be blamed.

From the night of that rainstorm in Cambridge, for weeks later, and even now, once in a while, I have dreamed of Sophronia and Helen, waking up sometimes so pleased that I try to go on with a dream that denies their death, at other times saddened by the dream because it seems a deep time-warning of my own age and death. When that happens, in argument with myself, I feel guilty because I did not know about Sophronia's death for two years after it happened, and had not forced Helen into the hospital that might have saved her. In fact, I had only been angry with her stubborn refusal to go. How often Helen had made me angry, but with Sophronia nothing had ever been bad. . . . But the answer there is easy: Sophronia was the anchor for a little girl, the beloved of a young woman, but by the time I had met the other, years had brought acid to a nature that hadn't begun that way—or is that a lie?—and in any case, what excuse did that give for irritation with a woman almost twenty years older than I, swollen in the legs and feet, marrow-weary with the struggle to live, bewildered, resentful, sometimes irrational in a changing world where the old, real-pretend love for white people forced her now into open recognition of the hate and contempt she had brought with her from South Carolina. She had not, could not have, guessed this conflict would ever come to more than the sad talk of black people over collard greens and potlikker, but now here it was on Harlem streets, in newspapers and churches, and how did you handle what you didn't understand except with the same martyr discipline that made you work when you were sick, made you try to forgive what you really never forgave, made you take a harsh nature and force it into words of piety that, in time, became almost true piety.

Why had these two women come together as one for me?

Sophronia had not been like that.

I don't know what year Helen came to work for me. We never agreed about the time, although when we felt most affectionate or tired we would argue about it. But it was, certainly, a long time ago. The first months had been veiled and edgy: her severe face, her oppressive silences made me think she was angry, and my nature, alternating from vagueness to rigid demands, made her unhappy, she told me years later. (She did not say it that way: she said, "It takes a searching wind to find the tree you sit in.")

Then one day, at the end of the first uncomfortable months, she said she was grateful, most deeply. I didn't know what she meant, didn't pay much attention, except that I knew she had grown affectionate toward me, even indulgent. Shortly after, she brought me three hundred dollars done up in tissue paper with a weary former Christmas ribbon. I asked her what it was, she said please to count it, I counted it, handed it back, she handed it back to me and said it was the return of the loan for her daughter. I said I didn't know what she was talking about. Her face changed to angry sternness as she said, "I want no charity. I pay my just debts, Miss Hellman. Mr. Hammett must have told you I said that to him."

Hammett hadn't told me she said anything, but it turned out that one night when he had come from the country to have dinner with me, and found he was too tired to return to the country—it was the early period of emphysema—he decided to spend the night in the library. He had been reading at about three in the morning when the phone rang and a frightened voice said there was an emergency, was it possible to call Helen? He had climbed four flights of steps to fetch her, and when she had finished with the phone she said her niece or her daughter or somebody-or-other had had a terrible accident and she would have to go immediately. He asked her if she needed money and, after the long wait she always took when pride was involved, she asked him for taxi money.

Hammett had said, "What about money for the hospital?"

She had said, "Black people don't have it easy in a hospital."

He had said, "I know. So a check won't do you any good. You'd better have cash."

I said to Hammett, "But what's this got to do with me?"

He said, "It's your money she's returning. I took it out of the safe."

He told me how disturbed she had been when he had opened

my safe and so he had said, "Don't worry. It's O.K. There's no sense waking Miss Hellman because she can't learn how to open the safe and that makes her angry."

For many years after, whenever I tried to open the safe, she would come as close to mirth as ever I saw her, saying always that I wasn't to get disturbed, she thought my fingers were too thin for such work, and then always reminding me of the night Hammett gave her the money, "before he even knew me, that is a Christian man."

I said to him, "Helen thinks you're a Christian man."

"Sure. She's a convert to my ex-church. We teach 'em to talk like that." . . .

[P]eople always came, in time, to like her and admire her, although her first impression on them was not always pleasant. The enormous figure, the stern face, the few, crisp words did not seem welcoming as she opened a door or offered a drink, but the greatest clod among them came to understand the instinctive good taste, the high-bred manners that once they flowered gave off so much true courtesy. And, in this period of nobody grows older or fatter, your mummie looks like your girl, there may be a need in many of us for the large, strong woman who takes us back to what most of us always wanted and few of us ever had.

It is difficult to date anything between people when they have lived together long enough, and so I can't remember when I knew, forgot, knew, doubted, and finally understood that her feelings for white people and black people were too complex to follow, because what had been said on one day would be denied on the next. In the early years, when she told me of the white family in whose house she had been raised in Charleston, her mother having been the cook there, I would dislike the Uncle-Tomism of the memories, and often when the newspapers carried a new indignity from the South we would both cluck about it, but she would turn away from my anger with talk about good and bad among white people, and she had only known the good. During the University of Mississippi mess, I asked her what she meant by good whites, good to her?

She said, "There's too much hate in this world."

I said, "Depends on where you carry the hate, doesn't it, what it's made of, how you use it?"

She shrugged. "I ain't ever hated."

I said, too fast, "Yes, you have. You just don't know it—" and stopped right before I said, You often hate me, I've known it for years and let you have it as a debt I wouldn't pay anybody else but Sophronia.

Oh, Sophronia, it's you I want back always. It's by you I still so often measure, guess, transmute, translate and act. What strange process made a little girl strain so hard to hear the few words that ever came, made the image of you, true or false, last a lifetime? I think my father knew about that very early, because five or six years after I was separated from Sophronia by our move to New York, when I saw her only during our yearly visits to New Orleans, he shouted at me one night, "To hell with Sophronia. I don't want to hear about her anymore." . . .

There has always been a picture of Sophronia in my house, all of them taken with me as a young child. Some years after Helen came to work for me, I came into the library to find her with one of the pictures in her hand.

I said, "My nurse, my friend. Handsome woman, wasn't she?"

"You look like a nice little girl."

"Maybe I was, but nobody thought so. I was trouble."

"She didn't think so."

I took the picture from Helen and, for the first time in the forty years since it had been taken, saw the affection the woman had for the child she stood behind.

I said, "It takes me too long to know things."

"What?"

"Nothing. I hadn't seen her for two years before she died."

"You didn't go to the funeral?"

"I didn't know she died. Her daughter didn't tell me."

"She was a light-skinned woman?"

I know about that question, I've known about it all my life.

"Yes, very. But she didn't use it, if that's what you mean."

"How old was she?"

"In the picture? I don't know. I—my God. She couldn't have been thirty. I can't believe it, but—"

"Black women get old fast."

"Yes," I said, "watching white women stay young."

"White women never been bad to me."

I was in a sudden bad humor, maybe because she wasn't Sophronia. I said, "Colored women who cook as well as you do never had a bad time. Not even in slavery. You were the darlings of every house. What about the others who weren't?"

She said, "You mean the good house nigger is king boy."

I said, "I mean a house nigger pay no mind to a field hand."

She laughed at the words we had both grown up on.

A half hour later I went down to the kitchen for a cup of coffee. She was using an electric beater and so neither of us tried to talk over the noise. Then she turned the beater off and, I think for the first time in her life, raised her voice in a shout.

"You ain't got no right to talk that way. No right at all. Down South, I cook. Nothing else, just cook. For you, I slave. You made a slave of me and you treat me like a slave."

I said, "Helen! Helen!"

"A slave. An old, broken slave."

"You're a liar," I said, "just a plain God-damned liar."

"God will punish you for those words."

"He is, right now."

She took a check from her apron pocket—her share of the last royalties from *Toys in the Attic*—tore it up, and held out the pieces to me.

"There. Take it. You think money and presents can buy me, you're wrong."

I said, "I'm going up to Katonah. That will give you a few days to move out."

That night, sitting on a pile of books that had become the only place one could sit in the depressing little cottage filled with furniture broken by the weight of phonograph records and books, ashtrays toppling on the edges of manuscripts, a giant desk loaded with unopened mail that had arrived that day or five years ago, facing a window that had been splintered by the gun of somebody who didn't like his politics, I told Hammett about the afternoon.

He said, "Why do you talk to her about the South?"

"I didn't think she hated me."

"She doesn't. She likes you very much and that scares her, because she hates white people. Every morning some priest or other tells her that's not Christian charity, and she goes home more mixed up than ever."

"I guess so. But I don't care about what she hates or doesn't. I care about what I said to her. I'll wait until she has left and then I'll write and say I'm sorry I screamed liar."

He stared at me and went back to reading. After a while he said, "You should have screamed at her years ago. But of course you never lose your temper at the right time. Then you feel guilty and are sure to apologize. I've always counted on that, it's never failed."

I said, "All these years, waiting to catch me out."

"Yep. And shall I tell you something else that goes hand in hand, kind of?"

"I am, as you know, grateful for all high-class revelations."

"Well," he said, "when you start out being angry, you're almost always right. But anybody with a small amount of sense learns fast that if they let you go on talking you come around to being wrong. So after you've slammed the door, or taken a plane, or whatever caper you're up to, that fine, upright, liberal old sense of justice begins to operate and you'll apologize not only for the nonsense part of what you've said but for the true and sensible part as well. It's an easy game—just a matter of patience."

I thanked him and went back to New York. It has long been my habit to enter the house on the bedroom floor, and on that day I did not wish to see the kitchen without Helen, did not wish to face a life without her, so it was four or five hours before I went downstairs. Helen was sitting in a chair, her Bible on the table.

She said, "Good evening. Your hair is wet."

"Yes," I said, "I'm trying to curl it."

We did learn something that day, maybe how much we needed each other, although knowing that often makes relations even more difficult. Our bad times came almost always on the theme of Negroes and whites. The white liberal attitude is, mostly, a well-intentioned fake, and black people should and do think it a sell. But mine was bred, literally, from Sophronia's milk, and thus I thought it exempt from such judgments except when I made the jokes about myself. But our bad times did not spring from such conclusions by Helen—they were too advanced, too unkind for her. They came, I think, because she did not think white people capable of dealing with trouble. I was, thus, an intruder, and in the autumn of 1963 she told me so.

I had gone down to Washington to write a magazine piece about the Washington March. Through Negro friends, through former Harvard students, through a disciple of Malcolm X, I had arranged to meet the delegations from Louisiana and Alabama.

Sophronia's grandson, whom I had never seen, was to arrive with the Alabama delegation. Many years before, I had had letters from his older sister, a teacher at Tuskegee. Now, when I wrote to ask if they would like to come to Washington, she had written back that they could not make the trip. Immediately after, I had a letter from Orin saying that he wanted to come if I would send the bus fare, but please not to tell his sister, because she did not approve. I had sent the money and, as far as I knew, he was on his way. . . .

At nine o'clock I went to look for the Alabama delegation. They had been in Washington for six hours, but nobody had heard of Orin and they were sure he had never been on the bus, never signed up to come. . . .

I wandered off looking for something to eat. I dropped my pocketbook, spilled the contents, and was helped by a small colored boy who, when I thanked him, said, "O.K., lady, courtesy of the Commonwealth." I laughed and found that his companion, a tall young Negro, was laughing, too.

I said, "What's that mean, courtesy of the Commonwealth?"

"Nothing," said the young man. "Old George tries to learn a new word every day. We were up around Boston last night so today it will be 'Commonwealth.'"

Old George turned out to be fourteen years old, small for his age, and the young man's name was Gene Carondelet.

I said, "That's the name of a street in New Orleans."

He said, "Yep. That's why I took it."

Old George weaved in and out of the crowd, bringing frankfurters and then coffee, while Carondelet told me he had been in jail seven times for trying to register Negroes in Greenwood, Mississippi, and for leading a march in Baton Rouge. He said he had never seen old George before McComb, Mississippi, where a policeman had hit George over the head and George's mother had hit the policeman. The next day George's mother said, "Take the boy with you. He's in danger here. Take him and teach him." . . .

About a week later, I came in the house to find Carondelet, George, and a gangly pop-eyed man of about twenty-four sitting in the living room with Helen. Carondelet said they'd been waiting for an hour and now they had to go because George was on his way to the doctor's. As I took them to the elevator, I did not notice that the strange man was still in the living room until George said, "You wanted him, you got him."

"Who?"

"That Orin something."

Carondelet said, "He's silly stuff."

Orin was, indeed, a dull young man, sleepy, overpolite, as anxious as I was to get the visit over with. He had been born long after Sophronia's death, had no memory of his mother's ever having talked about her. . . . Why hadn't he come to Washington with the Alabama delegation? They weren't his kind. He'd come to New York, been robbed, lost my address, hadn't eaten, where was the men's room? I pointed toward the kitchen, waited a long time, puzzled and sad that this man should be Sophronia's grandson. When he did come back, I said I had to go to work, and rose to shake his hand. He suddenly began to talk in a more animated way, although the words were now slurred. I had become Miss Hellmar or, more often, "man" in puzzling sentences like "Man, this is some town and they can take me to it any time they got enough, man," and "Man, where them two finkies I come here with, and where is here, just where is here at?" After a while I said I'd get him some money for the trip back home if he wanted to make it, and he began to laugh as I went into the hall to find Helen standing by the door.

She said, "He took a shot in the toilet."

"What do you mean?"

"A no good punkie-junkie. Maybe heroin."

The words were so modern, so unlike her, that I stared, amused and puzzled that there was a side of her I didn't know.

"I don't think so. He's just stupid, and uncomfortable with me."

When I came back down the steps, the phonograph was playing very loudly and Orin was moving around the room. I couldn't hear what Helen said, but his voice was very loud.

"Lady man, I'm stayin' right where I fall, see?"

Helen said, "You a sick boy. You going for a cure, or you going to hell."

"Lady man, hell's my place and you my girl, tired and old. Maybe even have to send you on a little errand soon—"

She crossed to him, pulled his arms behind his back, and stepped to one side as he tried to kick her. She held him easily, gracefully, as she pulled him toward a chair.

She said to me, "Go for a walk," and closed and locked the door.

The following morning she said, "You see, things happen to people."

I didn't answer her, and after an hour or so she appeared again—an old habit, conversation without prelude, in space, from hours or days or months before—"I locked the door 'cause I wanted you out of trouble."

"No," I said. "You just didn't think I'd be any good at it."

"Time I told you what I ain't told you. My daughter, same way, same thing."

After a while I said, "That shouldn't have happened to you."

"No good for colored people to come North, no good," she said. "Live like a slummy, die like one. South got its points, no matter what you think. Even if just trees."

I was never to see or hear from Orin again, but when George got out of the hospital he came to stay with us several times, appearing and disappearing without explanation. There was something odd about his relations with Helen, something teasing on his side, cautious on hers.

The next summer he came to stay with us for a few days on the Vineyard. He was romping with the poodle on the lawn outside her window, while I read on the porch above their heads.

He said to her, "Hey, Mrs. Jackson, your poodle got fleas."

"Lot of people got fleas," she said.

After a long pause, George called out, "I've been thinking about what you said, and I'm God-damned if I understand it."

"You been sleepin' here, Miss Hellman been sleepin' here. That's all I got to say."

George screamed with laughter. "You mean we give the dog the fleas? You some far-out lady, Mrs. Jackson." And a door slammed.

At dinner, a few weeks later, he said to Helen, "Could I have a piece of your cornbread?"

"Where you see cornbread?"

"Why you hide it where you do?"

It had long been her habit to hide any food that was fattening on the pretense that she ate very little and thus had inherited her "fat glands." Now she opened the stove, reached far back into the oven, and slammed down on the table a giant cornbread cake and a pot of greens and fatback.

"Can I have some," I said, knowing he had made a bad mistake—"nothing in the world like potlikker and corn—"

She said to George, "What you do all day, besides snoopin'? You know more about this island than we ever find out, or want to."

"Sure do," said George, "that my job. Got to find out before you organize. You, for example. Find out all about you being like crazy with your money. You got so much money, give it to SNCC instead of wasting it on that no good Almira family down in town."

Helen said, softly, "Eat your dinner, son."

George said to me, "Old man Almira leave his family for a fourteen-year-old girl, and Mrs. Jackson here, that makes her sad, so she send money all year round, *all year round,* to the wife and kiddies—"

Helen said, "No good men, that's what you all are."

George said, "And no good kiddies. You some fine picker, Mrs. Jackson. The Almira boy was the one set the fire last week and the girl whores all over the Cape."

"You lie, boy, and you a mighty dirty talker about your own people."

"First," said George, "they ain't my people 'cause they ain't all black, they part Portuguese. Two, bums is bums, forget the color. Three, a revolutionary got no right to defend the baddies even of his own color, kind, or faith. Otherwise it comes about—"

I said, "Oh, shut up, George," and Helen hit me on the arm, an old sign of affectionate approval.

George came to visit us the next summer for a few days but I did not see him at all in 1965, until the cold autumn day of Helen's funeral. That night, quite late, he rang the bell, a small suitcase in his hand.

He said, "I wouldn't have come like this, but I'm going back to Atlanta, and I wanted to— Well, I don't know."

We talked for a while about what he'd been doing, where he'd been and then he said, "You're worried, Miss Hellman."

"Yes," I said, "if that's the word."

"About the funeral. They didn't come to you?"

"I guess that's part of it, but not much. No, they didn't come to me, although they telephoned, the two nieces, and the daughter I'd never heard from before. They asked me what kind of funeral I wanted, but I didn't like to intrude, or maybe—I don't know."

"Stinking funeral."

I said, "It's hard to know what strong people would want. I've been there before. You think they're trying to tell you something, forbid you something, but you don't know—"

"Ah," he said, "the one thing they knew for sure was she didn't want that coffin, all done up for a bishop, with brass. Seventeen hundred dollars."

"My God, I didn't know that. What fools— Well, at least I talked them into burying her in South Carolina. That I know she wanted."

"It's my birthday," George said, so we had two drinks. When he got up to leave he said, "Don't worry about the funeral or the coffin. It's done, done."

"That's not what's worrying me. She got sick on Monday. I wanted her to go to the hospital. She wanted to go home. I was annoyed with her and went for a walk. When I came back she was gone. I phoned the next day and she said she was better, but might not be able to work for a while, and then as if she wanted to tell me something. The next morning she was dead."

"She did want to tell you something. She was getting ready to die."

I said, "You know too much, George, too much you're sure of. I don't believe she knew she was going to die. I won't believe it. And how do you know how much the coffin cost?"

"They told me," he said. "On Tuesday morning, Mrs. Jackson asked me to come round."

"She asked you, she didn't ask me. I'm jealous, George."

"She had things for me to do, errands."

I said, "She always had people doing secret errands. I didn't know you saw each other."

"Oh, sure, whenever I came up North, and then I always wrote to her. My second operation, I stayed in her place till I was better."

"You didn't tell me you had a second operation."

He smiled. "Anyway, there I am on Tuesday. She shows me two Savings Bank things and says they're for her grandchildren. Then she give me orders to pack her clothes and take 'em to the post office, all of them except one dress and shoes."

"Where did she send them?"

"Somebody in Augusta, Georgia. Then I take around the TV radio set and I sell that for her. When I come back, she asked me to make her a lemonade and said she wanted to sleep. I said I'd be back at night, but she said not to come, she wanted rest. Then she gave me one hundred dollars. Eighty-five for me, she said, or wherever I wanted to give it. Fifteen for Orin when I found him."

"*Orin? Orin?*"

"He's still hanging around. She always gave him a little money. But he ain't going to get this fifteen, 'cause I ain't going to find him. She was some far-out lady, Mrs. Jackson. Some far-out Christian lady."

[The closing segment of Hellman's memoir describes Hammett's death and her reactions.]

I would say I wanted to get everything straight for the days after his death when I would write his biography and he would say that I was not to bother writing his biography because it would turn out to be the history of Lillian Hellman with an occasional reference to a friend called Hammett.

The day of his death came on January 10, 1961. I will never write that biography because I cannot write about my closest, my most beloved friend. And maybe, too, because all those questions through all the thirty-one on and off years, and the sometime answers, got muddled, and life changed for both of us and the questions and answers became one in the end, flowing together from the days when I was young to the days when I was middle aged. And so this will be no attempt at a biography of Samuel Dashiell Hammett, born in St. Mary's County, Maryland, on May 27, 1894. Nor will it be a critical appraisal of his work. In 1966 I edited and published a collection of his stories. There was a day when I thought all of them very good. But all of them are not good, though most of them, I think, are very good. It is only right to say immediately that by publishing them at all I did what Hammett did not want to do: he turned down all offers to republish the stories, although I never knew the reason and never asked. I did know, from what he said about "Tulip," the unfinished novel that I included in the book, that he meant to start a new literary life and maybe didn't want the old work to get in the way. But sometimes I think he was just too ill to care, too worn out to listen to plans or read contracts. The fact of breathing, just breathing, took up all the days and nights.

In the First World War, in camp, influenza led to tuberculosis and Hammett was to spend years after in army hospitals. He came out of the Second World War with emphysema, but how he ever got into the Second World War at the age of forty-eight still bewilders me. He telephoned me the day the army accepted him to say it was the happiest day of his life, and before I could finish saying it wasn't the happiest day of mine and what about the old scars on his lungs, he laughed and hung up. His death was caused by cancer of the lungs, discovered only two months before he died. It was not operable—I doubt that he would have agreed to an operation even if it had been—and so I decided not to tell him about the cancer. The doctor said that when the pain came, it would come in the right chest and arm, but that the pain might never come. The doctor was wrong: only a few hours after he told me, the pain did come. Hammett had had self-diagnosed rheumatism in the right arm and had always said that was why he had given up hunting. On the day I heard about the cancer, he said his gun shoulder hurt him again, would I rub it for him. I remember sitting behind him, rubbing the shoulder and hoping he would always think it was rheumatism and remember only the autumn hunting days. But the pain never came again, or if it did he never mentioned it, or maybe death was so close that the shoulder pain faded into other pains.

He did not wish to die and I like to think he didn't know he was dying. But I keep from myself even now the possible meaning of a night, very late, a short time before his death. I came into his room, and for the only time in the years I knew him there were tears in his eyes and the book was lying unread. I sat down beside him and waited for a long time before I could say, "Do you want to talk about it?"

He said, almost with anger, "No. My only chance is not to talk about it."

And he never did. He had patience, courage, dignity in those last, awful months. It was as if all that makes a man's life had come together to prove itself: suffering was a private matter and there was to be no invasion of it. He would seldom even ask for anything he needed, and so the most we did—my secretary and Helen, who were devoted to him, as most women always had been—was to carry up the meals he barely touched, the books he now could hardly read, the afternoon coffee, and the martini that I insisted upon before the dinner that wasn't eaten.

One night of that last year, a bad night, I said, "Have another martini. It will make you feel better."

"No," he said, "I don't want it."

I said, "O.K., but I bet you never thought I'd urge you to have another drink."

He laughed for the first time that day. "Nope. And I never thought I'd turn it down."

Because on the night we had first met he was getting over a five-day drunk and he was to drink very heavily for the next eighteen years, and then one day, warned by a doctor, he said he would never have another drink and he kept his word except for the last year of the one martini, and that was my idea.

We met when I was twenty-four years old and he was thirty-six in a restaurant in Hollywood. The five-day drunk had left the wonderful face looking rumpled, and the very tall thin figure was tired and sagged. We talked of T. S. Eliot, although I no longer remember what we said, and then went and sat in his car and talked at each other and over each other until it was daylight. We were to meet again a few weeks later and, after that, on and sometimes off again for the rest of his life and thirty years of mine.

Thirty years is a long time, I guess, and yet as I come now to write about them the memories skip about and make no pattern and I know only certain of them are to be trusted. I know about that first meeting and the next, and there are many other pictures and sounds, but they are out of order and out of time, and I don't seem to want to put them into place. (I could have done a research job, I have on other people, but I didn't want to do one on Hammett, or to be a bookkeeper of my own life.) I don't want modesty for either of us, but I ask myself now if it can mean much to anybody but me that my second sharpest memory is of a day when we were living on a small island off the coast of Connecticut. It was six years after we had first met: six full, happy, unhappy years during which I had, with help from Hammett, written The Children's Hour, which was a success, and Days to Come, which was not. I was returning from the mainland in a catboat filled with marketing and Hammett had come down to the dock to tie me up. He had been sick that summer—the first of the sicknesses—and he was even thinner than usual. The white hair, the white pants, the white shirt made a straight, flat surface in the late sun. I thought: Maybe that's the handsomest sight I ever saw, that line of a man, the knife for a nose, and the sheet went out of my hand and the wind went out of the sail. Hammett laughed as I struggled to get back the sail. I don't know why, but I yelled angrily, "So you're a Dostoevsky sinner-saint. So you are." The laughter stopped, and when I finally came in to the dock we didn't speak as we carried up the packages and didn't speak through dinner.

Later that night, he said, "What did you say that for? What does it mean?"

I said I didn't know why I had said it and I didn't know what it meant.

Years later, when his life had changed, I did know what I had meant that day: I had seen the sinner—whatever is a sinner—and sensed the change before it came. When I told him that, Hammett said he didn't know what I was talking about, it was all too religious for him. But he did know what I was talking about and he was pleased.

But the fat, loose, wild years were over by the time we talked that way. When I first met Dash he had written four of the five novels and was the hottest thing in Hollywood and New York. It is not remarkable to be the hottest thing in either city—the hottest kid changes for each winter season—but in his case it was of extra interest to those who collect people that the ex-detective who had bad cuts on his legs and an indentation in his head from being scrappy with criminals was gentle in manner, well educated, elegant to look at, born of early settlers, was eccentric, witty, and spent so much money on women that they would have liked him even if he had been none of the good things. But as the years passed from 1930 to 1948, he wrote only one novel and a few short stories. By 1945, the drinking was no longer gay, the drinking bouts were longer and the moods darker. I was there off and on for most of those years, but in 1948 I didn't want to see the drinking anymore. I hadn't seen or spoken to Hammett for two months until the day when his devoted cleaning lady called to say she thought I had better come down to his apartment. I said I wouldn't, and then I did. She and I dressed a man who could barely lift an arm or a leg and brought him to my house, and that night I watched delirium tremens, although I didn't know what I was watching until the doctor told me the next day at the hospital. The doctor was an old friend. He said, "I'm going to tell Hammett that if he goes on drinking he'll be dead in a few months. It's my duty to say it, but it won't do any good." In a few minutes he came out of Dash's room and said, "I told him. Dash said O.K., he'd go on the wagon forever, but he can't and he won't."

But he could and he did. Five or six years later, I told Hammett that the doctor had said he wouldn't stay on the wagon.

Dash looked puzzled. "But I gave my word that day."

I said, "Have you always kept your word?"

"Most of the time," he said, "maybe because I've so seldom given it."

He had made up honor early in his life and stuck with his rules, fierce in the protection of them. In 1951 he went to jail because he and two other trustees of the bail bond fund of the Civil Rights Congress refused to reveal the names of the contributors to the fund. The truth was that Hammett had never been in the office of the Congress, did not know the name of a single contributor.

The night before he was to appear in court, I said, "Why don't you say that you don't know the names?"

"No," he said, "I can't say that."

"Why?"

"I don't know why. I guess it has something to do with keeping my word, but I don't want to talk about that. Nothing much will happen, although I think we'll go to jail for a while, but you're not to worry because"—and then suddenly I couldn't understand him because the voice had dropped and the words were coming in a most untypical nervous rush. I said I couldn't hear him, and he raised his voice and dropped his head. "I hate this damn kind of talk, but maybe I better tell you that if it were more than jail, if it were my life, I would give it for what I think democracy is, and I don't let cops or judges tell me what I think democracy is." Then he went home to bed, and the next day he went to jail. . . .

This memory of Hammett is being written in the summer. Maybe that's why most of what I remember about him has to do with summer, although like all people who live in the country, we were more closely thrown together in winter. Winter was the time of work for me and I worked better if Hammett was in the room. There he was, is, as I close my eyes and see another house, reading *The Autumn Garden*. I was, of course, nervous as I watched him. He had always been critical, I was used to that and wanted it, but now I sensed something new and was worried. He finished the play, came across the room, put the manuscript in my lap, went back to his chair and began to talk. It was not the usual criticism: it was sharp and angry, snarling. He spoke as if I had betrayed him. I was so shocked, so pained that I would not now remember the scene if it weren't for a diary that I've kept for each play. He said that day, "You started as a serious writer. That's what I liked, that's what I worked for. I don't know what's happened, but tear this up and throw it away. It's worse than bad—it's half good." He sat glaring at me and I ran from the room and went down to New York and didn't come back for a week. When I did come back I had torn up the play, put the scraps in a briefcase, put the briefcase outside his door. We never mentioned the play again until seven months later when I had rewritten it. I was no longer nervous as he read it: I was too tired to care and I went to sleep on the couch. I woke up because Hammett was sitting beside me, patting my hair, grinning at me and nodding.

After he had nodded for a long time, I said, "What's the matter with you?"

"Nice things. Because it's the best play anybody's written in a long time. Maybe longer. It's a good day. A good day."

I was so shocked with the kind of praise I had never heard before that I started out of the door to take a walk.

He said, "Nix. Come on back. There's a speech in the last act went sour. Do it again."

I said I wasn't going to do it again. He said O.K., he'd do it, and he did, working all through the night.

When *The Autumn Garden* was in rehearsal Dash came almost every day, even more disturbed than I was that something was happening to the play, life was going out of it, which can and does happen on the stage and once started can seldom be changed.

Yesterday I read three letters he wrote to a friend about his hopes for the play, the rehearsals, and the opening. His concern for me and the play was very great, but in time I came to learn that he was good to all writers who needed help, and that the generosity had less to do with the writer than with writing and the pains of writing. I knew, of course, about the generosity long before, but generosity and profligacy often intertwine and it took me a long time to tell them apart.

A few years after I met Dash the large Hollywood money was gone, given away, spent on me who didn't want it and on others who did. I think Hammett was the only person I ever met who really didn't care about money, made no complaints and had no regrets when it was gone. Maybe money is unreal for most of us, easier to give away than things we want. (But I didn't know that then, maybe confused it with showing off.) Once, years later, Hammett bought himself an expensive crossbow at a time when it meant giving up other things to have it. It had just arrived that day and he was testing it, fiddling with it, liking it very much, when friends arrived with their ten-year-old boy. Dash and the boy spent the afternoon with the crossbow and the child's face was awful when he had to leave it. Hammett opened the back door of the car, put in the crossbow, went hurriedly into the house, refusing all cries of "No, no" and such.

When our friends had gone, I said, "Was that necessary? You wanted it so much."

Hammett said, "The kid wanted it more. Things belong to people who want them most."

And thus it was, certainly, with money, and thus the troubles came, and suddenly there were days of no dinners, rent unpaid, and so on; there they were, the lean times, no worse than many other people have had, but the contrast of no dinner on Monday and a wine feast on Tuesday made me a kind of irritable he never understood.

When we were very broke, those first years in New York, Hammett got a modest advance from Knopf and began to write *The Thin Man*. He moved to what was jokingly called the Diplomat's Suite in a hotel run by our friend Nathanael West. It was a new hotel, but Pep West and the depression had managed to run it down immediately. Certainly Hammett's suite had never seen a diplomat, because even the smallest Oriental could not have functioned well in the space. But the rent was cheap, the awful food could be charged, and some part of my idle time could be spent with Pep snooping around the lives of the other rather strange guests. I had known Dash when he was writing short stories, but I had never been around for a long piece of work. Life changed: the drinking stopped, the parties were over. The locking-in time had come and nothing was allowed to disturb it until the book was finished. I had never seen anybody work that way: the care for every word, the pride in the neatness of the typed page itself, the refusal for ten days or two weeks to go out even for a walk for fear something would be lost. It was a good year for me and I learned from it and was, perhaps, frightened by a man who now did not need me. So it was a happy day when I was given half the manuscript to read and was told that I was Nora. It was nice to be Nora, married to

Nick Charles, maybe one of the few marriages in modern literature where the man and woman like each other and have a fine time together. But I was soon put back in place—Hammett said I was also the silly girl in the book and the villainess. I don't know now if he was joking, but in those days it worried me: I was very anxious that he think well of me. Most people wanted that from him. Years later, Richard Wilbur said that as you came toward Hammett to shake his hand in the first meeting, you wanted him to approve of you. There are such people and Hammett was one of them. I don't know what makes this quality in certain men—something floating around them that hasn't much to do with who they are or what they've done—but maybe it has to do with reserves so deep that we know we cannot touch them with charm or jokes or favors. It comes out as something more than dignity and shows on the face. In jail the guards called Hammett "sir" and out of jail other people came close to it. One night in the last years of his life, we walked into a restaurant, passing a group of young writers that I knew but he didn't. We stopped and I introduced him: these hip young men suddenly turned into deferential schoolboys and their faces became what they must have been at ten years old. It took me years of teasing to force out of Hammett that he knew what effect he had on many people. Then he told me that when he was fourteen years old and had his first job working for the Baltimore and Ohio Railroad, he had come late to work each day for a week. His employer told him he was fired. Hammett said he nodded, walked to the door, and was called back by a puzzled man who said, "If you give me your word it won't happen again, you can keep the job." Hammett said, "Thank you, but I can't do that." After a silence the man said, "O.K., keep the job anyway." Dash said that he didn't know what was right about what he had done, but he did know that it would always be useful.

When *The Thin Man* was sold to a magazine—most of the big slick magazines had turned it down for being too daring, although what they meant by daring was hard to understand—we got out of New York fast. . . .

[T]he years after the war, from 1945 to 1948, were not good years; the drinking grew wilder and there was a lost, thoughtless quality I had never seen before. I knew then that I had to go my own way. I do not mean that we were separated, I mean only that we saw less of each other, were less close to each other. But even in those years there still were wonderful days on the farm of autumn hunting and squirrel pies and sausage making and all the books he read as I tried to write a play. I can see him now, getting up to put a log on the fire and coming over to shake me. He swore that I would always say, "I haven't been sleeping: I've been thinking." He would laugh and say, "Sure. You've been asleep for an hour, but lots of people think best when they're asleep and you're one of them."

In 1952 I had to sell the farm. I moved to New York and Dash rented a small house in Katonah. I went once a week to see him, he came once a week to New York, and we talked on the phone every day. But he wanted to be alone—or so I thought then, but am now not so sure because I have learned that proud men who can ask for nothing may be fine characters, but they are difficult to live with or to understand. In any case, as the years went on he became a hermit, and the ugly little country cottage grew uglier with books piled on every chair and no place to sit, the desk a foot high with unanswered mail. The signs of sickness were all around: now the phonograph was unplayed, the typewriter untouched, the beloved, foolish gadgets unopened in their packages. When I went for my weekly visits we didn't talk much and when he came for his weekly visits to me he was worn out from the short journey.

Perhaps it took me too long to realize that he couldn't live alone anymore, and even after I realized it I didn't know how to say it. One day, immediately after he had made me promise to stop reading "L'il Abner," and I was laughing at his vehemence about it, he suddenly looked embarrassed—he always looked embarrassed when he had something emotional to say—and he said, "I can't live alone anymore. I've been falling. I'm going to a Veterans Hospital. It will be O.K., we'll see each other all the time, and I don't want any tears from you." But there were tears from me, two days of tears, and finally he consented to come and live in my apartment. (Even now, as I write this, I am still angry and amused that he always had to have things on his own terms: a few minutes ago I got up from the typewriter and railed against him for it, as if he could still hear me. I know as little about the nature of romantic love as I knew when I was eighteen, but I do know about the deep pleasure of continuing interest, the excitement of wanting to know what somebody else thinks, will do, will not do, the tricks played and unplayed, the short cord that the years make into rope and, in my case, is there, hanging loose, long after death. I am not sure what

Hammett would feel about the rest of these notes about him but I am sure that he would be pleased that I am angry with him today.) And so he lived with me for the last four years of his life. Not all of that time was easy, indeed some of it was very bad, but it was an unspoken pleasure that having come together so many years before, ruined so much, and repaired a little, we had endured. Sometimes I would resent the understated or seldom stated side of us and, guessing death wasn't too far away, I would try for something to have afterwards. One day I said, "We've done fine, haven't we?"

He said, "Fine's too big a word for me. Why don't we just say we've done better than most people?" . . .

Shirley Anita St. Hill Chisholm

(1924–   )

Shirley Anita St. Hill Chisholm was born in Brooklyn, one of two daughters of a Barbadian immigrant family struggling to make their way in New York. After the onset of the Depression it became clear that Chisholm's parents could not manage to raise and educate the children in the manner they thought appropriate, so Chisholm and her sister were sent back to Barbados to be raised under their maternal grandmother's stern but loving eye, and educated in British-style schools.

Chisholm was reunited with her parents by her high school years, during which she first learned that she had a penchant for asking difficult questions and a talent for public speaking. Her undergraduate years at Brooklyn College were a time of political awakening, delight in study, and warm relationships with white faculty who surprised her by recognizing her talents.

Once politically alert, Chisholm began to energize meetings of the Democratic political club of her ward, first by leading a rebellion of women members about the total lack of recognition of their fund-raising labors, and then by challenging the male regulars about the selection of candidates.

Like Rosemary Brown, Chisholm reveled in politics, relished a good fight, and throve on the demands of campaigning. While completing her M.A. in Education at Columbia and serving as director of the Friends Day Nursery, and then of the Hamilton-Madison Child Care Center, Chisholm was quietly building her political base. By the time she became education consultant to the Day-care Division of the New York Bureau of Child Welfare in 1959, Chisholm was well known in state Democratic circles, and ready to seize her opportunity, when the local state assembly seat became vacant in 1964.

Elected against high odds, Chisholm staked out a reputation for independence and common sense during her first legislative session, and earned recognition which quickly won her nomination to contest a spot on the state delegation to the House of Representatives. Elected a congresswoman in 1969, Chisholm was the first black woman to win national elective office.

Her election catapulted her to national prominence, and made her the national voice for those concerned with feminist and black issues. Her response was a matter-of-fact recognition of the reasons for her celebrity status, and a practical down-to-earth focus on the day-to-day logistics of drafting and piloting legislation through the Congress.

Her tone is matter-of-fact, wry, and disarming. She has a happy sense of the comedy of a youthful black woman of small stature taking on and defeating the old party hacks in her Brooklyn party organization. Yet beneath her comic vision is a strong moral sense, and the determination to see right done inherited from the Barbadian matriarchy of her childhood.

UNBOUGHT AND UNBOSSED

There are 435 members of the House of Representatives and 417 are white males. Ten of the others are women and nine are black. I belong to both of these minorities, which makes it add up right. That makes me a celebrity, a kind of side show attraction. I was the first American citizen to be elected to Congress in spite of the double drawbacks of being female and having skin darkened by melanin . . . .

Sometimes the media make me feel like a monkey in a cage. As soon as I was elected, the newspapers and networks started to besiege me. The first question was almost always, "How does it feel?" Naturally, it feels good. I am proud and honored that the people of my district believed in me enough to choose me to represent them. My Twelfth Congressional District of Brooklyn is mostly composed of poor neighborhoods with all the problems of poverty in an aggravated form . . . .

There was a large colony of Barbadians in Brooklyn, and it was there that my father, Charles St. Hill, and my mother, Ruby Seale, went—separately. He was a native of British Guiana who had grown up in Cuba and Barbados. She was a teen-aged Barbadian girl. They had known each other in Barbados, but not well; in Brooklyn they got better acquainted, fell in love, and married. I was born in 1924. My sister Odessa came about a year later, and two years later my sister Muriel. . . .

The middle 1920s may have been a time of legendary prosperity for some Americans, but not enough of it was rubbing off on young black immigrant couples in the big city. My father was unskilled. He worked as a baker's helper and later as a factory hand. His pay, even supplemented by what Mother could earn by sewing, was not much for a family of five. How could they ever save to buy a house and provide educations for their girls?

It is important to notice that they never questioned they had to do these things; Barbadians are like that. They are bright, thrifty, ambitious people. . . .

The Barbadians' drive to achieve and excel is almost an obsession and is a characteristic that other islanders do not share to the same degree. The Barbadians who came to Brooklyn all wanted, and most of them got, the same two things: a brownstone house and a college education for their children.

So early in 1928 a diminutive young black woman sailed out of New York Harbor on an old steamer named the *Vulcania* with her three little girls, three, two, and eight months, and ten trunks full of food and clothing bound for Barbados and her mother's farm. She planned to board us there until she and Father had saved enough to assure our future in the States. . . .

I still remember arriving: the delays for customs inspection and health clearance, the bus we boarded to ride to the village of Vauxhall where we were going to live. . . .

When the bus stopped, there was Grandmother—Mrs. Emily Seale, a tall, gaunt, erect, Indian-looking woman with her hair knotted on her neck. . . . [T]his . . . stately woman with a stentorian voice was going to be one of the few persons whose authority I would never dare to defy, or even question. . . .

The night noises bothered us city children for a long time: the clucking of chickens hit by cars when they dawdled in the road, the cows mooing and sheep bleating, the crickets, and all the unidentifiable sounds around a farm after dark. . . .

The kitchen had an old-fashioned coal range and innumerable cast-iron kettles, pots, and frying pans. The toilet was outdoors in the back yard. The furniture was sparse and plain, but we found Grandmother's house elaborately furnished with the two necessities: warmth and love.

Mother stayed for six months to help us get used to this new place, and there were many tears when she had to leave. . . .

Schooling is important on the islands. Teachers and parents are allied against children. "You are to pay attention to the teacher and learn," children are told sternly. Teachers are free to whip children, and use that freedom liberally. If a child comes home and reports that the teacher hit him, he can expect another beating, probably on his bare bottom. Psychologists now are sure this is bad for children. In my experience, it was not bad for us; I got my share of floggings, and it produced the effect that was desired. I went to school to pay attention and to learn. . . .

In the primer class, I learned to read and write before I was five. Theoretically, my eye and hand muscles were not developed enough at that age. Psychological theories did not get much attention then from educators in the British West Indies. I have always believed that many teachers underestimate the powers of children. . . .

The curriculum was austere: reading, writing, arithmetic, and history, meaning British history, naturally. The children ranged from four to about eleven. After the sixth form, most of them would go into apprenticeship in some trade like carpentry or shoe-making, or go to work on the family farm. Barbados is an island of small farms. Few would go to college, although there are two good colleges on the island. To go, they would have to take a preparatory course at a private school. To pay for that, some families made the ultimate sacrifice, selling a prized cow or brood sow.

We went to school from eight to four. When we came home, the first thing we had to do was take off our school clothes, which were issued clean on Monday and had to stay that way through Friday. Then we carried the water and helped with the other chores, feeding the chickens and ducks, gathering eggs, changing the straw bedding for the cattle and sheep. The sheep and goats were let out to graze on the abundant grass. There were no fences, so we children had to watch them, to keep them from straying into the road or the gullies, and bring them back at dark. . . .

Always a major part of our lives was the Caribbean, with its warm, blue and aquamarine, incredibly clear water, just a short run from the farm. We stripped and swam and rolled on the sand; the adults swam naked, too; there was perfect matter-of-factness about nudity. The most terrible punishment Grandmother could give us was to tell us we couldn't go to the beach. Almost as bad was to be kept home from a market day in the village, where you could snatch oranges or apples from a peddler who wasn't looking.

In Brooklyn, things had not been going the way Mother and

Father had planned. The depression had come, and their industry and frugality could not bring the security they had been counting on. But they missed us, Mother especially, who feared that her children would soon be grown and never really come to know her. At the end of 1933, the St. Hills decided that, come what may, it was time to get their family back together. . . .

Dinner together every night was an inflexible rule in our family . . . . Then [Papa] would lead the conversation, telling Mother about the events of his day and asking the children the inevitable question, "What did you learn in school?" It was no idle query; he wanted an answer. Papa harped on the theme, "You must make something of yourselves. You've got to go to school, and I'm not sending you to play either. Study and make something of yourselves. Remember, only the strong people survive in this world. God gave you a brain; use it."

Sometimes Papa would hold forth on his idol—hardly too strong a word—Marcus Garvey. . . . When any organization had a Marcus Garvey tribute, he would dress up and go. Sometimes he took me, and there I heard my first black nationalist oratory. . . .

"Bed-Stuy" was about 50 percent black in those days. After we moved there, I began to hear racial slurs and epithets for the first time—nigger, kike, Jew bastard, black son of a bitch. I was not used to black being used as a derogatory word.

Blacks were arriving in greater numbers from the South. But though their numbers were growing, there was no such thing as a black community. Most of the newcomers were passive and accommodating in the face of discrimination. They knew their place and stayed in it. . . .

Those were the hardest years of the depression. Dad had changed jobs and was working as a laborer in a burlap bag factory. He had expected to gain several dollars a week by the move, but it turned out that the work was not steady. Soon he was working as little as two days a week and bringing home sometimes no more than eighteen dollars. Mother had to do something she had always feared. She put a key on a string around my neck and went to work as a domestic for white families in Flatbush. Every noon I had to walk from junior high school to P.S. 28 and collect my sisters, take them home and feed them, and return them to school. I was usually late getting back, but the teachers knew why and made allowances. Lunch was usually a glass of milk and a bun. . . .

We had to read . . . even if we did not want to. We all had library cards and every other Saturday Mother took us to the library to check out the limit, three books each. Each of us had a dictionary, and our Christmas presents were books, often one of those endless "adventure" series such as the Nancy Drew or Bobbsey Twins stories.

When I graduated from junior high school in 1939 I went to Girls' High School, one of Brooklyn's oldest schools, on Nostrand Avenue in Bedford-Stuyvesant. We had moved again while I was in high school—to 316 Patchen Avenue, where my father worked as the janitor so we had a six-room apartment free, and Mother could stay home again—and it was only a short walk to school. Many of the other students walked or rode there from the farthest parts of Brooklyn. The school was highly regarded. As the name indicates, it was all girls; about half of them were white, but the neighborhood by now was nearly all black. . . .

When I graduated from Girls' High in 1942 I drew several scholarship offers. I wanted to accept either one from Vassar or one from Oberlin. But my parents argued that they could not afford my room and board at an out-of-town school. I had to admit they were right, and in the fall I went to Brooklyn College. . . .

If I had gone to Vassar, the rest of my life might have been different. Would I have become one of the pseudo-white upper-middle-class black women professionals, or a doctor's wife with furs, limousines, clubs, and airs?. . . At any rate, Brooklyn College changed my life. I was still naive about most things when I entered college, not quite eighteen. My fiercely protective parents had given me a sheltered upbringing that was incredible, considering the time and place in which I grew up. In school, my intelligence had put me in a special category. In college, I began to bump up against more of the world. . . .

Brooklyn was the largest of the five city-run colleges, and its campus was supposed to be especially for bright lower-class, poorer students. Tuition was free; it was a "subway campus," and one would have expected more black students. The trouble was, of course, that the grade and high schools they attended—then as now—did not do enough to overcome the handicaps of their background. So 98 percent of the students at the city colleges were white. . . .

I had already decided to become a teacher. There was no other road open to a young black woman. Law, medicine, even nursing were too expensive, and few schools would admit black men, much less a woman. Social work was not yet open to blacks in the early 1940s. If I had other ideas about what I might do, I dismissed them. My youth may have been sheltered from boys and some other realities, but I was black, and nobody needed to draw me a diagram. No matter how well I prepared myself, society wasn't going to give me a chance to do much of anything else. (My sister Muriel, who entered Brooklyn College a few years later, majored in physics and graduated magna cum laude. She was unable to find a job, even as a laboratory technician.) I knew it would have to be teaching for me; but I took no education courses, for some reason. I majored in sociology and minored in Spanish.

There was one all-black student group, the Harriet Tubman Society. Some upperclassmen had started it, about a year before I joined it in my sophomore year. There I first heard people other than my father talk about white oppression, black racial consciousness, and black pride. The black students kept to their own tables in the cafeteria. We talked. No one said "rap" then, but that's what we did. I had some things to contribute, more out of my reading than my experience. I knew about Harriet Tubman and Frederick Douglass, W. E. B. Du Bois and George W. Carver, and I had managed to find some books in the public library about our African heritage that few people then studied or talked about; I knew about the Ashanti kingdoms, for instance. . . .

Other experiences sharpened my feeling for how racism was woven through American life. I belonged to the Political Science Society, which naturally thought itself progressive. Some of its speakers, I became aware, looked at my people as another breed, less human than they. Politicians came to talk and gave us such liberal sentiments as, "We've got to help the Negro because the Negro is limited," or, "Of course, the Negro people have always been the laborers and will continue to be. So we've got to make it more comfortable for them.". . .

For a long time I watched such white people closely, listened to them, and observed silently the treatment blacks were given in social and political situations. It grew on me that we, black men especially, were expected to be subservient even in groups where ostensibly everyone was equal. Blacks played by those rules; if a white man walked in, they came subtly to attention. But I could see their fear, helplessness, and discomfort.

When I looked at the white people who were doing this, consciously or not, it made me angry because so many of them were baser, less intelligent, less talented than the people they were lording it over. But the whites were in control. We could do nothing about it. We had no power. . . .

I decided to devote my life to children. But the resolve was also there (I did not realize yet how fierce it had grown) to do something about the way whites treated my people. Political action was hardly even a fantasy for me at that time. But I decided that if I ever had a chance, somehow I would tell the world how things were as I saw them.

A blind political science professor, Louis Warsoff, became interested in me, and we had long talks. I called him "Proffy," affectionately. He was one of the first white men whom I ever really knew and trusted. . . . From Professor Warsoff I learned that white people were not really different from me. I loved formal debating particularly, and once after I starred in a match he told me, "You ought to go into politics." I was astonished at his naiveté.

"Proffy," I said, "you forget two things. I'm black—and I'm a woman."

"You really have deep feelings about that, haven't you?" he countered. The conversation stuck in my mind. I realized that I did have deep feelings, on both scores. . . .

Black students were not welcome in social clubs, so some friends and I formed a sorority-like black women students' society. . . .

I was still living at home, still going to church three times on Sundays, and still forbidden to date. I spent hours in the college library, and made no new, close friends in school. Naturally, the boys considered me a bookworm. It didn't bother me too much. They were surprised, though, when I showed up at parties and they discovered that I could dance, and loved to. . . .

When I graduated in 1946, cum laude, I was nearly twenty-two but I looked sixteen or seventeen; I weighed about ninety pounds. It made job hunting hard. School after school turned me down, even as a teacher's aide; I didn't look old enough to teach, and most of my interviewers told me so. Day after day I stomped the streets. Finally I blew up at one nursery school director. "At least you could try me!" I exploded. "Put me on as a probationer! Give me a chance to show you! Give me a chance to find out whether I can do the

job . . . don't judge me by my size." Mrs. Eula Hodges, director of
the Mt. Cavalry Child Care Center in Harlem, was persuaded. I
worked there for seven years. . . .

[T]o be as well prepared as possible, I enrolled in Columbia
University to work evenings for a master's degree in early childhood
education. It was about then that I had my own early education in
politics, in the toughest and most instructive school possible, New
York City's old-time clubhouses.

The political clubs are still there in New York, but things ain't
what they used to be for the clubhouse crowds, and I hope they
never are again. . . .

New York's clubs were organized by state Assembly districts.
Often the assemblyman was also the district leader and state com-
mitteeman. . . . Once a month the club had a membership meeting,
but the important meetings were the "club nights" on Monday and
Thursday evenings. Those were the nights people came in with their
problems. In the old Seventeenth Assembly District Democratic
Club, the leader, Vincent Carney, used to sit with his flunkies on a
dais at the far end of the room, while the voters came in and took
high-backed chairs to wait their turns for an audience.

The blacks sat at one side, the whites on the other. There was
no sign that said "Colored Side." It was an unwritten law. . . . You
could feel the men on each side daring those on the other to cross
the invisible line. The blacks did not go to club nights because they
felt wanted, or because they hoped to make any real inroads in the
organization. They went because they needed help.

The 17th A.D. at that time was probably two-thirds black, but
the all-white (mostly Irish) organization ran the district. It elected the
state senator, assemblyman, city councilman, and other local office-
holders and, by treaty with the similar clubs around it, picked the
men for congressional seats, judgeships, and other big-bore political
jobs.

During college, I had gone to a few club meetings when there
was a speaker I wanted to hear. After the city councilman or commissioner had finished, there was a question period. But hardly anyone ever asked questions. I did. I asked the sanitation commissioner
why trash wasn't picked up regularly in Bedford-Stuyvesant, as it
was in white neighborhoods. I asked councilmen why they hadn't

delivered on their promises. Such questions were unwelcome, and after the meeting someone was likely to tell me so. I pretended innocence: How do I know what kind of questions you're supposed to ask? . . .

One night I tried another challenge. I walked in the room and right past the rows of people waiting, black on one side and white on the other, and up on the dais. Two men blocked my way and told me I wasn't waiting my turn; I would have to go back to the end of the line and take a chair. I told them, "No. This is an urgent matter." I don't even remember now what it was, something for somebody else. I just wanted to see what they would do. I had been watching people sit and wait, evening after evening, and it had grown on me. It was insulting and degrading to them; they were being treated like cattle. Why should they have to sit there on hard, high-backed chairs, stiff, formal, and uncomfortable? They made an exception and talked to me. It didn't change the system though . . . .

My interest in politics grew gradually. I joined the Seventeenth Assembly District Democratic Club and scored my first political success there as a cigar box decorator.

When I began going to membership meetings regularly, they put me on the card party committee. The party and raffle formed the year's big fund-raising event. They were run by the women of the club, most of them wives of members. . . .

When the committee met to discuss the progress of the raffle ticket sales and so on, I went a little beyond the role they had assigned me and began to make suggestions. One turned out to be a real troublemaker.

The club . . . was exploiting the women. It lived on the proceeds of the annual raffle and card party that the women ran; its only other income was from dues. But the men never provided a budget to run the event, and the women had to beg money here and there to buy prizes and print raffle books.

"Why should we put up with it?" I asked them. "We bring in the money. Why shouldn't they give us five hundred dollars or a thousand, some definite sum, to do it with?" I was angry, and as we talked, some of the women got angry themselves. They brought it up at a club meeting. . . .

So at last, they gave us $700. The party, as it always did, brought in more than $8,000.

After that the women occasionally spoke up at meetings and raised questions. The reaction of the men became "Shirley is egging them on." Sometimes that was true. But I was not really there to make trouble; I thought I was trying to help. . . .

I was well on the way to forming my present attitude toward politics as it is practiced in the United States: it is a beautiful fraud that has been imposed on the people for years, whose practitioners exchange gilded promises for the most valuable thing their victims own, their votes. And who benefits most? The lawyers. This is true on any level, but at the district politics plane one sees it clearest. There are a few menial jobs for the doorbell ringers, the envelope stuffers, the petition carriers, and the car pool drivers who make the machine go. Some of them get to be charwomen in government buildings, or process servers, or guards. But without a legal background, the real patronage is out of their reach. . . .

[E]ven though I kept going to Democratic club meetings and irritating Carney and his crew by asking questions such as "Why can't Bedford-Stuyvesant have as much police protection as other parts of the city?" and "Why aren't the housing codes enforced?" I gradually became less active in the club. The NAACP, the League of Women Voters, the Stuyvesant Community Center, and, most of all, the Bedford-Stuyvesant Political League were taking too much of my time to leave any to waste on them. I was reaching positions of leadership in several of the groups and had become sort of a little local figure. . . .

I had already met the really important man in my life, the one who was eventually going to persuade me, with infinite gentleness and patience, to change my mind about being a spinster. At Columbia one night, running from a class to a meeting as I was always doing, a stocky, quiet, handsome Jamaican named Conrad Chisholm had stopped me and persuaded me to stand still long enough to get acquainted. . . .

Conrad . . . began to lay siege. I used every tactic I knew to drive him away: glacial aloofness, standing him up, angry sarcasm, avoiding him. He refused to be shaken by anything I did. It took months, during which he often came to the house and, reversing the previous situation, my mother welcomed him and I ignored him. Eventually his calm determination and his inexhaustible sympathy got through to me. I realized that this was a different kind of man. We were married in 1949.

The white organization was dead at last in Bedford-Stuyvesant. Its leaders were out of office, and the Unity Democratic Club was the official Democratic organization for the district. The election was an anticlimax. The Republican and Liberal parties had nominees, but, as usual, they were no threat. Our slate won easily. . . .

I was on the club's executive committee, just about back where I had started my political career. That seemed a little ironic, but of course there was an enormous difference. . . . This time I was one of the leaders of a group that was really representative of the district, and we were in a position, for the first time, to exert some leverage on the party and the state legislature in behalf of the people who had been second-class citizens all their lives.

Tom Jones served only one term in the Assembly. By 1964 a seat had opened up on the civil court bench in Brooklyn. The county organization, in a mood to make some accommodations with the black community, was willing to support him for it. Jones is an able and learned lawyer and was ideally suited for the bench. He deserved the opportunity. . . .

If Jones ran for judge, there was a vacancy in the state Assembly. I wanted it, and I told the club I felt I deserved it. This was unwelcome news to the county organization, and it did not appeal very much to some of the people in my own club. Some of the men fancied the nomination themselves. Others, who had had a taste of how I operated—a little woman who didn't know how to play the game or when to shut up—didn't want to see me in a position of any more importance than I already had.

For my part, I was not interested in listening to any reasons why I shouldn't run. By then I had spent about ten years in ward politics and had done everything else but run for office. . . . I was resolved that it was going to start changing right then. I was the best-qualified nominee, and I was not going to be denied because of my sex.

With noticeable reluctance by some of the members, the Unity Democratic Club endorsed me. Jones went to the county organization to report, "Shirley Chisholm is our Assembly candidate." We were the regular organization, and what we decided should have been the end of it, according to the rule book. . . .

I won the primary against token opposition, and my next problem was what to run my campaign with. The Unity Democratic Club had very little money although its organization would work for me, and that was invaluable. The county organization was not about to help us much. White clubs usually got more money than the black clubs. Mailings, posters, rallies, all the ways you get to the voters or get them out to hear you, cost money. I went to the bank four times that year and drew a total of $4,000 from my savings. It's not much by modern standards, but I made it do. . . .

I met with hostility because of my sex from the start of my first campaign. Even some women would greet me, "You ought to be home, not out here." Once, while I was collecting nominating petition signatures in the big Albany housing project—where Conrad and I had been captains for several years—one man about seventy lit into me. "Young woman, what are you doing out here in this cold? Did you get your husband's breakfast this morning? Did you straighten your house? What are you doing running for office? That is something for men."

A direct counterattack would have achieved nothing. I handled all such hecklers, male and female, the same way. I told them calmly that I had been serving the community for a number of years and now I would appreciate an opportunity to serve it on a higher level, in elected office. Many persons, both men and women, I said, felt that I was the person to protect their interests and I would like a chance to run and try to win.

The old man signed my petition. So did some of the others. I never struck back at the black men who wanted to argue with me in that vein. I understood too well their reasons for lashing out at black women; in a society that denied them real manhood, I was threatening their shaky self-esteem still more.

As a matter of fact, there is as much—it could even be more— panic among white men confronted by an able, determined female who refused to play the sex role they think is fitting. . . . [T]heir attack is indirect. They stress what are considered feminine foibles: "Women talk too much." "Women are illogical." "Women take everything personally." In politics, the men tell each other, "This isn't a game for women." Or, at parties, in asides that they allow one to hear, they talk about how "it has to be a certain kind of woman who goes in for politics. . . ."

[I]t was a long, hard summer and fall. I won by a satisfying margin, in a three-way contest, with 18,151 votes to 1893 for the Republican, Charles Lewis, and 913 for the Liberal, Simon Golar. . . .

When I went to Albany I went as one of eight, six black assemblymen and two state senators, the largest number by far in history. I was the only woman, but not the first. Mrs. Bessie Buchanan had represented an Assembly district in Harlem for a time, about ten years earlier. . . .

Most black politicians are no different from white ones. They're not their own bosses either. If they don't function within the framework, they're punished and, if possible, eliminated. The punishment is drastic. They assign you to committees that are not popular, or where no work is done. They don't invite you in on things, from dinner parties to drafting bills. Your own bills are doomed; bosses can tell a chairman to keep them bottled up in committee, or, if they get out, it only takes a hint dropped on the floor that the leadership would like to see this bill not pass.

The strange thing is that this hasn't happened to me, and I sometimes wonder why. Maybe I am just lucky, but being a maverick hasn't kept me from being an effective legislator. . . .

Out of fifty bills I introduced in the legislature, eight passed, a high score if one knows how many bills are introduced in Albany at every session and how few even reach the floor.

Two I was especially satisfied with. One reached a program called SEEK, to make it possible for young men and women from disadvantaged backgrounds to go to college, by seeking them out and assisting them while they go to school. . . . The other was a bill to set up the state's first unemployment insurance coverage for personal and domestic employees. Every employer who paid $500 or more had to make contributions to the unemployment insurance fund. It passed in my first year, and so did two of my other bills. . . .

The other black member with whom I worked most closely was Assemblyman Percy Sutton, now the Manhattan borough president, a man I came to admire greatly. The Associated Press called us the two most militant and effective black members of the Assembly. . . .

During four years in Albany, I had a liberal education in how politics is run in our country—a sort of graduate course to follow my basic education in ward and county politicking. I did not like a great deal of what I learned.

New York State legislators are part-time lawmakers. . . . For many, the legislative session is as much like a convention as it is a serious business. There is an active, shall we say, night life. . . .

Another lesson I learned was that if you decide to operate on the basis of your conscience, rather than your political advantage, you must be ready for the consequences and not complain when you suffer them.

In spite of this, I did manage to get some important things done in Albany. Was I less effective than I would have been if I had worked scrupulously within the system and played by all the rules? I don't think so. People who do that may be tossed a few bones, but their compromising really gets them nowhere. They make all the concessions, the bosses make none.

In Albany I learned how the processes of representative government work—or do not work. Often it was their failure that I saw. I do not want anyone to conclude that I have given up hope for our representative democracy; I have not, or I would not be where I am. It is because I value the idea so much that I am often keenly disappointed by the reality. . . .

But all this prepared me consummately well for Washington. That lesson was what I needed before I became a congresswoman. . . .

Another redistricting . . . made it possible for me to run for Congress. Brooklyn had been gerrymandered outrageously. The black vote had been split four ways into districts where black voters were snowed under. . . . After the Supreme Court ruled that districts must be of equal size and "compact and contiguous," that kind of outrageous districting disappeared (although the map makers are getting used to the new rules and are managing to invent new outrages without breaking them). . . .

The Kings County machine said it was going to keep its hands off the new "black" district and leave the choice of a nominee "up to the people." It sounded fine, but since when did a machine leave the choice of an important office up to the people? Shortly before Christmas 1967, months before the primary, a citizens' committee formed itself in the district. Their main concern was to prevent the choice of the kind of "Tom" that would appeal to the county organization.

The citizens' committee invited many of the potential candidates to come in for interviews, including me. I was the only woman. After all the interviews were over, they unanimously endorsed me. It was a big surprise. I had, I knew, been the only one of the potential candidates who talked back and disagreed with them about things they had said they would have to expect from a nominee. That was the reason they decided to pick me. Above everything, they wanted someone who would have the independence to refuse to be run by the machine. I did not go to them with my hat in my hand, and that was what they liked.

After the word leaked out, the politicians groaned. "If we couldn't control her in Albany, how are we going to in Washington?" The county organization, of course, did not abide by its pious intention to "leave it in the hands of the people." This was from the start their cop-out on endorsing me. It soon became well known in political circles and then in the district generally that Thompson was the organization's choice. The county machine never did endorse a candidate, but every action of its people showed, to the most unsophisticated resident of Bedford-Stuyvesant, that William C. Thompson was their man. White people think black people are stupid, but it came through to the community that the organization could not bring itself to endorse me because I would not submit to being bossed by any of them. It was interesting that, even among themselves, they never questioned my competence or dedication. What they said was always that I was "hard to handle." . . .

I faced a three-way primary. The Unity Democratic Club was for me; it was the base from which I started . . . I had a call from Mac Holder.

My old-time mentor and enemy in recent years wanted to work for me. Twenty years back, he had said he wanted to live to elect a black judge and a black congressman. Now he thought he saw a chance of reaching the second, greater goal with me but, he told me, I couldn't win without him and the people in the streets. Looking back on it, I think he was right.

Mac told me, "You're the easiest product to sell and I'm going to organize the campaign and sell you." He worked nineteen hours a day to do it.

The days I put in were just as long. I almost killed myself because I wanted to show the machine that a little black woman was going to beat it. Quite possibly no one but Mac and I . . .

believed I could do it. The organization believed, from its past experience and because the political columnists told it so, that it would win because it was the organization and it had what it took to deliver the votes in a primary. . . .

Starting in February, I spent ten months doing the only thing I could do: I tramped the streets of Williamsburg, Crown Heights, and Bedford-Stuyvesant, telling my story to the people. I didn't have the money for a conventional congressional campaign; I had to make up for it with hard work. But I was determined to show them. People had to know that it was possible for someone with decency and a fighting spirit to overcome the system by beating it with its own weapons. . . .

So I campaigned the hard way, in the streets. Indoors, with a selected audience, you have control. But out on the street corners with the people, in the housing projects, in parks, you are under fire constantly. If you are insincere or have something to hide, you will be found out.

I wrote a slogan that said it all: "Fighting Shirley Chisholm—Unbought and Unbossed." . . . On Friday nights and through Sunday evenings . . . I traveled with a caravan of twenty to fifty cars manned by volunteers—men, women, and children. On both sides of each car we put a picture with the legend VOTE FOR CHISHOLM FOR CONGRESS—UNBOUGHT AND UNBOSSED. We had shopping bags with the same inscriptions. All week long, on the street, in markets, at clinics, you could see people with my shopping bags. We gave them out to everyone who would take them, with a package of material on my biography and Assembly record and a souvenir—a pen or a handkerchief—inside. The main stops were at housing projects; there are ten big ones in the district. We also stopped at churches, at parks, and on street corners to talk to anyone who would listen. I shook hands, answered questions, and listened to what the people had to say.

During the week I went to endless little house parties and teas given by women. In the black neighborhood I ate chitlins, in the Jewish neighborhood bagels and lox, in the Puerto Rican neighborhood arroz con pollo. We contacted every neighborhood woman leader we could find. "Bring your women in," I would urge them. Sometimes a woman would tell me that she would like to have a party for me, but she just couldn't afford it, and I would provide the money. I went to all kinds of homes. I wasn't interested in style. . . .

When they counted the primary votes, with a very small turnout, I won by about 1000 votes. . . .

Immediately after the primary, I became seriously ill, completely without warning. . . .

I had been sleeping very little because I had to get up so many times each night. Finally, Conrad bullied me into going to a doctor. I had to miss three important meetings, and I was fussing and carrying on all the way there.

"Either you're pregnant or you have a tumor," the doctor said as soon as he looked at me.

"Doc, you'd better know what you're talking about," I told him, "because I am running for Congress and I am not going to have a baby."

He examined me thoroughly and dropped all pretense at humor. "You've got to take her to a gynecologist and a surgeon tonight," he told Conrad, and he picked up the telephone. "I'm sending over Congresswoman Chisholm," he told the specialist at the other end of the line, "the young black woman who is going to be the congressman. I'm quite sure she has a massive tumor." It was the first time I was ever called "congressman," and I still wonder why he said it. . . .

The biopsy showed no malignancy. But all the same, they had to operate. . . .

They had given me such a large dose of anesthetic that I didn't come to for thirteen hours. Conrad was walking up and down and sweating all that time. He knew I must be dead. The next day I was walking around the hospital. I was determined to get back on the streets.

It was August, though, when I got home. I looked at myself in the mirror and wept. I was so emaciated from the waist down that I looked like Twiggy. . . .

I took a big beach towel and wrapped it around my hips so my clothes wouldn't fall off. With that, I looked pretty good. . . .

I set up my own headquarters, at 1103 Bergen Street. . . . Mac took an unpaid leave from his job as statistician for the Brooklyn district attorney's office, and we got our own people, typewriters, and mimeograph machines and set up a campaign headquarters. He organized a regular assembly line for mailings. At details, there is no one like Mac. He seemed to remember everything. "That is how you keep your mind free for the important matters," he told me.

But Mac's important contribution to the campaign was not in organization alone. It came when I found that Farmer* and his people were using my sex against me. To the black men—even some of those supposedly supporting me—sensitive about female domination, they were running me down as a bossy female, a would-be matriarch. . . . But that was exactly what wise and wily Mac realized I had going for me. He had studied the voter rolls and found that for each man registered in the district there were 2.5 women. This is something not found in white communities. He and I realized that what Farmer thought was his strength was his Achilles' heel.

Men always underestimate women. They underestimated me, and they underestimated the women like me. If they had thought about it, they would have realized that many of the homes in black neighborhoods are headed by women. They stay put, raise their families—and register to vote in greater numbers. The women are always organizing for something, even if it is only a bridge club. They run the PTA, they are the backbone of the social groups and civic clubs, more than the men. So the organization was already there. All I had to do was get its help. I went to the presidents and leaders and asked, "Can you help me?" If I succeeded in convincing them, they were ready to help—and able.

It was not my original strategy to organize womanpower to elect me; it was forced on me by the time, place, and circumstances. I never meant and never mean to start a war between women and men. It is true that women are second-class citizens, just as black people are. Tremendous amounts of talent are being lost to our society just because that talent wears a skirt. This is stupid and wrong, and I want the time to come when we can be as blind to sex as we are to color. But that time is not here, and when someone tries to use my sex against me, I delight in being able to turn the tables on him, as I did in my congressional campaign. . . .

I decided my staff would be composed of young women, for the most part, from the receptionist to my top assistants. Capitol Hill offices swarm with intelligent, Washington-wise, college-trained—and attractive—young women who do most of the work that makes a congressman look good, but often get substandard pay for it and

---

* Chisholm's opponent. Ed.

have little hope of advancing to a top staff job. The procedure in my office, I decided, would be different. I have never regretted it. Since then, I have also hired some outstanding young men, on my district and Washington staffs, but the majority is still female. More than half are black, but there has been pressure on me from some of my constituents to hire an all-black staff. "If you don't, who will?" I have been asked. What I have done is to hire the best applicants I can get. If they are black, so much the better. But the young white women on my staff are every bit as dedicated and hard working. Even the most suspicious folks from Bedford-Stuyvesant, once they come in contact with them and see how they are working for me and my district, are won over. One constituent paid one of the girls what he thought was the ultimate compliment. "She's black inside," he said.

The first big event in a freshman congressman's career is his assignment to a committee. He is not likely to get the one he wants because length of service, seniority, counts more than anything else and there are several hundred more senior members ahead of him. But for the sake of courtesy the leaders of his party ask him which one he prefers. Democrats in the House leave the power to assign members to committees in the hands of the fifteen Democrats who form the majority of the Ways and Means Committee. The Republicans have a special Committee on Committees that does the same thing. Why they need so many people to do the job is hard to understand. The only criterion that matters in picking members for committee vacancies is their length of service in Congress. Congress calls it the seniority system.

I call it the senility system.

My first choice, naturally, was the Education and Labor Committee, because I am an educator and because I had worked on and for educational legislation in the New York State Assembly. There were some vacancies on the Democratic side, and it would have made sense to take advantage of my twenty years' experience in education by appointing me to one of them. Next I would have liked to have been appointed to the Banking and Currency Committee, because it holds the purse strings for housing construction, and, next to education and employment, housing is the major need of poor people, black and white. The Post Office and Civil Service Committee would also have been relevant to my interests to some extent. A large part of post office employees are blacks or from other minority groups. Failing all those, I would have welcomed appointment to the Government Operations Committee. I thought it would be a chance to satisfy my curiosity about how government decisions are made and how federal money is spent. . . .

I learned by the grapevine that the committee had met and assigned me to the Agriculture Committee. Gilbert* assured me he had tried to get me a better assignment, but other members confided that he hadn't tried very hard.

The Agriculture Committee sounded like a ridiculous assignment for a black member from one of the country's most deprived city neighborhoods, but as a matter of fact it might not have been completely out of line. I had grown up on a farm. . . . [M]ore than that, the committee has jurisdiction over food stamp and surplus food programs and is concerned with migrant labor—subjects with which I am concerned and to which I could make a contribution.

Then I found out what my subcommittee assignments were to be: rural development and forestry. Forestry! That did it. I called Speaker McCormack. . . .

"I don't know if this is protocol, Mr. Speaker," I told him, "but I wanted to talk to you because I feel my committee and subcommittee assignments do not make much sense." John McCormack was cordial and sympathetic. His manners never fail him. Could he help me get my assignment changed to one with some relevance to my district?

"Mrs. Chisholm, this is the way it is," the Speaker said. "You have to be a good soldier."

After I was a good solider for a few years, my reward would come, he assured me.

"All my forty-three years I have been a good soldier," I said. "The time is growing late, and I can't be a good soldier any longer. It does not make sense to put a black woman representative on a subcommittee dealing with forestry. If you do not assist me, I will have to do my own thing." . . .

What he thought I meant, I will never know. . . .

There was one avenue of attack left. The committee assignments still had to be approved by the full Democratic majority at a caucus. I appealed to some of the more experienced members for

---

* Representative Jacob H. Gilbert from the Bronx, New York. Ed.

advice on how to move that my assignment be reconsidered. Representative Brock Adams of Washington coached me but warned, "The way they operate, you won't get recognized to make your motion."

He was almost right. Every time I rose, two or three men jumped up. The senior member standing is always recognized first, so they never got to me. They probably expected that I would be discouraged after a while. Men were smiling and nudging each other as I stood there trying to get the floor.

After six or seven attempts, I walked down an aisle to the "well," the open space between the front row of seats and the Speaker's dais, and stood there. I was half afraid and half enjoying the situation, as Mr. Mills,* who was in the chair, conferred with the majority leader, Carl Albert of Oklahoma. They must have been talking about what to do with me, because after the huddle ended I was recognized.

"For what purpose is the gentlewoman from New York standing in the well?" Mr. Mills asked.

"I'd been trying to get recognized for half an hour, Mr. Chairman," I said, "but evidently you were unable to see me, so I came down to the well. I would just like to tell the caucus why I vehemently reject my committee assignment."

I had a short speech prepared. It said that even though I had spent twenty years in education and served on the Education Committee of the New York Assembly for four years, I understood that geography and seniority make it difficult for a first-term representative to get his first choice of a committee assignment.

"But I think it would be hard to imagine an assignment that is less relevant to my background or to the needs of the predominately black and Puerto Rican people who elected me, many of whom are unemployed, hungry, and badly housed, than the one I was given."

I pointed out that there were only nine black members of the House, although in terms of the percentage of the population that is black there should be more than forty (I underestimated—I should have said fifty-five). So, I said, the House leadership "has a moral duty to somewhat right the balance by the putting of the nine members it has in positions where they can work effectively to help

---

* Wilbur Mills, chairman of the Ways and Means Committee. Ed.

this nation meet its critical problems of racism, deprivation, and urban decay." ...

The seniority system keeps a handful of old men, many of them southern whites hostile to every progressive trend, in control of the Congress. These old men stand implacably across the paths that could lead us toward a better future. But worse than they, I think, are the majority of members of both houses who continue to submit to the senility system. Apparently, they hope they, too, will grow to be old. ...

I knew from the start that the Washington social whirl was not for me. In Albany and New York, I had seen the political party circuit. I stayed away from it in those places and I came to Washington determined to do the same thing. Quite a few people think I'm aloof and antisocial. Actually I'm gregarious, but I am selective about whom I want to be with. ... My weekly routine, like that of most members of Congress who are within traveling distance of their home districts, is to spend four long days in the capital and three longer ones back home. I leave my office as a rule no earlier than 7:30 in the evening, later when a House session runs late. Occasionally I have a speaking engagement in the Washington area, and more rarely a television show to tape; unless there is some such obligation to discharge, I go home, have dinner, and get in bed with the memorandums, reports, and letters I will have to know about the next day. On Thursday evenings, unless there is a Friday session of the House (there seldom is unless Congress is bearing down to clear up its work for adjournment), I fly back to Brooklyn. The three-day weekends are not a time for rest. At least one full day is spent in my district office. On top of that, I have a heavy speaking schedule, taking me to all parts of the country. Nearly every Sunday morning I appear as the speaker at some church. It's a good thing I'm *not* a party type, because I just don't have the time for it. ...

Our representative democracy is not working because the Congress that is supposed to represent the voter does not respond to their needs. I believe the chief reason is that it is ruled by a small group of old men. The majority of members of the House have surrendered their power to a tiny minority—the Speaker, the party organization leaders, and the chairmen of the committees. They could take it back at any time, but apparently they are afraid to. ...

So our troubled, embattled, urban society, looking to Washington for wisdom and help, finds that the processes of change are thwarted by the control of old men whose values are those of a small-town lawyer or a feed-store operator. If they react at all to the challenge of our age, it is with incomprehension and irritation. Congress seems drugged and inert most of the time. Even when the problems it ignores build up to crises and erupt in strikes, riots, and demonstrations, it is not moved. Its idea of meeting a problem is to hold hearings or, in extreme cases, to appoint a commission. . . .

The liberals in the House strongly resemble liberals I have known through the last two decades in the civil rights conflict. When it comes time to show on which side they will be counted, they suddenly excuse themselves. Black people have come to expect this kind of betrayal. As an example, there was a time when open housing committees were fashionable in the New York City area, making an effort to pry open the barriers of bigotry that confine black and brown Americans to the city slums. Some of my liberal friends were on these committees. One suburban woman I knew well was president of a housing conference, ostensibly trying to integrate her community. Her husband, a realtor, was on a real estate men's board that was protesting against "flooding" the area with "certain kinds of people." My friend's efforts for the cause were, you can imagine, quite feeble.

When morality comes up against profit, it is seldom that profit loses. The liberal civil rights campaigners in the suburbs usually shied away when they were asked to take a firm stand that might make someone else angry, and the excuse they gave was, all too often, "We have to do business with these people." It has begun to occur to me that liberals in Congress are not very different. They say all the right things, their hearts are in the right place, but they keep trying to do things without ever actually doing anything. Without a deeper and more sincere commitment by some of its members, it will never be possible to get enough bodies and minds together to make the Congress of the United States more relevant to the times and meaningful to its constituents. . . .

At meetings of the "black delegation"—and we do meet, more than most people know—I have said, "Who needs a leader for nine people?" We each have our individual strengths. Some of us, like me, are talkers, persuaders, preachers. Others can work with other members of Congress, even conservative whites, in a way that I cannot. Others are researchers, creators, organizers. There is a danger that we will fall into the trap of not cooperating for fear of projecting one member into the limelight to the dismay of the others. Certainly I do not want that one to be me. I do not want to be the "black leader" in the House. Unfortunately, because I have national recognition thanks to the accident of being the only black woman member, at press conferences the television cameras and reporters seldom fail to cluster around me. I have seen the unhappy looks on the other members' faces when this happens, and one result is that I have sometimes ducked meetings with the media in order to stay more in the background. . . .

Sometimes southern members stop to talk to me, and I feel they wish they had a knife to open me up down the middle and see what's inside. I know they think, as many people do, that I don't understand politics. I understand it too damned well, after all my years in it, and that's why I want to change it. I did not come to Congress to behave myself and stay away from explosive issues so I can keep coming back. Under the circumstances, it's hard for me to imagine I will stay here long. There isn't much that I can do inside Congress in a legislative way. There is a great deal I can do for the people of my district by using my office and the resources it opens up to me in helping individuals and groups. I can investigate the unfair treatment of a black sergeant in the air force, and I can help a black businessman in Brooklyn apply for a Small Business Administration loan, and do so successfully in a satisfying number of cases. This kind of work is important, and it occupies a lot of my time and most of the time of my staff.

But beyond that, my most valuable function, I think, is as a voice. The accident of my prominence at this period in the struggle of my race for justice and equality can be a good thing if I use it well. I work to be a major force for change outside the House, even if I cannot be one within it. I still believe that our system of representative government can work. It deserves another chance. I feel change will come, sooner or later. . . .

Most Americans have never seen the ignorance, degradation, hunger, sickness, and futility in which many other Americans live. Until a problem reaches their doorsteps, they're not going to understand. They won't become involved in economic or political change until something brings the seriousness of the situation home to them. Until they are threatened, why should they change a system that has been fairly beneficial for a fairly large number of people? It is going to have to be the have-nots—the blacks, browns, reds, yellows, and whites who do not share in the good life that most Americans lead—who somehow arouse the conscience of the nation and thus create a conscience in the Congress. My role, as I see it, is to help them do so, working outside of Washington, perhaps, as much as inside it. . . .

[W]hen NARAL* asked me to lead its campaign, I gave it serious thought. For me to take the lead in abortion repeal would be an even more serious step than for a white politician to do so, because there is a deep and angry suspicion among many blacks that even birth control clinics are a plot by the white power structure to keep down the number of blacks, and this opinion is even more strongly held by some in regard to legalizing abortions. But I do not know any black or Puerto Rican *women* who feel that way. To label family planning and legal abortion programs "genocide" is male rhetoric, for male ears. It falls flat to female listeners, and to thoughtful male ones. Women know, and so do many men, that two or three children who are wanted, prepared for, reared amid love and stability, and educated to the limit of their ability will mean more for the future of the black and brown races from which they come than any number of neglected, hungry, ill-housed, and ill-clothed youngsters. Pride in one's race, as well as simple humanity, supports this view. Poor women of every race feel as I do, I believe. . . .

[T]ime did not permit me to be an active president of NARAL, so I asked to be made an honorary president. My appearances on television in September 1969, when the association's formation was announced, touched off one of the heaviest flows of mail to my Washington office that I have experienced. What surprised me was that it was overwhelmingly in favor of repeal. Most of the letters that disagreed with me were from Catholics, and most of them were temperate and reasoned. We sent those writers a reply that said in part, "No one should be forced to have an abortion or to use birth control methods for religious or personal reasons they oppose. But neither should others who have different views be forced to abide by what they do not and cannot believe in." Some of the mail was from desperate women who thought I could help them. "I am forty-five years old," one wrote, "and have raised a family already. Now

---

* National Abortion Rights Action League. Ed.

I find that I am pregnant and I need help. Please send me all the information." . . .

The reaction of a number of my fellow members of Congress seemed to me a little strange. Several said to me, "This abortion business . . . my God, what are you doing? That's not politically wise." It was the same old story; they were not thinking in terms of right or wrong, they were considering only whether taking a side of the issue would help them stay in office—or in this case, whether taking a stand would help me get reelected. They concluded that it would not help me, so it was a bad position for me to take. My advisers were, of course, all men. So I decided to shake them up a little with a feminist line of counterattack. "Who told you I shouldn't do this?" I asked them. "Women are dying every day, did you know that? They're being butchered and maimed. No matter what men think, abortion is a fact of life. Women will have them; they always have and always will. Are they going to have good ones or bad ones? Will the good ones be reserved for the rich while poor women have to go to quacks? . . ."

Brotherhood Week makes me sick. The original idea may have been fine, but it was naive. I have seen too many racists serve on Brotherhood Week committees, pretending to be decent human beings for seven days. What about all the other fifty-one weeks of the year? When people asked me to speak at Brotherhood Week events, I used to ask them, "What else are you doing? What are you doing about open housing? About schools? About fair employment and job training?" Now I don't get into that. I just say, "No thanks. Invite me to speak at some other event and I'll try to make it then." I'm not going to take part in a sterile ceremony by which hypocrites pretend to be cleansing themselves of the guilt of the racism they practice the rest of the time.

Much of the hypocrisy of Americans on the subject of race seems to be unconscious. Perhaps self-deception would be a better word for it. Racism is so universal in this country, so widespread and deep-seated, that it is invisible because it is so normal. . . .

On a speaking date in 1969 in St. Louis, a white member of the audience asked me a question that I have heard repeatedly. It makes me more furious each time I hear it, until I think it's a good thing I don't have a gun, or I would use it. "What do you Negroes want now?" he asked me. "You all aren't doing too bad. As a matter of fact, you're doing a lot better than some of the white people."

My God, what do we want? What does any human being want? Take away an accident of pigmentation of a thin layer of our outer skin and there is no difference between me and anyone else. All we want is for that trivial difference to make no difference. What can I say to a man who asks that? All I can do is try to explain to him why he asks the question.

"You have looked at us for years as different from you that you may never see us really. You don't understand because you think of us as second-class humans. We have been passive and accommodating through so many years of your insults and delays that you think the way things used to be is normal. When the good-natured, spiritual-singing boys and girls rise up against the white man and demand to be treated like he is, you are bewildered. All we want is what you want, no less and no more."

At one time a lot of us hoped that all it would take was to convince the white majority of the simple truth and justice of our cause, and the day of equality would dawn. That was the faith that created and sustained the civil rights movement of the 1950s and early 1960s. The movement was a failure. Everyone who was deeply involved in it hates to admit that. When one remembers the exhilaration that came from linking hands and singing, "Black and white together . . . We shall overcome," it is hard to believe that in spite of all the passion, the sacrifices, and the idealism that the civil rights movement called forth, it left little behind it but some new laws that have yet to be really enforced. The goal of the movement—integration—was not accomplished. It was not even brought closer, and that fact has at least temporarily discredited the goal.

Frustration at its failure split the civil rights movement. . . .

The reign of Jim Crow was a long and bloody one, and it is far from over yet, as the brutal killings of black students at Jackson State College reminded white America in the spring of 1970. But even when Jim Crow was at its height, there were southern whites who saw farther ahead than their neighbors, although they were equally unreconstructed. Their view, more subtle and dangerous, is still current, in the North as much as anywhere. Between the poles of complete repression and complete freedom for blacks and for any of our other racial minorities, there is another approach, that of using education as a means of continuing control over the lives of black people . . . .

The days of mind-deadening "industrial education" and of turning out half-trained black professionals to practice in the black community are not yet past, and it is time that they were. This chapter in the history of black America is another proof of the justice of black demands for control of their own institutions, particularly the schools. How can we trust even the most benevolent-appearing white, when we have seen through the years how a trap was concealed in nearly every "gift" we have been offered?

There is no longer any alternative for black Americans but to unite and fight together for their own advancement as a group. Everything else has been tried, and it has failed. This brings us again to the hardest question: How shall that fight be waged? Must it be with bullets, bombs, and guerrilla armies? God help me if I ever decide that there is no course left but that of destruction. I can feel in myself sometimes an anger that wants only to destroy everything in its path. There is a point at which passions as great as those that burn in the hearts of black Americans will not be frustrated any longer. . . . [E]verywhere, particularly in city neighborhoods like my district, there are thousands of young people who are almost ready to break loose, and there are militant groups urging them to do it. Unlike many black politicians, I still have an open line to them. The Panthers, the Moslems (black and orthodox), the Republic of New Africa, and other groups grow stronger and stronger. . . .

I used to be a moderate. I spent twenty years going to all kinds of meetings, trying to find ways all of us, black and white, could work together. Thousands like me kept saying, "Let us in a little. Give us a piece of the pie." What happened? Watts, Newark, Hartford. And what was the reaction? We started to hear a new jargon about "the urban crisis" and "law and order" and "crime in the streets."

Today I am a militant. Basically I agree with what many of the extremist groups are saying—*except* that their tactics are wrong and too often they have no program. But people had better start to understand that if this country's basic racism is not quickly and completely abolished—or at least controlled—there will be real, full-scale revolution in the streets. I do not want to see that day come. But I think often of what Malcolm once said about freedom: "You get your freedom by letting your enemy know that you'll do anything to get your freedom. Then you'll get it. It's the only way you'll get it." ...

When we look at the condition of black Americans in a historic context, we are forced to conclude that there has been relatively little change in our condition. Worse yet, we are forced to realize that there are relatively few means that we can use to change our position in the society. We are not the only ones, if you consider that roughly 2 percent of the people of this country control 80 percent of the resources and wealth. One has to be very good at make-believe to think that the remaining 98 percent are controlling anything. They are, in fact, being controlled by others. Just because all the hands on the reins of power are white, it does not follow that all whites have their hands on that power. But they feel that they do. This fact is important, because it reveals to us one of the major functions of racism in this society.

Racism keeps people who are being managed from finding out the truth through contact with each other. It serves the insidious purpose of the wars in George Orwell's novel *1984*. Orwell's imaginary world is a lot like the real world for black Americans today. But many of us, and most whites, have consistently refused to accept that they live in a managed society where conflict between the races is maintained and managed because it serves a purpose. ...

How can we define a role in this society for the black politician? First, whether he represents an urban or a rural black district or a racially split one, there is one thing he should never forget—that he is black. Because his opponents won't forget it, nor will the electorate. ...

We have no adequate profile of the average black elected official yet, but it is apparent that they are overwhelmingly male—a trend that I have to deplore, because the most disenfranchised and exploited minority in this country is still its women. More women must come to the forefront, but I do not think that they have to do so at the expense of black male candidates. There are too many offices held by the declared enemies of both groups for blacks and women to fight over who is going to run. We should be concerned with finding and running every qualified candidate we can for every office that is open, from county commissioner to U.S. senator and for President and Vice President.

The majority of black elected officials are registered either as

Democrats or Independents. Only about fifty to fifty-five, it is esti-
mated, are Republicans. But under whatever label, most of them
seem to share a distaste for following the old party lines. The average age of black elected officials is somewhat lower than that of
white ones, and that may be because the growing tone of militancy
in the black community demands youth. There are still old-line
black politicians around whose primary interest is lining their pockets, but it seems that the political atmosphere is growing more
hostile to them and more friendly to candidates who are ready
to question priorities, fight for what they believe, and refuse to
compromise when they believe that a compromise is not good
enough for those whom they represent. If it is true that the black
electorate is becoming more sophisticated and more militant about
positive change, as I am sure it is, the effect will be to demand that
candidates be the best choice available to the community at the
time. . . .

Of course, all this theoretical discussion should not lead anyone
to lose sight of the three basic elements of political action—registration, financing, and campaigning. Without these three founda-
tions, successful political activity is impossible no matter how
sophisticated its theoretical basis. People often ask me how I burst
on the national political scene so quickly. What they fail to realize
is that in Brooklyn there have been black people working toward
political freedom for more than twenty years. They do not know
the efforts of groups like the Bedford-Stuyvesant Political League,
the Unity Democratic Club, and others that in all the Bedford-
Stuyvesants of this country have been working, organizing, collecting, and fighting toward freedom from white political control of
black communities.

From the beginning I felt that there were only two ways to create change for black people in this country—either politically or by
open armed revolution. Malcolm defined it succinctly—the ballot
or the bullet. Since I believe that human life is uniquely valuable
and important, for me the choice had to be the creative use of the
ballot. I still believe I was right. I hope America never succeeds in
changing my mind. . . .

We must become revolutionaries in the style of Gandhi and
King. Then, working toward our own freedom, we can help the
others work free from the traps of their stereotypes. In the end,

antiblack, antifemale, and all forms of discrimination are equivalent to the same thing—antihumanism. The values of life must be maintained against the enemies in every guise. We can do it by confronting people with their own humanity and their own inhumanity whenever we meet them, in the streets, in school, in church, in bars, in the halls of legislatures. We must reject not only the stereotypes that others have of us but also those we have of ourselves and others.

In particular, I am certain that more and more American women must become involved in politics. It could be the salvation of our nation. If there were more women in politics, it would be possible to start cleaning it up. Women I have known in government have seemed to me to be much more apt to act for the sake of a principle or moral purpose. They are not as likely as men to engage in deals, manipulations, and sharp tactics. A larger proportion of women in Congress and every other legislative body would serve as a reminder that the real purpose of politicians is to work for the people.

The woman who gets into politics will find that the men who are already there will treat her as the high school counselor treats girls. They see her as someone who is obviously just playing at politics part-time, because, after all, her real place is at home being a wife and mother. I suggested a bright young woman as a candidate in New York City a while ago; she had unlimited potential and with good management and some breaks could become an important person to the city. A political leader rejected her. "Why invest all the time and effort to build up the gal into a household name," he asked me, "when she's pretty sure to drop out of the game to have a couple of kids at just about the time we're ready to run her for mayor?"

Many women have given their lives to political organizations, laboring anonymously in the background while men of far less ability managed and mismanaged the public trust. These women hung back because they knew the men would not give them a chance. They knew their place and stayed in it. The amount of talent that has been lost to our country that way is appalling. I think one of my major uses is as an example to the women of our country, to show them that if a woman has ability, stamina, organizational skill, and a knowledge of the issues she can win public office. And if I can do it, how much more hope should that give to white women, who have only one handicap?

One distressing thing is the way men react to women who assert their equality: their ultimate weapon is to call them unfeminine. They think she is antimale; they even whisper that she's probably a lesbian, a tactic some of the Women's Liberation Front have encountered. I am not antimale any more than I am antiwhite, and I am not antiwhite, because I understand that white people, like black ones, are victims of a racist society. They are products of their time and place. It's the same with men. This society is as antiwoman as it is antiblack. It has forced males to adopt discriminatory attitudes toward females. Getting rid of them will be very hard for most men—too hard, for many of them.

Women are challenged now as never before. Their numbers in public office, in the professions, and in other key fields are declining, not increasing. The decline has been gradual and steady for the last twenty years. It will be difficult to reverse at first. The women who undertake to do it will be stigmatized as "odd" and "unfeminine" and must be prepared to endure such punishment. Eventually the point will be made that women are not different from men in their intelligence and ability and that women who aspire to important jobs—president of the company, member of Congress, and so on—are *not* odd and unfeminine. They aspire for the same reasons as any man—they think they can do the job and they want to try.

For years to come, most men will jeer at the women's liberation groups that are springing up. But they will someday realize that countless women, including their own wives and especially their daughters, silently applaud the liberation groups and share their goals, even if they are unable to bring themselves to rebel openly. American women are beginning to respond to our oppression. While most of us are not yet revolutionaries, the time is coming when we will be. The world must be taught that, to use the words of Women's Liberation activist Robin Morgan, "Women are not inherently passive or peaceful. We're not inherently anything but human. And like every other oppressed people rising up today, we're out for our freedom by any means necessary." . . .

If my story has any importance, apart from its curiosity value—the fascination of being a "first" at anything is a durable one—it is,

her process of reconciliation with her mother, a process accelerated by her father's death in an automobile accident in 1967.

Her memoir opens with one of her visits home. Chernin evokes with painful vividness the tension of mother, daughter, and granddaughter, each fighting for control, each wanting to see her view of the world vindicated. The rest of *In My Mother's House* chronicles the final skirmishes that end the war between mother and daughter, and captures the storytelling capacity of both mother and daughter as they relive the life of four generations of the family. Chernin is a poet, and the language of *In My Mother's House* swings between lyrical and tense political polemic.

Chernin now works as a psychiatrist in Berkeley, and shares her life with Renate Stendahl. From her poetry and prose it is clear that being Jewish, and what her imaginative life can draw from those roots, is her central concern as a writer. Her poetry is devoted to mysticism, to the interpretation of the female experience, and to exploring the meaning of the female in traditional Judaism.

Chernin's technique of having the mother in this duo tell her own story in the author's words works well, and is reminiscent of Sally Morgan's use of the storytelling mode to recapture her Aboriginal past. Its only defect is that the reader is never told what the basis for reconciliation between the generations really is, and so cannot judge whether it is real and will continue in the future.

IN MY MOTHER'S HOUSE

July 1974

Since I was a small girl I have been fighting with my mother. When the family was eating dinner some petty disagreement would arise and I'd jump up from the table, pick up a plate and smash it against the wall. I'd go running from the room, slamming doors behind me.

By the age of thirteen I insisted that Hegel was right and not Marx. "The Idea came first," I cried out from the bathroom, which had the only door in the house that locked. "The Spirit came before material existence."

In the afternoons I read books. I started on the left side of the bookcase, at the top shelf, and thumbed my way through every book in the library. *The Classics of Marxism, Scottsboro Boy, State and Revolution* by Lenin, a story about the Huck Bella Hak in the Philippines, stories about the Spanish civil war.

I understood little of what I read, but I built a vocabulary, a mighty arsenal of weapons to use against my mother.

Then, when she came into the house, I was ready for her. Any opinion she uttered, I took the opposite point of view. If she liked realism, I preferred abstract art. If she believed in internationalism, I spoke about the necessity to concentrate on local conditions.

Twenty years later nothing has changed. We still refuse to understand one another, both of us still protesting the fact we are so little alike.

Her voice rises; she has clenched her jaw. "You're going to tell me about the exploitation of the workers?"

I answer belligerently, shaking with passion. "There is the same defiance of authority in the scholarship I do, the same passion for truth in the poetry I write as there has been in your life."

"Truth? We're going to discuss truth now?"

"And it changes, doesn't it? From generation to generation?"

The silence that follows this outburst is filled up through every cubic inch of itself by my shame. We are not even out of the airport and already I've lost my temper. And this time especially I had wanted so much to draw close to her. Surely, it must be possible after all these years. . . .

She takes a deep breath, looks around the room as if she has misplaced something, and then delivers herself of one of those weighty utterances which have been troubling the atmosphere all day. . . .

My mother's conversation frequently assumes this rhetorical tone. It comes, I suppose, from the many years she has been a public speaker. Even her English changes at such moments. It loses its Yiddish inflection and her voice rings out as if she were speaking through a megaphone. But today I know that all these statements are intended for me.

"Never mind how old I am," she says. "Never mind when I was born. Or where, or to what mother. There's only one important fact about a life. And that one is always a beginning. A woman who lives for a cause, a woman with dedication and unbreakable devotion—that's a woman who deserves the name of woman."

Has she been rehearsing this little speech? I ask myself. Has she been going over it again and again in her mind, as she waited for me at the airport? . . .

She is standing next to the fire . . . and now she says, "My mother knew how to read and to write. Isn't it so, Gertrude? Mama was a literate woman."

This fact makes no impression upon my daughter. She has no context for wondering at this achievement, so rare, so remarkable in a Jewish woman of the shtetl. On me, however, these words make a tremendous impression. The tone in which my mother speaks them moves me even to tears. "Mama was a literate woman," she repeats with a strangely wistful pride. Now she looks significantly at me and I know that we have come finally to the end of all this hinting.

"You are a writer," she says. "So, do you want to take down the story of my life?"

I am torn by contradiction. I love this woman. She was my first great aching love. All my life I have wanted to do whatever she asked of me, in spite of our quarreling.

She's old, I say to myself. What will it take from you? Give this to her. She's never asked anything from you as a writer before. Give this. You can always go back to your own work later. . . .

I'm afraid. I fear, as any daughter would, losing myself back into the mother.

I sit down on the edge of the gray chair that used to be my father's favorite reading place. It occurs to me that I should reason with her, tell her how much it means to me now to go on my own way. "Mama," I say, intending to bring everything out into the open. And then she turns toward me expectantly, a raw look of hope and longing in her eyes.

I learned to understand my mother's life when I was a small girl, waiting for her to come home in the afternoons. Each night I would set the table carefully, filling three small glasses with tomato juice while my father tossed a salad. Then we would hear my mother's car pull up in front of the house and I could go into the living room and kneel on the gray couch in front of the window to watch her come across the lawn, weighed down with newspapers and pamphlets and large blue boxes of envelopes for the mailing I would help to get out that night. . . .

The twilight comes into the room. It spreads itself out on the stacks of magazines, the lacquered Chinese dish, the little carved man with a blue patch in his wooden trousers. Everyone begins to look as if they have been brushed with understanding. For here finally is the clear shape of the story my mother wants me to write down—this tale of four generations, immigrants who have come to take possession of a new world. It is a tale of transformation and development—the female reversal of that patriarchal story in which the power of the family's founder is lost and dissipated as the inheriting generations decline and fall to ruin. A story of power. . . .

Now we are making the bed together, smoothing the sheet and tucking it with careful folds at the corners, while my mother discourses upon women and the making of beds. Listening, half-listening to her, I observe the way she never loses an opportunity for giving instruction. "My own mother," she says, "told me not to learn to cook or to sew. 'You'll marry a rich man, then you won't need it. If he's a poor man, better you don't know how to become his slave.'"

Now she is telling us, as the blanket flaps up into the air, and, laughing, we take hold of the corners and spread it out, the way the world is ordered by these smoothings and tuckings. The way, as I remind her, I needed her there at night when I was a child because no one else could tuck me in tightly enough. How, when she was arrested during the McCarthy time and went to jail, it seemed that my father, no matter how hard he tried, could not make the bed covers smooth, and could not braid my hair so that the braids were tight enough. The way, without her, things always seemed to come undone.

Now we pull the corners taut and slip them under the mattress. My mother passes her hand over the blanket and I recall how much I loved this gesture when I was a girl, believing it made sleep possible and kept it peaceful. . . .

ROSE CHERNIN'S STORY

We easily got used to life in America but the misery in our home we could never get used to. My father beat my mother. Always he would yell at her. There were terrible scenes. . . . She was a gentle person and he broke her spirit. He broke her mind. . . .

My mother found it easier when I started to work. I was earning twenty-nine dollars a week. The wages were high for those times. There were no deductions, except for war bonds. They were a form of savings. So, I was taking home about twenty-five dollars a week for five and a half days' work. Naturally, I gave the money to my mother for the family. "Now we can live a little," she said.

I loved my mother, I wanted to help her. I would lie awake at night and remember those fists beating at her, breaking her down. Destroying her. . . .

The factories in Waterbury at that time were producing ammunition twenty-four hours a day. Mama rented out our bedrooms to the night-shift workers. When we would get up in the morning they would go into our beds. The months passed, our lives took on a pattern.

In bed I would sit with my book, falling asleep on the first pages. . . .

Then came my break. Because of the shortage of labor, they needed high-school children in war industries. They shortened the school day so the students could get out by one o'clock from school and still put in a full day at the factory. It was a grueling schedule, let me tell you. . . .

So I went down to register at Crosby. It was the college-preparatory high school. Very high up. I put on my best clothes. When I got there I talked to the principal. "I'm a factory worker," I said. "I want to go into the high school." But then suddenly I lost my nerve. He was looking at me. "Maybe," I said, "I should go over and register at Welby." Welby was the commercial school. I felt I was stepping beyond myself.

Meanwhile, he's giving a long look at me. And he says, "Go into Crosby."

I will never forget it. I looked up at him. I said, "I don't have money for college."

"Listen to me, young lady. You came to this country in 1914. (This was 1917.) If you can learn English the way you did, you don't know what will happen in four years. You're an intelligent girl. Go to school. Maybe some good luck will make it possible for you to go to college."

I, Rose Chernin, go to college? Think who I was. An immigrant girl, fourteen years old, a factory worker, without a future. But now I stood there. In the office of an American high school. I heard the possibility I might go to college. . . .

In this way I went to school and I could still earn the twenty-five dollars a week. You think my father gave us money? We never knew what he did with his money and by that time, let me tell you, we never cared. All we wanted was for him to leave Mama alone. One day, finally, I said to him, "If you ever hit my mother again I am going to hit you back." . . .

After that childhood everything was easy. Nobody could break me. I knew, even as a child, that this would be so. . . .

By that time I had already met your father. He and his brother Max were in the same school with my sister Celia and me. We all lived on the same block and often we went to school together. . . .

Paul Kusnitz was three years older than me, already a senior in high school when I was a freshman. And a senior doesn't bother much with a freshman, of course. But because we were neighbors and we were Jewish, and our families both came from Russia, and because my mother was a friend of his mother, this walking together occurred. We very seldom talked together. The girls walked by themselves and the boys walked alongside or in back of us.

But one day Paul Kusnitz suddenly asks me if I'd be interested in reading something. He came right up to me and gave me some material. It was the *New York Call*. He stood next to me and he said, "You ought to read this."

So I said, "What kind of paper is this?"

"It's a socialist paper," he told me. . . .

So I read the paper. Why not? It made sense to me. For the first time I learned that there were classes. I found out that there were people struggling for a better system than capitalism. . . .

[O]ne day Paul Kusnitz comes again. This time he asks me to go with him to hear a conscientious objector who would lecture, a woman speaker named Kate Richards O'Hare, who had served some time in prison. She was coming to speak in the workers' hall and I decided right away I would go with him. From the moment Paul Kusnitz mentioned this woman I thought about nothing else. I felt, something is coming here, something from the world, to this little town. . . .

So the night arrived. We walked into that meeting and it was packed. It was the first time in my life I heard the voice of a radical woman. It stirred me. I sat at the edge of my seat. I held my breath. I didn't want to miss a word. Who ever heard of such a woman before? I wanted to be just like her. And I thought I could be. . . .

One day my father left us. He sold his store to an auctioneer and left for Pennsylvania where those Jerome relatives were living.

He never wrote to us, he never made an effort to contact us. By then, a fourth girl, Lillian, was born in our family. There were five children at home now and Lillian was only a baby. At first, it was just terrible, and especially for me as the eldest. Onto my shoulders came now the responsibility for Mama and the children. How long had we been in the country by then? Five years? So consider. . . .

[Rose Chernin and her family settle in New York. Ed.]

[W]hen I was twenty-two years old, a young man came to New York. My phone rang one night. I heard a voice asking if I was Rose Chernin. So who else would I be?

The voice said, "I am Paul Kusnitz, from Waterbury." It was he who had given me the socialist material while we walked to school. "Do you remember me?"

"Of course, Paul Kusnitz. Are you still reading the *Call*?"

"I just came to New York a few weeks ago. I graduated from MIT, I'm an engineer. I've been looking for a job but it's not so easy to find anything in engineering."

Now Paul Kusnitz was something special. Not everybody goes to MIT. He got a scholarship to study there, but MIT only admitted so many Jews a year. And they never filled the quota because the Jewish men wouldn't go into engineering. After they graduated they were discriminated against. Paul was living in Brooklyn, with another Crosby student.

I said to him, "Well, do you want to come over?"

"Of course. I'll come on Saturday."

So it began. Paul Kusnitz made a tremendous impression on me. He was a very handsome young man and he dressed in the latest fashion. He wore spats, he had a waxed mustache; he was more mature, of course, but his eyes still twinkled the way they did in Waterbury. . . .

I asked him why he had chosen engineering.

"I'm good in math," he said. We were sitting in the kitchen at the table. "I have always liked the idea of building something. I thought that as an engineer I would be able to travel. I want to make a contribution to the underdeveloped countries of the world."

I stopped stirring my tea. This man, I thought, is somebody you look at twice. "So which underdeveloped countries, Paul?" I asked. . . .

"I want to go to the Soviet Union." . . .

One day he asked me to marry him, but I felt that I was not ready for marriage. Behind me was the example of my father and mother. . . .

Paul found a job as an engineer, working for the city. He came to tell me and he asked me to marry him again. So I agreed, we would marry but we did not decide upon a date. Paul went home to tell his people. He was supposed to stay in Waterbury for a week. But after two days he called up and said to me, "I'm coming home."

I met him at the train, I looked at him and I thought an avalanche had hit him. He was pale and he looked very sad. I asked him what had happened and he said, "Don't ask. My family just let me have it when I told them I was going to marry you."

You can imagine the objection they would have to me. I was a woman living alone, going out with men and doing everything else they could imagine for a girl who lives in New York. . . .

"Paul," I said to him, "you didn't marry me yet. I'm not holding you to any promises. You're a free man, Paul Kusnitz. You can change your mind."

You should have seen the look on his face. For this look he won from me a friend for the rest of his life. "You think," he says, "I would ask for their permission?"

Now Paul cut his family off completely. His mother began writing letters right away. But Paul would not answer. He pressed me to set a date for our marriage but I was still hesitating. . . .

A few years went by, I no longer remember how many. Paul Kusnitz and I got married; we went to live in the Bronx. Paul was working by then on the Eighth Avenue subway. One afternoon he took a half day from work, we went down to City Hall and we got married. That's how it happened, completely natural. And for this, believe me, I have been happy all my life. If I kept on drifting, who knows? . . .

I read Marxism with your father, I went out to the Russian Club, we supported the strikes of the workers, but something held me back.

Already in the shtetl we were thinking about this country. There we will get an education, when Papa sends for us we will go to America, there we won't be poor anymore.

But now I was hearing about things; I was learning about the exploitation of the workers and we heard about the way Negroes were living in the South. If a Negro man looked at a white woman he would be lynched. We heard stories about the Ku Klux Klan and these bothered me, they really bothered me. All this reminded me of the pogrom; this we were used to for the Jews in Russia. But here in America? . . .

[T]hen it was 1931 or 1932, the beginning of the Great Depression. Millions of workers were unemployed. There was no social security, no unemployment insurance. . . .

[O]ne day, the Communist Party called a mass demonstration in Union Square. One hundred thousand men and women came out. William Foster was the main speaker. Mounted police surrounded the crowd. The slogans we carried read: JOBS OR WAGES. . . .

But then something happened I will never forget. The police rode into the crowd and scattered the people. In America, police on horseback rode into the crowd. . . .

That is how I remember it. His words showed us the way out. I felt the justice of what he said. We could not wait for someone to give to us what we needed. We, the workers, had to make demands. Then I looked up and I could see those horses coming. It was a nightmare. And we were paralyzed. They were riding straight toward us, riding us down. Suddenly someone screamed. It was, how can I tell you? Never in my life, before or since, have I heard anything like that shriek. I heard, in that cry . . . to me it seemed we were standing in a village and the Cossacks were riding down. You could go so far back in Jewish history and always you would find that cry. . . . I stood there, looking out at the crowd. My fear was gone. I felt angry, I felt exhilarated, and I felt purposeful. That was the day I joined the Communist Party. . . .

We were poor. Your father was always worried about what would happen if he lost the job. He talked and thought about it constantly. This worry began to characterize his life. I hated the system for doing this to him. We lived in a small apartment, six floors up. I was a mother, I was active in various political organizations, and your father earned the money to support us. He read and studied Marxism, he belonged to a study club and at night he taught a class in Marxist theory. After dinner, you could see him there, at the kitchen table, the sleeves rolled up. He and another man would be playing chess. Sometimes, when I was going out the door, I'd turn back. There he'd be, a man with such a gentle look on his face. Imagine, I'd think to myself, this is Paul Kusnitz. This man is my husband.

Always, we respected each other. I was proud of his education. I was proud of his understanding. And he admired me for the way I could speak to people and organize. In our home there was, between the husband and wife, something never known in our family before. . . .

[W]e began to organize. We formed Unemployed Councils. They were spontaneous people's organizations and I want you to know about them because I helped to organize them from the first day. In this activity I was already involved before I joined the Communist Party. . . .

We would go about the streets advertising the neighborhood councils. We'd ask people to come and told them to bring whatever they could spare. There was always something to eat in the councils. People would drop in, we'd get them to work on a pamphlet, we would involve them in a conversation. Coming off the street in those days, out of that despair, you can imagine the impact the council made upon them.

The women were organized to monitor the prices of food all the time. If an item became too expensive in a particular store, we immediately went on strike. Again, we came with the children in the carriage. We picketed with the sign: DON'T PATRONIZE THIS GROCERY. THEY ARE CHARGING TOO MUCH FOR BREAD.

These strikes were very successful. Nobody would cross our picket lines. . . .

I went to California with Nina, for a rest and to visit my family.

There everything was the same. But now it was a terrible shock to me. I had forgotten about it. Here was my life. Such purpose it had. In this small life of a person, was something so big, maybe already the future of the world. . . .

I had come from New York, from the campaign, the strikes, the council, from all our activity. And there was Celia, sitting in the delicatessen store, selling salami. . . .

Then, I heard from your father; he was working for the city of New York, on the Eighth Avenue subway. The work was completed and all the engineers were laid off. So, finally it had happened. Everything we feared. Now, what would happen?

In New York the only jobs available for the engineers were in those cubbyholes in the subway, exchanging dimes for nickels. Paul couldn't accept the job; none of the engineers would accept it, they agreed.

He was the sort of man who didn't like to show he was upset. But this time he couldn't hide it. We talked many times, from Los Angeles to New York, and one time he said there was maybe the possibility of finding work, as an engineer, in the Soviet Union. He had been down to Amtorg, the American Trading Company, and he heard they were starting to build a subway in Moscow.

Finally, he came to me in Los Angeles. We took an apartment together and tried to find work. And meanwhile, we were waiting to hear about the Soviet Union. . . .

We had, at the time, about two hundred dollars in savings. Food was very cheap. The government was giving away beans and canned milk for children. You could live on three or four dollars a week. Everything was cheaper than in New York, especially the fruits and vegetables. The Kusnitz family was still in the meat business and most of them had already moved to California. We lived on our savings and we waited. . . .

Then, one day, we received notice that jobs were open in the Soviet Union. In New York a group of engineers was forming. We were going to Moscow!

We went to say good-bye to my mother and we told her that we're leaving for the Soviet Union. She said, "Where will you live?"

"We're going to live in Moscow, Mama. Paul is going to build a subway."

"In Moscow!" she says. "You can't live in Moscow!"

"Mama," I said to her, "what do you mean?"

"No Jews are allowed to live in Moscow."

The world hadn't changed for her. For her, it was all exactly the way she had left it twenty years before. I said, "Mama, there was a revolution. And now we're going to live in Moscow and work on the subway." . . .

[Kim Chernin hears her mother's story differently. Ed.]

[F]or an instant, I am standing outside myself. We see the world differently. What of that? We're not enemies. We're only, of necessity, a mother and daughter.

"I know there was poverty in the shtetl, Mama." My voice

speaks these words calmly as if they were facts. "I know that I can't easily explain the nostalgia I feel for that vanished world."

She is sitting forward in her chair, her eyes narrowing. But now she tilts her head to the side, listening the way I have seen birds listen to what the world around them is saying.

And I know that between us the time has finally come. I will tell her, simply, the way the world looks to me. And she will listen.

"What we—my generation—long for, grew up in the shtetl in spite of hunger and dust; a sacred dimension to daily life, which held its own alongside the terror and violence."

For a moment, she says nothing. I have the curious sensation that I have spoken in some strange tongue that is incomprehensible to her.

But then, clearing her throat, she says, "This is a different shtetl than the one I knew. Or maybe," she whispers, and a look of great weariness comes into her eyes, "maybe I have forgotten." . . .

I find it impossible to talk. One false move and I shall lose her again. But how can I remain silent in the face of this terrible vulnerability? There must be some right word, a gesture, something so perfectly modulated it will be neither too little nor too much. . . .

I am stunned to silence by the fact that she has not closed me out of her despair. And now, raising her fists to her temples, she hammers upon them in a sudden excess of grief. She says, echoing me: "Mama." She says it once, softly. Then there is that closing down in her face, a look of rage that her secrets have been exposed, a flash of accusation, of warning. Our intimacy is gone.

But in the silence that pushes itself between us there is a new sensation. She has given me this moment of truth. . . .

SHE COMES TO VISIT

June 1978

I stand with my hands in my pockets, trying not to look excited. What a foolish person I am, I think to myself, as I notice how fast my heart is beating. It is four years since I last saw her. Dry mouth, moist palms, I have all the symptoms of a young woman in love. But I am thirty-eight years old. And now as I glance over at the passengers it is my mother I catch sight of, a small white suitcase in her hand, her red cape folded neatly over her arm, as she comes down the steps from the airplane.

Suddenly, I am overcome by feeling; the years during which I have kept myself from her rise up aching and roaring in my cheeks. This is love I feel, forgetting my embarrassment, pushing past the small crowd of people gathering at the gate, and I run now, opening my arms to her. She is frowning in the light, the recognition dawning as I sweep her against me, rocking her. "Kimmie, Kimmie," she is saying, her hand against my cheek, refusing to let me take the suitcase out of her hand, slipping her arm through mine.

Soon, she will tell me that I have grown taller. "You're so thin," she says and stops walking although the other passengers press up behind her. "And you know," she muses, her voice full of astonishment, as if what she is about to say had not been said every time she has seen me over the years, "you've grown taller."

"Mama," I say, still trying to get the suitcase away from her through every sort of subterfuge. But she holds on with a mighty grip, refusing to be distracted by my hand slipping over hers, affectionately. "I can manage," she says. "I can manage."

I have parked my car in the red zone but there is no ticket. I drive too fast going to the freeway but she is too excited to notice. "Are you hungry?" she asks. "Are you?" "I could eat," she says, "if you could." "Well," I say, "if you're hungry, why shouldn't we eat?" . . .

[S]he suddenly . . . says in a loud voice, "It's been too long." And her words have all the solidity of simple, factual statement. Then, hurrying, in case I think she is reproaching me: "I understand," she says. "A writer needs time alone, without distraction, to work on the material." . . .

When we are leaving the car I lock her suitcase into the trunk but I take along with me the manuscript on which I have been working. She raises her eyebrows, whispering, as if we were conspirators. "Our book?" she says.

As we walk through Jack London Square she takes it from my hands, folds her arms across it, and carries it against her breast. . . .

The First and Last Chance Bar is a tiny room. The floor slopes at a steep angle and she, determined not to spoil our day, laughs as she takes my arm. "You remember," she says, "the way we read *call of the wild* when you were eight years old?"

"Jack London used to come to this place. Now it's only for tourists. But I always promised myself to bring you here one day."

"Never mind," she says, patting me confidingly on the hand. "Am I too proud to be a tourist?"

"Well, girls," the bartender says, "what will it be?"

Oh, mister, I think, you don't know what you're asking for.

"Pardon me," she says, "you are talking to two women."

"Well, ladies," he answers, "no insult intended," and turns his back to prepare the drinks I order.

She takes a matchbook out of an ashtray, turns it up and down on the bar. Finally: "You're a nice man," she says to his back. "Why shouldn't you be careful what you say?"

But now she thumbs through the manuscript, her face furrowed. I notice that I am as eager still for her judgment as I was when I used to bring my school essays to her for approval, proud and terrified as I set my writing down on the kitchen table with a thump. But I am interrupted in my recollection by the return of the bartender. "You live around here?" he says to me, setting down the frosted glasses of tomato juice and vodka.

"She's a writer," my mother answers. "She lives in Berkeley. And this," she says, lifting up the manuscript, "is a book she's writing about my life."

After dinner, she wanders through my house, strolling along with me as if we were on tour together through some famous villa that does not really interest us now. Her hand passes over the Tiffany lamp, she touches the chain, moves on and stands in front of the grand piano, touching the keys without making a sound. . . .

A ship moves out under the Golden Gate Bridge. A late bird passes over the holly tree below us and my mother sighs. "One day we'll be done with this," she says. "My whole life will be in the story. And then we'll have to start all over again. But this time you will be telling. Everything I don't know about you. . . ."

And so we sit down in the rattan chair and the blue swing. Again, she bends over and touches the large black purse that always stands next to her. "You see," she says, "I have been making preparations." Very carefully she takes out a pad of yellow paper, folded into thirds and tied with a ribbon. Holding it at a slant, to catch the light from the window behind her, she reads, "It was November, the early winter of 1932. We were on our way to the Soviet Union. . . .

"They were building the great subway. And how was Paul

going to Moscow? As a professional man he was going, as an engineer, to make an important contribution. Now I, too, of course was happy. How else could it be? But for me all this would not be so easy. What did I have to offer? This used to worry me. I talked it over with Paul. 'I am an organizer,' I said. 'And who needs rent strikes and Unemployed Councils in the Soviet Union?'"

There are times when I am sorely tempted to answer these rhetorical questions. But that of course is only my playfulness, and just now it has to wrestle with a growing sense of dread. Coming soon, out of these stories, although she pretends not to be aware of it, is our most serious confrontation. Her voice, however, gives no sign of this: "It was, after all, a big thing that was happening to us. We were, as you know, poor people. For us travel was always out of the question. But now, what happened? We went to Europe in tourist class on the *Aquitania*. It was the same boat that brought my family to America in steerage almost twenty years before. The same boat!

"You see? I was going back to Russia. And in Russia, there was no more Czar. The Soviet Union in 1932 was something new in the world. In the whole history of humankind, who had seen such an experiment before?"

Here she breaks off and frowns at me. But I expect this. I have heard the story so many times before and am familiar with all its ritual interruptions.

"You maybe don't see it like this," she says and we are both aware that we stand, once again, at the edge of our interminable quarrel.

But this time she stops herself, willing her own silence. And now, when she speaks, her voice seems to search for a new way, something never tried by her before. It falters, it confesses: "I'll never forget the day," she says, "I came into your room. You remember?"

She expects me to know what she is talking about and, in fact, I know. But she has never mentioned this before.

"You were maybe sixteen years old. 'So what's wrong?' I say to you. Then, I notice you're holding a book. And you're shaking, literally shaking. 'Tell me, what is it?' Nothing, not a word from you.

"Okay, I go out, I shut the door. Later, after dinner I go to see what you were reading. You never mentioned a word, never told me what you were thinking. The Khrushchev report. But I knew. That's when all the trouble began."

For both of us this memory cuts. It reminds me of the time I told her I was no longer a Marxist and she stood with her hands on the ironing board and wept. It reminds me of the way I myself wept, in front of a university bulletin board, looking at the face of a Jewish woman imprisoned in the Soviet Union.

I look at my mother. She is watching me with her hawk's eyes. More than anything in the world I want us to agree, to share a vision, to experience the world identically.

The moment breaks open, it seems to tear from our hands all that we have accomplished so far together. We can't go on, the story ends. To tell her life I would have to be able to listen to these stories about the Soviet Union the way I listened as a child. But now I can only hear them through my disillusion.

For a moment I think she is going to sigh, but she only straightens her shoulders. And then, in the same instant, we are talking.

"Mama, I want you to understand . . ."

"It's not your fault," she answers, simultaneously.

Then her words come more easily. Her conviction carries them, giving them a power they would not have if they were spoken by another person.

"By the time you came into the world a person could take for granted the socialist revolution. But for us the Soviet Union was . . . what should I say? In that underdeveloped country, the impossible was happening. This made you feel that even to a worker, to a poor Jew, even to a woman, the world, history even, the whole future belonged."

She stops, looking at me with an eagerness that breaks my heart. I see that now, for the first time in our life together, she acknowledges, without blaming me, the differences between us. And, in the wonder of this, I find myself as open and innocent as a child. . . .

For a moment, completely revealed, I see the truth of her life in her eyes, in all its severe, problematical beauty, willing the world to fit the architecture of her dream. . . .

"We were very busy before we left for the Soviet Union. . . . We were buying clothes. We knew the winters were cold in the Soviet Union and of course we heard there were shortages in consumer goods. And so we were traveling there with twenty-two crates of belongings.

"Well, the day comes and we are arriving in the Soviet Union. Can you imagine? Where will you look first? What will you talk about? . . .

"Now began our life in Moscow. But this life, I tell you, was not like anything we lived before. We would walk in Red Square, looking at the walls of the Kremlin. Here was a city where a Jew could hardly even walk before. And so we would marvel, all this which belonged once to the Czar was now for the people. . . .

"The trade unions gave free tickets to all the cultural events. The Moscow Art Theater, the greatest theater in the world. The Bolshoi Ballet, where else could you see such dancing?

"But even this was not for us the most important thing in the Soviet Union. You must have security in life. In the United States, when your father was working he used to say, 'Well I don't know whether I'll be working very long.' This was something you didn't hear in the Soviet Union. On the job you had all the conditions a worker seeks. These maybe couldn't be so important to you. An eight-hour day, extra pay for overtime, free health care, four weeks vacation every year. But for us, it was everything, everything we always wanted. . . .

"Why did I leave the Soviet Union?" she asks, as if no time had passed since she fell silent late last night. "To that question you won't get an answer in three words. People ask me. But to you I want to be certain the answer I give is the right one. I have to go looking, after all this time. . . ."

I look at my mother. A fine point of light opens into her eyes. And now she stares at me as if she could find the truth of her own life in my face.

"I remember, in 1934, the International Longshoremen's Union called for a general strike. This I read about when I was in Moscow. Right away I thought, Oh my God, we should go home. I wanted to get on a boat and go back to California. You see what I'm trying to tell you? The longshoremen were the most underpaid workers in the class."

Her voice is rising now. It is louder than the voice that has been in her mouth all morning. The soapbox voice, I used to call it. "For years," she says, "the longshoremen were never organized. They finished up a job and then maybe they would be without work for weeks. But now, these same men were able to get the support of the other unions. They could lead a successful strike."

Suddenly I feel an immense rush of love for her, this woman struggling so hard to remain more powerful than what she feels. But I am afraid to touch her. . . . "Can you imagine what this meant?" she says. "I thought something we were waiting for, working for, dreaming for in America was now going to occur."

She stops walking. Her voice, even louder than before, comes in a rush. "As you know, we had a three-year contract with the Moscow subway. Your father was happy in Moscow. There he wanted to remain for the rest of his life." . . .

[Rose Chernin returns to California on vacation—but really searching for a way to reconnect with the American labor movement. Ed.]

"So there I am, on . . . vacation from the Soviet Union. And here are the organizers, our own people. I knew some of them. They were Communists. I met them before we left for the Soviet Union. . . .

"Of course your father was upset when I told him I was going to stay in America and organize a defense for the [strikers*]. We spoke about it. This talking went on for weeks. But you know how I am, I had an argument for every argument he raised up. I was very happy with your father. But I was thinking, the revolution will occur any day now. I was afraid I would miss it.

"To you this is perhaps something to laugh at now. But America in those days you can't understand from your own experience of life. For us in those years it felt like the last days of the capitalist system. The way workers were treated in America made you feel they just couldn't go on without a revolution. Even to strike took an act of courage. The workers were beaten, dumped into a police wagon, they were shut up in a jail cell, they lost their jobs, they were fined. Even to join a union meant a worker would be spied on, blacklisted, discriminated against in hiring. How can I tell you what it was like to be alive in that time? All this that is so familiar to you— strikes, unions, organized labor, decent conditions on the job—was then still a very revolutionary thing. . . .

---

* Communist union organizers imprisoned for promoting strikes. Ed.

"Finally your father said to me, 'Rose. Don't you know I would miss you?'

"'Paul,' I said to him, 'did you marry just a woman or did you marry also a Communist?'

"Your father had a habit when he was thinking. He would pass his finger across his mustache. This he did. And then he said, 'I'm not going to interfere with you. I understand your thinking. But . . . it will be hard for you.' . . .

"This was a big moment in my life. I knew the consequences. Maybe I would never see your father again. He loved the life in the Soviet Union. He had work there. Could I expect him to give this up for me? We parted for one year. Already I told you the way the women would go after him. Who knew what would happen afterwards? I thought about this, I was worrying but I said to myself, Rose, you are an organizer. Stay here and do your work. Your father returned alone to Moscow and my work in California began.

"Right from the beginning our organization began to grow. The farmworkers would come into our office. We kept it open night and day. There was always someone to answer a telephone, or write out a leaflet. People came in from other organizations to offer support. That's how it was. In those days from every action we made the larger struggle."

[Eventually Paul Kusnitz returns from Moscow and the family settles in New York. Ed.]

"When your father came off the boat he was wearing a thick Russian coat. . . . We walked all over New York together. After Moscow it looked so dirty. Paper all over the street, clothes hanging from the windows. The people coming by with weary expressions on their face. Everything we saw looked to us tired, old, worn out. . . .

"Later, when we were sitting down your father said to me, 'Well,' he said, 'I didn't yet miss the revolution, anyway.' . . .

"Your father got a job as an engineer, he was active in the union, he taught classes in Marxism. We found an apartment in the Bronx, next to the park, on the fifth floor. We had a small elevator in the building. But the Third Avenue El ran right past our window. We learned to fill the glasses only halfway up. Every time we would sit down at the table the train would go by and everything would begin shaking. . . .

"We wanted to make a decent life for the workingman, a decent life for the workingwoman, for their children and for their children's children. Nina understood this. Naturally, she forgot Russian. But how could she forget her life in the Soviet Union? . . .

"This was our life. We were a powerful movement. The future was our future; we were making it ourselves. . . . Your sister believed it. Her education, her social activity, her whole life was in the movement. At school she wore her Young Pioneer's scarf, a young Communist she called herself, very proudly. She was the future we were building, in her we saw the outcome of our work. . . .

"Of course, we did not know she would die so young. Who could have known it?"

"We were going forward. Every leaflet, every telephone call, every strike was to make this future come along a little bit faster. That is why you could not grow tired. You came home from a meeting. Maybe, it was late. Maybe you have been out speaking. The phone rings. Somebody didn't write a leaflet, and so they are asking, could you come down there, could you do this thing? Naturally, you are falling off your feet—but you think, maybe, from this, it will come . . . the revolution, a little bit faster. With this thought, where is the tiredness? You get on your hat, you put on the coat, you go out into the street. That was our dream. Our wonderful dream. Even today, who has lost it? This dream, I tell you, I believe in still." . . .

Something is happening between us that makes possible these silences we have avoided all our lives, which might have healed us. And suddenly I understand. This precisely is what we feared—this knowledge of loving, the depth of this love, our love so terrifying for us both. The last time, in childhood, we loved like this we both lost so bitterly. Finally now I understand my mother, this woman who was once a child. Now I hear this history of separations in her life, the loss of her first home, the shtetl, grandfather. The loss of her mother, who could not be a mother to her in America. And I think how very courageous we are to take upon ourselves this unmerciful greatness of loving.

"This part of my life," she says, "I never wanted to talk about.

I didn't want to remember. The whole thing I wanted to cut away from me and be done with it. But the past holds on. We've gone this far, we have to go further. I'm ready. . . ."

She says this without looking at me, but I know she is making good the promise we have both felt from the moment she arrived. Her fingers trace a line of blue thread in the arm of the couch and I watch her features set and grow firm.

"This," she says, "is the story in which you are born. You begin to grow up, you take your place in the family. After this story, you must start talking. What happens in my life after this, who I am, what sort of person I am in the world, we must hear later from you."

She clasps her hands in her lap and sits very still, her shoulders hunched. She has the look of a small girl, listening. And now when her words come it is clear to both of us they have been there, beneath everything else she has ever said, waiting for this moment. . . .

"You were born in May of 1940. The early years of your life were filled with the war. Every evening, each morning, we were glued to the radio. . . .

"I had serious doubts about bringing another human being into the world. I want you to know this. With the loss of the war in Spain, the success of Hitler, the formation of the fascist parties in Europe, everything we lived for disappeared. Instead of the revolution there came fascism to the world. We knew our struggle as Communists was going to be more difficult. We knew, as Jews, we faced a terrible catastrophe. The fear of pogrom was something we lived through already as children.

"Many times, even today, I ask myself why in a time like this I gave birth to another child. I had doubts about myself as a mother. I wasn't sure I was capable of raising another child and still going on with my organizing. . . .

"I was very busy during the pregnancy, active in the Party, making speeches, picketing, distributing material. I thought I was prepared for giving birth. I was a mother already, I was a strong woman. But I felt apprehensive. In my generation we always heard stories that glorified childbirth by describing how horrendous it was. . . .

"The day you were born it was hot. Before Paul left for work in the morning I told him I would be giving birth. Nina went off to school. Don't be so certain, Rose, I said to myself. You can't know everything. But still, somehow I knew. I packed up a few things in a bag. I canceled my meetings. . . .

"You were a beautiful baby. You had blond hair, like white silk. Your whole face was ringed with curls.

"I stayed home with you for the first year and a half after you were born. It couldn't be otherwise. We didn't have the money to bring somebody in the house. There was a nursery for the people who lived in the cooperative, but otherwise there was none available in New York. And now I'm going to tell you something a mother can't usually say. It wasn't so easy for me after your birth. Should I lie about it? I loved you, of course, it's not a question of loving. . . . [N]ow it was I who had to sit home all day with a new baby. Of course, I wanted to be a mother who likes to stay home with her children. You think anybody wants to feel like an unnatural person? But if you can't make a meaningful life from diapers and nursing, what's to be done? I ask you, what is to be done? . . .

"At home, I'd sit there while you were taking a nap. I'd get depressed. I had the feeling my life was over, I had accomplished everything I would ever accomplish. There was nothing more to look forward to, only the washing and the shopping and the cleaning and the cooking.

"One day a leading woman in the Party came over to me and said, 'Rose, we've been watching your work and we'd like you to return to full-time organizing. . . .

" 'Listen, Rose,' she says. 'We know that Paul will support you. . . . We want you to be the organizational secretary of the Bronx.'

"Well, when I heard that I gave her a good look and I started laughing. It was just like the time in the Soviet Union, when I was offered the job in the publishing house. How could I believe what I was hearing? We had five thousand members in the Bronx. I would be responsible for the entire Party membership and of course as the organizational secretary I would sit on the board. This position, let me tell you, was not often given to a woman.

"But now I found myself on my feet. This time I knew it was a serious offer. And I saw that if I accepted I would have to get some kind of child care for you. I put on my coat. I saw exactly what I had to do. I was an organizer. So why hadn't it occurred to me before?

"'Rose,' says this woman, 'where are you going? We need an answer from you right away.'

"I knew by then I could not blame my life on circumstance. I knew it was essential to fight for what you wanted from life. If you have doubt and conflict you have to master them.

"'Sadie,' I said, 'you ask where I'm going. I'll tell you. My daughter needs a nursery. I'm going out to make one.'

"Naturally, there were other mothers to help me with this. It was a need we all felt, and now we acted. We rented the building, we paid for the teacher. A month later we had a nursery. That's how it was, that's how I became the organizational secretary for the Communist Party in the Bronx. . . .

"When Nina was a senior in high school she received a prize, on May first, for being the healthiest girl in her class. She had never missed a day of school because of illness. But shortly after this she began to complain of an itching on her legs. She began to lose weight and she had many sleepless nights. She would wake me and I would sit with her. You and she shared a room; we would cover the light with a blanket and whisper together in the dark. At first I thought she might have been worried about something; she was an adolescent and that can be a difficult time. But when she continued to complain about the itching on her legs I took her to our doctor. He assured me that it was an ordinary skin rash and gave her medication. But the rash did not disappear. It became worse and worse. Then we took her to a specialist. It was wartime and the doctors were all mobilized for the war. It was very difficult to get someone to see her but we managed it through Party channels. He examined her but could not find the cause of the rash. They took some tests and shortly afterwards I came into the office to get the results. The doctor was white as a sheet.

"'But what are you suspecting, Doctor? Is it tuberculosis?' That was the worst thing I could think of.

"'I wish it were, Rose. I wish it were.'

"He told me that she had cancer, Hodgkin's disease, that it was incurable, and that she was in a terminal stage. I thought, He has given me my death sentence. I sat there and felt that I was dying. Then I realized it was even worse than that. I was going to lose Nina and survive!

"I stopped all my political work to stay home with her. The dis-

ease advanced very rapidly. We had no time to get used to the idea
she was dying. I have not got used to it yet. Thirty years have passed
and the idea still haunts me. I thought I had known what difficulty
was but I had no idea. Nothing in my experience had prepared me.
I thought I was a strong woman but I didn't think I could survive. . . . [S]even months passed and she was dead.

"Then I felt that I had no strength left to live. . . . The shadow
that fell on the world at the end of the thirties dropped down on my
life, too, and I could not shake it off. . . .

"At last, finally, I decided we should move to California to get
away from the place where she died. We didn't know if it would be
a visit or a permanent settlement there. We weren't sure Dad could
find a job. We arrived in February. The weather was very mild, it
was warm and beautiful. It seemed to me that we had left New
York far behind and that here I could begin to involve myself in the
world again.

"But grief comes with you. If I forgot for a minute, I felt something running to catch up with me, I could not escape. I gave myself
tasks, I forced myself to do them, the grief accompanied me.

"The people in the Party were pulling me back into activity.
They were afraid that I would go down into a constant depression.
But I had no heart left for struggling. If I couldn't save my daughter
what was I capable of?

"I didn't think I could ever begin again.

"But then, you know how it is, the months passed and I began
to notice things. I saw that something was happening in our community. When we moved in there were many Jews in the neighborhood. Your father's family lived all around us. But now, very slowly,
Negroes were beginning to move into the community and the white
people began to move out. Soon, only Barney and Sara were left,
your father's oldest brother and his wife. And they were Communists. You could walk in the neighborhood and see all these nice little houses with a sign. It seemed to happen overnight. First there
would be one house for sale, three days later six houses, after a
week there were a dozen.

"Every time a Negro family moved into our community there
was a struggle in the neighborhood. One day a cross was burned on
the lawn in front of a house several blocks from where we lived.
When I heard about it I became enraged. I rushed out of the house,
I took you with me. I ran down the block. You remember, when my

mother moved to Cannonsville, the neighbors burned a cross because she was a Jew? And now, in my own neighborhood, in 1946, the same thing was happening all over again against blacks.

"That night and for many nights following we threw up a marching line around the house to protect the occupants. I organized for this. Many neighbors joined us and a community organization came into existence. When I came home the next morning, very tired, my hands sore from carrying the sign, I knew my life had returned to the struggle.

"Without realizing it, I had been drawn back. I would go out to meet a family moving into the neighborhood and make them feel welcome. We began to organize the community to protect the Negro people who were moving in. And then we moved out into other communities, protesting the restrictive covenants, agreements drawn up among neighbors and realtors that no houses would be sold to minority people.

"I took you on picket lines with me. I began to attend meetings at night. People stopped by the house, we made plans, the coffee pot was always brewing, we drew up leaflets, we called press conferences, and very slowly life began again." . . .

Seven o'clock. The bell rings. Larissa races for the door. I hear her slow down as she crosses the tile entryway. . . .

My mother is standing in front of the mirror in my downstairs bedroom, where guests stay. It's a large room, looking out on the garden. Rain is dripping from the upstairs deck onto the porch. She's frowning at herself, putting on her lipstick. "How do I look?" She checks the buttons on the front of her dark dress. She looks formal, the way she always used to look when she was preparing to make a speech.

"Tonight," she says, suddenly serious, "is an important occasion." I wait, but I feel my face becoming tender.

"Tonight, for the first time, you are the one who will tell about our family."

I nod, keeping my face grave.

"And tonight, for the first time," she continues, "you are introducing me to a group of your friends."

"That's not possible. It can't be the first time."

"Don't I know what I'm talking about? I always thought you were ashamed of me."

"Ashamed of you? Me, ashamed of you?"

"So, why not? You are a very intellectual person. An accomplished woman. And your friends are cut from the same cloth."

I stand there, staring down at her with astonishment. And then I feel that something is about to be said which has never been spoken between us.

"Listen to me," I say, "and you'll hear the truth. If I never introduced you to my friends it's because I thought you wouldn't like them. I thought they wouldn't be political enough for you. I thought you'd disapprove of us."

She raises her eyebrows and straightens her shoulders. Her head tips back. I can see she is about to disagree violently with me. But then she says, "Who knows? Maybe," and her voice is quiet, matter-of-fact. "Maybe that's what I used to be like." . . .

And then, for an instant, all of us are silent, my closest friends gathered here, with my mother and me. We are sitting together on the small sofa in front of the window, the manuscript lying quietly on our knees.

"My mother and I want to speak to you tonight about a book we've been working on together for the last six years."

My voice is surprisingly calm, but my lips are dry and my heart is pounding so hard I can scarcely hear my words.

"Tonight my mother will introduce the story I'm going to tell about our experience during the McCarthy years." . . .

"My daughter Nina died in 1945. She was sixteen years old. By then, the war was over. But we, in America, did not come out of the war and move in the way some of us hoped. We, the Communists, thought maybe with the victory over fascism, the United States and all the Western countries will move toward socialism. That's how it is, you make mistakes.

"And I, who had seen with my own eyes life for the worker under socialism, should I blame myself that I began to hope?

"What am I trying to tell you? Am I saying this hope for humanity brought me finally out of my own grief? Maybe.

"Am I trying to tell you my life as a Communist, a fighter for justice, saved me? Perhaps.

"Grief is a very selfish thing, very private. For me, the despair I felt was something to drive me away from people.

"So it was. For four years, after we moved away from New York, my life was recovering. I worked, I organized in the community, I involved myself with people, but in those years, to tell you the truth, I was not completely alive.

"Then came October 1950. . . ."

I watch my friends as my mother talks. She, too, is looking at them, weighing her words. . . .

"In 1950," she says, "the government passed the Internal Security Act. Would you believe it? They make a law stating that the Communist Party advocated the violent overthrow of the government, and never mind whether they have to prove it. So here suddenly we have a piece of legislation that allows for the deportation of any foreign-born person who has been a member of a so-called subversive organization. The act was passed in October and in that same month we had already four people arrested for deportation in Los Angeles."

My mother's voice breaks off as we go right on listening. But I know why she hesitates; soon she will catch herself up, she will continue, overcoming her resistance.

"I don't like people to think I'm boasting," she says. "But if I tell people about the McCarthy period, and I don't tell them what I've done, they begin to look at me. So, why not? After all, only two kinds of people have these facts sitting in the pocket. You know what I mean? Radicals and stool pigeons. So, I figure I'd better tell you which I am."

Now, she glances over at me and winks. Storytelling makes her playful, the way she never is at any other time.

"In 1950," she repeats, and I can hear how many times she's used that date before, "I founded an organization to protect the people arrested for deportation. It was called the Los Angeles Committee for the Protection of the Foreign-Born. At that time, we already had a national organization, active since 1941. But now I established a committee to handle the cases of people arrested on the West Coast. And believe me, we had our hands full. . . . And then, before the McCarthy period was over, we had almost two hundred denaturalization and deportation cases. But I am proud to tell you, most of these we fought right up to the Supreme Court. We stopped the deportations. So I ask you, who had time for personal troubles?"

My mother is no longer talking. Slowly she moves her gaze around the room, a conductor in that moment of acute suspense before the baton is lifted. And now when she knows that we are all perfectly attentive, she turns toward me, a deliberate gesture. She intends to remind me, my turn is coming soon, the story has led back out of history into our own personal lives.

And then she says, "There's another date I'll always remember. July 26, 1951," with that cadence of the storyteller who has come upon a tale that has long since proved to be everyone's favorite. "July 26, 1951, is an important date in my life."

But now, at the second repetition of this date something happens to me. Recalling it later, it seems to me that the room disappeared for a moment. And then I see the door to the house in which we lived when I was a girl. I see the red steps leading up to it. A child in braids runs up the steps, shouting something. The door swings open and the image fades.

My mother's hand rises to her earlobe, toying with an earring. Her eyes are cast toward the ceiling. "I got up early," she says. "Paul and I had breakfast together, he prepared his lunch and I read the newspaper aloud to him. Who could have expected it? He left for work. I began to straighten up around the house. I prepared something for dinner and then . . . I heard a knock at the door.

"I opened the door. I saw two men standing there. They were dressed very conservatively. They asked me if I was Rose Chernin.

"'Yes,' I said, 'I am Rose Chernin. But who, gentlemen, are you?'

"The men showed me a warrant. I looked it over, I was satisfied. FBI. I was arrested. And for what? For forming a conspiracy, they said, and advocating the overthrow of the government. By force and violence, no less. That was the Smith Act. But of course I knew at once it was all because of my work with the Foreign-Born Committee.

"Well, I said to them, 'Gentlemen, I am going into the house to change my clothes and to say good-bye to my daughter.'

"They agreed, they began to follow me into the house. But I said to them, 'Gentlemen, stay right where you are. Into this house you are not taking one single step.'

"'Oh no? Then you're not going in either.'

"They arrested me.

"I looked behind me. I saw the gate to our back yard was open. Three men were standing there, with rifles. I walked out onto the porch. Our entire block closed off. It was early in the morning. But most of the neighbors were on their porches, watching. There were some men, they were walking up and down the block. These, I thought, are FBI agents. A car was parked across the street. From that car emerged a nurse in a white uniform and two men. They were coming toward us. We met in the middle of the street. They got into another car with us and then we were driving away.

"Kim was asleep when they came to arrest me. Everything happened so quickly. I couldn't say good-bye. I hoped our neighbors would see what was happening, they would go and tell her. But their faces didn't look familiar. I thought, they are all strangers.

"That was July 26, 1951. That summer my daughter became eleven years old."

I am aware of a desire not to cry. I am in the grip of something. It is old, it is powerful, it makes me want to turn away and to go toward it. It is fearful, I lost it long ago, and I desire it.

"What was it like for her? How did she first learn I was arrested? Had she expected this thing? That is what she will tell us now."

It's called memory, the child rushing up the steps, the door swinging open. But to me it seems an immense, inarticulate rush of feeling. At first I am afraid it will eat up my words. Then, I open my lips and it makes language:

"I heard them talking. I heard them, even before my mother was arrested." ...

There were ... words. People used them and their voices had an edge. The Attorney General's List. The Blacklist. McCarthy. Red-baiting. Witch Hunts. The Loyalty Oath, they said. These were words they didn't want children to hear. ...

I divided my life. On the surface there was a little girl. I made a mess in my room and straightened it up when my mother yelled at me. I taught my dog Lucky to play dead. In the mornings my mother braided my hair.

But inside I had already grown old. There, I figured out my sister was never coming back. The dying, that no one had talked about, had gone so far it couldn't turn around anymore.

I figured things out. I figured out there was some new danger in the world. The fascists had gone. The concentration camps were gone. The Jews had gone to Israel. Now it was the turn of the Communists. We were Communists, it was our turn. ...

One night I began to pray. I knew my parents did not approve of praying. I hid my folded hands under the covers. "God, keep my mother and father safe."

I had learned to pray in the boarding school where they sent me, after Nina died, when we first moved to California. . . .

Then I was a Communist and at that time you could tell it to other people. It was something, my mother told me, to be proud of. . . .

Now it changed. It was 1950. I was ten years old. I wasn't supposed to open the door to strangers. I had to ask first, making sure, before I opened the door. I wasn't supposed to tell the kids at school. I shouldn't repeat anything I heard my parents say at home. The kids said they were Democrats, they were Republicans. I said nothing.

The second time the committee came to town my prayers grew longer. "God, keep Aunt Lillian, Uncle Norman, Aunt Sara Barney safe. God, keep Lucky safe. God protect the other Lillian, and Dorothy, Sam and Eva, Helen and Ben."

I was horrified about my prayers. Did they work? Did they help? I began to repeat them, beneath my breath, even at the dinner table. . . .

I stopped sleeping. I lay awake and kept watch on things. I kept watch on the shadows that filled up my closet. I kept watch to make certain someone had left the light on in the hall. I listened to my mother and father whispering in their bedroom. . . .

I crept back down the hall, I closed the door to my room. Inside, it was dark. I opened the curtain next to my bed. The light came in from Crenshaw Boulevard. Very quietly I started packing. I put an old pair of jeans, a sweater with a hole in the sleeve, and a heavy flannel shirt into the gym bag I made at school. I added a book by Laura Ingalls Wilder. The next day I added a chocolate bar.

Every night, before I said my prayers, I checked to make sure everything was okay in that bag. I never ate the chocolate bar.

My prayers grew longer. Sometimes I would fall asleep in the middle of my list but I woke up a few hours later, in the dark. I was covered in sweat. I started reciting. "Dear God, keep Sonia and Peter and Freddie safe." . . .

The next day I was late for school. For weeks now I had been coming late so that I could miss Current Events. Usually, if I came too early I raised my hand and went out to the bathroom.

In Current Events they said there were prison camps in Russia.

In Current Events they said reds were a menace. They said Communism was spreading out all over the world.

That day, in Current Events, they said that five Commies had been arrested. The teacher said it was a good thing. Now, she said, they could be deported.

One of those Commies she named was my friend. He was a Korean architect, he used to come over once a week in the late afternoon to give me art lessons. Sometimes, we went to his house for dinner. They served us spicy food in little bowls and David Hyun taught me how to eat with chopsticks. My mother had told me that if David and his wife were sent back to South Korea they would both be killed. I thought maybe I should raise my hand and say that to the class. But I looked around at them, these kids I'd gone to school with since the first grade. What difference would it make to them that David Hyun taught me to draw? . . .

One day when I woke up in the morning a neighbor was standing next to my bed. I reached up to hug her. My mind raced. Our neighbor began to speak. I knew, even before she said a word to me. They had taken my mother. I was eleven years old.

It was summer, I put on my shorts. I got my bike and rode over to my friend's house. Her parents were Communists, we went to day camp together.

"Jessie, they arrested my mother. She didn't even get to say good-bye. No, I'm not kidding, are you kidding?"

Sara Kahen came out of the kitchen. "What are you whispering about?"

"They arrested my mother. This morning. I was asleep."

She got on the phone. "Sam? Rose was arrested. This morning. No, she's fine, she's not even crying."

Jessie and I got on our bicycles. Sara Kahen made us a big lunch. She chucked me under the chin. "What's the matter? You don't miss your mother?"

"I never cry."

In the afternoon the newspapers had the headline. Jessie and I saw it when we were riding home from camp. FIFTEEN COMMIE LEADERS ARRESTED IN CALIFORNIA. There were names, pictures. I saw my mother, wearing my flannel shirt.

"Jesus, Jessie, look at that. They didn't even let her change her clothes."

Jessie Kahen used to call herself my cousin. We had known each other since grammar school, we were best friends. But the day after my mother was arrested, Jessie Kahen told all the kids at camp we weren't really cousins.

"The hell with her," I said to myself three times. Then, I rode home from camp alone, without crying. . . .

Aunt Lillian had brought dinner for me and my father. She was gathering up clothes for my mother, in jail. "What do you think?" she said, holding up a polka-dot dress. "Does she like this one?"

My father warmed up the dinner. "Lillian," he said, "you'll understand, I'm not very hungry."

I was very hungry. I ate more than they ever saw me eat before. I ate my dinner, and my father's dinner and Aunt Lillian's dinner.

"Look at her," Lillian said. "She'll eat for all of us."

The telephone kept ringing.

"Eight o'clock this morning," I said. "Sure I was at home."

People kept coming to the house. Aunt Sara came, with a dish of stuffed cabbage.

My father gave her a hug. "Thank you, Sara," he said, "but you'll understand. Tonight I'm not very hungry."

Sara was plump. She carried a red purse. When she came in the door you could go over and take a look into her purse. There was always something, a cookie wrapped in a napkin, some chocolate, a little game.

I loved Sara. She never forgot. "So come," she said, when she saw me looking. "You're too old all of a sudden to give a look in the purse?"

In Sara's arms, for the first time, I cried. With my father, alone, I wouldn't cry. "Tell me," he'd say. "Talk to me. Why should you have this all alone? Tell me, what are you feeling?"

"I'm all right," I'd say in a furious voice. He had let me down when my sister died. "Just leave me alone," I'd say, "I'm okay." Now he couldn't even keep my mother safe. Why should I talk to him?

One night he told me that bail for my mother and the other defendants was one hundred thousand dollars. He told me that meant they couldn't get out of jail. They had to stay there until the bail was reduced. He said, "How could we raise one hundred thousand dollars?"

"Well," I said, figuring quickly. "We'd have to divide it by fifteen, right? That means, for each one, less than seven thousand dollars." I went right on thinking. It didn't seem so bad. There was Uncle Max and Aunt Anne. They were wealthy. There was cousin Sol, who had bought the shopping center. There was Dorothy in New York, who had loaned us the money to buy our house. I became excited. I couldn't figure out why he looked so grim. "Come on, Dad. You're making a big deal. You could get on the phone, start calling, you'll have the money like that." I snapped my fingers. I began to prance around.

"Listen, listen," he said, trying to grab me. "You don't understand."

"What? What?" I was scared now.

"One hundred thousand dollars each."

"Come on." I couldn't believe it. "Just come on. They couldn't do that. It's not fair."

"Ach, fair." He sat down at the table and looked tired. "A fair world we haven't yet been able to make."

I shook him by the shoulder. I didn't want to see him like that. It was the same when Nina was dying. I began to shout.

"Goddamn it," I yelled and my voice thundered. "We won't let them get away with that." I was eleven years old, I knew something about the law. "It's unconstitutional," I screamed. "And we're going to fight it."

We fought. The hearings lasted six months. The lawyers also thought it was not constitutional. My father said, "In these times, who's going to protect the Constitution?"

"Daddy," I shouted at him. "We're going to protect it."

We were standing in the garage, stacking up newspapers for the school paper drive. "Daddy," I yelled, and I just kept on yelling. "We won't let them get away with that shit." He looked up startled. Then he smiled. That night, he talked to his brother Max on the telephone. "A fiery one," he said, and he had the same smile on his face. "Just like her mother."

I didn't tell him I hated going to school. I didn't tell him how one day, when I walked up to the school, I saw my friends gathered together, standing in a little group, whispering. . . .

The kids were all smiling. Then someone was holding the newspaper clipping in his hand. Oh yeah, of course, it had to happen. ROSE CHERNIN, COMMIE LEADER, ARRESTED IN LOS ANGELES. Sooner or later someone had to figure it out.

Who cares? I walked away, shrugging my shoulders. Then it came to me: Now things were different. If I denied who we were, that was betrayal. It was not keeping her safe. I turned back. "Rose Chernin," I said. My voice was loud. "My mother's maiden name is Rose Chernin."

I never told anybody how much I hated going to school. Every day I passed through the front gate and my eyes itched. My mother said I was a fighter. I made a fist. The other kids, their gossip, that passed over. But my biggest fear was, I knew things I shouldn't know and I was afraid I might tell.

I knew the name of a man who had been deported. I knew he had come back secretly and was living in Los Angeles again. I heard them talking. He was underground, they said. If anyone found out, my mother said, he'd be sent back to South Korea. They kill Communists there. . . .

Would they torture my mother in jail? Would they torture me? Would I tell the names I knew? Would they put needles under my nails? Would they hold a burning match under my chin?

I knew the name of everybody who came to our house. I knew if you started talking you'd tell everything. "He sang his heart out," my mother had said one night at dinner before she was arrested. "Once he started, he never stopped. He gave even his wife's name. The name of his sister."

Once a week I wrote her a letter. "Dear Mama," I said. "Everything's just great here."

I didn't want my father to find out and tell her. I didn't want her to worry about me. . . .

[F]or a while, I didn't have any friends at school. I didn't try to catch up with the other kids in the morning. At lunchtime, I sneaked out of the playground, so I wouldn't have to sit by myself eating my lunch. Tonio no longer picked me up in the afternoon. I hung around in the halls, or I sat by myself on the back staircase. That way no one would see me walking home alone. At home, in the afternoon, I clipped articles about my mother out of the newspaper and pasted them into my scrapbook. My dog Lucky and I went out for a walk in the Baldwin Hills.

But then one day everything changed. One day in class there was an incident. A boy hadn't done his homework. The teacher was exasperated. She turned away from the blackboard and she said: "Keep on like this and you'll end up collecting garbage." Before she could turn back to the board a book was flying across the room. There was a silence and then she went over and took the boy, James Grove, by the shoulder. She pulled his sweater and dragged him over to the door.

"Take your hands off him." I was on my feet shouting. My voice cut the other voices in the room. "I threw that book."

"Sit down," she yelled back. "Don't even try. I saw him."

"I threw that book. If someone's going to the principal, it better be me."

That boy had a strange look on his face. He had light skin and gray eyes and we thought he was real cute. . . .

[N]ow it was awfully quiet in the class. Everyone was looking at me and the teacher.

"Prove it," I said. "Prove he threw the book and I didn't."

"All right," she said. "If you're so eager to go to the principal, you come, too." . . .

"Who threw the book?" the principal said.

"I did," said James Grove and I.

"You both threw the same book! Okay, you're both suspended. Tell your mothers to come to school." . . .

But something happened to the principal's face. Before I could say a word a look crossed over it. James Grove saw it and I saw him see it.

She knew already that my mother was in jail.

She fiddled about with the charts. She looked inside and read over our records. "Well," she said, "you have good grades. Both of you. Take this as a warning."

James Grove put his arm around me when we walked back to class. James Grove opened the door for me when we came to the room. The teacher was at the blackboard and some of the Negro kids got to their feet. They stood there, girls and boys I hardly knew, cheering as we walked into the room.

In our school the white kids all left by the front gate. The Negro kids and the Mexican kids and the tougher Oriental kids went out through the back gate. James Grove was a Negro kid. And now I went out through the back gate with him. There, behind the school, were older boys from the neighboring high school. Policemen often came cruising by in patrol cars. Fights broke out. There were knives, gangs, secret clubs, violence. . . .

My new friends never asked me about my mother. They never

whispered about me. I went to parties and the boys lined up to dance with me. . . .

Then, one day, the teacher called on a white boy for Current Events. James Grove stood up by his desk. "Ah, shit, teacher," he said, "ain't nothin' new 'bout this ol' world."

The next day, she called on someone again. James Grove was on his feet. "Didn't I tell you, teacher?" A white girl was standing up, her newspaper clipping pasted on a piece of yellow paper. She looked at James Grove. "You hear?" he said. And she sat down again. . . .

The next day and the day after and then every day for a week the teacher called for Current Events. But each day one of my friends stood up. "Teacher, don't you know by now? Ain't nothin' new in this ol' world." . . .

Sometimes I had to call out for my father at night. He came and sat next to me on the bed. He didn't know any Russian lullabies. "What's wrong with you?" I yelled. "Is something wrong with you? Didn't you have a Mama? Couldn't she sing?"

At my uncle's house, where my father and I went for dinner on Sunday nights, I yelled at my father. "You old goat," I shouted, for no reason at all.

I ran out of the room, no one came after me. I ran into the bathroom and locked the door. "You old goat," I screamed again. But that time I was crying. I sat right down in a heap on the tile floor, my shoulders started shaking. "It's not fair," yelled a hoarse voice. "It's not fair," it shouted in a terrified whisper. "It's not fair, it's not fair, it's not fair, it's not fair . . ."

I stayed in that bathroom for a long time. After a while, I heard them talking. "How can you blame the child?" my father said. "Six years ago she lost her sister. Now, her mother's in jail. Did you ever think," he said to his brother, "how the world must look in the eyes of this child?"

One day he came home early from work. He parked his car in front of the house and he came up the driveway practically running.

"She's coming home," he said. "She's coming home."

"Hey, what happened? She escape from jail?"

"The bail's reduced. She's coming home."

My father had bought me a new dress, organdy.

"Come on, Daddy, I'll wear jeans."

He bought me a pair of patent-leather shoes.

"You kidding, Daddy? I'm twelve years old."

"You're happy?" he said, and he touched my hair.

"Sure I'm happy, what d'ya think?"

The day my mother got out of jail I wore the organdy dress and patent-leather shoes my father bought for me.

I smiled and I kept on smiling, letting my father hold my hand as the elevator door opened and a group of men and women came down from the Federal Building, and one of them was my mother.

She was different than I remembered. She was not taller or shorter, or plumper or thinner. Her face was, I suppose, the same. But something inside me, bravely smiling, was saying: Who is she? What does she want of me?

This woman, with gray hair, wearing a neat dress with a belt, walking with a good, firm, dignified stride into my father's arms; taking my hand to draw me along beside them; this woman, who spoke my name twice and pulled me against her, was an acceptable person to be proud of (and I was). But the woman who had gone away to jail, six months before, had taken my feelings along with her. And now, having by this time forgotten how to feel, I had lost my mother.

We could hold hands, we could walk cheerfully down the street, waving good-bye to the others. We could get into the car the way we'd always done, my mother in the front, I kicking my heels in the back. But it was only pretending. This woman, coming home with us, was not my mother.

During the six months my mother was in jail my father and I had roast beef every night for dinner, except for the nights we had dinner out. We had roast beef warm, roast beef warmed over, roast beef in cold pink slices, roast beef cut into small pieces and stirred in the pan with onion. For six months we had roast beef. And that night, in celebration of my mother's homecoming, we had roast beef.

I set the table, putting out rye bread and butter, the tomato juice in little glasses. My mother went in to change her clothes and when she came back into the kitchen I could tell from one look at her face that she wasn't happy to be at home with us.

"Good to be home?" my father said, taking her hand.

My mother stiffened. "Of course, Paul, what do you think?"

I watched her. I kept my eyes on her all through dinner. She liked it better in jail, I thought to myself, she can't fool me.

There was, without a doubt, a strain in our little family gathering. The conversation just couldn't get going. My father talked to her about the prospects for the trial.

"They'll have paid witnesses, what else?" my mother said.

We heard the sound of knives and plates. My dog came over to beg at the table. I threw him a piece of roast beef.

"You feed the dog now at the table?"

My father put out his hand to touch my mother on the arm. "All right, Paul," she said, impatiently.

I saw what I shouldn't see. That was the problem. Before, when she was in jail, I knew what I shouldn't know and I felt what I shouldn't be feeling. But now, I just could not stop my eyes from seeing. They saw the way my father jingled the coins in his pocket all the time. They saw he was afraid to lose his job. He smiled too much and when he said something he put his hand to his mustache and stroked the hair back from his lips. He did that a lot; before he only used to do it when he was nervous.

My mother didn't like roast beef. I could tell. She was cutting irritably at the tough meat.

[After Kim Chernin's reading her mother withdraws into silence. Ed.]

"Mama," I say, and I try to forgive myself the eagerness in my voice. "Talk to me."

"Talk to you." She repeats the words with her flat, despairing tone, and I see in this one moment everything that has gone wrong between us, repeating itself, again.

The kettle begins to whistle. She gets up to turn it off and stands next to the stove watching the steam. She is trying to straighten her shoulders, but the effort it takes makes her look crushed and broken. This powerful woman, so completely helpless. And still so sternly, so militantly refusing to share her mood. . . .

I have never been able to forgive her for this insistence upon bravery. Now, I put my arms around her. She stiffens, drawing away, but I hold on to her.

"Talk to me."

She touches my hand; her fingers are very cold.

"If I hurt you I want you to tell me." My voice is scarcely more than a whisper.

But now I can feel her gathering herself, focusing. I can feel that my struggle has reached her. She, too, wants us to change. Her whole body becomes taut and finally she says, "I don't want to make life hard for you."

So that's it? That's why she withdrew? I should have known it. She has carried this guilt, as a mother, even before I was born. This awful sense that she has hurt her children by being a Communist. But I had wanted to give her this story of our life as a gift; as a reparation even for Nina's death. And now it turns out that what I have just read to her she sees as her public condemnation.

We are both sinking; it is a perceptible sensation; we are falling back into that silence which used to be so terrible between us.

"Listen," I say, "it can't end here." My voice cracks, breaking through its hostility. "I'm thirty-nine years old. And I don't blame you for being a Communist. I never did. No one has an easy adolescence. I, at least, had a mother I could be proud of."

She turns around and looks at me, straightening her shoulders, as if she were making a speech. "I closed you out. From the time Nina died. I know, you don't have to tell. How could I tell a five-year-old child about such grief?"

But her voice is not the voice of an orator. It is simple and naked. It speaks what we have both been waiting a lifetime to hear.

And now I hear in my voice the same simplicity, a truth, spoken with feeling. "I couldn't forgive you for letting Nina die. I hated you for falling apart. I hated you because you loved her better. I thought I killed her."

"You?" she says. And then she repeats the word in a tone of stunned and urgent disbelief. "You?" We do not look at each other, but we both hear, in this single word, the echo of all the lonely guilt and horror that always, until now, divided us. She, too, blamed herself for Nina's death.

I would like to put my arm around her and look out into the night.

"We're not done yet," she says. "There's more coming. I know it."

I glance at the clock. It is still early, not yet nine-thirty. Only an hour has passed since Larissa shut the door behind her, calling out, "Don't stay up talking all night this time."

"I gave you the impression I wasn't a strong woman?" she asks.

"You want me to read?"

"Read, tell, what does it matter?"

I smile, almost convinced. There is so much I still want to tell her. But I don't go down into the living room for the manuscript. She watches me, that stern, self-mastering look in her eyes. And then she says, very seriously, "I want you to do something for me first."

"Anything. Just ask."

I stand there, my whole being reaching out to her with eager hands. I would fly up the chimney if she wished for it.

"So, sit," she says. And then she's on her feet, moving over to the stove. "You'll eat a bite first. What will it hurt you?" . . .

As children of the left we had always known we had a meaningful place in the Communist vision. We were the hope and the promise; it was we who carried the hope of the revolution they had expected in their youth. Later, when for some of us the vision collapsed, it left an emptiness that reached back into the earliest experience of childhood and shook the very fundaments of memory.

It would be hard to forget the Sunday afternoons, walking between my parents down Pico Boulevard, where there was a cinema that showed Soviet films. And yet, for many years after I gave up being a Marxist, I had to make myself forget the happiness I felt as we strolled along there, catching sight of one friend after another, waving, calling out greetings, gathering in little clusters of two and three to exchange comments about the world situation.

"So, Rose," people would say, hurrying to catch up with us, "what do you think about the situation in ———?" We would stop, my father would look thoughtful, my mother would make her pronouncement, and on we would go, drawing further with each step into that safe and familiar world of radical feeling and thought. . . .

In the smaller world, I felt safe and secure. I was very popular, my mother was admired, and I would go home from a weekend or an event feeling very courageous and optimistic about the future. I took my radical commitment very seriously in those days, and planned to become a civil-rights lawyer. Of course, it didn't work out that way. But how could I foresee the terribly difficult times my mother and I would pass through as I tried to turn away from political life and become a poet? That was several years ahead of us.

Now, during the McCarthy period, if we were ever tempted to draw too far apart, the political danger she faced always reunited us. We would be sitting at the table and every time there was a knock at the door we would fall silent and look at one another. By then my own feelings had begun to run ahead of events, and I could frequently sense trouble or danger before anyone had spoken about it. I remember one night when she came in late for dinner. . . .

"So, I've been subpoenaed. What could you expect?"

My mother's appearance before the House Un-American Activities Committee became a source of stories we would tell over and over again. . . .

My mother's denaturalization trial lasted for seven days. The government had to prove that in 1928, when she applied for citizenship, she was already intending to join the Communist Party. Therefore, they claimed, she had perjured herself when she swore on her citizenship application that she was not a member of a subversive organization.

It was, even for those years, an outrageous charge, and it required the government to prove, beyond reasonable doubt, that they knew her state of mind almost thirty years earlier. At any other period in American history a case like that could never come to court.

My mother and father discussed these things with me every night at dinner. And I myself was in court one day when the government witness, who claimed to have known my mother during the twenties, insisted that he could easily identify her even today. My mother frankly could not remember the man and we decided he was probably confusing her with some other organizer from the Bronx. Or maybe, my father suggested, he was paid to lie and it simply didn't matter whether he ever knew her at all. For my father, that was a severe degree of cynicism and he spoke it with the first edge of bitterness I'd ever heard in his voice.

Unfortunately, he wasn't with us that day in court when the witness stood up and went striding through the courtroom, to stand, his finger pointing, before a small, gray-haired woman. "This," he boomed out triumphantly, "is Rose Chernin."

"Will you stand please," the judge requested, nodding his head at the woman who had been identified.

She stood up, clearly struggling not to smile. "Are you Rose Chernin?" the judge asked.

"Lord no," she cried out, putting her hand to her cheeks, and all of us burst out laughing.

Because of course we had planned it that way. "That stool pigeon," my mother had said. "You think he would know me from Karl Liebknecht?" And her friend Frances Williams added, "Let's try him." And so another middle-aged woman, with gray hair, had been found to sit in my mother's place. And now the government witness carried himself back across the courtroom with a distinct air of deflation. . . .

I listened to his testimony with a feeling of outrage. I was fourteen years old, and it scared me. The government of the United States dared to come into a federal court and present this man, this paid, professional liar, as their witness against my mother?

John Porter, her attorney again for this trial, was cross-examining the man. He was asking whether he'd noticed anything different about my mother during 1928. But the witness shook his head and said there had been no significant change in her.

I could scarcely sit still while the cross-examination was proceeding. What changes had taken place in 1928, which the witness should have remembered if he'd known my mother? Baby books were brought into court; they were submitted as evidence and it was established beyond any doubt that in 1928 my mother had become pregnant with my sister Nina.

The trail was a mockery, and after seven days the judge refused to denaturalize her. The newspaper said: RED LEADER TO KEEP CITIZENSHIP. The judge told the government that it could not prove its case against her and had presented no evidence of guilt. Then he went further, and I cheered for him under my breath. He reprimanded the government and cautioned them to be more careful how they handled citizenship. It was, he said, a very sacred right.

I'd give a great deal to be able to describe my mother's face at that moment. Triumph? Vindication? Relief? No doubt all of that was apparent. But I saw something else, which affected me deeply. It was, I think, the rebirth of her optimism after a time of unacknowledged doubt. There was a clear, fierce light in her eyes. A return of belief in her own power to fight, to overcome, to beat back institutional injustice. She looked over at me, her eyebrows raised. I lifted my hands over my head. And silently, from opposite sides of the courtroom, we shared this feeling of victory.

But for us, in those years, such moments were rare. . . .

I . . . decided . . . to attend the Seventh World Youth Festival in Moscow. For weeks I had been counting the days until I could leave Los Angeles. Now there were five left. I got up early and went downtown with my mother. Years before, whenever I was off school, I used to meet her at her office and we'd go out for lunch. . . .

Now, a few days before I was leaving home, we decided to go into all the old places we'd gone to when I was a kid. We stopped at the juice bar, we went into Clifton's Cafeteria, where the water was still pouring into the fake stone fountains. When we had finished lunch I suggested to my mother that we stop in for a movie. We checked the papers, but Roy Rogers had long since gone out of style.

Instead, we went shopping. I needed clothes for my trip to Europe, and the two of us needed to spend time together before I left. She knew something was going on for me at school, but she had never asked me about it. I took her arm when we crossed the street. And suddenly she said, "So who ever told you it was easy to be the exception? At your age, especially? But a year from now you'll look back, you'll be with a whole new group at college, and all this will be something to smile at."

She was wrong; she, who never needed to be told, who could always figure it out, was wrong. I would never forgive myself for that one. The dread of it ran too deeply through the generations of our family, this repetition of the impulse to make a sacrifice of the mother. . . .

Occasionally, when the fog is heavy late at night, it is possible to hear sounds from a great distance. The cars on the boulevard near the bay seem to be passing along my own street. Voices, a loud knocking at an unknown door, a child waking in an invisible house, footsteps that seem to be walking up my own stairs, or the sound of a train from the old station that was torn down, more than twenty years ago. . . .

Tonight I hear the bells on a church across town. It is very late and I have been sleeping fitfully. The heater comes on with a subdued roar. I am tired, I don't want to risk more. I have spent almost seven years on this work, in order to make her a gift. And now that we have accomplished so much, I find myself suddenly aware of a danger larger than any we have faced so far. There is a story I did not want ever to tell her. I found it so difficult to write down that once, a few weeks ago, I actually left my notebook in a gas station where I'd gone inside to make a telephone call. The owner came running after me as I was walking down the block, but I had already turned back, my shoulders aching with the awareness of what I had almost done. And then, a few days later, when my story about my trip to the Soviet Union was complete, I left the manuscript in a coffee shop. That day, I got all the way back to my car before I realized that I'd gathered up my empty notebooks but left the written pages behind.

Since then, I've taken the notebook with me when I move about from room to room. When I go out at night I wrap it in tin foil and put it in the freezer, in case a fire should break out in my house. I am terrified of my impulse to destroy this confession. It is the story of how I stopped being a Communist.

Why is it so hard for me to tell her the truth? Is it because, after a lifetime of faith, she needs to believe as she does about the Soviet Union? Because she was persecuted, jailed, and tried for her belief during the McCarthy period? . . . All my life I have admired her loyalty to the ideal, the dream vision of world peace and justice, decency and freedom. The trials and purges of the thirties, Hungary, the Khrushchev report, the work camps, the gulags. It took strength, I thought, the power of sustained belief, to remain loyal no matter how hard the jagged failures of reality pushed her. . . .

The manuscript, typed in its first draft, is on my desk. I pull the papers together and write down a title. I have been considering it for days, but have resisted it. Now, it makes clear that on my journey to the Soviet Union I saw everything she was unable to see twenty-five years earlier. I'm moving fast. When the time comes to risk, I don't know how to move with care. I lose all sense of delicacy and timing. There is, I know, much to criticize in this impulsiveness that insists on waking up an old woman who has had a long and difficult day. But I'm going to do it.

The door to the downstairs room is not locked. There is a crescent of light on the stairs, and I make my way easily. I walk softly, but I hope that my footsteps will wake her. Or maybe she's not yet asleep? I've known her to lie awake reading a newspaper or a book until the early hours of the morning.

Tonight she sleeps. The lamp is on next to her bed, the newspaper is open on the pillow beside her. She is propped up in bed, frowning, her glasses atilt at the end of her nose. She looks much older than I've ever seen her. I stare at the wrinkled skin on her breast, where the pink nightgown opens below her neck. Her hand is clenched tight, balling up the blanket.

I sit down in the wicker chair next to her bed. Carefully, I place the manuscript on the chair beside me. I cannot regain a sense of my own life. This room, where I once hammered up the oak walls, seems strange to me. Suddenly I remember a critic saying that no real woman would ever burn a manuscript, the way Hedda Gabler had done.

And then, she turns toward me. The newspaper crackles. I reach out and very gently remove her glasses. I put a lace cloth over the lamp but I do not turn it off. My tenderness has released me.

When I look back from the staircase I see this little composition I have arranged. The veiled light, the old woman asleep in the large bed near the window, the manuscript waiting on the wicker chair, her glasses resting beside it.

I can feel from my own love for her the certainty that nothing can destroy the bond between us. It is stronger than ideology, unshakable in its binding. It is not the birth bond which made us a mother and daughter; that we could have trampled down, in our impatience and confusion. This bond is a comradeship, won from the work we have done together. It comes so rarely to a mother and daughter, but once it is achieved it tangles itself in with all the nature and shared flesh. And then even they, if they wished, could no longer pull it down. . . .

She will read my story in the morning.

Long ago, long after the time I ceased to think of myself as a Marxist, for years past that time, the words *Soviet Union* brought tears to my eyes. But that had begun when I was a little girl and my mother would say to me, in that way she had: "So guess what? We have a surprise for you. Do you know what it is?"

"Something to eat?"

"Even better."

"To see?"

"Yes, to see."

"From the Soviet Union?"

"What else?"

Usually it was a film, sometimes a dancer or a musician. When the pianist Emil Gilels came to Los Angeles for the first time, she got me a box seat so that I could sit on the left side and watch his hands.

"Someday we're all going to the Soviet Union," she'd say, and I believed her. "Someday, we, too, will have a worker's revolution just like the Soviet Union." That, too, I believed. "While we were living in the Soviet Union, during the thirties," she'd say, and then I could go over and sit next to her on the gray couch and put my head in her lap.

Then, the day came. I graduated from high school and left for the Soviet Union. Falling asleep on the train that crossed through Poland I heard her voice and it spoke clearly. It murmured again between dream and awakening, repeating its stories. I was going home.

It struck me suddenly when we changed trains near the Polish border. All at once I knew that I would cross the border and be at home. Everything looked familiar, the landscape drawing away into the distance, the trees around the station, the plump women dancing together, the steaming samovar: Russia near the Polish border, Vitebsk, Chasnik, my mother's home—wasn't it somewhere near?

I stood in the open space between the cars, holding myself in a precarious balance so that I could be away from the others, undisturbed in my contemplation of this extraordinary landscape, the likes of which I had never seen before and yet seemed always to have known: forests of white trees, stirring up in me a feeling so profound I suddenly did not know who I was; surely it could not be I who felt this way?

One of our interpreters came looking for me, to tell me that we had crossed the border and were now in the Soviet Union. But I had known it and had already begun to cry. The young man put his arms around me and I wept against his shoulder, trying to tell him something I could never possibly have expressed. . . .

In Moscow the ecstasy continued. We had arrived several days before the official opening of the Youth Festival, and I used them to explore Moscow. Here, too, everything was just like my mother had told me. I saw the gleaming steel of the Mayakovski subway station, and I told everyone, very proudly, that my father had worked on its design. I walked in Red Square, I looked at the Kremlin. Here the May First Celebration had taken place. I stood in line to see Stalin and Lenin, lying in state, in the Mausoleum. The crowd of people moved steadily past the biers, but I stopped dead in my tracks and stood there, looking at the waxen face of Stalin, with his big mustache. Was it possible? He looked just like the pictures my mother had shown me when I was a child. And I remembered my sister had been invited into the Kremlin to meet this man. . . .

One day several people from our delegation went to call on Madame Kozmodemyanskaya, the mother of Zoya, the partisan girl who had been tortured and killed by the Germans during the Second World War. I was beside myself when I heard that she was still alive. Zoya's mother? My heroine's mother, still living? We carried huge bouquets of flowers and stood in the street below her window, singing to her, while she leaned forward and looked down at us. In that moment, I felt that my whole life came together and made sense. My old childhood idealism came back to me and I felt that I, too, would be capable of the heroism and sacrifice Zoya had shown.

But then, one night, two days before the opening celebration of the festival, something happened. At the time, I did not consider it very important, and was completely unaware that it had any lasting significance. If it had taken a physical form I could now say that it shattered me. But it was instead an emotional blow and its effects went so deep I couldn't afford to know they had occurred.

On the surface, the event was slight—such events usually are. One of the girls in the English delegation had relatives in the Soviet Union. They were Jewish and one night after dinner we set out across Moscow to visit them. It took us time, of course, because people kept stopping us and inviting us to join them for drinks. But finally we were walking up the steps of a large apartment block. Several floors above us we heard a door open, and then the head of a girl about our age leaned over the railing and called down. Soon, the whole family was trooping down the stairs, their arms open. There was an initial confusion about which of us was the niece, but then no one seemed to mind very much or to pay much attention to the distinction. When we got in the door, the commotion grew even greater; everyone had to be hugged and kissed all over again, the table was covered with food, we were eating dark bread and cheese, drinking tea in glasses, the spoons were tinkling and we were shouting in Russian and Yiddish and English, everyone talking at the same time.

The mother of the family was handicapped, she had been injured on her job and after dinner she showed us the work she did at home, for full pay, sorting colored bits of industrial glass. Then letters were brought out; they were carefully stacked in wooden boxes, and they went back to the beginning of the century, when Hyla's family had gone to England. Each one was carefully dated in ink, on the envelope, and we could see how often the family had moved around from the repeated changes of address. But I could also see that the mood in the room was changing. Hyla's aunt was becoming more and more silent. Her two daughters were trying to keep up the conversation, but their English wasn't very good. Her son, a boy of seven or eight, translated for us, but it made him impatient, and he would suddenly turn and glare at his sisters for talking too fast. Then, in an uncomfortable silence, Hyla's aunt sighed. She said, "So, you're here. You've come. It's good." She leaned forward and took both of us by the hand. But then she said, "It's good you're here and it's good you'll be going away again."

We both looked at her with astonishment. What did she mean? I said, putting my hand to my heart, fervently, "I could stay here forever."

"You like Moscow?"

"I love it. It's my home. I've never been happier."

"You're a foreigner. Don't believe everything you see."

Hyla and I looked at each other. We were both part of the Young Communist movement. And now we were proudly wearing the festival pin on our collars next to a Soviet Young Communist badge. Hyla laughed. She patted her aunt on the hand. "Just like Mama," she said affectionately, "always looking on the dark side of things."

But it was clear to me that something serious had been said. The young boy was whispering with his sisters, translating our conversation. I looked over at the older girl, a beautiful woman with blond hair and blue eyes. It was hard to believe she was Jewish. She nodded her head vigorously at me while her brother was talking.

"What?" I said to her. "The Khrushchev report?"

I had read it, of course, several months earlier, and it had made me shake. But why now? Why should we be cautious now not to receive the wrong impression?

She looked right at me and spoke to me in Russian. And then her brother's shrill voice repeated everything. I'll never forget it, such a terrible meaning from a child's lips. "So you think now that we've had Khrushchev everything's changed? Don't you believe it.

To be a Jew in the Soviet Union I wouldn't wish on my worst enemy. What's changed? So now they'll take Stalin out of the Mausoleum, maybe, and put him in the Kremlin walls. Who cares?" . . .

Fresh tea was poured, little candies in colored wrapping were passed out, and the conversation drifted back to family gossip. But the bitterness in the cousin's voice had chilled me. Because of it I now recalled the day I read the Khrushchev report a few months before, alone in my room. It was the first time in my life I did not turn to my mother for reassurance about the politics we shared. I had stayed there, frozen on my bed, watching the dust in a beam of sunlight. Could I believe that in the Soviet Union, in that world of justice and equality I had loved since childhood, millions of innocent people had been killed? By the Communist Party? By Stalin? . . .

I wrote enthusiastic letters to my parents and I told them the whole story of the festival. But that was the official version; what I left out was the real story, and it is difficult for me to write even today. For I was, in the next weeks, to learn even more about this country that had once inspired my greatest childhood passion.

Traveling in a bus with Tolya, one night I saw two women standing outside the subway station. He told me they were prostitutes and . . . at first I wouldn't believe him. How could there be prostitution in a socialist country? I looked back, and what he said seemed true. They looked like prostitutes anywhere. For a minute I closed my eyes and put my hands over my face. "Shtotakoy? What is it, little friend?" he asked. "Something hurts you?" "Prostitutes," was all I could say, but there was a lot in my voice if he cared to hear it. . . .

[W]hen I returned to California I . . . had . . . let my hair grow and I had a certain carefully cultivated way of tossing back my head to get my hair out of my eyes.

I had developed an enthusiasm for abstract art, had begun to read Sartre, and came home talking about existential angst.

My parents sat at the table during dinner and listened to me in silence. Of course, they did not understand that by advancing this image of myself to them, as an explanation for what had happened to me in Moscow, I was trying to save them from a confrontation with my own doubts and disillusions about Communism. How could they? I myself refused to understand. Once, in a wild moment, I screamed at my mother about my change of heart. But usually, I never mentioned it.

"Don't tell me about Marx," I shouted. "Or Lenin. Or any other of their theories. Lenin is to Marx what the New Testament is to the Old. It's a completely new departure. The most revisionist doctrine in the world."

"Listen to her, will you listen," she yelled back, banging the door to the refrigerator. "She's unlearned everything we taught her."

My father stood in the doorway, looking nervous. This sort of yelling match was not for him. Later, I knew, when I'd gone to bed, he'd knock at the door to my room and want to talk to me. But now he stood there, shaking his head and looking mournful.

"The revolution cannot take place in one country," I yelled, advancing an idea I had worked out for myself, in an effort to explain what had happened in the Soviet Union. "We will not have socialism until revolutions take place all over the world, simultaneously." At the time, this was as far as I could go.

"Hah," my mother shouted, pointing her finger at the ceiling, "so there it is. That's what has happened. She met Trotskyists." . . .

I had only a few weeks with them before I left for the university in Berkeley. Most of the time I spent out of the house, running around with my old friends. Because I was in the first group of Americans to go to China after the revolution, my picture had been in the newspaper; there had been a television segment of me on the ABC news. I had become a minor celebrity and everyone was happy to know me now. I stayed out late, made lists of all the boys who called me for dates, and briefly I fell back into my old way of distracting myself from whatever troubled me.

But now, because I was older, it was harder to pretend. I knew that something had happened. Something had changed me. I had become a poet. By the time I came home from college for Easter vacation I had perfected my new role.

"These clothes," my mother would say, watching me with her hands on her hips. "You're going to a costume party, maybe?"

I always played dumb. "What's wrong with them? Everybody dresses like this."

"Show me please this everybody."

The next time I came home for a visit, one long weekend toward the middle of my freshman year, I wrote poetry with soap all over the mirror on my dressing table. Then, I began to recite poetry as I walked about the house, doing my chores. Poetry consumed me. I barely ate a meal. I learned a poem by Walter de la Mare and repeated it at every opportunity. "Very old are the woods; / And the buds that break / Out of the briar's boughs, / When March winds wake, / So old with their beauty are / Oh, no man knows / Through what wild centuries / Roves back the rose."

"What's this?" my mother would say. "Can't take anything into the mouth but poetry now?"

One night, when my mother invited me to a political rally where she was going to speak, I said I had to stay home and finish a poem I was writing.

And so we had an argument which was repeated, again and again, without much variation over the years. You could have heard it the night before my wedding, or the day my husband and I left for Oxford, a year or so later. When I finally moved back to America after four years of living abroad, I spent the summer in Los Angeles. And of course the argument broke out again.

In retrospect, I see that it was a separation ritual, a way we had evolved to speak the central issue between us. For, whatever else we shouted or declaimed, a single idea was at the heart of our quarrel. I mean of course the fact that we thought different thoughts, and experienced the world differently. That we were no longer the same person. . . .

[D]uring the next two years, before my father died, I gave even him cause to worry about me because of the way my life seemed to be going. Peter* and I separated; we never talked about why. . . . I got a job teaching remedial reading to adults. I took care of children after school in the playground of Larissa's kindergarten. Peter began to pay child support when our savings ran out and I lived from month to month, terrified at times by a sense of insecurity, but at times elated by the first real freedom I had known.

Then, for several months I spent most of my time walking about in Golden Gate Park. Once or twice during my long walks I actually went down on my knees to worship . . . God, or something nameless that seemed to be looking out at me from everything I saw. But kneeling there, I would suddenly become aware of my mother's attitude toward such things and I would scramble to my feet. . . .

---

* Chernin's husband. Ed.

[B]y ... 1965 ... in Berkeley, across the Bay, the Free Speech Movement had begun. I went over there one day out of curiosity and watched the strike that emptied the classrooms and the libraries. But now, as a generation of students turned political, I found myself refusing to do what I knew my mother would have done. While the others marched I went into the library and sat there for several hours, reading Nietzsche and listening to the muted sounds of the students chanting outside the window. . . .

During those months it was my father who called me regularly. . . .

He understood me. I don't know how or why, but he understood. Sometimes, he'd call me quite late at night, when he was at home alone. I once told him that I was reading about Saint Theresa and I thought I was a little like her. He answered, "For us, Marx expressed the truth when he said religion was the opiate of the people. But you, it seems, are a poet. We know, for a poet the world is different. In the Soviet Union I knew a man who claimed he could talk to the birds. Of course, everyone laughed at him, how else? But I did not laugh. Maybe, I thought, he can talk to the birds. How should I know?"

Perhaps he understood that I was, during the first year of my separation from Peter, working out the style of life I would live; hanging up pictures of Rilke and Lou Salome and Jesus in my study, aggravating my mother, bewildering myself, a woman in her middle twenties who did not seem to be growing out of her youth; who wrote and wept and laughed and ran about with men, and became solitary again. And who managed, briefly as I say, to communicate something of all this to her father, who never judged her.

Then, one Sunday in June, in 1967, on the last day of the Six-Day War between Israel and the Arabs, when Larissa was almost four years old, I got a call. It was my father's doctor, and closest friend, telling me that my father had been killed in an automobile accident. He had been on his way, with my mother, to the Festival of Nationalities.

"No," I said, "it can't be."

Murray was silent.

"She's fine?" I asked, knowing she was.

"Not a scratch," he said, "although, you know, she was sitting beside him."

I grieved then, for the passage of a very gentle soul; he had lived his whole life according to a simple wisdom of the heart. He found it easy to love, he had never hated anyone. He once said to me, "I am a socialist man in a land where socialism has not yet been accomplished." He seemed to regard that as a sufficient statement about his life, and I agree with him. If we had buried him that would have been a good epitaph, although he spoke it in a rare, melancholy moment. . . .

He was cremated and my mother held a memorial for him. To my surprise, hundreds of people came. Who would have thought this quiet man had touched so many hearts? We sat together, in the front row of the hall, and people filed past, many of them weeping, to shake our hands and embrace us.

That night, at home alone, after our guests had gone, she sat in bed and I came to sit beside her. . . .

She had cried before, but now she wasn't crying. She sat straight up in bed. By then, each time I saw her, I thought she had grown smaller. Now, I looked at her little hands, bunched into fists.

"We did not make life easy for him," she said. At first, her voice was tense, caught somewhere between guilt and accusation. But then she repeated herself and I heard tenderness. "We didn't make his life easy, I tell you."

Maybe our reconciliation dated from that moment. . . .

I can say, in truth, on that night, sitting beside my mother in the bedroom she had shared with my father since we moved to Los Angeles twenty-two years before, I felt the first sense of something peaceful between us. No doubt, my own prolonged youth came to an end that night. I was twenty-seven years old and for the first time in many years I put my arms around her.

"Well," I said, "we don't exactly make life easy for ourselves either." And then we both laughed and rocked each other and wept.

And she said, looking up sideways for my embrace, "So, who said it's too late to learn something?" . . .

EDITIONS CITED

Pasty Adam-Smith, *Hear the Train Blow* (Ringwood, Australia: Penguin Books Australia Ltd, 1987).

Rosemary Brown, *Being Brown: A Very Public Life* (Toronto: Ballantine Books, 1990).

Kim Chernin, *In My Mother's House* (New Haven: Ticknor & Fields, 1983).

Shirley Chisholm, *Unbought and Unbossed* (Boston: Houghton Mifflin Company, 1970).

Lauris Edmond, *Bonfires in the Rain* (Wellington, New Zealand: Bridget Williams Books Limited, 1991).

Janet Frame, *An Autobiography* (New York: George Braziller, Inc., 1991).

Lillian Hellman, *An Unfinished Woman: A Memoir* (Boston: Little, Brown and Company, 1969).

Dorothy Hewett, *Wild Card: An Autobiography, 1923–1958* (Ringwood, Australia: McPhee Gribble, 1990).

Robin Hyde, *A Home in This World* (Auckland, New Zealand: Longman Paul Limited, 1984).

Dorothy Livesay, *Journey with My Selves: A Memoir, 1909–1963* (Vancouver: Douglas & McIntyre Ltd., 1991).

Sally Morgan, *My Place* (Boston: Little, Brown and Company, 1990).

Gabrielle Roy, *Enchantment and Sorrow: The Autobiography of Gabrielle Roy* (Toronto: Lester & Orpen Dennys Limited, 1987).